Fundamentals of Behavior Pathology

Fundamentals of
Behavior Pathology

RICHARD M. SUINN

Professor of Psychology
Colorado State University

JOHN WILEY & SONS, INC.   NEW YORK · LONDON
SYDNEY · TORONTO

Cover and frontispiece: Photo by Wayne Miller, Magnum Photos

Library of Congress Catalogue Card Number: 70-109431

SBN 471 83544 7

Printed in the United States of America

10 9 8 7 6 5 4 3 2 1

To: *Grace,* for endurance throughout her husband's toils.

         Randall, Susan, Stacy, & Bradley, my rambunctious offspring.

         An ever patient mother, *Edith.*

         And my *students,* always a source of inspiration.

Preface

Fundamentals of Behavior Pathology has been written for those who are most concerned with an introduction to the topic of abnormal psychology: the beginning student and his instructor. The interested student will discover the world of abnormality unfolding in the following pages in a form designed to provide maximum clarity and understanding. Fundamentals are always presented before details. Illustrations, case histories, and research add a concrete dimension to the text narrative. Instructors will find that the book consistently offers breadth of coverage rather than a limited orientation to the field. A substantive attention to research is included as an aid in understanding topics; however, the data presented should not distract the undergraduate student from the basic area under discussion. Scientific data permit the reader to become aware of the current state of knowledge and challenges yet to be resolved, and it is in this spirit that special attention is given to data on genetics, cross-cultural material, family relationships, interpersonal experiences, biological findings, physiology, personality theory, and experimental psychopathology. A further effort to aid in instruction is seen in the chapter-by-chapter glossary and the listing of the basic symptoms of pathologies in outline form for easier reading and retention. For a shorter course, the text has been organized to permit faculty to exclude some sections of the book without harming the continuity of other sections.

The book is organized in three parts. Part I traces the historical influences on modern psychopathology, clarifies common misconceptions about mental illness, copes with the problem of definitions, introduces the student to the classification scheme, and orients him to the mental health professions. Part II is somewhat unique in that it makes the student aware of the possible multifactorial origins of mental illness by discussing genetic, sociocultural, familial, biophysiological, and psychological factors. Part III is primarily concerned with the pathologies themselves, listing their characteristics, probable etiologies, and common modes of treatment. The entire organization, therefore, is from an overview to details, from the basics of personality theory to the complexities of personality disorganization, and from the overall data on causative factors to the specific etiologies of designated syndromes.

In addition to the more traditional areas of discussion, the text includes chapters that are often overlooked in books on this topic. Included are chapters on childhood pathology and mental retardation. In addition, the medical therapies and pyschotherapies are described and analyzed in an objective fashion. Psychoanalysis, client-centered therapy, and behavior therapy are all given equal attention. The values of chemotherapy and psychotherapy are discussed along with research evidence associated with such evaluation. Major social and medical problems of our time, namely alcoholism and drugs, are given careful attention.

The author is indebted particularly to Dr. Brendan Maher, Wiley advisor in clinical psychology, for his constructive comments on earlier drafts of the manuscript. Appreciation is also due Dr. David Marlowe, University of California, Santa Cruz and Dr. Jerry Higgins, University of California, Santa Barbara for their constructive and encouraging comments. Special thanks go to Roger T. Holloway, Wiley editor, Mrs. Olivia Buehl and Stella Kupferberg, Wiley picture researchers, for the type of assistance so necessary for a work such as this. Recognition for invaluable service must be given to Brenda Tracy and Susan Peterson. Finally, but most importantly, the author is deeply grateful for the patience and understanding of his wife during the seemingly infinite number of hours involved in the preparation of this manuscript.

RICHARD M. SUINN

Contents

PART I

History and Orientation to Abnormal Psychology

The two chapters that follow present a brief history of abnormal psychology and a general orientation to psychopathology. In order to fully appreciate the progress achieved in the identification and treatment of psychopathology, a historical review of earlier views and methods is necessary. In some cases, certain continuing trends may be noticed, while in others, distinctive new directions have been taken. The progress of a science is inevitably rooted in its past. Sciences are made up of people and their contributions, and the accomplishments of people before them. Chapter 1, on history, focuses on some of these people.

Chapter 2 is a general introduction to abnormal psychology. Throughout the course of man's concern about deviant or seemingly unexplainable behavior, certain "facts" and beliefs have been offered. Chapter 2 distinguishes between fact and fallacy in order to remove misconceptions that interfere with an accurate understanding of psychopathology. Following this, the difficult but fundamental question of how to define and classify abnormality is approached. The reader will note the varied definitions that have been offered; each has separate implications for understanding and treatment of the abnormal. The task of reaching a satisfactory definition is a major one, yet an extremely difficult one. In fact, some experts suggest that abnormal *persons* do not really exist, only problems of *habits* that interfere with adequate living. Chapter 2 emphasizes defining abnormality through comparison with the characteristics of normal behavior.

Part of the general orientation involves acquainting the reader with the extent of the problem of mental illness is society. Finally, the different mental health professions are described to provide a familiarization with the training and contributions of each.

1 *History*

PRIMITIVE POSSESSION

There can be little doubt that primitive man experienced stresses, anxieties, and psychological pain. But because of the very primitive nature of his mental development, distinctions between the real and unreal, the somatic and the psychic, the feeling and the thought, were probably vaguely, if at all, present. Studies of modern primitive tribes and anthropological findings suggest that mental illness did exist in early prehistoric man. The form that it took would be a function of the stage of man's mental development, the particular stresses characteristic of survival, the resources permitted by whatever presocietal or cultural organization existed. Skull remains suggest that a primitive form of surgery—trephining—may have been used in ritualistic treatment. This was comprised of chipping through the skull in circular form with the available crude cutting implements. In all likelihood, the hope was to release whatever evil existed within the sick person through the gap in the skull.

As man's own physical evolution progressed, his explanations for illness took a more distinct shape in demonology, a belief that sources external to the body were the origins. Just as the early Chinese, Egyptians, and Hebrews turned to the belief in spirits or God to lend meaning to their physical world, so did they refer to evil spirits, demons, and possession as a way of explaining sickness. A daughter of the Pharaohs was said to have been possessed by an evil spirit and cured by a benign spirit. Biblical sources are full of references to madness attributed to Satanic control, or considered consequences of moral wrongdoing. In most instances, the treatment reflected the prevailing attitude: the suffering person was stoned or banished to do penance. Reactions were hostile rather than sympathetic. However, some exceptions did occur that showed attitudes completely antithetical to this punitive, vengeful position—the prophets and disciples were often sought after with awe *because of* their special possessions. Similarly, conversions following periods of severe mental disturbance were common, as are reports of visions and mood changes. Gradually, the belief that treatment could be prescribed was formulated, and this power was invested in certain persons. Since the origin of the illness was a spirit or god, evil though it be, then the treatment should logically come from a person who was especially in communication with

Archeological evidence of *trephining*, a primitive form of treatment of illness. Holes are made in the skull apparently to permit the evil spirits or demons to leave. (The University Museum, Philadelphia)

the god or gods, the priest. Crude attempts to exorcise the evil spirit often made the unfortunate human victim more uncomfortable than the demon he was supposed to be housing.

GRECO-ROMAN MEDICINE: EARLY INSIGHTS

Pre-Hippocratic Greece embellished on the theme of mental illness and mythology: madness was attributed to divine power and influence. Hercules was mad, it is said, because Lyssa, the goddess of night and madness so decided. The daughters of Proteus became delusional and acted like cows because of the wrath of the gods. Mysticism and medicine were indistinguishable. And as is typical of the superstitious, paradoxes in beliefs existed, such that some mentally ill were sought after as oracles and soothsayers while others were stoned, feared, and hated.

With Hippocrates (about 460–357 B.C.), a marked change in medical thought occurred. This Greek physician was trained in the traditional thinking of ancient medicine, but his own intense drive for knowledge enabled him to progress far beyond the limited level of his medical contemporaries. This remarkable man, known primarily as the Father of Medicine, may well have been also the Father of Psychiatry. As a person who believed in the value of keen and systematic observation, it was inevitable that he recorded the first diagnostic description of melan-

cholia. In addition, he provided written descriptions of postpartum psychoses, phobias, delirium states associated with certain infections, and other psychological states linked to medical origins. Through his busy clinical work, he recognized hysteria, mania, epilepsy, and mental deterioration. He not only differed from his predecessors in his interest in careful description, he also spearheaded a concern about causation. He stressed the physical-medical origins of psychological symptoms, such as symptoms caused by injury, infection, and physiological changes, in an era when the belief in divine causation was still dominant. Regarding epilepsy, an ailment considered sacred, he sharply denounced that "It is not, in my opinion, any more divine or sacred than other diseases, but has a natural cause and its supposed divine origin is due to men's inexperience, and to their wonder at its peculiar character" (Jones, 1959, p. 139). Even then he did not limit himself to purely physical causes but was an exponent of environmental stress as a factor. Thus, he explained that a fair-skinned woman who was on trial could well have conceived a dark-skinned child as a reflection of her deep emotional stress at her first sight of an Ethiopian tribe.

Hippocrates was an original thinker groping in the darkness surrounded by mysticism, biases, and lack of systematic medical knowledge. Thus, despite his own intellect and skill, he was also influenced by the basic lack of knowledge of his time

The Greek physician and Father of Medicine, *Hippocrates*. A noted original theorist and careful diagnostician, he is pictured at the bedside of a patient. (Bettmann Archive)

—a time that saw Socrates clearly described as exhibiting catatoniclike symptoms, yet refused to accept these signs as indices of mental disturbance; instead, the great philosopher was tried rather than treated for his actions. Hippocrates himself believed that man reflected the four principal elements of the universe—earth, water, fire, and air (*Nature of Man*). Fluids in the human body were said to represent these elements with yellow bile being derived from the earth, black bile from the water, blood from fire, and phlegm or mucous from air. Mental illness was a product of an imbalance of the bodily fluids, for example, an excess of black bile would lead to melancholia. Similarly, although he shifted the emphasis from the heart to the brain as the important source of complex processes, he was still willing to accept the mistaken be- lief that air carried intelligence and feeling through the mouth and then to the brain (the *Sacred Disease*).

Two other Greeks bear brief mention: Plato (about 427-347 B.C.) as a regressive influence and Aristotle (384-322 B.C.) as a progressive thinker. Plato's psychology (*Republic*) returned to the accepted importance of the divine: the rational soul was divine; the irrational soul was animal, mortal, the source of all impulses and feelings, the cause of madness, or irrationality. Mental illness and, in effect, all human emotions, were relegated to a lower level of humanity and, by implication, to be despised. Aristotle strove mightily to develop a philosophy embracing all of science and his psychology reflects this search for unity. He viewed man, animals, and plants in a fashion reminiscent of evolutionary thinking, seeing the behavior

5

The Greek philosopher, *Aristotle*, attempted to develop a unified view of life. Because he believed the mind to be impregnable to illness, he proposed that abnormal mental states must be derived from illnesses of the body. (Bettmann Archive)

and reactions of man as existing on a scale that links him to those of other living creatures (*De Partibus Animalium*). He established the point of view that all of the material or physical world was worthy of study by man through use of his senses, and human senses were there because they were needed and used by the soul or the mind—a concept that serves as an early prototype of Lamarkian genetics. Finally, Aristotle tendered the premise that psychological reactions were linked together in a succession of interrelated events, thereby dispelling any categorizing of reactions as healthy or unhealthy. An unhealthy reaction may well show a transition and change in a healthy personality, and could well serve as a necessary first stage of productive functioning. Thus, for example, the poet Marascos was able to write brilliantly only when suffering from mania (Isensee, 1845). Unfortunately, Aristotle was also responsible for other lines of thinking that served to hinder the development of psychological thought. He maintained a viewpoint that insisted that all psychological illnesses have an organic or physical basis. The mind was conceived of as impregnable to illness, hence, environmental or cultural factors could not affect the mind directly (*De Anima*). This leaves the body as the only agent through which abnormal mental states could be derived, a view which is reflected in modern day search for physiological or anatomical causative factors of mental illness, and for chemical agents for treatment.

The Romans were more concerned with their refinement of skills related to the rule of their vast empire. In medicine, they were content to borrow rather than speculate or invent. From the historical treatises of Celsus (*De re Medica*) it is possible to review the medical atmosphere of the Romans. Superstition and mysticism returned to the extent that special citizens meetings were called if a bad omen appeared, such as the sight of a citizen during an epileptic seizure. The numbers of persons diagnosed as mentally ill increased, partially because of the better diagnostic skills of the physicians who were able to recognize more of the signs of mental illness. In turn, more attention was necessarily paid to treatment processes, mainly the use of "harsh, corrective measures" such as the application of fetters for restraint. The insane person had to be taught to attend so that he could learn and remember what he was doing, through the use of hunger, punishment, even fear. In effect, he had to be brought to his senses.

An outstanding contributor in the Roman Empire was Aretaeus (first century

Galen, the most advanced Roman physician, developed the principle that a symptom can develop in a part of the body separate from the diseased area. He is shown lecturing before Emperor Marc Anthony and Empress Faustine. (Bettmann Archive)

A.D.). He believed that mania and melancholia were both representations of the same basic illness, while yet accepting that the pathological state of euphoria could also derive separately (Arnold, 1806). He fostered the view that severe mental states are but the exaggerations of the person's normal personality disposition and temperament. In addition, Aretaeus devoted his attention to the question of prognosis —what is the likely outcome of a given illness—and differential diagnosis—what is the difference in clinical symptoms that distinguishes one illness from another, for example, the euphoria associated with mania from that connected with alcoholic inebriation.

If Hippocrates represented the apex of Grecian medicine, Galen (130-200) was the zenith of the Roman world. Seven centuries separated these two men who were temperamentally so much alike: both were vehement in their attacks and outspoken in their beliefs. Galen was an eclectic, a person who neither preached a single theory nor denounced a single theory, but who selected, collected, and coordinated the best of all accumulated knowledge. Galen is known for his development of the insight that an affected part need not be the part where the disease resides (*De locis Affectis*). The principle of *consensus* or symptom developed in "sympathy" allowed for a symptom to appear in a part of the body separate from the diseased area. This point of view leads directly to the modern-day treatment dictum: Treat the illness, not the symptom. This is especially true in cases of hysteria, where it is obvious that the symptom such as blindness does not originate in the retina or optic nerve but in deeper emotional areas. Overall, Galen contributed little that was original to medical thought or practice. However, he did much to synthesize views concerning the brain as the center of sensation and the soul, the role of the physical and environmental state as they affect the mind, and the relationship between mental illness and the rational or animal soul.

A woodcut illustrating the treatment of witches in the 16th century. Women were considered special targets for possession by the Devil, pictured here as a serpent. (New York Public Library Picture Collection)

THE DARK AGES: THE RETURN OF DEMONOLOGY

With the death of Galen in 200 A.D., medical advances ceased and the dark era of medical ignorance and fearful superstition returned to blanket the civilized world. The teachings of the Greco-Romans were banned as pagan, mental illness was again seen as a form of possession, laws were passed at synods pronouncing the view that the possessed and any who attempted to treat the possessed were to be condemned. Medical psychology ceased to exist, and the struggling roots of psychiatry were supplanted by demonology. Psychiatry had become theology, the learned physician was replaced by the blessed priest. At the peak of this era, St. Gregory of Tours (d. 594), when treating a headache, "touched the disordered spot with the sombre pall of St. Martin's sepulchre and petitioned forgiveness of the holy martyr for applying profane medication" (Fort, 1883, p. 136). Incantations and invocations were as crucial a part of the armamentarium of a physician as medicinal preparations. Diagnosis was directed toward identifying the signs that showed the presence of the devil rather than identifying those symptoms that indicated a person in need of medical attention. Earlier, records of anesthesias were relied upon as evidence of diabolic collaboration and possession; these same signs were to later form the clinical symptomatology of hysteria in Charcot's time. In fact, these *stigmata diaboli* were deliberately sought by inquisitors through the use of sharp implements for poking a suspect until an insensitive area was found. Detailed descriptions of the types of devils responsible for troubling the soul were developed to enable further diagnosis and "treatment." An encyclopedic work is attributed along these lines to Psellus (1020-1105), a monk who seemed particularly suited to the task since he himself was plagued by hallucinations.

By the thirteenth century the struggle between the religious and the secular interpretations of man and illness led to dramatic inconsistencies. These were especially reflected in the behavior of Frederick II who established the funda-

A modern day Italian *Flagellant* bloodied from a crown of thorns and other self-inflicted punishment. (David Seymour/Magnum)

mentals of medical education maintained to this day: five years of academic work, one year of internship, and a state qualifying examination before certification for practice. On the other hand, it was also Frederick II who condemned all heretics to the fiery stake with imprisonment, loss of property and home, and denial of status to the offspring, for those who renounced their sins. The only originality in treatment methods existed in terms of inventing newer ways of creating discomfort for the demon and his human host, for example, dunking in a pond in between special masses, whipping with the skin of a porpoise, and fumigation with burning wood. A rise in miraculous cures through religion occurred as an offshoot of the growing social tensions created by these severe threats and channeled by the pronounced encouragement of religious ecstacy and glory. In addition, a new type of religion arose, combining the belief in the value of punishment with the spiritual seeking of the Lord; it reached its peak in the wierd, self-torturing, *Flagellants* who achieved a state of ecstacy through self-inflicted whippings.

By the middle of the fifteenth century, the hold of religious emotionalism over medical and legal thought was supreme. "Fact" was founded not on careful observation and objective analysis, but on religious documents such as *Malleus Maleficarum,* the Witches' Hammer (Summers, 1928). This text, born out of the zealous fervor of Inquisitors, marked the end of all prior gains in psychiatric medicine. The simple phrase, "this is contrary to true faith" once and for all eliminated any doubt that devils and witches existed and were responsible for the inhuman symptoms appearing in man; "It is contrary to true faith" became the authoritative

9

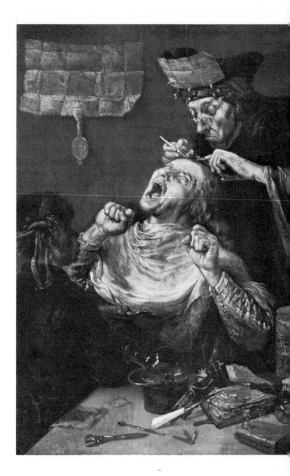

An early painting illustrating the primitive stage of medicine. Patient is being operated on for treatment without anesthesia. The quack is removing what he claims to be a stone in the head causing the mental illness. (Museum Boymans-van Beuningen, Rotterdam)

decree that dispensed with any heretic who would believe that there were natural explanations for mental illness; "It is contrary to true faith" proclaimed "diagnosis" as the identification of the varieties of demons and their nefarious ways of injuring man. It is amusing to note that one sufferer actually had 6670 such evil demons cast from his body during course of "treatment."

The medical profession was by no means innocent of the guild of ignorance and superstition. As distinguished a physician as John Lange (1485-1565) was convinced of the reality of the supernatural when he removed wood segments, iron, and hair from the stomach of a patient. Fernel (1497-1558) considered lycanthropy, the transformation of a human into a werewolf, as a legitimate medical entity. Felix Plater (1536-1614) offered a progressive

classification of mental illness, yet adhered to the belief that the originator of the illnesses was the devil himself (Plater, 1583). In all, the physician had little to say, little to contribute to new knowledge, and even less power to initiate any change in beliefs.

THE PSYCHIATRIC REVOLUTION: THE INTELLECT OVER THE INQUISITION

The seeds for a revolution that would come bursting through were quietly planted while the darkness still enveloped science. From the pens of nonmedical scholars came the first interest in a true science of behavior. The word "psychology" appeared for the first time with manuscripts by Goeckel (*Psychologia-Hoc Est de Hominis Perfectione,* 1590) and Casmann (*Psychologia Anthropologica,* 1594) offering a return to humanistic views of mankind. Francis Bacon (1561-1626) helped forge a major new orientation in separating the mind from the soul. He argued that the mind had characteristics and functions that were linked to the body, and not the spirit. In addition the human mind could be studied through empirical rather than metaphysical methods (Bacon, 1620). The mind was now free to become an entity to be studied for its own sake, and not for the sake of demonstrating the divine nature of man.

Juan Luis Vives (1492-1540) represented a second major breakthrough from metaphysical misconceptions. A devout Roman Catholic already known for his inspired private prayers, Vives argued for social change in attitudes toward treatment. The insane could be restored to sanity by gentle treatment, not harsh condemnations. Reason regressed in the face of punishment, but was regained in the air of tranquility. Of additional significance were the dynamic formulations of human processes which Vives developed (*De Anima et Vita,* 1538). With admirable insight in a time where original thinking was suppressed, he outlined the relationship between emotions and memory and discussed the basic drives in such modern tones as to foreshadow the eventual proposals of Freud. He described examples of contiguity as a factor in associations, and emotions as they influence recollection; he was on the threshold of identifying the unconscious, and faced the issues of the dynamic drives that move man.

The greatest contributor to psychiatry of the revolutionary period known as the Renaissance was Johann Weyer (1515-1588). Unlike many of his vituperous medical predecessors, Weyer was a tranquil, composed, sedate man, unshaken by the swirls and struggles of ignorance that went on around him. Well versed in literature and the Bible, he slowly and methodically removed the aura of authority from the *Malleus Maleficarum,* repeatedly referring to the Bible itself to refute the Inquisitors' document (*De Praestigiis Daemonum,* 1563). Weyer is credited with breaking the grip that theology had on medical psychology, thereby permitting the renewal of interest in mental illness as sickness rather than sinfulness or possession. He was also the first physician to "specialize" in mental illness, and in this sense was the first psychiatrist. He gave to the profession complete descriptions of psychopathology, drawing time and time again from personal experiences, and couching them in a language that would stir interest and understanding instead of abhorrence and fright. For example, he implores, "I beg you to examine closely the thoughts of those melancholic people their words, their visions and their actions . . . (that) burdens their minds to such a degree that some of them imagine themselves to be animals the gestures and voices of which they try to imitate" (Weyer, 1886, p. 303). Weyer's impact was unfortunately minimized by the very subject that was his strength: abnormal behavior. As personal physician to Duke William, Weyer was assigned full responsibility for the Duke's health when a cerebral hemorrhage struck. Duke William developed the mental symptoms associated with a stroke, and others were quick to seize the opportunity to conclude that Weyer was indeed a sorcerer. It was a full century before Weyer's writings were to truly impress the world.

THE SEVENTEENTH CENTURY: THE ORGANIC HYPOTHESIS RETURNS

With the loss of Weyer's influence there were few who remained humanistic in their treatment of the mentally disturbed. Cases of the mentally ill being mistreated were common; in Konigsberg, a psychotic man with delusions of being God had his tongue removed, his head cut off, and his body burned; a woman of striking beauty lost her mania and her life through excessive bloodletting as a curative measure; in Normandy, 500 people were charged as a group with witchcraft and when the king opposed the ruling, his own parliament took it upon itself to reprimand their sovereign.

Many Europeans still believed in the reality of possession as well as the existence of dark alliances between man and devil. In Loudun, a dwarfed prioress of an Ursuline convent, Sister Jeanne, attempted to gain the favor of a handsome new priest Father Urbaine Grandier. Grandier's reputation as an ardent lover had reached and captivated Sister Jeanne. Upon being turned down, Sister Jeanne reported to the other nuns her dreams of being seduced by the priest, whereupon they in turn began experiencing similar dreams. Soon the nuns were beset with convulsions; Sister Jeanne herself rolled on the floor howling and gnashing her teeth as Satan blasphemed through her mouth. Father Grandier was accused and found guilty of causing these possessions and burnt at the stake. Numerous holy men were brought in to exorcise the demons, only to fail. Father Jean-Joseph Surin attempted his best, only to fall victim himself. He later reported: "I have engaged in combat with four of the most potent and malicious devils in hell . . . both by night and day in a thousand different ways . . . for the last three and a half months . . . . Things have gone so far that God has permitted, I think for my sins, what has perhaps never been seen in the Church, that in the exercise of my ministry the devil passes out of the body of the possessed woman and entering into mine, assaults and confounds me. . . ." Father Surin remained completely conscious and alert during these seizures, and reported seeming to be two distinct persons: "I

even feel that the same cries which issue from my mouth come equally from the two souls, and am at a loss to discern whether they be caused by joy or by the extreme fury with which I am filled. . . . When I desire by the motion of one of these two souls to make the sign of the cross on my mouth, the other averts my hands with great swiftness and grips my finger in its teeth to bite me with rage" (Aubin, 1716).

Where mental illness was seen as worthy of a physician's attention, it was attributed to anatomical or physical abnormalities requiring physical treatment. This organic viewpoint ascribed mental symptoms to faulty flow of blood or nervous fluid, the influence of bad ferments circulating in the brain, or gross physical abnormalities, but never to purely emotional or psychological causes. As a logical outcome of this viewpoint, and in the face of lack of theoretical understanding, it was quite natural that bloodletting, emetics, cathartics, and even animal-to-human tranfusions were the treatments of the day.

Theories about the mind began appearing in earnest among philosophers. These ideas were to become a necessary background for those who eventually wished to understand the normal mind, while the progress in medical thinking was to provide a foundation for those who would treat the abnormal mind. Thus, the philosophical thought of the Renaissance influenced the development of modern psychology while the medical advances were to form the framework for psychiatry and clinical psychology. The French philosopher and mathematician Descartes (1596-1650) agreed to the dualistic belief that mind and body were separate; but he proffered the view that the two interacted with each other, the notion of interactionism. The anatomical site of the interaction was the pineal gland at the base of the cerebrum (Descartes, 1649).

Although his literal acceptance of an anatomical link between mind and body is no longer accepted today, the mind-reacts-to-body/body-reacts-to-mind conception is reflected in modern psychosomatic medicine. Hobbes (1588-1679) stressed the theory that the origin of the mind is in sense impressions that build up in complexity through associations. This view has carried over to the problems of learning in psychological thought, and has relevance for the use of free-association or word-association in mental diagnosis. Of pertinence to abnormal psychology were Locke (1632-1704) and Berkeley (1685-1753) who spearheaded the views that physical reality may well be less significant for understanding the human than the reality *as experienced* by man (Locke, 1700; Berkeley, 1709). Viewed in the context of abnormal behavior, a hallucination is often more real an influence on a psychotic's behavior than his real life surroundings.

THE EIGHTEENTH CENTURY: NOSOLOGIES AND REFORMS ABOUND

The desire to systematize, to classify into orderly categories (nosologies), prevaded the eighteenth century. Stahl (1660-1734), an opinionated and often morose man was the first to divide mental illness into those of organic origin, and those of functional or psychological origin. Others added their schemas until a proliferation of diagnostic systems developed, including such refinements as the distinctions between melancholia *hypochondriaca,* depression with gastrointestinal complaints; melancholia *thanatophobia,* depression with fear of death; and melancholia *demonomania,* depression with fear of the devil (Erhard, 1794). One earnest physician wrote three volumes with three hundred and twenty-six pages devoted to identifying various forms of mental illness.

Others added their own unique principles for diagnosis—Gall (1758-1828), a believer in the major role of the brain, stressed the diagnostic signs presented by bumps in the cranium (phrenology) (Gall, 1825), while Lavater authored the science of physiognomy by which diagnoses were made from inspection of facial features and expressions (Lavater, 1775). Certainly progress in psychiatry was hindered rather than helped by this overabundance of highly inventive, but confusing productivity. However, the activity does reflect the return of medical interest in clinical observation of mental disturbances. In addition, such overenthusiasm still does represent a demonstration of the start of psychiatry as a specialized branch of medicine.

Until the end of the eighteenth century, formal treatment centers were nonexistent. Those who could afford it or who showed symptoms that were intriguing received the private services of physicians. For the majority, hospitalization or imprisonment were still all they could hope for, and hospitals and prisons were often indistinguishable from one another. The infamous Bedlam Hospital, actually the Hospital of St. Mary of *Bethlehem,* and Bicetre Hospital were places where the insane were kept in darkness, without nourishment, or attention for their basic needs. Patients were known to live in their own excrement. Guards considered the inmates as exhibits rather than human equals and supplemented their income by charging a fee to those who wished to be entertained by the sight of a madman's antics. This was the "progress" that was made from the Dark Ages, the mentally ill finally escaped "treatment" by burning at the stake, only to fall into the dungeons of despair and isolation.

The most dramatic hospital reform was spearheaded by Pinel (1745-1826). In the fall of 1793, he took over Bicetre and proceeded to follow his conviction that the

Tickets of this type were often sold to persons wishing to view the "antics" of mental patients during the 18th and 19th centuries. (British Museum, and, R. Hunter and I. Macalpine, *Three Hundred Years of Psychiatry, 1535-1860,* Oxford, 1963)

insane needed only "Fresh air and . . . their liberty." He carried his plea to the Commune officers only to be met with suspicion and doubt regarding his political motives in seeking such reforms. However, although no permission was given, he was not expressly forbidden to carry out his plans provided he accepted full individual responsibility. True to his convictions, he released a small group from their chains. Among these were an English officer who had not seen the sun in 40 years of internment, and a French soldier who was feared as insanely violent. Pinel's handling of this Frenchman is revealing: he quietly promised to free the soldier if the man would reciprocate by behaving himself. As a further expression of good faith, Pinel employed the former madman as a personal manservant. Ultimately, Pinel was to be later saved from a lynch mob by the courageousness and strength of this loyal servant-patient. Another astounding example of Pinel's effectiveness was the priest who had believed himself to be Christ for 12 *years.* Pinel helped him to recover in 10 *months* (Zilboorg and Henry, 1941).

Two years after the American Revolution, a unique new form of therapy appeared, with dramatic cures in Vienna and then Paris. Anton Mesmer (1734-1815) induced cures by bringing people to a "crises," evidenced by sudden convulsions, fits of crying, clairvoyance. He was able to restore the sight to a patient, induced crises in groups of patients at a time, and to show that there was no trickery involved, he performed his "mesmerism" in public. All but the scientific world flocked to his side. When the medical world finally looked his way, it was with a suspicious eye. An investigatory committee was charged with the task of passing judgment on Mesmer's claims. Among the members were Benjamin Franklin; Lavoisier, the renowned chemist; Bailly, one time mayor of Paris and an esteemed scientist; and Guillotine, the man who invented the execution device for "humanizing" court execution methods. What they saw was a volatile, egotistical, aggressive man whose ambition was for fame and fortune through capitalizing on his "miraculous powers"; he used an instrument called the "baquet" comprised of mirrors and iron rods being touched by a magnetic wand, and a seance of patients forming a human chain around the contraption of metal and glass. They heard a flowing explanation that the imbalance of magnetic fluid from the universe in the human body caused illnesses that could be cured by restoring the proper balance. The commit-

14

Progressive mental hospital reforms were initiated by *Pinel* at Bicetre Hospital. He is shown releasing mental patients from manacles common to hospitals of the 18th century. (Bulloz / Art Reference Bureau)

Mesmer attending to a woman experiencing a "crises," a fainting spell considered a part of the animal magnetism cure. In the picture are two groups with baquets; in the background an orchestra plays music to set the mood. (University of Chicago Press)

tee condemned the man as a charlatan, proclaiming that "imagination without magnetism produces convulsions . . . (but) magnetism without imagination produces nothing" (Bailly, 1784).

Mesmerism continued to hold Europe spellbound for 40 years because of its dramatic appeal, the seemingly miraculous cures, and Mesmer himself. Anton Mesmer can only be described as a significant public spectacle: he possessed a turbulent, relentless, electrifying will to exaggerate, to proclaim his beliefs to commoner and court, to demonstrate that his cures were unquestionable, his theory unassailable, and his own power unequaled. But the scientific world was not seduced by such appeals and maintained its air of skepticism. For example, a patient was amputated at the thigh in 1842 with the help of no anesthetic other than that provided by the hypnotic trance. This case was presented to the Royal Medical Society and was immediately denounced as fraud! Either the physician in question was falsifying his report, or he was naively tricked by his patient (who really felt pain but refused to admit it) (Bramwell, 1930).

THE NINETEENTH CENTURY: THE BEGINNING OF MODERN PSYCHIATRY

Psychiatry was to be the first to strip the gaudy unessentials from mesmerism and examine it for its real value. Elliotson (1791-1868) considered the value of mesmerism to be in the treatment of hysteria. Braid (1795-1860), a surgeon and not well informed in psychological thinking, nevertheless had the insight to realize that the effectiveness of mesmerism was *not* in the magnetic powers of man or machine. Substituting the term hypnotize for mesmerize, he concluded that the effects resulted from the arousal of ideas in the patient by the suggestion of the mesmerist or hypnotist (Braid, 1843).

The Nancy School

A French country doctor, Liebeault (1823-1904) is considered to be the founder of the Nancy School, although strictly speaking, he established a workaday clinic and not a school. He was a new type of physician—unassuming, concerned **not** with the whys of hypnosis, but with the careful improvement on method to increase its effectiveness as a tool. His was a service function, to treat those who could not afford special care. Modest and unpretentious, he stood in contrast to the aggressive figure of Mesmer, yet accomplished more toward the acceptance of hypnotism than its founder. Working a step at a time, Liebeault empirically tried different modifications, cautiously testing and retesting. His school emphasized empiricism, a therapeutic environment, and humanitarianism. Along with Braid, Liebeault has often been viewed as the founder of psychotherapy. In addition, Liebeault (1866) and Bernheim (1886) helped to unravel some of the mysteries of hysteria—that strange malady involving paralysis or anesthesia and considered somehow linked to abnormality of the uterus (the Greek name for uterus was hystera). They concluded that hysteria and hypnotism were closely related, that the symptoms in hysterical patients were produced by the suggestibility of the afflicted. In effect, hysteria was self-induced hypnosis or auto-suggestion. In this way, the Nancy School differed from the nearest rival, the Salpetriere School.

The Salpetriere School

Charcot (1825-1893) directed the Salpetriere School, known for its stress on organic explanations of hysteria and hypnosis. This school is considered the first postgraduate center of formal psychiatric education. It was Charcot who finally put the superstitions of demonology to rest by

Charcot, the director of the Salpetriere School, argued that both hysteria and hypnotic phenomena were due to organic disturbances. He is shown giving a demonstration to postgraduate students in medicine. (Bettmann Archive)

presenting a psychological explanation for possession. Those signs mistakenly taken as possession, he explained, were really symptoms of hysteria. On the other hand, he firmly believed that hysteria was grounded in organic disturbances, and that hypnotic phenomena were themselves symptoms of organic abnormality (Charcot, 1882). Many professional arguments transpired between Bernheim and Charcot on these issues. Ultimately, the logic of Bernheim based on his careful analysis of nearly 10,000 cases of hypnosis won over Charcot (Bernheim, 1886).

Although the leaders of both schools appeared within a fraction of a step from recognizing the influence of the unconscious, the insight was not developed at this time. Pierre Janet (1859-1947) was to come the closest as he described the "automatic" characteristic of hysterical behavior and even referred to it as "unconscious" but failed to elaborate further (Janet,

1911). Janet shared the organic viewpoint of the Salpetriere group and even felt that hysteria was caused by a constitutional weakness. Paradoxically, Janet is honored today as the first to offer a psychological theory of neurosis. He suggested that a degree of mental energy was necessary to maintain a state of adjustment. If this is exhausted, then mental breakdown occurs and neurotic symptoms develop.

While the French were making headway in understanding the neuroses and in therapy, Kraepelin (1855-1926) in Germany was establishing the guidelines for a system of psychoses. As Charcot captured the symptoms of hysteria away from demonology, Kraepelin was victorious in winning a place for mental disease in medicine. Psychiatry became a legitimate branch of medicine rather than a bastard offshoot reflecting the interests of a few. He accomplished this by detailing a concise and clear classification system (Krae-

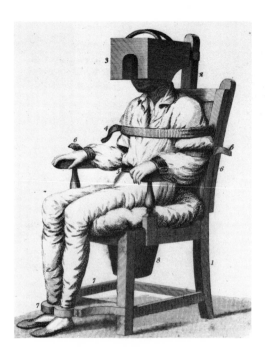

Dr. Benjamin Rush is known as the Father of American Psychiatry and for his contributions to hospital reform. Despite his progressive ideas, he still believed in restraints and invented the "tranquilizing chair" illustrated above. *Legend:* (1) sturdy wooden chair, (2) brace for helmet, (3) wooden helmet to keep out distractions and calm the patient, (4) chest straps, (5) strap around the abdomen, (6) wrist leather restraints, (7) restraints for the legs. (The Historical Society of Pennsylvania)

pelin, 1883) based on the disease entity supposition: mental illness exists as a separate and distinct disease and all the rules that apply to physical diseases also apply to mental diseases. There are separate clusters of symptoms that characterize and distinguish one mental disease from another in the same manner that the symptoms of mumps differentiate it from meningitis. In addition, once a disease begins its course, it follows a rigid, predictable unvarying sequence such that a prognosis can be made even during the early stages of the disease. Detailed descriptions of dementia praecox and manic-depressive psychoses were presented by Kraepelin in his discussion of what he

felt to be the two major psychoses. Writing from the disease entity attitude, he stressed the symptoms, the course of the disease, the prognosis or outcome. Manic-depressive psychosis was more favorable in outcome, while dementia praecox invariably led to mental deterioration from which recovery was impossible. Kraepelin accepted and recorded the classification of the psychoses into endogenous and exogenous diseases. The endogenous were of internal origin, caused by factors such as organic brain changes. The exogenous were of external origin, caused by factors unrelated to heredity, metabolic differences, or constitutional defects. Kraepelin's treatises had a profound effect particularly on American psychiatry. The impact of his disease entity views and his clinical descriptions of the major psychoses can be felt to the present day in much of psychiatric thought.

American psychiatry of the nineteenth century owed much to Dr. Benjamin Rush (1745-1813), the Father of American Psychiatry and the American equivalent of Pinel in terms of hospital reform. As was typical of the other psychiatric pioneers into new territory, Rush still could not let loose entirely of misdirected beliefs of his time. He remained a firm user of purgatives, and bloodletting techniques and even invented two diabolic "curative" devices: The gyrator designed to increase cerebral circulation by spinning the patient, and the tranquilizer to restrain the patient "comfortably" by leather straps and a wooden helmet not unlike a modern electric chair.

: American hospital conditions were of concern to the administrators themselves as well as to lay persons. The current American Psychiatric Association, the professional organization for the advancement of psychiatry, had its beginnings through the efforts of the "Original 13" —the thirteen hospital superintendents who met to share their concerns. Of the

A scene in a 20th century mental hospital illustrating the despairing conditions that provoked modern reform movements. (Jerry Cooke)

lay public, Dorothea Dix (1802-1887) stands as a significant figure in hospital reform. A retired schoolteacher, she carried on a personal crusade across the United States and Europe and is credited for the expansion of over 30 state hospital facilities.

In addition to the contributions of medical men to abnormal psychology, psychologists were laying the groundwork for understanding the normal personality, and hence in comparison, the abnormal mind. Psychologists of the nineteenth century were working to establish a method and a viewpoint that would finally separate them from the influence of philosophy. The scientific method of hypothesis formation, observation, quantitative measurement, and experimental control received a strong impetus through the efforts of Fechner (1801-1887) and Galton (1822-1911). Fechner's psychophysical methods and mathematical skills turned psychology for the first time into an exact science; Wundt's psychological laboratory, the first of its kind (est. 1875), demonstrated that human experience could be subjected to experimental study; and Galton stirred the movement toward measuring the ways in which humans differ from one another by means of mental tests. William James (1842-1910) was soon to add his analysis of emotions and instincts. Life is a process of adjustment; irrational purposes as well as the search for pleasure and the most utilitarian means serve as basic motives;

emotions are the expected end products of bodily changes. Lighter Witmer (1867-1956) opened the first psychological clinic in the United States in 1896 and initiated the specialty of clinical psychology, that area of psychology particularly devoted to the diagnosis and treatment of abnormal human behavior.

THE TWENTIETH CENTURY: REVOLUTIONARY INSIGHTS

It is difficult to neatly classify the trends and contributions of the twentieth century. From the standpoint of diagnosis, the following developments are relevant: the psychodynamic formulations of Freud; the acceptance of pluristic determinants (biological, social, sociological) of illness proposed by Meyer; the interpersonal analysis of Sullivan which disputes the disease entity conception; the medical evidence that lends support to the view that organic factors cause mental illness, such as the discovery of the spirochete causing syphilis and general paresis; and the building evidence for possible genetic factors suggested by the twin studies of Kallman, and the discovery of chromosomal aberrations in mental retardation. Regarding the treatment of mental illness, unquestionably significant gains have occurred because of progress in mental health movements, and in psychopharmacology and pioneers in new methods in psychotherapy, such as group psychotherapy, client-centered therapy, and family therapy. The details of most of these developments will be treated in later chapters. This discussion shall be limited to two fundamental pathways opened during the twentieth century: psychoanalysis, and experimental psychopathology.

Psychoanalysis

Sigmund Freud (1856-1939) was a young physician who made his most important discovery in the nineteenth century when he co-authored a manuscript with Breuer and introduced the idea of the unconscious. His creativity and profound influence on other brilliant men reached a peak in the 1900's, and hence the twentieth century can lay legitimate claim to him. It is of side interest that Freud entered medicine without any great sense of attractiveness to the discipline. Yet, his talent displayed itself early in his student career with major discoveries in zoological evolutionary trends, in nerve fiber analysis, and in the development of an improved method of histological study. He came within a stone's throw of being the founder of neurone theory, and within a hair's breadth of establishing the anesthetizing properties of cocaine as valuable for eye surgery.

Sigmund Freud, who was to so profoundly influence the lives of others, was himself deeply affected by three men: the personable and dynamic Charcot who was at the peak of his career, the keenly insightful Bernheim, and the inventive Breuer (1842-1925). Freud's early attempt to become closely associated with Charcot was discouraging because of Charcot's fame. Eventually, and because of his ability to translate into German, Freud was accepted into the inner circle of friends and colleagues by Charcot. Like many others, Freud later left Paris deeply impressed by the demonstrations of hypnosis on hysterical symptoms. Less than five years later, while the work of Charcot was still vivid in his memory, Freud was to see and be further astonished by Bernheim's work and the implication that strong, hidden mental forces existed within men. In addition, Breuer had been diligently at work with a classical case of hysteria compounded by a double personality syndrome. The latter symptoms showed Breuer how to relieve the former—during a period when the patient's second personality gained control, she spilled forth all the unhappy feelings and experiences connected with a hysterical symptom . . . and suddenly, the symptom vanished! Hypnosis was used to bring about further occurrences of this "talking cure," "chimney sweeping" treatment known eventually as catharsis, or the method for relief of symptoms through the release of the unpleasant feelings. Breuer and Freud collaborated on a manuscript discussing catharsis (Breuer and Freud, 1895), and expanded the first truly psychological explanation for a neurosis. Freud was to later discard hypnosis in favor of a "concentration" technique and finally to invent the free-association method, considered one of his greatest developments to methodology. It is said that one of the reasons for Freud's disillusionment with hypnosis was his inability to effectively hypnotize a number of patients. By 1896, free association had become integrated into that unique form of psychotherapy fathered by Freud, psychoanalysis.

In addition to his contribution to therapy, Freud was to revolutionize psychiatric thought by his theory of neuroses (Freud, 1953). He was deterministic in that he proposed that all events, including the irrational symptom, could be traced to a specifiable origin. Seemingly meaningless symptoms were said to have understandable relationships. Mental illness was seen as related to disturbances and distortions from the unconscious, developmental difficulties in psychic growth and maturation, conflicts over sexual and self-destructive instincts, and traumatic experiences. The concept of repression was introduced to explain the difficulty one experiences in retrieving material from the unconscious. And ultimately, Freud was led to apply his theory of abnormality to understanding normal behavior, the development of societies, art, religion, and literature. Freud was even to undertake and publish an analysis of Leonardo da Vinci which served to horrify Freud's

Dr. Sigmund Freud, the founder of psychoanalysis, at age 66. **(Max Halberstadt)**

friends, but which nevertheless soon sold out (Freud, 1910).

Freud, the founder of psychoanalysis, endured a tragic bout with cancer insidiously eating through his cheek. Although he courageously operated on himself several times, the sickness took his life in 1939. He was to leave a distinctive contribution through numerous lectures and manuscripts. However, his image was to be also carried forward by his disciples in psychoanalysis, Jung, Adler, and Rank, as well as Abraham, Ferenczi, Jones, and Brill. Of the early "inner circle" members, Jung, Adler, and Rank broke off their relationships with their master to form revised offshoots of Freudian theory. Each break was accompanied by feelings of anguish by both Freud and disciple. Firm bonds of intense friendship were brought into conflict with intellectual doubts over the validity of Freudian theory. Jung (1875-1961) established a school of An-

Dr. Carl Jung, the founder of Analytic Psychology. (Karsh/Rapho Guillumette)

strives to overcome an inferiority complex, searching for experiences and developing a style of living to obtain this goal (Adler, 1927). As with most of Freud's errant disciples, Otto Rank (1884-1939) devised a theory basically founded on Freud's original ideas but with significant deviations. Rank is best known for his belief that the profound shock of birth (the birth trauma) continues to influence man as he strives to regain control and self-development (Rank, 1929).

An even more decisive split from traditional Freudian views has taken place in the formation of the "neo-Freudian school" of thought centered at the Washington School of Psychiatry and the William Alanson White Institute in the United States. This group is generally characterized by a stress on sociological factors, and a basic belief in the positive features of man. Harry Stack Sullivan (1892-1949), the first American psychiatrist to develop a significant theory, stressed the concept of interpersonal relations (Sullivan, 1953). This view removed the emphasis on examining the patient as the source of the disease, and broadened the outlook to examining the *interaction* between the patient and others. Karen Horney's (1885-1952) views centered around the interplay between neurotic defenses and cultural forces. She developed the analysis that normal adjustments to others involve moving toward, moving against, and also at times moving away from other people (Horney, 1945). Erich Fromm (1900-), a psychoanalyst who had never been trained in medicine, applied his previous background in sociology to Freudian concepts. He strongly argued for viewing man in the context of anthropological data and social philosophy. Religious and humanistic ideals become as relevant for understanding human illness as the satisfaction of needs for love and basic organic demands (Fromm, 1955).

While such movements to *improve* on

alytic Psychology not long after being appointed as the first president of the International Psychoanalytic Association. The views that he proposed were soon to lead to his voluntary resignation, his stepping down as the potential successor to Freud's leadership, and his ultimate separation, even socially, from Freud. Jung believed in a larger life energy motive force instead of the sexual instincts; he emphasized the role of unconscious racial experiences, divided personality into several groups (e.g., introversive and extraversive types), and contributed the word association test as a means of drawing forth individual "complexes" (Jung, 1953). Adler (1870-1937), also a onetime president of an analytic society, had his views roundly denounced as misleading and invalid. He terminated his formal connection with the Freudians and developed the theory of Individual Psychology. Adler substituted social urges for Freud's sexual motive with an emphasis on the will to power and conscious efforts. Man

22

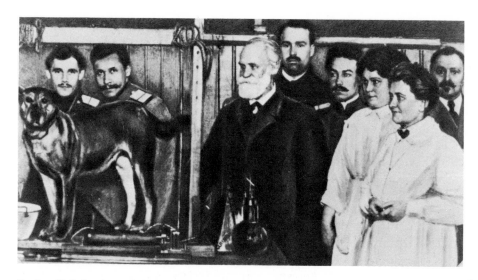

Pavlov, **Nobel prize recipient, shown with a dog used in his experiments and students at the Military Medical Academy. (Culver Pictures, Inc.)**

basic Freudian *theory* were underway, *extensions* of the *application* of Freudian thought were also progressing. The application of the psychoanalytic method to children was pursued by Melanie Klein (1882-1960), and Anna Freud (1895-), the daughter of Sigmund Freud. Flanders Dunbar (1902-1959) defended the value of the method in the field of psychosomatic medicine (Dunbar, 1954). Frieda Fromm-Reichman (1890-1957) carried psychoanalysis to the psychotics, a patient group for which the method was previously considered too dangerous (Fromm-Reichman, 1950). Karl Abraham (1877-1925), one of Freud's most brilliant pupils, and Kardiner (1891-), took psychoanalytic theory into anthropological work (Abraham, 1913; Kardiner, et al., 1945).

Any survey of the early twentieth century, even a brief one, cannot overlook the greatest contribution to diagnosis of the era: Bleuler's monograph (1911) on dementia praecox. Guided by Freud's influence, Bleuler (1857-1939) focused on the ideational components and emotional reactions of this patient group. He substituted the term "schizophrenia" to indicate that there were several classes instead of a single disease. He isolated a crucial symptom of schizophrenics: disturbance of thought processes shown in the loose, associational thoughts and the autistic thinking—thinking tied to private meanings instead of reality-based definitions. In addition, Bleuler did away with the pessimism implicit in the old dementia praecox classification by demonstrating that these patients were in fact curable.

Experimental Psychopathology

Pavlov (1849-1936) was a Russian physiologist who spent the better part of sixty years in scientific experimentation and writing. He devised a totally new operative-surgical method, demonstrated the chemical regulation of digestion, detailed the sequence of digestive processes in different parts of the gastrointestinal system, and offered significant views on the circulatory and the nervous systems. In 1904, Pavlov was honored with the Nobel prize in physiology and medicine, with a citation that this was in recognition of "his work on the physiology of digestion."

During his study of digestion in dogs, Pavlov discovered a phenomenon that has become a significant part of modern psy-

23

chology. He was fully aware of the ability of food placed in the mouth to stimulate salivation, but he also observed that the laboratory dogs were salivating before the food reached their mouths. Because these secretions were not connected with direct stimulation of digestive-linked senses, he initially called them "psychical secretions" (1897). He later discarded any explanations based on psychical or "mentalistic" ideas in favor of physiological terms. He continued his careful experimentation, but now referred to the phenomenon as a "conditioned reflex" (Pavlov, 1904). The procedure used in his laboratory is known today as classical conditioning: a neutral cue such as a light is paired with a cue that is part of a reflex, such as the presentation of food to the mouth; with continued pairings, the neutral cue is able to elicit the same reflex response, such as salivation.

Of significance to psychopathology is an incident that occurred during a later training trial. A dog was being presented with the task of discriminating between a circle and an ellipse, with the ellipse being gradually modified so as to become more and more similar to the circle. Suddenly, the animal which had hitherto been quite calm, began to bite, tear at the restraining harness, and squeal. This dramatic event laid the foundation for the experimental development of conflict and pathology. Pavlov's own explanation remained physiologically oriented and non-mentalistic: he maintained that pathological behavior could be induced whenever excitatory states existed in the organism along with strong inhibitory states. Liddell (1895-1962) developed neuroses in sheep, pigs, and goats by shocking the animals to encourage them to learn to discriminate, then making the discrimination task impossible (Liddell, 1944). While Pavlov's procedure demonstrated the role of conflict, and Liddell showed the impact of trauma or punishment in conflict

situations, Masserman (1905-) demonstrated the equally disturbing results where the conflict involved threat associated with a goal. Hungry cats were first permitted to eat, but later subjected to a nerve-shattering blast of air just as they were about to reach the food. This frustrating situation which draws, yet repels, created chronic anxiety, phobia to the extent of self-starvation, and regression (Masserman, 1943).

John B. Watson (1878-1958), the controversial founder of Behaviorism in psychology, expounded the view that all references to "consciousness" must be discarded, that observable behavior was the only critical unit for study, that man should be studied and viewed in the same fashion as the brute animal, and that ultimately, all behavior will be predictable if there is knowledge of what stimuli are presented (Watson, 1919). His major contribution to psychopathology was in his classical laboratory study of Albert, a normal young infant (Watson and Raynor, 1920). Watson reports that Albert was without fears of any type and responded with naive infantile interest when shown a white rat. After some hesitation, Watson assured himself that an experiment in conditioning would be acceptable. For seven trials, Albert was shown the rat but also severely frightened at the same time by the experimenter's sudden banging on a metal bar. This pairing of the neutral cue of the animal with the fear-producing sound followed the traditional Pavlovian model. The outcome: Albert not only became fearful of the little white rat, but also generalized his fear to a rabbit, a dog, a fur coat, and even a ball of wool. Albert did not remain long enough for Watson to continue his study and determine the methods for eliminating the fear. However, Mary Cover Jones (1924), with the advice of Watson, did apply the methods of conditioning to the removal of an animal phobia in a boy named Peter. Young Peter, aged two, showed a remarkable similarity to Albert in his fear of white rats, rabbits, furs, and cotton wool. In her treatment of this modern case of "Peter and the Rabbit," Jones removed the fear of the rabbit by introducing it when Peter was happily engaged in play with three other children. By the forty-fifth session, Peter's tolerance of the rabbit extended to the point where he was actually willing to fondle the animal and allow it to nibble on his fingers without fear. This shift of concern to the problem of the removal of abnormal behavior by application of conditioning methods was applied by Mowrer and Mowrer to enuresis (Mowrer & Mowrer, 1938). Bedwetting, they felt, was attributable to the child's inability to respond to the minimal cues of a full bladder when he is asleep. They believed that a system for awakening the child in response to bladder tension would be extremely valuable. Once awake, the child would naturally inhibit further urination. The problem was therefore to design a method for conditioning the waking response to the bladder tension. The ringing of a bell was selected as the stimulus that would arouse the reflex response, awakening. The apparatus for triggering the bell when bladder tension was high depended upon an electric circuit that was completed by the electrolytic properties of urine. The moment the child released a little urine, it was absorbed by a pad containing the electrical wires, the circuit was completed and the bell rung. Mowrer and Mowrer used this device with 30 children and reported cures in *all* cases. Oddly enough, although progress with the Pavlovian model was impressive, its impact on the field of psychiatry and psychopathology was minimal. Psychiatry was more entranced by the dynamic formulations of Freud and his followers who offered a greater feeling for the "real" substance of

human nature than the apparently sterile, seemingly superficial material of the reflex and behaviorist school. Abnormal behavior was best understood by looking beyond superficial exteriors and delving into the swirls and conflicts in the inner man. Freud himself demonstrated the power of the unconscious, and the error in treating merely the external symptoms. Moreover, psychologists themselves were still debating the value of Behaviorism, and psychological theory was still being revised, refined, and reviewed.

A separate school was soon to develop in the United States. As with classical conditioning, the major initial concern was the understanding of the learning process. Thorndike (1874-1949) initiated the movement in his cat-in-the-box studies by offering some new principles whereby behavior is acquired. Of these, his law of effect is th most famous: behaviors that are *followed* by satisfaction tend to be strengthened, those followed by discomfort are weakened (Thorndike, 1905). The full development of this law was reached in the works of Clark Hull (1884-1952). Hull presented a highly systematic series of principles in the form of postulates regarding behavior (Hull, 1943). These rules of behavioral acquisition and elimination are stated in mathematical and logical statements permitting scientific study. Among his more crucial insights are: the belief that rewards and motivational level influence the strength of a response, the information that the removal of a reward (i.e., reinforcement) leads to the elimination or extinction of the response, the concept that responses are cued by stimuli as a result of the presence of reinforcement, and the view that a response may be weakened or inhibited by repetition without reward, or interference from a competing response. The greatest value of Hullian reinforcement theory was the fact that it encouraged those who wished a theory precise enough to permit predictions, and objective enough to allow for experimental proof or disproof. A commonly raised criticism of Freudian-based analyses of behavior is the difficulty of subjecting its predictions to experimental study. For these critics, the potentials of Hullian theory were enormous as soon as its application to the learning of *all*-types of behavior was accepted. If abnormal *symptoms* could be viewed as abnormal *responses,* and if abnormal responses could be viewed as subject to the same principles of learning as other acquired responses, then the key to the mystery of psychopathology and its development had indeed been found. It will be remembered that the spread of Freudian theory to the field of abnormality was mainly the result of those in the *medical* profession who were specialists in psychopathology, the psychiatrists. The demonstration of the value of reinforcement theory and other forms of learning theory to psychopathology was to come from psychologists interested in abnormal behavior. In many instances, the early impetus came from those psychologists who wished to combine the best insights of Freud with the rigorous qualities of Hull. As psychology developed its own additional insights and confidence in its contributions, other psychologists separated themselves from Freudian foundations and developed ideas and treatment methods based solely on learning theory. Of the former group, pioneers include John Dollard, Neal Miller, O. Hobart Mowrer, and Robert R. Sears. Of the latter, major contributions have come from Hans Eysenck (1916-), B. F. Skinner (1904-), and Joseph Wolpe (1915-).

The learning-oriented theorists have offered a new conception of the origin of abnormality, and more recently, unique approaches to cure. According to Dollard and Miller (1950), neuroses are learned in the same ways that normal behaviors are acquired. A child learns to speak a specific language because in so doing he receives a reward that reduces a drive such as hunger. The child says "I'm hungry" and he is fed. In the same way, a soldier may develop an hysterical paralysis "because" it serves as a need and is reinforcing. It is not necessary that the person *know* what is happening; the soldier may be entirely unaware of the relationship between his symptom and need reduction. In fact, all of the evidence on learning indicates that a behavior, even an annoying symptom, is strengthened as long as reinforcement occurs. In addition, research shows that learning without awareness does occur. In many cases of neuroses, the critical reinforcing event is simply the reduction of anxiety or fears from conflict. As long as the reinforcement continues, the neurotic solutions will persist.

An entirely new psychotherapeutic method has been developed by learning psychologists. Pavlovian representatives stress the reflex quality of certain symptoms and propose classical conditioning methods to establish new more normal reflexes. Mowrer and Mowrer's bedwetting treatment method followed this format. Sears and Cohen (1933), and Hilgard and Marquis (1940) reinstated feeling and movement in two women with hysterical disorders of the arm and hand. Salter (1961) agrees with Pavlov's view that the excess of inhibitory traits serves as a primary cause of symptoms. As a counteractant, he has patients engage in assertive, noninhibitory behaviors. However, the greatest stir of activity has developed out of Hullian orientations. Leaders in this exciting area are Hans Eysenck in England, and Joseph Wolpe originally of South Africa. Eysenck (1960) has been instrumental in bringing about the acceptance of behavioristic psychotherapy through his scholarly publications. Wolpe (1958) has stimulated much attention to the *method* of behavior modification by introducing the psychotherapy of "reciprocal inhibition." Wolpe devised by far the most widely used and most successful form of behavior therapy for phobias. He reports a case of a woman who was so fearful of traffic that she would panic at the mere sight of an approaching car as much as a block away. She was treated by systematic desensitization: a method for counteracting the fear response by evoking an incompatible response of relaxation. The patient was asked to provide a ranked list of fear-fear situation on the list. Although a complete life history could have been available that would have been considered highly important to a Freudian therapist, this material was of no relevance to the behavioristic therapist.

Within five months she was completely free not only from the fear but also from headaches that she had been having as a result of emotional tension. Behavior therapy has been successfully used for a variety of pathological conditions: negative practice (based on the inhibition ideas of Hull) was used by Dunlap (1932) and Yates (1958) on tics and obsessive-compulsive behavior; reinforcement conditioning cured a functionally blind man (Brady and Lind, 1961) and a five-year-old girl who suffered from anorexia nervosa (White, 1959); and both adult (Isaacs, et al., 1960) and child (Ferster and DeMyer, 1961) psychotics have shown gains after behavior therapy.

Glossary

Abreaction: The expression of charged emotions.

Analytic psychology: Founded by Jung as a theory of personality.

Anorexia nervosa: The lack of appetite for food leading to starvation.

Autistic: The tendency to misperceive or to think in ways that are more in accordance with wishfulness than with reality.

Baquet: A device of mirrors and rods used by Mesmer to bring about mesmerism.

Bedlam: Corruption of the name Bethlehem, and referring to the asylum St. Mary of Bethlehem.

Behaviorism: A school of psychology emphasizing the observable, nonsubjective aspects of humans.

Behavior therapy: A group of psychological therapies based on the belief that maladjustment is learned and can be eliminated in accordance with the principles of learning.

Catatonia: A psychotic condition marked by extreme lethargy, and immobility, alternating with excitability.

Catharsis: The discharge of emotional tension by reliving or talking out repressed material.

Chromosome: Structures within body cells which are present in pairs and which are composed of substances, *genes,* involved in hereditary transmission.

Client-centered psychotherapy: The psychological treatment based on the theory of Carl Rogers which stresses the strengths of the individual and his capability to develop toward adjustment.

Clinical psychology: The area of psychology specializing in the identification and treatment of mental illness.

Conditioning: A form of learning whereby a stimulus becomes associated with a response by being paired with the original stimulus eliciting the response.

Contiguity: Being next to or near another event or object in time or space. A principle of learning that suggests that events near to one another become strongly associated.

Delirium: A state involving mental confusion, disorientation, restlessness, and often hallucinations.

Dementia praecox: Early term for schizophrenia, an illness characterized by social withdrawal, thought disturbance, and emotional blunting. Dementia praecox was once believed to be an affliction of youth.

Demonology: The belief that spirit sources external to man are the source of events.

Determinism: A belief that all events can be explained or understood by examining their antecedents.

Diagnosis: The identification of the nature and extent of a specific illness.

Disease entity hypothesis: The belief that mental illnesses are analogous to physical diseases in that each has symptoms which cluster together, a causative factor, a distinctive course, and a predictable outcome.

Electrolytic: The capability of carrying an electrical current through chemical action.

Empiricism: The valuing of facts derived from experience rather than relying upon theory or speculation.

Endogenous: Originating from within the individual.

Enuresis: Wetting of the bed through uncontrolled discharge of urine.

Epilepsy: A condition involving convulsions and sometimes disturbance in consciousness, associated with abnormal brain wave patterns.

Euphoria: An exaggerated sense of well-being and happiness.

Exogenous: Originating from factors external to the individual.

Exorcism: Religious rituals for casting out the demons believed to be present in possessed persons.

Extinction: The weakening or elimination of a response.

Family psychotherapy: The psychological treatment of members of the family instead of the single patient with the symptoms.

Free association: A technique used in psychoanalysis involving the reporting of thoughts immediately upon their arousal and without censorship.

General paresis: An organic type of mental illness caused by syphilitic infection.

Group psychotherapy: The psychological treatment of patients in a group setting.

Hallucination: A sensory disturbance in which a sensory experience appears but without an appropriate external stimulus.

Histology: The study of the structure of bodily tissues.

Hysteria: A previous term for conversion reaction, a form of mental illness characterized by bodily symptoms without an organic foundation.

Ideational: Pertaining to thoughts or ideas.

Individual psychology: Founded by Adler as a theory of personality.

Instinct: A pattern of behavior which is present in all animals in the same species and is unlearned.

Lamarkian genetics: A theory that acquired human characteristics may be transmitted genetically.

Law of effect: The principle that an organism learns those responses followed by a satisfying event and eliminates those followed by discomfort.

Learning theorists: Those who rely upon the principles of learning to understand human behavior.

Mania: A condition involving excitability and impulsive behavior.

Manic-depressive psychosis: A type of mental illness characterized by exaggerated mood states. The patient may show euphoria and excitability, depression and inhibition, or alternating cycles of both.

Melancholia: A form of mental illness characterized by severe depression.

Mesmerism: Now known as hypnotism. Originally introduced by Anton Mesmer as a means of curing illnesses through animal magnetism.

Neuron theory: The belief that the neuron is the basic histological and metabolic unit of the nervous tissue.

Obsessive-compulsive behavior: Maladaptive behavior involving repetitiousness of ideas or activities.

Organic viewpoint: The theory that organic factors are the cause of all mental illnesses.

Pathology: The study of diseased or abnormal conditions. Sometimes used to refer to these conditions themselves.

Phobia: A psychoneurotic reaction characterized by excessive, irrational fears.

Phrenology: A procedure attempting to distinguish personality traits by the examination of topological features of the cranium.

Physiognomy: A procedure attempting to identify personality traits by the examination of the facial features.

Possession: An archaic belief that deviant behavior was due to the presence of an evil spirit possessing the patient. Sometimes present in contemporary superstitions among primitive peoples.

Post partum psychosis: (Puerperal psychosis) A psychotic condition precipitated by childbirth.

Psychiatrist: A medical specialist in the identification and treatment of mental illness. All psychiatrists are medical doctors.

Psychiatry: An area of medicine devoted to the identification and treatment of mental illnesses.

Psychoanalysis: Founded by Freud, and referring to either a theory of personality or a special psychotherapeutic approach.

Psychodynamic: The complex interaction between emotions, motivations, and behaviors underlying normal or abnormal patterns.

Psychoneurosis: A form of mental illness involving anxiety that is experienced or defended against. Personality disorganization or loss of contact with reality is not present.

Psychopathology: The study of abnormal behaviors, their causes and characteristics. Sometimes used to refer to the psychological disorders themselves.

Psychopharmacology: The study of the effects of chemicals on mental processes, or the treatment of mental illness through the use of drugs.

Psychophysical methods: An experimental procedure for quantifying human experience.

Psychosis: A form of mental illness involving loss of contact with reality, severe personality disorganization, sensory distortion, and lack of insight. Hospitalization is often required.

Psychosomatic medicine: An area of medical practice concerned with the diseases which are attributable to emotional stresses.

Psychotherapy: A method for treatment of mental illness by psychological techniques.

Reciprocal inhibition: A behavior therapy involving the elimination of maladaptive responses by the development of competing adaptive behavior.

Regression: The return to behaviors appropriate for a previous stage of maturity.

Reinforcement: An event that increases the strength of a response when it is presented following the response.

Reinforcement theory: A theory based on the idea that responses can be modified through the use of reinforcement.

Repression: The exclusion of threatening material from conscious awareness.

Spirochete: A microorganism shaped like a corkscrew. The spirochete *Treponema pallidum* is the cause of syphilitic infection.

Systematic desensitization: A behavior therapy involving the elimination of maladaptive responses by the development of competing adaptive behavior.

Tics: Involuntary spasms or muscle twitches.

Trauma: Medically, a severe injury or blow; psychologically, a severe stress.

Trephining: A primitive surgical method involving entering the skull with a crude instrument.

Unconscious: A premise that indicates that behaviors may be motivated by forces of which the individual is unaware.

References

Abraham, K. Dream and myths. *Nerv. ment. dis. Monogr. Series,* 1913, No. 15.

Adler, A. *The practice and theory of individual psychology.* New York: Harcourt, Brace, 1927.

Arnold, T. *Observations on the nature, kinds, causes and prevention of insanity.* London, 1806.

Aubin, *Cruels effets de la vengeance du Cardinal Richelieu ou Histoire de diables de Loudun.* Amsterdam, 1716.

Bacon, F. *Novum organum sive indica de interpretatione naturae.* London, 1620.

Bailly, J. *Rapport des commissaires chargés par le roi, de l'éxamen du magnétisme animal.* Paris: L'imprimerie royale, 1784.

Berkeley, G. *An essay toward a new theory of vision.* Dublin, 1709.

Bernheim, H. *De la suggestion et de ses applications à la thérapeutique.* Paris, 1886.

Bleuler, E. *Dementia Praecox oder die Gruppe der Schizophrenien.* Leipzig, 1911.

Brady, J., and Lind, D. Experimental analysis of hysterical blindness. *Arch. gen. Psychiat.,* 1961, 4, 331.

Braid, J. *Neurypnology, or the rationale of nervous sleep.* London: Churchill, 1843.

Bramwell, J. *Hypnotism, its history, practice and theory.* Philadelphia: Lippincott, 1930.

Breuer, J., and Freud, S. *Studien über Hysterie.* Vienna, 1895.

Celsus, A. C. *De re medica.*

Charcot, J. Essai d'une distinction nosographique des divers états compris sous le nom d'hypnotisme. *Compt. rend. acad. Sc.,* 1882, 44.

Descartes, R. *Passions of the soul.* Amsterdam, 1649.

Dollard, J., and Miller, N. *Personality and psychotherapy: an analysis in terms of learning, thinking and culture.* New York: McGraw-Hill, 1950.

Dunbar, F. *Emotions and bodily changes.* New York: Columbia University Press, 1954.

Dunlap, K. *Habits: their making and unmaking.* New York: Liveright, 1932.

Erhard, J. Über die Melancholie. In Wagner's *Beitr. zur phil. Anthro.* Vienna, 1794-1796.

Eysenck, H. *Behaviour therapy and the neuroses.* New York: Pergamon, 1960.

Ferster, C., and DeMyer, M. The development of performances in autistic children in an automatically controlled environment. *J. ch. Dis.,* 1961, 13, 312.

Fort, G. *Medical economy during the Middle Ages.* New York, 1883.

Freud, S. *The standard edition of the complete psychological works.* J. Strachey (Ed.). London: Hogarth Press, 1953.

Freud, S. *Leonardo Da Vinci: a study in psychosexuality.* New York: Random House, 1947. (First German edition, 1910.)

Fromm, E. *The sane society.* New York: Rinehart, 1955.

Fromm-Reichman, F. *Principles of intensive psychotherapy.* Chicago: University of Chicago Press, 1950.

Gall, F. *Sur les fonctions du cerveau.* Paris: Baillière, 1825.

Hilgard, E., and Marquis, D. *Conditioning and learning.* New York: Appleton-Century-Crofts, 1940.

Horney, K. *Our inner conflicts.* New York: Norton, 1945.

Hull, C. *Principles of behavior.* New York: Appleton-Century-Crofts, 1943.

Isaacs, W., Thomas, J., and Goldiamond, I. Application of operant conditioning to reinstate verbal behavior in psychotics. *J. speech hear. Disorder,* 1960, **25**, 8.

Isensee, E. *Geschichte der Medicin,* Part II, Book 6. Berlin, 1845.

Janet, P. *L'état mental des hystériques.* Paris, 1911.

Jones, M. C. A laboratory study of fear: the case of Peter. *Pedagog. Sem.,* 1924, **31**, 308.

Jones, W. *Hippocrates.* Cambridge, Mass.: Harvard University Press, 1959.

Jung, C. *Collected works.* New York: Pantheon Press, 1953.

Kardiner, A., Linton, R., DuBois, C., and West, J. *The psychological frontiers of society.* New York: Columbia University Press, 1945.

Kraepelin, E. *Lehrbuch der psychiatrie.* Germany, 1883.

Lavater, J. Physiognomische fragmente zur Beförderung der Menschenkenntniss und Menschenliebe von Johann Casper Lavater. Leipzig: 1775.

Liddell, H. Conditioned reflex method and experimental neurosis. In J. Hunt (Ed.) *Personality and the behavior disorders: Vol. 1.* New York: Ronald Press, 1944.

Liebault, A. *Du Somneil et des états analogues considérés surtout au point de vue de l'action du moral sur le physique.* Paris: Masson, 1866.

Locke, J. Essay concerning human understanding (1700). In J. St. John (Ed.), *The Philosophical works of John Locke.* London: Bell & Sons, 1913.

Masserman, J. *Behavior and neurosis: an experimental psychoanalytic approach to psycho-biologic principles.* Chicago: University of Chicago Press, 1943.

Mowrer, O., and Mowrer, W. Enuresis: A method for its study and treatment. *Amer. J. Orthopsychiat.,* 1938, **8**, 436.

Pavlov, I. *Lectures on the work of the principal digestive glands,* 1897.

Pavlov, I. *Lectures on conditioned reflexes.* Moscow and Leningrad: State Publishing House, 1904.

Plater, F. *De partium corporis humani structura.* Basel, 1583.

Plato. *Republic.*

Rank, O. *The trauma of birth.* New York: Harcourt, Brace, 1929.

Salter, A. *Conditioned reflex therapy.* New York: Putnam, 1961.

Sears, R., and Cohen, L. Hysterical anesthesia, analgesia, and astereognosis. *A.M.A. Arch. neurol. Psychiat.,* 1933, **29**, 260.

Sullivan, H. S. *The interpersonal theory of psychiatry.* New York: Norton, 1953.

Summers, M. (transl.) of Sprenger, J. & Kraemer, H. *Malleus malificarum.* London: Rodker, 1928.

Thorndike, E. *The elements of psychology.* New York: Seiler, 1905.

Vives, J. *De Anima et vita.* Basel, 1538.

Watson, J. *Psychology from the standpoint of a behaviorist.* Philadelphia: Lippincott, 1919.

Watson, J., and Raynor, R. Conditioned emotional reactions. *J. exp. Psychol.,* 1920, 3, 1.

Weyer, J. *Histoires, disputes et discours des illusions et impostures des diables, etc.* Vol. I. Paris: Bibliothèque Diabolique, 1886.

White, J. The use of learning theory in the psychological treatment of children. *J. clin. Psychol.,* 1959, **15**, 227.

Wolpe, J. *Psychotherapy by reciprocal inhibition.* Stanford: Stanford University Press, 1958.

Yates, A. The application of learning theory to the treatment of tics. *J. abnorm. soc. Psychol.,* 1958, **56**, 175.

Zilboorg, G., and Henry, G. *A history of medical psychology.* New York: Norton, 1941.

2 *Introduction to the Abnormal Personality*

SOME COMMONLY ENCOUNTERED MISCONCEPTIONS

The history in Chapter 1 indicates that the abnormal person has always been with us. The ability to identify abnormal behavior has not always been associated with understanding. In one period of modern man's history, the abnormal person was viewed with suspicion, superstition, and horror. Although much of the superstitious fear has been swept away by modern science, some misconceptions still persist regarding abnormality. Some of these misconceptions are spread by well-meaning people who lack facts, others are accepted as explanations by those with a great anxiety to know something about the unknown, while still others are perpetuated by those with an eye toward the commercial appeal of the melodramatic.

Several of the rather common misconceptions that continue in spite of facts to the contrary are given below.

1. FALLACY: The abnormal person is strange, violent, a different breed from the normal person.

FACT: Only the severely disturbed exhibit behavior that is not like that of normal persons, and even such disturbed people have frequent periods of highly normal behavior. The belief that the abnormal person is strangely different is probably a remnant of the earlier beliefs in demoniacal possession, which stressed that the possessed individual was in fact "not himself" and certainly "not human." There is more reason to believe that many of the characteristics of abnormal persons are also shown by normals, for example, severe depression or obsessive-compulsive behavior. In fact, Freud himself has written about the "abnormal" behavior shown in normals in a treatise called *The Psychopatho'ogy of Everyday Life* (1938). The difference between the behavior of abnormals and that of normals is mainly in intensity and appropriateness rather than in quality or type. Thus, compulsive behavior may be shown in some degree by a bank teller in his everyday dealings with large sums of money. Similarly, children often show compulsive characteristics in their play at certain age levels. A depression is a normal display of emotion following a serious loss and, in fact, the *lack* of appropriate grief and mourning would be considered abnormal.

2. FALLACY: Because the abnormal person is different from you and me, they

must be reacted to differently, for example, pampered, humored along.

FACT: Although it is true that the severely disturbed person is likely to be hypersensitive and often misinterprets or misperceives the actions and motives of others, nevertheless, even the most severely ill person will appreciate being treated normally, without fear, without cringing, without extra-special treatment. Pinel's success with the "violent" soldier was a dramatic example of this (Zilboorg and Henry, 1941). Even normal individuals will resent being "handled" and will feel concerned if others appear tense in their presence. Anxiety breeds anxiety, aversion fosters withdrawal, fearfulness encourages resentment.

3. FALLACY: Mental illness is a sign of weakness, something inherent that affects the nerves, a defect in character or in will power.

FACT: In fact, mental illness is a function of many circumstances interacting, such as the person's early experiences, learning conditions, perhaps emotional makeup, stresses, etc. Evidence indicates that even the strongest have breaking points, as seen in combat fatigue. There are some illnesses where the premise of a defect is being theorized, such as in early infantile autism, but even here the view is that the person has a *predisposition* to react unfavorably under certain abnormal family conditions—the interaction between temperament and home environment are *both* considered necessary for the symptoms to appear. An analogy will be helpful: people differ in the number of tasks they can attend to at a time; some can carry on a conversation and read a newspaper at the same time, others can only do one or the other. It would be erroneous to suggest that the one person is weak or exhibits a defect. Similarly, it is misleading to consider a neurotic weak because of his neurosis; he

may be ineffective in life problems, or inefficient, but no "weaker" than the person who happens to process information at a slower rate.

4. FALLACY: All mental illnesses are inherited; a person is born crazy and will transmit his insanity to his offspring.

FACT: Only amaurotic idiocy (Tay-Sachs disease), phenylketonuria, and Huntington's chorea have been definitely proved to be genetically transmitted. The former two represent cases of mental retardation, the last is a form of neurological deterioration first traced by an American country doctor. There is a strong movement to treat manic-depressive psychosis and schizophrenia as inherited illnesses, but the evidence is still controversial and the topic remains an open question. To date, none of the neuroses have been considered inherited.

5. FALLACY: Mental illness is incurable; even if the symptoms diminish, the person will never be the same again.

FACT: Cures do occur. And *permanent* cures do occur. The incidence of recovery varies with the nature of the disorder, as well as with other facets of the problem. There is increasing evidence that infantile autism is responsive to certain modes of treatment, and recovery from the major nonorganic psychoses is common. Of course, only limited recovery is possible where there are metabolic changes, genetic anomalies, or cerebral injuries. In most instances, control is feasible through drugs and physical therapy which provide temporary relief while the patient is participating in more permanent forms of treatment. The greatest issues involve the prevention of mental illness, and the determination of the best mode of treatment for each type of special disturbance.

6. FALLACY: The insane can be normal if they only try or exercise their will-power.

FALLACY: The mentally disturbed person is helpless and will recover only if someone does something *to* him.

FACT: The above two fallacies are grouped together since they represent opposite ends of the same misconception about what is needed for recovery. The first assumes that the patient will recover through his own efforts, and stresses the lack of self-motivation. The second indicates that the "spirit is willing but the flesh is weak," and the patient is seen as a passive recipient of psychological medication. Neither viewpoint is correct. The neurotic firmly wishes he were different and could rid himself of energy-consuming fears and tensions. Frequently, his feelings are triggered off by circumstances which he cannot identify. Even if he tried his utmost to change, his path would be blocked by unconscious determinants such as conflicts. Masserman's (1943) cats would have been delighted to rid themselves of their conflict and settle down to a tension-free meal and a placid nap. It is sometimes appropriate to speak of "secondary-gains," that is, fringe rewards which sometimes accompany abnormal symptoms such as the sympathy or attention the patient receives. However, the conscious desire to get rid of the symptom is more characteristic of the sufferer.

The opposite belief is often implicitly maintained by those who seek therapeutic help. Patients and family alike desire a quick and simple solution whereby the burden would be magically absolved and vanish. We all wish to be cured when we are afflicted with a physical ailment, but we reject the bad tasting medicine that is required, or the restrictive diet, or the lengthy treatment. Similarly, the neurotic may harbor a desire for a painless and effortless cure without having to work through his anxieties, develop new ways of relating, face his fears, or join in extensive therapy. The view that the patient is not responsible for his illness is expressed on a sophisticated level by those who maintain that the patient is solely a victim of his environment, his culture, his background, and so forth. The fact is that even with drug and shock therapies where something is *done to* the patient, follow-up participation by the patient in psychotherapy is needed to prevent recurrence and to maximize gains.

7. FALLACY: The abnormal person develops differently from the normal person. The development of a normal life follows a different process from the development of an abnormal life.

FACT: Modern evidence suggests that the rules and principles governing the development of abnormal behavior are the same as those associated with normal development. Freud's classic discussion of the "pathology" of everyday life is again pertinent. Unconscious wishes affect normal behavior as well as lead to abnormal symptoms. Forgetting a despised person's name occurs through the same process as the pathological forgetting in fugue states. The experimental psychopathologists and learning psychologists (Dollard and Miller, 1950, Bandura and Walters, 1963) have also demonstrated that much of abnormal behavior is learned in the same way as normal behavior is learned. There is no more mystery about why a superstitious belief persists than there is about why a person continues to play the slot machine in the face of heavy losses; both continue because of intermittent reinforcement. Physicians have long studied the abnormal body to understand the functioning of the normal body, psychologists are now understanding the psychology of the abnormal through their knowledge of the normal human psychology.

8. FALLACY: Abnormality and creativity or intellectual genius go hand in hand.

FACT: There is little reason to believe that the creative person or the intelligent person is more susceptible to mental illness. In fact, evidence gathered systematically over forty years on the intellectually gifted demonstrate their greater *resistance* to mental illness (Terman and Oden, 1959). In addition, intensive studies of the creative person, such as the creative writers seen at the Institute for Personality Research in Berkeley (1961; also Barron, 1963), are characterized by greater resources for maintaining psychological health than their less creative peers. It is a moot question as to whether Van Gogh was creative *because* he was disturbed, or whether he was creative *and* later disturbed. The drugged experiences of Coleridge may have been no more than the medium through which he expressed himself. Psychotherapy has as much potential for releasing creative energies as it has for diverting them.

9. FALLACY: Insanity is caused entirely by the stresses of civilization. There are cultures free from the blight of mental illness.

FACT: Although early explorations tended to suggest that an "ideal" illness-free culture does exist in a group known as the Hutterites (Eaton and Weil, 1955), more careful study proved otherwise. Differences do seem to exist in the type of symptoms or the form of the illness, for example, modern-day man has incorporated the television set into his delusions. However, there is little chance that a truly neuroses- or psychoses-free environment will be discovered.

10. FALLACY: All mentally ill persons are mentally retarded.

FACT: Mental illness tends to drain energies and resources; the anxieties become the primary focus of attention and divert problem-solving efforts away from more appropriate issues at hand, and in extreme cases, the patient is so out of contact with reality that he appears to be intellectually incompetent. With the ex-

ception of the abnormalities associated with neurological deterioration, the mentally ill person does not lose his intellectual capacities. On the other hand, his ability to effectively and efficiently make use of his abilities may be blocked, interfered with, or masked by his psychological concerns.

The lower intelligence test scores sometimes seen in a depressed patient reflect the inability of the patient to feel interested enough to perform at his best level. Once the depression lifts, the cognitive tasks may again represent a meaningful challenge, and the test scores are improved. In cases of paranoia, the intellect is often enlisted by the patient in support of his delusion, and except for the initial assumption, the delusional material is logically quite sound.

11. FALLACY: All mentally ill persons are irrational.

FACT: Only in the severely disturbed, the psychotic, is there any reason to stress the reasoning power of the patient. In the schizophrenias, logical thinking is disturbed, private rules for drawing conclusions are established, and personal associations replace culturally agreed-upon definitions. However, *paranoia* is a type of mental illness that is characterized by retention of rational thought. In addition, other forms of psychoses are characterized more by the inappropriateness or flightiness of ideas than by lack of reason. Moreover, many psychotics show prolonged periods of highly normal behavior, demonstrating their symptoms only when emotionally charged topics are introduced. It is instructive to distinguish between *irrationality* and *inappropriateness:* irrational behavior involves thought processes that fail to follow the accepted rules of reason or logic; inappropriate behavior is behavior that does not fit or is unsuited to the circumstance at hand. There are fewer cases of abnormality where the *process* of thinking, that is, reasoning, is affected and more where the *appropriateness* of the behavior is in question. For example, a neurotic who has an extreme fear of open spaces can rationally discuss the inappropriateness of the phobia. His thinking is clear, and his arguments rational. Yet, he retains an emotional reaction that is entirely inappropriate to the situation.

WHAT IS ABNORMAL BEHAVIOR?

The problem of defining abnormal behavior has not been a simple one. Attempts to provide suitable definitions have included a *statistical* definition, a *cultural* definition, and a *legal* definition.

The *statistical* definition depends on a mathematical model shown by the normal distribution curve. This curve represents the frequency, or incidence, of appearance of a characteristic among a large group of people. The curve is typically said to be bell-shaped, with a bulge at the middle, tapering off at the extremes. Most people, for example, are between 5 and 6 feet in height with fewer and fewer people either shorter or taller than this "average" height. There *are* people who do fall at these extremes and who may therefore be considered as statistically deviant or abnormal. These abnormal persons are the dwarfs or giants seen in carnivals. By the

statistical definition, therefore, any person who is "average" is normal, and anyone who is deviant from the average is abnormal. Any human characteristic that can be identified and measured can be subjected to this type of analysis by simply counting up the numbers of people showing degrees of the characteristic. It is possible to speak of those who are "abnormally" tall, "abnormally" small, as well as those with "abnormal" blood pressure readings or body temperatures.

The main problem with the statistical definition is exemplified in viewing intelligence. Normal curves can be and, in fact, are calculated for intelligence scores (see Fig. 2-1). Most people have average intellectual ability reflected in I.Q. test scores of 100. Relatively fewer people achieve scores far below 100, and relatively few obtain scores far above 100. It makes some sense to consider the low scorers as in a sense "abnormal" for these are the mental defectives. However, by the statistical model, the intellectually gifted would also be considered "abnormal" since they are deviant from the average. Clearly, this would be a misnomer.

In addition, the statistical definition suffers from the fact that high incidence of a trait is not necessarily an index of health. Cancer and heart disease afflict great numbers in our society. Influenza

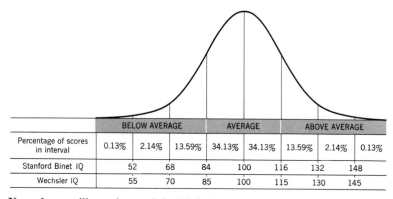

Figure 2-1. Normal curve illustrating statistical definition of normal (average) intelligence.

and the common cold occur frequently enough to be considered the "average" illnesses during winter. Neuroses plague millions. Yet none of these conditions would be accepted as normal simply by virtue of frequency.

A second definition is the *cultural* definition of abnormality. In a sense, it is statistical since it is partly dependent upon numbers of people. But, where the statistical definition involves the number of people who *possess* the trait, the cultural definition involves the trait *accepted* by the greatest number of people. In this sense, a trait that appears with high frequency may still be considered abnormal if the majority of people in the culture so agree. Thus, the problem of the statistical approach is resolved. In the American culture, hallucinations, homosexuality, exaggerated suspiciousness, and irrational violence are all treated as symptoms of abnormality. For those who belong to the society, these are such "obvious" indications of abnormal behavior that the handling of people with such traits has been turned over to the law. The strength of the cultural definition lies in its societal consensus, yet this is also the source of its greatest weakness for entirely opposite behaviors can be found in cultures only short distances away in space or time. Hallucinations and trance states were normal among the Plains Indians and the Yogis; the world of Plato admired homosexuality as a sign of virility; the natives of Dobu are by nature filled with suspicion; and the tribe of Malays once called Amuco were so noted for the frenzied attack of their warriors that they are remembered in the English language ("to run amok"). The immense influence of the Inquisition over the beliefs of the masses, and today's sweeping waves of fads in styles and songs are convincing enough evidence that cultural consensus can be misleading. In fact, a new viewpoint called psychosocial medicine has been developed to study the health of societies, based on the premise that sick individuals are merely representative of sick societies.

In the United States, prosecution of criminal cases upholds the principle that the accused is still a citizen with rights, including the right to a just decision whether or not he is convicted. If the accused is mentally "insane" then it is his right to be so treated. Because of this critical issue, *legal definitions* of abnormality have evolved through the courts. The definition of criminal responsibility prevailing in the United States is known as the M'Naghten Rule (1843) and states that the insane person suffers "such a defect of reason . . . as not to know the nature and quality of the act he was doing or if he did know it that he did not know he was doing what was wrong." The M'Naghton Rule is the final result of one of the most famous forensic-psychiatric cases in Anglo-American law, the trial of Daniel M'Naghton. M'Naghton shot and killed Drummond, private secretary to Sir Robert Peel, the man M'Naghton really intended to kill. The jury found him not guity by reason of insanity, and the defendant was sent to a mental institution where he eventually died after twenty-two years of incarceration. In some states the *irresistable impulse* definition is acceptable as a defense providing that the temporary disturbance prevented the accused from exercising his free will or his ability to restrain himself. Psychiatrists themselves have rejected both definitions; the former because it focused entirely on the reason to the exclusion of emotional factors, the latter because it failed to give recognition to types of mental illnesses characterized by brooding and reflection, e.g., as in the case of Sirhan Sirhan, Senator Kennedy's assassin. Moreover, psychiatric experts felt called upon to answer questions that were not within their field on such issues as malice, intent to commit crime, right versus wrong, and morality. On the whole, it has been felt that courts have been too judgment-oriented by trying to set up rules or "tests" of a person's mental state. Mental illness should be diagnosed by a psychiatric specialist in accordance with psychiatric criteria and not legal rules; the jury's responsibility should be limited to the disposition of the case. It should be noted that this is the case under a noncriminal proceeding, the *commitment*. The exact process differs from state to state, but generally one or two physicians certify that the patient belongs in a mental hospital. The qualifications of these physicians are carefully prescribed by law, as are the persons permitted to petition for commitment. Typically, the decision is made by the judge on the basis of the physician's medical opinion and certifying evidence.

A number of other approaches have also been offered in attempts to define abnormality.

1. *Subjective pain*—An abnormal person is sometimes seen as an individual who is in psychological pain. He is subjectively uncomfortable, feels tense or unhappy, is troubled or in conflict. His exterior behavior may or may not reflect his feeling state: he may *appear* outwardly calm but *feel* inwardly upset, or he may show exactly how he feels. This approach to defining abnormality must rely heavily on the ability of the person to express how he feels. In fact, if the individual behaves in a deviant fashion but feels little or no subjective discomfort, then he would be considered normal. Such a definition, of course, runs into difficulty in dealing with pathologies where exaggerated euphoria prevails or where the individual loses touch with or is isolated from his own emotions.

2. *Irrationality or unpredictability*—A person may be judged as abnormal if his behavior is seemingly irrational or un-predictable. Basically, this means that the observer, from what he knows of the circumstances, finds himself unable to find any logic or meaning to the actions of the patient. The abnormal person is considered "out of his mind," and the implication is that reason has been replaced by disruptive emotionality. Incoherent speech is often accepted as a sign of irrationality since speech reflects thought processes and is based on some logical rules. This definition becomes inadequate in cases where the patient's behavior becomes quite logical when his frame of mind is understood, for example, acting secretively when confronted by a stranger may seem irrational, until it is explained that the visitor was mistaken for a bill collector. In paranoia, too much rationality is exhibited in that affected persons go through excessive and detailed deductions; a man may accuse his wife of faithlessness upon noting that the gas mileage was lower one week, thus implying that she had traveled faster to get home on time because she had been visiting another man.

3. *Undergoing psychiatric treatment*—A person may be considered to be abnormal if he voluntarily or involuntarily seeks treatment. By this approach, it is suggested that "only sick people need therapy." At one time, and in some cultures, this is generally true since seeking out a therapist is perceived as an admission of a problem. In the past, one did not call on a physician unless ill health was involved. However, current attitudes encourage such checkups more to certify health than to restore health, to prevent illness instead of to cure illness. For some, appointments with mental health personnel may be made for the sake of clarifying one's goals in life. For others, the purpose of a psychiatric consultation may be to prove sanity for legal matters. Thus, simply being in treatment may not be evidence of abnormality. In fact, some workers feel that the nature of psycho-

therapy and its goals are changing such that "treatment" may be directed toward bettering the interpersonal skills of normal persons.

4. *The ipsative definition*—Typically, the statistical approach compares the traits of a person against its appearance in other people; if it is uncommon or rarely appears in most other people, then the trait might be considered deviant or abnormal. This is called a *normative* approach. By the *ipsative* method, the person is compared against himself, perhaps because the trait in question is so idiosyncratic that there is no value in comparing that person with others. A person, for example, may have a high pulse rate as a standing characteristic, yet be perfectly healthy. In order to tell whether this individual is showing an abnormal pulse rate in the future, it is necessary to compare the rate with that which is normal *for this person*. Parents are always aware of behavior that is uncharacteristic for their child and therefore symptomatic, such as a sudden disinterest in communicating in a normally verbose youngster. A major problem of the ipsative approach is the fact that there are certain allowable limits to individual differences which are accepted. Extreme idiosyncracy becomes deviancy. Friends of a mentally retarded person may attest to the fact that "he was below average in doing things all through his life"; however, this consistency of behavior does not change the fact that such behavior is retarded and not normal.

THE CLASSIFICATION OF ABNORMAL BEHAVIOR

The previous section dealt with the general rules for defining abnormality. Once a set of rules has been agreed upon for determining which behaviors are deviant, it is then meaningful to refer to such behaviors as *symptoms*. Symptoms are subjective or objective characteristics which can be considered as signs of illness. The classification of such symptoms into orderly groups has been a task of great concern to many professional workers. Such classification could provide a useful means for identifying different types of disorders, as well as suggesting a variety of cues regarding the possible causation and treatment for such disorders. The achievement of a completely satisfactory classification scheme has thus far eluded psychopathologists. The American Psychiatric Association (1968) engaged in a major effort to arrive at a consistent classification that could serve as a standard method for use all over the United States. This approach serves as the general basis for the classification of the mentally ill in American mental hospitals today. Although this scheme has had wide acceptance, it has nevertheless been subject to criticism. Some, for example, maintain that the classification relies too heavily on the disease entity notion, the assumption that mental illness is akin to physical disease in that symptoms can be identified, specific causative factors exist for each type of illness, and a predictable course of symptom development will occur. Such critics are concerned that the *illness* analogy might be stretched too far, and that the "mentally sick" will be viewed as a person infected by some foreign virus or substance, or treatment would be devoted solely to doing something *to the patient* instead of attending to familial or interpersonal relationships, cultural, or other external factors (see Zigler & Phillips, 1961; Szasz, 1961; Sarason & Ganzer, 1968). Significant changes in classification is a certainty in the future, for example, the possibility that schizophrenia must be viewed as encompassing two distinctly different types, the process schizophrenias (caused by organic factors) and the reactive schizophrenias (caused by environmental stress factors).

A variety of new classification schemes

have been offered (e.g., Bandura, 1968; Cattell, 1957; Eysenck, 1952; Staats & Staats, 1963; Thorne, 1953; Wittman & Sheldon, 1948), but none has yet reached the wide adoption of the American Psychiatric Association model. Thus far, the official scheme of the American Psychiatric Association has proved valuable in differentiating reasonably well among the mental disorders, in covering fairly comprehensively the types of conditions afflicting American patients, and in providing significant clues regarding treatment. This classification scheme, with some modifications,* will form the basis for this text. The major groups of disorders are as follows:

I. **Disorders of Psychological (Psychogenic) Origin.** These are conditions in which there is no proven physical cause or brain pathology.

A. *The Psychoneurotic Disorders:* These are very prevalent disorders generally characterized by anxiety which is either directly experienced or controlled by defense mechanisms. There is no gross distortion of reality, no disorganization of personality, and hospitalization is ordinarily not required. Among the neuroses are:

>Traumatic neuroses
>Anxiety reaction
>Hypochondriasis
>Conversion reaction
>Dissociative reactions

Phobias
Obsessive-compulsive neurosis
Reactive depression

B. *The Psychophysiologic Disorders:* These are conditions characterized by structural changes in the body attributable to emotional disturbances. Among the psychophysiologic reactions are:

>Skin reactions
>Musculoskeletal reactions
>Respiratory reactions
>Cardiovascular reactions
>Gastrointestinal reactions

C. *The Conduct Disorders:* These are conditions characterized by the tendency to act out conflict through behaviors that violate the code of conduct of the society. Little, if any, anxiety is experienced. Impairment of personality development rather than severe emotional stress is the apparent cause. Among the conduct disorders are:

>Antisocial reactions
>Dyssocial reactions
>Addictions
>Sexual deviations

D. *The Psychotic Disorders:* These are conditions characterized by profound disturbance and disability, often requiring hospitalization. Loss of contact with reality and sensory distortions often occur. In addition, there may be a lack of insight into the nature and severity of the disturbance by the patient. Among the psychotic disorders are:

>Affective disorders
>Paranoid disorders
>Schizophrenic disorders

II. **Disorders of Organic Origin.** These are conditions caused by impairment of brain functioning. Among the organic disorders are those resulting from:

>Infections
>Toxic factors
>Traumas (head injuries)
>Aging
>Convulsive reactions

---

* The classification terminology used in this text and outlined in the appendix follows more closely the diagnostic scheme first published by the American Psychiatric Association in 1952. Most of the research on psychopathology and a majority of the theoretical literature were based on this earlier standard. In addition, most of the clinicians and practitioners are familiar with the 1952 classification or minor modifications of it. A final reason for using the earlier guidelines is the fact that the newer version has apparently created more controversy than ready acceptance (Fish, 1969; Jackson, 1969; McCall, 1969; Menninger, 1969; Talbott, 1969).

III. **Mental Retardation.** These are conditions involving a significant deficit in intellectual functioning or development. Among the types of mental retardation are those resulting from:

>Infections
>Traumas
>Disorders of metabolism, growth, or nutrition
>Prenatal influence

These different types of disorders will be discussed in detail in Part III of this book. The general evidence regarding the contribution of genetic, sociocultural, familial, biophysiological, and psychological factors to mental illness and personality development will be presented in Part II. The specific relationship between such factors and each of the various disorders will be reviewed in Part III in the chapters devoted to each group of disorders.

It must be stressed that the classification scheme and the descriptions of the disorders represent statements of the *predominant* symptom patterns. To the degree to which each patient is a unique human being, such patterns may vary from the common pattern. A patient may show a majority, or only some, of the symptoms and still be classified within one type of disorder; he need not exhibit all of the symptoms. Occasionally, the patient shows some of the symptoms during one examination period, and others during another session. In some instances, a single patient may show symptoms suggestive of multiple affliction; thus, he may be both psychotic and have a conduct disorder. It is possible for a patient to be born mentally retarded, to progress through an antisocial reaction, and to end up schizophrenic.

WHAT IS NORMAL BEHAVIOR?

Although the statistical and cultural approaches provide much of the bases for understanding abnormality, a complete picture must include a description of the normal personality for comparison. Being normal involves much more than the absence of abnormal traits. To be normal is to be:

1. *Effective*—A normal person shows instrumental behavior, behavior directed toward solutions by direct attack on the source of problems or stresses. He seeks to diminish the stresses that mount into emotional blockades, he develops positive measures to strengthen those means for overcoming tensions and fears, he attempts to reach goals in spite of tensions when such goals are meaningful and valuable.

2. *Efficient*—An adjusted person utilizes his energies without wasted effort. He is realistic enough to realize when strivings will be ineffective, when obstacles are insurmountable, when goals are unrealistic. Under these conditions, he accepts frustrations and loss of goals and redirects his energies. Energy resources seem more available since less are consumed in the ravenous maws of anxiety, ceaseless worries, and emotional conflict. In addition, the lack of need for erecting and maintaining costly defensive behaviors releases energies for more adaptive responses.

3. *Appropriate*—A normal individual demonstrates thoughts, feelings, and actions that are appropriate. His perceptions reflect reality, his judgments are conclusions drawn from relevant information. The neurotic and psychotic misinterpret their environment, or they draw conclusions before even facing the facts; many behave in ways that suggest that they are really responding to their own inner anticipations of rejection, failure, or humiliation, rather than the reality of the circumstance.

The normal person experiences fear, or worry, or anger, or distress, but these are all appropriately related to the circumstances he faces. And they diminish and disappear when the circumstances change.

Or he controls their overt expression and prevents himself from becoming overwhelmed if such control is needed for effective performance. Yet he accepts his feelings, and for this reason he is spontaneous.

Not only are his behaviors appropriate for the setting, they are also appropriate for his age and maturity level. A normal child may exhibit a low frustration tolerance and weep readily, but a normal adult must endure much more and react with greater composure and maturity. A neurotic person often behaves in an immature way, showing actions or attitudes that are inappropriate to his age level. Some psychoses are characterized by age inappropriateness to such a degree that age-regression has been hypothesized.

4. *Flexible*—A normal individual is adaptable. When faced with conflict and frustration, he seeks new ways of solving problems instead of persisting in old ways. A willingness to learn, to change, to engage the new is also a part of flexibility. To bend as the reed in the gale when forces are too strong, to float over the threatening wave, or to seek a passage through rather than over a mountainside, is to adapt.

5. *Able to profit from experience*— One overpowering trait of the neurotic is his seeming inability to profit from experience as he permits himself to become entangled over and over again in the same anxiety-provoking, self-defeating situations. This is because his life is so cluttered up with misperceptions, anxieties, hostilities, distorted self-evaluations, and excess attention to self-needs that he can concentrate very little on cues that would enable him to learn and differentiate.

6. *Interpersonally effective*—The bulk of human life is composed of human interpersonal interactions and the adjusted person participates to the fullest. He relates well without either excessive dependence on others or extreme withdrawal. He is emancipated enough to avoid being directed solely by what others say or do, yet he is sensitive and empathic enough to respond to their demands and needs. He can accept others as separate identities. And finally, he can enjoy the presence of others while also appreciating the need for solitude.

7. *Self-secure*—The well-adjusted person possesses a sense of self-esteem, of self-worth, of security. This is founded on a realistic appraisal of his weaknesses *and* strengths, on what he is and what he can become, on what is expected and his own self-determinism. Such a person knows and accepts what he is. Or if he perceives a change as more desirable, he views such a process of change as self-motivated and self-controlled. Frequently, the neurotic is bitter over his lot in life, sees himself as incapable of controlling the forces that make him the kind of person he is, or considers change as something forced upon him by others.

Several others have offered descriptions of the mentally healthy person. Kenneth E. Appel, a past president of the American Psychiatric Association, considers the sound person as having the ability "to meet and handle problems; to make choices and decisions; to find satisfaction in accepting tasks; to do jobs without avoiding them and without pushing them onto others; to carry on without undue dependency on others; to live effectively and satisfactorily with others without crippling complications; to contribute one's share in life; to enjoy life and to be able to love and be loved." (Appel, 1957, p. 363).

Jahoda (1958) established a multiple sign approach to mental health with six major categories of concern:

1. Attitudes toward the self—accuracy of the self-concept, self-acceptance, self-identity, and self-awareness.

2. Self-actualization—the growth and development of one's fullest potentials.

3. Autonomy—the conscious identifying of social forces and the capacity to be free from social influences.

4. Integration—a unifying outlook on life, resistance to stress, balance of psychological forces.

5. Reality perception—the freedom from a need to distort reality, the capacity to be empathetic and socially sensitive.

6. Mastery of the environment—the ability to live; to be adequate in work and recreation, in interpersonal relations, and in problem solving; the capacity to meet situational demands, to adapt and to adjust.

THE SEVERITY OF THE PROBLEM OF MENTAL ILLNESS

The magnitude of the problem of mental illness can be appreciated by a look at some upsetting figures announced by the Joint Commission on Mental Illness and Health (1961):

Nearly half of all hospital beds in all types of hospitals are occupied by the mentally ill.

One out of every ten children born will experience either a major or a minor mental disorder.

One of every hundred persons will become so severely disturbed as to require hospitalization.

Once a person is hospitalized, the chances of his being released decrease drastically with his length of stay: within 1 year, he has an even chance; after 2 years, the odds are 5 to 1 *against* his recovery, and after 5 years, the odds are *99* to 1 against him.

Public mental hospital inpatient populations quadrupled during the previous half-century while the general population itself only doubled. The U.S. Department of Health, Education and Welfare (1964) figures on patients in mental institutions are somewhat encouraging (see Fig. 2-2): in 1903, there were 185.5 inpatients per 100,000 civilians; by 1940 this rose to 363.7 per 100,000; reaching a peak in

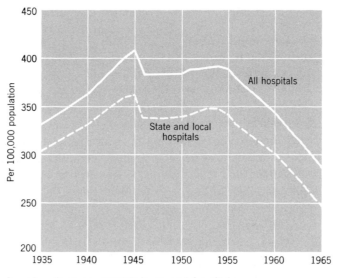

Figure 2-2. **Number of patients per 100,000 in mental hospitals.**
SOURCE: Adapted from U.S. Department of Health, Education ,and Welfare, *Health, education, and welfare trends.* Washington, D.C.: Government Printing Office, 1967.

1945 at 409 per 100,000 as a result of the unusual stresses of the war. After the disturbing influence of the war had settled, the upward trend was again re-established with the rates being 383.7 in 1948, increasing to 384.9 in 1950, rising to 389.0 in 1952, and finally 391.3 in 1954. From this period on, a reversal occurred with declines occurring steadily such that the 1965 rate (286.5 per 100,000) was near that registered in the 1930's. However, this decline is only somewhat encouraging. A closer look at the information indicates that the reduction represents a decrease in patient residents because of increased discharge rates and not a lower incidence in mental illness (Fig. 2-3). The discovery of tranquilizers, the increase in hospital personnel, the establishment of more liberal discharge policies, and the availability of community clinics, nursing homes, and protected environments have all contributed to the decrease in the total hospital population. However, admissions rates have continued to increase over the same periods and nearly a third of those discharged return as readmission cases.

Surveys of the general population rather than just mental hospital residents are even more appalling. The Joint Commission reported to the U.S. Congress in 1960 (Ewalt et al., 1960) that an estimated 17.5 million people suffered from severe enough illness to require treatment. Of these, a mere 1.8 million were actually able to obtain therapy: 1 million through hospitals (leaving 2 to 3 million more who should have been but were not hospitalized), 380,000 through clinics, and 400,000 through private arrangements with psychiatrists or psychologists. At least 4 million are chronic alcoholics, nearly 50,000 are addicted to narcotics, and more than 400,000 couples seek divorces for personal reasons. It stretches the imagination to realize that some 2 million young men were either rejected or discharged from the military during World War II for emotional disorders (Hadley et al., 1944).

Sometimes such statistics fail to impress the occasional skeptic who claims that they reflect those special people in hospitals, or clinics, or in private analysis, but certainly not the everyday person. Figures (Gurin et al., 1960) are available on this group as well . . . and they are as disheartening. In another portion of the

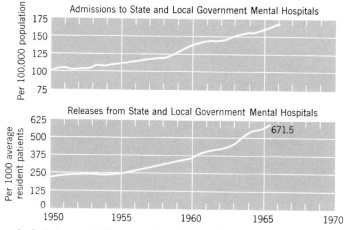

Figure 2-3. **Rates of admissions and discharges of mental patients.**
SOURCE: U.S. Department of Health, Education and Welfare, *Health, education and welfare trends.* Washington, D.C.: Government Printing Office, 1967.

Joint Commission's exhaustive study, a nationwide survey was conducted. The results show that 1 out of every 5 adults answered affirmatively to the question "Have you every felt that you were going to have a nervous breakdown?" And nearly half of these felt concerned enough that they sought professional help. An interesting sidelight was the dispersal of another fallacy: fears of atomic holocaust engulfing the world, anxieties over international tensions, concerns stemming from the state of the world were *not* prominent or common causes for the anticipated breakdown. Rather, sources were more related to the imminent problems of everyday living, the day-to-day stresses of work, marital relations, interpersonal demands, or family life.

A somewhat different perspective leading to the same conclusions is observed when the economics of mental illness are analyzed (Fein, 1958). Mental disturbances cause undue personal grief and suffering to the individual plagued. In addition to the drain on his emotions and personal relationships, mental illness is also a drain on finances. The United States is spending 1.7 billion dollars annually on the care

and treatment of patients. Losses in current and future earning power and production setbacks amount to another .7 billion. In 1961, Congress allocated over 100 million dollars for the National Institute of Mental Health; this is 12 times the amount that had been appropriated when this separate mental health institute was established only 11 years previous. The average amount spent by hospitals daily for the care of each patient in 1960

TABLE 2-1. *Types of Mental Illness of Private Mental Hospital Patients, First Admissions*

ILLNESS	MALES	FEMALES	TOTAL
Organic disorders	2,154	2,119	4,273
Psychotic disorders	5,204	10,701	15,905
Psychophysiologic disorders	53	165	218
Psychoneurotic disorders	4,732	10,394	15,126
Conduct disorders	3,217	2,356	5,573
Mental retardation	88	42	130
Undiagnosed	391	533	924

SOURCE: Adapted from U.S. Dept. of Health, Education, and Welfare, *Patients in mental institutions, 1966, Part III.* Washington, D.C.: U.S. Government Printing Office, 1968.

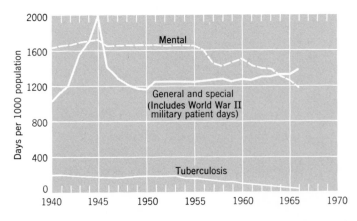

Figure 2-4. **Use of hospitals by mental patients as compared with patients with other illnesses.**
SOURCE: U.S. Department of Health, Education and Welfare, *Health, education and welfare trends. Washington,* D.C.: Government Printing Office, 1967.

was $4.44 for state, county, and city psychiatric hospitals, $16.72 for voluntary psychiatric hospitals, $17.33 for proprietary psychiatric hospitals, and as high as $66 for private sanitariums (Joint Commission, 1961). The bill for the hospitalization of patients in state hospitals has amounted to as much as a third of the operating budget of some of the largest and wealthiest states in the union (Gorman, 1956).

The most depressing of all statistics on mental illness are those that reflect the extreme shortages in trained personnel to help those in need. The Joint Information Service (1962) sponsored by the American Psychiatric Association and the National Association for Mental Health reported the following:

1. The number of physicians working in public mental hospitals in 1958 was only up to 57% adequacy. In addition, only one-half of the states reached at least 50% adequacy.

2. The number of psychologists reached

75% adequacy, registered nurses were at the 23% adequacy level, and social workers at the 40% level.

3. In terms of professional man-hours spent in mental health clinics by psychiatrists, psychologists, and social workers, the overall figure was 147 man-hours per 100,000 population. But some states showed as low as 10 hours spent with clinic patients.

More recently, Albee (1959) has concluded that the manpower shortage has persisted and will continue to persist. In many states there is on the average 1 psychiatrist for each 18,000 people but in some regions of the South the ratio diminishes to 1 for each 34,000. Approximately 450 new psychiatrists are added each year, yet by 1965 an estimated 6000 new psychiatrists was judged needed to man the clinics. The picture is somewhat brighter for psychologists since there are over 25,000 professionals in that field. Unfortunately, only a third are in clinical work where they would be of direct ser-

TABLE 2-2. *Rates per 100,000 Population of First Admissions to Private Mental Hospitals*

ILLNESS	UNITED STATES	GEOGRAPHIC LOCALE[a]					
		NEW ENGLAND	MID-ATLANTIC	MIDWEST	SOUTH	MOUNTAIN	PACIFIC
Organic disorders	2.9	3.9	3.0	2.6	4.8	6.7	1.8
Psychotic disorders	10.5	13.7	14.0	10.3	9.9	16.5	7.7
Psychophysiologic disorders	.1	.2	.1	.1	.2	.6	.1
Psychoneurotic disorders	10.1	13.8	7.8	10.6	12.6	34.3	8.3
Conduct disorders	3.8	9.2	3.4	3.5	3.9	8.7	2.8
Mental retardation	.1	.1	.1	.2	0.0	.2	0.0

a New England—Maine, New Hampshire, Vermont, Massachusetts, Rhode Island, Connecticut
Mid-Atlantic—New York, New Jersey, Pennsylvania
Midwest—Ohio, Indiana, Illinois, Michigan, Wisconsin
South—Kentucky, Tennessee, Alabama, Mississippi
Mountain—Montana, Idaho, Wyoming, Colorado, New Mexico, Arizona, Utah, Nevada
Pacific—Washington, Oregon, California, Alaska, Hawaii
SOURCE: Adapted from U.S. Department of Health, Education, and Welfare, *Patients in mental hospitals, 1966, Part III*. Washington, D.C.: U.S. Government Printing Office, 1968.

vice to the mental patient. And many have been limited in function to diagnostic psychological testing rather than permitted to practice psychotherapy or counseling. Ten percent of the casework positions were left unfilled by social workers in a single year, compounded by the fact that over a fourth left their jobs by the end of the same year. Moreover, they tended to cluster in certain geographic areas, e.g., 85 percent live in urban areas even though only one-half of the general population live in the same region. There is typically one nurse for every three patients in a general hospital. But one psychiatric nurse must care for fifty-three mental patients. To make matters worse, the pyschiatric nurse is generally required to split her time between administration, teaching, supervision, or other duties which limit the amount of her actual contact with patients.

What Must Be Done?

The solutions of the staggering problem of mental illness must attend to several areas: manpower, the expansion of knowledge, the promotion of newer concepts, the development of more adequate facilities, and an increased concern for prevention.

Manpower shortages will continue to plague us as the population grows. The time invested in training, the lack of either material or status rewards, the personal financial costs of education, and the ambivalence of experts over curriculum practices all contribute to the lag in attracting and producing qualified personnel. Training institutions must commit themselves to clear-cut goals, distinctive rewards for those who enter and qualify, objective and relevant criteria for selection, and an organized curriculum plan which maintains the student's involvement in and personal contact with patients. New rules are demanded permitting the trained professional, be he psychiatrist or psychologist or social worker or behavioral scientist, to contribute his most to the mentally disturbed. The facts no longer allow the medically trained person to retain personal control over who is permitted to practice psychotherapy, or even who is charged with prime responsibility for patient care. If the available manpower is to be maximized, then historical divisions of labor must give way to scientific fact. A truly team approach is desirable with professionally qualified members serving as consultants or advisors to less intensely trained but equally sensitive personnel. Teachers, employers, welfare workers, and judges should all be aware of their involvement in the mental health process and be willing to participate and profit as members.

TABLE 2-3. *Mental Patients in Hospitals and Treatment Centers in the United States*

CENTER	CAUCASIAN			NON-CAUCASIAN		
	MALE	FEMALE	TOTAL	MALE	FEMALE	TOTAL
Federal hospitals	58,256	4,970	63,226	8,772	1,771	10,543
State, county, city hospitals	267,350	276,062	543,412	39,959	33,750	73,709
Private hospitals, residential centers	9,986	13,422	23,408	723	458	1,181
Total	335,592	294,454	630,046	49,454	35,979	85,433

SOURCE: U.S. Bureau of the Census, *U.S. census of the population, 1960. Subject reports. Inmates in institutions.* Washington, D.C.: U.S. Government Printing Office, 1963.

Finally, *all* of society should be educated in the dynamic effects of group forces on behavioral change. The effectiveness of the "therapeutic community" on the individual patient has been clearly demonstrated—it now needs broadening and expansion such that all communities inside and outside the professional region became therapeutic.

There is little doubt that the fund of knowledge regarding psychopathology is shockingly meager. The discovery of the usefulness of tranquilizers is a recent affair. Yet even here, there is a limitation to its value for these drugs do not cure, nor does their use shed any light on the question of etiology. We have yet to resolve the controversy on the genetic or non-genetic origin of schizophrenia although the disease has been recognized for half a century now. The precise role of society in creating or precipitating illness is still unclear. The same is true, with some exceptions, for genetic, constitutional, or biochemical variables. The strange and fascinating world of genetic transmission of coded information is only now slowly opening. The astounding data on sensory deprivation, and early infantile deprivation, arouse further questions to be explored. But perhaps the greatest deficit is in the realm of curative processes. Readmission rates, and the comparative data on the results of psychotherapy versus no therapy, raise serious questions regarding our treatment methods.

The mental health movement stimulated by Clifford Beers (1908) at the beginning of the century seems to have lost some of its momentum. It is true that national associations exist, and mental health clinics are being built, and educational programs are in effect, but the impact nowhere matches the need. There is a clear lack of concern by the public. Of the ten national voluntary health fund-raising campaigns, mental health ranks a sorry eighth. In a survey (Univ. of Michigan, 1958) of the ability of people to recall various news items relating to medicine, there was a 32 % recall for items on heart disease but only 5 % for mental illness items. An integrated plan for mass education and arousal of concern for the care and prevention of mental illness is greatly needed. In addition, mental health clinics based on new concepts must be developed. Some are already being tried in the form of living arrangements which permit the patient to enter for day care and treatment and return home evenings, or to work during the day while residing in a therapeutic environment. The encouragement of *family* units to participate in mental health discussions or psycho-therapeutic meetings provides a departure from the archaic orientation which accuses the patient of being solely responsible for his illness. The firm lines dividing the mentally healthy from the mentally unhealthy need to be gradually dissolved in one respect—counseling and therapeutic meetings must no longer be seen as limited to "those with problems." Stresses and strains exist for all people, and professional advice or a therapeutic environment can be most helpful in preventing future breakdown. Strengthening mental *health* is as critical as treating mental *illness.* Finally, mental health programs must reach out into the surrounding neighborhood. Attention to housing, educational needs, recreational and work opportunities, is needed in order to remove those factors that contribute either directly or indirectly to breakdown. The underprivileged may fall short of mental health goals because of direct exposure to certain socioeconomic stresses, or he may be unable to cope with common stresses because of a lack of opportunity to develop inner resources.

Facilities for the care of those requiring specialized treatment must be developed. Centers for treatment and rehabilitation must be constructed which remove the awe or aura of stigma often attached to mental institutions. The opportunity to seek help without being helpless, to accept treatment without social rejection for doing so, and to receive help when the need arises, are integral parts of the atmosphere of such planned centers. Emergency service should be available for "crises reactions"—those occasions when a critical event occurring in a person's life demands immediate resolution. Specialized personnel and equipment for providing "tailor-made" treatment schedules for each patient are a necessity where severe disturbance is evidenced. Combinations of physical-pharmacological-psychological programs must be worked out so as to maximize the effects of each, thereby avoiding the conceptual trap of considering any single approach as the only suitable method. A rudimentary proposal would include behavior therapy for phobias, shock therapies for depressions, and pharmacological therapies for the situational anxiety reactions.

Prevention develops from programs of education, early identification, and early treatment. Education in the signs of disturbance, in the development of psychological resources for coping with stress, in self-awareness and social sensitivity, in how to achieve help when needed, forms a firm foundation to prevention. Child development information will become increasingly more helpful in preventive work as the relationships between early childhood practices and later adult disturbances are uncovered. Aid to parents in child-rearing techniques and in airing their feelings about parenthood are important. Early identification of personal danger signs, and early recognition of oncoming stresses can enable prudent planning for minimizing psychological injury. Mental health consultants specializing in the problems of labor, management, military life, and rural community living, may be placed in locations within easy access to enable early discussion of those problems uniquely experienced by individuals in such environments.

THE HELPING PROFESSIONS

For those who wish to become active participants in those services for the mentally ill, there are a number of professions from which to choose. The major disciplines include psychiatry, psychoanalysis, clinical psychology, social work, and psychiatric nursing.

Psychiatrists are physicians who specialize in emotional illnesses. As is characteristic of all physicians, the psychiatrist first enters four years of college, four more years of medical school, and one year of on-the-job training called an internship. Upon completion of this internship, he is licensed by a state medical board to practice medicine although not as a specialist. Most doctors elect to specialize and enter a residency in an approved hospital or agency. Psychiatrists take their residency in a placement which centers around the diagnosis and treatment of mental disorders. Within approximately three years, the residency is completed. Relatively few physicians select psychiatry for their specialty—only about 8 to 9 percent of all new medical school graduates. Although psychiatrists in practice before World War II tended to be introspective, theoretical, and preoccupied with psychoanalytic literature, today they are more conventional, less concerned with theory, and intent on completing their training so as to open a private practice.

Psychoanalysts represent an even more specialized aspect of medicine. Just as psychiatry was once split off from the rest of medicine, so was there once a cleavage between psychoanalysis and psychiatry. The psychoanalyst tends to shy away from a somatic, neurological, or biochemical approach, and is unlike the psychiatrist in preferring the psychological approach

A *psychiatrist* is a physician specializing in the diagnosis and treatment of mental illness. He may prescribe drugs, or as illustrated above, he may rely upon psychotherapy to help the disturbed. (Lee Lockwood / Black Star)

to treatment rather than relying upon drugs or physical procedures. In addition, this psychological approach is quite carefully prescribed in doctrine and includes the analysis of dreams, the belief in Freudian-related explanations of abnormality, the use of free-association, and a prolonged, exhaustive therapy program over long periods of time. Prospective psychoanalysts are selected by training institutes from those physicians who have completed a year of residency in psychiatry. Although nonmedical candidates have been accepted for analytic training, this is the rare exception. A basic requirement which must be completed by the analyst in training is his own personal analysis. In addition, he must pay for at least 200 hours of supervised or control analysis in which he is supervised as he conducts treatment sessions. Because the training is extremely lengthy and expensive, few are able to pursue this type of specialty.

Clinical psychologists are specialists in psychology concerned with the diagnosis and treatment of mental disorders. Psychology itself is a branch of science concerned with the study of human behavior of all types. As a science it has its own methods for observing, collecting, and analyzing data. A high percentage of psychologists first considered it to be of interest to them in college, but not all who are interested are capable of completing the training requirements. Only 12 percent of those who major in psychology in undergraduate work go on for further training as professional psychologists. Beyond the bachelor's degree, advanced training typically means graduate school courses in psychopathology, pyschodynamics, psychotherapy or behavioral modification, intellectual and personality assessment, statistics, research design, personality theory, and a core of courses designed to acquaint the student with other basic information in psychology. In addition, the clinical psychologist completes 1 to 2 years of internship in the form of supervised experience in mental hospitals, mental health clinics, or counseling centers. For practical reasons, the

53

Clinical psychologists are trained in the diagnosis and treatment of mental illness. As illustrated above, psychological tests have been a prime tool of the psychologist along with a wide variety of other diagnostic techniques. In a similar way, psychologists are skilled in many approaches in their psychotherapeutic practice. (Ken Heyman)

Ph.D. degree is frequently sought since job opportunities tend to be limited without this level of training. Generally, the graduate school curriculum is completed within 4 to 5 years. The clinical psychologist may select placements in mental hospitals or clinics, general medical and surgical wards, rehabilitation centers for the physically disabled, Job and Peace Corps assessment programs, educational settings, and research centers.

Social workers are men and women who are concerned with the problems of individuals, groups, and communities. They engage in diverse activities such as psychotherapy with families, cooperation with the courts over cases of child neglect, supervision of residents in correctional institutions, participation in child welfare planning, providing financial arrangements for medical expenses, attending to recreational needs, and alleviating socially derived stress. A two-year period of grad-

uate training is recommended at one of the fifty approved schools of social work in the United States. Candidates are selected on the basis of intellectual promise, emotional maturity, and the potential for tolerating stress. The desire to help others must be tempered by an ability to let others help themselves rather than to control or dominate. The social work curriculum includes training in the casework interview method and fieldwork experience. Of all the psychiatric disciplines, the social worker is most identified with the image of warmth and sensitivity toward people.

Psychiatric nurses are nurses who aid the psychiatrist in the medical treatment and supervision of patients. A large percentage engage in teaching, administrative, and other nonpatient care activities, and nearly a third of those employed in hospitals are in the position of head nurses. Oddly enough, most psychiatric nurses had planned on nursing for a career early in their lives, but had not considered psychiatric nursing. In addition, many experienced some dissatisfaction with their field partly because of social attitudes. Yet, because of the opportunity for prolonged and intense contact with the patient throughout his hospitalization, psychiatric nursing has the greatest potential for contributing to patient welfare. Nursing education is available in three forms: (1) the three-year program connected with a hospital school following high school, (2) the four- to five-year bachelor's degree program in colleges, and (3) the two-year community college certification program. In actuality, a large proportion of psychiatric nurses received no basic psychiatric nursing experience other than the general nursing clinical training connected with all degree programs. Yet those who did receive training in psychiatric hospital units or psychiatric research centers tended to orient themselves earlier toward their eventual careers in psychiatric nursing.

Glossary

Age regression: The return to behaviors characteristic of an earlier age level.

Amaurotic idiocy: Also known as Tay-Sach's Disease. This is a central nervous system disease resulting from a recessive gene; characterized by mental deficiency and early death.

Antisocial reaction: A form of personality disturbance characterized by impulsive actions and the inability to profit from experience.

Behavior modification: The systematic application of learning principles to the strengthening or elimination of unwanted behaviors.

Combat fatigue: An early term for the traumatic reactions to combat experienced by soldiers. Also referred to as shell shock, war neuroses, and combat exhaustion.

Cognitive: Referring to activities involving reasoning, judgment, perception, and conceptualizing.

Delusion: A belief that is tenaciously held in the face of evidence to the contrary.

Depression: An emotional state characterized by sadness and gloom.

Early infantile autism: A form of severe mental illness appearing early in life and classified as a psychosis.

Frustration tolerance: The capacity to experience frustrations without disruption or disorder to one's behavior.

Fugue states: A psychoneurotic condition characterized by amnesia without loss of habits and skills. The patient usually leaves home and lives a different life elsewhere.

Huntington's chorea: An inherited form of mental illness characterized by brain atrophy, involuntary jerky movements, distractibility, apathy, and loss of coordination.

Intermittent reinforcement: Also referred to as partial reinforcement. The occurrence of a reward at irregular periods following an activity.

Mental retardation: Deficit in intellectual capacity leading to impairments of academic, social, and vocational abilities.

Neurotic: Shortened term for psychoneurotic. Persons with mental disturbance of a mild nature. No personality disorganization is involved.

Normal curve: A statistical representation of the distribution of characteristics among people. This frequency curve is bell-shaped since most people fall in the middle, with fewer and fewer persons possessing either a greater or lesser amount of the trait.

Obsessive-compulsive: A psychoneurotic person characterized by repetitive thoughts or actions over which he has little control.

Paranoia: A psychotic condition characterized by a systematized, logical delusion.

Phenylketonuria: A type of mental retardation caused by the lack of an enzyme.

Schizophrenia: A psychosis characterized by social withdrawal, emotional blunting, and thought disturbance.

Schizophrenia, process: Evidence is building that this group of psychotics has a case history with early signs of pathology that become progressively worse. It is suggested that this is a genetically associated illness.

Schizophrenia, reactive: This group appears to have a healthy early history, but with a later onset of psychosis following a precipitating stress.

Secondary gain: The extra rewards that accrue from symptoms, such as attention from others, sympathy, or relief from responsibility.

Symptoms: The signs associated with an illness.

References

Albee, G. *Mental health manpower trends.* New York: Basic Books, 1959.

American Psychiatric Association. *Diagnostic and statistical manual, mental disorders* (2nd ed.). Washington, D.C.: American Psychiatric Association, 1968.

Appel, K. Mental health and mental illness. In R. Kurtz (Ed.), *Social Work Yearbook.* New York: National Association of Social Workers, 1957.

Bandura, A. A social learning interpretation of psychological dysfunctions. In P. London and D. Rosenhan (Eds.), *Foundations of abnormal psychology.* New York: Holt, Rinehart, & Winston, 1968.

Bandura, A., and Walters, R. *Social learning and personality development.* New York: Holt, Rinehart, and Winston, 1963.

Barron, F. *Creativity and psychological health.* New Jersey: Van Nostrand, 1963.

Beers, C. *A mind that found itself.* New York: Doubleday, Doran, 1908.

Cattell, R. *Personality and motivation structure and measurement.* New York: World Book, 1957.

Dollard, J., and Miller, N. *Personality and psychotherapy: an analysis in terms of learning, thinking, and culture.* New York: McGraw-Hill, 1950.

Eaton, J., and Weil, R. *Culture and mental disorders.* Glencoe, Ill.: Free Press, 1955.

Ewalt, J., Schwartz, S., Appel, K., Bartemeier, L., and Schlaifer, C. Joint commission on mental illness and health. *Amer. J. Psychiat.,* 1960, **116,** 782.

Eysenck, H. *The scientific study of personality.* London: Routledge & Kegan Paul, 1952.

Fein, R. *Economics of mental illness.* New York: Basic Books, 1958.

Fish, B. Limitations of the new nomenclature for children's disorders. *Intern. J. Psychiat.,* 1969, **7,** 393.

Freud, S. *Psychopathology of everyday life.* In A. Brill (Ed.), *The basic writings of Sigmund Freud.* New York: Random House, 1938.

Gorman, M. *Every other bed.* New York: World, 1956.

Gurin, G., Veroff, J., and Feld, S. *Americans view their mental health.* New York: Basic Books, 1960.

Hadley, E., et al. Military psychiatry. *Psychiatry,* 1944, **7,** 379.

Institute for Personality Assessment and Research. University of California, Berkeley. *The creative person.* Berkeley: University Extension, University of California, 1961.

Jackson, B. Reflections on DSM-II. *Intern. J. Psychiat.,* 1969, **7,** 385.

Jahoda, M. *Current concepts of positive mental health.* New York: Basic Books, 1958.

Joint Commission on Mental Illness and Health, *Action for mental health.* New York: Basic Books, 1961.

Joint Information Service. *Fifteen indices: an aid in reviewing state and local mental health and hospital programs.* Washington, D.C.: Joint Information Service, American Psychiatric Association, National Association for Mental Health, 1962.

Masserman, J. *Behavior and neurosis: an experimental psychoanalytic approach to psycho-biologic principles.* Chicago: University of Chicago Press, 1943.

McCall, R. The dispensable and the indispensable in psychopathological classification: neurosis and character disorder in the 1952 and 1968 DSM'S. *Intern. J. Psychiat.,* 1969, **7**, 399.

Menninger, K. Sheer verbal Mickey Mouse. *Intern. J. Psychiat.,* 1969, **7**, 415.

M'Naghten's case. 8 Eng. Rep. 718, 1843.

Sarason, I., and Ganzer, V. Concerning the medical model. *Amer. Psychol.,* 1968, **23**, 507.

Staats, A., and Staats, C. *Complex human behavior.* New York: Holt, Rinehart, & Winston, 1963.

Szasz, T. *The myth of mental illness: foundations of a theory of personal conduct.* New York: Hoeber-Harper, 1961.

Talbott, J. An inch, not a mile—comments on DSM-II. *Intern. J. Psychiat.,* 1969, **7**, 382.

Terman, L., and Oden, M. *The gifted group at mid-life. Vol. 5, Genetic studies of genius.* Stanford: Stanford University Press, 1959.

Thorne, F. Back to fundamentals. *J. Clin. Psychol.,* 1953, **9**, 89.

University of Michigan, Survey Research Center. *The public impact of science in mass media.* Michigan: Institute of Social Research, University of Michigan, 1958.

U.S. Department of Health, Education, and Welfare, *Health, Education and Welfare Trends.* Washington, D.C.: Government Printing Office, 1964.

Wittman, P., and Sheldon, W. A proposed classification of psychotic behavior reactions. *Amer. J. Psychiat.,* 1948, **105**, 124.

Zigler, E., and Phillips, L. Psychiatric diagnosis: A critique. *J. abnorm. soc. Psychol.,* 1961, **3**, 607.

Zilboorg, G., and Henry, G. *A history of medical psychology.* New York: Norton, 1941.

PART II

The Factors Contributing to Abnormal Development

As is evident from the historical developments traced in Chapter 1, scientific progress in understanding psychopathology has been outstanding. As new insights and new technologies develop, great strides are being made toward the unraveling of the origins of abnormal behavior. The following chapters outline some findings and their implications. As the careful reader will note, these chapters do not attempt to offer a conclusive or dogmatic statement regarding "the" causation of mental illnesses. Rather, each chapter will review a cause or a factor that could conceivably be a contributor to pathology. It is perhaps more accurate to refer to the "Genetic hypothesis, the Sociocultural hypothesis, the Familial hypothesis, the Biophysiological hypothesis, and the Psychological hypothesis" of mental illness in each of the folowing chapters, instead of discussing the genetic factor contributing to mental illness, the sociocultural factor, etc. The evidence on each of these topics varies; the genetic foundation of Huntington's chorea is clearly supported, the genetic factor in some forms of schizophrenia has been convincing for many but not all researchers, the role of the family has been controversial, and physiological variables have been elusive.

3 Contributor to Personality: The Genetic Factor

Although much is known about the role of genetics in lower animals, the great puzzle regarding its contribution to psychological traits in humans has plagued psychologist and geneticist alike. It is conclusive that heredity is the major determinant of physical traits, such as sex, height, weight, skin color, and even taste (three out of very ten people are unable to taste a chemical PTC, phenylthiocarbamide, because they possess a recessive "nontasting" gene). Similarly, certain physical or medical abnormalities have proved to be directly linked to genetics, for example, red-green color blindness, hemophilia, and diabetes mellitus. Nevertheless, great controversies have arisen over the place of genetics in influencing psychological characteristics such as intelligence. The "nature-nurture" issue caused learned men to separate into opposing camps depending on their belief in the critical importance of heredity or of environment in intellectual behavior.

In general, the environmental approach has been received more favorably by the psychopathologist. Admittedly, certainly psychological abnormalities (Huntington's chorea, phenylketonuria, amaurotic idiocy) have dominant genetic etiologies, yet the majority of the neuroses and psychoses are better understood through the use of the environment premise. Arguments that have strengthened the preference for non-genetic analyses have included: the immense obstacles to carefully controlled scientific studies of human breeding which might demonstrate the importance of inheritance on personality; the seemingly appropriate analyses and results from the case history-psychodynamic approach; the impressive demonstration of behavior change through the application of environmental manipulation and reinforcement; and the conclusive data regarding the formation of experimental neuroses. Several events have developed that refocus attention on genetics and personality. The onset of nuclear discovery and nuclear destructiveness as well as nuclear usefulness have made radiation a constant companion to mankind. The radiation risk of mutation changes have spurred a concern for increasing the knowledge surrounding man's genetic foundation. It has become paradoxical that man, the intellectual master in the evolutionary ladder, should know so little about the sources of his own human traits. Yet, developments are speedily reaching fruition including the provocative discovery of causal relations between genetic elements and metabolic and hematologic functions (Haldane, 1952; Pauling and Itano, 1957; Race and Sanger, 1954). The high degree of specificity found between certain physiological functions and the properties of genetic molecules is a major step forward. Most significant is the development of technology and biostatistics necessary for the precise identification and interpretation of the incredibly complex material.

FUNDAMENTALS OF HUMAN HEREDITY

Modern genetics holds that the human being is constructed of cells which contain elongated, microscopic substances called *chromosomes*. With the exception of the male sperm and the female ovum, each human cell contains 23 pairs of these chromosomes arranged in a spirally twisted fashion. Of these pairs, half represent the chromosomes contributed by the individ-

ual's father while the other half represents the corresponding chromosomes coming from the mother. In reality, each chromosome is itself composed of several jellylike parts responsible for determining human traits. These parts, called *genes,* are living molecules of a protein with the vital substance known as *DNA*—deoxyribonucleic acid. The total number of genes is yet unknown, but present estimates range from between 40,000 to 80,000 minimum in the 23 pairs of chromosomes.

Physical characteristics are determined by these genes, sometimes by only a single pair, although most traits are multiply determined (see Table 3-1). Blood type, for example, is determined by the presence or absence of the type A gene, the type B gene, or the type O gene (see Fig. 3-1). Every gene in any one chromosome has its corresponding partner in the paired chromosome. When both are the same, for example, if both are type A (written AA), then the person is said to be *homozygous* for these genes. When there is a

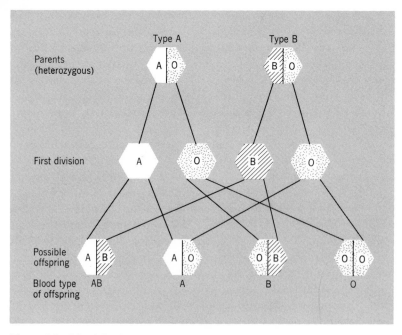

Figure 3-1. **The inheritance of blood type.**

TABLE 3-1. *Some Dominant and Recessive Characteristics*

CAUSED BY DOMINANT GENES	CAUSED BY RECESSIVE GENES
Dark hair	Blond hair
Curly hair	Straight hair
Black skin	White skin
Normal hair	Baldness
Short stature	Tall stature
Nearsightedness	Normal vision
Double-jointedness	Normal joints
Normal color vision	Color blindness
Normal blood clotting	Hemophilia
Fused fingers or toes	Normal fingers or toes
Immunity to poison ivy	Susceptibility to poison ivy
Blood type A, B, and AB	Blood type O
Brown, green, or hazel eyes	Blue or gray eyes

mixture, for example, if one gene is type A and the other in the pair is type B (written AB), then the person is said to be *heterozygous* for these genes.

What physical characteristics the person will actually exhibit is not only determined by what *type* of genes are present but also by the genes' *penetrance,* that is, the power to become expressed. Some genes are *dominant*: they are so powerful that they will always show up and will suppress lesser genes in heterozygous pairs. Others are *recessive*: they require a partner recessive gene of the same type (i.e., a homozygous condition) before they can penetrate (see Fig. 3-2). Human traits associated with a recessive gene will therefore never be shown until it is paired with another recessive. Many genes that produce pathological conditions are presumed

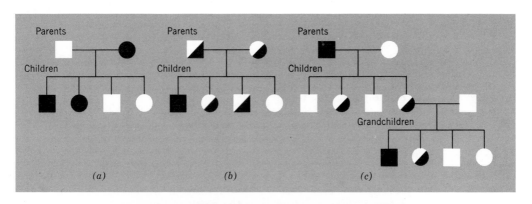

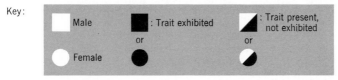

Figure 3-2. **Inheritance of dominant, recessive, and sex-linked genes. (a) Dominant pedigree (Heterozygous parents illustrated): Parent who carries a dominant gene will exhibit the trait, and will have an average of one in two children also showing the trait. If parent carries two dominant genes for the illness, all children will exhibit the trait. (b) Recessive pedigree (Heterozygous parents illustrated): For the trait to be exhibited in the offspring, both parents must each carry a recessive gene. On the average, one in four children will carry both genes and exhibit the trait; two in four will carry one gene and be carriers but will not exhibit the trait; and one in four will be entirely free of the gene and therefore the trait. (c) Sex-linked pedigree: Father with trait passes on gene to all daughters who do not exhibit trait but act as carriers. In the grandchildren, chances are one in two that any grandson will exhibit the trait; and one in two that any granddaughter will be a carrier.**

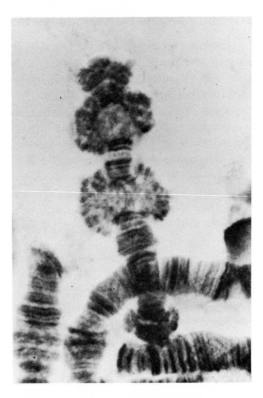

Chromosomes contain the basic elements of heredity. The above is a photograph of the chromosomes of a midge fly; the dark bands mark the location of genes; the puffed areas produce RNA, the substance that acts as a messenger carrying the coded commands of the genes. (**Dr. Ulrich Clever**)

to be recessive and will not lead to the appearance of the trait unless the person is homozygous for these genes. The person may be a carrier of the pathology while remaining himself free of symptoms. An interesting example involves the genes controlling the ability to taste a chemical substance called PTC. Assume that your father lacked the ability to taste the chemical. Since this is a recessive condition, he would be homozygous—call his gene pair *tt*. Assume your mother is homozygous but with the dominant ability-to-taste genes—call her gene pair *TT*. Since you receive one gene from your father and one from your mother you would be heterozygous for this condition, or *Tt*. Because tasting is dominant, you would show the normal

ability to taste PTC but you would also be a carrier for the taste deficiency. Unlike all other human cells, the sex cells (sperm in males; ova in females) carry only 23 single chromosomes and therefore half the genes. If you are a male, some of your sperms will carry the *T* and others will carry the *t* gene; if you are a female, some of your ova will have the *T* and others the *t* gene. If you marry a person who is also heterozygous for PTC tasting, some of your spouse's sex cells will carry the *T* and others will carry the *t* gene (see Fig. 3-3). When a sperm unites with an ovum to produce your offspring, four possible combinations may occur from this mating: a *T* sperm with a *T* ovum (*TT*), a *T* sperm with a *t* ovum (*Tt*), a *t* sperm with a *T* ovum (*tT*), and a *t* sperm with a *t* ovum (*tt*). The homozygous dominant (*TT*) and the heterozygous offspring (*Tt* or *tT*) will be normal tasters, and only the homozygous recessive child (*tt*) will exhibit the taste deficiency.

The inheritance of traits is not always as simple as the case just discussed. *Intermediate* genes, which are neither dominant nor recessive, are known to exist and are found in cases where an effect is exhibited to a greater or lesser degree instead of in an all-or-none present versus absent manner. Skin color is a trait illustrating incomplete dominance. A mulatto is the result of the mating of a Negro and a white, with the mulatto's skin color being somewhere in between that of his parents. It is plausible to also assume the presence of *polygenes*. These are genes that must combine in a cumulative effort to control a characteristic. Basically, it is believed that each of these genes individually fail to have sufficient penetrating power to be expressed, but collectively are able to exert an influence. In some cases, a small collection will lead to the appearance of a lesser amount of a trait, with greater and greater collections leading to more and more amounts. For example, the level of one's intelligence may result from this type of arrangement; the premise is that retarded, dull normal, average, bright average, and superior intelligence are re-flections of the combined effects of poly-genes (Gottesman, 1963). In other cases, the polygenes collectively still fail to lead to the appearance of a trait. However,

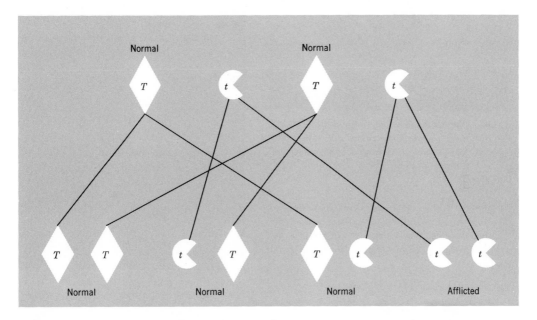

Figure 3-3. **Diagram showing the inheritance of a recessive trait for an illness (t) among offspring of parents heterozygous for the trait.**

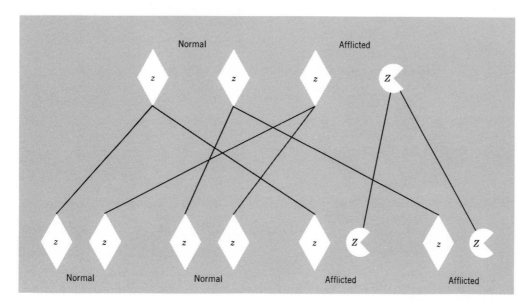

Figure 3-4. **Diagram showing the inheritance of a dominant trait for an illness (Z) among offspring of a normal and an affected parent.**

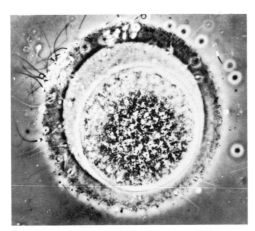

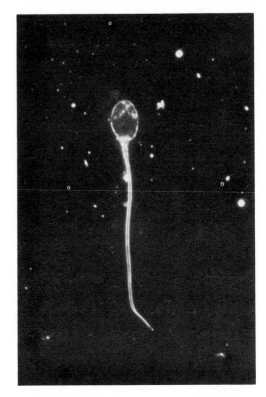

(Above:) Photograph of a living human ovum at the moment of *fertilization*. Of the many sperms surrounding the ovum, only one penetrates to begin a new human life. (Dr. L. B. Shettles)

(Right:) A living human *sperm* magnified several hundred times. Within the head are packed the 23 chromosomes. The elongated tail propels the sperm through a lashing motion. (Lester V. Bergman)

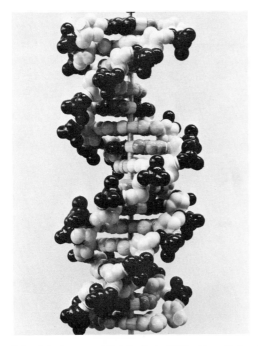

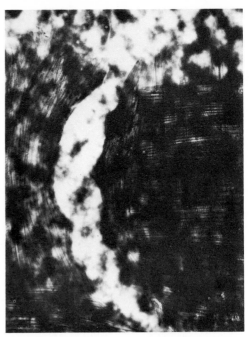

Scientists have predicted that *DNA*, the vital substance of genes, should look like the spirally twisted model at the left above. This was finally confirmed when the first actual photograph of DNA shown at the right above was obtained and released in 1969, 16 years after the prediction. (Left: John Oldenkamp / Psychology Today) (Right: Wide World Photos)

their presence makes the individual more susceptible or *predisposed* to exhibit the trait under the proper circumstances. Schizophrenia, for example, may be thought of as involving the inheritance of a number of faulty genes which predisposes the person to a mental breakdown under the proper conditions of stress. Thus, the occurrence of a schizophrenic break would be a function of the degree of his polygenic predisposition and the severity of his life stresses (Rosenthal, 1963).

The occurrence of sex-linked traits further complicates the issues of heredity such that the patterns of trait inheritance evade identification until sex differences are taken into account. *Hemophilia* is a sex-linked characteristic confined almost entirely to males and passed along to sons through their carrier mothers. Hemophilia is an abnormal condition in which the body is unable to stem the flow of bleeding. Blood-clotting fails to occur and the victim may bleed to death. Only a few rare cases of hemophilia have been found in women. Records indicate that the gene for hemophilia which arose in the royal families of Europe developed first in Queen Victoria (see Fig. 3-5, page 68) or her mother as a mutation, a sudden alteration on gene properties.

Identical twins (monozygotic twins) are individuals who possess the same genes. The union of a sperm and an ovum is called a zygote. With fertilization, the zygote first divides into two daughter cells, each of which is the perfect replica of the other. Ordinarily, the two daughter cells remain attached and again divide and subdivide to form millions of cells. Ultimately, these cells differentiate into the nerves, muscles, connective tissue, skin, etc., of the embryo. In some instances, the first two daughter cells do not stay attached but actually separate. After separation, the usual process of multiplication and differentiation occurs, but this time two embryos are formed each with the identical genetic structure. These persons are called identical twins. *Fraternal twins* (dizygotic twins), on the other hand, arise from the fertilization of two separate ova by two separate sperms at the same time. The two zygotes do not share any genes and the embryos are no more similar to one another than brothers or sisters who are born at separate times. Fraternal twins simply happen to share a common intrauterine environment.

Monozygotic twins are of interest in our study of genetics and personality because we can be sure of their genetic similarity. Therefore, similarities in mental characteristics could be attributed to genetic factors just as are similarities in their physical characteristics. Of course, one is never absolutely certain that other factors can be ruled out, such as environmental conditions. The case is strengthened, however, if identical twins continue to show the same or similar personality traits when reared in separate environments. We shall see in a later section how the study of twins in comparison with nontwins can contribute valuable information about psychoses.

Evidence of Genetic Influence on Personality

Data of varying types have been gathered in attempts to prove the importance of heredity. The research approaches might be grouped under five categories: animal studies involving controlled breeding, human family history studies, human population studies, human studies involving morbidity risk estimates and chromosome studies.

Animal Studies. Although animal studies should present an ideal condition for genetic work, there has been, in fact, a paucity of sound research devoted to the direct issue under discussion. Of note are the intelligence studies of Tryon (1940) and Thompson (1954), the experiments on emotionality of Hall (1934) and Searle (1949), Tinbergen (1951) and Lorenz's (1935) classic works on instinct and imprinting, and more recently, Scott and Fuller's (1965) carefully controlled research on psychological behavior of canines. Some causes of the lack of research production were: the rise of the racist extremisms of Nazi Germany, the exaggerated and premature claims of the early eugenic movement, and the psychological controversy over the value of the term "instinct" in psychology. Those studies which were accomplished

dealt with the laboratory rat, various breeds of dogs, or members of the bird family. However, breed differences in animal "personality" have also been demonstrated for cattle (Holsteins and Ayrshires tend to be dominant over Jerseys) and rabbits (Race X rabbits are more aggressive than Race III).

Among the rodent studies, those of Tryon and Hall stand out. Tryon took a random group of rats and tested their abilities in maze learning. He then selected the "brightest" and the "dullest" per-

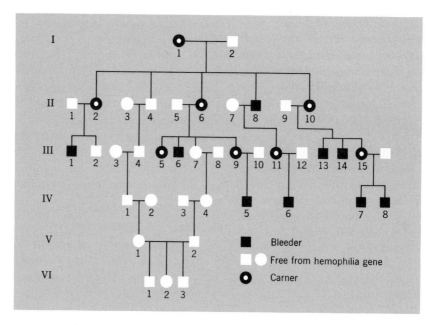

Figure 3-5. Inheritance of hemophilia in royal families. KEY: I-1, Queen Victoria of England; I-2, Prince Albert; II-1, Frederick X, Emperor of Germany; II-2, Victoria, Empress of Germany; II-3, Queen Alexandria; II-4, Edward VII of England; II-5, Ludwig IV of Hesse; II-6, Alice; II-7, Helen of Waldeck; II-8, Leopold of Albany; II-9, Henry, Prince of Battenberg; II-10, Beatrice; III-1, Boy died in early childhood; III-2, Prince Henry of Prussia; III-3, Queen Mary of England; III-4, George V of England; III-5, Irene of Hesse; III-6, Prince Frederick; III-7, Victoria; III-8, Prince Louis of Battenberg; III-9, Alexandrovna, Czarina of Russia; III-10, Czar Nicholas II of Russia; III-11, Alice; III-12, Alexander of Tech; III-13 and III-14, died young; III-15, Victoria, Queen of Spain; III-16, Alfonzo VIII, King of Spain; IV-1, George VI of England; IV-2, Queen Elizabeth; IV-3, Prince Andrew of Greece; IV-4, Lady Alice Mountbatten; IV-5, Alexi; IV-6, Lord Trematon; IV-7, Alfonzo Pio; IV-8, Gonzalo Manuel; V-1, Queen Elizabeth; V-2, Prince Phillip Mountbatten; VI-1, Prince Charles; VI-2, Princess Anne; VI-3, Prince Andrew.

SOURCE: E. Gardner, *Principles of genetics,* New York: Wiley, 1968.

formers and rewarded them by permitting them to breed with mates of similar maze performance ability. Each generation was similarly evaluated, segregated, and inbred. By the ninth rat generation, those offspring of the bright parents were indeed clearly superior on the maze than those less fortunate rats whose heredity traced back to line after line of dull parents (Fig. 3-6, page 70). Similar results were obtained by Thompson. Hall, a student of Tryon, confronted his rats with a circumstance arousing fearfulness or emotionality. His animals were placed in an open field test situation which elicits emotional responses in the naive rat. Such upset is shown by refusals to eat and nervous loss of bladder and bowel control. Again through selective inbreeding, Hall was able to demonstrate the impact of genetics on behavior. Whereas the parent generation showed a mean emotionality score of four, the ninth generation offspring of *fearful* parents showed an average score of ten. The development of the nonemotional strain showed a slightly different course although still significant. By the very *first* generation, the offspring showed a decline in fearfulness with a mean score of below 0.5 indicating almost no signs of urinary or bowel incontinence from fright. Further inbreeding, however, appeared unable to perfect this performance and occasional cases of disturbed offspring were produced within this nonemotional strain. Nevertheless, the average score of the ninth to the twelfth generation only reached the level of 1.4.

Fearfulness is not the only psychological trait in rats that has been experimentally studied; the primary influence of genetics on aggression has also been documented. Ginsburg and Allee (1942) raised the following question: Can rearing by a non-aggressive mother eradicate the influence of inheritance? A strain of black mice known for their aggressiveness and a strain of albino mice known for their greater passivity were selected. A litter of blacks and a litter of whites, born on the same day, were split and raised by a "foster" mother such that each mother raised both black and albino youngsters. Although one would hope that the more peaceful disposition of the albino foster mother would serve as a prevailing influence on the innately aggressive adopted offspring, this was *not* the outcome. The aggressive strain of mice remained aggressive. Scott (1947) studied the possibility that substituting a punitive experience for the albino mother's permissive one would do more toward discouraging the influence of inheritance. His C57 mice (the black aggressive strain) were raised in isolation and exposed to the highly punishing experience of facing another mouse carefully selected for its highly successful fighting behavior. For 30 minutes per session, this fighter battled and subdued the experimental animals. Hopefully, all aggressive instincts would be literally beaten out of the normally aggressive experimental mice. Again, genetics proved a more powerful determinant of behavior as Scott found that the experimental animals showed *increased* aggressiveness when later paired with a helpless subject.

Of final interest from the rodent family studies are those of the "alcoholic" mice. Rodgers and McClearn (1962) were able to identify strains of mice who showed quite distinct preferences for alcohol when permitted to choose their drink, as well as mice who were "teetotalers" in the sense of preferring water to the alcohol solution. In such studies, the "drinking" mice show a minimum of 30-50% alcohol in their bloodstream at the height of their drinking "episodes." In addition, there was a high relationship between drinking and sleep, with the nondrinking strains reacting more to injected alcohol by spending more time "sleeping it off." The "drinkers" slept for a shorter period, per-

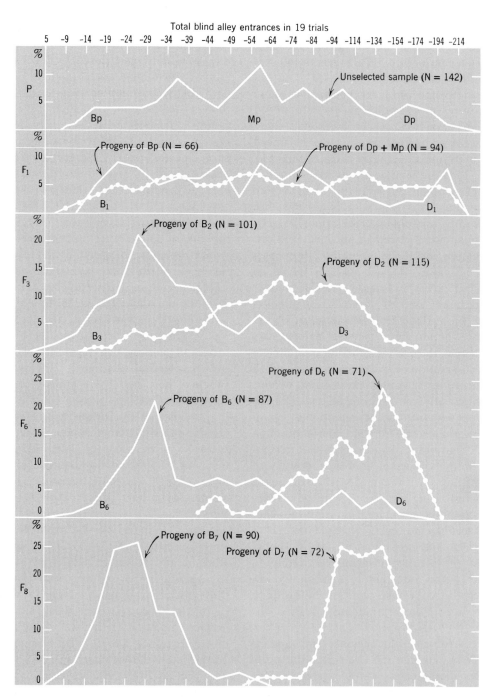

Figure 3-6. **Differences between maze-bright and maze-dull animals in successive generations.**
SOURCE: F. Moss (Ed.), *Comparative psychology.* © 1934. Reprinted by permission of Prentice-Hall, Inc., Englewood Cliffs, N.J.

haps as a result of the more rapid oxidation of the alcohol from the action of the liver enzyme found in their system.

Of all the animals with whom man has interacted, the dog has attained the highest peak of affection and acceptance. Dogs have been bred and crossbred for show and for more functional purposes. The German shepherd and the doberman make excellent guard dogs because of their strong physique and aggressive territorial defense behavior, the fox terrier and dachshund were deliberately bred for aggressive temperaments and size compact enough to search and seize vermin and badgers, the basenjis are noted for their "active defense reflexes" of attack, while the Alsatian breed is characterized by the "passive defense reflex" of cowardice and withdrawal. Dog breeders and handlers are also familiar with breed differences in fear of loud sounds, pain hypersensitivity, shyness to being touched, and certain innate behavioral patterns such as baying, retrieving, swimming, and setting. Scott and Fuller (1965) have reported on an extensive study spanning a 13-year period at the Jackson Laboratories in Bar Harbor, Maine. Five breeds were selected for their well-controlled study: basenjis, beagles, American cocker spaniels, Shetland sheep dogs (shelties), and wire-haired fox terriers. Because they wished to study the influence of genetic factors alone, the researchers kept strict control over the influences of nongenetic factors such as physiological characteristics, social environmental variables, and the physical conditions during rearing. Thus, all animals underwent carefully prescribed contacts with humans and other dogs, lived in the same types of draft-free insulated dog houses with attached sun porches, and played in identical nurseries equipped with the same "toys" such as tire casings to chew on and steps and ramps to clamber on. Two types of results are of interest: those on emotionality and those

on problem-solving skills. Using behavioral measures and physiological indices, the authors found "that heredity greatly affects the expression of emotional behavior and also that differences in emotional behavior form a prominent part of the characteristic behavior of breeds. . . ." (p. 204). Overall, the terriers proved to be most emotional, closely followed by the beagles and basenjis, then the shepherds, and finally the cockers. On problem-solving tasks, differences were also consistently found attributable to heredity (breed) differences. In the Barrier or Detour Test, the animal is permitted to see the food goal but prevented from reaching it via a direct route. To solve the problem, the animal must go against his instincts and move *away* from the food until he passes around the U-shaped barrier. Basenjis proved most competent, while the cockers and shepherds were least capable. A Maze Test with six different choice points also pointed out breed differences after differences in conditions of testing and in rearing were held constant. Beagles showed the most outstanding performances in terms of speed and the ability to avoid developing strong incorrect stereotyped habits in turning. The shelties were again the poorest performers. Of note was the interaction between emotions (timidity) and the ability to follow a scented trail—the worst performances were shown by the basenjis because they seemed actually afraid of the scent itself, a case in some ways similar to the problems of those neurotic persons whose capacity to function are blocked by their emotions. Their findings on the effects of practice observable in one test were of particular importance. Practice served to *increase* the stability of the observed differences between breeds, leading the researchers to comment, "One must conclude that training does not decrease, and possibly stabilizes, the contribution of heredity to individual variation. The point is important, for it is sometimes assumed that . . . demonstration of modifiability by training makes is unnecessary to account for any variance for heredity. The logic of this argument is clearly false and experimental data contradict it" (pp. 254–255).

Human Family History Studies. In the family history method, the investigator looks backward into the family trees of individuals with certain psychological abnormalities. Since we cannot systematically mate humans according to predetermined scientific patterns, the next nearest thing is to trace the results of marriages for which there is information on several generations of offspring. Typically, such "pedigree" studies have involved cases of pathological traits easily traced genealogically, in families prolific enough to produce sufficient offspring to allow some analysis. The prime examples of this type of evidence are connected with Huntington's chorea, and defects of intelligence. Huntington's chorea is named after a country doctor whose physician-father and physician-grandfather before him had noted the disease symptoms in generation after generation of certain families. Sjögren (1935) systematically documented (see Fig. 3-7) the family tree of a case of Huntington's chorea appearing in a male. During five generations of marriages where all spouses were normal, two offspring in the first generation were affected, seven were affected in the next, fifteen in the third, and two in the fourth. In comparison, the pedigree for a schizophrenic family is included (Fig. 3-8). Here too, the high incidence of illness in the offsprings is striking.

The notorious families of the Jukes and the Kallikaks have often served as examples of what can happen from the transmission of defective genes. Both passed on generations of feeblemindedness and "degeneracy." The original Jukes (Estabrook, 1916; Dugdale, 1877) were five sisters who produced legitimate and illegitimate offspring traceable for at least seven generations. They were first officially noticed when six members of the same family were found in prison in a single county in New York in 1874. Follow up pedigrees unfolded a history of 540 per-

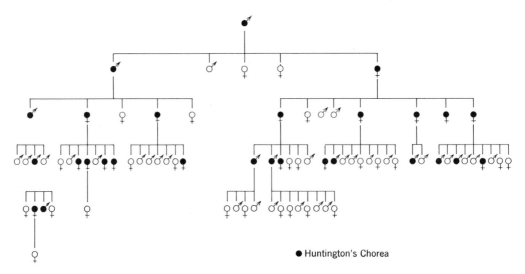

● Huntington's Chorea

Figure 3-7. **Inheritance of Huntington's Chorea in a family.**
SOURCE: T. Sjögren, Vererbungsmedizinishe Untersuchunger über Huntington's Chorea in einer schwedischen Bauernpopulation. In *Zeitschrift für menschliche Vererbungs-und Konstitutions-lehre.* Bd. 19, S.131-165. Berlin: Springer, 1936.

sons with extensive histories of disease, degeneracy, crime, and pauperism. The Kallikaks (Goddard, 1919) were not better: they represented two genealogical family lines originally fathered by a military man of the American Revolution, Martik Kallikak, Sr. During his military career, he started one lineage by impregnating a feebleminded tavern maid. Later, he married an intellectually capable girl of his own social status to begin a legitimate line of progeny. As with the Jukes, the offspring of Kallikak's feebleminded mate abounded in mental deficiency, immorality, alcoholism, and character defect (see Fig. 3-9, page 74). On the other hand, the results of the legitimized mating were normal, self-respecting persons, many of whom achieved distinction. Both reports have subsequently been soundly criticized for the conclusion drawn—that they represent incontroversial proof of the strength of heredity over environment. There were no controls over the types of environment

to which the various offspring were exposed, a problem characteristic of pedigree studies when one must accept the conditions as presented by Nature. In addition, psychologists have felt highly dubious about the genetic transmission of such traits as "degeneracy" and "immorality."

Human Population Studies. In these studies, the influence of heredity is explored through census taking, vital statistics, or registries of reportable diseases. Examination of data repeatedly obtained from a population can indicate trends in the development of that group. Mental health data may be obtained from all persons living in areas with a high degree of environmental and social stability, such as rural towns. By tracing the year-by-year changes in the incidence of specific mental illnesses, and examining these rates in relation to other data such as consanguinity rate in marriage, or genealogical research, it is possible to improve on the limited pedigree approach. This method

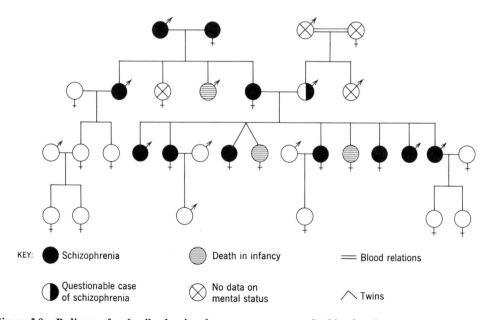

Figure 3-8. **Pedigree of a family showing frequent occurrence of schizophrenia.**
SOURCE: F. J. Kallmann, The genetic theory of schizophrenia. *American Journal of Psychiatry,* 1946, **103**, 309-322. Copyright 1946, American Psychiatric Association.

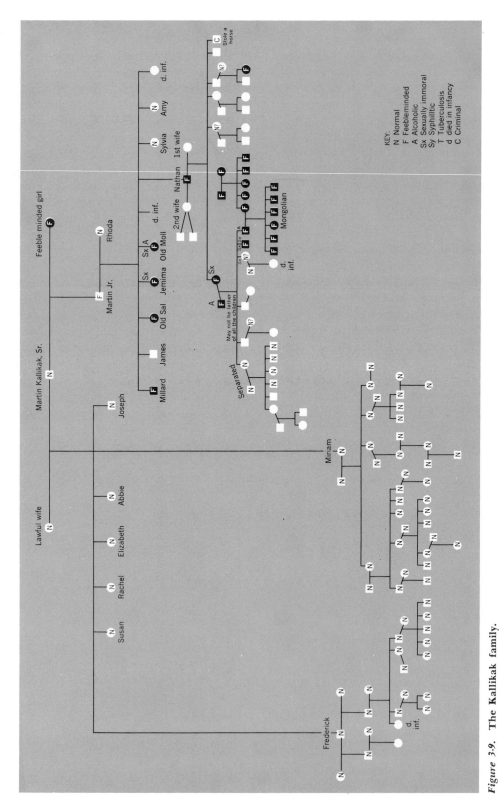

Figure 3-9. **The Kallikak family.**

SOURCE: Adapted from H. Goddard. *The Kallikak family*. New York: Macmillan, 1912.

Two members of the *Hutterites*, a religious sect with its own customs. Because of their isolation and within-group marriages, study of their mental health characteristics contributes to understanding the role of genetics in psychopathology. (Lloyd Knight/Professor Joseph W. Eaton)

has real advantages when *isolates* are discovered; those groups of people living in isolated communities are often characterized by a high rate of inbreeding. Böök (1953) undertook the incredible task of studying three complete parishes of isolated folk living thirty miles beyond the Arctic Circle. His prevalence rates involving schizophrenia and schizoid traits suggested the presence of an intermediate type gene. Another group of isolates called the Hutterities (Eaton and Weil, 1955) exist in the United States and Canada. A religious sect with beliefs in the sinfulness of marrying outsiders, all members can claim direct descendants from the founding 101 married couples who settled in South Dakota in the 1870's. Three surnames—Hofer, Waldner, and Wipt—accounted for nearly half of all families in 1950. When studies were conducted on the incidence of mental illness in this group, it was found that manic-depression was the most common form of psychoses in contrast to all other populations (in which schizophrenia has found to reign supreme). The rigidity and stability over time of the Hutterite's social order, and the high inbreeding, plus the prescribed isolation from outside influences of any significance, all argue for a genetic explanation.

Human Morbidity Risk Studies. In morbidity risk studies, the researcher calculates the chances of varying members of a family becoming ill in the same manner as a selected relative. These risk figures are taken with reference to the risk of becoming ill among nonrelatives, that is, by the general population. If the illness is inherited, then the blood relatives of the patient should be more affected with the same ailment than nonrelatives, therefore showing a higher risk or incidence rate.

There are two approaches in reporting risk data: one is to report the incidences of the illness in offspring of varying parental matings (one parent ill, both parents ill), the other is to report the incidences in persons of varying degrees of blood relationships (twins, full-siblings, half-siblings, step-siblings).

Elsässer (1952) calculated the risks for varying parental matings where psychosis was involved. In 34 cases of schizophrenic marrying schizophrenic, 39.2% of the children also became schizophrenic. In 20 cases of manic-depressives marrying another manic-depressive, the risk rate was 44.4% with nearly all affected children showing the same type of psychosis as their parents. Kallmann (1946) reports that 68.1% of the children of two schizophrenic parents in his sample became schizophrenic as compared to 16.4% of the offspring where one parent was schizophrenic and one normal. In addition, Kallmann reports the risk rate for schizophrenia to be 0.9% when both parents are normal. The results of these two reports indicate that the chances of a psychosis developing in a child born from two psychotic parents increases by two to threefold over the risk rate when at least one parent is normal.

The incidence is even more incredible when compared with the rate in the general population of two normal parents.

Kallmann (1946, 1953) is responsible for the classic research on varying risks as a result of the differing degree of blood relationships with an affected patient (called the "proband" or "index case"). He obtained information on 691 families involving 1382 twins, 2741 full-siblings, 134 half-siblings, and 74 step-siblings. In all instances, the index case had been hospitalized for schizophrenia. If psychosis is affected by heredity, then the risk figures should be increasingly higher for those persons who share a greater similarity to the index case. Thus, the incidence should be highest among identical twins (monozygotic twins), next among fraternal twins (dizygotic twins), next among full siblings, then half-siblings, step-siblings, and finally lowest for nonrelatives (see Fig. 3-11). Kallmann's results confirmed this, and appeared as follows (figures in parentheses represent later estimates):

Identical twins	85.8 (86.2)
Fraternal twins	14.7 (14.5)
Full-siblings	14.3 (14.2)
Half-siblings	7.0 (7.1)

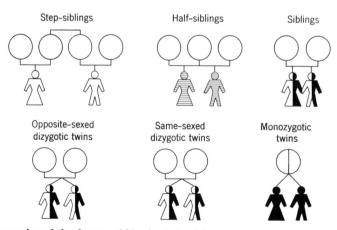

Figure 3-10. **Illustration of the degrees of blood relationship among various relatives.**
SOURCE: F. J. Kallmann, The genetic theory of schizophrenia. *American Journal of Psychiatry,* **103**, 1946, 309-322. Copyright 1946, American Psychiatric Association.

Step-siblings	1.8	(1.8)
General population	0.9	(0.9)

The following conclusions can be drawn:

1. All persons with some blood ties with the proband showed higher incidence of the same illness than nonrelatives, and the closer the relationship, the higher the incidence.

2. Approximately 85% of the siblings and fraternal twins did *not* develop schizophrenia even though 10% had a schizophrenic parent and all had a schizophrenic brother or sister (the index case) and most shared the *same* family environment—if schizophrenia is caused by psychological or environmental factors alone, how did these normal siblings escape, and why were fewer of the identical twins able to avoid being affected?

3. Among the monozygotic twins who were also affected, 17.6% had their breakdowns on *exactly* the *same* day as their proband sibling, and altogether 70.5% occurred before four years had gone by.

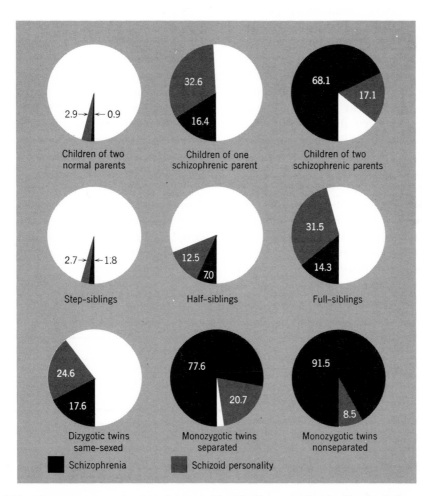

Figure 3-11. **The expectancy of schizophrenia and schizoid personality in blood relatives of schizophrenic patients.**
SOURCE: F. J. Kallmann, The genetic theory of schizophrenia. *American Journal of Psychiatry,* 103, 1946, 309-322. Copyright 1946, American Psychiatric Association.

In addition, dissimilarities in symptoms occurred *only* when there was dissimilarities in age of onset.

4. In the monozygotic twins who lived together, the incidence figure was 91.5%, and the risk figure was 77.6 for twins who had been separated, thus confirming the power of the genetic influence even with changes in the environment.

Similar risk data suggest genetic factors in other types of psychiatric states (see Table 3-2), including manic-depressive psychosis (Kallmann, 1953; Luxemburger, 1942), childhood schizophrenia (Kallmann and Roth, 1956), involutional psychosis (Kallmann, 1950), and senile psychosis (Kallmann, 1950). It is intriguing to note that schizophrenia and manic-depressive psychosis appear to be clearly distinct from one another; whatever genetic mechanism is involved in the one illness is specific only to that illness. Thus, Hurst (1952) was unable to find any case among 1232 index cases where the twins exhibited nonidentical psychoses.

Many reports on risk have concentrated on the twin groups alone. Typically, they concern the chances of a twin being affected by the same illness as the proband. Cases where there is such agreement are called *concordant*. Where a genetic factor is present, the concordance rates are expected to be higher for the monozygotic twins than for the dizygotic pairs because the members of the first group actually possess the same gene structure while the members of the latter simply shared the same uterine environment (see Table 3-3). Zygosity is determined by comparing certain physical characteristics such as earlobes, fingerprints, blood group, and dental features. For example, Kallmann, Feingold and Body (1951) were able to determine that such physical similarities persisted into old age, such that their sample of 108 twins over the age of 60 showed similarities in size, the amount of baldness, and even the amount and location of wrinkles. Using the concordance approach, Slater (1953) confirmed Kallmann's earlier work with schizophrenics, and Da Fonseca (1959) added supporting data on manic-depressives. Among twin pairs where both were ill, remarkable resemblances were found in their general symptoms, tendencies toward self-injury, age of onset of the illness, type of onset (gradual or sudden), and course (one or more attacks). Rosenthal (1963) was involved in the incredible discovery of identical quadruplet girls all concordant for schizophrenia, an occurrence that takes

TABLE 3-2. *The Expectancy of Various Types of Mental Illness in Blood Relatives of an Afflicted Person*

FAMILY RELATIONSHIP	MENTAL ILLNESS				
	SCHIZO-PHRENIA	MANIC-DEPRESSION	CHILDHOOD SCHIZO-PHRENIA	INVOLUTIONAL PSYCHOSES	SENILE PSYCHOSES
Monozygotic twins	86.2%	95.7%	70.6%	60.9%	42.8%
Dizygotic twins	14.5%	26.3%	17.1%	6.0%	8.0%
Full-siblings	14.2%	23.0%	12.2%	6.0%	6.5%
Half-siblings	7.1%	16.7%	—	4.5%	—
Step-siblings	1.8%	—	—	—	—
Unrelated (gen. popul.)	0.9%	0.4%	—	1.0%	<1.0%

SOURCE: Adapted from L. Hurst, Classification of psychotic disorders from a genetic point of view. *Proceed. Second Intern. Congr. of Human Genet.* Vol. III. Rome: Instituto G. Mendel, 1963.

place only once in every billion and a half births. Intensive psychological study of these girls showed that they had similar personality traits before their illnesses, and similar symptoms during the course of their illnesses.

It is interesting to note that although twins show exceptional similarities in many aspects of their psychoses, distinct differences often exist in the durations of the illnesses and the chances for recovery (Slater, 1953; Essen-Moller, 1941; Rosenthal, 1963). This points to the possibility that environmental factors are still important in determining the outcomes of genetically based illnesses. Shields and Slater (1960) reported on twins reared apart with distances ranging from living in the same neighborhood to being raised in different continents. Their results suggest that twins brought up in different homes can still resemble one another to a high degree in personality and temperament because of their genetic commonality. However, these scientists also concluded that "On the whole the kind of home made a bigger difference than the degree of separation. In pairs that differed most psychiatrically there was generally some definitely unsatisfactory feature in the early enviroment of the twin who had the poorer mental health" (p. 324).

Although not a morbidity risk study, the work of Gottesman on the "Hered-

itability of Personality" (1963) deserves mention. Starting with the names of over 31,000 schoolchildren, he identified and contacted 163 pairs of same-sex twins. Of these, 68 pairs were able to cooperate in the research. These twins were carefully diagnosed for zygosity on the basis of blood type, with half of the group being identified as monozygotic twins and the other half being dizygotic. Personality traits were then assessed by psychological tests and the results statistically analyzed to determine which traits seemed to be most influenced by a genetic component. A trait was considered to be genetically related if the degree of similarity between the scores of identical twins was significantly higher than that between fraternal twins. Extraversion-introversion and social withdrawal were among the traits identified as genetically influenced. In addition, scores representing the psychiatric disorders of depression, schizophrenia, psychasthenia, and psychopathic personality appeared significantly affected by inheritance. Gottesman suggests that these findings lend some "support to the general idea that in human beings psychopathology, especially psychosis, has a substantial genetic component" (p. 16). It should be noted, however, that he himself cautions earlier in his report that such conclusions are based on many methodological assumptions, and that the results should

TABLE 3-3. *Concordance Rates for Mental Illness for Monozygotic and Dizygotic Twins*

FORM OF ILLNESS	MONOZYGOTIC TWINS		DIZYGOTIC TWINS	
	RATE	N	RATE	N
Schizophrenia	86.2%	268	14.5%	685
Childhood schizophrenia	70.6%	17	17.1%	35
Manic-depression	95.7%	23	26.3%	52
Senile psychosis	42.8%	33	8.0%	75
Involutional melancholia	60.9%	29	6.0%	67

SOURCE: J. Shields & E. Slater, Heredity and psychological abnormality. From H. Eysenck (Ed.), *A handbook of abnormal psychology.* © 1960, Pitman Medical Publishing Co., Inc. New York: Basic Books, 1961.

therefore be "recognized as suggestive and heuristic rather than definitive" (p. 15).

The question of the relative contribution of genetics and environment to the formation of psychopathology has been asked by many and studied by many for a long time. The work of Shields and Slater previously mentioned, along with the contributions of others (Rosenthal, 1959; Brackbill and Fine, 1956; Gottesman and Shields, 1966) make it clear that the riddle of genetics versus environmental contributions to mental illness is still far from being resolved. It is possible that two forms of schizophrenia exist, one as an inherited variety and another with similar symptoms but resulting from psychological factors. Another possibility that bears intensive exploration is Kallmann's belief that a defense system is also inherited and interacts with the schizophrenia gene factor, permitting some persons to show greater resistence to this mental illness. This inherited resistence factor explains the differences in severity of symptoms and outcomes and those cases of discordance where the symptoms are completely suppressed in one twin. Kallmann writes, "The marked differences in the penetrance and expressivity of the schizophrenic genotype may be interpreted as being controlled by a genetically non-specific constitutional defense mechanism . . . which . . . may . . . be identical with or related to . . . (those defenses which also prevent) the multiplication of tubercle bacilli" (Kallmann, 1953, p. 153). A third possible way of resolving the genetic-environment question is to integrate the two. Rosenthal proposes in his *diathesis-stress* theory that schizophrenia is caused by an interaction between heredity and environment. What is inherited is a predisposition to mental illness, perhaps as a result of polygenes which accumulate to determine differences in symptom severity. Environmental stresses serve to activate the predisposition, leading to the expression of the illness in symptoms. Thus, it is possible for the individual to remain symptom-free for years in the absence of the appropriate stressors. Most genetic-oriented workers favor the diathesis-stress type belief in multifactorial genetic mechanisms and polygene influences of explanation (Essen-Möller, 1941; Gottesman and Shields, 1966; Meehl, 1962; Rosenthal, 1963).

The current state of knowledge is perhaps best reflected in remarks by Rainer (1962) during the anniversary symposium of the Department of Medical Genetics at the New York State Psychiatric Institute—Kallmann's primary base of activities. Dr. Rainer said, "Operating by means of a long series of interactions and feedback mechanisms, the development of schizophrenia most certainly includes biochemical, neurological and psychological alterations. Therefore, it is to specialists in these fields that one turns for further elucidation of the problems of specificity and pathogenesis in this disorder" (p. 6).

Chromosome Studies. The direct examination of chromosomes has recently been made more precise through the introduction of skillfull photographic methods. It is now possible to actually obtain a picture of chromosomes, called a karyotype. The chromosomes are photographed in sequential order. They are then identified by a sequence number in accordance with an international classification scheme adopted in 1960 at a conference in Denver. Karyotypes of abnormal persons can now be compared with those of normal persons to determine if genetic abberations are present. Several types of chromosomal abberrations have been discovered, many of which are associated with physical abnormalities but not necessarily with psychological abnormalities. Among such aberrations are abnormalities in the number of chromosomes.

Mongolism, or Down's syndrome, is a type of mental retardation that will be discussed in more detail in Chapter 17.

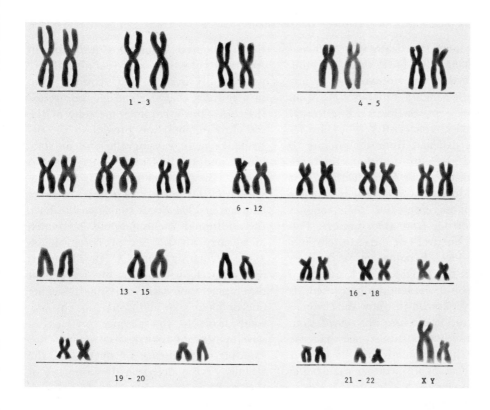

An example of the normal pairs of chromosomes of the author appears in the top photograph. Below it is an illustration of the abnormal set (#21) of a *Mongoloid* with three instead of two chromosomes. (Top: Courtesy of R. Brannon, and W. Dewey, Department of Radiation Biology, Colorado State University) (Below: From *Principles of Genetics*, 3rd Ed., by Eldon J. Gardner, John Wiley and Sons.)

Current evidence indicates that afflicted individuals usually have three chromosomes instead of the normal two in one of the sets (sequence number 21). Mongoloids have very distinctive intellectual and physical characteristics. They are intellectually deficient from a moderate to a severe degree. In addition, they are small in stature, have facial features that make them look somewhat Oriental (hence the term, mongolism), and their tongues tend to protrude from their mouths. Following the discovery of the extra chromosome in 1959 (Lejeune, et al.), many believe that this provides conclusive proof that mongolism is genetically caused. It is still not yet known just how the chromosomal aberration produces the retardation. In fact, another possibility is that the additional chromosome is in itself another symptom of mongolism rather than being a causative agent.

Two recently publicized court cases emphasize another chromosomal aberration and its relationship to pathology. In 1968,

the Melbourne Criminal Court jury in Australia ruled that a 21-year-old laborer was "legally insane," and acquitted him of a murder charge. The defense argued that an extra Y chromosome (one of the sex chromosomes) was present in the defendant's cells, causing the violent stabbing crime. In the United States, Richard Speck, tall and mentally dull, was convicted of the murder of eight nurses in Chicago in 1966. Speck is also said to have the additional Y chromosome. Normally, men carry an XY set of chromosomes while women have an XX set. These sets determine the sex and the physical sexual development of each individual; lacking one or having an additional sex chromosome leads to the absence or lack of development of sexual chracteristics, for example, the absence of ovaries in the female, or the defective development of the testes in the male. In 1962, Court Brown noted that delinquency seemed to be high among his own patients with sex chromosome aberrations. Since then, a

TABLE 3-4.   *The XYY Chromosome Aberration and Aggressive Behavior*

NUMBER OF PERSONS EXAMINED	POPULATION	CHARACTERISTICS	NUMBER OF XYY	INVESTIGATOR
10,725	Newborn		0	Maclean et al. (1964)
2607	Retarded	Intellectually deficient	0	Maclean et al. (1962)
197	Institutionalized	Intellectually deficient, criminal	7	Jacobs et al. (1965)
942	Institutionalized	Intellectually deficient, criminal	12	Casey et al. (1966)
315	Institutionalized	Criminal	9	Price et al. (1966)
19	Detention center	Criminal	1	Telfer et al. (1968a)
129	Institutionalized	Criminal	5	Telfer et al. (1968b)
34	Prison	Criminal	3	Wiener et al. (1968)
1021	Institutionalized	Delinquent	3	Hunter (1968)

number of researchers have looked for such anomalies among patients known for aggressive behavior or prisoners guilty of violent crimes. To date, results have shown that a greater proportion of patients and prisoners possess extra chromosomes than tends to occur in normal persons (see Table 3-4) (Forssman and Hambert, 1963; Moor, 1967; Price, Strong, Whatmore, and McClemont, 1966). The most prominent abberation in such males seems to be the presence of an extra Y chromosome, or XYY. Jacobs et al. (1965) found 7 cases of XYY among 197 retarded persons kept in maximum security because of their aggressive actions, Wiener, et al. (1968) discovered 3 out of 34 men in a penal institution. In contrast, Maclean et al. (1964) reported no cases of XYY among 10,725 newborn and none among 2607 mentally retarded without aggressive behaviors, while Court Brown et al. (1964) noticed only 1 in 2000 men in Edinburgh. The presence of the extra Y chromosome also seems to be associated with tall stature, with the XYY men generally measuring well over six feet (see Table 3-5). In addition, some but not all of these men are mentally retarded. Of significance is the presence of abnormal electroencephalographic records (brain wave) taken from individuals with supernumery chromosomes (Hambert, 1966; Hambert and Frey, 1964). Such evidence is highly suggestive of a possible relationship between aggressive behavior and chromosomal aberration. Much more research is necessary before such a relationship can be considered a conclusive and invariant one (Suinn, 1969). An important piece of information is yet to be gathered: the frequency with which the XYY appears in prisoners convicted of nonviolent crimes. Basically, we must determine whether the XYY condition *invariably* leads to violence, or whether the XYY aberration must be paired with other factors to produce violence, or finally (as is the question with mongolism) whether the XYY condition is a remarkable coincidental occurrence and has little or no influence on violence.

TABLE 3-5. *Heights of Normal Versus XYY Chromosome Men in a State Hospital*

MEN	HEIGHT (INCHES)						
	57-59	60-62	63-65	66-68	69-71	72-74	75 AND ABOVE
Normal (XY)[a]	2	18	63	134	73	13	1
Aberrant (XYY or XXYY)[b]	0	0	0	1	2	6	1

[a] The average height of the XY men was 67.2 inches.
[b] The average height of the XYY men was 71.8 inches.
SOURCE: Adapted from W. Court Brown, *Human population cytogenetics*. New York: Wiley, 1967.

Glossary

Childhood schizophrenia: Schizophrenia occurring early in life.

Chromosome: Elongated, microscopic substances present in cells as 23 pairs. Responsible for genetic transmission.

Chromosomal aberration: An abnormality in chromosomes either in structure or in numbers.

Concordance: Cases are considered concordant if both persons studied share a common illness. Used in twin studies, where one is mentally ill, to determine the influence of genetics.

Consanguinity rate: The rate of occurrence of an illness in relatives of a patient under study.

Diabetes mellitus: One type of disease involving the deficiency of insulin; this type is believed to be inherited.

Diathesis-stress theory: The theory that mental illness is a result of a predisposition caused genetically, but triggered by environmental stress.

D.N.A.: Deoxyribonucleic acid, a substance directly involved in genetic coding and transmission.

Etiology: The origins or causes of an illness.

Eugenics: The attempt to improve on human characteristics by selective mating.

Gene: Protein molecules containing the substance D.N.A. involved in genetic transmission.

Gene, dominant: A gene that predominates and can therefore have an effect when singly represented.

Gene, recessive: A gene that requires a matching similar gene for expression.

Gene, intermediate: Genes whose effects are neither dominant nor recessive, but of an in-between effect.

Hematology: The study of blood and its diseases.

Hemophilia: A sex-linked disease involving the failure of the blood to clot. Persons with hemophilia can bleed to death from even minor cuts.

Heterozygous: For a given pair of chromosomes, the lack of similarity within the pair.

Homozygous: Both chromosomes within a pair match.

Hutterites: A religious sect living in self-imposed isolation with prohibitions against marrying outsiders.

Imprinting: The acquisition of complex behaviors in early life through the presentation of a triggering cue. These behaviors become highly resistant to change.

Incidence: The number of new cases of an illness appearing during a given period.

Involutional melancholia: A form of mental illness occurring during the "change of life" and characterized by depression.

Karyotype: A photograph of chromosomes.

Mongolism: Also known as Down's syndrome. A type of mental retardation characterized by short stature, protruding tongue, Oriental-looking eyes, and intellectual deficit.

Ovum: Female egg.

Penetrance: The ability of a gene to be expressed in overt characteristics.

Polygene: Genes that have no effects alone but that join with other genes to have a cumulative effect.

Prevalence: The total number of all existing cases of an illness during a given period.

Proband case: Also called Index case. In genetic studies, this is the reference case.

Psychasthenia: A term, seldom used currently, referring to a neurosis marked by anxiety, obsessions, or fixed ideas. Often corresponds to anxiety reaction.

Psychopathic personality: A seldom-used term corresponding to antisocial disorder.

P.T.C.: Phenylthiocarbamide, a substance that tastes bitter to some persons but has no taste to others.

Senile psychosis: A type of psychosis caused by aging and deterioration and characterized by emotional blunting, faulty memory, loss of self-care habits, and intellectual deficit.

Sperm: The male sex organism involved in reproduction and fertilization.

Twins, monozygotic: Persons sharing the same chromosomal makeup and the same intrauterine environment.

Twins, dizygotic: Persons sharing the same intrauterine environment but having different chromosomal makeups.

Zygote: An egg fertilized by a sperm.

References

Böök, J. A genetic and neuropsychiatric investigation of a North Swedish population. I. Psychoses, *Acta Genetic.,* 1953, 4, 1.

Brackbill, G. & Fine, H. Schizophrenia and central nervous system pathology. *J. abnorm. soc. Psychol.,* 1956, **52**, 310.

Casey, M., Blank, C., Street, D., Segall, L., McDougall, J., McGrath, P., & Skinner, J. YY chromosomes and anti-social behavior. *Lancet,* 1966, 2, 859.

Casey, M., Segall, L., Street, D., & Blank, C. Sex chromosome abnormalities in two state hospitals for patients requiring special security. *Nature,* 1966, **209**, 641.

Court Brown, W. Sex chromosomes and the law. *Lancet,* 1962, 2, 508.

Court Brown, W., Harnden, D., Jacobs, P., Maclean, N., & Mantle, D. *Abnormalities of the sex chromosome complement in man.* Special Report Series No. 305. Medical Research Council. London: H. M. Stationery Office, 1964.

Da Fonseca, A. *Analyse heredo-clinica das perturbacoes affectivas atraves de 60 pares de gemeos.* Oporto: Faculdade de Mecina, 1959.

Dugdale, R. *The Jukes: a study in crime, pauperism, disease, and heredity.* New York: Putnam, 1877.

Eaton, J. & Weil, R. *Culture and mental disorders.* Glencoe Ill.: Free Press, 1955.

Elsässer, G. *Die Nachkommen geisteskranker Elternpaare.* New York: Grune & Stratton, 1952.

Essen-Möller, E. Psychiatrische Untersuchungen an einer Serie von Zwillingen. *Acta Psychiat. Scandinavica,* 1941, Suppl. 23.

Estabrook, A. *The Jukes in 1915.* Washington, D.C.: Carnegie Institute, 1916.

Forssman, H. & Hambert, G. Incidence of Klinefelter's syndrome among mental patients. *Lancet,* 1963, 1, 1327.

Ginsburg, B. & Allee, W. Some effects of conditioning on social dominance and subordination in inbred strains of mice. *Physiol. Zool.,* 1942, **12**, 585.

Goddard, H. *The Kallikak family.* New York: MacMillan, 1919.

Gottesman, I. Genetic aspects of intelligent behavior. In N. Ellis (Ed.), *The handbook in mental deficiency.* New York: McGraw-Hill, 1963.

Gottesman, I. Heritability of personality, *Psychol. Monogr.,* 1963, **77**, no. 572.

Gottesman, I. & Shields, J. Contributions of twin studies to perspectives on schizophrenia. In B. Maher (Ed.) *Progress in experimental personality research, Vol. 3.* New York: Academic Press, 1966.

Haldane, J. *The biochemistry of genetics.* London: Allen, 1952.

Hall, C. Emotional behavior in the rat: I. Defecation and urination as measures of individual differences in emotionality. *J. comp. Psychol.,* 1934, **18**, 385.

Hambert, G. *Males with positive sex chromatin.* Gothenburg: Akademiförlaget, 1966.

Hunter, H. Chromatin-positive and XYY boys in approved schools. *Lancet,* 1968, 2, 816.

Hurst, L. Research in genetics and psychiatry. *Eugen. News,* 1952, 4, 86.

Jacobs, P., Brunton, M., Melville, M., Brittain, R., & McClemont, W. Aggressive behavior, mental subnormality and the XYY male. *Nature,* 1965, 208, 1351.

Kallmann, F. The genetic theory of schizophrenia. *Amer. J. Psychiat.,* 1946, 103, 309.

Kallmann, F. *Heredity in health and mental disorder.* New York: Norton, 1953.

Kallmann, F. The genetics of psychoses: an analysis of 1,232 twin index families. *Congr. int. psychiat. Rapports.* 1950, 6, 1.

Kallmann, F., Feingold, L., & Body, E. Comparative adaptional, social and psychometric data on the life histories of senescent twin pairs. *Amer. J. hum. Genet.,* 1951, 3, 65.

Kallmann, F. & Roth, B. Genetic aspects of preadolescent schizophrenia. *Amer. J. Psychiat.,* 1956, 112, 599.

Lejeune, J., Turpin, R., & Gautier, M. Le mongolisme, premier example d'aberration autosomique humaine. *Ann. Genetique,* 1959, 2, 41.

Lorenz, K. Der kumpan in der unwelt des vogels. *J. Ornith,* 1935, 83, 289.

Luxemburger, J. Das zirkulare Irresein. In A. Gutt (Ed.), *Handbuch der Erbkrankheiten.* Vol. 4. Leipzig: Thieme, 1942.

Maclean, N., Harnden, D., Court Brown, W., Bond, J., & Mantle, D. Sex chromosome abnormalities in newborn babies. *Lancet,* 1964, 1, 286.

Maclean, N., Mitchell, J., Harnden, D., Williams, J., Jacobs, P., Buckton, K., Baikie, A., Court Brown, W., McBride, J., Strong, J., Close, H., & Jones, D. A survey of sex chromosome abnormalities among 4514 mental defectives. *Lancet,* 1962, 1, 293.

Meehl, P. Schizotaxia, schizotypy, schizophrenia. *Amer. Psychol.,* 1962, 17, 827.

Moor, T. Sex chromosomal aberrations and antisocial behavior, present stage of knowledge. *Ann. intern. de Criminol.,* 1967, 6, 459.

Pauling, L. & Itano, H. (Eds.) *Molecular structure and biological specificity.* Washington, D.C.: *Amer. Instit. Biol. Sci.,* 1957.

Price, W., Strong J., Whatmore, P., & McClemont, W. Criminal patients with XYY sex-chromosome complement. *Lancet,* 1966, 1, 565.

Race, R. & Sanger, R. *Blood groups in man.* (2nd ed.). Springfield, Ill.: Thomas, 1954.

Rainer, J. Studies in the genetics of disordered behavior: methods and objectives. In F. Kallmann (Ed.), *Expanding goals of genetics in Psychiatry.* New York: Grune & Stratton, 1962.

Rodgers, D. & McClearn, G. Mouse strain differences in preference for various concentrations of alcohol. *J. stud. Alcohol,* 1962, 23, 26.

Rosenthal, D. Familial concordance by sex with respect to schizophrenia. *Psychol. Bull.,* 1962, 59, 401.

Rosenthal, D. (Ed.) *The Genain quadruplets.* New York: Basic Books, 1963.

Rosenthal, D. Some factors associated with concordance and discordance with respect to schizophrenia in monozygotic twins. *J. nerv. ment. Dis.,* 1959, 129, 1.

Scott, J. Emotional behavior of fighting mice caused by conflict between weak stimulatory and weak inhibitory training. *J. comp. physiol. Psychol.,* 1947, 40, 275.

Scott, J. & Fuller. J. *Genetics and the social behavior of the dog.* Chicago: University of Chicago Press, 1965.

Searle, L. The organization of hereditary maze-brightness and maze-dullness. *Genet. psychol. Monogr.,* 1949, 39, 270.

Shields, J. & Slater, E. Heredity and psychological abnormality. In H. J. Eysenck (Ed.), *Handbook of abnormal psychology.* New York: Basic Books, 1960.

Sjögren, T. Vererbungsmedizinische untersuchungen über Huntington's Chorea in einer schwedischen Bauernpopulation. *A. menschl. Vereb. -u. Konstitlehre,* 1935, 19, 131.

Slater, E. *Psychotic and neurotic illnesses in twins.* London: H. M. Stationery Office, 1953.

Suinn, R. The need for data on false positives among the XYY chromosomal aberrants. *Lancet,* 1969, 1, 157.

Telfer, M., Baker, D., & Lontin, L. YY syndrome in an American negro. *Lancet,* 1968, 1, 95 (a).

Telfer, M., Baker, D., Clark, G., & Richardson, C. Incidence of gross chromosomal errors among tall criminal American males. *Science,* 1968, 159, 1249 (b).

Thompson, W. The inheritance and development of intelligence. *Proceed. Assoc. res. nerv. mental Dis.,* 1954, 33, 209.

Tinbergen, N. *The study of instinct.* London: Oxford University Press, 1951.

Tryon, R. Genetic differences in maze-learning ability in rats. *39th Yearbook, Nat. Soc. Stud. Educ.,* Part I, 1940, 111.

Wiener, S., Sutherland, G., Bartholomew, A., & Hudson, B. XYY males in a Melbourne prison. *Lancet,* 1968, 1, 816.

4 Contributors to Personality: Sociocultural Factors

In direct opposition to the position that personality is genetically determined is the viewpoint that society molds man's nature, that man is a product of his social environment. There is no doubt that man is a social being: he chooses for the most part to live near others, thinks up ways of increasing the means for communicating with others, and establishes codes for behaving so as to facilitate societal living. This characteristic of man-as-a-social-being has caused scholars to develop a discipline, *sociology*, devoted to the study of man in his social environment. We shall summarize some of their ideas as the background for the discussion on sociocultural factors which will appear later in this chapter.

FUNDAMENTALS OF THE STUDY OF SOCIETY

A *society* includes the organized population of people living together and sharing a mutual sense of belonging. In the modern world today, society has become nearly synonymous with the word *nation*. Each society or nation exposes its members to specific cultural influences. A *culture* is the socially transmitted mass of attitudes, ideas, values, practices, and beliefs of the society; another term for culture is *social heritage*. Whether we realize it or not, our culture is continuously impressed upon us, preparing us to think and act and feel in ways that are consistent with the identity of our society. Our social heritage is omnipresent, repeating its themes over and over again through every advertisement, every value preached in church and school, every law controlling our behaviors.

Early in life, the child is exposed to the task of learning his culture. This training is facilitated through the establishment of such institutions as the family, the school, the church, the state. This acquisition process is referred to as *socialization*. The child may become aware of what his culture demands in a very direct way, for example, through his parent's admonition: "We just don't *do* things *that* way, that's barbaric, let's be more civilized." Or he may acquire the elements of his social heritage indirectly, for example, what is right and what is wrong is often transmitted in fairy tales, bedtime stories with "good" being embodied in the heroes and heroines, and "bad" being exhibited by the villains.

Each society establishes its customs and values along with different degrees of sanction for violations. A *sanction* is the punishment invoked when a custom is broken; it enables the society to retain social control over individuals. A folkway is that type of social heritage which is passed on from generation to generation but which has only mild sanctions. An example is the rule governing the use of the knife: we are expected to use a knife as an implement for cutting and not for carrying food. A person violating this rule of etiquette may be viewed as uncouth, but never severely punished, and we may even be willing to engage in a discussion with him on the meaningfulness of the rule. *Mores,* on the other hand, are unquestionable standards of behavior that are strictly followed and strictly enforced. The willful destruction of another's life or property is strictly taboo in our society unless done in accordance with certain set rules (of warfare or self-protection).

Social control is brought about through other ways, such as stratification or the assignment of status and roles. *Stratification* involves the assignment of people to different levels or strata. Another word for these levels is *status;* a person's status is his position in the social system. A person's status or position or level may be defined in terms of social class, socioeconomic or occupational class, and even religion or race. Members of each level are deeply affected by their class; for example, one's social class limits and defines the social contacts he will have, his attitudes toward himself and others, his values and interests, motivations, and even his behavior. Upper and middle class children, for example, are molded to have good manners, to study hard, to be unaggressive, and to avoid making friends with lower class children (Hollingshead, 1949).

A *role* involves patterns of behaviors associated with a given status. A person in a given position is expected to act in certain ways by reason of his status, and he in turn expects others to behave toward him in specific ways. These behaviors are more in the order of obligations since all persons identified with the same status are expected to show the same patterns or roles. A minister is expected to be dignified and kindly and to avoid excesses, and others are expected to treat him with respect. Because of these expectations or obligations, those who accept a particular status automatically come under social control since their roles are now defined for them.

There are many advantages of having cultures and mores and status and roles. Social control has already been mentioned; those within the same society can expect a certain degree of cooperativeness and harmoniousness of life with one another. Another significant advantage is the promotion of a sense of stability within the society. Everyone in the society knows what to expect of others, the mores and sanctions explicitly control any deviations from the norm, and roles help an unfamiliar position. Unfortunately, as we shall see later, this same advantage can turn into a major disadvantage for a person moving to a different society. For a person who has lived all his life knowing what to expect and how to behave, the mores and role arrangements of a foreign society may be so deviant from his own as to make it impossible for him to adapt.

As we might expect from the discussion thus far, each society impresses itself on the very personality of its members. The majority of those within a society embody in their personalities the dominant motivations, values, ways of thinking, and traits of the society. An Asian acts, feels, and thinks pretty much like others of his society and a European tends to maintain a belief and behavioral system more like those of other Europeans. The Dobu natives of New Guinea as a group are secretive, treacherous, and violent (Benedict,

1934); but those who are members of the Alorese society are anxious, insecure, and suffer from inferiority feelings (Kardiner, 1945). Among the Tchambuli, the mores of the society act to produce a role reversal such that the women behave like men and the men like women. Tchambuli women are dominant and manage all affairs while the men are emotionally dependent and less responsible (Mead, 1935).

The evidence for the impact of sociocultural factors on personality comes from two sources: (1) the material on cross-cultural comparisons, and (2) the information from intracultural studies.

CROSS-CULTURAL COMPARISONS

It has long been a belief that temperamental differences existed across cultures. Thus, we tend to speak of the "fighting Irish," "emotional Italian," "fiery Spaniard," "autocratic Prussian," or "inscrutable Oriental." In fact, there does tend to be some truth to the existence of cultural differences in normal personality traits. The pre-World War II *Japanese* were noted for their self-discipline, imperturbability, sense of honor, obedience, and ability to accept the consequences of actions as natural consequences (Hopkins, 1945; Benedict, 1946). The *Russian* of this same period was considered from the scanty information available to be typified by a lack of interpersonal trust, little individual interest in personal planning or self-control (Mead, 1951), and a sense of acquiescence to strong authoritarian leadership (Dicks, 1952). Later study also suggested that the Russian was greatly concerned over receiving loyalty, respect, and sincerity from his group, had a strong interest in people and human affairs, evaluated others for their own merit instead of being influenced by stereotype evaluations, and was more likely to seek underlying motivations for actions (Hanfmann, 1957; Inkeles et al.,

1958). Even the *American* has been shown to possess characteristic traits. For example, Williams (1951) proposed that the American is a believer in the "personal success story," oriented toward active mastery and away from passivity, desirous of altering the status quo, overwhelmed by his own sense of generosity toward others almost as a sense of duty, concerned over moral and ethical justifications for his actions, fearful of being guilty of hypocrisy, a defender of the right to individual freedom, and uncomfortable when idle. Margaret Mead described the American national character as "a character in which aggressiveness is uncertain and undefined, to which readiness to fight anyone who starts a fight and unreadiness to engage in violence have both been held up as virtues; a character which measures its successes and failures only against near contemporaries and engages in various quantitative devices for reducing every contemporary to its own stature; a character which sees success as the reward of virtue and failure as the stigma for not being good enough . . ." (1942, pp. 193-194).

In addition to these cultural differences in normal traits, there is also evidence that certain variations of differences exist in abnormal behaviors. The *Indians* of northeastern Canada were subject to an illness called *windigo psychosis,* based on a belief in a superhuman, man-eating, fearsome giant (the "windigo") who preyed on human flesh. This grotesque monster, some twenty to thirty feet tall, was believed to have a heart of ice. Persons suffering from windigo psychosis were said to be possessed by the giant-spirit and therefore turned into cannibals often with hearts of ice.

The *Ethiopian* of the Zar cult were reported as "roaming with the hyenas" (Messing, 1959) and the *Zulu* were afflicted by an illness called ufufunyana characterized by the appearance of stereotyped dreams of flooded rivers (Loudon, 1959). The *French* and *Italian* have described *Capgras' syndrome,* a European condition whereby the patient, on meeting someone he knows well, will insist that the person is an imposter who has assumed this person's appearance (Capgras, 1924). The *Eskimos,* mainly women, have been afflicted by *pibloktoq.* The victim shows sudden fits of shouting, tearing of clothes, frantic plunges across the snowdrifts, followed by convulsive seizures and finally stuporous sleep or coma. Eight of seventeen Eskimo women associated with Peary's 1908 expedition were afflicted during one winter season.

Latah known to exist for many centuries in Malaya has recently been found in other non-Western countries such as northern Japan, Siam, the Philippines, and the Congo. Those affected, often middle-aged women of dull intelligence and compliant natures, uncontrollably mimic in pantomime the acts of others. This often leads to personal harm to the patient from those who become irritated by this behavior (Yap, 1952). Among the *Chinese* and natives of the Celebes and West Borneo, a sadly ludicrous phobia exists called *shook yong* or *karo* (Linton, 1956; Stitt and Strong, 1945). The fear is of death . . . unless the person prevents his penis from becoming inverted into his body. The analogue in women is the fear of death if the breasts are not prevented from disappearing into the chest. The fear is so

Case History 4-1

CASES OF WINDIGO PSYCHOSES

Swift Runner had taken the police to a little grave near his camp. . . . He had killed his wife and eaten her; he had forced one of his boys to kill a younger brother and cut him up, and this one he had eaten; he had then killed his baby by hanging it to a lodge pole, and while at his supper had pulled the baby's legs to hasten its strangulation. In this manner he had turned for food not only to the body of his helpmate but to his living children. He also confessed that he had done away with his mother-in-law, who, he acknowledged, was a bit tough. It was said by neighboring Indians that a brother had met the same fate. What made his act even more barbarous was the fact that while he was indulging in his ghastly orgy he had plenty of dried meat hanging around the camp.

Source: J. Turner, *The North-West Mounted Police.* Ottawa: King's Printer, 1950.

This woman was named Saweyal-nok which means streak of daylight. She was an old lady who feared that she was becoming a windigo and who, accordingly, asked her sons to kill her. She was shot by her youngest son. The oldest son cut open her body, took out the heart and split it open. He found that the heart had begun to turn to ice. The body was burned, but the oldest son was not satisfied; he took her bones, already whitened in the fire, and he pounded them to ashes.

Source: A. Hallowell, unpublished field notes. In Morton Teicher, Windigo Psychosis. *Proceed. of the 1960 Annual Spring Meeting of the Amer. Ethnol. Society,* Seattle: Amer. Ethnol. Soc., 1960.

---

intense that members of the family are desperately enlisted to grip and retain the sex organ. The *Japanese* are affected by *taijin kyofusho* (anthrophobia), manifested by feelings of inadequacy, fear of meeting people, flushing, stuttering, and other signs of anxiety. The *Ashanti* of Africa accept paranoia to such an extent that "nobody looks twice at a lorry announcement in big letters, 'Enemies all about me,' or 'Suro nnipa' (Be afraid of people)" (Field, 1960, p. 296). Epidemiological studies across the world suggest that schizophrenia is ubiquitous, however obsessional neuroses appear to be rare in the Orient (LaBarre, 1946), and manic-depressive psychosis seems uncommon in the southern Bantu African (Carothers, 1953).

Cross-cultural differences in the mode of treatment offered the mentally ill are also clearly definable. The *Iroquois* Indian believed that the soul expressed its un-conscious wishes in dreams or that the dream was used by a supernatural spirit to convey its wishes. To prevent being plagued by illness or death by an unsatiated spirit, compliance to the dream wish was therefore demanded. A council of chiefs was often convened to decide on the best means for gratifying the spirit without harming the host. Thus, a warrior who dreamed of being tortured by his tribal enemies was routinely put through part of the torture cycle thereby satisfying the dream demand without real personal danger (Wallace, 1958). The Zar cult doctor of *Ethiopia* first lures his own Zar spirit into taking possession of himself, then the doctor-spirit cajoles, prods, and threatens the spirit inhabiting the patient until this spirit identifies itself. A sequence of lengthy financial bartering then transpires between the doctor-spirit and the patient-spirit until an agreement is reached and the patient is enrolled for life

Case History 4-2

A CASE OF PIBLOKTOQ

In July 1901 I was witness of such an attack in the woman Inadtliak. It lasted 25 minutes. She sat on the ground with the legs stretched out, swaying her body to and fro, sometimes rapidly, sometimes more slowly, from side to side and tortuously, whilst she kept her hands comparatively still and only now and then moved her elbows in to her sides. She stared out in front of her quite regardless of the surroundings, and sang and screamed occasionally, changing the tone, iah-iah-iaha-ha . . . , now and then she interjected a sentence, e.g., that the Danish had at last come to them, and again the great happiness this gave her now in the glad summer-time and so on. Her two small children sat and played about her, whilst the members of the tribe scarcely looked at her during the attacks; they seemed to be very well acquainted with such things. She recovered quite suddenly and only some hectic, red spots on her cheeks indicated anything unusual. Without so much as looking about her or betraying a sign of anything unusual she began, literally with the same movement, to give her youngest child milk and then went quickly on to chew a skin.

Source: H. P. Steensby in Z. Gussow, Pibloktoq (hysteria) among the polar eskimo. In W. Muensterberger and S. Axelrad (Eds.) *The psychoanalytic study of society.* Vol. I. New York, 1960, p. 222.

Arctic expedition photograph showing an Eskimo woman during an attack of *Pibloktoq* or arctic hysteria. (The American Museum of Natural History)

into a cult of fellow sufferers. Although the patient is never offered a complete cure, membership does provide him with some status and temporary freedom from possession and illness during his periods of worship of the Zar spirit of his group (Messing, 1959). A form of treatment in modern *Japan* includes isolation in an empty room for a week, communication with the therapist through means of a diary, the assignment of simple manual tasks, and the stress on the curative forces of nature (Kora, 1965).

It has been suggested that psychopathology exists in all cultures with each society adding its own distinctive "flavor" to the psychodynamics of the illness. Thus Schooler and Caudill (1964) hypothesize that the symptoms of schizophrenia reflect each patient's strong negative reaction to the major expectations of his own culture. They support this view by noting that Japanese schizophrenics are physically assaultive in contrast to their normal interpersonal decorum, while the normally cognitively controlled American becomes bizarre and loses control over his percep-

tions and thoughts. The Japanese society enforces self-control and prevents the expression of guilt feelings. At the same time, the mores foster guilt and shame. For example, the Japanese mother assumes the personal burden of responsibility for the failure of any of her children to conduct themselves properly. Any person who fails to achieve or meet community standards must not only cope with the embarrassment of failure, but also with the additional guilt of seeing his mother shamed (De Vos, 1960; Babcock and Caudill, 1958). It is instructive to note that the Japanese who is raised in a Westernized culture (the Japanese-American or *"Nisei"*) escapes from this type of stress and shows more flexibility and less maladjustment than his brethren living in America, but originally reared in Japan and its culture (the *"Issei"*) (De Vos, 1955). The British and the American also show differences in guilt which may be attributable to cultural differences. American students were found to be clearly more anxious and prone to guilt than British students. In addition, Americans appeared

Different societies hold different beliefs about the cause and treatment of illness. Pictured is a *witch doctor* shopping for cola nuts to be used in divination. He carries under his arm other fetishes essential for his medicinal and therapeutic practice. (Marc & Evelyne Bernheim / Rapho Guillumette)

more extraverted, while the British were more introverted. When viewed in the context of the cultures, the greater anxiety and disposition to guilt has been attributed to the "rigid convictions which the society of saints planted in New England . . . the fundamentalist religious education of the (Americans)" (Cattell, 1964, pp. 561, 563). On the other hand, the British appeared to be persons who expressed their anxiety through fantasy activity; this tendency has been interpreted as a result of the greater inhibition imposed by the British culture which stresses the development of "the polish of the gentleman" (Cattell, 1964, p. 561). Perhaps the best summary of the relationship between culture and personality is that of Spiro (1959):

It is my guess . . . that each culture creates stresses and strains—some of them universal, some unique—with which the personality must cope; that the cultural heritage provides, to a greater or lesser degree, institutional techniques for their reduction, if not resolution; that the incidence of psychopathology in any society is a function not merely of the strains produced by its culture but also of the institutional means which its cultural heritage provides for the resolution of strain; that those individuals who, for whatever the reasons, cannot resolve the culturally created strains by means of the culturally provided instruments of resolution resolve them in idiosyncratic ways (neuroses and psychoses); and that to the extent that different cultures create different types of strain, idiosyncratic resolution of strain (neuroses and psychoses) will reveal cultural variability. This general theory, it need not be emphasized, does not deny the importance of idiosyncratic experiences in the development of mental illness. . . . In general, however, these experiences, though pathogenic, contribute to psychopathology because of the absence of institutionalized means for tension reduction (p. 142).

The contribution of culture on psychopathology can be seen in frequency figures for members of different societies. Laubscher (1937), a psychiatrist who did pioneer work living among the tribes of South Africa, discovered a lower rate of suicide (1 per 100,000 per year) for the Africans than for either the British (10 per 100,000) or Americans (11 per 100,000). He also noted the frequent appearance of mythical creatures in the dreams of normals, in the delusions of psychotics, and in attempts to explain psychotic behavior. Hypersexual dwarfs, blood-eating and hypersexual birds, and snakes were viewed as living in female organs to provide gratification for extramarital sexual cravings.

When the numbers of hospital admissions for mental illness are examined, there is again evidence for significant diferences across cultures. A report commissioned by the World Health Organization showed an annual admissions rate for schizophrenia in Nairobi, *East Africa* to be 1.1 per 100,000 (Carothers, 1948). In contrast, Negroes in Massachusetts were being admitted at the rate of 161 per 100,000. The report suggested that contact with other cultures was influential in the development of psychopathology. Nearly 50 percent of the Nairobi hospital admissions were natives derived from the 10 percent of the population who worked in cities or on European-owned plantations and who had lost touch with their traditional culture.

Tooth (1950) conducted a highly relevant survey of the Gold Coast region of *West Africa* (now called Ghana). Part of his data shows an annual rate of admissions to the Accra Asylum to be 3.3 per 100,000. In comparison, in *New York,* Malzberg (1940) found an admissions rate of 150.6 per 100,000 for Negroes and 73.7 for whites. Before any conclusions are drawn about the Negro-white racial discrepancy, it must be noted that socioeconomic factors played a prominent role in producing such a difference. When allowances are made for socioeconomic and urbanization variables, the differences in rates diminish. Moreover, an analysis of data on approximately seven thousand Negro and white patients in New Orleans led one researcher to conclude that "no evidence could be found of the relevance of biological-racial determinants for the incidence of neuropsychiatric conditions" (Carothers, 1953, p. 163).

It is important to note that such cross-cultural comparisons can only be considered suggestive information. Careful, systematic data is extremely difficult to obtain for a variety of reasons: the accuracy of rates varies with the ability of the investigator to obtain cooperation from tribesmen; estimates obtained from one country or even one region are not always comparable nor as reliable as data from other areas; language handicaps present real barriers; definitions of illness and methods of observation may differ for different investigators; and hospital rates may be affected by the artifact of differences in the willingness to keep at home or to hospitalize the mentally ill.

An additional area in which gross cultural differences affect mental health is seen in instances of "culture shock." For those who leave their native countries to live abroad, the impact of the foreign culture can become traumatic: the mores and roles are different, socialization techniques vary, and sanctions are provided for different behaviors. Part of the shock is due to the loss of identity that occurs when the immigrant is faced with new values, part of it derives from the intense feeling of isolation from others because of language barriers, and part of it is related to the loss of self-worth associated with a lack of the type of skills demanded for employment and status in the new society. Loneliness builds on frustration, insecurity seizes on helplessness, and tension weakens the capacity to cope. Faced with such acculturation demands, the immigrant is faced with four alternatives: (1) he can devote his fullest efforts toward becoming assimilated and acquire a new identity acceptable to his adopted country; (2) he can refuse to adapt, restrict or narrow his contact with the alien environment, and live a marginal existence on the fringe of the society; (3) he can give up entirely by returning to his native country; or (4) he can give up psychologically by escaping into mental illness. A survey of various countries indicated that many immigrants accept the last alternative and become ill with what has been called the "psychosomatic disadaption syndrome" (Fried, 1959; Seguin, 1956). In a questionnaire survey (Fried, 1959, p. 120) sent to 38 countries, the following remarkably similar comments were received:

Formosa. "The outstanding characteristic of the clinical picture of both neurotics and psychotics among the group of migrated patients (i.e., Mainland Chinese) as compared with the group of Formosan born (is the) . . . great tendency to utilize somatic symptoms. . . ."—Dr. Eng Kung Yeh.

Israel. "There are indications of psychosomatic diseases among certain groups of the population; for instance . . . among immigrants from Iran"—Dr. Abraham Weinberg.

Australia. "There is a substantially higher percentage of Polish immigrants in mental hospitals than would be expected from the incidence rate for the country as a whole"—Dr. O. C. Maddison.

INTRA-CULTURAL STUDIES

For several decades, sociologists and other scientists have conducted large scale surveys in attempts to determine the incidence (number of new cases of an illness) or prevalence (total number of existing cases) of mental illness in the United States with particular reference to identifying possible social factors contributing to mental illness. Social stratification, neighborhood, urbanization, religion, ethnic or minority group membership, marital status, and migration status, have been examined. These will be reviewed in the following sections.

Social Stratification

Hollingshead, a sociologist, and Redlich, a psychiatrist teamed up to examine the New Haven, Connecticut community with an emphasis on socioeconomic class (Hollingshead and Redlich, 1958). Five classes were identified with class I representing those coming from well-established family lineages, with college educations, employed in executive and professional occupations, while class V was composed of those factory hands and unskilled laborers who claimed for the most part only a sixth-grade education. These authors distinguished between *prevalence*—the number of active cases of a disease present in a particular population, and *incidence*—the number of new cases of the disease. The prevalence rate provides an index of the total number of people who are ill, while the incidence figure provides an index of the current rate of breakdown. Figures for this study showed that the lower class persons exhibited not only the highest prevalence but also the highest incidence of mental illness (Fig. 4-1). Moreover, there appeared to be class-typed neuroses in that antisocial and immature reactions were concentrated in classes III and V, phobias, anxiety and psychosomatic reactions clustered among class IV members, and the depressive reactions tended to affect the class I and II persons. In a thumbnail summary of this, the authors

described the class members in the following way: "the class V neurotic behaves badly, the class IV neurotic aches physically, the class III patient defends fearfully, and the class I-II patient is dissatisfied with himself" (p. 240). The incidence of psychosis for the class V members was nearly three times that of classes I and II combined. Manic-depressive psychosis was more common among class I and II members, although schizophrenia was found to be a nondiscriminator of class as it appeared as prevalent in all classes (Table 4-1).

The Midtown Manhattan Study (Srole, et al., 1962) was another investigation of significance. It was an eight-year investigation of mental health in an area within New York City. From 110,000 adults living in the area, a total of 1660 were extensively interviewed. Each person interviewed was then classified into one of six socioeconomic levels and one of four mental health categories (well, mild symptoms, moderate symptoms, impaired). Definite impairment in mental health was noted for 33 percent of the persons in the lowest socioeconomic level as compared with 18 percent of those in the highest level (see Table 4-2). On

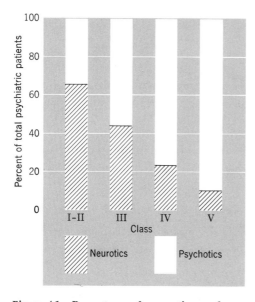

Figure 4-1. **Percentage of neurotics and psychotics found in each social class.**
SOURCE: A. Hollingshead and F. Redlich, *Social class and mental illness.* New York: Wiley, 1958.

TABLE 4-1. *Percentage of Types of Psychotics Found in Each Social Class*

	CLASS			
DIAGNOSTIC CATEGORY	I-II	III	IV	V
Affective psychoses	21	14	14	7
Psychoses resulting from alcoholism and drug addiction	8	10	4	8
Organic psychoses	5	8	9	16
Schizophrenic psychoses	55	57	61	85
Senile psychoses	11	11	12	11
$n =$	53	142	584	672

SOURCE: A. Hollingshead & F. Redlich, *Social class and mental illness.* New York: Wiley, 1958.

the other hand, 24 percent of the highest socioeconomic level persons were symptom free, but only 10 percent of the lowest level people could claim to be well.

Supportive data have also been obtained in Japan (Ministry of Health and Welfare, 1954), Singapore (Murphy, 1959), Formosa (Lin, 1953), and South America (Stainbrook, 1952). In Japan, psychosis rates were greatest in lower income groups. In Singapore, the business and professional class showed a much lower rate of hospitalization for mental illness than the unskilled laboring class. In Formosa, the upper class showed a prevalence rate of 3.5 schizophrenics per 1000 as compared with 1.2 per 1000 for the middle class and 4.5 per 1000 for the lower class. South American lower class men, and lower and middle class women, express their feelings of persecution through religious concerns. On the other hand, the middle class men "secularize" their delusions and focus on economic fears.

Neighborhood

The pioneering study of Faris and Dunham (1939) of Chicago in the 1930's dem-

onstrated that cases of mental disorder decrease from the center of the city to the periphery in much the same fashion as do delinquency rates, unemployment, and communicable disease (see Fig. 4-2). Mental breakdown was less common among residents of the outlying residential districts as compared to those living in the center. Thus, the rate of mental disorders was 48 per 100,000 in the outlying residential areas as compared to 499 per 100,000 for the downtown district. In addition, some relationship was found between living area and the symptoms or type of mental illness. Manic-depressives were more common among those who were able to afford the apartments in the higher

TABLE 4-2. *Mental Health and Socioeconomic Status in the Midtown Manhattan Study*

MENTAL HEALTH CLASSIFICATION	SOCIOECONOMIC STATUS		
	HIGHEST STRATUM	MIDDLE STRATUM	LOWEST STRATUM
Well	24%	20%	10%
Mild symptoms	36	37	33
Moderate symptoms	22	23	25
Impaired	18	21	33

NOTE: Because of rounding of decimals, columns do not always add to 100%.
SOURCE: Adapted from L. Srole et al., *Mental health in the metropolis: the midtown Manhattan study*, Vol. 1. Copyright 1962, McGraw-Hill. Used with permission of McGraw-Hill Book Company.

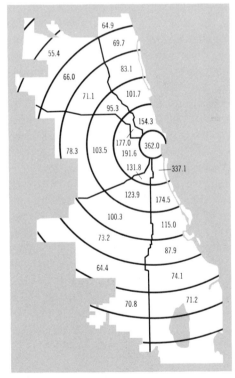

Figure 4-2. **A Census map of Chicago showing the decrease in mental illness rates from the center to the periphery of the city.**
SOURCE: R. Faris and H. Dunham, *Mental disorders in urban areas.* Chicago: University of Chicago Press, 1939.

price district, while paranoid schizophrenia was more prevalent among the rooming house tenants. The authors offer the explanation that a chain of events leads ultimately to breakdown: disorganized community life promotes social isolation, social isolation encourages extreme seclusiveness, and this break of successful and normal interaction with the society ends in mental illness. In this sense, social isolation is the result of neighborhood disintegration and, in turn, is the cause of mental disorganization.

An alternative interpretation of the Faris and Dunham material has sometimes been suggested. The *downward drift* hypothesis argues that the inverse relationship between the rates of psychosis and living area or socioeconomic level results from the inability of the mentally ill person to maintain his previous level of achievement. As he becomes progressively worse mentally, he drifts further and further into the lower class environment. This hypothesis appears to be refuted by the Hollingshead and Redlich work. They demonstrated that the highest class subjects of the study had always lived in the best areas while the lowest class persons had always lived in the slums. Moreover, 91 percent of the patients were still in the same class as their parents, only 1.3 percent were in a lower class than their parents, 89 percent of class V patients came from class V families, and only 69 percent of classes I-II patients originally belonged to class I-II families. Thus, the lower class patients did not appear to "drift" downward and, in fact, some of the upper class patients were mobile upward.

Urbanization

For all types of mental illness, the rates for urban residents are clearly higher than those for rural residents. Jaco (1960) has reported that urban areas contribute over two times as many first admissions to mental hospitals as rural regions. The previously mentioned work of Carothers in Nigeria suggested that higher rates were associated with life in cities. Lin (1953) interviewed nearly 20,000 Formosans living in a rural village, a small town, and an urban community and found the prevalence rates for schizophrenia to be 1.8 per 1000 for the rural area, 2.5 per 1000 for the small town, and 2.1 per 1000 for the city. Cases of schizophrenia tended to concentrate in the most densely populated centers of each of these regions.

Suicide rates show an increase as a function of the size of the community (Schroeder & Beegle, 1955). Cities of from 10,000 to 25,000 population have 15.9 suicides per 100,000 as compared with 19.9 per 100,000 in cities of 250,000 to 500,000 population. Chronic alcoholism appears twice as frequent among city dwellers than rural people (Jellinek, 1947).

Those who accept these rate differences point to the stresses involved in urban living, such as the loss of personal relationships and the extreme competitiveness. The technological advancements existent in cities press workers to keep up with their field or be displaced. Higher cost of living, greater material needs, and increased taxation may all add burdens characteristic of more complex living arrangements.

The urbanization figures appear on the surface to be convincing. However, critics point to the detailed population studies of Sjögren and Larrson (1954) which failed to confirm the higher urban rates. Whatever differences occur may be attributable to a number of factors not necessarily associated with greater stresses of urban living. For example, higher rates of admission may reflect the greater availability of hospital resources or the greater willingness of families to rely upon hospitalization in the cities than in the rural zones. One possibility is that rates are lower in the rural areas because it is easier to care for a patient in the home in these regions. Another possibility is that older persons move into the cities as they retire from agricultural labors but find the drastic shift too stressful.

Religious Affiliation

Psychotic disorders appear to be more prevalent among Protestants than among Catholics or Jews (Frumkin and Frumkin, 1957; Hollingshead and Redlich, 1958). On the other hand, for the more moderate types of illnesses seen in mental hygiene clinics, the number of Jewish patients in treatment was double their proportionate number in the population. Catholics were next, followed by Protestants (Eichler and Lirtzman, 1956). The Midtown Manhattan Study confirmed the fact that Jews have a lower frequency of the severe disorders but a higher frequency of the mild and moderate symptoms. Overall, they counted more persons in the "impaired," "moderate symptom," and "mild symptom" groups and therefore less in the "well" category. On the other hand, Jews have a low number of persons troubled with alcoholism (Malzberg, 1936), with the orthodox Jew having the lowest rate among the Jewish groups and the Jewish secular persons showing the highest (Snyder, 1955). Concerning sex offenses, Catholics were found to comprise a majority of patients (Hirning, 1945), the estimate being up to 53 percent of all sex offenders. In addition, Catholics comprised the highest numbers of alcoholics (Malzberg, 1936). The Jewish mores against excessive drinking and the Catholic atmosphere of harsh suppression may be explanatory factors in these differences.

Ethnic Group

The study of ethnic group differences in mental illness is extremely difficult because of the frequent association between racial background and other factors, such as socioeconomic level, education, occupational status, etc. In addition, "ethnic origin" and "race" are words which have different meanings for different people. For example, a Filipino man born in the Hawaiian Islands may be considered of Filipino origin by one person but of Hawaiian origin by another.

As was mentioned in a previous section, some reports have found higher admissions rates for Negroes than for Caucasians (Crawford et al., 1960; Dreger and Miller, 1960; Gorwitz, 1964; Malzberg, 1963) while others have found no significant differences (Carothers, 1953; Pasamanick, 1962). In fact, in one study (Jaco, 1960) in which the entire state of Texas was canvassed, Anglo-Saxon whites were found to have a higher incidence of psychosis than either non-Whites (Negroes, Indians, Orientals) or Spanish-Americans. On the other hand, in Hawaii the rates for Caucasians or for part Hawaiians were lower than for Japanese or Filipinos (Kimmich, 1960).

Interesting information on the relationship between ethnic background and the type of symptoms exhibited was reported by Opler and Singer (1956). Such material is consistent with the cross-cultural data reported at the start of this chapter indicating that different cultures expressed mental illness in differing ways. Opler and Singer examined Irish and Italian schizophrenic patients matched for age, intelligence, education, length of hospitalization, and marital status. The Italians showed more overt homosexuality, acting-out behavior, rejection of authority, and bodily complaints. The Irish patients were more preoccupied with sin and guilt feelings, were compliant, fixed in their delusions, and had more alcoholics and latent homosexuals. This study demonstrates the difficulty of using ethnic origin as a meaningful variable for understanding mental illness. It is useful only in that it provides some clues regarding the effects of culture; the relationship between ethnic origin and schizophrenic symptoms in this study certainly cannot be interpreted to mean a genetic relationship. The greater acting out, hyperactivity, emotional outbursts of the Italian schizophrenics was more likely a product of their cultural background; the Italian culture tends to sanction free expression of emotions and encourage the release of such emotions through bodily action.

Marital Status

Marital status is another factor found to be associated with mental illness and for which several interpretations may be offered. A number of studies have shown that married persons are less susceptible to mental illness than persons without a marital partner (Jaco, 1960; Ödegaard, 1946; Srole et al., 1962). Persons without a mate either by choice, by divorce, or by death, tend to show higher rates of illness. For example, the rates for first admissions to hospitals in Canada were as follows: married persons—56 per 100,000, single persons—115 per 100,000, divorced persons—286 per 100,000, widowed persons—89 per 100,000 (Rosen and Gregory, 1965).

Marital status may be as much a cause as it is a result of emotional instability. The married state may bring with it certain stabilizing features such as positive interpersonal relationships, a sense of belonging and worth, and reassuring companionship. In addition, marriage may provide the outlet for sexual and social desires for both partners. On the other hand, the single life, divorce, widowhood, are states that may provoke certain stresses, such as feelings of alienation from others, isolation, rejection, incompetence. The antagonistic system adopted by courts in handling divorce cases is often criticized for encouraging these attitudes of rejection and condemnation of one's marital partner. Another possibility exists that emotional instability prevents the attaining of a successful marital life as such individuals may be less attractive as po-

tential mates or unlikely to adjust well to married life. Widowhood can be considered to be the end result of a traumatic event, death of a loved one. In this sense, the widowed person is more vulnerable to emotional disturbance.

Migratory Status

Modern travel has made mobility from state to state, country to country, a more common part of life. Admission rates in the United States are higher among the immigrant than among native residents. The difference may be due to a selective factor in that those who chose to leave their home country might do so because they are personally unable to adapt. The departure is an attempt to escape from personal failure. Ödegaard (1932) found a higher rate of hospitalization for Norwegians living in Minnesota than for those in Norway. Moreover, he found no evidence that the stress of immigration itself contributed to the development of the symptoms. He concluded that, in cases of schizophrenia, the illness was already present before the immigration took place.

It is still possible that the relationship is due to factors other than selection. The "culture shock" phenomenon mentioned earlier may be a contributing factor. An immigrant is basically faced with minority group standing, lack of economic status, and interpersonal isolation because of language barriers. Conflict of cultural standards and mores may make life stressful.

SUMMARY

No man exists in a cultural vacuum. He exists surrounded by and is deeply involved in society. No conclusive data is yet available to determine whether certain societies are more or less susceptible to mental illness than others. Yet it can be stated with reasonable assurance that mental illness is a universal ailment.

Where man exists, psychopathology will exist. In all likelihood, the particular contributions of the cultural heritage lies in providing the *conditions of stress* which precipitate breakdown, the various *modes* through which the patient *expresses* his illness, the belief systems called upon by the therapists to explain the illness and hence their choice of *treatment technique* and, of course, the *avenues for releasing* tensions or receiving emotional support. Finally, it might be noted that societies may contribute to emotional breakdown in many ways. For example,

1. By the direct introduction of stress —for example, through encouraging incompatible desires, through conditions of acute unemployment, or through breakdown of the society itself.

2. Through increasing the vulnerability of members to stress—for example, membership in a minority group may mean limited life experiences such that the person never develops the mental health skills that permit him to cope with stress.

3. By the direct encouragement of agents leading to illness—for example, the participation in rituals involving hallucinatory or addictive drugs.

4. Through the influence of child-rearing practice—personality differences appear quite clearly related to the maternal socialization practices accepted by each culture.

5. By the indirect effects of the stage of progress of the society—for example, underdeveloped countries are more likely to have a high incidence of organic mental illness because of poor medical facilities, on the other hand, mental symptoms associated with aging are more likely to increase in societies with advanced medical knowledge that leads to prolonging the life span.

Glossary

Alcoholism: The excessive use of and reliance upon alcohol.

Anxiety reaction: A type of psychoneurosis characterized by a sense of imminent danger, increased heart rate, and other physiological reactions to threat.

Culture: The socially transmitted system of attitudes, ideas, values, practices, and beliefs.

Capgras' syndrome: A form of mental illness characterized by distrusting the identity of friends.

Immature reaction: A type of disorder involving emotional immaturity and therefore the inability to adapt to stress.

Latah: A form of mental illness in which the individual mimics others.

Latent homosexuality: Latent refers to the absence of outward expression of a trait. Homosexuality involves the selection of a same sex person as a love object. Latent homosexuals do not display their homosexuality and may even be completely unaware of their tendencies.

Mores: The unquestioned standards of a society which are strictly enforced.

Paranoid schizophrenia: A subgroup of schizophrenia characterized by suspiciousness and delusions of persecution.

Pibloktoq: An Arctic-based type of mental illness believed to involve hysteria.

Psychosomatic illness: A form of mental illness involving actual organ damage caused by emotional factors.

Sanction: The punishment invoked by a society for unacceptable behaviors.

Shook yong: Also known as karo. The fear of death from inversion of sex organs.

Socialization: The process of acquiring the characteristics in accordance with the patterns of a society.

Status: A person's position in a social system.

Stratification: The assignment of individuals to different social levels.

Taijin kyofusho: A mental illness involving fear of people and feelings of inadequacy.

Ufufunyana: A form of mental illness involving repeated dreams of a sexual nature.

Windigo: A form of mental illness involving cannibalism.

References

Babcock, C., and Caudill, W. Personal and cultural factors in treating a Nisei man. In G. Seward (Ed.), *Clinical studies in culture conflict.* New York: Ronald Press, 1958.

Benedict, R. *Patterns of culture.* Boston: Houghton Mifflin, 1934.

Benedict, R. *The chrysanthemum and the sword.* Boston: Houghton Mifflin, 1946.

Capgras, J., Lucchini, P., and Schiff, P. Du sentiment d'éstrangeté á l'illusion des sosies. *So. clinic. med. Ment., Paris,* 1924, **12,** 210.

Carothers, J. *The African mind in health and disease.* Geneva: World Health Organization, 1953.

Carothers, J. A study of mental derangement in Africans and an attempt to explain its peculiarities, more especially in relation to the African attitude of life. *Psychiat.,* 1948, **11,** 47.

Cattell, R. *Personality and social psychology.* San Diego: Robert R. Knapp, 1964.

Crawford, F., Rollins, G., and Sutherland, R. Variations between Negroes and whites in concepts of mental illness and its treatment. *Annals N.Y. Acad. Science,* 1960, **84,** 918.

De Vos, G. The relation of guilt towards parents to achievement and arranged marriage among the Japanese. *Psychiat.,* 1960, **23,** no. 3.

De Vos, G. A quantitative Rorschach assessment of maladjustment and rigidity in acculturating Japanese Americans. *Genet. Psychol. Monogr.* 1955, 52, 51.

Dicks, H. Observations on contemporary Russian behavior. *Hum. Relat.,* 1952, **5,** 75.

Dreger, R., and Miller, K. Comparative psychological studies of Negroes and whites in the United States. *Psychol. Bull.,* 1960, **57,** 361.

Dunham, H. *Community and schizophrenia, an epidemiological analysis.* Detroit: Wayne State University Press, 1965.

Eichler, R., and Lirtzman, S. Religious background of patients in a mental hygiene setting. *J. nerv. ment. Dis.,* 1956, **124,** 514.

Faris, R., and Dunham, H. *Mental disorders in urban areas.* Chicago: University of Chicago Press, 1939.

Field, M. *Search for security: an ethno-psychiatric study of rural Ghana.* Evanston, Ill.: Northwestern University Press, 1960.

Fried, J. Acculturation and mental health among Indian migrants in Peru. In M. Opler (Ed.), *Culture and mental health,* New York: Macmillan, 1959.

Frumkin, R., and Frumkin, M. Religion, occupation, and major mental disorders. *J. hum. Rel.,* 1957, **6,** 98.

Glueck, S. *Mental disorder and the criminal law.* Boston: Little, Brown, 1925.

Gorwitz, K. The demography of mental illness in Maryland. Paper presented at the meeting of the Phipps Psychiatric Unit of Johns Hopkins Hospital, Nov., 1964.

Hanfmann, E. Social perceptions in Russian displaced persons and an American comparison group. *Psychiat.*, 1957, **20**, 131.

Hirning, J. Indecent exposure and other sex offenses. *J. clin. psychopath. Psychother.*, 1945, **7**, 105.

Hollingshead, A. *Elmtown's youth.* New York: Wiley, 1949.

Hollingshead, A., and Redlich, F. *Social class and mental illness.* New York: Wiley, 1958.

Hopkins, P. The problem of Japan. In G. Murphy (Ed.), *Human nature and enduring peace.* Boston: Houghton Mifflin, 1945.

Inkeles, A., Hanfmann, E., and Beier, H. Modal personality and adjustment to the Soviet socio-political system. *Human Relations*, 1958, **11**, 3.

Jaco, E. *The social epidemiology of mental disorders: a psychiatric survey of Texas.* New York: Russell Sage Foundation, 1960.

Jaco, E. *The social epidemiology of mental disorders.* New York: Russell Sage Found., 1960.

Japanese Ministry of Health and Welfare. *Factual Survey of Mental Hygiene.* Tokyo: Ministry of Health and Welfare, 1954.

Jellinek, E. Recent trends in alcoholism and alcohol consumption. *Quart. J. Stud. Alcohol*, 1947, **8**, 23.

Kardiner, A. *Psychological frontiers of society.* New York: Columbia University Press, 1945.

Kimmich, R. Ethnic aspects of schizophrenia in Hawaii. *Psychiat.*, 1960, **23**, 97.

Kora, R. Morita therapy. *Intern. J. Psychiat.*, 1965, **1**, 611.

La Barre, W. Some observations on character structure in the Orient, II. the Chinese. *Psychiat.*, 1946, **9**, 378.

Landes, R. The abnormal among the Ojibwa. *J. abnorm. soc. Psychol.*, 1938, **33**, 14.

Laubscher, B. *Sex, custom and psychopathology.* London: Routledge, 1937.

Lin, T. A study of the incidence of mental disorder in Chinese and other cultures. *Psychiat.*, 1953, **16**, 313.

Linton, R. *Culture and mental disorders.* Springfield, Ill.: Thomas, 1956.

Loudon, J. Psychogenic disorder and social conflict among the Zulu. In M. Opler (Ed.), *Culture and mental health.* New York: Macmillan, 1959.

Malzberg, B. *The mental health of the Negro.* Albany, N.Y.: Research Foundation for Mental Hygiene, Inc., 1963.

Malzberg, B. New data relative to incidence of mental disease among Jews. *Mental Hygiene, N.Y.*, 1936, **20**, 280.

Malzberg, B. *Social and biological aspects of mental disease.* Utica, N.Y.: State Hospitals Press, 1940.

Mead, M. *Soviet attitudes towards authority.* New York: McGraw-Hill, 1951.

Mead, M. *And keep your powder dry.* New York: Wm. Morrow, 1942.

Mead, M. *Sex and temperament in three primitive societies.* New York: Wm. Morrow, 1935.

Messing, S. Group therapy and social status in the Zar cult of Ethiopia. In M. Opler (Ed.), *Culture and mental health.* New York: Macmillan, 1959.

Murphy, H. Culture and mental disorder in Singapore. In M. Opler (Ed.), *Culture and mental health.* New York: Macmillan, 1959.

Ödegaard, O. Marriage and mental disease: study of social psychopathology. *J. Ment. Sci.*, 1946, **92**, 35.

Ödegaard, O. Emigration and insanity. *Acta Psychiat. et Neurol.*, Suppl. 4, 1932.

Opler, M. *Culture and social psychiatry.* New York: Atherton Press, 1967.

Opler, M., and Singer, J. Ethnic differences in behavior and psychopathology: Italian and Irish. *Intern. J. Soc. Psychiat.,* 1956, **2**, 11.

Pasamanick, B. A survey of mental disease in an urban population. VII. An approach to total prevalence by race. *Amer. J. Psychiat.,* 1962, **119**, 299.

Rosen, E., and Gregory. I. *Abnormal psychology.* Philadelphia: Saunders, 1965.

Schooler, C., and Caudill, W. Symptomatology in Japanese and American schizophrenics. *Ethnology,* 1964, **3**, 172.

Schroeder, W., and Beegle, J. Suicide: an instance of high rural rates. In A. Rose (Ed.), *Mental health and mental disorder.* New York: Norton, 1955.

Seguin, C. Migration and psychosomatic disadaptation. *Psychosom. Med.,* 1956, **18**, 404.

Sjögren, T., and Larrson, T. A methodological, psychiatric and statistical study of a large Swedish rural population. *Acta Psychiat. et Neurol. Scand.,* Suppl. 89, 1954.

Snyder, C. Culture and sobriety: a study of drinking patterns and socio-cultural factors related to sobriety among Jews. *Quart. J. Stud. Alcohol,* 1955, **16**, 101.

Spiro, M. Cultural heritage, personal tensions, and mental illness in a south sea culture. In M. Opler (Ed.), *Culture and mental health.* New York: Macmillan, 1959.

Srole, L. et al. *Mental health in the metropolis: the midtown Manhattan study.* Vol. I. New York: McGraw-Hill, 1962.

Stainbrook, E. Some characteristics of the psychopathology of schizophrenic behavior in Bahian society. *Amer. J. Psychiat.,* 1952, **109**, 330.

Stitt, E., and Strong, R. *Diagnosis, prevention and treatment of tropical diseases.* New York: Blakiston, 1945.

Tooth, G. *Studies in mental illness in the Gold Coast.* London: H.M. Stat. Office, 1950.

Wallace, R. Dreams and the wishes of the soul: a type of psychoanalytic theory among the seventeenth-century Iroquois. *Amer. Anthrop.,* 1958, **60**, 234.

Williams, R. *American society, a sociological interpretation.* New York: Knopf, 1951.

Yap, P. The latah reaction: its pathodynamics and nosological position. *J. Ment. Sci.,* 1952, **98**, 515.

5 Contributors to Personality: The Family

Unlike any other animal, the human being experiences a period of growth and development that is extraordinarily long. Many mammals are born fully developed and independent of their parents, but the human being must wait many years before his physical and mental capacities completely mature. A child is highly dependent on his parents through these formative years, and consequently they play a significant role in the personality development of their offspring. These adults help determine the type of environment in which the child will grow up: whether it will be one of harshness and rejection or warmth and acceptance, security and comfort or anxiety and uncertainty, a healthy home atmosphere or a distorted environment. Some aspects of the family that critically affect the child include *parental presence*, the *personality* of the parental figures, and the *behavior of the parent* toward the child (child-rearing practice).

PARENTAL PRESENCE

For a child to develop normally, an adult must be present. Where all adults are absent during infancy or childhood,

the child shows subhuman traits; where the one crucial adult—the mother—is absent, the child shows pathological human traits. The "feral children" are good examples of the former. Such cases as the "Wild Boy of Aveyron" and the "Wolf Children" of India (Singh and Zingg, 1942) involved children raised in the wilds without human companionship or care. Such children are said in reports to have survived either through their own efforts or through the aid of wild beasts who adopted them as part of the litter. When finally retrieved from this animal upbringing and life, the child typically showed more similarity to his adopted animal brethren than to his human counterparts. The feral child was found to have difficulty in walking erect, in speaking intelligibly, and in acquiring human social skills. In one instance, it was said that the child was able to run faster on all fours than he could walk standing erect. More recently and with more detailed and sounder reporting, the necessity of parental presence has again been documented through studies of *maternal deprivation*. In contrast to the feral children, the youngsters of this group did experience human companionship, human care, and the physical comforts and medical care of city living. However, they lacked the presence of their own mothers and were either being raised in institutions or separated momentarily from their true mother because of illness. Scientists associated with maternal deprivation studies have included Bowlby (1944), Spitz and Wolf (1946), Robertson (1952), and Goldfarb (1943, 1945). In all cases of either institutional care or maternal separation examined by them the effects attributed to deprivation have been appalling. Major deviations in personality of such children involve:

1. "Affect hunger" (Goldfarb, 1945; Freud and Burlingham, 1944)—In some cases, the children developed an insatiable and indiscriminate demand for attention and affection when near others as if to compensate for their deprived life.

2. The "affectionless character" (Bowlby, 1944)—In a larger number of cases, an avoidance of or indifference to social approaches have been apparent along with a social apathy, and a lack of the capacity to form meaningful relationships with people.

3. "Anaclitic depression" or "mourning" (Spitz and Wolf, 1946; Robertson and Bowlby, 1952)—This deviation, particularly noted in cases of separation, involves a dramatic sequence of behavior that begins with initial protest and efforts to recapture the lost mother, followed by mourning and despair accompanied by decreased activity level, and finally either complete physical and intellectual deterioration or, in older children, a denial of the need for a mother such that the child may even refuse to recognize his own parent upon later reunion.

Many significant questions remain unresolved from these studies and some major attacks have been directed toward the soundness of the research. However,

close evaluation of the material to date suggests some tentative trends.

1. Single, brief, separation experiences occurring in a healthy family is recovered from fairly promptly and completely although there is some possibility that a "hidden" scar remains to make the person more vulnerable to future threats, for example, susceptibility to later depressions.

2. Brief separation leads to overanxious overdependency and clinging following reunion, while severe separation leads to detachment and affectionless withdrawal.

3. Fairly prolonged deprivation experiences in early infancy followed by reunion can result in dramatic improvements in social and intellectual functioning although speech appears to be retarded.

4. Prolonged and severe deprivation beginning early in the first year of life (from third month on) and continuing for as long as three years usually leads to severe intellectual and personality deficits that appear irreversible.

5. Severe and prolonged deprivation beginning in the second year of life leads to grave effects on personality development that are apparently irreversible, but the effects on intellectual functioning seem to be reversible.

6. The child is less able to sustain separation experiences before 5 years of age than after.

7. Impairments in language, abstraction and the capacity for meaningful interpersonal attachments are most resistent to recovery.

8. In general, the effects of deprivation or separation vary with the nature and duration of experience, the quality of parental substitute figures, the age of development of the infant at the time of the experience, the quality of mothering received before (see Table 5-1) and after the separation, and the child's physical

and psychological inner resources available for coping with the stress.

Why is the presence of a parent so crucial to the normal development of the human child? No one yet knows the precise answer. Perhaps the traumatic experience of separation is too extreme for the infant's immature system to adequately react to. But this does not explain the equally drastic effects where institutional deprivation occurs but not separation from a loved object. Another answer that might be offered draws from information on animal developmental studies (Scott, 1962). In the animal kingdom, a process called *imprinting* has been identified. This process involves two characteristics:

1. The triggering of whole patterns of actions in a young animal by an environmental cue.

2. The establishment of a primary socialization object.

The case of the "ducklings-who-follow" can illustrate this process: ducklings follow their parent in an orderly fashion early in life without any special training from the mother duck; yet it is possible to induce these very ducklings to follow any substitute object if it is presented during the critical period in development that such imprinting occurs; and once the substitute object is selected by the ducklings, they will refuse any association with others of their own kind. An additional informa-

tion from the study of animals involves the fact that once a behavioral pattern becomes organized, it becomes progressively more difficult to reorganize the system—*organization inhibits reorganization.* For example, up to a certain age, a chaffinch can learn to sing a variety of songs characteristic of neighbor birds, but once this occurs, the chaffinch then ceases to be able to acquire any new song patterns (Thorpe, 1961). One might conclude, therefore, that *certain behavior patterns can be stimulated during critical periods in life, that primary socialization choice occurs during this early period,* and that *once a behavioral pattern is initiated, reorganization or acquisition of substitute patterns becomes difficult.* Applied to the maternal deprivation data previously discussed, one might hypothesize the following:

1. Man acquires the "normal" ways of acting, feeling, and thinking through social interaction with others of his culture.

2. Typically, the parent is the primary agent of socialization and the first person other than himself which the infant experiences.

3. In an adequate family relationship, the infant will respond to and be responded to by the parent thereby increasing the already intimate interpersonal relationship now existent. This occurs around the age of three months.

TABLE 5-1. *The Influence of Mother-Child Relation Prior to Separation on Degree of Child's Depressive Reaction*

| | MOTHER-CHILD RELATION | | | | | |
| | GOOD | | | BAD | | |
	INTENSE	MODERATE	WEAK	INTENSE	MODERATE	WEAK
Severe depression	6	11	—	—	—	—
Mild depression	4	—	3	7	—	—
No depression	—	—	2	11	2	14

SOURCE: R. Spitz & K. Wolf. Anaclitic depression. *Psychoanal. Stud. Child.,* 1946, **2**, 313.

4. Because of the mutually rewarding results, the infant begins to develop more and more of the interest in relating to others, and in acquiring the means for improving this relationship, for example, through language or attending to the presence of others.

5. Once the infant has been thus oriented toward others in his environment, he continues to be responsive to the patterns represented or encouraged by them and resists "reorganization" away from people or toward isolation.

6. Unless the mother herself exhibits deviate or pathological behavior patterns, the infant will soon acquire the overall "imprint" of normalcy.

7. In the pathological condition of deprivation, the infant is never stimulated by the social environment nor adequately rewarded for responding to become attached to, and hence to acquire the behavior patterns characteristic of, other people. *This* organization of resistance to *normal* communication or social approach also resists reorganization. The loss of socialization in turn leads to further isolation, and as the child thereby becomes further out of touch with social reality, he also becomes increasingly vulnerable to a break with psychological reality. Thus, we have the pattern of social apathy and indifference to meaningful interpersonal relations found in the maternal deprivation studies.

8. In cases of separation where mourning occurs, one might presuppose that an early primary object choice had been induced in the child in the form of the mother. As with imprinting in the ducklings, once formed, such a relationship is extremely resistant to change and the traumatic aspects of the separation experience becomes magnified. Ultimately, even the mother is given up rather than allow a reorganization to occur in the figure of a substitute mother.

PARENTAL PERSONALITY

In cases of pathology in a *child,* pathology in the parent is a significant factor. In cases of pathology exhibited by an *adult,* it can also be argued that the spectre of parental influence exists in a high proportion of cases. Wordsworth (1807) was quite observant in remarking that the "child is the father of the man" —the mold of personality structure is poured in infancy and becomes firm during childhood. Mind and body develop rapidly during the formative years of life and are especially responsive to external and internal influences. Significant figures during this period help to form attitudes, perceptions of others, and interpersonal skills that become the prototype for adult life. The family is the primary social group for the young child and is the crux of his contact with the world. His social, emotional, and cognitive development depends on the figures within his family. It is they who will provide him with the essential external guides necessary for early learning and adaptation.

There are three possible ways in which the pathology of parents becomes instrumental in the development of pathology in the offspring: (1) the child develops the same symptoms as the parent through direct *learning or identification;* (2) the child exhibits the conflicts, unacceptable needs, or problems of the parents upon *instigation by the parents;* (3) the child is a member of a *pathological family unit.*

1. *The learning identification process* —Children will show a remarkable similarity to their parents in habit patterns, interests, and mannerisms as a result of the two processes of learning and identification. Specific responses shown by the child are reinforced by the beaming parent, especially when the responses are imitative of the parent's own traits, for who can resist this form of flattery? Even

Most fears are *learned*, including phobia of snakes. The child pictured above has not yet learned to be afraid of his plaything, a live snake. (David Seymour/Magnum)

the amount of smiling by an infant—and thus perhaps "good humor"—is subject to reward control (Brackbill, 1958). Unfortunately, it appears also true that fears are acquired in the same fashion from parents. Thus, the nature and number of fears expressed by a child have been found directly correlated with that of his parent (Hagman, 1932). On a more complex level, larger patterns of emotional and behavioral traits may be acquired by the child through identification. Here, the child becomes a miniature version of the parent either for defensive reasons, or because the parent has been associated with positive reinforcement. In the first instance, called *identification with the aggressor*, the identification is with a feared model since this permits one to be "on the same side" or to have better control (at

least in fantasy) of the feared person. Bettelheim (1958), for example, reports on the tendency of concentration camp prisoners to imitate their Nazi guards. In the second instance, sometimes called *primary identification* or *developmental identification*, the child associates the parent with pleasant, nurturant, rewarding events and identifies in order to prolong or reestablish these cues when the parent is absent. By acting like the parent in the parent's absence, the child can restir those positive feelings associated with the parent's characteristics. Bandura and Huston (1961) were able to produce such developmental identification experimentally by having the experimenter-model assume a nurturant role toward the child before enacting the behaviors that they wished the child to acquire. In all cases

113

of identification, it is clear that the child will assume the entire behavioral pattern of the parent including pathological behaviors. Over and over again, it has been shown that irrelevant, meaningless behaviors as well as antisocial responses may be indiscriminately imitated. For example, Bandura and Huston (1961) demonstrated that children would imitate nonsense behavior of the experimenter-model, such as chanting. In addition, Lovaas (1961), and Bandura, Ross, and Ross (1961) have provoked much concern over mass media in their reports which show that children will imitate aggressive behavior when shown movies of an adult or a cartoon character aggressing.

2. *The parental instigation process*—Cases exist where the pathological behavior exhibited by the child is apparently not imitative of or congruent with the behavior of the parents. These are the cases where attention is then focused on the patient or on factors external to the family in the search for causality. In some of these cases, the parents are in fact quite deeply influential in the symptom expression. Typically the child serves as a "representative" of the parents' own neuroses, in a sense, the "spokesman." Sperling (1951) has convincingly described such a setting whereby the child senses certain repressed needs of the mother and acts them out in a literal fashion. Powdermaker and Frank (1953) noted many occasions where group therapy members who harbor hostile feelings toward the therapist pressure one member of the group, disturbing him to such a point as to incite him to do what they all wish to do, that is, aggress toward the therapist. The significance of this type of symptom development is in pointing out the necessity of either removing the patient from the influence of the others, or extending the treatment to include the parent-instigator. Of course, this type of process can occur whenever two or more indi-

viduals establish a close and relatively permanent interpersonal relationship with one another, and would include child-parent relationships, spouse-spouse relationships, roommate-roommate relationships, etc. An unusual variation occurs in some of the cases included by Josephine Hilgard (1951) as the "anniversary reactions." Under this circumstance, a mother may promote a mental breakdown in her offspring when the child reaches the same age the parent was when she experienced a severe trauma. It is as if the parent "celebrates" the anniversary by recreating the event using the child to play the role that the parent once assumed.

3. *The pathological family unit*—It has become more and more common to examine the workings of the family as a unit rather than to single out a particular member, the patient, for analysis. In this sense, the patient is no more nor less responsible for his illness than the other members of the unit. He is no more or less "ill" than the family unit. In some cases, the members of a family over several generations seem to show the same pathogenic modes of interaction, perpetuating a neurosis from generation to generation. For example, personality test results revealed that members of one family showed highly similar fears over body image and feelings of unusual body distortion, while the members of another family seemed to perseverate over concerns of death and destruction (Fisher and Mendell, 1956). In other cases, the parents are at odds with one another and the child is confronted with a "double-bind," that is, a situation where the child is faced with messages that are directly contradictory (Bateson et al., 1956). For example, a father may condemn the worth of women, including his own wife, yet feel the need for retaining the adulation of his daughter. This need is connected to his fearfulness that the daughter might choose to identify with the mother, there-

by demonstrating the mother's greater worth than his own. At the same time, his own basic hostility and devaluation of women is also directed toward the daughter. For the daughter, this situation represents a tragic dilemma: if she attempts to identify and side with the father, she will be faced with his hostility; yet if she refuses to do so and attempts to join with her mother, she will arouse her father's fears and again come under pressure. She is condemned if she does and condemned if she does not. If she correctly interprets the messages from her father, she must accept the fact that she is being rejected, and is being deceived by her father's *apparent* affection for her. A critical element of the double-bind is that the parent denies any inconsistency to his behavior, thus preventing the child from any possibility of a direct solution. This particular pattern has been identified as one of several *patterns* in families of schizophrenic patients. The particular *personality* traits of the "schizophrenogenic" mother or father have yet to be consistently identified. One reviewer of the literature has even decided that "there is no such thing as a schizophrenogenic or a neurotogenic mother or family" (Frank, 1965). The mothers of schizophrenic patients have been reported as being rejecting by some researchers (Clardy, 1957; Despert, 1942; Tietze, 1949) but overprotective and more devoted by others (Gerard and Siegel, 1950; Despert, 1938), aloof and cold by some (Abrahams and Varon, 1953; Hill, 1955) yet overinvolved and intrusive by others (Jenkins, 1950; Freeman and Grayson, 1955; Prout and White, 1950). One earlier study concluded that the mothers were both excessively devoted and cooly detached (Mark, 1953). Other traits attributed to mothers by researchers (Tietze, 1949; Jenkins, 1950; Behrens and Goldfarb, 1958; Mark, 1953) included high restrictiveness and control, anxiety over sexual information, insecu-

rity with the role of womanhood, self-sacrificing martyrdom, subtle domination, control through emphasis on moral conviction and conformity, lack of spontaneity and pleasure over traditional family roles, and an air of confusion and disorganization. Fathers have been described as distant, aloof, passive, neglecting, in conflict with their wives, weak and ineffectual, and unable to assume the adaptive-instrumental role (Donnelly, 1960; Tietze, 1949; Lidz et al., 1957a; Behrens and Goldfarb, 1958).

It is entirely possible that the search for a single type of trait, or even a consistent cluster of traits, which characterizes *all* schizophrenogenic mothers or fathers will always be futile simply because this approach is too narrow. In effect, this orientation fails in the same way as earlier studies which focused on finding out what was "wrong" with the patient, to the neglect of the significant role of the parents. Perhaps more conclusive results will derive from examining the family dynamics that produce schizophrenia, the "schizophrenogenic *family*," rather than the traits of the schizophrenic, the schizophrenogenic mother or father. However, this task presents many problems for research methods, and as yet no fully rigorous study has been completed. Suggestive material has been reported by Lidz and his collaborators (1957a, 1957b), Farina (1960, 1963), and Behrens and Goldfarb (1958), all of whom have attempted assessments of the family observed together as a unit. From intensive contacts with 14 fathers of schizophrenic patients, Lidz et al. (1957a), identified five overlapping patterns or types of fathers.

1. Fathers of female patients characterized by extreme antagonism toward women and inconsistent and unrealistic demands —the daughter who identifies with him becomes psychotic as she attempts the

impossible task of seeking his love and meeting his chaotic demands.

2. Fathers of male patients who direct their hostility toward their son as a pseudo-rival for the attention and affection of the mother—these fathers tend to interfere with the mother's attempt to carry through her role as a mother, yet do not contribute anything constructive.

3. Fathers with an exaggerated sense of self-exaltation whose offspring feel unable to ever attain the stature of their aloof parent—mothers are either adulatory admirers at the foot of their husband and thereby inattentive to their children, or isolated by their husband's distance and substitute an attachment to their offspring.

4. Fathers who are failures in life's achievements, nonentities in their own homes, unable to cope either with life or the excluding coldness of their spouse—they lack prestige even in the eyes of their own offspring.

5. Fathers who are passive, undemanding, unable to assert their own needs or express their ideas about child rearing, and incapable of countering the bizarre child-rearing patterns of their wives—they are content to assume the role of lesser siblings to their own children, and accept their wives as grown-up authorities.

Fleck, in collaboration with Lidz and Cornelison (1963), pursued the study of the family milieu and discovered a basically distorted family structure with one or both parents exhibiting serious psychopathology. The marriages are either "schismatic" with the parental hostilities and recriminations dividing the family into opposing factions, or "skewed" such that one spouse passively goes along with the aberrant ways and child-rearing practices of the more disturbed parent. The children are thus raised in an atmosphere permeated by irrationality, distortions,

role uncertainties, and lack the culturally adaptive and instrumentally valid role models with which to identify. Unlike other parent pairs, no compensatory or ameliorative role is assumed by the more normal parent to balance off the idiosyncratic deficiencies of the disturbed parent. The parental patterns of female patients appear to be different from that of the male patient. In the family of the female schizophrenic, the dominant figure is the father. He is highly narcissistic, derogating of his wife and women in general, and has turned to his daughter as a wife-substitute. The mother is unable to serve as a model for her daughter because she accepts her low status position, living in insecurity and low esteem, unable to maintain ground in the face of her dominant spouse. A schism exists in that both parents are isolated from one another. For the daughter, an alliance with one is therefore at the expense of any relationship with the other. The schizophrenic patients were found to have sided with their fathers. In the family of the male schizophrenic, the dominant role was occupied by a seriously disturbed mother. She is openly dissatisfied with her ineffectual husband and communicates this to her son along with an implied directive that he must grow up different from his father. This type of mother experienced difficulty in being close to her son as an infant, but has subsequently become over-solicitous and overprotecting. Her earlier lack of warmth has turned into the engulfing, restrictive emotion sometimes aptly caricatured as "smother love."

PARENTAL ATTITUDES AND CHILD-REARING BEHAVIORS

Parental attitudes toward their children have broadened considerably in comparison with the past (Table 5-2). Whereas at one period "children should be seen and not heard" might have been the accepted

TABLE 5-2.   *Changes in Child-rearing Attitudes*

SEVERITY IN THE HANDLING OF	TIME PERIOD				
	1914 TO 1921	1921 TO 1929	1929 TO 1938	1938 TO 1942-1945	1942-1945 TO 1951
Masturbation	*Decreases*	*Decreases*	Constant	*Decreases*	Constant
Thumb-sucking	Constant	*Decreases*	Constant	*Decreases*	*Decreases*
Weaning	Increases	Increases	Constant	*Decreases*	Constant
Bowel training	Increases	Increases	*Decreases*	*Decreases*	*Decreases*
Bladder training	Increases	*Decreases*	*Decreases*	*Decreases*	*Decreases*

SOURCE: M. Wolfenstein, Trends in infant care. *Amer. J. Orthopsychiat.*, 1953, **23**, 120. Copyright, the American Orthopsychiatric Association, Inc. Reproduced by permission.

slogan, modern parents appear more aware of their children as individual personalities. This greater awareness has been stimulated in part by the growing educational and developmental literature directed toward the lay public. Such attempts by professionals to share their knowledge has not been without drawbacks. Initially, parents eagerly absorbed the "What-To-Do," "How-To-Do" publications as infallible guides to relieve themselves of the responsibility of decision making. But the lay parent was soon to become disappointed by the apparent inability of the experts to agree among themselves. First there were warnings from Freud and Watson about the dangers of too much parental love, then came similar warnings that not enough love and mothering was equally dangerous (neither camp bothered to point out of course that *both* extremes are undesirable). And so some parents return to relating in ways that reflect their own adjustment (or maladjustment) to life and marriage and children, while others continue to seek advice from expert sources to supplement their own decisions. Several types of attitudes have been identified and found to influence both the way a parent treats his child and the personality of the child (see Table 5-3, page 118):

1. *Overprotectiveness*—This attitude consists of an excessive concern for their child's behavior. "Pure" overprotectiveness is evidenced in four ways: excessive physical contact, prolongation of treatment of the child as if he were still an infant, prevention of the development of independent behavior, and excessive maternal control. The first three stem from the mother's own needs, the last from the child's activity which triggers off her fears. Maternal control could be either indulgent or dominating: the overprotective, indulgent mother capitulates to the child as a love-object, the overprotective, dominating mother shows an exaggerated possessiveness toward her child. Overprotection stems from reality conditions (previous miscarriages, inability to conceive, physical disabilities, or susceptibility to illness in the child) or psychological conditions (social isolation, parent's own impoverished upbringing, marital conflict leading the mother to transfer her love to the child, guilt feelings over underlying attitudes of rejection). Levy's work (1943) showed that the overprotected, indulged children were disobedient and tyrannical at home, had temper tantrums and showed uncontrollable behavior, but were generally well behaved in school and did well in classwork. On the other hand, the dominated, overprotected children were submissive at home, had eating difficulties, and generally found it difficult to make friends.

2. *Domination*—Although this has been touched on in the previous section as a possible adjunct to overprotectiveness, a dominating attitude can also exist alone. Dominant parents tend to be authoritative with the child, establishig standards that are not appropriate to the child's level of maturity, and criticizing or punitive when the child is unable to meet the demands. The dominant parent comes from a dominant family. As a child, this parent had also been dominated and now he treats his

TABLE 5-3. *Summary of Investigations of Impact of Parent Behavior on Child Personality*

TYPE OF HOME	TYPE OF CHILD BEHAVIOR ASSOCIATED WITH IT	
Rejective	Submissive	Sadistic
	Aggressive[a]	Nervous
	Adjustment difficulties	Shy, stubborn
	Feelings of insecurity[a]	Noncompliant
Overprotective, babying	Infantile and withdrawing[a]	Jealous
	Submissive[a]	Difficult adjustment[a]
	Feelings of insecurity[a]	Nervous
	Aggressive	
Dominating parent	Dependable	Uncooperative
	Shy	Tense
	Submissive	Bold
	Polite	Quarrelsome
	Self-conscious	Disinterested
Submissive parent, permissive	Aggressive[a]	Self-confident[a]
	Careless[a]	Forward in making
	Disobedient[a]	friends[a]
		Noncompliant
Inharmonious	Aggressive[a]	Delinquent[a]
	Neurotic	Uncooperative
	Jealous[a]	
Defective discipline	Poor adjustment[a]	Delinquent
	Aggressive	Neurotic
	Jealous	
Harmonious, well-adjusted	Submissive	Good adjustment
Calm, happy, compatible	Cooperative[a]	Independent
	Superior adjustment	
Child accepted	Socially acceptable	Faces future confidently
Logical scientific approach	Self-reliant	Responsible
	Cooperative	
Consistent strict discipline	Good adjustment	
Child given responsibilities	Good adjustment	
	Self-reliant	Security feelings
Parents play with child	Security feelings	Self-reliant

a These findings are from several studies.
SOURCE: Adapted from M. J. Radke, *The relation of parental authority to children's behavior and attitudes.* Institute of Child Welfare Monograph # 22, University of Minnesota Press, Minneapolis, © Copyright 1946 University of Minnesota.

own offspring as he was treated. Thus, a self-perpetuating pattern is established. The immediate results of domination is a heightened socialization: these children tend to be polite, careful, honest, docile, dependable. However, they are also self-conscious, sensitive, and insecure (Symonds, 1939; Baldwin, 1948).

3. *Permissiveness*—This attitude is the opposite of overprotectiveness and may turn into indulgence if carried to its extreme. It involves giving maximum freedom and encouragement to the child. Parents with this attitude show high tolerance for the weaknesses of their offspring and acceptance of the child's early ambitions. Although the lives of these parents are often disrupted by their children's activity level, the ultimate results of the permissiveness are satisfying. The children grow up to be resourceful, cooperative, self-reliant, socially adjusted and popular (Hurlock, 1964; Radke, 1946).

4. *Rejection*—Parental rejection is a severe and continuing trauma for children since it deprives them of the comforting sense of security which they derive from having a home. Rejected children develop nervous problems when young such as enuresis, nail biting, and poor eating habits, and antisocial behavior when older such as lying, stealing, swearing, and cruelty. Showing off and attention seeking is common (MacFarland et al., 1954). Emotional instability to the point of requiring psychiatric care has been found to characterize those children from severely rejecting families (Newell, 1934; Newell, 1936). Rejected children also tend to be in a hurry to grow up and leave school; they are realistic, shrewd, alert, and likely to become independent of others (Hurlock, 1964).

5. *Acceptance*—The accepting parent creates a warm and loving home atmosphere for the child. The child is treated as an independent person who partici-

pates in family affairs. He is wanted and more often than not the parents planned for the birth. The results of this attitude are gratifying: the accepted child is not only socialized, but happy and secure as well. He is cooperative, friendly, loyal, cheerful, dependable, honest, emotionally stable, and able to appraise himself realistically (Symonds, 1939).

The parental attitudes mentioned above determine the child-rearing methods used. One overall controversy that has occupied the attention of parents and professionals alike is the question: Should parents be permissive or restrictive in child rearing? The answer to this question has proven very elusive. It is not a simple matter to define what is meant by "permissive" or by "restrictive"—does permissiveness imply laxness, indulgence, low control, acceptance, or close rapport; does restrictiveness mean severity, autocratic discipline, rejection, overprotection, rigid control, or simply consistent rule enforcement? In addition, the parental attitude must be taken into account since the results of strict upbringing seem to vary with whether the parents are "warm" or "cold" (Sears, 1961) and even maternal rejection is reacted to differently where the father is accepting and warm (McCord and McCord, 1961). A summary of the effects of different types of discipline in different home atmospheres is found in Table 5-4 (page 120). This table suggests that restrictiveness along with warmth leads to highly socialized but perhaps overcompliant children, while the same disciplinary orientation in an atmosphere of rejection and hostility breeds inner-directed conflicts exhibited by personal problems and loss of esteem. On the other hand, permissiveness in an environment of warmth facilitates the development of assertiveness, sociability, and a "bossiness" expressed within an acceptable context. Coupled with rejection, however, permissive disci-

TABLE 5-4. *Interactions in the Consequence of Warmth vs. Hostility and Restrictiveness vs. Permissiveness*

	RESTRICTIVENESS	PERMISSIVENESS
Warmth	Submissive, dependent, polite, neat, obedient (Levy) Minimal aggression (Sears) Maximum rule enforcement, boys (Maccoby) Dependent, not friendly, not creative (Watson) Maximal compliance (Meyers)	Active socially, outgoing, creative, successfully aggressive (Baldwin) Minimal rule enforcement, boys (Maccoby) Facilitates adult role taking (Levin) Minimal self-aggression, boys (Sears) Independent, friendly, creative, low projective hostility (Watson)
Hostility	"Neurotic problems" (clinical studies) More quarreling and shyness with peers (Watson) Socially withdrawn (Baldwin) Low in adult role taking (Levin) Maximal self-aggression, boys (Sears)	Delinquency (Glueck, Bandura, and Walters) Noncompliance (Meyers) Maximal aggression (Sears)

SOURCE: W. Becker, Consequences of different kinds of parental discipline. In H. Hoffman and L. Hoffman, (Eds.), *Review of Child Development research*. New York: Russell Sage Foundation, 1964.

pline becomes a license for outwardly-directed conflict, especially antisocial aggression. Even here the picture is still incomplete since severe punishment for aggression appears to have completely opposite effects at different ages; for example, it incites further antisocial aggression in the child at age 5 but inhibits antisocial aggression in the same child from the same family at age 12 (Sears, 1961).

Many child-rearing concerns have been directly stimulated by the works of Freud. Working from a theory of development, he suggested that the child passed through several stages or phases and that excessive gratification or extreme deprivation during any stage causes fixation and failure in further development. For example, gratifying the infant during the oral stage was said to lead to the persistence of oral traits such as dependency, optimism, receptivity, while deprivation was said to lead to selfishness, impatience, insecurity (Freud, 1938). Many practical concerns arose from these writings and related works: Is too early weaning dangerous? Is demand feeding more desirable than schedule feeding? Is thumbsucking a part of the oral signs? How severely should an infant be weaned from the bottle? The search for conclusive information has consumed many man-hours of research time, stimulated the devising of ingenious methods for testing theories, and resulted in the publication of volumes—of inconclusive results. While some studies showed a definite relationship between severity of weaning and dependency (Sears et al., 1953), later studies by the same authors

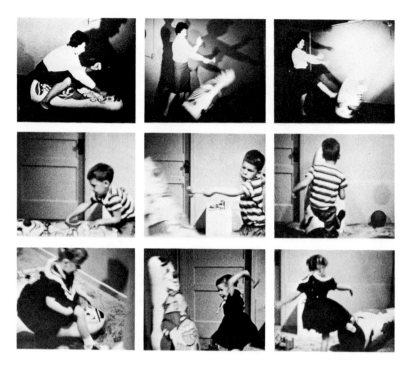

Children can learn aggressive behavior through observing adult *models*. The children shown above are using the identical aggressive acts on the inflated doll that they observed in the adult model. (Courtesy of Albert Bandura, Stanford University)

failed to confirm the association (Sears et al., 1957). When one researcher (Levy, 1934) demonstrated that the frustration of the oral drive leads to nonnutritive sucking (e.g., thumbsucking), another demonstrated that the prolonged satisfaction of the drive led to greater signs of disturbance (Sears and Wise, 1950). It may be that such inconsistencies again prove the complex nature of personality rather than disproving the Freudian theory. Examining each major variable by itself, such as severity of weaning, may be too artificial and simple an approach. Perhaps again the age of the child, the nature of the home atmosphere, and the previous experiences of the youngster interact with the child-rearing technique in varying ways to produce varying results. Murphy (1962) and Yarrow (1954) propose that oral gratification leads to different results if satisfied during a critical period of life, and Heinstein (1963) has demon-

strated that the efficacy of bottle feeding depends upon the warmth of the mother.

Brief mention should be made of a modern development in child rearing: the use of the television for "baby-sitting services." Color screens and cartoon films enhance the attention value of this electronic miracle and can capture the child in a way that is remarkable. It is estimated that children may spend 14-20 hours per week watching television. Although educational televised series have contributed immensely to instruction, it is the influence on personality of films during casual home-viewing time that has implications for this discussion. Plots involving villains and violence invariably have an impact on youngsters. Murray (1933) developed his conception of *complementary projection* through examining the effects of such suspenseful storytelling on judgments of the degree of hostility of others. He was able to show that the fearfulness stirred

121

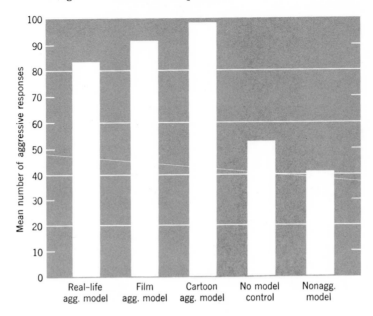

Figure 5-1. **The average number of aggressive responses performed by children in each of five groups.**
SOURCE: Reprinted with permission from "The role of modeling processes in personality development" by Albert Bandura. In *The young child: Reviews of research.* Willard W. Hartup and Nancy L. Smothergill (Eds.). Copyright © 1967, National Association for the Education of Young Children, 1834 Connecticut Avenue, N.W., Washington, D.C. 20009.

by such stories remained in the listeners, leading them to assign sinister and hostile intent to their surroundings. Similarly, Emery and Martin (1957) found that the themes depicted in western movies were incorporated by boys into their perceptions of life, leading them to fantasy about being victims of a powerful and hostile environment. Perhaps the most provocative results were those pinpointing the *behavioral* results of film-viewing. Bandura, Ross, and Ross (1961) prepared films showing adults and cartoon characters aggressing in specific ways. Those children who saw these films exhibited nearly twice as much aggression as control subjects (see Fig. 5-1), and their aggressive be-

haviors were duplicates of that shown by the film models. Lovaas (1961) also demonstrated the aggressive-stimulating influence of cartoons on children. Although it is not claimed that exposure will inevitably lead to indiscriminate displays of aggression, children do seem more likely to show aggression following movie-viewing and given an appropriate circumstance. It is also likely that such imitation will be even more encouraged if the film "heroes" are portrayed as justified and even praiseworthy for their actions. Finally, if the aggressive acts are perceived as instrumental in achieving a goal, then the films cannot help but be a stimulus toward aggression.

Glossary

Affect hunger: A disturbance in children following maternal deprivation involving a heightened search for affection from others.

Affectionless character: A disturbance in children following maternal deprivation involving the lack of normal display or need for affection.

Anaclitic depression: A disturbance in children following maternal deprivation involving a mourning for the parent, followed by denial of recognition of the parent.

Complementary projection: The attributing of a trait to others that will justify or complement the feeling or emotions that one possesses.

Double-bind hypothesis: The hypothesis that an individual may communicate conflicting demands without admitting to the inconsistency.

Enuresis: Bed-wetting.

Feral children: Children said to have been raised by wild animals.

Identification with the aggressor: Acquiring the characteristics of another person who is threatening.

Imprinting: In some animals, the acquisition of complex behavioral patterns at a critical time in development.

Maternal deprivation: In psychopathology, the absence of the mother for prolonged periods, leading to intellectual and emotional difficulties in the child.

Primary identification: Also called developmental identification. The acquisition of the characteristics of another person who is associated with nurturance or reward.

Schismatic family: A disturbed family characterized by hostilities dividing the family into factions.

Schizophrenogenic: Producing the conditions leading to the development of schizophrenia.

Skewed family: A disturbed family characterized by one spouse going along passively with the aberrant ways of the other.

References

Abrahams, J. & Varon, E. *Maternal dependency and schizophrenia: mother and daughter in a therapeutic group.* New York: International University Press, 1953.

Baldwin, A. Socialization and the parent-child relationship. *Child Develpm.,* 1948, **19**, 127.

Bandura, A. & Huston, A. Identification as a process of incidental learning. *J. abnorm. soc. Psychol.,* 1961, **63**, 311.

Bandura, A., Ross, D., & Ross, S. Transmission of aggression through imitation of aggressive models. *J. abnorm. soc. Psychol.,* 1961, **63**, 575.

Bateson, G., Jackson, D., Haley, J., & Weakland, J. Towards a theory of schizophrenia. *Beh. Sci.,* 1956, **1**, 251.

Behrens, M. & Goldfarb, W. A study of patterns of interaction of families of schizophrenic children in residential treatment. *Amer. J. Orthopsychiat.,* 1958, **28**, 300.

Bettelheim, B. Individual and mass behavior in extreme situations. In E. Maccoby, et al. (Eds.), *Readings in social psychology.* (3rd ed.). New York: Holt, Rinehart & Winston, 1958.

Bowlby, J. Forty-four juvenile thieves. *Int. J. Psycho-Anal.,* 1944, **25**, 1.

Brackbill, Y. Extinction of the smiling response in infants as a function of reinforcement schedule. *Child Develpm.,* 1958, **29**, 115.

Clardy, E. A study of the development and course of schizophrenic children. *Psychiat. Quart.,* 1951, **25**, 81.

Despert, J. Schizophrenia in children. *Psychiat. Quart.,* 1938, **12**, 366.

Despert, J. Prophylactic aspects of schizophrenia in childhood. *Nerv. Child,* 1942, **1**, 199.

Donnelly, E. The quantitative analysis of parent behavior toward psychotic children and their siblings. *Genet. Psychol. Monogr.,* 1960, **62**, 331.

Emery, F. & Martin, D. Psychological effects of the western film: a study in television viewing. Melbourne: Dept. of Audio Visual Aides, 1957.

Farina, A. Patterns of role dominance and conflict in parents of schizophrenic patients. *J. abnorm. soc. Psychol.,* 1960, **61**, 31.

Farina, A. & Dunham, R. Measurement of family relationships and their effects. *Arch. gen. Psychiat.,* 1963, **9**, 31.

Fisher, S. & Mendell, D. The communication of neurotic patterns over two and three generations. *Psychiatry,* 1956, **19**, 41.

Fleck, S., Lidz, T., & Cornelison, A. Comparison of parent-child relationships of male and female schizophrenic patients. *Arch. gen. Psychiat.,* 1963, **8**, 1.

Frank, G. The role of the family in the development of psychopathology. *Psychol. Bull.*, 1965, **64**, 191.

Freeman, R. & Grayson, H. Maternal attitudes in schizophrenia. *J. abnorm. soc. Psychol.*, 1955, **50**, 45.

Freud, A. & Burlingham, D. *Infants without families.* New York: International University Press, 1944.

Freud, S. *Basic writings of Sigmund Freud.* New York: Random House, 1938.

Gerard, D. & Siegel, J. The family background in schizophrenia. *Psychiat. Quart.*, 1950, **24**, 45.

Goldfarb, W. Effects of early institutional care on adolescent personality (graphic Rorschach data). *Child Develpm.*, 1943, **14**, 213.

Goldfarb, W. Psychological privation in infancy and subsequent adjustment. *Amer. J. Orthopsychiat.* 1945, **15**, 247.

Hagman, R. A study of fears of children of preschool age. *J. exp. Educ.*, 1932, **1**, 111.

Heinstein, M. Behavioral correlates of breast-bottle regimes under varying parent-infant relationships. *Monogr. Soc. Res. Child Develpm.*, 1963, **28**, No. 4.

Hess, E. Imprinting. *Science,* 1959, **130**, 130.

Hilgard, J. Sibling rivalry and social heredity. *Psychiatry,* 1951, **14**, 315.

Hill, L. *Psychotherapeutic interaction in schizophrenia.* Chicago: University of Chicago Press, 1955.

Hurlock, E. *Child development* (4th ed.). New York: McGraw-Hill, 1964.

Jenkins, R. Nature of the schizophrenic process. *Arch. neurol. Psychiat.*, 1950, **64**, 243.

Levy, D. Experiments on the sucking reflex and social behavior in dogs. *Arch. J. Orthopsychiat.*, 1934, **4**, 203.

Levy, D. *Maternal overprotection.* New York: Columbia University Press, 1943.

Lidz, T., Cornelison, A., Fleck, S., & Terry, D. The intrafamilial environment of the schizophrenic patient: I. The father. *Psychiatry,* 1957, **20**, 329.

Lidz, T., Cornelison, A., Fleck, S., & Terry, D. The intrafamilial environment of the schizophrenic patient: II. Marital schizm and marital skew. *Amer. J. Psychiat.*, 1957, **114**, 241.

Lovaas, O. Effect of exposure to symbolic aggression on aggressive behavior. *Child Develpm.* 1961, **32**, 37.

MacFarlane, J., Allen, L., & Honzik, M. A developmental study of the behavior problems of normal children between twenty-one months and fourteen years. Berkeley, California: University of California Press, 1954.

Mark, J. The attitudes of the mothers of male schizophrenics toward child behavior. *J. abnorm. social Psychol.*, 1953, **48**, 185.

McCord, W., McCord, J., & Howard, A. Familial correlates of aggression in nondelinquent male children. *J. abnorm. soc. Psychol.*, 1961, **62**, 79.

Murphy, L., et al. *The widening world of childhood.* New York: Basic Books, 1962.

Murray, H. The effect of fear upon estimates of the maliciousness of other personalities. *J. soc. Psychol.*, 1933, **4**, 310.

Newell, H. The psycho-dynamics of maternal rejection. *Amer. J. Orthopsychiat.*, 1934, **4**, 387.

Newell, H. A further study of maternal rejection. *Amer. J. Orthopsychiat.*, 1936, **6**, 576.

Powdermaker, F. & Frank, J. *Group psychotherapy: studies in methodology of research and therapy.* Cambridge: Harvard University Press, 1953.

Prout, C. & White, M. A controlled study of personality relationships in mothers of schizophrenic male patients. *Amer. J. Psychiat.*, 1950, **107**, 251.

Radke, M. The relationship of parental authority to children's behavior attitudes. Minnesota: University of Minnesota. *Child Welf. Monogr.*, No. 22, 1946.

Robertson, J. & Bowlby, J. Responses of young children to separation from their mothers: II. Observation of sequences of response of children aged 18-24 months during course of separation. *Courr. cent. int. l'Enfance,* 1952, **2**, 131.

Scott, J. Critical periods in behavioral development. *Science,* 1962, **138**, 949.

Sears, R. Relation of early socialization experiences to aggression in middle childhood. *J. abnorm. soc. Psychol.,* 1961, **63**, 466.

Sears, R., Maccoby, E., & Levin, H. *Patterns of child rearing.* Evanston, Illinois: Row Peterson, 1957.

Sears, R., Whiting, J., Nowlis, W., & Sears, P. Some child-rearing antecedents of aggression and dependency in young children. *Genet. Psychol. Monogr.,* 1953, **47**, 135.

Sears, R. & Wise, G. Relation of cup feeding in infancy to thumb-sucking and the oral drive. *Amer. J. Orthopsychiat.,* 1950, **20**, 123.

Singh, J. & Zingg, R. *Wolf Child and Feral Man.* New York: Harper, 1942.

Sperling, M. The neurotic child and his mother: a psychoanalytic study. *Amer. J. Orthopsychiat.,* 1951, **21**, 351.

Spitz, R. & Wolf, K. Anaclitic depression. *Psychoanal. stud. Child.,* 1946, **2**, 313.

Symonds, P. *The psychology of parent-child relationships.* New York: Appleton Century, 1939.

Thorpe, W. Sensitive periods in the learning of animals and men: a study of imprinting with special reference to the induction of cyclic behavior. In W. Thorpe & O. Zangwill (Eds.), *Current problems in animal behavior.* Cambridge: Cambridge University Press, 1961.

Tietze, T. A study of mothers of schizophrenic patients. *Psychiatry,* 1949, **12**, 55.

Wordsworth, W. My heart leaps up. In E. de Selinicourt (Ed.), *The poetical works of William Wordsworth.* London: Oxford University Press, 1940.

Yarrow, L. The relationship between nutritive sucking experiences in infancy and non-nutritive sucking in childhood. *J. Genet. Psychol.,* 1954, **84**, 149.

6 Contributors to Personality: The Biophysiological Factors

I. Introduction

There is no question that man is made of flesh and blood; he is a creature composed of a bony structure of calcium within a sheath of epidermal tissue filled out with muscles and fatty substance and interlaced with a network of nerves and blood vessel canals. Our basic biological needs have the power to influence our thoughts and fantasies—view what happens when appetite turns into hunger and takes over our senses. Our endocrine glands produce biochemical substances that affect our emotional state; for example, they release adrenaline into the system and the results are subjectively similar to anxiety and fear experiences. Our bodies are kept sound by very delicately balanced machinery; a single disturbance in the basic physiology of the person and the effects may appear in intellectual retardation or personality instabilities. Such a close linkage between the psychology of man and his physiology has encouraged many to seek the answers to mental pathology through the study of physiological and biological factors. Before exploring the results of these quests, we must first briefly outline some of the relevant aspects of human physiology in the normal state.

THE INTERNAL STATE OF NEEDS AND HOMEOSTASIS

The human body functions internally to maintain a continuous state of stability or equilibrium, referred to as *homeostasis.* Temperature, nutrition, oxygen, and other internal conditions are automatically regulated for purposes of survival. Certain basic physiological and biological needs must be fulfilled, among these being the need for oxygen, the need for sleep, the need for food and water, and the need for the elimination of body wastes. Disruption of the homeostatic condition in the direction of either deprivation or excesses can produce abnormal effects. Thus, oxygen *insufficiency* may produce severe brain injury and personality changes, while the *accumulation* of waste products can produce a toxic or poisoning effect.

Among the systems within the human body which serve to preserve the homeostasis are the endocrine glands and the nervous system. The endocrines are those glands which secrete chemical substances into the blood stream. These chemical products are carried to certain organs of the body where they may accelerate or retard various functions. The nervous system is a complex network of nervous tissue that includes the brain, the spinal cord, and innumerable fibers spreading throughout the body. Although the endocrine glands are known to influence the growth of the nervous system early in life, the nervous system ultimately attains at least partial control over the activity of the glands. The nervous system is also involved in the integration and coordination of many mechanisms directly responsible for the maintenance of homeostasis.

The Endocrine Glands

Several important glands are distributed throughout the body: the pituitary in the center of the head, the thyroid and parathyroids in the neck, the adrenals near the kidneys, the pancreas along the stomach, and the gonads (Fig. 6-1). Very briefly, these glands serve the following functions:

The Pituitary. This is often called the "master gland" because of its controlling effect on growth and on the activity of other glands such as the thyroid, the adrenals, and the gonads. Excessive activity produces excessive growth leading to the physical stature often seen in circus giants. Personality changes can also accompany malfunctioning of the pituitary.

The Thyroids. They regulate the production of heat and the release of energy within the cells of the body. In addition, the hormone produced by the thyroid gland is essential for the normal physical and intellectual development of the young. Thyroid deficiency in infancy leads to cretinism, a condition of mental retardation associated with lethargy, dwarfism, and other distinctive physical characteristics (see Chapter 16).

The Parathyroids. These are glands that appear to regulate the balance of calcium in the blood and in the bones. Bone and tooth growth and maintenance are associated with parathyroid functioning. These glands also indirectly affect nerve and muscle irritability (manifested by involun-

tary "twitchings" or contractions of the muscles) through their effects on blood-calcium concentration.

The Adrenals. These paired glands are responsible for the production of epinephrine (also called adrenaline). It is sometimes hypothesized that epinephrine helps prepare the organism for emergency situations, a type of "flight or fight" reaction, involving elevated blood sugar (presumably enabling more fuel to be available for the emergency), increased heart rate and blood pressure (making more blood available to the brain and muscles), greater resistence to fatigue (for more intensive effort), and increased blood coagulation (to help in a quicker stopping of bleeding from possible wounds).

The Pancreas. This stretches along the lower border of the stomach. It produces an important digestive secretion and, more important, a hormone that prevents the occurrence of diabetes.

The Gonads. These are the sexual glands, the testes in the male and the ovaries in the female. They are responsible for the production of sperms and eggs, respectively. In addition, the sexual hormones are responsible for the development of sexual physical characteristics, and control the menstrual cycle in the woman.

The Nervous System

The nervous system is composed of cells called *neurons*, each having a cell body and fibrous projections called *axons* and *dendrites*. Neural impulses are carried away from the cell body by way of the axons while incoming impulses are transmitted through the dendrites. Neurons do not actually touch one another; the small gap separating neurons is called a *synapse*. It has been speculated that a neural impulse is transmitted across the synapse via the release of a chemical, acetylcholine, at the neuron endings. Neurons may be found bundled together much like wires in a telephone cable; these bundles are the *nerves* of the human body and are arranged in long columns. The simplest functional arrangement of neurons is the *reflex arc;* here, three neurons are linked together, an *afferent* (incoming) neuron which is excited into action by a

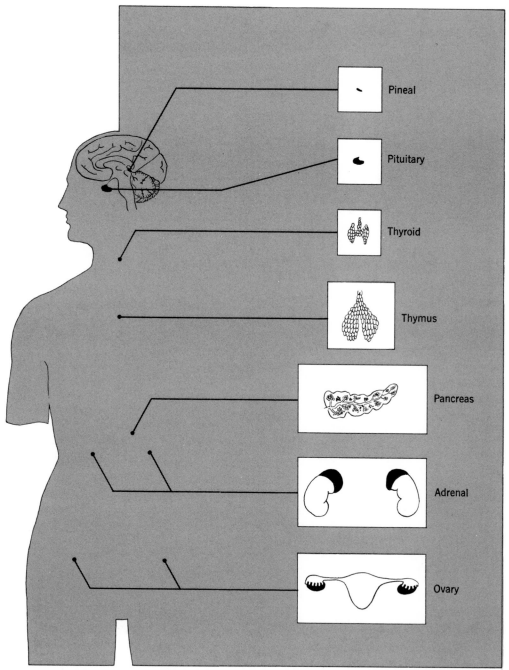

Figure 6-1. **Schematic representation of the endocrine system.**

stimulus, an *internuncial* (connecting) neuron which transmits the impulse onward, and an *efferent* (outgoing) neuron which triggers some type of activity. Thus, for example, a person touches a hot object: the pain receptors send an impulse through the afferent neuron, across the spinal cord through an internuncial neuron, and back out through an efferent neuron to the muscles of the hand, leading to a hasty hand withdrawal.

The nervous system is classified into two major divisions: the *central nervous system* and the *peripheral nervous system*. The central nervous system is composed of the brain and the spinal cord; the peripheral nervous system is composed of the *autonomic nervous system* and the *somatic nervous system*. The autonomic nervous system is a set of nerve fibers that run parallel to the spinal cord and that reach into and control many of the glands and organs of the body. The autonomic system is actually made up of the *sympathetic nervous system* and the *parasympathetic nervous system*. Typically, the

sympathetic and the parasympathetic systems have reciprocal effects; the sympathetic generally activates an organ or gland, while the parasympathetic usually inhibits that same organ or gland. The somatic nervous system includes those nerves which terminate in muscles, sensory cells, and sensory organs and therefore is associated with sensory and motor activities.

The Central Nervous System. The brain is the most fascinating structure in this system. Viewing it from the top, it forms two distinguishable halves called the *cerebral hemispheres* or the *cerebrum*. As we look at it from the side (as in Fig. 6-2), two large grooves can be seen with one coming down from the top and the other proceeding from the bottom upward diagonally. The top central groove is known as the *central fissure* or the *fissure of Rolando;* the lower groove is called the *lateral fissure* or the *fissure of Sylvius*. These landmarks aid as reference points in identifying functional parts of the brain. The

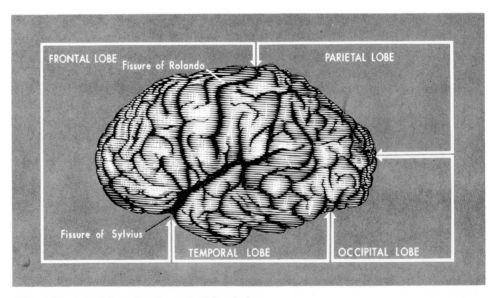

Figure 6-2. **The lobes of each cerebral hemisphere.**
SOURCE: From *Basic psychology,* by Howard J. Kendler. Copyright © 1963, Meredith Corporation. Reproduced by permission of Appleton-Century-Crofts.

four principal lobes are the *frontal lobe* located in front of the central fissure, the *parietal lobe* immediately to the rear of the central fissure, the *temporal lobe* situated below the lateral fissure, and the *occipital lobe* at the very rear of the brain (Fig. 6-2 will help in these locations). Functionally, the frontal lobe appears to control motor behavior and appears to be important for higher mental processes such as reasoning and memory. However, cases have been reported involving surgical removal of large portions of this lobe without significant damage to the patient's intellect. In fact, this type of operation has been prescribed as a method of treatment of certain mental disorders. Such surgery often decreases the patient's anxieties, and he seems to be less self-conscious and more satisfied with life. The parietal lobe is connected with body sensations and movement receptors. It has been possible for surgeons to actually stimulate this lobe with an electric probe and to obtain a direct report from the patient. Reports have included statements such as "I suddenly felt a warm feeling" and "I thought my leg was moving." The temporal lobe is involved with hearing; stimulation of this area produces buzzing or ringing sounds in the ears. Persons with epilepsy, a condition involving convulsions and often associated with irritability or damage to the brain, sometimes experience an auditory reaction just prior to another seizure. The occipital lobe is directly connected to vision; destruction of this region will lead to complete blindness even though the person's eyes are normal. It has also been noticed that epileptics may experience visual sensations such as flashing colors before a seizure, suggesting that the occipital lobe is involved.

The cerebral hemispheres are covered by a layer called the *cerebral cortex,* literally meaning the "brain's bark." This covering is convoluted and ranges in thickness from one-eighth to one-fourth of an inch. The cerebrum and its cortex form the most significant differences between the brain of man and those of other mammals. In a man they form the largest and most visible part of the brain, obscuring most of the other parts. The motor area of the brain is actually centralized in the cortex, in the part located just in front of the central fissure. Surgeons have actually mapped out this area and can identify which portion will cause the toes to move, which will move the tongue, etc. (see Fig. 6-3). Of greater importance is the role that the cortex plays in higher mental activities. Approximately three-fourths of the cortex is believed to be connected with learning, memory, and thinking. Damage to parts of the cortex may, for example, lead to strange disturbances in speech. The patient may be able to pronounce a simple word or sentence, but not be able to comprehend its meaning.

Among the other parts of the brain are several that are tucked in under the cerebrum. Briefly, the major parts of the brain include (Fig. 6-4):

The forebrain (prosecephalon)—involving the cerebral hemispheres themselves and the diencephalon. The diencephalon contains the thalamus and the hypothalamus.

The midbrain (mesencephalon)—an area controlling visual and auditory reflexes.

The "nosebrain" (rhinencephalon)—located between the cerebral cortex and the midbrain. Contained here are the septal area and the amygdala, both important in emotions and motivation.

The hindbrain (rhombencephalon)—divided into the cerebellum (necessary for body posture and coordination), the pons (the link between the cerebellum and the cerebrum), and the medulla (the mediator of reflex activities such as breathing, and heart rate).

The hypothalamus, the septal area, and the amygdala, have prominent roles in emotions. The hypothalamus has in fact been credited by some with having the major responsibility for the integration and control over emotions. Extensive observations have been made of animals whose cortex has been surgically removed, leaving the hypothalamus intact (Goltz, 1892; Cannon, 1925). Such animals showed violent rage reactions without any appropriate cause; it was as if the hypothalamus went berserk in releasing rage patterns when uninhibited by the restraining influence of the cortex. Direct stimulation of the hypothalamus has been found to suddenly release rage behavior or fearful behavior. On the other hand, electrical stimulation of the septal area seems to produce a pleasurable emotion (rats will continue to press a bar for no other reward than the sensation of a shock to the septum) (Olds, 1956). Destruction of the septal area just in front of the hypothalamus has resulted in a mixture of fear and rage responses (Brady and Nauta, 1953). Interestingly enough, destruction of the amygdala, another portion of the rhinencephalon, will cause wild animals to stop biting and scratching. Such animals become abnormally tame even when mishandled or pinched (Schreiner and Kling, 1953). Of relevance to the study of mental illness is the fact that tranquilizers (calming drugs) such as reserpine and chlorpromazine appear to inhibit the action of the hypothalamus. Chlorpromazine also appears to inhibit the reticular activating system, a system of nerve fibers intricately connected with the hypothalamus and the cortex (Himwich, 1955).

The Autonomic Nervous System. This system is also critically connected with

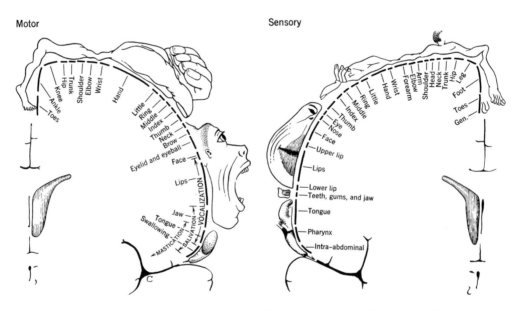

Figure 6-3. **The cerebral cortex of man showing localization of sensory and motor function.** SOURCE: Adapted from W. Penfield and T. Rasmussen, *The cerebral cortex of man.* New York: Macmillan, 1950. Copyright 1950, Macmillan.

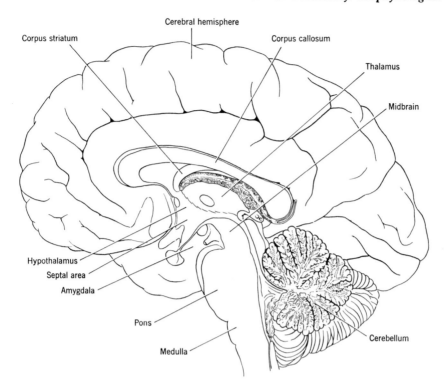

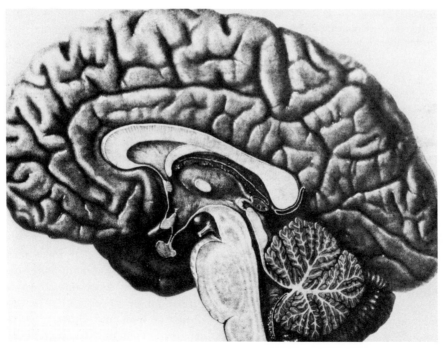

Figure 6-4. **Lateral views of the human brain showing major areas.**
SOURCE: G. Wolf-Heidegger, *Atlas of systematic human anatomy. Vol. 3.* (2nd ed.) New York: Karger, Basel, 1962.

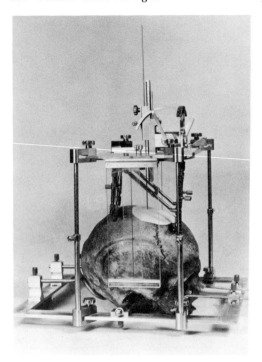

Research on *electrical stimulation* of the brain demands preciseness in the technique of electrode implantation. **The above shows a device that permits the exact alignment needed for implantation in the human brain. (Dr. Adolph Spiegel)**

emotional activity. It was called *autonomic* because it was originally believed that the system functioned autonomously or independently. It now seems established that higher centers, particularly the hypothalamus, exert some control over this system. The endocrine glands and their secretions, and the functioning of many important organs such as the heart and the lungs, are dependent upon the autonomic system (see Fig. 6-5). Under the control of the parasympathetic system, the continuous biological and physiological activities necessary for life are maintained without conscious effort. Without thinking about it, we breathe in air and expel carbon dioxide from our lungs, our stomach and intestines carry out the task of

breaking down food and eliminating waste, and our heart continues to pump and circulate blood. The sympathetic nervous system becomes dominant under emergency conditions. Because of its overall effects, it has been supposed that the sympathetic system acts to prepare the person for fight or flight, for coping with danger. The pupil of the eye enlarges, the adrenals release epinephrine, blood is rerouted from the skin and stomach to the muscles of the limbs, heart rate is increased, and blood pressure rises..

II. *The Biophysiological Hypotheses*

The previous introduction to the endocrine glands and the central nervous system will help the reader to more fully understand the complexities involved in the search for clues to mental disorders. In this chapter, we shall be referring to investigations directed to the examination of physiological or biological factors. From time to time, significant breakthroughs have apparently been achieved, such as the identification of a toxic (poisonous) factor in the blood of schizophrenics, only to be discounted by further investigations. Because of this, it is more relevant to speak of physiological or biological *hypotheses* pertaining to mental illness rather than the physiological or biological *origins* of mental abnormality. Among the leading physiological hypotheses are those concerning the functioning of major glandular systems, and those that focus on finding toxic substances. Among the biological hypotheses are those related to the constitutional or phenotypic structure (physique) of man and those related to the genotypic (genetic) structure. The former will be discussed in this chapter, the latter was discussed in Chapter Three.

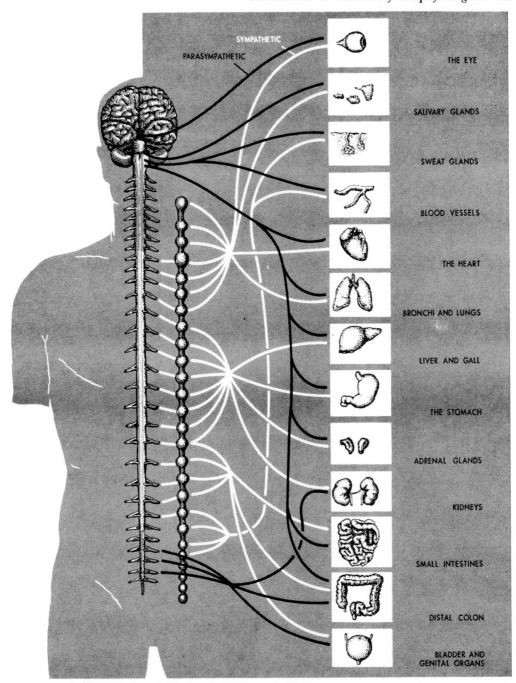

SYMPATHETIC

PARASYMPATHETIC

THE EYE

SALIVARY GLANDS

SWEAT GLANDS

BLOOD VESSELS

THE HEART

BRONCHI AND LUNGS

LIVER AND GALL

THE STOMACH

ADRENAL GLANDS

KIDNEYS

SMALL INTESTINES

DISTAL COLON

BLADDER AND
GENITAL ORGANS

Figure 6-5. **Schematic representation of the autonomic nervous system.**
SOURCE: From *Basic psychology,* by Howard J. Kendler. Copyright © 1963, Meredith Corporation. Reproduced by permission of Appleton-Century-Crofts.

THE ENDOCRINE GLAND HYPOTHESES

The Adrenal Glands

These are small, paired organs lying anterior to the kidneys. The inner portion is called the adrenal medulla and secretes epinephrine (adrenaline) and norepinephrine (noradrenaline); the outer portion is called the adrenal cortex and its secretions are called steroids or corticoids. The role of epinephrine and norepinephrine as possible factors in psychoses will be examined later. The adrenal cortex can malfunction and either degenerate or become overactive (hyperfunction); the former is associated with Addison's disease, the latter with Cushing's disease. Both physical illnesses commonly involve mental symptoms. Addison's disease is characterized by general muscular weakness, digestive upsets, a unique bronzing of the skin, and:

apathy	apprehension
depression	hallucinations
delirium	irritability
delusions	restlessness
confusion	difficulty in
	concentration

Unless properly treated, the ultimate outcome is death.

In Cushing's disease, commonly reported mental states include:

irritability
uncooperativeness
crying spells
agitation

Of greater interest is the apparent role that the adrenals play in stress tolerance. In rats, exposure to stress leads to increased output by the adrenals. Where the animal is prevented from producing such secretions because of an adrenalectomy, the result is death. Similar enhancement

in adrenal secretion appears to occur in humans in the face of stress. Medical students about to take examinations showed a demonstrable increase in steroid excretion (Schwartz and Shields, 1956) as did naval submarine candidates undergoing stressful training and evaluational procedures (Cook and Wherry, 1950). Similarly, subjects who were faced with discrepancies between their aspiration level and their actual achievement levels on a task also showed increased adrenal activity (Berkeley, 1952). Finally, it has been found that schizophrenics tend to be underreactive in comparison with normals in their adrenal response to stress and in some instances a fall in output was identified rather than simply a lack of increase (Pincus and Hoagland, 1950). These studies suggest a close tie between the adrenals and reactivity to stress. In animals, at least, this close association appears to be relevant to adapting. In the human, it is still difficult to determine whether the relationship is functional or incidental. Thus, it is possible that a malfunctioning of the adrenals is the *origin* of misadapting in the schizophrenic. On the other hand, it is also possible that the schizophrenic is a person faced with so much intense psychological conflict and stress in his life that he experiences not only a mental but a physical breakdown. His adrenals are overloaded by the continuous and intense stimulation into activity. In this sense, the adrenal deficiency is the by-product but not the cause of the mental pathology.

The Thyroid Glands

The effects of underproductivity of the thyroid are well known. Such deficiency leads to a form of mental retardation known as cretinism (see Chapter 16). Hyperthyroidism in Basedow's disease is associated with thyroid enlargement, elevated basal metabolism, and mental symptoms such as:

anxiety
mood swings
irritability
excitability

No consistent or well-defined relationship has been proved between the thyroid gland and the psychoses. Hoskins (1954) once found an increased tolerance by schizophrenics to thyroid extracts, and Reiss (1954) reported an over-and under-activity of the thyroid gland in depressives. However, few have viewed the thyroid as a significant factor in the major mental illnesses.

The Pancreatic Gland

Although the disturbed functioning of the pancreas is best identified with the physical symptoms of diabetes, certain results are suggestive for psychology. In some instances, diabetics show depressions beyond that realistic for the illness, along with a continuing feeling of deprivation. Furthermore, it is agreed that conscious fears can lead to hyperglycemia (Eiduson, et al., 1964), which, in turn, has been associated with depression or anxiety. Treatment with insulin, a refined extract of the pancreas, has of course proved a useful procedure in psychoses (see Chapter 17).

The Parathyroid Glands

In approximately half of the known cases of parathyroidism, some psychiatric symptoms have appeared that range from intellectual impairment and organic brain syndrome to pseudoneurotic and pseudo-psychotic states (Denko and Kaelbling, 1962; Bartter, 1953). Nearly every conceivable type of neurotic symptom has been connected with parathyroid disturbances, stretching from obsessional states to anxiety states. This very diversity of the mental picture must necessarily rule out this gland as involved in other than a general influence on psychopathology.

THE TOXIC FACTOR HYPOTHESES

The hypotheses that presuppose that mental illnesses are caused by toxic substances seem at first glance to be a natural line of thought. Such views are predicted on the disease entity orientation—that diseases of the body are attributable to invasion by foreign agents such as bacteria; symptoms are in part reflections of the action of the disease-carrying agent, and in part the reactions of the body in its attempt to counteract the infection. It seems logical to carry this analogy over to mental illness and to search for the invading agent. The first step in this search requires the demonstration that the infectious substance, taken from a "diseased" person, will in fact show up as potently harmful. When the medical literature is examined regarding such a step, an impressively long list of material can be cited. As early as 1903, Berger attempted to determine whether the blood of schizophrenics contained anything that might prove infectious. Using himself as a human guinea pig, he injected blood taken from acutely ill schizophrenics into his own bloodstream on seven different occasions. For four trials nothing happened, but on the fifth he felt a transient vertigo within fifteen minutes of the injection (of five milliliters), within two hours he experienced increased salivation, within four hours palpitations and headache, and by evening he felt a severe and aimless depression. Following the seventh injection, he experienced a slight deafness after fifteen minutes and he fainted three hours later; he remained weak and could not shake a persistent headache for eight days. Such studies have continued in many forms by other researchers: blood sera have been found lethal to mice (Kastan, 1926), toxic to certain cells in tissue cultures (Fedoroff and Hoffer, 1956), an inhibitor of the growth of plants (Herz and

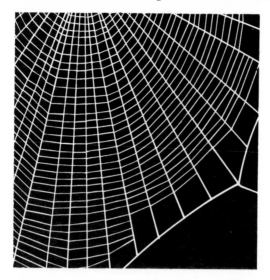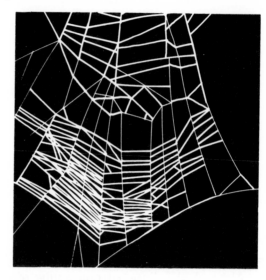

Web-building in spiders is studied to determine the effects of certain drugs. Illustrated are (a) marked exactitude in a web built under the influence of LSD, and (b) an erratic, bizarrely constructed web built under the influence of mescaline. (The Schering Company)

Weichbrodt, 1924), an obstacle to the rope-climbing behavior of trained rats (Sanders, et al., 1959, 1962), and a cause of aberrant web-spinning in spiders (Witt, 1956); the bile from catatonic schizophrenics have been injected into pigeons, cats, and mice and reported to lead to catatoniclike symptoms—plasticity of body position, loss of spontaneous body movements, and prolonged suspension of posture (Baruk and Camus, 1949); and finally, the urine of psychotics has been used and cited as leading to behavioral changes in monkeys, cats, and spiders and lethal to rabbits and mice (Wada and Gibson, 1959; Rieder, 1957; Moya, et al., 1958; Gamper and Kral, 1934). Unfortunately, the promise of these works has never become fruitful. Toxicity is at best a highly crude measure and literally hundreds of unrelated factors may produce essentially indistinguishable toxic effects. It is difficult to know, for example, whether Berger experienced the effects of a toxic factor within the blood, or whether he experi-

enced the side effects connected with a blood transfusion of any type under such conditions, or whether he was simply the victim of his own expectations. It is now known that the "placebo effect" exists, whereby subjects show all the *expected* effects of a certain drug even though they received in reality a pill with no effects (a placebo). In addition, such studies are often complicated by the lack of control of other factors that may be important in explaining apparent differences between the products of psychotics and normals. Differences in diet, activity, and general health can all lead to significant differences in body products when patients and normals are compared. At one time, a strange factor was identified in the bloodstream of patients (Freud and Dingemanse, 1932; DeJong, 1934) which was believed responsible for their illness. One can imagine the excitement aroused by this finding. Since the substance was found to exist in the blood of schizophrenics, it was called "catatonine." Further study ultimately led to the correct identification of this factor —to the obvious disappointment and embarrassment of the researchers—as the catatonine was more correctly named *nicotine* (Dingemanse and Freud, 1933)! This by-product of smoking showed up as a "toxic" factor in the blood and was related to smoking habits rather than to mental disease. A similar story is sometimes told of the discovery of peculiar phenolic acids in the urine of schizophrenics but not in that of control subjects. As luck would have it, later observation uncovered the fact that the patients had been drinking much more coffee, and phenolic acids are known to derive from coffee! A complicating influence making the task of modern researchers even more difficult is the free use of tranquilizers and energizers as part of the treatment program. Many patients who comprise study groups for research are on drug treatment (chemotherapy); the by-product effects of such drugs are not yet fully known. Even if the patients are removed from chemotherapy for a month prior to study, there is still a distinct possibility that the metabolic effects of the drugs still persist. Perhaps the most telling argument for caution in the interpretation of reports on toxicity results is the contradictory evidence of later studies. For example, other equally competent researchers have failed to confirm the lethal effect of psychotic blood serum or urine on cell cultures (Reiter, 1938), plants (Freeman and Looney, 1934), or rabbits (Goldner and Ricketts, 1942; Harris, 1942) nor has there been support for the reported behavioral changes in spiders, or catatonia in mice, pigeons, cats, rats, or guinea pigs from either bile, urine, blood, or cerebrospinal fluid (Guilmot, 1952; Rieder, 1957; Shapiro, 1957; Sogliani, 1934; Tinel and Eck, 1933; Tomescu, 1937).

In spite of such incredible obstacles and inconsistencies, several major works continue to show promise. One line of study represented by research teams at Tulane (Heath, et al., 1957), the Lafayette Clinic (Frohman, et al., 1962), the Worcester Foundation (Bergen, et al., 1966), and the laboratories of Merck, Sharp and Dohme (Sanders, et al., 1959) is the search for a unique factor in blood serum. A separate line, epitomized by the efforts of Woolley (1962), has restricted the search to specific neurohormones such as serotonin, acetylcholine, and epinephrine or its by-products (adrenolutin and adrenochrome).

The Serum Factors

The work of Heath and his group at Tulane University School of Medicine deserves attention. They were initially involved in a comprehensive program directed toward correlating brain activity and behavior (Heath, 1954; Heath, 1955; Heath and Mickle, 1960). Working with animals and then with humans, electrodes were implanted deep within the brain and maintained for periods of up to two years. Electrical stimulation was attempted in some cases and improvement in patients' symptoms was noted. Most pertinent to their later work was the analysis of electroencephalographic (EEG) data which showed a relationship between EEG abnormalities from the septal region of the brain and psychotic behavior (Heath, 1954). The research team then began to search for the factor that might account for such abnormalities in brain function. During this same period, much excitement was being stirred by the identification and purifying of a blue plasma protein called *ceruloplasmin*. A flood of reports first added support to the role of this protein in abnormality (Akerfeldt, 1957; Leach, et al., 1956; Abood, et al., 1957). However, other reports soon left the issue in doubt (Yuwiler, Jenkins, and Dukay, 1961; Maas, Gleser, and Gottschalk, 1961). Some of the Tulane group had been involved in ceruloplasmin research including Heath himself. Thus, Heath turned again to biochemical analyses in his attempt to find an explanation for the abnormal EEG records. Schizophrenic serum was analyzed and a substance resembling ceruloplasmin but not identical to it was found. It was assigned the name *taraxein* (from the Greek *Tarasso,* mind disturbing). Introduction of this serum fraction into monkeys or humans was found to lead to abnormal EEG patterns—an effect consistent with the researchers' premise that a toxic factor is responsible for the abnormal brainwave patterns recorded from their patients. They were also able to elicit abnormal behavioral effects by administering taraxein. Behavioral symptoms included depersonalization, autistic feelings, delusions of persecution, auditory hallucinations, as well as catatonic and hebephrenic signs. The story of taraxein is still incomplete. The extraction and purification of this substance has been greatly improved. However, taraxein has proved to be a highly unstable substance and its toxic properties are extremely sensitive to temperature and temporal changes. Furthermore, other scientists have failed to confirm the psychological effects of taraxein administration even when using extracts prepared and supplied directly by Heath (Robins, et al., 1957). Perhaps the best evaluation of the current status of taraxein is that supplied by Heath himself when he wrote: "These studies, as well as earlier studies, are provocative but inconclusive" (1966, p. 387).

Also worthy of mention is the work of the Lafayette Clinic. This group also accepts the premise that the source of mental disease will be found in biochemical factors. In addition, they have postulated that the abnormal serum factor is a result of maturation; failure to receive such stimulation results in the development of a maladaptive biological mechanism that could result in psychosis. Therefore, the abnormal serum factor represents the biochemical immaturity or maldevelopment

due to the lack of stimulation. The first stage of this group's research was a quest for a consistent laboratory indicator of the presence of the hypothesized serum factor. They derived a technique called the L/P ratio (actually, an index of cellular metabolism) and ultimately isolated small quantities of a serum factor associated with the L/P ratio for schizophrenics (Frohman, et al., 1960, 1962). A second stage was the examination of the L/P ratios of various subjects to prove that the hypothesized factor was present in patient groups as opposed to normals. Their results were significant for the schizophrenic group but not for the normals, alcoholics, manic-depressives, or diabetic groups. Thus, the factor seems to be illness-specific, that is, related to the presence of a single illness, schizophrenia. However, major differences were found within the schizophrenic group itself leading the researchers to conclude that schizophrenia is made up of four different entities:

Schizophrenia, Vera, Type I—characterized by an active serum substance that is responsible for a metabolic disturbance and possibly a cause of the disorder.

Schizophrenia, Vera, Type II—not characterized by an active serum substance and with no known signs of biochemical or physiological pathology.

Schizophrenia, Childhood—not characterized by an active serum substance. Abnormal EEG records suggest physiological pathology.

Schizophrenia, Temporal Lobe Type —characterized by seizures and temporal lobe EEG abnormalities suggesting physiological pathology.

This clinical-entities classification is still, of course, highly tentative. Another stage of research adding support to the

Lafayette hypotheses was derived from the Primate Laboratory operated by Harlow (Beckett, et al., 1963). Here, monkeys were raised with their own mothers, with terrycloth mother surrogates, or without mothers or mother surrogates. The last group was subdivided into two further groups: those who were stimulated by a shock to the feet and those who received no tactual stimulation at all. Blood plasma was sent to the Lafayette Clinic for L/P ratio. It was immediately evident that the animals who totally lacked any form of stimulation, the no-shock, no-mother group had the highest abnormal L/P ratio (Fig. 6-6). This was interpreted as supporting the researchers' premise that the presence of the serum factor is attributable to maturational defect due to early sensory deprivation. As with taraxein, the story is still unfolding. An attempt was made at the National Institute of Health to repeat the work involving schizophrenics with careful control over medication, general health, and diet. This replication study was considered successful. However,

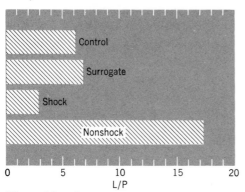

Figure 6-6. The average level of L/P ratios for rhesus monkeys under varying degrees of maternal deprivation and stimulation.
SOURCE: J. Gottlieb, C. Frohman, and P. Beckett, The characteristics of a serum factor in schizophrenia. In M. Rinkel (Ed.), *Biological treatment of mental illness*. New York: L. C. Page, 1966. Reprinted with the permission of Farrar, Straus, and Giroux, Inc. From *Biological treatment of mental illness*, copyright © 1966 by the Manfred Sakel Foundation.

it was later reported that differences in serum samples could be related to differences in the physical state of the subject. Blood samples of patients differed from that of normals only under certain conditions involving physical exercise. Thus, it is possible that the spectre that haunted "catatonine" is now haunting the L/P ratio—could it be that the observed difference between patients and nonpatients is more related to activity habits than to the disease process?

The Neurohormone Factors

A *neurohormone* is a secretion that affects the nerves in the body. Some neurohormones, such as epinephrine, are produced by the endocrine glands. The attention to neurohormones is not a recent development, although the current attitude of acceptance and respectability is new. Sir Henry Dale (1954) once described the earlier attitudes toward neurohormonal study as follows: "Transmission by chemical mediators was like a lady with whom the neurophysiologist was willing to live and to consort in private, but with whom he was reluctant to be seen in public." Refinements in technique, advances in understanding of organic biochemistry, and increased knowledge of physiology have all stimulated intensive study of these substances. Neurohormones are considered *essential metabolites*—that is, compounds which occur naturally in living creatures and which are necessary for specific normal life processes. They perform special functions such as acting as a base for some special enzyme (a facilitant of chemical reactions) or as a receptor in a chemical reaction. The functioning of a metabolite can be blocked by other compounds known as *antimetabolites*. Antimetabolites are structurally similar to metabolites in their molecular shape in that they can combine with the enzyme, but are sufficiently different so that chemical processes are prevented and a deficiency exists. An antimetabolite has been likened to an imperfectly formed key that can be made to fit the lock but cannot turn, and since it is jammed in the keyhole it prevents the correct key from being inserted and used. This structural analysis has been used as one of the steps in proving the linkage between certain neurohormones and psychosis.

Serotonin is a substance in blood serum responsible for constriction of blood vessels and, therefore, for increases in blood pressure. It is not found in all tissues, but is present in the gastrointestinal tract, the spleen, in blood platelets, and certain parts of the brain. Most of the sum total of serotonin in the central nervous system is in the *brain stem.* The major structures of the brain stem are the medulla, the pons, the midbrain, the thalamus, and that important component, the hypothalamus. Woolley and Shaw (1954) were the first to provide evidence for the participation of serotonin in mental illness. They demonstrated that a number of drugs that produced psychotic symptoms (called *psychotomimetic* drugs) in normals were structurally similar to serotonin and acted as antimetabolites. Among the most readily recognized of this group of drugs is *psilocybin,* the extract from the sacred mushrooms used in primitive rituals. *Lysergic acid diethylamide* (LSD) is another psychotomimetic drug found to be structurally similar to serotonin (see Fig. 6-7). This substance is so powerful that an oral dose as low as 1 to 2 micrograms per kilogram of body weight will produce vivid changes in a person. Further evidence for the importance of serotonin in pathology also comes from structural comparisons, this time between serotonin and tranquilizers. Reserpine is a tranquilizing drug that was once heavily relied upon in the treatment of chronic psychoses. Structurally, it is a derivative of another substance which is an antimetabolite of serotonin and which therefore displaces serotonin in the human system. Chlorpromazine is another tranquilizer used more frequently today. Although structurally it is neither an antimetabolite of serotonin nor is it capable of displacing this hormone, chlorpromazine has been found to be a potent inhibitor of the action of serotonin. Finally, it has been found that the administration of serotonin leads to a worsening of the condition of schizophrenic patients. Woolley (1962) has

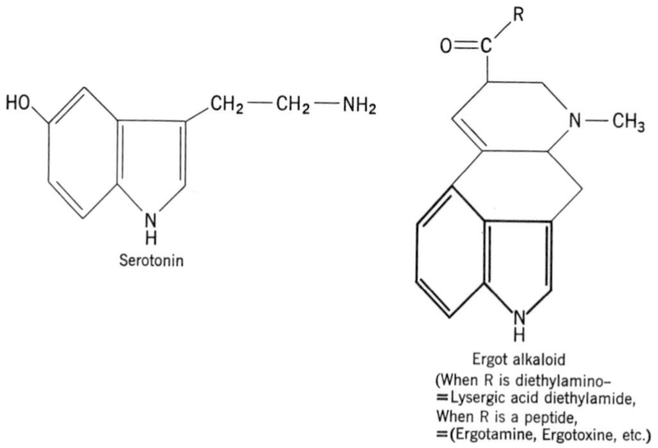

Figure 6-7. **Structure of lysergic acid diethylamide (LSD) emphasizing the relationship to serotonin.**

brought together all the evidence and analyzed the data in great detail offering some convincing argument for the serotonin hypothesis. As the most vocal believer in the importance of serotonin, he has sketched out a theory about its influence. This theory hypothesizes that mental illness reflects an improper balance of serotonin in the brain such that both excesses and deficiencies can trigger symptoms. Increases in serotonin production is said to excite states of psychosis, for example, hallucinatory states, while decrements in serotonin level is believed to lead to depressive or inhibitory states. Such abnormal serotonin levels result in changes in the functions of cells in the central nervous system which in turn are responsible for the abnormal mental condition. Finally, the metabolic imbalance is viewed as similar to diabetes mellitus, a disease affecting metabolism which does not express itself until adulthood. In the same way, schizophrenia is more likely to appear in adults than in children.

Epinephrine (adrenaline) and norepinephrine (noradrenaline) are two hormones that are found in the adrenal glands and in the brain. Epinephrine is formed from norepinephrine, and both have similar effects on man. It is interesting to note that these hormones have effects similar to serotonin, for example, in their effect on blood pressure. In fact, some of the same arguments in support of serotonin as the factor in abnormality also apply to norepinephrine:

1. The psychotomimetic drug *mescaline* which produces feelings of depersonalization, auditory hallucinations, and depression or euphoria is structurally similar to norepinephrine (see Fig. 6-8). It is important to note that mescaline is one of the potent hallucinogenic drugs which is not similar in organic structure to serotonin.

2. Tranquilizers such as reserpine appear to displace norepinephrine from the brain structures connected with rage and pleasure emotions. Chlorpromazine is not only an antagonist to serotonin, but is also known to block norepinephrine.

3. The introduction of epinephrine commonly leads to an emotional reaction often subjectively described as "anxiety" and encompassing such feelings as tenseness, restlessness, agitation, and excitability (Jersild and Thomas, 1931; Basowitz, et al., 1956). It also seems to have some effects on EEG activity (Gibbs and Mattby, 1943; Porter, 1952). Of even greater interest are the results of certain products of epinephrine, such as *adrenochrome*. Intravenous injection of such substances produce schizopheniclike symptoms (Hoffer, 1958; Hoffer and Osmond, 1959), impair web spinning in spiders (Hoffer and Osmond, 1959) and lead to catatonia in pigeons. Since adrenochrome is formed by the oxidation of epinephrine, further support for its role in abnormality was sought through attempting to prove that adrenochrome is formed more readily by mental patients. Preliminary results

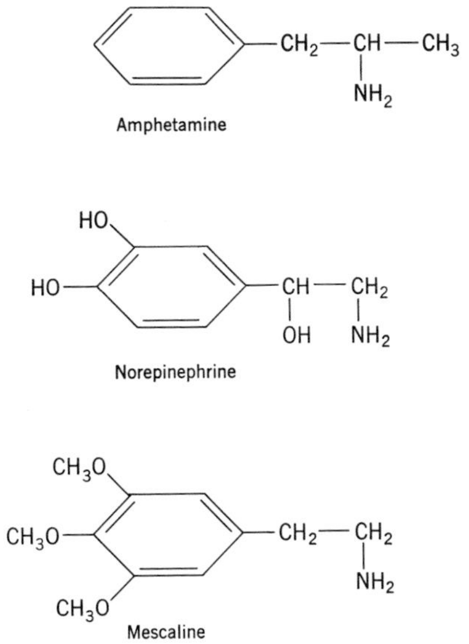

Figure 6-8. **Structure of amphetamine and mescaline emphasizing the relationship to norepinephrine.**

showed that the blood plasma of schizo-phrenics did oxidize epinephrine more rapidly than the plasma of normals (Leach and Heath, 1956). Even stronger support was claimed with further reports announc-ing that adrenochrome appeared in higher concentrations in schizophrenic blood, and in increased amounts after the injection of LSD (Hoffer, et al., 1960). Such infor-mation has been accepted as strong ev-idence for the hypothesis extended by Hoffer and Osmond (1960), that mental illness is caused by a metabolic distur-bance in which epinephrine becomes ox-idized and produces abnormal quantities of adrenochrome. Those who maintain the epinephrine hypothesis are as certain that it is the key to the riddle of mental illness as those exponents of the serotonin hypothesis. To date, however, there have been more failures to replicate the types of data cited in support of epinephrine. Controversial and inconsistent results have stirred dispute over the adrenochrome for-mation theory and the early reports. For example, sophisticated methods of high sensitivity have failed to confirm the pres-ence of even traces of adrenochrome in the blood of acute or chronic schizo-phrenics (Szara, et al., 1958).

Evaluation of the Toxic Factor Hypotheses

The search for a toxic substance, either foreign or a product of the body's own neurohormone system, is an incredibly complex task. Among the neurohormones themselves there exists highly involved interrelationships. Serotonin and norepi-nephrine both compete for the same en-zyme for their formation; norepinephrine can act as a powerful antagonist to sero-tonin and thus may determine the level of serotonin; reserpine blocks the action of both hormones, yet amphetamine (a drug with psychotomimetic properties) will decrease the level of norepinephrine but increase the level of serotonin; acetyl-

choline and serotonin are both rendered ineffective when epinephrine is applied to certain tissues, and the combination of serotonin plus acetylcholine will pre-vent the action of LSD (in mice) whereas neither used alone has an effect. Even the psychotomimetic drugs reflect the same array of unbelievably complicated facts. In the first place, these drugs do seem to mimic the signs rather than cause mental disturbance. A delusion that appears with LSD is recognized as a delusion by the subject and not accepted as reality as would be the case with a schizophrenic. Furthermore, the drugs bring forth differ-ing reactions—LSD elicits visual distor-tions rather than visual hallucinations, mescaline is more likely to stimulate audi-tory hallucinations, while adrenochrome distorts thoughts into delusions but rarely leads to hallucinations. Finally, the action of the psychotomimetic drugs is consid-erable—LSD increases acetylcholine, po-tentiates epinephrine, inhibits serotonin action, acts on the sympathetic and para-sympathetic nervous system, influences energy metabolism and EEG activity; and the effects of LSD are in turn distinctly modified by chloropromazine, a combina-tion of serotonin and acetylcholine, and the personality, predrug expectations, and even the immediate surroundings during the drug state. With such widespread effects, who can quickly pinpoint the locus of LSD effects?

The overall stage of accomplishment reached by researchers is less than astound-ing. When a complete survey of all per-tinent studies is undertaken, one is struck by the number of statements that reflect the highly tentative nature of the data and incomplete level of understanding. Phrases such as "this may mean . . . ," "perhaps the action is due to . . . ," "pro-vocative but yet inconclusive," "a confus-ing factor was . . . ," "on the other hand, others fail to confirm . . . ," abound in the literature. The toxic effects of taraxein, the Lafayette Clinic's factor, and serotonin have not been consistently duplicated. The reported presence of adrenochrome in the blood of schizophrenics and the early evidence for defect in glucose metabolism has not been replicated to any satisfactory degree. On top of it all, the much sought after serum factors have been found to be so unstable that they have been known to become impotent after a bouncing trip from laboratory to laboratory. One reviewer (Quastel, 1966) in fact expresses a sense of amazement that such sensitive substances could survive the jostling and bouncing which the human body undergoes in an ordinary day of activity. Another source of concern about the research claims by those knowledgeable but without so personal an investment is the issue of the elusive third factor, the extraneous uncontrolled variable. Diet differences have always been a problem, in fact, one well-equipped hospital was found with patients with major dietary deficiencies. Psychotic patients and severely disturbed neurotics are not likely to be concerned with food even if a well-balanced and attractive meal were offered them. It is no wonder that many reported differences between patients and nonpatients are ultimately explained by differences in food intake. It will be recalled that other secondary factors in the lives of patients have also been found to be the real explanations for seemingly significant results, for example, smoking habits, activity level, perhaps even the residual effects of therapeutic drugs.

It should be emphasized that gains have been made even though we are obviously far from an understanding of biochemistry and abnormal behavior. It is discouraging to be continuously faced with exciting results that stir the imagination only to be again disappointed by the lack of repetition of the finding by others, or the immense complications involved in data interpretation. Yet it is significant

that some serum factors have been identified by several groups of researchers working independently. Similarly, it is encouraging to note that the neurohormones do show a complex interrelationship with one another. In addition, these substances often have powerful effects on brain centers of emotion, such as the hypothalamus. Such recurring themes and overlapping effects as these, along with the remarkable structural similarities between neurohormones and psychotomimetics and tranquilizers seem to occur too frequently to be written off completely as coincidences, and misleading coincidences. It would not be surprising if the toxic-factor scientists were to ultimately discover that they were distilling out the same factor by different methods and with different tests. And it would be quite consistent with other information to find that mental illness in man is a function of a complex interaction involving many steps for, after all, the human has been found to be a complex creature. In fact, causation in psychopathology is nearly always multiple, and schizophrenia itself is not one entity but in all likelihood several. It seems inevitable that the mysteries of life and of abnormal life will continue to resist quick and simple answers and will await those solutions based on painstaking fundamental work carefully and systematically intertwined with advanced classification and research techniques and woven into a framework that accepts the dynamic and complex nature of man.

THE CONSTITUTIONAL HYPOTHESIS

An hypothesis that has intrigued man for a long time is the premise that physical and mental abnormality go hand in hand. A person's physical appearance is what strikes us upon first meetings; perhaps this is the history behind the hypothesis. It takes some perspicuity to learn about a person's inner motives and temperament,

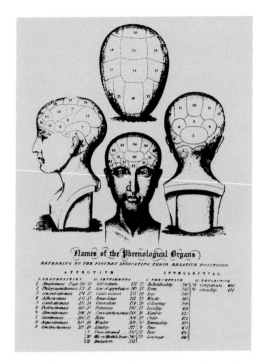

Phrenology was an early attempt to determine character from physical characteristics. Charts such as that illustrated above indicated to the phrenologist the traits associated with various areas on the skull. (G. Combe, *A System of Phrenology*, 1836, frontispiece)

but few can avoid the impressions and impact of another's physical presence. The assumed correlation between one's *physical* character and one's *mental* character is reflected in an old English adage: "Fat and merry, lean and sad." Literature, and especially Shakespeare, abounds in such derived associations, for example the famed quote: "Yon'd Cassius has a lean and hungry look. He thinks too much: such men are dangerous . . . would he be fatter!" (Julius Caesar, Act I, Scene ii). A varied form of this type of hypothesis was espoused by phrenologists such as Gall (1825) who pronounced that cranial configuration reflected character, and physiognomists like Lavater (1775) who were equally certain that facial features were diagnostic. Certainly, some interchange between mental and physical state occurs. This is clearly evidenced when we

notice the way in which a happy disposition seems to somehow be expressed in a buoyant walk while a depressive mood is easily detected through one's dragging gait. Famous experts of the art of mime (or pantomime) such as Marcelle Marceau can create vivid moods and convey complete plots by the use of bodily movements alone.

Investigations into the morphology of mankind has led to a variety of body classifications, some of which are summarized in Table 6-1. Kretschmer's work is of historical significance because of its effect in spurring studies in psychopathology and physique. He developed an elaborate inventory of physical traits and with camera, scale, and caliper proceeded to measure and record. From these records, he concluded that there are four general body types:

1. The aesthenic or leptosomatic type —noted for a deficiency in thickness in all body parts combined with average length. The aesthenic looks lean and narrowly built, seems taller than he is, has skin poor in blood system, delicately boned hands, lean arms, and a long, narrow chest.

2. The athletic type—noted for strong development of skeletal and muscular systems, wide shoulders, well-developed chest, and a tapered trunk.

3. The pyknic type—noted for pronounced body cavities, tendency toward fat distribution around the trunk, smooth and well-fitting skin of moderate thickness, broad hands and feet, and short extremities.

4. The dysplastic type—noted for pronounced deviations from the typical forms included in the other three body types.

As a psychiatrist, Kretschmer was concerned with the biological relationship between physique and psychoses with emphasis on the manic-depressive and schizophrenic illnesses. He examined 85 manic-depressive psychotics and 175 schizophrenics and discovered that:

> Manic-depressive patients tend to be pyknic in physique.
> Schizophrenics are diverse in body types but are mainly aesthenic.

More recently, a new approach to classification and measurements has been described by Sheldon (Sheldon, Stevens, and Tucker, 1940). Physiques are rated on three basic characteristics or somatotypes: endomorphy, mesomorphy, and ectomorphy (Fig. 6-9). The ratings are on a 7-point scale used to describe a person's position on each somatotype, for example, an extreme endomorph would show a rating of 7-1-1. Sheldon assumed that the somatotype was basically derived from the three primary germinal layers of the body, the endoderm believed to form the digestive layer, the mesoderm believed to be the component of the blood vessels, the bone, the muscles, and connective tissue, and the ectoderm believed to form the outer

layer of skin and the nervous tissue. The somatotypes are defined as follows:

1. The endomorph—shows predominance of soft roundness throughout various regions of the body, with digestive viscera being massive and tending to dominate the body.

2. The mesomorph—shows predominance of muscle, bone, and connective tissue, with erect bearing, the domination by bone and muscle, and thickness of the skin because of heavy underlying connective tissue.

3. The ectomorph—shows predominance of linearity and fragility, with the largest surface area, brain, and central nervous system in proportion to mass of all groups.

In addition to demonstrating the use of this measurement technique by classifying photographs of 4000 students, Sheldon also proposed that certain primary temperaments exist. These components of temperament were arrived at through factor analysis (a statistical method) and

TABLE 6-1. *Classifications of Body Types*

NATIONALITY OF SCHOOL	NAME OF MAIN INVESTIGATOR	NAME OF CONSTITUTIONAL TYPES			
		TYPE I	TYPE II	TYPE III	TYPE IV
Roman	Hippocrates Galen	apoplecticus sanguine	phthisicus melancholic	— phlegmatic	— choleric
French	Rostan	digestive	respiratory-cerebral	muscular	
Italian	De Giovanni Viola	megalosplanchnic brachymorphic	microsplanchnic dolichomorphic	normosplanchnic eumorphic	
German	Gall-Beneke Kretschmer Stockard	hyperplastic pyknic lateral	hypoplastic asthenic linear	athletic	dysplastic
Anglo-American	Rees-Eysenck Sheldon	eurymorphic endomorphic (viscerotonic)	leptomorphic ectomorphic (cerebrotonic)	mesomorphic mesomorphic (somatotonic)	dysplastic

SOURCE: Reprinted from *Heredity in health and mental disorder* by F. J. Kallman, M.D. By permission of W. W. Norton & Co., Inc. Copyright 1953 by W. W. Norton & Co., Inc.

sifting from over 650 trait names said to refer to types of temperament. From these analyses, Sheldon identified three clusters of traits that appeared to be primary:

1. Viscerotonia—the complex of temperament traits closely associated with dominance by the digestive viscera. The life of the viscerotonic is organized "primarily to serve the gut." The traits involved in this component are:

Love of physical comfort
Love of eating
Love of company
Desire for approval and affection
Indiscriminate amiability
Tolerance and easy-going nature
Complacence and smugness
Free outgoingness, extraversion
Need for others when troubled

2. Somatotonia—this complex is associated with dominance of the moving parts of the body such as the musculature. The somatotonic person lives for physical excitement and exertion. The traits involved in this component are:

Assertiveness and readiness to act
Love of adventure for its own sake
Love of domination and power
Recklessness, love of risk
Boldness, courage, confidence
Callousness, insensitivity
Lack of inner-directedness, extraversion
Need for action when troubled

3. Cerebrotonia—this complex is associated with a dominance of mental attentiveness, or cerebration although not

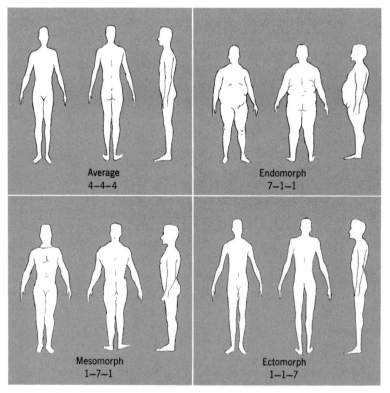

Figure 6-9. **Sketches of Sheldon's three body types and of an average combination of the three extremes.**

SOURCE: From *Abnormal psychology* by J. Strange. Copyright 1965, McGraw-Hill. Used with permission of McGraw-Hill Book Company.

necessarily intelligence. The traits in this component are:

Restraint, tenseness
Love of privacy
Apprehensiveness, attentiveness
Emotional control
Inner-oriented, introversion
Overly sensitive and responsive
Need of solitude when troubled

In relating physique to temperament, Sheldon reports highly significant associations between:

endomorphy and viscerotonia
mesomorphy and somatotonia
ectomorphy and cerebrotonia

Child (1950) followed up on these relationships by asking 414 students or former students of Yale University to describe themselves on traits drawn from Sheldon's definitions of the three temperaments. These subjects had previously been somatotyped by Sheldon himself. The major purpose of this approach was to eliminate the investigator bias possibly present when both the somatotyping and the temperament ratings are done by the same person. This flaw in design was particularly evident in Sheldon's work since he not only derived the theory but did all the ratings of physique and temperament. Child's results were supportive of Sheldon's original work. However, the correlations obtained were much lower (see Table 6-2).

The constitutional hypothesis has had its share of severe criticism as well as earnest support. Critics point out the cause-and-effect or chicken-and-egg issue: even if an association existed between adult physique and temperament, who is to know which caused what? Sheldon would hold that somatotype is a very direct determinant of temperament. Others would interpret the relationship as an indirect one—the chubby youngster learns to exhibit a good-natured tolerance because he can't fight and he can't run. Still others can as easily point out the possible involvement of cultural stereotypes—we *expect* the fat man to be jolly and our expectations may well shape this man's attitudes toward himself. Critics also emphasize that the temperament trait clusters include many items that are not truly independent in that they also include physical characteristics, for example, love of eating. The most telling criticism comes from studies which prove that body type is subject to change and therefore is not a stable characteristic. Lasker (1947) demonstrated that somatotype changes after partial starvation, and Newman (1952) found that simply growing older produces somatotypic change. On the other hand, sympathizers with the constitutional theory continue to use somatotyping in their search for correlates of personality. Extraversion seems to appear with high frequency in the endomorph-pyknic type, while introversion appears to characterize the ectomorph-aesthenic type (Burt, 1949; Rees, 1950). Glueck and

TABLE 6-2. *Degree of Association Between Physique and Temperament*

	ENDOMORPHY		MESOMORPHY		ECTOMORPHY	
Temperament Cluster	S[a]	C[b]	S	C	S	C
Viscerotonia	.70	.13	−.23	.13	−.40	−.15
Somatotonia	−.29	.03	.82	.38	−.53	−.37
Cerebrotonia	−.32	−.03	−.58	−.38	.83	.27

[a] S = Sheldon's study, N = 200.
[b] C = Child's study, N = 414.

Glueck (1962), in a classic extensive study of delinquents and nondelinquents, add supportive results showing:

endomorphs as more—
    submissive to authority
    dependent on others
mesomorphs as more—
    extroversive
    unconventional
    energetic
    likely to seek action when tense
ectomorphs as more—
    inclined to fantasy
    sensitive and acutely aware
    inhibitive of action

They also reported that delinquents were mainly mesomorphs. However, they also showed the complexity of the somato-type-personality relationship. Boys who are mesomorphs, who have a feeling of not being appreciated and who have a father who is himself a criminal are likely to become delinquent. But, regardless of physique, delinquency is also likely to occur as long as the latter two conditions are present. Another example of the complex interaction between physique, personality, and environment is seen in the data on unconventionality. This trait is more characteristics of ectomorphs; however, being reared in a noncohesive family has more of an influence on the development of unconventionality among endomorphs than ectomorphs. Supporters of body-typing have also continued to examine psychotic populations to determine the role of physique. Among the schizophrenics, a greater proportion of the aesthenic (ectomorph) build is found while manic-depressives seem to be more of the endomorphic (pyknic) build (see Table 6-3). In addition, Kallmann reports that a greater number of monozygotic twins who were obese were concordant for manic-depression; and where obesity occurred in twins who were discordant for manic-depression, it was in the psychotic twin.

Evaluation of the Constitutional Hypothesis

In an area as complex as the human mind, there can be no definitive study, only suggestive results. Some association between physique and personality appears to exist, but such is also the case between personality and many other variables. It may be possible to demonstrate a relation-

TABLE 6-3. *Somatotype and Psychoses*

PATIENT GROUP	SOMATOTYPE	RESEARCHER
Schizophrenics	Greater proportion of aesthenic	Betz (1942)
	Lower proportion of pyknic	
Schizophrenics	Leptosomate	Rees (1943)
Schizophrenics	Ectomorph	Bellak and Holt (1948)
Nonparanoid schizophrenics	Leptosomate	Moore and Hsu (1946)
Nonparanoid schizophrenics (from China and India)	Ectomorph	Morris (1951)
Paranoid schizophrenics	Mesomorph	Wittman, et al. (1948)
Paranoid schizophrenics	Mesomorph	Morris (1951)
Paranoid schizophrenics	Mesomorph	Kline and Tenney (1950)
Manic-depression	Eurymorph	Rees (1943)
Manic-depression	Endomorph	Wittman, et al. (1948)
Manic-depression	Mesomorph	Morris (1951)

ship between length of hair, clothing style, and personality, but such findings would be useless and meaningless in understanding the determinants of mental illness. A correlation between physique and personality or temperament appears to exist, although a smaller relationship than originally reported. Of greater significance is the incidence of certain body types in patients with varying psychoses, and in delinquents. The lean and frail tend to be nonparanoid schizophrenics, the athletic tend toward paranoid schizophrenia or delinquency, and the overweight tend toward manic-depression. Is it that the genetic fault that limits body development also generates schizophrenia? Or is it that the frail person meets up with so much failure because of his body limitations that he withdraws into the unreality of his own fantasy? Even incidence figures are only suggestive and not conclusive. It is only apparent that there are more manic-depressives who are endomorphic than there are manic-depressives who are mesomorphic; it is not that *all* manic-depressives are endomorphs. In fact, an association has also been found between manic-depression and mesomorphy, although to a lower degree than between manic-depression and endomorphy (Wittman, Sheldon and Katz, 1948). Similarly, ectomorphs are more *likely* to become delinquents than other boys of other body builds raised in the *same* environment since they are more prone to destructiveness in deleterious home atmospheres (Glueck and Glueck, 1962). And previous study has shown that eurymorphy (endomorphy) was a common body type in delinquents (Epps and Parnell, 1952). To be successful, and indeed to be useful, investigations of physique and personality must go beyond the earlier studies comparing traits to body build in adults. Longitudinal work is needed to at least partially deal with the issue of early identification and prediction. How early can a child be accurately somatotyped? Does early body classification enable prediction of later personality breakdown? Multivariable study is demanded—what is the nature of the interaction between learning experiences, sociocultural stereotyping, physique, and later personality? What different blending of factors leads one mesomorph to become delinquent, another to become manic-depressive, and another to become paranoid (all found to be correlates of mesomorphy)? The inverse relationship between ectomorphy and manic-depression, and endomorphy and schizophrenia raises another desirable line of pursuit. This is consistent with Kallmann's conclusion that the two psychoses are derived from different genetic origins; a close relative of a manic-depressive is likely to also become manic-depressive rather than schizophrenic and vice versa. To add to this, significant associations between various biochemical measures and somatotypes in schizophrenic patients have been reported (Kline, Wertheimer, Dyer, Schenker, Rubin, and Sniffen, 1953). All of which raises the possibility that body typology may be *symptomatic* of the existence of other factors involved in mental illness. Thus, physique itself has no direct or indirect significance in the development of mental abnormality. At best it might only serve as an additional aggravation. At worst, it might be no more than another sign that a genetic error is existent, or that a biochemical abnormality is present. One does not become mentally disturbed because of his body structure; rather, his body structure is another symptom of the effects of certain causative factors just as the mental symptoms are the effects of the same factors. In all likelihood, the role of somatotypology will prove to be relevant but minor. As a contributor to mental illness, it may be more akin to the "straw that breaks the camel's back" than it is a major determinant.

Glossary

Adrenal glands: Endocrine glands producing adrenaline and noradrenaline, and apparently involved in stress reactions.

Aesthenic body type: Also called leptosomatic. Physique characterized by thinness and delicate features.

Amygdala: A part of the brain whose destruction leads to elimination of rage reactions, even when the animal is mishandled.

Antimetabolite: Compounds that are structurally similar to essential metabolites, but which do not contribute to normal metabolism.

Athletic body type: Physique characterized by strongly developed musculature and skeletal system.

Auditory hallucination: A sensory experience involving hearing without any basis in reality.

Autistic feelings: Reactions influenced by internal needs and fantasies.

Autonomic nervous system: Part of the peripheral nervous system governing internal organs; involves the sympathetic nervous system and the parasympathetic nervous system.

Catatonic symptoms: Symptoms associated with a form of psychosis, including rigidity or heightened flexibility of muscles.

Central nervous system: Part of the nervous system involving the brain and the spinal cord.

Cerebral cortex: Layer covering the cerebral hemispheres and involved in motor control and certain higher mental activities.

Cerebral hemispheres: Also called the cerebrum. The two halves of the brain taken in totality.

Cerebrotonia: Temperament believed to be associated with the ectomorph body type.

Ceruloplasmin: A substance once believed to be the causative factor in psychosis.

Constitutional hypothesis: The view that personality and mental illness are directly associated with physique.

Cretinism: A form of mental retardation caused by malfunctioning of the thyroid glands.

Delusions of persecution: A false belief that one is being persecuted.

Depersonalization: A state of feeling that one's body is unreal.

Ectomorph body type: Sheldon's term for the linear, fragile body type.

Endocrine glands: Organs within the body that secrete chemical substances necessary for metabolic functioning.

Endomorph: Sheldon's term for the round, soft, viscerally-dominant body type.

Epilepsy: A disorder characterized by convulsions.

Epinephrine: Also called adrenalin. The secretions of the adrenal glands.

Essential metabolites: Compounds necessary for metabolic processes.

Forebrain: Also called the prosencephalon. The part of the brain that includes the cerebrum, the thalamus, and the hypothalamus.

Frontal lobe: One of the principal lobes of the brain involved in reasoning and memory.

Genotype: Genetically transmittable traits. May not be manifested outwardly in the person.

Gonads: Human sexual glands.

Hallucinogenic: Producing hallucinations.

Hebephrenic symptoms: Symptoms associated with a form of psychosis and involving silliness, grimacing, regressive behavior.

Hindbrain: Also called the rhombencephalon. The part of the brain that includes the cerebellum, the pons, and the medulla.

Homeostasis: A state of stability or equilibrium maintained by bodily functions.

Hypothalamus: A part of the brain apparently controlling rage or fear behavior.

Lysergic acid diethylamide: Also called LSD. A drug that produces a psychoticlike condition.

Mesomorph body type: Sheldon's term for muscular body type.

Midbrain: Also called the mesencephalon. The part of the brain that controls visual and auditory reflexes.

Neurohormone: Secretions affecting the nerves in the body and necessary for normal metabolic functioning.

Neuron: The single cell composing the structure of nervous tissue.

Norepinephrine: Also called noradrenaline. A secretion of the adrenal gland.

Nosebrain: Also called the rhinencephalon. The part of the brain that includes the septal area and the amygdala.

Occipital lobe: One of the principal lobes of the brain involved in vision.

Pancreas: An organ that contains tissue secreting insulin.

Parasympathetic nervous system: Part of the autonomic nervous system often working during related states, and in opposition to the sympathetic nervous system on organs and glands.

Parathyroid glands: Endocrine glands whose major function is the maintenance of calcium and phosphorous balance in the blood.

Parietal lobe: One of the principal lobes of the brain involved in bodily sensations and movement.

Peripheral nervous system: Part of the nervous system involving the autonomic nervous system and the somatic nervous system.

Phenotype: The actually observed or manifested trait regardless of genetic origin.

Phrenology: The attempt to identify personality traits through examination of the skull.

Physiognomy: The attempt to identify personality traits through the examination of facial features.

Pituitary gland: An endocrine gland controlling growth and the activty of other glands such as the thyroid, the adrenals, and the gonads.

Placebo effect: The improvement of a patient who believes he has received medicine when in fact he has been given a preparation containing no medicine.

Psilocybin: A drug producing psychoticlike effects.

Psychotomimetic: Capable of producing psychoticlike states.

Pyknic body type: Physique characterized by fat distribution, enlarged body cavity, stubby appearance.

Reflex arc: The simplest type of nervous system pathway involving a sensory neuron, a connecting neuron, and a motor neuron.

Septal area: A part of the brain believed associated with pleasurable and painful emotions.

Serotonin: A neurohormone hypothesized to be involved in psychosis.

Somatic nervous system: Part of the peripheral nervous system involving sensory and motor parts of the body.

Somatotonia: Temperament believed to be associated with the mesomorph body type.

Sympathetic nervous system: Part of the autonomic nervous system often working during emergency states and in opposition to the parasympathetic nervous system on organs and glands.

Taraxein: A substance believed to be involved in psychosis.

Temporal lobe: One of the principal lobes of the brain involved in hearing.

Thyroid glands: Endocrine glands influencing cell organization, metabolism, and the secretion of thyroxin.

Tranquilizers: Chemical substances used medically to bring about a calming state.

Viscerotonia: Temperament believed to be associated with the endomorph body type.

References

Abood, L., Gibbs, F., & Gibbs, E. Comparative study of blood ceruloplasmin in schizophrenia and other disorders. *A.M.A. Arch. neurol. Psychiat.,* 1957, **77**, 643.

Agnew, N., & Hoffer, A. Nicotinic acid modified lysergic acid diethylamide psychosis. *J. ment. Science,* 1955, **101**, 12.

Akerfeldt, S. Oxidation of N, N-dimethyl-p-phenylenediamine by serum from patients with mental disease. *Science,* 1951, **125**, 117.

Bartter, F. The parathyroid gland and its relationship to diseases of the nervous system. *Res. Pub. Assn. Res. Nerv. Ment. Dis.* 1953, **32**, 1.

Baruk, H., & Camus, L. Le principe toxique cataleptisant de la bile humaine; nouvelles études sur la catatonie biliaire expérimentale, *Presse méd.,* 1949, **57**, 1065.

Basowitz, H., Korchin, S., Olsen, D., Goldstein, M., & Gussoch, H. Anxiety and performance changes with minimal dose of epinephrine. *Arch. neurol. Psychiat.,* 1956, **76**, 98.

Beckett, P., Frohman, C., Gottlieb, J., Mowbry, J., & Wolf, R. Schizophrenic-like mechanisms in monkeys. *Amer. J. Psychiat.,* 1963, **119**, 835.

Bellak, L., & Holt, R. Somatotypes in relation to dementia praecox. *Amer. J. Psychiat.,* 1948, **104**, 713.

Berger, H. *Experimentelle Studien zur Pathogenese acuter Psychosen.* Berlin: Klin. Wschr. No. 30, 1903.

Bergen, J., Pennell, R., Saravis, C., Freeman, H., & Hoagland, H. Human plasma protein factors possibly related to schizophrenia. In M. Rinkel, (Ed.), *Biological treatment of mental illness.* New York: L. C. Page, 1966.

Berkeley, A. Level of aspiration in relation to adrenal cortical activity and concept of stress. *J. comp. physiol. Psychol.,* 1952, **45**, 443.

Betz, B. Somatology of the schizophrenic patient. *Hum. Biol.,* 1942, **14**, 192.

Brady, J., & Nauta, W. Subcortical mechanisms in emotional behavior: affective changes following septal forebrain lesions in the albino rat. *J. comp. physiol. Psychol.,* 1953, **46**, 339.

Burt, C. Subdivided factors. *Brit. J. Psychol.* (Stat. Sect.), 1949, **2**, 41.

Cannon, W., & Britton, S. Studies on the conditions of activity in endocrine glands. *Amer. J. Physiol.,* 1925, **72**, 283.

Child, I. The relation of somatotype to self-ratings on Sheldon's temperament traits. *J. Person.,* 1950, **18**, 440.

Cook, E., & Wherry, R. Urinary 17-kestosteroid output of naval submarine enlisted candidates during two stressful situations. *Hum. Biol.,* 1950, **22**, 104.

Dale, H. Beginnings and prospects of neurohumoral transmission. *Pharmacol. Rev.,* 1954, **6**, 7.

De Jong, H. Presence in urine of substance which may produce catatonic symptoms. *Psychiat. en neurol. bl.,* 1934, **38**, 914.

Denko, H., & Kaelbling, R. The psychiatric aspects of hypoparathyroidism. *Acta Psychiat. Scand.,* 1962, **38**, Suppl. 164, 1.

Dingemanse, E., & Freud, J. Identification of catatonine. *J. Acta Brevia Neerland. Physiol. Pharmacol Microbiol.,* 1933, **3**, 49.

Eiduson, S., Geller, E., Yuwiler, A., & Eiduson, B. *Biochemistry and behavior.* New Jersey: Van Nostrand, 1964.

Epps, P., & Parnell, R. Physique and temperament of women delinquents compared with women undergraduates. *Brit. J. med. Psychol.,* 1952, **25**, 249.

Fedoroff, S., & Hoffer, A. Toxicity of blood serum from schizophrenic and non-schizophrenic subjects. *J. nerv. ment. Dis.,* 1956, **124**, 396.

Freeman, H., & Zabarenko, R. Relation of changes in carbohydrate metabolism to psychotic states. *Arch. neurol. Psychiat.,* 1949, **19**, 569.

Freeman, W., & Looney, J. Phytotoxic index; results of studies with 68 male schizophrenic patients. *Arch. neurol. Psychiat.,* 1934, **32**, 554.

Freud, J., and Dingemanse, E. Über Katatonin, einen giftigen Stoff im Lipoid extrakt von Harm, Gewebsflussigkeiten und Organen. *Biochem. Zeitschr.,* 1932, **255**, 464.

Frohman, C., Goodman, M., Beckett, P., Latham, L., Senf, R., & Gottlieb, J. The isolation of an active factor from serum of schizophrenic patients. *Ann. N.Y. Acad. Sci.,* 1962, **96**, 438.

Frohman, C., Latham, L., Beckett, P., & Gottlieb, J. Evidence of a plasma factor in schizophrenia. *A.M.A. Arch. gen. Psychiat.,* 1960, **2**, 255.

Frohman, C., Tourney, G., Beckett, P., Rees, H., Latham, L., & Gottlieb, J. Biochemical identification of schizophrenia. *A.M.A. Arch. gen. Psychiat.,* 1961, 4, 404.

Gall, F. *Sur les fonctions du cerveau.* Paris: Bailliere, 1825.

Gamper, E., & Kral, A. Weitere experimentellbiologische, Untersuchungen zum Schizophrenieproblem. *Zeitschr. f.d. ges. Neurol. u. Psychiat.,* 1934, **150**, 252.

Ghent, L., & Freedman, A. Comparison of effects of normal and schizophrenic serum on motor performance in rats. *Amer. J. Psychiat.,* 1958, **115**, 465.

Gibbs, F., & Mattby, G. Effect on electrical activity of cortex of certain depressant and stimulant drugs—barbiturates, morphine, caffeine, benzedrine and adrenaline. *J. Pharmacol.,* 1943, **78**, 1.

Glueck, S., & Glueck, E. *Family environment and delinquency.* Great Britain: Houghton Mifflin, 1962.

Goldner, M., & Ricketts, H. Significance of insulin inhibition by blood of schizophrenic patients. *Arch. neurol. Psychiat.,* 1942, **48**, 552.

Goltz, F. Der Hund ohne Grosshirn. *Arch. ges Physiol.,* 1892, **15**, 570.

Gottlieb, J., Frohman, C., & Beckett, P. The characteristics of a serum factor in schizophrenia. In M. Rinkel (Ed.), *Biological treatment of mental illness.* New York: L. C. Page, 1966.

Guilmot, P. Contribution expérimentale préliminaire à l'étude pathogenique de la catatonie humaine. *Acta neurol. Psychiat. Belg.,* 1952, **52**, 81.

Halstead, W. *Brain and intelligence: a qualitative study of the frontal lobes.* Chicago: University of Chicago Press, 1947.

Harris, M. Insulin sensitivity of patients with mental disease; factors in their serum affecting action of insulin. *Arch. neurol. Psychiat.,* 1942, **48**, 761.

Heath, R. (Ed.), *Studies in schizophrenia.* Cambridge: Harvard University Press, 1954.

Heath, R. Correlations between levels of psychological awareness and physiological activity in the central nervous system. *Psychosom. Med.,* 1955, **17**, 383.

Heath, R., Cohen, S., Silva, F., Leach, B., & Cohen, M. Administration of taraxein in humans. *Dis. nerv. Syst.,* 1959, **20**, 206.

Heath, R., Leach, B., Byers, L., Martens, S., & Leiley, C. Pharmacological and biological psychopathology. *Amer. J. Psychiat.*, 1958, 114, 683.

Heath, R., Leach, B., Oerster, F., & Bayers, C. Serum fractions in schizophrenia. In M. Rinkel (Ed.), *Biological treatment of mental illness.* New York: L. C. Page, 1966.

Heath, R., Martens, S., Leach, B., Cohen, M., & Angel, C. Effect on behavior in humans with the administration of taraxein. *Amer. J. Psychiat.*, 1957, 114, 14.

Heath, R., & Mickle, W. Evaluation of seven years' experience with depth electrode studies in human patients. In E. Ramey, and D. O'Doherty (Eds.), *Electrical studies on the unanesthetized brain,* New York: Paul Hoeber, 1960.

Herz, E. & Weichbrodt, R. Toxicity of serum. *Deutsche Med. Wochenschr.* 1924, 50, 1210.

Himwich, H. The new psychiatric drugs. *Scient. Amer.*, 1955, 193, 80.

Hoffer, A. Effect of niacin and nicotinamide on leukocytes and some urinary constituents. *Canad. med. ass. J.*, 1956, 74, 448.

Hoffer, A. Adrenochrome in blood plasma. *Amer. J. Psychiat.*, 1958, 114, 752.

Hoffer, A., & Osmond, H. Schizophrenia; an autonomic disease. *J. nerv. ment. Dis.*, 1955, 122, 448.

Hoffer, A., & Osmond, H. The adrenochrome model and schizophrenia. *J. nerv. ment. Dis.*, 1959, 128, 18.

Hoffer, A., & Osmond, H. *The chemical basis of clinical psychology.* Springfield, Ill.: C. C. Thomas, 1960.

Hoffer, A., Osmond, H., & Smythies, J. Schizophrenia: a new approach. II. Results of a year's research. *J. ment. Sci.*, 1954, 100, 29.

Hoffer, A., Osmond, H., Callbeck, M., & Kahan, I. Treatment of schizophrenia: with nicotinic acid and nicotinamine. *J. clin. exptl. Psychopath. and Quart. rev. psychiat. Neurol.*, 1957, 18, 131.

Hoffer, A., Payza, A., Szara, S., & Axelrod, J. The presence of adrenochrome in blood. *Amer. J. Psychiat.*, 1960, 116, 664.

Hoskins, R. Hormone therapy, *J. clin. exptl. Psychopath.*, 1954, 15, 363.

Jersild, A. & Thomas, W. Influence of adrenal extract on behavior and mental efficiency. *Amer. J. Psychol.*, 1931, 43, 447.

Kallmann, F. *Heredity in health and mental disorder.* New York: Norton, 1953.

Kastan, M. Die Toxizität des Serums der Geisteskranken. *Arch. f. Psychiat.*, 1926, 78, 637.

Kline, N., & Tenney, A. Constitutional factors in the prognosis of schizophrenia. *Amer. J. Psychiat.*, 1950, 107, 434.

Kline, N., Wertheimer, N., Dyer, C., Schencker, A., Rubin, B., & Sniffen, R. Patterns of biochemical organization related to morphology, *Amer. J. Psychiat.*, 1953, 109, 603.

Kooy, F. Hyperglycemia in mental disorders. *Brain,* 1919, 42, 214.

Kretschmer, E. *Physique and character.* New York: Harcourt Brace, 1925.

Lasker, G. The effects of partial starvation on somatotype. *Amer. J. phys. Anthrop.*, 1947, 5, 323.

Latham, L., Warner, K., Frohman, C., & Gottlieb, J. The effect of exercise on the serum factor in schizophrenic subjects. *J. S. Fed. Proceedings,* 1962, 21, 415.

Lavater, J. Physiognomische Fragmente zur Beförderung der Menschkenntniss und Menschenliebe von Johann Caspar Lavater, Leipzig: 1775.

Leach, B., Cohen, M., Heath, R., & Martens, S. Studies of the role of the ceruloplasmin and albumin in adrenaline metabolism. *A.M.A. Arch. neurol. Psychiat.*, 1956, 76, 635.

Leach, B., & Heath, R. The vetro-oxidation of epinephrine in plasma. *A.M.A. Arch. neur. Psychiat.*, 1956, **76**, 444.

Looney, J., Freeman, W., & Small, R. Studies in phytotoxic index; evaluation of method with reference to depressed psychotic patients. *Amer. J. med. Sci.*, 1939, **198**, 528.

Maas, J., Gleser, G., & Gottschalk, L. Schizophrenia, anxiety, and biochemical factors. The rate of oxidation of N, N-dimethyl-p-phenylenediamine by plasma and levels of serum copper and plasma ascorbic acid. *A.M.A. Arch. gen. Psychiat.*, 1961, 4, 109.

Mann, S. Blood-sugar studies in mental disorders. *J. ment. Sci.*, 1925, **71**, 443.

Moore, T., & Hsu, E. Factorial analysis of anthropological measurements in psychotic patients. *Hum. Biol.*, 1946, **18**, 133.

Morris, C. Similarity of constitutional factors in psychotic behavior in India, China, and the United States. *Amer. J. Psychiat.*, 1951, **108**, 143.

Moya, F., Dewar, J., MacIntosh, M., Hirsch, S., & Townsend, R. Hyperglycemic action and toxicity of the urine of schizophrenic patients. *Canad. J. biochem. Physiol.*, 1958, **36**, 505.

Newman, R. Age changes in body build, *Amer. J. phys. Anthrop.*, 1952, **10**, 75.

Olds, J. A preliminary mapping of electrical reinforcing effects in the rat brain. *J. comp. physiol. Psychol.*, 1956, **49**, 281.

Pincus, G., & Hoaglund, H. Adrenal cortical responses to stress in normal men and in those with personality disorders. I. Some stress responses in normal and psychotic subjects. *Amer. J. Psychiat.*, 1950, **106**, 641.

Porter, R. Abberations in electrical activity of hypothalamus induced by stress stimuli. *Amer. J. Physiol.*, 1952, **169**, 629.

Quastel, S. Formal discussion. In M. Rinkel (Ed.), *Biological treatment of mental illness.* New York: L. C. Page, 1966.

Rees, L. Physical constitution in relation to effort syndrome, neurotic and psychotic types. M.D. thesis, University of Wales, 1943.

Rees, L. Body build, personality and neurosis in women. *J. ment. Sci.*, 1950, **96**, 426.

Reiss, M. Investigations of hormone equilibria during depression. In P. Hoch, & J. Zubin (Eds.), *Depression.* New York: Grune & Stratton, 1954.

Reiter, P. Untersuchungen zur Beleachtung der Intoxikations—theorie bei der Dementia praecox mit besonderer Berucksichtigung der Versuche mit totaltransfusionen. *Zeitschr. f.d. ges. Neurol. u. Psychiat.*, 1938, **160**, 598.

Rieder, H. Biological determinations of toxicity of pathologic body fluids. III. Examination of urinary extracts of mental patients with the help of the spider web test. *Psychiat. et Neurol.* (Basel), 1957, **134**, 387.

Rinkel, M. *Biological treatment of mental illness.* New York: L. C. Page, 1966.

Robins, E., Smith, K., & Lowe, I. Neuropharmacology, in *Transactions of the Josiah Macy, Jr. Foundation,* 4th Conference, 1957.

Sanders, B., Flataker, L., Boger, W., Smith, E., & Winter, C. Effect of protein fractions of normal and schizophrenic serum on rat performance. *Vox Sanguinis*, 1959, 4, 68.

Sanders, B., Smith, E., Flataker, L., & Winter, C. Fractionation studies of human serum factors affecting motor activity in trained rats. *N.Y. Acad. Sci.*, 1962, **96**, 448.

Schreiner, L., & Kling, A. Behavioral changes following rhinencephalic injury in cats. *J. Neurophysiol.*, 1953, **16**, 643.

Schwartz, T., & Shields, D. Urinary excretion of formaldehyogenic steroids and creatinine; a reflection of emotional tension. *Psychosom. Med.*, 1956, **18**, 159.

Shapiro, A. Attempt to demonstrate catatonigenic agent in cerebrospinal fluid to catatonic schizophrenic patients. *J. nerv. ment. Dis.*, 1956, **123**, 65.

Sheldon, W., Stevens, S., & Tucker, W. *The varieties of human physique.* New York: Harper, 1940.

Sogliani, G. Ricerca di proprietà catatonigene nel siero di sanque e nel liquor cefalo-rachidiano umano. *Il Cervello,* 1938, **17,** 253.

Szara, S., Axelrod, J., & Perlin, S. Is adrenochrome present in the blood? *Amer. J. Psychiat.,* 1958, **115,** 162.

Tinel, J., Eck, M., & Eck, M. Toxines urinaires et catatonine de De Jong. Pouvoir neutralisant du serum humain. Dissociation "in vivo" par le choc de la combinaison toxine-antitoxine. *Ann. Med.-Psychol.,* Ser. 14, 1933, **91,** 710.

Tomescu, P., Badenski, G., & Cosmulesco, I. Considérations à propos de l'action catatonisante passagère de l'urine d'une schizophrénique catatonique et colibacillurgique. *Bull. Soc. de Feat. de Burcarest,* 1937, **2,** 175.

Wada, J., & Gibson, W. Behavioral and EEG changes induced by injection of schizophrenic urine extract. *A.M.A. Arch. neurol. Psychiat.,* 1959, **81,** 747.

Witt, P. *Die Wirkung von Substanzen auf den Netzbau von Spinne als biologischer Test.* Berlin: Springer, 1956.

Wittman, P., Sheldon, W., & Katz, C. A study of the relationship between constitutional variations and fundamental psychotic behavior reactions. *J. nerv. ment. Dis.,* 1948, **108,** 470.

Woolley, D. Participation of serotonin in mental processes. In M. Rinkel, & H. Denber (Eds.), *Chemical concepts of psychoses.* New York: McDowell, Obolensky, 1958.

Woolley, D. *The biochemical bases of psychoses.* New York: John Wiley, 1962.

Woolley, D., & Shaw, E. A biochemical and pharmacological suggestion about certain mental disorders. *Science,* 1954, **119,** 587.

Yuwiler, A., Jenkins, I., & Dukay, A. Serum oxidase tests and schizophrenia. *A.M.A. Arch. neurol. Psychiat.,* 1961, **4,** 395.

7 *Contributors to Personality: The Psychological Factors*

THE FREUDIAN VIEW

Sigmund Freud broke with the tradition of medicine by offering an outlook based on psychological rather than physical factors. Though a combination of keen observation and personal insight, he developed a description of the human psyche or mind, its normal development, and malfunctioning. Freud (1953) established many principles regarding personality development which he deemed universal. Although Freudian theory is considered controversial in many respects, it has been and still remains among the leading forces directed toward identifying the psychological factors connected with human personality.

Human Motivation

Psychological motives, termed instincts, are driving forces directing man's efforts. These instincts have several important characteristics:

Instincts are believed to be quantities of *energy*.

As energy, instincts exert pressure for release as they increase in intensity.

The *source* of such energy is traceable to bodily states.

Such psychic energy is goal-oriented

—the ultimate *aim* is to produce effects that reduce the intensity or quantity of accumulated energy.

The activities that lead to acquiring the goal, and the goal itself are known as the *object* of the instinct. Therefore instincts serve to guide behavior, impel behavior, and may do so by affecting the senses through heightening their sensitivity to certain environmental cues. A hungry person is aroused to activity that is oriented toward obtaining food. In addition, he is more sensitive to signs connected with food. Basically, it can be said that the Freudian theory of instincts is a tension-reduction one in that the tendency to return to an earlier state of equilibrium is stressed. New instincts may appear as new bodily needs develop; however, the overall goal is still to keep the intensity of these instincts reduced. To accomplish this, it is sometimes necessary to release the energy by investment in a substitute object. That is, psychic energy is displaceable. For example, a child may displace his love away from his mother and toward a teacher. It is entirely possible that displacement is absent or prevented because release of an instinct in any form is too threatening to the individual. Such a person may then be faced with a neurotic conflict—a battle between the instinct that continually presses for expression and release, and the efforts of the person to deny and prevent this from happening. Such efforts are extremely wearing and fatigue-producing. Displacement can, of course, lead to neurosis. In sexual perversions, the element of displacement toward less threatening substitute objects is a primary factor.

Freud grouped the human instincts into two large categories: the *life instincts* (Eros) and the *death instincts* (Thanatos). The life instincts are those directed toward the protection and preservation of the individual and the race. Such preservative instincts include thirst, hunger, and other physiological urges which lead to behaviors that maintain life. The sexual instincts also belong in this group. These sexual instincts are not simply erotic-genital in nature, but are more broadly defined as involving pleasurable sensations arising from the reduction of tensions particularly around the erogenous zones. During the first year of life, the sensitive erogenous zone centers around the mouth. Toward the end of the first year, the anus and anal activities are the center of satisfactions. The genitals become a source for pleasurable sensation later, at age three.

In opposition to the life instincts are the death instincts. The death instinct is but a reflection of a universal principle of life—that all organic processes will return ultimately to an inorganic state. Anabolism (life-building, constructive processes) exists side by side with catabolism (destructive processes). **Of significance is the Freudian belief that aggressivity is derived from the death instinct and is therefore a natural and powerful urge.** In essence, aggression toward others is the displacement of the self-destructive instinct toward an external object. Where this is not permitted, and where the life instincts are too weak to counterbalance

the death instinct, self-destructiveness takes hold either in the insidious form of masochism, or the suppressive form of depression.

The Structure of the Psyche

Freud conceptualized the human personality as divided into three systems: the *id,* the *ego,* and the *superego.* The id is everything that exists of personality at birth. It includes all psychological processes, including the instincts, in their most primitive and early form. If one visualizes a hungry newborn infant, all the properties of the id can be imagined:

> Demands for immediate gratification —the id is characterized by attempts to seek *immediate* discharge of tension through whatever means available (the *pleasure principle*).
>
> Ineffective acceptance of unreal substitutes—the id may momentarily reduce its efforts through forming a mental image of a tension-reducing object such as food.
>
> Irrational, or nonrational thinking pervades—thought patterns are alogical with contradictory needs and demands existing side by side, susceptible to magical beliefs, more replete with unordered image-events than sequentially ordered verbal thoughts.

As the human organism matures, other psychological processes become differentiated such as the ability to distinguish between the real and the imagined, the capacity to think in verbal terms and to call forth memory residues to determine courses of action. The ego is now said to exist. It is characterized by:

> The capacity to delay immediate gratification, or to elect avenues for instinctual satisfaction along socially acceptable lines (the *reality principle*).

The ability to differentiate between mental images of desired objects and the real presence of such objects.

The competency to take into account and cope with the realities of the environment at hand instead of being dominated by instinctual demands.

The differentiation of self-identity as contrasted with the identity of the other. The person is aware that others exist, that the universe goes beyond himself, that crucial events take place outside of his own unique subjective experiences.

As the ego enables the person to become aware of and appraise the presence of others, a third system is stimulated into development. The superego is the internal representation of the moral values, code of ethics, rules for living established by parents and other significant figures. If the ego is concerned with the terms of reality, the superego is more concerned with the attainment of the ideal. If the id is continuously striving after pleasure, the superego is continuously pressing for perfection. If the ego evaluates the *environmental situation* in order to determine the least dangerous course of action, the superego evaluates the *course of action* itself to determine its acceptability according to moral standards. The superego is characterized by:

An ever-watchful concern for the "rightness" or "wrongness" of activities.

Demands to live up to the high standards without regard for the reasonableness of such expectations.

Efforts to control instinctual gratification through the powerful tool of guilt.

A continuous upholding of ideals as guiding forces in replacement of instinctual aims.

Circumstances that weaken the development or functioning of any of these psychological processes are responsible for neurotic conditions. In addition, any misbalance of strength among the id, ego, and superego will mean that the personality is dominated by whichever is the strongest. A neurotic condition again develops. Overly powerful id impulses may force primitive, impulsive, thoughtless, unplanned acts unless checked by an effective ego. Yet, an overly rigorous ego control may so override the id forces as to remove all traces of human spontaneity, resulting in a mannequinlike person of carefully prescribed moves and countermoves. If the superego is overly developed, it becomes a harsh, perfectionistic taskmaster plaguing the person with guilt, inhibitions, fear of punishment, and rigidity.

The warning signals of anxiety are intimately connected to the id, ego, and superego. Anxiety is a condition of tension and as such it motivates the person to behaviors that reduce the tension, for example, the defense mechanisms (see Chapter 8). *Neurotic* or *id anxiety* stems from a concern that the instincts will become so powerful as to overwhelm the person, forcing actions geared to impulsive gratification. *Reality* or *ego anxiety* derives from the dangers that ensue from the world, such as punishment by parents. *Moral* or *superego anxiety* is less concerned with externally based punishment and more oriented toward the threat of internal punishment, guilt feelings.

The Developmental Stages

Freud observed certain stages or phases of psychological growth:

The Oral Phase. In infancy, the primary source of instinctual gratification and pleasure is obtained on an oral level

(Top) An integrated personality system is a requisite for mental health. Expressive works, such as the clay sculpture above, often mirror the condition of the *personality structure*. This sculpture reflects the lack of integration and poor ego control of the client.

(Bottom) Powerful *instinctual impulses* of a destructive nature are emphasized in this sketch by the same client who created the clay sculpture above. Art work in therapy often permits an insight into unconscious factors. This sketch symbolizes the weakened ego defense which often fails to control the aggressive outbursts of the client's id. (Courtesy of J. Denny & A. Fagen, University of Hawaii)

through sucking, swallowing, and later, through chewing and biting. The latter is known as the oral-aggressive stage. Prolongation into adulthood of the traits of this phase is possible and may influence habits, character structure, and needs; thumbsucking and other oral acts may carry over into adult life as excessive drinking, eating, smoking. Oral-aggressiveness may be exhibited as a trait of sarcasm, "biting" criticism, verbal (oral) argumentativeness. The nurturant life of this period where one is cared for may increase the need for dependency and a desire to be again nurtured by others.

The Anal Phase. As the erogenous zones shift, the satisfactions of anal stimulation dominate. Both retention of waste-products and the expulsion of such become associated with pleasant feelings. Parental concerns over cleanliness and bowel control interact with instinctual pleasure-seeking with the resolution leaving a mark on the adult personality.

Anal retention leads to psychological retention expressed in obstinacy, stinginess.

Anal expulsion turns to explosive fury, disorderliness, wasteful destructiveness, cruelty.

Anal excretion under conditions of praise can encourage generalized productivity and creativity.

The Phallic Phase. For the first time, the child directs his emotional drives toward others in his environment with the first glimmerings of affection-seeking and vague genital sexuality. The three- to five-year old desires to possess the total love of his opposite sex parent and is envious and hostile toward his competitor, the other parent. This is called the *Oedipus complex* after the mythical Greek hero Oedipus who killed his father and married his mother. The guilt that accompanies these incestuous and hostile feelings

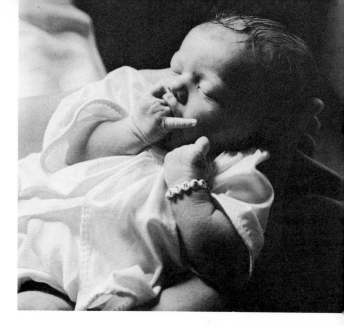

According to Freudian theory, instinctual gratification and pleasure are achieved through *oral stimulation*. This may be the explanation for the orally centered behaviors observed in infants and young children, such as the one above. (Fritz Henle/Photo Researchers)

becomes associated with a fear of retaliation. The child's fantasies envision such counteraggression in the form of castration, thereby producing *castration anxiety*. Boys deal with the conflict by repressing (denying to consciousness) their sexual feelings, and by identifying with their fathers. This emulation of the father figure is the method whereby masculine sexual traits are acquired. Failure to identify, the lack of a satisfactory male model, or the failure to resolve the sexual conflict are all causes of future psychopathology.

The girl also develops erotic feelings toward her opposite sex parent, mainly through recognizing the father's possession of an object she lacks, a penis. This *penis envy* is the female corollary of castration anxiety. Ultimately, she seeks vicarious satisfaction for her desire to possess the father and identifies with her mother. Failures in conflict resolution may show up as masculine protest, whereby the woman continues to envy the role of the male and begins to actively compete with them in business ventures, politics, etc. Feelings of inadequacy, sexual confusion, and sexual promiscuity may all be consequences of Oedipal problems.

The Latency Phase. Prior to puberty, a period of quiescence appears whereby instinctual strivings and sexual concerns decline in importance. Interpersonal activity is confined to members of the same sex, often with feelings of aversion toward those of the opposite sex. It is as if a phase of consolidation and taking stock occurs. The practice of sex-role behaviors is strengthened with boys engaging in masculine interests and endeavors, and girls playing house, grooming dolls, and participating in other feminine role patterns.

The Genital Phase. The adolescent re-experiences the stirrings of sexuality, but proceeds to handle them adaptively if the Oedipal conflict has been properly resolved. True feelings of concern for others, altruism, and the development of mature genital love appear. The peak of psychological development has occurred with each of the earlier steps contributing its share to this ultimate end phase. Failures to develop through and beyond any early phase (*fixations*) can block the achievement of this genital phase. In addition, if the genital phase has been just barely achieved through a series of borderline adjustments and completions of earlier phases, a return to an earlier stage (*regression*) under conditions of stress is more likely to occur. Similarly, too extravagant gratification during earlier phases increases the person's susceptibility to withdrawing to this less mature state.

THE LEARNING VIEW OF DOLLARD AND MILLER

Although there are many approaches to psychopathology based on learning (Mowrer, 1950; Wolpe, 1958; Eysenck, 1959; Rotter, 1954), one of the earliest efforts to bridge the gap between Freudian psychiatric thought and psychological learning theory was spearheaded by Dollard and Miller (1950). John Dollard, a cultural anthropologist, and Neal E. Miller, an experimental psychologist, essentially translated Freud's theory into terms that made it possible to draw upon the enormous fund of knowledge from the experimental psychological laboratory. More specifically, they emphasized the psychological data on human learning and learning theory. Learning theory is basically the study of the circumstances under which habits are formed or eliminated.

The Basic Elements of Learning

Four elements are conceptualized as important in human learning: the *cue,* the *response,* the *drive,* and *reinforcement* (reward).

A cue is an event that directs the response of the person. Such cues or stimuli may be external to the individual (e.g., the sight of food), or internal (e.g., the anticipation of food). Cues of different intensity may trigger off different responses. Thus, the mild call of a child by his parent may lead to no response in the busy youngster, while the loud, imperative, I-mean-business shout will lead to an immediate reaction. Naturally, differences in type of stimulus events may also be responded to differentially—the sound of music versus the sight of a marching band. Stimuli may involve single discrete events such as a gunshot, as well as more complex patterns of stimuli such as the configuration of sight (cloud formations), feeling (temperature change), and sound (of winds) which signify a storm. Responses themselves can also serve as cues and are best seen in the learning of complex sequences such as the memorizing of a musical score, or in performances involving many decisions such as negotiating a highway trip with many turns. Of great significance for psychopathology is the evidence that emotions and drives (motives) serve as distinctive cues for specific responses. Anxiety and fear can serve to cue off avoidance and withdrawal response.

A response is an activity that occurs and is attached to a cue. For any one stimulus situation, there are actually a number of responses that may be potentially released. These have different likelihoods of actually being called forth, and hence can be arranged in a *hierarchy of responses,* with the most dominant response being at the top of the hierarchy. If the circumstances are such that the dominant response is prevented from occurring, then the next response in line may be substituted. In pathological states, such severe emotional blocking may occur that a response very low in the hierarchy may be forced to appear. On the other hand, in normal problem solving, or "brain-storming" individuals attempt to encourage alternative responses to appear in the search for newer solutions. In this latter sense, thoughts and ideas are themselves treated as responses. Emotions can also be conceptualized as responses. A phobia, for example, involves the appearance of a fear response when certain environmental cues are presented.

Drives involve motivation and are actually strong stimuli that impel action. *Primary drives* are those such as hunger, thirst, pain. *Secondary drives* are acquired through being associated with primary

Remarkable new behaviors can be acquired through the use of *reinforcement*. Tuffy, the porpoise, is shown receiving his reward as he learns to carry messages in the Navy's Sealab II project. Divers living for 30 days underwater use Tuffy as their link with the surface. (DPI)

drive situations. *Secondary drives* differ from primary drives in that:

> Their strength is independent of the physiological state of the person.
>
> Their strength will dissipate unless there is periodic reassociation with the appropriate primary drive.
>
> They do not appear in periodic cycles as do the primary drives.

For most modern men who have their basic or primary drives essentially cared for, the secondary drives are of greater concern. The desire to be recognized, the need to achieve a position of status, the search for wealth or power, are more salient driving forces. Most socially oriented motives are acquired—the need for independence or nurturance, the simple wish to be with others (gregariousness), the desire for approval, the pursuit for nonconformity.

A reinforcement is an event that comes after the occurrence of a response, reducing the drive, and thereby increasing the strength of the cue-response connection. The work of Dollard and Miller indicates that simple repetition of responses does not serve to strengthen them. The more intense the drive that is reduced, and the more frequently drives are reduced by the response, the greater will be the strength of that response. The reinforcing event may have the innate capacity to reduce the drive, for example, food possesses the properties for directly reducing hunger. Other objects or events

167

can also acquire such drive-reducing properties if they are associated with primary reinforcers. Most common among the learned reinforcers are the various forms of money. In America, coins are accepted in exchange for food which reduces one's hunger. Such coins thereby acquire reinforcing value and can be given to a person as a means of rewarding him for showing desired responses. On the other hand, American coins may have no reinforcing value in primitive native cultures where other objects are used in bartering for food. In psychopathology, bizarre items may have reinforcing value because they serve to reduce the anxieties or fears of the person. In addition, maladaptive responses may be learned and may persist because they have been associated with drive reduction. Repression is an act of not-thinking or not-labeling. It is reinforced because it prevents an unpleasant impulse or thought from appearing and enables the person to reduce his tensions, anxieties, or guilt feelings. As long as this response is reinforced it will persist. In fact, no new behavior occurs unless a *learning dilemma* develops. A learning dilemma is a circumstance in which the usual responses do *not* lead to drive reduction. Under such a condition, the person is forced toward other behaviors. Lacking such a condition, the old behavior will be relied upon even though it is not the most effective or efficient mode of activity.

Basic Principles of Learning

The principles of learning are those basic rules that have been formulated through careful scientific experimentation. Systematic observations under controlled conditions of how behavior is acquired or eliminated form the basis for these principles. Although most of their observations were based on animal work, or on motor responses in humans, the learning theorists feel that the principles have clear application to all aspects of human development and performance. Some basic principles are given below.

1. The association between a cue and a response is strengthened each time the response is followed by reinforcement (this has been stated previously). This is acquisition.

2. The association is weakened each time the response occurs and is *not* followed by reinforcement. This is extinction. Thus, disuse alone does not lead to extinction.

3. A response to a given cue may be seen to recur after complete extinction when the stimulus is re-presented. This phenomenon is known as spontaneous recovery.

4. Once a specific cue-response habit has been acquired, another cue which is similar in some way to the original cue can also elicit the learned response. This is stimulus generalization.

5. Responses that occurred just prior to the reinforced (learned) response will also be strengthened, those nearest in time being strengthened more than those further away. This is the gradient of reinforcement.

6. Responses nearer to the point of occurrence of reinforcement tend to occur before their original time in the response sequence and crowd out earlier (useless) behaviors. This is the development of anticipatory responses.

7. Drives can act as cues (and elicit specific learned responses) or as responses (and become elicited by certain cues, and strengthened by reinforcement).

The Learning of Disorder

A neurosis develops through learning that is faulty and maladaptive. Conflicts are acquired and involve typically the presence of powerful but incompatible drives. The lack of thought-cues (repression) for identifying the elements of the conflict prevents the acquisition of more adaptive behavior. Frequently, the drive of fear is a critical element of the conflict. Neurotic symptoms often involve responses that have been maintained only because they are followed by the reduction of this drive. This process, whereby mental disorders develop, may be detailed as follows:

1. Inadequate training takes place early in life when children are taught by parents —persons who are relatively ineffective teachers because of their own backgrounds. The major areas in which emotional conflict is learned include: feeding, elimination, sexual behavior, and anger. The learned patterns that are shaped around these situations persist throughout the child's adult life.

2. Various types of intense drives are aroused during these periods of training. For example, premature or severe toilet training may arouse strong emotions of apprehension as the child finds himself incapable of acquiescing to the parental demands. Severe punishment for the display of sexual behavior can lead to sex-fear conflict. The neurotic is faced with the conflict aroused by the existence of two or more drives leading to incompatible responses.

3. Specific neurotic symptoms are acquired since they momentarily serve to reduce drives. For example, problem drinking behavior may be strengthened because alcohol reduces the person's fears or tensions. Of course, some sets of symptoms are unlearned and involve the unpleasant physiological reactions that often accompany intense emotional or drive states.

4. Repression is a response that greatly contributes to the development of neurosis. It is essentially the automatic response of not-attending, not-thinking, not-labeling. Although a great deal of repression occurs before the child had acquired the language to provide labels to identify the conflict, the act of repressing can also exclude once verbalized events. Each time an unpleasant drive is reduced by repression, the act of repression is strengthened. A child may be spanked for an act and have his fear generalize from the act to his thinking of the act. Repression of the thought reduces the fear and is thus reinforced. Or the parent may actually threaten the child with punishment if he "even thinks of doing that again" and thereby actually encourage the child to learn how to repress.

5. Other learning phenomena such as generalization or the development of anticipatory responses also help to explain neurosis. Fear originally attached to the cue of behaving angrily may generalize and be elicited by mild feelings of anger, or even by vaguely similar feelings such as competitiveness or assertiveness. If the person has learned to inhibit angry feelings, this could lead to overcontrol and inhibition of all traits. Because labeling is an aid to preventing generalization, repression serves to increase maladaptive generalizing.

THE SOCIAL LEARNING VIEWPOINT

An increasing number of psychologists (Bandura, 1968; Eysenck, 1960; Ferster, 1961; Staats and Staats, 1963) have been dissatisfied with the Freudian viewpoint. Their criticisms include the Freudian reliance upon "fanciful" hypotheses about inner forces, the heavy dependence upon the disease entity analogy, and the tendency to lose sight of identifying more concrete factors in pathology that can be subject to immediate change. This group believes that similar problems beset other psychodynamic viewpoints as well, such as the nondirective or Rogerian personality theorists (a major psychological approach stressing the role of the self-concept in psychopathology) (Rogers, 1951). They consider the Dollard and Miller analysis of pathology a major step forward; however, even this approach is seen as being somewhat more reliant upon psychiatric hypotheses rather than psychological laboratory evidence. Albert Bandura, Arthur Staats, and Carolyn Staats have offered a system for understanding psychopathology which they feel is more valuable. This social learning viewpoint relies entirely upon the basic principles of learning to provide an interpretation of pathology. Pathological behavior is examined strictly and solely from the standpoint of learning data without reference to Freudian, Rogerian, or any other psychodynamic points of view. The social learning theory psychologists do not characterize persons as possessing varying types or degrees of "mental illness" or disease, and refuse to limit their analyses to examination of subject variables, that is, the characteristics of the *persons* involved rather than the *stimulus situations*. Bandura writes:

> In view of the demonstrated importance of stimulus control over behavior, a social learning taxonomy (classification) of psychopathology must attend to the interaction between behavioral predispositions (subject variables), on the one hand, and stimulus events, on the other. This type of analysis can help both to explain the acquisition and maintenance of deviant response patterns and to guide therapeutic practices (1968, p. 298).

One such classification scheme (Bandura, 1968; Staats and Staats, 1963) is presented in the sections to follow.

Behavioral deviations refer to those psychological difficulties that do not have an organic cause; this term replaces the psychiatric classification "functional mental illnesses" and is used by social learning theorists to eliminate the unnecessary connotations implicit in the psychiatric system. The behavioral deviations are of several major types:

Behavioral deficits

Defective stimulus control of behavior

Inappropriate stimulus control of behavior

Defective or inappropriate incentive systems

Aversive behavioral repertoires

Aversive self-reinforcing systems

Behavioral Deficits

Some individuals are considered maladjusted by reason of the absence of skills normally expected. For example, an autistic child (one who is severely disturbed) may lack the ability to speak, fail to respond socially to people, or demonstrate poor emotional responsiveness. In effect, the main difference between the autistic child's behavior and that of normal children is the fact that the normal behavior occurs with less frequency in the disturbed child (Ferster, 1961). The abnormal behavior of children separated from their parents (see Chapter 5), such as the "affectionless character," can be explained in this manner.

Behavioral deficits occur through a variety of conditions. The presence of a physical disability from birth defects, disease, or injury, can prevent the person from learning a skill (Meyerson, et al., 1962). A deaf child may show speech deficits because of his inability to hear words. Since patterns of behavior are acquired through the imitation of social models (Bandura and Walters, 1963), the absence of good models can lead to behavioral deficits. Reinforcement for demonstrating desired behaviors is necessary if those behaviors are to be maintained. Therefore, insufficient rewards are likely to produce deficits. This might be the circumstance when the parent is too preoccupied to respond to the child, or too disinterested in the child to show approval. Punishment (the use of an aversive stimulus) has been known to lead to inhibition or suppression of behavior. Staats and Staats indicate:

> In general, it may be said that when chil-

dren develop adjustive behaviors later than usual, they are subject to aversive social stimuli of various kinds, such as derision. The child who does not develop independent toilet habits, who does not speak well enough, who stutters past an acceptable age, who lacks motor skill, and so on, receives much social punishment as a consequence. This state of affairs would be expected to continue throughout life (p. 468).

Defective Stimulus Control of Behavior

A wide number of normal responses are normal in the sense that they are immediately triggered off or controlled by specific stimuli. Thus, a "normal" person approaches to the verbal stimuli, "Come here, please"; inhibits his activity to the posted sign, "Do not walk"; and is properly respectful when in the presence of a person in grief over a death. On the other hand, "abnormal" individuals sometimes appear to be oblivious of the stimuli in their environment, even those specifically directed toward them. Thus, hospitalized psychotics may fail to respond to the announcement that meals were being served (Ayllon and Haughton, 1962). Neurotics will often exhibit deviant behavior in spite of appeals and pleas by others that they change. Criminals continue to break the law despite their awareness of the rules which say, "Do not . . . on penalty of punishment." A person who expresses merriment during a funeral service is certainly not under stimulus control, and may be risking commitment to a mental institution.

Basically, defective stimulus control of behavior involves the failure to respond in a *discriminating* fashion to important cues. Much of human learning involves responding one way to one stimulus, and another way to a different stimulus. This is referred to as *discrimination*. Discrimination is developed if there are differing consequences of performances to different stimuli, for example, if the person is rewarded when one stimulus is present and

punished or not rewarded when he responds to a different stimulus. A good example is braking an automobile when the red stoplight is on and accelerating when the green light is presented; in this case, our driving behavior comes under discriminative stimulus control. Failure to learn discrimination (and therefore failure of stimulus control to develop) may occur because of faulty learning conditions. In effect, if the consequences of our behaviors do *not* differ when the stimuli differ, then we will not learn to discriminate. If driving through stoplights was never penalized by a traffic ticket or by an accident, then drivers would soon ignore traffic lights. If a parent never followed through on her directive to her child, the child would soon pay her no heed. Failures in reading may result from a failure to discriminate between relevant differences in letters or words; when one is scanning a novel such discrimination may be unimportant, but it can be critical if one is preparing a drug from a prescription for medicinal purposes.

Inappropriate Stimulus Control of Behavior

Another class of maladaptive circumstances are those involving the inappropriate association between certain stimuli and certain responses. Typically the stimuli are innocuous in nature, but have acquired the ability to elicit intense emotional reactions. Phobias are a good example; a phobia involves the arousal of intense fear by inappropriate stimuli, such as harmless animals. Observation of persons suffering from phobias make it clear that the individuals are under stimulus control: they often rearrange their lives and go out of their way to avoid encountering the feared object. Pervasive and continuing arousal of anxiety (anxiety reactions) can be viewed as another form of inappropriate stimulus control of behavior. In an anxiety reaction, so many cues in the patient's environment are able to elicit tension that he lives in a state of chronic anxiety. Psychosomatic complaints are also better understood in terms of stimulus control. Studies have shown that it is possible to precipitate asthmatic attacks through the presentation of innocuous stimuli under the proper learning conditions. Dekker, et al. (1957) had two asthmatic patients inhale certain allergens to which they were hypersensitive. Using these allergens as the unconditioned stimulus, the investigators were able to cause an asthmatic attack by just presenting the inhaling mouthpiece.

In the above conditions, the common learning condition is classical conditioning. This involves the identification of a stimulus capable of eliciting a specific response, then pairing this stimulus (the unconditioned stimulus) with a neutral cue (the conditioned stimulus). Continued pairing leads to the formerly ineffective stimulus acquiring the ability to evoke the same response. Research in Russia (Razran, 1961) has shown that autonomic nervous system responses can be conditioned to many cues. In fact, visceral responses can themselves act as stimuli which can evoke other internal responses. Constriction of the blood vessels, for example, can be conditioned to breathing. This evidence, along with such works as Watson and Raynor's (1920) on conditioning of fear (see section on Experimental Studies in Psychopathology, in this chapter), strongly suggest that classical conditioning may account for a number of types of abnormal behaviors.

Defective or Inappropriate Incentive Systems

In *defective incentive systems,* those rewards which are ordinarily capable of establishing and maintaining behavior, fail to be influential for the patient. Praise, parental attention, and group recognition, do not seem to affect the person; conversely, verbal censure, criticism, and so-cial ostracism fail as negative stimuli. The common picture is that of a person who is not responsive to the rewards offered by his social environment. In its extreme, we have a person who is nonresponsive to his surroundings, for example, the adult schizophrenic or the autistic child. A less extreme form appears in the individual who is described as listless, apathetic, bored, uninvolved, unmotivated; such persons can be found among students who are disinterested in schoolwork, housewives who are continuously fatigued before they start their chores, wealthy men who experience ennui. The so-called habitual criminal or antisocial person may well be one who not only does not respond to social rewards, but who also reacts adversely to such reinforcers. Cairns (1961) found that delinquent boys who strongly inhibited dependency reacted toward social reinforcers as if they were aversive.

The failure of social reinforcers is connected with inadequacies of early learning. Much of our social incentives, such as praise or recognition, acquire their reinforcing value through early association with primary reinforcers (events that are rewarding without prior learning experiences, e.g., food). Reinforcers that have acquired their reward value through previous pairing with primary reinforcers are called secondary reinforcers. Deficient development of social incentives is the result of factors such as the absence of such early associations, infrequent associations, or extreme delays in time between the primary reinforcer and the secondary reinforcer. For a child, praise from a stranger is meaningless as compared with praise from the parent, who gives praise along with warmth, comfort, love, and a special dessert. Seashells are valueless as reinforcers unless one lives in a culture where they are associated with food that can be purchased. We may work hard for the reward of extra trading stamps until the redemption company goes out of business, making the stamps worthless.

In the problems of *inappropriate incentive systems,* certain inappropriate stimuli acquire reinforcing value. Sexual perversions involve the responsiveness to unusual cues as rewards, for example, obtaining satisfaction from articles of clothing, animals, or members of the same sex. The male transvestite experiences a reward whenever he dresses in women's clothes, and may feel especially complimented when told how feminine he looks. Seeing others happy is reinforcing for the normal person, whereas the maladaptive person may find it rewarding to see others in pain.

The development of a *defective* incentive system is due to the lack of adequate association between a primary reinforcer and a socially common stimulus (secondary reinforcer); the development of an *inappropriate* incentive system is due to the presence of an association between primary reinforcer and a socially uncommon or deviant stimulus. A parent, for example, might always give her child a stuffed animal to hold when she comforts and carries him; this animal will acquire secondary reinforcing value. Had the parent instead provided him with a doll, or a shoe, or a scarf, he would develop a positive association with these other items. As might be guessed, activities can themselves acquire reinforcing value. The well-built athlete may achieve a sense of satisfaction whenever he displays his muscle development to others, lifts weights, or engages in physical fitness exercises. In a similar fashion, the exhibitionist might find it personally rewarding to display his genitals to young children.

Aversive Behavioral Repertoires

Under this class are behaviors that lead to aversive consequences to others, such as aggressive actions, dependency behaviors, and attention-seeking activities. The way in which aggression becomes part of a person's behavioral repertoire is becoming better known. Certainly one of the most common reactions to a frustrating circumstance is aggression (Dollard, et al., 1939). The young child who faces an obstacle to his goal, and who is yet ill-equipped to resolve the problem, will throw a tantrum or attack the obstacle in his way. Although there are other responses that can be cued by frustration, some form of aggressiveness is often rewarded since the parent will quickly remove the obstacle for the child. Loud arguments and fights among offspring are poorly tolerated by many parents, and it is too often simpler to make peace by giving in than by trying more positive tactics. In delinquents, the achievement of peer approval from the gang is derived through the display of strength and aggressiveness. Even in the world of business, one is often impressed by the role of reinforcement in the maintenance of controlled aggression. The persistent, demanding, sometimes insulting salesman is reinforced each time this approach leads to a sale; one second-hand automobile dealer admits to continuing his "hard-sell" television commercials because they improved his sales record. It is important to note that as long as reinforcement occurs for aggressive behavior, such behavior will persist even in the face of punishment. Basically, reinforcement strengthens the aggressive responses such that they become the most frequent and most relied upon actions within the person's repertoire. Punishment alone may momentarily suppress the response but will not eliminate it totally. Before modern penal rehabilitation methods, many criminals were known to return immediately to their former illegal activities upon release. In fact, many never did change their behavior, but simply continued on with the same activities within the prison itself.

A number of studies have demonstrated

the influence of reinforcement in the development of aggression. Davitz (1952) exposed half of a group of children to praise for displaying competitive and aggressive responses, and the other half to approval for showing cooperative and constructive behaviors. Both groups were then subjected to frustration and observed for their reactions. The aggression-rewarded children responded with aggression, while the cooperation-rewarded children reacted with constructive behaviors. Patterson, et al. (1961), Lovaas (1961), and Walters and Brown (1963) all obtained similar results demonstrating that aggression when reinforced increases in strength, persists over time, and even is used in new circumstances not related to the original learning conditions.

Recent work has made it quite clear that aggression can be acquired without being instigated by frustration. Aggressive behavior can be elicited simply through exposing the individual to an aggressive model, and particularly a successful model (Bandura, 1965). Children who observed an adult whose aggressive behavior resulted in gaining rewards imitated this model even though they disapproved of his actions. Even cartoon models were imitated in very precise fashion by the viewers (Bandura, et al., 1963). Exposure to aggressive models can also weaken the inhibitory behaviors of the observer. Children who watched an aggressive adult subsequently showed nearly twice as much aggression as control subjects, while viewing a nonaggressive model tended to decrease the display of aggression during frustration. The open use of physical aggression appears to be inversely associated with socioeconomic status. In effect this may be a self-perpetuating system: the lower class parent uses aggression in his discipline and serves as a model for the child, the child acquires the aggressive behavioral pattern, the child grows up and becomes a parent and is a model for his child, and so on.

Aversive Self-reinforcing Systems

Although reinforcers examined thus far are socially transmitted, that is, provided by others, the human is also capable of self-transmitted reinforcement. Man is self-aware, can evaluate his own performance, and can think well or poorly of himself. Although such activity usually takes place covertly, some individuals are more overt and can be observed monitoring themselves. Athletes in the midst of competition can be seen talking to themselves, encouraging themselves, applauding a good move, condemning a bad one. A housewife may buy herself a new hat in celebration of a job well done, and a businessman may spend an evening "on the town" after closing a difficult transaction. Self-reward involves self-evaluation which is in turn associated with standards of performance. In socially transmitted reinforcement the individual undertakes an activity, but the standard of performance required and the reward contingent upon this standard are determined by others. In self-reinforcement, the behaviors, the standard, and the reward may all be within the control of the individual himself. In some individuals, such a self-oriented system may be a source of maladjustment. Their behavioral patterns may be adequate, their responses may be both subject to stimulus control and linked to appropriate stimuli, and their actions might be generally socially competent. In all respects they may be considered to be adjusted by others observing their actions. However, the individual might still experience self-dissatisfaction, unhappiness, and a sense of maladjustment. That is to say, the person views his own behavior as not reaching standard and therefore withholds reward and, in fact, self-administers punishment. Such characteristics are often found in persons who become depressed, who bemoan their worthlessness, who seek escape from their own devaluation through drugs or alcohol or suicide, or who are extremely low in self-confidence.

Self-evaluation and self-rewarding actions may be viewed as behavior patterns, just as the evaluation of others and the dispensing of rewards to others are behaviors. As such, self-evaluation and self-reinforcement are learned patterns. It would be expected that a person who experiences the conditions of learning that would encourage indulgent self-reward would be more lenient toward his own performances; conversely, the person who learned more strict self-evaluation would tend to be more demanding. Kanfer and Marston (1963) exposed subjects to a task in which there was no apparent correct response nor way of determining their accuracy. One group of subjects was freely and generously rewarded and approved of whenever they expressed confidence that their response on a given trial was correct, that is, whenever they showed positive self-evaluation. The other group was continuously cautioned against requesting approval for undeserving performances and rewarded only grudgingly. Immediately following this learning experience, the subjects of both groups were then tested on another task for which correct answers were available. The subjects were placed on a self-reinforcing schedule, being told to reward themselves whenever they thought their answers were correct. Although both groups were equally accurate on the task, the indulgent-treated group were much more willing to reinforce themselves for their performances than the strictly-treated group: the indulgent group administered 58 percent self-reinforcements as compared with 0.2 percent by the strict group. It is apparent that self-evaluative, self-reinforcing activities are subject to learning experiences.

EXPERIMENTAL STUDIES IN PSYCHOPATHOLOGY

It is appropriate at this point to briefly review some of the evidence in support of the view that psychological factors play a critical role in mental pathology. The data come from studies which were stimulated by a variety of psychological theories; they have in common the fact that they all involve psychological variables.

Frustration and Conflict

A number of studies exposed animals to irresolvable conflicts; the result: experimental neurosis. Possibly the earliest experiment of this type was that conducted by Pavlov on the basis of his conditioned reflex method. When a stimulus, such as a circle, is presented during the feeding of a dog, the animal soon begins to respond to the sight of the circle by salivating. The circle is thus considered an excitatory stimulus, triggering off activity in the dog. If a different stimulus, such as an ellipse, is presented and the animal is consistently not fed during this time, the dog soon learns to inhibit his activity. Hence, the ellipse may be considered an inhibitory stimulus. In a classic experiment, Pavlov first developed the ability of the circle to arouse an excitatory state and the ellipse to arouse an inhibitory state. He then created a circumstance whereby both excitatory and inhibitory states were simultaneously aroused. This was done by changing the shape of the ellipse until it was so similar to the shape of the circle that the dog could not tell the difference. The effects were impressive: the dog began to howl, struggle, rip at the restraining harness with his teeth. All previous learning was lost and the animal was unable to respond correctly even when the ellipse was restored to its original distinctive shape. Pavlov concluded that an acute neurotic condition had been duplicated. This general type of procedure has

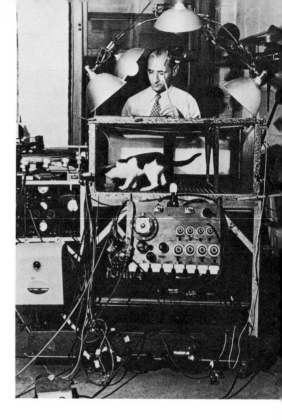

Experimental neuroses, involving phobias, psychosomatic ailments, withdrawal, or obsessive-compulsive behaviors, have been produced in cats. Masserman (pictured above) accomplished this by subjecting the animals to an approach-avoidance conflict in the food box. (Courtesy—Dr. Jules Masserman)

subsequently been repeated in other laboratories, including that of Gantt (1942). This psychologist conducted the most prolonged single case history study of experimental neurosis. He worked with Nick, a dog, for over nine years reporting on the pathological, psychological, and physiological effects of conflict. He even attempted a form of therapy—a rest cure in the country (which had little lasting effect on the neurosis).

The Conflict of Stress

The experimental neurosis of Pavlov and Gantt were produced by impossible discrimination tasks and without other external stress. Later scientists, such as Maier and Masserman, produced breakdowns by introducing an aversive aspect to the conflict situation. Maier (1939) placed rats on a stand and trained them to jump toward one of two windows facing them. If the animals chose the correct window (identified by some visual cue such as a black circle) they reached a feeding platform. The incorrect windows were fastened

shut so that the rats bumped and fell into a net below if they jumped toward these windows. During the experimental condition, the rats were faced with insoluble decisions and forced to jump by the use of either shock or a blast of compressed air. Within a very short period, a number of animals developed symptoms including frantic running in circles, convulsions, and a catatonic state in which the rats remained motionless in bizarre positions (for example, lying on their backs with hind feet and rump rolled upward into the air).

Masserman (1943) trained cats to obtain food by manipulating a switch. For a period of months, the animals were routinely provided with pellets of breaded salmon whenever they pressed the switch. When the cats had become thoroughly accustomed to this procedure, the experimenter added a new element—a mild blast of compressed air across the snout. In earlier trials, the cats were quite startled by the unexpected event and would withdraw, inspect the switch from afar, but eventually return hesitantly to the food-bin. They were allowed to feed again uninterrupted for a few more trials but then subjected again to the air blast. After two to seven such experiences, the cats began to show aberrant patterns which Masserman describes as markedly similar to human neurotic symptoms. Some of the symptoms included:

> Irrational fears of harmless sounds, lights, closed spaces, caged mice, the food and food-bin, and even air currents.
>
> Psychosomatic illnesses such as gastro-intestinal disturbances, asthma, convulsions, and increased blood pressure.
>
> Peculiar ritualistic or compulsive behavior such as circling the food-bin three times to the left and head-bowing prior to eating.
>
> Loss of responsiveness to the environment, including a refusal to acknowledge food in a nearby plate, ignoring mice in a cage, and remaining motionless as if paralyzed.

Like Gantt, Masserman also tried rest cures by transferring the cats to a home setting for prolonged rests of three to twelve months. This "treatment" led to reduction in symptoms while the animals were away but the neuroses reappeared as soon as the cats were returned to the laboratory. The experience of viewing a normal cat at work with the switch, the use of sedatives, and mild cerebral electro-shock all acted as transient but not complete therapeutic agents. Alcohol ingestion also served to reduce the cats' conflicts to an extent that they could again eat albeit in a somewhat tipsy fashion. Significantly, about half of the cats showed a distinct preference for alcohol to the point of becoming "problem-drinkers." Such alcoholic addiction continued until the underlying conflicts were reduced by other non-alcoholic therapy techniques.

Need Deprivations

Pathological states have also been produced in man and monkeys through deprivation: of sensory experiences, social experiences, and in monkeys, of tactual contact experiences. The Canadian psychologists, Bexton, Heron, and Scott (1954) quite accidentally became aware of some peculiar effects of sensory deprivation in humans. They were originally conducting a study related to a practical problem of the military: the effects of prolonged monotony (such as radar screen watching). Subjects were paid $20.00 a day for nothing, that is, they had nothing to do other than remain quiet on a comfortable bed for as long as they cared to remain. They wore translucent goggles, gloves, and cuffs to prevent sensory variation. Sounds were masked by an air-conditioner hum. Earlier in the isolation period, the subjects simply took advantage of the quiet surroundings and slept. Before long, however, they began to become extremely uncomfortable, restless, irritable, and showed impairment in their ability to think on simple problems. A majority experienced hallucinatory types of experiences ranging from seeing light changes with eyes closed, to seeing a "procession of squirrels with sacks over their shoulders marching 'purposefully' across a snow field" (p. 74). Similar emotional effects have been subsequently obtained by others, including Lilly (1956), Suinn (1969), and Hebb, Heath, and Stuart (1954). Suinn observed hallucinatorylike reactions in some subjects undergoing brief sensory limitation of one hour's duration. Hebb, Heath, and Stuart (1954) stuffed the ears of paid subjects with cotton impregnated with petroleum jelly. This did not completely prevent all hearing, but normal audition and conversation was accomplished only with effort. Variable amounts and types of personality changes occurred in these subjects. One reacted with marked irritability to the point of nearly hitting a

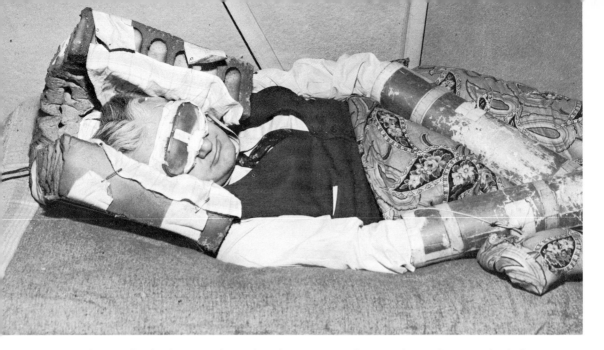

Sensory deprivation research restricts the amount and types of sensations permitted the subjects. The subject in the photograph above is fitted with goggles to limit his vision, gloves and cuffs to prevent tactual stimulation, and rests on a sound-deadening pillow. (Montreal Star-Canada Wide)

woman. Another developed overwhelming feelings of personal inadequacy, and although he denied being seclusive or irritable, his girl friend maintained that he had become quite withdrawn and terse. Other subjects appeared to have only minor emotional reactions. In addition to such laboratory-produced isolation, many cases of naturally caused sensory deprivation have taken place with similar effects. Christine Ritter, alone in the Arctic for long periods, reported hallucinatory experiences such as seeing a monster and hearing ski strokes in the snow (1900). Captain John Slocum, sailing alone around the world, "saw" a man take over the tiller during a vicious galestorm (1900).

Social deprivation seems to be as upsetting as sensory deprivation. Rowland (1964) raised groups of infant monkeys in total social but not sensory deprivation. One group was raised in isolation for their first six months of life, while another group was isolated for the first twelve months. Each monkey was raised in a solid, illuminated cage and never saw any other living creature. Through remote-control techniques, sensory experiences and testing for learning and food responsiveness were made possible. Physically, the animals appeared to have developed normally, but psychologically, the monkeys seemed to have been affected. For example, when they were given their first glimpse at the world outside their quarters by the removal of the opaque screen, profound terror gripped the young monkeys. A typical reaction pattern was self-clutching, freezing, and hiding head-covered in a corner. When placed with other monkeys, the deprived ones were totally unresponsive socially as if their capacity for social activity was completely obliterated. When subjected to abusive and even dangerous aggression by others, the deprived monkeys remain passive and vulnerable. Similar results regarding pain were obtained by Melzack and Scott (1957). Six litters of terriers were divided into two groups, one raised in a sensory and socially deprived environment. At maturity the animals were tested. In two

Young monkeys raised under *social deprivation* conditions appear to become psychologically maladjusted. A typical response when taken out of isolation is the self-clutching fearful behavior shown above. (Dr. Harry Harlow / Regional Primate Research Center)

of the pain tests, being jabbed by a dissecting needle and being burned with a match, the deprived dogs accepted the painful stimulus passively without any attempts to move away. They acted as if they were totally oblivious, did not have to be restrained, and in fact even *approached* the pain-provoking stimulus.

Of final interest in the deprivation type studies is the work of Harlow (1958) in exploring the contact-comfort hypothesis. After observations of the seeming attachment of infant monkeys to dummy mothers made of terry cloth, Harlow concluded that intimate physical contact is necessary for the animal to acquire security feelings, particularly security from a mother figure. In the experiments, two surrogate-mother monkeys were constructed: one of bare welded wire, the other with the wire sheathed with terry cloth. Infant rhesus monkeys were raised either with a wire or a cloth mother. Testing involved placing the infants in a strange environment with unfamiliar objects. Those monkeys raised without the benefit of the terry cloth mother showed significantly higher emotional reactions than those raised in the security of the cloth mothers. Even the presence of their mother-surrogate failed to create a sense of security in the wire-mothered monkeys. Whereas the cloth-reared infants rushed to their mother-surrogates and gradually clamed down, the wire-reared animals often clutched themselves, held their heads in their arms and engaged in convulsive jerking and rocking movements. These ritualistic rocking movements are also found to characterize pathological states in human children deprived of maternal care.

The Learning of Neurosis

The classic human case of laboratory-induced symptoms is that conducted by Dr. John B. Watson and his associate Rosalie Rayner in 1920. Albert, an infant of nine months, was selected because of his emotional stability which, it was felt, would protect him from serious harm due to the experiment. He was a stolid, phlegmatic youngster afraid of nothing under the sun. However, he did show a fear reaction if a steel bar was suddenly struck, making a loud and unexpected sound. This fear was a quite natural reaction in a youngster of this age. When Albert was 11 months of age, he was presented with a white rat. It had been demonstrated previously that the infant had no fear of such animals, and in fact he would reach out for them. On the first day of the crucial experimental period, as Albert reached for the white rat, the steel bar was struck immediately behind the infant's head thereby eliciting a fear reaction. This was repeated once more before tests were suspended for a week so as not to disturb the child too seriously. One week later, the following was recorded:

(1) White rat presented . . . without sound . . . tentative reaching movements began (by Albert).

(2) Joint stimulation with rat and sound. Started, then fell over immediately to right side. No crying.

(3) Joint stimulation. Fell to right . . . No crying.

(4) Joint stimulation. Same reaction.

(5) Rat . . . presented alone . . . whimpered and withdrew body . . .

(6) Joint stimulation. Fell over . . . began to whimper.

(7) Joint stimulation . . . cried.

(8) Rat alone. *The instant the rat was shown the baby began to cry. Almost instantly he . . . began to crawl away so rapidly that he was caught with difficulty . . .* (Eysenck, 1960, p. 30).

This case quite clearly demonstrated that a specific course of learning, classical conditioning, could lead to the development of phobias. It has been cited in support of the belief that many, if not all, phobias are acquired through a paired association between an originally neutral cue (such as the rat) and a fear-producing cue (such as the startling sound). Such learning via joint stimulation has long been offered as a process whereby many normal behaviors are acquired, for example, learning to withdraw when someone warns "That's hot" or when we see a sign "Danger." Watson's work now adds another dimension to the application of this type of learning process.

Instrumental, or operant, learning is another type of learning process involved in the acquisition of normal behaviors. This is the reinforcement learning applied by Dollard and Miller to psychopathology. A response is strengthened whenever it is followed by reinforcement. Masserman used this type of learning procedure to develop apparent masochistic behavior in his cats. As will be recalled, Masserman's cats showed intense dislike and fear of sudden blasts of air. Yet he was able to train these animals to actually administer these air blasts to themselves (the equivalent to a human being slapping himself in the face, or hitting his head against the wall). The cats were taught to depress a pedestal switch, after which they received food reward. Once the switch-pressing was established, a very light current of air was released each time the switch was depressed in later trials. Reinforcement was always presented after the response. The air pressure was increased progressively until the cats were actually presenting themselves with what ordinarily was an intolerable blast. Moreover, animals can be trained to "seek" severe electric shock, loud noises, rancid odors, provided that reinforcement followed the behavior that triggered off the painful stimuli (Masserman, 1961). Perhaps this is all akin to the story of the woman who chose to wear extremely tight shoes two sizes too small despite the excruciating pain; her explanation—"I do it because I feel so good when I finally take them off!"

The Dream State of Existence

Dreams have long been considered a psychological phenomenon rather than a physiological one. Freud relied heavily upon the interpretation of dreams as the "royal road to the unconscious." In addition he believed that dreams were necessary in that sleep was protected while yet permitting sexual or aggressive drives to be free (Freud, 1900). Adler hypothesized that dreams occur as a means of solving unresolved problems from waking life (Ullman, 1962). It has been demonstrated that dreams do in fact occur with regularity and predictability. Adult humans spend about 20 percent of their sleep time dreaming, with a dream occurring about every 80-90 minutes and lasting for a period of approximately 14 minutes (Hartmann, 1966). Dreaming is unlike wakefulness, yet different enough from sleep that it has been designated as the third state of existence. Robert (1886) proposed that dreams serve as safety valves permitted pressures and tensions of the day to be discharged. Moreover, he believed that a human deprived of dreaming would become mentally disturbed. His first premise has received but little support. Rechtschaffen and Verdone (1964) found a slight but significant correlation between anxiety in college students and amount of dreaming, and Suinn (1967) noted a relationship between anxiety and color dreaming. However, Robert's second premise has received some intriguing support:

A number of studies (West, Janszen, Lester, and Cornelisoon, Jr., 1962; Luby, Grissell, Frohman, Lees, Cohen, and Gottlieb, 1962) have reported on the *sleep*-deprivation-psychosis. As a function of loss of sleep, subjects undergo certain predictable changes ending in a psychotic-like condition:

1. Progressive lapses of attention.

2. Loss of fine movements of the eyes and hands leading to staring; increased hand steadiness but gross tremors.

3. Illusory sensations such as tingling, feeling a tightness around the forehead (the "hat illusion").

4. More and more prominent intrusive thoughts.

5. Hallucinations first of rhythmic movements in stationary objects, then patterns (geometric designs, lace, cobwebs).

6. Increase in need for oral activities although appetite is not increased.

7. Gradual appearance of psychotic signs:

    a. Hallucinations become more vivid, prolonged, and insight into their unreality is lost.

    b. Paranoid delusions of persecution, or grandiose ideas develop.

    c. Confusion and disorientation takes place.

    d. The strain appears in facial features in the hollow-eye, suspicious stare nicknamed the "Mindzenti look" after the pictures of the Cardinal taken at his trial and public confession as a spy (West, et al.).

Sleep deprivation has been reported to exacerbate the illness of chronic schizophrenics and even cause the return of symptoms which had not been seen since their first admission (Karanyi and Lehman, 1960). Many cases of psychotic episodes are known to have been preceded by prolonged insomnia (Bliss, Clark, and West, 1959).

Of course, the sleep-deprivation psychoses may be a product of loss of sleep and fatigue alone and not necessarily due to the loss of dreaming. Dement (1960, 1965) conducted experiments with humans and cats in which sleeping was permitted but dreaming was prevented. The dream state is identifiable by the occurrence of

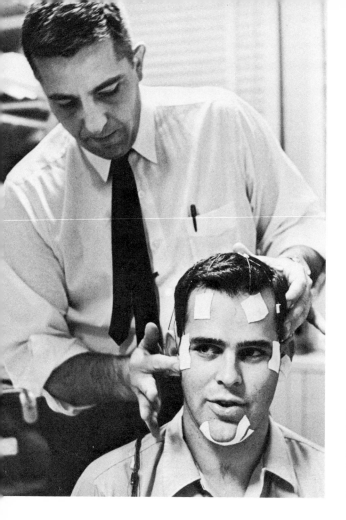

Research on Rapid-Eye-Movement (*REM*)*sleep* has contributed much to understanding the value of dreams. Dr. William Dement, a noted scientist, is shown attaching electrodes which will signify the onset of dreams *(REM sleep)* in the subject. (Dr. William Dement/Stanford University School of Medicine)

rapid eye movements (REM) (Aserinsky, and Kleitman, 1953). Sleep during which no dreams occur lack rapid eye movements (NREM). Using brain-wave recordings to identify the REM and the NREM sleep, Dement systematically interrupted human subjects when they began to dream but allowed them to remain asleep as long as they did not have a dream. Several things happened:

1. One subject became disturbed enough after three nights of dream deprivation that he left in a flurry of contrived excuses.

2. Two others insisted they could not go another night after having slept for four nights during which they were dream-deprived.

3. Personality changes were apparent

although not catastrophic—anxiety, irritability, and difficulties in concentration occurred (one subject became seriously agitated).

4. Marked eating behavior occurred along with weight gains up to five pounds from the increased food intake.

Of importance was the fact that none of these results occurred when subjects experienced the same number of interrupted awakenings during the evening *provided that the awakenings occurred after a dream had run its natural course* (Dement, 1960). Dement continued this dream-deprivation work on cats, permitting them all the sleep they needed but prodding them to wakefulness whenever a dream began to appear (Dement, 1965). Dement has now reversed his earlier position and concluded from this study that REM sleep is not required, at least in the adult cat, and that serious impairment does not occur. He did admit, however, that certain unique behavioral changes occurred in his dream-deprived cats and not in other cats. The dream-deprived animals prowled more, seemed restless, and showed a marked increase in sexual activity. They also showed difficulty in learning which arm of a simple Y maze to take to obtain food, with one cat requiring *5000 trials* before he learned although he was "obviously an intelligent cat" (p. 406).

The dream-state, or D-state, or REM-state is still a controversial and exciting area. Is it a psychological event as Freud and Adler supposed, or is it a neurochemical state as Hartmann and Dement argue? How critical is it that a person be permitted to dream? What exactly is the function of the dream-state: to release tensions of the day, to resolve psychological conflicts, to metabolize or discharge an accumulating substance (serotonin, perhaps)? What is the answer to the old yet elusive riddle of the meaning of the content of dreams? How do everyday events in the waking-state influence the need to dream? And finally, the most intriguing and tantalizing question of all: What is the nature of the relationship between dream-deprivation and mental illness?

Glossary

Acquisition: The learning process whereby responses are strengthened or stimulus-response associations are formed.

Anal phase: The Freudian stage of development characterized by a shift of the erogenous zones to the anal area.

Aversive behavioral repertoire: Learning theory classification of disorders involving response patterns that have noxious consequences for others, such as aggression.

Aversive self-reinforcing system: Learning theory classification of disorders involving self-administering condemnation, as seen for example in low self-confidence or depression.

Behavioral deficit: Learning theory classification of disorders involving the absence or infrequent appearance of certain responses, such as emotional responsiveness to others.

Castration anxiety: The Freudian premise that boys undergo a fantasied fear of castration; a premise important in the Oedipal complex.

Classical conditioning: A form of learning involving the pairing of a neutral cue with one already associated with a response.

Cue: Sometimes called stimulus. An event or change capable of initiating a response.

Death instinct: Also called Thanatos. The Freudian motive reflecting the destructive aspect of life.

Defective or inappropriate incentive system: Learning theory classification of disorders involving failure to respond to typical rewards, or the response to atypical rewards, for example as seen in the person who is reinforced for sexual exhibition.

Defective stimulus control of behavior: Learning theory classification of disorders involving the failure to respond to given stimuli, as seen for example in the failure to heed lawful commands.

Displacement: The shifting away of emotion from one object and toward another.

Discrimination: In learning terms, the selective responding to differences in stimulus characteristics.

Drive: In learning terms, a motive.

Ego: The Freudian term for psychological processes including reasoning, reality testing, coping behavior, and other higher mental processes.

Ego anxiety: Also called reality anxiety. The anxiety associated with a fear of aversive consequences from the environment.

Eros: Also called the life instinct. A major motive in Freudian theory.

Extinction: The process whereby responses are weakened or eliminated through the removal of reinforcement.

Fixation: The Freudian term for the failure to progress beyond an early developmental phase.

Frustration: The blocking of ongoing, goal-directed behavior.

Genital phase: The Freudian stage of development characterized by the shift to adult genital love.

Hierarchy of responses: The learning term for the arrangement of different responses associated with a stimulus in order of increasing likelihood of expression.

Id: The Freudian term for infantile psychological processes including impulses demanding immediate gratification.

Id anxiety: Also called neurotic anxiety. The anxiety associated with a fear of being overwhelmed by inner impulses.

Inappropriate stimulus control of behavior: Learning theory classification of disorders involving the inappropriate association between certain stimuli and responses, for example, as seen in phobic reactions to innocuous stimuli.

Instinct: Innate motives.

Latency phase: The Freudian stage of development characterized by a temporary repression of conflict.

Learning dilemma: The learning term for a circumstance in which drive reduction does not occur following a response.

Life instinct: Also called Eros. The Freudian motive reflecting the constructive, self-preservative, aspects of life.

Operant learning: A form of learning involving the presentation of a reward following the response to be strengthened.

Oedipus complex: The Freudian term for the boy's repressed love for his mother.

Oral phase: The Freudian stage of development characterized by a focus of the erogenous zones around the oral areas.

Penis envy: The Freudian premise that girls undergo an admiration and a repressed desire to possess the male sexual organ.

Phallic phase: The Freudian stage of development characterized by the Oedipus complex.

Pleasure principle: The Freudian term for the tendency to seek immediate discharge of tension without attention to the consequences.

Primary drive: Motives that are innate.

Primary reinforcer: An incentive that has reward value without previous learning.

Reality principle: The Freudian term for the capacity to delay gratification, or to elect socially approved means for gratification.

Regression: The return to earlier, typically less mature, behavior patterns.

Reinforcement: In operant learning, the presentation of a reward; in classical conditioning, the pairing of the neutral stimulus with the stimulus normally associated with a response.

Repression: The exclusion of psychological activities or contents from awareness.

Secondary drive: A motive that is acquired through learning.

Spontaneous recovery: The return of a response that has been extinguished upon the presentation of the stimulus after a delay.

Stimulus generalization: The tendency for a response to be evoked by stimuli that are similar to the stimulus associated with that response.

Superego: The Freudian term for psychological process involved in the setting of moral standards.

Superego anxiety. Also called moral anxiety. The anxiety associated with a fear of guilt reactions.

Thanatos: Also called the death instinct. A major motive in Freudian theory.

References

Aserinsky, E., & Kleitman, N. Regularly occurring periods of eye motility and concomitant phenomena during sleep. *Science,* 1953, 118, 273.

Ayllon, T., & Haughton, E. Control of the behavior of schizophrenic patients by food. *J. exper. anal. Behav.,* 1962, 5, 343.

Bandura, A. Influence of models' reinforcement contingencies on the acquisition of imitative responses. *J. person. soc. Psychol.,* 1965, 1, 589.

Bandura, A. A social learning interpretation of psychological dysfunctions. In P. London and D. Rosenhan, (Eds.). *Foundations of abnormal psychology.* New York: Holt, Rinehart, and Winston, 1968.

Bandura, A., Ross, D., and Ross, S. Imitation of film-mediated aggressive models. *J. abnorm. soc. Psychol,* 1963, 66, 3.

Bandura, A., & Walters, R. *Social learning and personality development.* New York: Holt, Rinehart and Winston, 1963.

Bexton, W., Heron, W., & Scott, T. Effects of decreased variation in the sensory environment, *Canad. J. Psychol.,* 1954, 8, 7076.

Bliss, E., Clark, L., & West, L. Studies of sleep deprivation-relationship to schizophrenia. *A.M.A. Arch. neur. Psychiat.,* 1959, 81, 348.

Cairns, R. The influence of dependency inhibition on the effectiveness of social reinforcers. *J. Personal.,* 1961, 29, 466.

Davitz, J. The effects of previous training on postfrustration behavior. *J. aborm. soc. Psychol.,* 1952, 47, 309.

Dekker, E., Pelser, H., & Groen, J. Conditioning as a cause of asthmatic attacks. *J. psychosom. Res.,* 1957, 2, 97.

Dement, W. The effect of dream deprivation. *Science,* 1960, 131, 1705.

Dement, W. Recent studies on the biological role of rapid eye movement sleep. *Amer. J. Psychiatry,* 1965, 122, 404.

Dollard, J., Doob, L., Miller, N., Mowrer, O., & Sears, R. *Frustration and aggression.* New Haven, Conn.: Yale University Press, 1939.

Dollard, J., & Miller, N. *Personality and psychotherapy.* New York: McGraw-Hill, 1950.

Eysenck, H. Learning theory and behavior therapy. *J. ment. Sci.,* 1959, 105, 61.

Eysenck, H. *Behaviour therapy and the neuroses.* New York: Pergamon Press, 1960.

Ferster, C. Positive reinforcement and behavioral deficits of autistic children. *Child Develop.,* 1961, 32, 327.

Freud, S. *The standard edition of the complete psychological works.* J. Strachey (Ed.) London: Hogarth Press, 1953.

Freud, S. *The interpretation of dreams.* New York: Basic Books, 1956.

Gantt, W. The origin and development of nervous disturbances experimentally produced. *Amer. J. Psychiat.,* 1942, **98**, 475.

Harlow, H. The nature of love. *Amer. Psychol.,* 1958, **13**, 673.

Hartmann, E. The D-state: a review and discussion of studies on the physiologic state concomitant with dreaming. *Intern. J. Psychiat.,* 1966, **2**, 11.

Hebb, D., Heath, E., & Stuart, E. Experimental deafness. *Canadian. J. Psychol.,* 1954, **8**, 152.

Kanfer, F., & Marston, A. The conditioning of self-reinforcing responses: An analogue to self-confidence training. *Psychol. Rep.,* 1963, **13**, 63.

Karanyi, E. & Lehman, H. Experimental sleep deprivation in schizophrenic patients. *A.M.A. Arch. gen. Psychiat.,* 1960, **2**, 534.

Lilly, J. Mental effects of reduction of ordinary levels of physical stimulus on intact, healthy person. *Psychiat. Res. Rep.,* 1956, **5**, 1.

Lovaas, O. Effect of exposure to symbolic aggression on aggressive behavior. *Child Develop.,* 1961, **32**, 37.

Luby, E., Grissell, J., Frohman, C., Lees, H., Cohen, B., & Gottlieb, J. Biochemical, psychological and behavioral responses to sleep deprivation. *Ann. N.Y. Acad. Sci.,* 1962, **96**, 71.

Maier, N. *Studies of abnormal behavior in the rat.* New York: Harper, 1939.

Masserman, J. *Behavior and neurosis.* Chicago: University of Chicago Press, 1943.

Masserman, J. *Principles of dynamic psychiatry.* Philadelphia: Saunders, 1961.

Melzack, R., & Scott, T. The effects of early experience on the response to pain. *J. comp. physiol. Psychol.,* 1957, **50**, 155.

Meyerson, L., Michael, J., Mowrer, O., Osgood, C., & Staats, W. Learning, behavior and rehabilitation. In L. Loftquist (Ed.), *Psychological research in rehabilitation.* Washington, D.C.: American Psychological Association, 1962.

Mowrer, O. *Learning theory and personality dynamics.* New York: Ronald, 1950.

Patterson, G., Ludwig, M., & Sonoda, B. Reinforcement of aggression in children. Unpubl. manus., Eugene, Ore.: University Oregon, 1961.

Pavlov, I. *Conditioned reflexes* (translated by G. V. Anrep) London: Oxford University Press, 1927.

Razran, G. The observable unconscious and the inferable conscious in current Soviet psychophysiology. *Psychol. Rep.,* 1961, **68**, 81.

Rechtschaffen, A. & Verdone, P. Amount of dreaming: effect of incentive, adaptation to laboratory, and individual differences. *Percep. motor Skills,* 1964, **19**, 947.

Ritter, C. *A woman in the polar night.* New York: The Century Co., 1900.

Robert, W. *Der Traum als Naturnotwendigkeit Erklart.* Hamburg: H. Seippel, 1886.

Rogers, C. *Client-centered therapy; its current practice, implications, and theory.* Boston: Houghton, Mifflin, 1951.

Rotter, J. *Social learning and clinical psychology.* New Jersey: Prentice-Hall, 1954.

Rowland, G. *The effects of total social isolation upon learning and social behavior of rhesus monkeys.* (Doctoral dissertation, University of Wisconsin) Ann Arbor, Mich.: University Microfilms, 1964, No. 64-9690.

Slocum, J. *Sailing alone around the world.* New York: The Century Co., 1900.

Staats, A. & Staats, C. *Complex human behavior.* New York: Holt, Rinehart, and Winston, 1963.

Suinn, R. Anxiety and color dreaming. *Mental Hygiene,* 1967, **51**, 27.

Suinn, R. Limited sensory and social deprivation and operant control of affiliation and deference responses. *J. proj. Tech.,* 1969, **33**, 535.

Ullman, M. Dreaming, life-style, and physiology: A comment on Adler's view of the dream. *J. ind. Psychol.,* 1962, **18**, 18.

Walters, R., & Brown, M. Studies of reinforcement of aggression: III. Transfer of responses to an interpersonal situation. *Child Develop.,* 1963, **34**, 563.

Watson, J., & Rayner, R. Conditioned emotional reactions. *J. exper. Psychol.,* 1920, **3**, 1.

West, J., Janszen, H., Lester, B., & Cornelison, Jr., F. Psychoses of sleep deprivation. *Ann. N.Y. Acad. Sci.,* 1962, **96**, 66.

Wolpe, J. *Psychotherapy by reciprocal inhibition.* Stanford: Stanford University Press, 1958.

PART III

Types of Abnormal Conditions, Their Dynamics and Treatment

The following chapters cover three topics: (1) basic concepts to provide an understanding of the normal personality, and an aid to understanding more about the abnormal personality, (2) descriptions of certain types of abnormal conditions, their probable origins, characteristic treatment for such disorders, and case histories representative of such conditions, and (3) an overall discussion and evaluation of modes of treatment.

The reader should take special note of the orientation of this text toward the treatment of disorders. Each of the discussions of therapy programs that follow each section of disorders emphasizes the modes of treatment with the greatest history of success. Thus, a pragmatic orientation was adopted: the depressions seem to be particularly responsive to electroshock therapy and therefore shock treatment is discussed in some detail, on the other hand, since phobias are most responsive to behavior therapy, this mode of treatment is given primary attention. Also included are discussions of those additional modes of therapy for each disorder which appear to have been successful to some degree in bringing about improvement in patients.

In a similar fashion, an attempt is made to provide the reader with an understanding of the meaning and origins of the various disorders; this is offered in the sections called "Dynamics" immediately following the descriptions of each disorder. Again, the discussions are not limited to providing a single point of view. Most explanations about the circumstances leading to the expression of a particular type of disorder might be seen as theories rather than proven fact. The supporting evidence that any one theory is appropriate for explaining any one disorder varies among theories and disorders. Since no one theory has yet proved to be suitable for explaining all types of disorders equally well, this text restricts itself to tracing the dynamics of *each* disorder using the theoretical explanation which provides the greatest meaning and which receives substantial support when applied to *that* disorder. If a different disorder is better understood from another approach, then that theoretical frame of reference will be provided. In one sense, the orientation is eclectic in that the reader is not burdened with persistent reliance upon one theory to explain all types of disorders. At the same time, the discussions of dynamics and of therapy are limited to those approaches which, on a pragmatic basis, present the most meaningful and useful information for each disorder considered separately. This orientation is more in keeping with the current state of knowledge; it is hoped that matters will change soon so that texts may provide a single, unified point of view that is neither eclectic nor foolishly biased.

8 Basic Concepts in Personality and Psychopathology

In order to fully comprehend pathology certain basic aspects of human personality must be understood. Needs, frustration, conflict, anxiety, defense mechanisms, and the self-concept will each be discussed in the sections to follow. Each relates to the other in an endless sequence of dynamic interactions, for the human personality is a complex, fluid system.

NEEDS

The forces that motivate man may be referred to as needs. Needs possess the following characteristics:

An energic quality—needs pressure for release, push for action.

A directional influence—while the need is pressing, it directs the individual toward activities that are pertinent to need-satisfaction. A hungry person seeks food, a thirsty one seeks drink.*

A sensitizing effect—individuals in need appear sensitized to events related to need-satisfaction. A road-

---

* There are some distinct exceptions. Vitamin deficiencies do not exert pressure for action, and infants tend to react to needs by diffuse and undirected activity.

---

weary traveler is quickly alert to signs of motel vacancies; a famished traveler is more perceptive of signs of food than of lodging.

In general, it is useful to conceive of needs as following an overall principle of homeostasis (Cannon, 1939). This principle operates most clearly in physiological functions, for example, in the mechanisms for maintenance of a constant body temperature. In a similar way, certain psychologically related needs appear to involve a search for a state of equilibrium, for example, deprivation of sensory stimulation and excessive sensory stimulation are both undesirable and promote efforts directed toward their removal. An interesting consideration is the possibility that a disequilibrium may be only a *perceived* disequilibrium, where a person believes himself to be deprived but in reality is not. Under such a condition, the individual would be expected to act in every way as if a need state existed. Perhaps this explains the miser who continues to hoard even after a fortune has accumulated or a businessman who continues to labor despite all outward signs that indicate he has arrived at the peak of success.

Many efforts have been devoted to

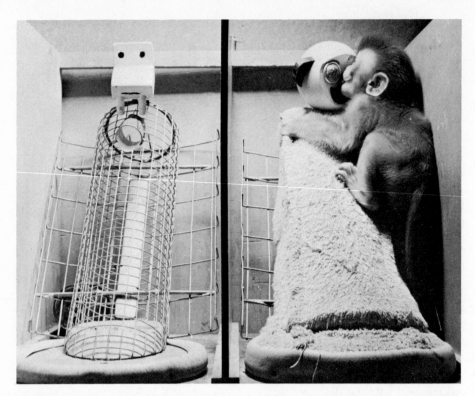

Dr. Harry Harlow provided infant monkeys with two surrogate mothers, one of wire, which provided food, and another of terrycloth, but no food. The monkeys preferred the terrycloth mother, leading Harlow to conclude that tactual or *contact-comfort* is an important primate need. (Dr. Harry F. Harlow, Regional Primate Research Center)

classifying the needs that characterize man. Some of the more significant ones are given below.

1. The need for "mothering"—For want of a better term, "mothering" is used to refer to that special need exhibited by infants and young children. In humans, it is the need for the intimate contact with a mothering figure which protects the child from the effects reported in the maternal deprivation works, for example, anaclitic depression, the affectionless character, and affect hunger (see Chapter 5). In primates such as monkeys, it is the need for a mother figure which provides the tactual comfort that leads to monkey security.

2. The need for sensory and social stimulation—This need is epitomized in the previously mentioned works on sensory

deprivation in humans and social deprivation in dogs (see Chapter 7). Inadequate sensory input or variability leads to abnormal personality development in the young, and a search for sensory stimulation in the adult. It is entirely possible that the hallucinatory behavior of those undergoing severe deprivation is an internal attempt to provide for the lack of external stimulation.

3. The need for nurturance, dependency gratification—This need is part of the foundation stones for personality growth. Out of this, the child acquires the sense of belonging, of being cared for, of security. Through being nurtured the child is able to later offer care and love to others, and after being dependent the youngster derives the confidence to seek independence.

The *need to achieve* has prompted man toward unbelievable scientific accomplishments. Man's footsteps are now imprinted on the moon as a result of this motivation. (NASA)

4. The need for autonomy, mastery—Overlapping with dependency needs is the often conflicting need for independence, autonomy, self-reliance. Mastering oneself and one's environment is satisfying. Proving one's adequacy in standing alone, in being alone in one's accomplishments is a tremendous aid in the development of self-esteem. Learning to walk is an incredibly difficult task for the one year old, fraught with many pitfalls. Yet the tumbles and discouragements seem more than made up for by the sense of accomplishment derived from the achievement of self-mastery.

5. The need for achievement—This need has received much recent attention as a major motive (McClelland, Atkinson, Clark, and Lowell, 1953). It is associated with making good, getting ahead, excelling, and surpassing others. It serves as a constant spur to performance in work, competitive, and problem-solving settings (French and Thomas, 1958; Suinn, 1966a).

6. The need for approval, acceptance—Man *is* a social being responsive to the attitudes, opinions, and regard of others (Crowne and Marlowe, 1964). One of the strongest forms of punishment is social ostracism; the most gratifying reward is

193

the unqualified acceptance by one's peers. A nod of acceptance or an approving word has as much power to influence behavior as material reward (Krasner, 1958).

7. The need for self-esteem—Closely related to autonomy, achievement, and approval is the desire to feel of value, worthy of respect. This self-approval is sometimes more difficult to obtain than the approval from mothers because of the high inner standards set by many for themselves. Many are driven by the eternal search for that sense of self-contentment, self-acceptance, worthwhileness.

8. The need for structure and meaning —This need represents a higher order motive, perhaps reflecting man's developed intellect. Ambiguity, lack of explanation for the unexpected, vague structure are poorly tolerated (Stagner, 1961). Superstitions are often primitive attempts at explaining events that are not understood. Rumors frequently spread quickly in situations that appear otherwise illogical, inexplicable, and inconsistent (Festinger, 1957).

Although the primary biological needs such as hunger, thirst, and respiration, remain essentially unchanged throughout life, the psychological needs are subject to changes. Some needs appear for the first time later in life, others show decreases in intensity, some are modified, and others are controlled. Maturation serves a significant role in such changes. As implied in the previous listing of needs, certain developmental sequences exist. Roughly speaking, needs such as "mothering" and sensory social stimulation appear during infancy; needs involving dependency and autonomy develop during early childhood; and needs for achievement and peer approval occur during later childhood. With maturation, some needs tend to diminish, for example, the amount of sleep demanded decreases with age. The process of socialization also contributes to change.

Parents direct much of their energies toward encouraging, modifying, or discouraging need states in their offspring. Psychological needs are particularly susceptible to external influences as witnessed by the great value placed on self-reliance, achievement, and status recognition in our society. New motives may be developed and fostered by the close association with reinforcement. In a sense, it might well be possible to define socialization as involving the process whereby: socially disapproved motives are prevented or discouraged, infantile motives are eliminated, need-satisfactions are postponed until certain cues are present (as in the case of toilet training), the behaviors for need-satisfactions are altered and more "civilized" or adult actions encouraged, and the objects suitable for need-satisfaction are changed (as is the case in weaning from liquids to solids). Several factors influence the ease with which needs are modified:

1. The abruptness of change—Gradual modifications of needs are much better tolerated than sudden demands. The birth of a second child frequently leads to changes in the family abruptly affecting the needs of the firstborn. A nurturing mother must now devote her attentions to the newborn child and may discourage further dependency in the elder child. Sudden shifts from dependency gratification to independence training represent a difficult task for the child. In a remarkable study of cultures, Whiting and Child (1953) discovered that severe demands for motive modification in children led to socialization anxiety which carried into adulthood in the form of fears.

2. The amount of past gratification— A person with a history of high reinforcement for needs such as dependency will find it quite difficult to change. Research has shown that punishment for dependency leads to *increases* in dependency

Partial reinforcement, whereby rewards occur intermittently, is responsible for learned behaviors which are extremely difficult to eliminate. Slot machines capitalize on this principle with the intermittent payoffs maintaining the gambling habits of the players. (Fred Grunsweig/Photo Researchers, Inc.)

seeking, with this relationship being particularly evident in those children who had previously experienced gratification for their dependency needs (Sears, Maccoby, and Levin, 1957). Many psychological motives are said to be acquired in the same way habits develop with continued reinforcement leading to strengthening of the motives. And, of course, the stronger the motive becomes the more resistent it is to change.

3. The expectation of renewed gratification—A principle of psychology states that behavioral patterns that are sometimes rewarded and sometimes not resist elimination more than behaviors that are always rewarded. This pattern of issuance of reward is called partial reinforcement (when rewards occur intermittently) or regular reinforcement (when rewards occur every time the behavior is shown). When partial reinforcement is terminated, it is as if the individual continues to expect that rewards will again reappear . . .

as they did in the past. In a similar way, a child who has received inconsistent gratification for his needs will take longer to change even after need-satisfaction is terminated by his parents.

4. The presence of reminders of lost gratifications—Needs are aroused by internal and external cues. In biological needs, the cues are mainly internal such as changes in the biochemistry of the body. However, even in such physically based needs, external cues are capable of arousing states quite similar to biological needs. One's appetite for food can be stimulated by the sight of a steak, the smell of simmering sauce, or the sound of bacon frying. In a similar fashion, a child who has given up his need to be nurtured may have his desire restirred by the sight of a younger sibling being comforted and cared for by a parent. Such regression is a common experience in families where an only child is confronted by reminders of his infantile past.

195

5. The strength of competing needs—Part of growing up involves the giving up of infantile needs in favor of more mature needs. In some instances, an infantile need is modified into a more socially acceptable form (this is called sublimation). If the change requires the substitution of a newer motive for a previously held one, then the relative strengths of the two motives will affect the ease of the transition. The newer motive must be more satisfying, more desirable, more likely to be satisfied for it to compete successfully with an established motive. Parents help to make the desired motive more attractive by setting up obstacles that prevent the child from obtaining satisfaction of the undesired motive. Punishment and reprimands are resorted to in an attempt to reduce the sense of satisfaction. And although such techniques fail as far as being permanently effective, they help in momentarily channeling the child toward other more acceptable needs.

6. The blockage of an ongoing motive—Once a need state is instigated, interruption before gratification is obtained is usually strongly resisted. The well-known Zeigarnik (1927) effect demonstrated that interrupted tasks were more remembered than completed ones. However, the tendency to persist can be altered under the following conditions:

a. When the interruption is perceived as a signal of the start of a desirable event. For example, if a person is told that he will be stopped before he completes a task as soon as it is evident that he is working *successfully* in its solution, he can be interrupted with little frustration.

b. When the significance of the task is minimal. If the need being blocked has little significance to the person, interruption will be better tolerated.

c. When the motive was instigated by someone other than the subject.

A child whose achievement orientation is a result of parental pressure will accept obstacles more readily.

An important aspect of motivation is the fact that needs may operate without the individual being aware of their influence. This has been called *unconscious motivation.* Individuals often say or do things for which they have no explanation. It is as if another part of themselves were responsible for the actions. Even when the obvious reasons are pointed out to them, they are not able to accept the connections. Reactions such as, "No, I am not capable of that" or "That's the last thing I had in mind" are common. Slips of the tongue, lapses of memory, inadvertent double *entendres,* all involve to some extent unconsciously motivated behavior. A name may be forgotten, not by chance, but by intention—an unconscious wish to remove all traces of an unhappy experience. Freud (1914) elaborated on many such examples of unconscious motivation occurring in everyday life in his treatise, *The Psychopathology of Everyday Life.* Moreover, it was Freud who first recognized the significance of the unconscious in psychopathology and who must be credited with providing the most detailed and influential discussion of the topic (Freud, 1900).

Without the concept of unconscious motivation much of human behavior would remain inexplicable and seemingly irrational. Yet the actual proof of its significance is extremely difficult. Because of the unconscious nature of the motive, it is impossible to rely upon the person himself for confirmation. The search for proof is similar to that taken by scientists in their pursuit of electrons—no one can point to one yet everyone can detect their presence. Identification is by inference—if one sees a trail left in a miniature cloud, it is possible to infer that something passed through the cloud. If a bachelor continues to verbalize his desire to wed, yet avoids dating eligible girls and antagonizes those to whom he becomes attracted, one may infer that he is unconsciously motivated by a desire to remain single. Through hypnosis it is possible to create an experimental situation demonstrating the workings of unconscious motivation. For example, Erickson reports on a subject who was placed in a trance and instructed that upon awakening he would have a great desire to have his borrowed cigarettes returned but would not be able to directly ask for them back. Furthermore, he would begin a conversation on any topic but the thought of his cigarettes would prey on his mind continuously. The brand of cigarettes was *Camels*. The following is what occurred:

He began chatting casually, wandering from one topic to another, always mentioning in some indirect but relevant fashion the word "smoking." For example, he talked about a boat on the bay at New Haven, commenting on the fact that the sight of water always made him thirsty, as did smoking. He then told a story about how the dromedary got one hump and the *camel* two. When the question of travel was raised he immediately pictured . . . rocking . . . on a *camel*. Next he told a tale of Syrian folklore in which again a camel played a role. . . . Asked what he would like to do, he commented on the pleasant weather and said there was nothing more glorious than paddling in a canoe or floating at ease on the water, smoking (Erickson, 1939).

The capacity of the human being to show highly complex behavior without being aware of what he is doing is not restricted to the area of unconscious motivation. There are many overlearned tasks which we undertake without paying much attention to our movements. We have all had the experience of being fatigued to the point of barely staying awake yet somehow driving home safely and without wrong turns. Workers skilled on routine manual jobs soon find themselves day-dreaming, planning the weekend outing, or conversing, while their hands continue to go through the intricate movements in production. Another common event related to the characteristics of unconscious motivation is the lack of awareness of the obvious. A person whose acts are unconsciously motivated fails to perceive his own motive and will deny its existence although the motive may be quite obvious to an onlooker. In the same way, we are oblivious to many aspects of our immediate environment. The sounds of traffic in the street outside, the hum of a fan, the books on the desk, the color of the walls may all be quite distinct parts of one's surroundings. Yet until attention is again called to them, their presence quickly fades out of our awareness. And in some instances, we are never fully attentive to features which by all rights should be unavoidable, such as the color of a spouse's dress or a traffic light. Of course, these examples of behavior without awareness or inattentiveness are typically not unconsciously motivated. The difference is that unconsciously motivated effects are due to an active process, whereas failure to recognize a traffic signal is more connected to a passive process. Putting it another way, if we fail to see a traffic light because we dislike any reminder of authority and law, then unconscious motivation may be suspected. On the other hand, if we fail to see a traffic light simply because we were too busy talking or too engrossed in admiring a pretty woman in the crosswalk, then other explanations are called for. In addition, an individual involved in *unconsciously* motivated activity *is* unconscious of his motives and often resists recognizing the motive, whereas behavior due to inattentiveness is readily understood by the individual.

FRUSTRATION

Frustration occurs when obstacles to need-satisfaction are encountered. Such obstacles deter or prevent an individual from reducing his needs and may derive from several sources:

1. Economic—Loss of income or lack of sufficient income to purchase what is desired. In some cases, income itself is what is desired as it might symbolically represent security, prestige, or power.

2. Physical—A physical disability, intellectual limitations, geographical distance, tangible barriers such as a fence, aging.

3. Societal—Rules and laws, customs, institutional standards, prejudicial attitudes.

4. Occupational—Working conditions, requirements for promotion, production demands, employer-employee relations.

5. Interpersonal — Competitiveness from others, lack of empathy or understanding, excessive concern by parents, the very fact that others have needs as well.

Frustration is important not only because of the psychological discomfort it results in, but because of certain other effects. It seems clear now that there is no single immediate result of frustration but that a number of differing things may happen. Frustration can lead to:

> need or goal enhancement
> aggression
> regression

The need, or objects that satisfy the need (goals), are *enhanced* in situations of mild frustration. Somehow the "grass is greener on the other side of the fence." It is as if the characteristic of being *less* easily obtained increases the attractiveness of goals. The *too easily* reached is scorned, the *impossible* to reach is often forgotten. The date-wise coed says "maybe," the promoter points out the limited availability of his product, the club president emphasizes the probationary status required before full privileges are achieved by the new member. Wright (1937) found that adults sought after the harder-to-reach

dessert dishes in a cafeteria and that children rated toys as more desirable when they were enclosed than when they were easily available on a table.

Aggression has also been found to be a reaction commonly triggered by frustration. We kick the car that won't run, curse the rain that spoils the picnic, and struggle to keep from hitting the person who stands in our way. The aggression itself may be frustrated by physical, psychological, or social barriers, in which case the attack may be shifted to a substitute and often innocent object. This is *displaced aggression*. For example, boys at a camp showed significantly higher hostility toward minority groups (Mexican, Japanese) after they were deprived of their weekly movie night. The frustrating agent was neither Mexican nor Japanese, but the boys were not permitted to be critical of him, hence the displacement occurred (Miller and Bugelski, 1948). In a similar fashion, historical data show that lynchings used to increase whenever financial returns decreased, for example, when the value of cotton dropped (see Figure 8-1) (Hovland and Sears, 1940). Raccoons that were taught to climb their cage for food when a certain card was displayed, tore up the card in displaced fury when deprived of their usual reward (Masserman, 1961). With such evidence, one wonders how often military and political decisions are linked to frustrations rather than sound planning. Suinn (1966b) found that subjects engaged in war-games were more likely to initiate "nuclear warfare" when faced with overwhelming odds even though to do so removed all chances for any outcome other than certain defeat.

Regression can also occur in the face of frustration. Regression is the return to earlier, less adaptive ways of behaving. It may involve a return to earlier forms of activity to reach a current goal (*instrumental act regression*), or selection of a goal once held at an earlier time (*object regression*), or a reversion to earlier, less mature needs (*need regression*). The following are examples:

Instrumental act regression—An older child reverts to baby talk to regain his parent's attention from a younger sibling.

Object regression—A married woman returns to her mother for love when faced with a frustrated attempt to gain gratification from her husband.

Need regression—A child gives up his independence strivings and renews his search for dependency satisfactions.

In its severest form, regression can of course be so complete that all three types are shown. This may be referred to as *age regression*. Where age regression occurs, the total personality seems to have taken a backward step in time.

CONFLICT

Whereas frustration involves the presence of obstacles to needs, conflict involves the presence of antagonistic needs or goals. Conflicts are therefore a special type of obstacle producing frustration. In a conflict situation, a person is faced with opposing needs or goals each pulling for opposing behaviors. Many adolescents are torn by a dependency-independency conflict. On the one hand they wish to be cared for, yet they simultaneously reject offers of help. A college student may rebel against authority direction yet be unable to accept personal responsibility. An executive may wish to retire yet find it impossible to enjoy recreation. Conflicts can be grouped into some basic categories with associated outcomes (see Figure 8-2):

1. The approach-approach conflict— This involves the presence of two or more mutually exclusive positive goals. It is

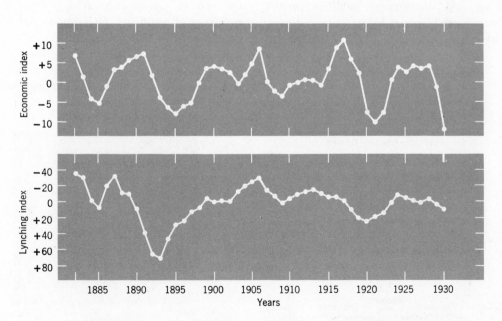

Figure 8-1. **Relationship of lynchings and the economy, an example of displaced aggression.** SOURCE: C. Hovland, and R. Sears, Minor studies of aggression: VI. Correlations of lynchings with economic indices. *Journal of psychology*, 1949, 9, 301. Copyright Journal Press, Provincetown, Mass.

epitomized by the fable of the donkey standing equidistant between two tantalizing bales of hay. The story says that the animal is so unable to make up its mind that it starves in its indecision. In reality, humans vacillate only a little but tend to resolve the issue quickly through the selection of one goal.

2. The avoidance-avoidance conflict— This involves the presence of two or more equally undesirable choices. In this situation the individual is motivated to escape from both horns of the dilemma. He is "between the devil and the deep blue sea." Where a realistic escape is impossible, a psychological escape frequently occurs: the individual may retreat into fantasy, into a psychosis, or into an intellectual denial that any danger is involved (e.g., combat flying personnel report feeling that "it will never happen to you, always to the other guy, but never to you").

3. The approach-avoidance conflict— This involves the presence of both satisfying and threatening qualities to the same goal. The goal is attractive, yet anxiety-producing; desired, yet feared. Investi-

gations have shown that the attractiveness of the goal decreases while its threat increases with nearness (see Figure 8-3). Such conflicts are never resolved satisfactorily: the person may ruminate about the advantages and disadvantages and even repeatedly approach the goal, but he will stop just short of decisive action. Vacillation, ambivalence, and immobility are common.

The intensity or severity of conflicts varies with the strength of the needs in question. A conflict over sleeping late or getting up for an employment interview becomes much more severe as the need for sleep is heightened and as regaining a steady income becomes critical. Moreover, the strengths of the needs relative to one another are important (see Figure 8-4). A starving man will be prompted to approach many acts that he would normally avoid for reasons of risk or conscience or distaste. One can well envision the excruciating conflict that preceded the acts of cannibalism among trapped survivors of accidents. It is important to note that the influence of conflict is not dissipated by impulsive action (the approach-approach conflict is an exception). Those who chose to eat human flesh to

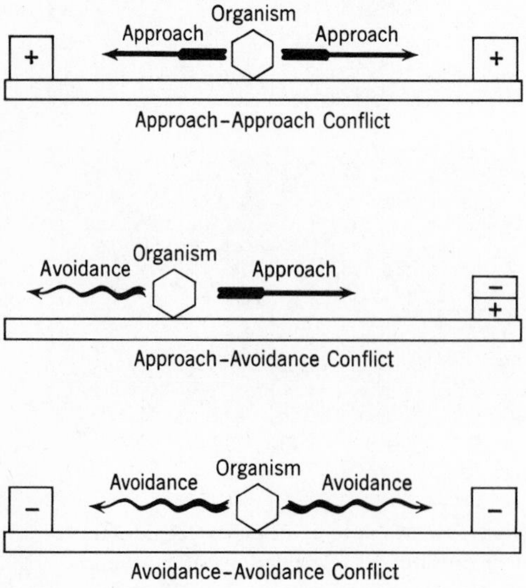

Figure 8-2. **Types of conflict situations schematically represented.**

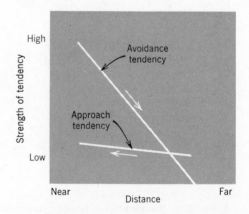

Figure 8-3. **Approach and avoidance gradients compared: approach or avoidance tendencies increase with nearness, with avoidance showing a steeper increase.**

survive may have felt physically satiated but were prone to suffer from guilt feelings. In fact, a modern theory of motivation—Festinger's *cognitive dissonance* theory (1957)—makes it clear that commitment to a decision is the beginning not the end of conflict. Briefly, the theory is as follows:

1. Dissonance is aroused in an individual when a person possesses two cognitive elements (information) about himself or his environment and where one is the obverse of the other. For example, knowledge that one has *eaten* a disliked substance would be clearly dissonant with knowledge that the substance is disliked.

2. Dissonance arouses tension (Suinn, 1965a) and motivates individuals to seek ways of reducing the dissonance. The greater the magnitude of the existing dissonance, the greater is the motivation. The more important the cognitions are, the greater the magnitude of the dissonance. The greater the ratio of dissonant to consonant cognitions already present, the greater is the magnitude of added dissonance.

3. Some means for reducing dissonance include: behavioral change, addition of evidence justifying one's decision, changing one's attitude about one's act, distorting the information.

Close examination of dissonance theory and research shows that cognitive-based tension occurs after the person has committed himself to a choice, while conflict-based tension occurs prior to decision making (Brehm and Cohen, 1962). In food aversions, for example, persons may experience the discomfort connected with approach-avoidance conflict when encouraged by an authority to eat a distasteful food. They are attracted toward the act because of the positive facet of approval from the authority. They are also repelled by the food itself. On the other hand, once they have chosen to go ahead with the repulsive behavior and have eaten, the discomfort of dissonance is aroused. This dissonance pressures in turn for reduction. In an experiment with junior high school students, Brehm (1960) induced students to eat different disliked and supposedly nonnutritious vegetables. He found that these students were impelled to actually change their previously held attitude of dislike for the food the more they were committed to eating. A fascinating finding was reported later by Smith (1961) who used a survival training program as a

 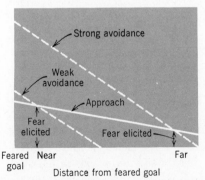

Figure 8-4. **Approach-avoidance conflict. To the left is a representation of how an approach-avoidance conflict is affected by increasing the strength of approach by increase in needs. To the right is shown how the conflict is affected by decreasing the strength of avoidance.**

SOURCE: Neal E. Miller, Experimental studies of conflict. In J. McV. Hunt (Ed.), *Personality and the behavior disorders.* Copyright 1944, The Ronald Press Company, New York.

means of getting soldiers to eat grasshoppers. One group was induced into the act by a friendly, warm experimenter while the other group was led by a researcher who was cool, formal and abrupt. Once having eaten the grasshoppers, those soldiers in the negative-inducer group showed a greater change in their attitudes toward grasshoppers than those in the positive-experimenter group. It appeared as though once a conflict was acted upon, dissonance tensions became even greater when elements were added that increased the negative components of the act.

Conflict situations may develop and be responded to without the awareness of the individual. Baker (1938) in some unique experiments used a conditioning procedure whereby a physiological response was elicited during the presentation of an irrelevant stimulus (the conditioned stimulus). In one study, the subjects were rapidly conditioned even when the physiological response was elicited by a subliminal shock and the conditioned stimulus was a sound they did not consciously hear. In another study, the conditioning technique enabled the experimenter to trigger emotional responses whenever a faint buzzer went off without the subjects ever being aware of the sound or its connection with their suddenly felt anxieties. Diven (1937) instructed subjects to give as many word-associations as they could to each of a series of stimulus-words. At the end of some of these associations, the subjects received an electric shock. Each shocked stimulus-word thus represented an approach-avoidance conflict—the approach aspect because of the desire to cooperate with the experimenter, the avoidance aspect because of the electric shock. Analysis showed that the shocked-words called forth an anxiety reaction as measured by the galvanic skin response. Of importance is the finding that the subjects were not aware of the source of their anxiety since none were able to identify which stimulus-words had been routinely followed by shock. Such experiments demonstrate that conflicts and anxiety can well develop under situations outside of the conscious control of an individual. Such unconscious conflicts may have developed because the person was inattentive to the situational cues, or because he was too young to have a suitable language system to identify the cues or because he was actually trained to avoid being attentive to his environment. In any case, such conflicts will continue to persist and will affect the adjustment of the individual.

ANXIETY

Anxiety is the cornerstone of all psychopathology. Its presence signals danger—to one's security, to one's psychological safety, to one's self-esteem, to one's sense of well-being. It is a concomitant of conflict and is itself associated with physiological concomitants. The most important symptoms of mental illness are maneuvers to cope with anxiety, attempts to discharge its intolerable pressure, or a sign that the personality has been overwhelmed by the force of anxiety. Yet anxiety can be a helpful ally rather than a fearful foe. Under normal conditions, anxiety stimulates learning, prepares a person for coping with challenges of his environment, and encourages optimum performance.

Anxiety may be defined as an unpleasant emotional state cued off by the presence of a threat and associated with subjective feelings of tension and apprehension. Physiological changes resulting from anxiety involve the sympathetic and parasympathetic nervous systems and include pupillary dilation, palmar perspiration, increased heart rate, and rapid respiration. This state is referred to as *state anxiety* and is conceptualized as a transitory experience that varies in intensity and fluctuates over time. When it is used to characterize or describe the basic personality of an individual, then the term *trait anxiety* is employed (Cattell, 1966). Thus, all people have experienced the state of anxiety but a few do so to such a chronic extent that they are said to possess the trait of anxiety. Fear and anxiety differ in that:

> Fear derives from a threat from an identifiable object while anxiety is diffuse and not directly related to any situation.
>
> Fear reactions dissipate upon the withdrawal from or disappearance of the feared object. Anxiety reactions persist over a much longer period and can therefore become attached to new triggering cues.
>
> Fear mobilizes efforts appropriate to coping with the feared object such as preparations to fight, flight, reassurance, or reevaluation of the situation. Severe anxiety is disruptive and excites a wide variety of behaviors including irrelevant, disorganized, inappropriate responses.

Positive Effects of Anxiety

Anxiety may be viewed as serving useful functions under normal conditions. As a signal of danger or threat, it activates the organism and serves as a sort of psychological "early warning system." Once alerted, the process of adapting to the environment is helped in that the individual is more perceptive of his surroundings. For example, it has been shown that rats made more anxious by punishment in a jumping-stand discrimination situation took more time in making their choices. This extra delay occurred as the animals appeared to "inspect" or "study" the situation to determine the cues associated with the correct choice—they literally began to "look before they leaped" (Munn, 1931). More recently, additional insights regarding the warning effects of anxiety have been reported from data based on perception studies. In some instances anxiety protects the individual by dulling his awareness, while in other instances the presence of anxiety acts to heighten an individual's sensitivity to cues. These effects have been referred to as *perceptual defense* and *perceptual vigilance*. Studies of this area have been concerned with subliminal perception or *subception,** the responsiveness to a stimulus below the threshold for conscious detection. A typical study on perceptual defense is reported by Eriksen (1951). Mental hospital patients were asked to create stories from four pictures that usually evoked aggressive stories in most people. Some patients were found to be ready-producers of overtly hostile themes while others avoided aggressive stories to the point of actually distorting the stimulus content of the picture in their avoidance. When their perceptual recognition thresholds for aggressive cartoons were examined, Eriksen found that the freely-aggressive patients showed a lower threshold for the aggressive cartoons than for neutral ones. In addition, the aggression-avoidance patients showed a higher recognition threshold for the aggressive cartoons. In a study of perceptual vigilance, McClelland and Liberman (1949) exposed subjects to tachistoscopic viewing of achievement- and security-related words. The researchers found that subjects with a high need to achieve had low recognition thresholds for achievement-related words, compared to low achievers who were more sensitive to security-related words. What appears to be happening is the functioning of a dynamic self-protection and need-oriented system. The perceptual defense phenomenon suggests a mechanism involving discrimination at an unconscious level as to the nature of a stimulus. Where the stim-

---

* For detailed reviews of the controversial area of subception studies, see Erikson (1960).

ulus is adjudged threatening, defenses are mobilized to prevent a conscious encounter. The perceptual vigilance phenomenon suggests that the mechanism sharpens responsiveness to need-related cues thereby enabling the person to obtain gratification.

Anxiety is also an effective facilitator of learning and performance. Any activity that serves to reduce anxiety is quickly learned. In fact, anxiety reduction has been used as a reinforcer in many animal studies. Mowrer, for example, taught laboratory rats to recognize that a tone signifies danger (an oncoming electric shock) and to run at once to another section of the cage in order to avoid the shock. These animals learned much more rapidly than those animals who were not permitted to avoid the shock and reduce the anxiety (Mowrer, 1940). Defense mechanisms, which will be discussed in a later section, are developed in the same manner. In fact, the main function of defense mechanisms is the reduction or avoidance of anxiety. And humans are no different from rats in this respect: any behavior that reduces anxiety is quickly learned.

In addition to defensive behavior, anxiety also facilitates the learning of other types of behavior. Among these are:

Simple, uncomplicated tasks such as eyelid conditioning or the learning of nonsense syllables of low complexity (Farber and Spence, 1953; Taylor and Spence, 1958; Montague, 1953).

Verbal memory tasks where there is an initial high degree of association between the cues and the memorized responses as in paired-associate learning (Spence, Farber, and McFann, 1956).

Overlearned, meaningful academic material as reflected by grades in college. This effect appears restricted to the more generalized state anxiety and does not apply to the test-taking anxiety state (Sarason, 1957; Suinn, 1965b).

Complex perceptual tasks where deliberate, cautious attention is required such as the location of a hidden figure imbedded in a puzzle (Ruebush, 1960).

Concept formation material when the persons with high anxiety are also of high intelligence as measured by College Entrance Examination Board (CEEB) scores. The concept-formation task involved the deduction of attributes from an increasing set of information representative of the attribute (Denny, 1963).

The Negative Effects of Anxiety

Anxiety, like radiation, is useful when controlled but extremely harmful if allowed to run rampant. In addition, once trait anxiety of one type exists the individual is prone to other types of anxiety. Thus, a person who experiences the vague tensions characteristic of neurotic anxiety is also susceptible to being anxious in the specific situation of test taking. Moreover, persons who suffer from test anxiety are also likely to react with other anxieties which interfere with adjustment in other settings. Such persons are unfortunately less likely to experience the facilitating effects of anxiety (Suinn, 1965c).

In a sense, the negative effects of anxiety are a result of having "too much of a good thing," that is, the very effects that prove helpful in moderation turn harmful in excess. The momentary delay to permit inspection of the situation before action turns into prolonged inhibition and freezing. The lessened perceptual recognition of cues quickly forces even slightly discomforting material into the unconscious. The behaviors learned through anxiety-reduction become more and more directed toward the dismissal of tension and less and less directed toward problem solving. Excessive anxiety facilitates the appearance of such a wide variety of random, irrational, undirected activity that it can only be labeled panic reaction. The alerting function of mild anxiety turns into a disturbing wakefulness and insomnia under severe tension. If sleep is finally achieved, the dream state is blocked thereby contributing to further anxiety. In addition, where dreams finally do occur, anxiety continues to exert its influence through the expression of color nuances (Suinn, 1967a).

The interfering aspects of high anxiety has been of recent interest to many experimentalists. Through continuing programs of research, it has been suggested by psychologists at the University of Iowa that anxiety has motivational properties (Spence and Spence, 1966). The belief is that anxiety energizes activity producing a quickness to respond. In the case of simple learning situations, this energizing effect facilitates learning. However, when the learning is more complex, anxiety may also energize incorrect responses which then interfere with the appearance of correct responses. From their work and the contribution of others, the following picture of the interfering effects of anxiety emerges:

> High anxiety is a hindrance to learning of complex tasks where incorrect responses are initially dominant. This has been shown on serial verbal learning in which subjects must anticipate the next item on a list (Montague, 1953), maze learning requiring a "left" or "right" decision at each choice point (Farber and Spence, 1953), and paired-associates learning in which the subject must give the appropriate word paired with each word presented (Spence, Farber, and McFann, 1956).

> High anxiety lowers performance on timed intelligence tests while facil-

itating performance on untimed tasks (Siegman, 1956).

High anxiety in subjects of lower intelligence faced with a concept formation task hinders performance (Denny, 1963).

High anxiety lowers the capacity to discriminate among similar objects in the environment, reduces the number of responses the individual employs in new settings and thereby leads to response stereotypy (Eriksen and Wechsler, 1955).

High anxiety interferes with effective communication. This appears to be true of all individuals who are faced with state anxiety, for example, during an oral examination involving extremely difficult questions. Communication effectiveness is also deterred in trait anxious persons and often is evident in stuttering, flustering, and blocked speech patterns (Gynther, 1957; Kasl and Mahl, 1965).

Excessive anxiety provokes primitivization of behavior to the point of temporary loss of rationality in problem solving. In an early work, Hamilton challenged rats and humans with the following problem: to discover which of four doors served as the exit from the enclosure in which the subject was placed. Since the same door was never unlocked on successive trials, the most efficient solution had to involve the avoidance of the previously correct door. Under Hamilton's no stress study, humans showed highly adaptive, efficient behavior while rats showed the opposite and perseverated in trying to open the same now-incorrect door. In a dramatic study by Patrick involving severe physical stress (electric shock, intense and irritating noise, and splashes of cold water), the humans reverted to exactly the same type of primitive, irrational, completely incompetent behavior as the rats (see Figure 8-5) (Hamilton, 1916; Patrick, 1934a, 1934b).

DEFENSE MECHANISMS

Once one experiences the state of anxiety, the role of defense mechanisms becomes immediately apparent. The onset of anxiety is the signal that a threat is present; defensive behaviors are operations to protect, prevent, and thwart the danger. Defense mechanisms are also appropriately called security mechanisms since

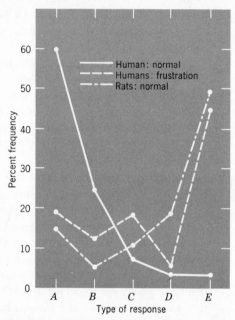

Figure 8-5. Effect of naturalistic stress on problem solving of humans and rats. KEY: *A:* Subject ignores previously unlocked door and tries each of the other three exits once, in a regular order. *B:* Subject attempts to open each of the four doors once in random order. The previously unlocked door may or may not be ignored. *C:* Subject tries all four doors once in regular order, clearly including the previously open door. *D:* Subject tries a door, then another, then returns to try the first door. *E:* Subject attempts to open the same door several times before trying any other one.
SOURCE: From *Experimental psychology: an introduction* by Benton J. Underwood. Copyright 1949, Meredith Corporation. Reproduced by permission of Appleton-Century-Crofts.

they are also involved in securing the personality from further threats. They must be continuously maintained in order to preserve one's sense of security and well-being. When anxiety-coping mechanisms are successfully in operation they can modify and even prevent the negative effects of anxiety (Suinn, 1965d). It must be recognized, however, that defenses are erected for one sole purpose—that of preventing or reducing anxiety. This, of course, can be helpful in freeing the person from the debilitating effects of anxiety such that he may attempt to adapt to the stress. Yet defenses are more often a mixed blessing since they often may in turn become obstacles to adjustment. Repression, for example, involves the denial to consciousness of anxiety-associated information. Once repression occurs, the information is essentially irretrievable and hence for all practical purposes the individual must function without the advantage of the material. Furthermore, defense mechanisms cannot be readily modified because their strength is firmly established through anxiety-reduction. Moreover, defenses are said to typically involve a denial, falsification or denial of reality and operate unconsciously so that the individual is quite unaware of what is happening. In fact, it is pertinent to suggest that defense mechanisms not only defend against the onslaught of anxiety, but they also defend against their own removal.

Some of the more commonly relied upon defense mechanisms will be listed and described in the discussion to follow.

Denial

A simple, primitive form of defense is the denial of the existence of an anxiety-provoking situation. It is one of the few security mechanisms that functions at the conscious and semiconscious (preconscious) levels. It is quite apparent in children who pretend that something undesirable does not exist. In adults, it is particularly evident in protective mothers who are blind to the obvious shortcomings of their offspring. The grief-stricken person who cries "Oh no, it can't be happening to me" is seeking the reprieve through denial. It is a characteristic early method used by the physically disabled to cope with the traumatic impact of their handicap (Suinn, 1967b). It is a favorite of community groups who are afraid to look for fear of what they might see, and so they prefer to say, "Surely you must be mistaken, there is no prejudice in *our* community."

Denial may take the form of fantasy in which we construct the type of life and world we prefer in place of reality. Instead of simply verbalizing "No, it is not so," the use of fantasy affords a more refined "No, that is not so, the *opposite* is." Daydreaming, wishful thinking, identifying with make-believe heroes enable some escape from the discomfortable truth of reality. Unfortunately, fantasy is made of fragile framework and one must soon pay attention to the insistent demands of fact.

Repression

Repression is a much more powerful defense, possibly the most powerful of all security mechanisms. Repression is frequently the first line of defense upon which other defenses are built. It involves the complete exclusion from consciousness of material that is so threatening, so damaging to the esteem, and so repugnant to recognize that banishment to the unconscious occurs. And as seen by the information on perceptual defense, this banishment itself takes place without the individual being in the slightest bit aware of what has happened. Selective forgetting of a past event, the failure to recognize an acquaintance, the absence of emotion, even the loss of sexual potency, are attributable to repression.

Repression requires considerable effort. Sometimes the effort is not enough and the repressed information begins to show itself—in dreams, slips of the tongue, vague feelings of uneasiness or guilt. When the repressed material is crucial for progress in therapy, the removal of repression is encouraged through drugs such as sodium pentothal or through hypnosis. Repression is also weakened by fatigue and alcohol.

Suppression

Repression is an entirely unconscious process, suppression is a deliberate effort of the conscious mind. The individual willfully and methodically prevents the thought or impulse from being expressed and diverts his attention elsewhere: "Count to ten" and avoid being angry, repeat over and over again to yourself "I will not be annoyed." Suppression is a relatively short term defense and depends upon the ability of the individual to first be forewarned of the imminent arrival of an unacceptable thought or impulse. He can then engage in suppressive behavior until the "storm blows over" or until the impulse turns out to be too much to handle by this technique and bowls him over. We all know of circumstances where counting to ten became simply the prelude to an emotional tirade that was only momentarily inhibited.

Rationalization

Rationalization is another form of defense that is preconscious. It involves attempts at providing a justification for otherwise unacceptable thoughts, feelings, or actions. As the name implies, a rational approach is used although this approach tends to be a misuse of logic—reason is enlisted to justify a decision already made, not to help in arriving at the best decision. What seems like objectivity proves to be distortion for subjective purposes. And in many instances, the reasons issued do have a ring of truth, the deception is the discussion of these reasons as if they had really been the motivations preceding the act. Persons relying upon rationalization cannot bear close scrutiny; they give the impression that the issue is closed once they have stated their rationale. In fact, they resist alternative evidence and become upset when inconsistencies are pointed out. As previously mentioned, the rationalizations are means of ending, not opening a discussion.

Among some of the more common rationalizations are the "sour grapes" and "sweet lemon" arguments. In the sour grapes fable, a fox struggles mightily to obtain a cluster of tasty grapes, fails miserably in his efforts, then slinks away muttering that it was a good thing he didn't get the grapes because they were probably sour anyway. The woman who says "I'm glad I didn't buy that dress, it'll fall apart in the first washing" instead of admitting that she couldn't afford it, is guilty of a sour grapes attitude. The sour grapes attitude attacks the item that we can't obtain, the sweet lemon attitude focuses on the advantages of items we already possess. The sweet lemon argument is a lengthy discourse on how much better, more desirable, more important, more valuable, etc., *our* possessions are. After the struggle to acquire ends in failure, the person pronounces "I wouldn't give up my —— for the world! It beats anything on the market now." The desired object may be a material substance such as a new car, or less material, such as an invitation to a dance, the love or respect of another, the status of an honor, or the advance to a higher occupational level.

Identification

Identification is a way of obtaining the unobtainable. It is considered by the Freudians as a critical step in the normal development of the child. In order to cope with castration anxiety, the youngster identifies with his father thereby relieving his tensions and obtaining vi-

carious gratification for his needs. Fantasy heroes may be selected for identification, such as the glamorous woman in a movie or the exciting international agent in a novel. When this occurs, the individual literally becomes the person he identifies with, suffering from all the agonies and glorifying in all the pleasures that affect the hero. Real-life persons may also be chosen for identification, such as movie stars, astronauts, athletes. The individual may go through great lengths to become just like his hero, dressing like him, imitating his mannerisms, talking like him, and compiling detailed accounts of the hero's life. Another source for identification may be an institution or a group. The aging alumnus who relives his youth by identifying with his university, the sorority girl who is indistinguishable from her group, and the football fan who returns home flushed with the sense of "our victory." Some unexpected identifications may also occur such as the mother who lives through the successes of her now-grown offspring, or the businessman who identifies himself with an unpopular cause. Identification in its extreme form is found in psychotic conditions in which a completely new identity is assumed, for example, in the patient who believes himself to be Jesus Christ.

Through identification with others, we can share in the rewards without participating in the efforts; we can make up for feelings of personal inadequacy and loss of esteem; we can achieve a sense of status, pride, accomplishment. Identification can also serve another function—that of coping with a feared rather than a desired environment. In what is known as identification with the aggressor, a person protects himself from danger from others. Generally, the circumstances involve a feared attack from a more powerful enemy. The emphasis here is not on identifying in order to obtain something desirable, but in order to prevent a feared event from happening. By identifying with the aggressor, the aggression is then perceived as now coming from oneself and therefore as being under own's own control. In addition, the victim can now feel as though he is the ally rather than the enemy of the aggressor.

Reaction Formation

Reaction formation is a defense against the discomfort of the unattainable goal as well as the anxiety connected with the wish itself. The possession of an impulse, a need, a wish, a desire, which is unacceptable to the person can trigger off not only repression but also the development of completely opposite behaviors. The person reacts against himself. Instead of feeling a need to drink, the person expresses an abhorrence of all forms of "stimulants" and wages a campaign against alcohol. Rather than attend to the inner stirrings of sexuality, the individual becomes a self-appointed committee to stir up the community against immoral and degrading literature and pledges himself to combat sex in any guise, shape, or form. Usually, reaction formation is suspected when the professed intolerance reaches a magnitude out of proportion with reality. In addition, the person becomes extremely insulted if faced with the suggestion that perhaps he is in some ways attracted to the very "vices" he so vigorously crusades against. It must be remembered that reaction formation takes place unconsciously; therefore, the individual is to a great extent truly unaware of his own real desires.

Reaction formation can often be observed in children. In response to the parental taboos against dirt and grime, the child must learn to control his forbidden urge to experiment with grease, to frolic in the grass, and to crawl through the earth. He may show a reaction formation that involves impeccable cleanliness and fastidious dress. However, since his urges have merely been blocked and not altered,

given the opportunity, they will return. It is a common experience for therapists to see the once-spotless child turn into an incredible mess of paints, mud, and chalk. This transformation takes place only after the child is assured that it is safe to recognize and release his inner impulses. As soon as there is even the slightest hint of adult disapproval, the defense is again erected.

Projection

Projection is a defense which is also directed against a trait that is possessed but unacceptable. In projection, the trait is repressed and then attributed to others. According to Freud, it has the advantage "that from an external danger protection may be gained through flight and the avoidance of the perception of it, whereas against a danger from within, flight is of no avail" (Freud, 1936). The defense makes it possible to see one's faults as belonging to someone else. The person cannot tolerate the trait in himself and drives it out of consciousness, yet he cannot escape and becomes preoccupied in seeing it in others. The person with homosexual tendencies who uses projection becomes appalled at the number of men whom he meets who make furtive "passes" at him. The basically hostile person may see himself as warm and peaceful but feel that he is surrounded by a hostile world. Basically the individual is saying "I am not like that, but there sure are many people around me who are."

Although the primary form of this defense is attributing to others the very trait that one possesses, another form also exists called *complementary projection*. As will be recalled from an earlier chapter, complementary projection involves attributing to the environment a quality that helps to justify one's own traits. Thus, the person who is ashamed of being frightened without good reason starts to read hostility and maliciousness into the gestures of others. He does not feel any less frightened, but at least he can anchor his fear to something or someone specific. A small community began preparations for certain destruction from an earthquake which miraculously bypassed them. Rather than celebrating the unexpected safety, the frightened villages became even more fearful and actually started their own rumors of greater destruction to come (Prasad, 1950). It was as if all their hysteria and fear would go for naught unless they continued to imagine themselves threatened. In this modern day of "over-kill" weapons and international tensions, perhaps complementary projection has been triggered by our generalized discomfort and is the explanation for the many extremist "witch-hunting" groups in existence.

Displacement

In displacement, impulses are discharged by means of a substitute object. Direct release is too unacceptable or too dangerous. An employee who is refused a raise by his boss may take out his frustration on his family. An angry young man may recklessly weave his car in traffic in a manner to antagonize other drivers. A child may throw his toys against the wall after being scolded. A person who is a failure in life may direct his tauntings and criticisms toward a minority group. In all of these situations, the emotion is being released at a person, object, or group not originally responsible for the individual's pent-up feelings. In this respect it involves scapegoating. Frequently, the release of feeling occurs so suddenly and violently that it is obviously out of proportion to the immediate circumstances. What has happened is that the unwitting victim simply served as the convenient target for the already overflowing emotions.

Displacements are rarely as satisfying as direct release of the emotion toward the original object. We all acknowledge this when we hear someone say "Boy, am I

going to be glad when my last day of work comes and I can go up to that no-good so and so and really tell him what I think of him." Yet, this defense does have its value. Displacement can serve as a minor safety valve permitting the release of some tension. In children, it enables the avoidance of further punishment or loss of love from the parent which would occur if the parents were directly attacked.

Sublimation

Displacement that is routed into more socially acceptable and culturally creative channels is called sublimation. The impulses that drive for release are transformed, tamed, and channeled so that they are now acceptable for direct release. Freud originally conceived of it as the factor that enabled primitive man to develop a civilized culture. In what proved to be a bestseller for Freud when it was originally published, he interpreted Leonardo da Vinci's Madonna paintings as a sublimated longing for intimate relations with a lost mother (Freud, 1910). The spinster who lacks a love-partner may sublimate her sexual needs by channeling her attention to nursing. The antagonistic man may turn his talents to becoming an aggressive salesman. Sadistic tendencies may be transformed into beneficial skills as in dentistry, surgery, and police work.

Sublimation has often been considered a higher order defense. Although there is doubt as to whether complete gratification of the original need is ever achieved, sublimation nevertheless provides for a greater degree and a more continuous need-satisfaction than any other defense. Sublimation is a response that recognizes the realities of acculturation pressures and offers an attempt at adjustment. As with most defenses, the adoption of a sublimated approach is unwitting rather than deliberately planned. In the event that the original impulse is an aberrant one, the existence of the defense does not resolve the difficulty but merely offers a means for limited discharge.

Isolation

Isolation involves a compartmentalizing of life events or of thought-feeling associations. By keeping job and family separate, the same man can be a brutal business competitor in one life situation and a warm and loving parent in the other. Normal emotions may be dissociated from distasteful or anxiety-producing acts so that the person can carry out his chore. In its severe form, isolation leaves a person devoid of emotion or even split into multiple personalities.

A type of isolation is accomplished by intellectualization. This defense is a preconscious reliance upon thinking and pseudointellectual verbalizing. The normal feeling tone is cut off as the person engages in discourse and debate. He may have all the right intellectual answers and scientific labels for his conflict but still be unable to solve his problem because the intellectualizing is used as a way of avoiding rather than confronting the conflict.

Regression

Regression involves the return to an older established pattern of behavior. It may or may not involve a reversion in time. When current experiences arouse anxiety or behaviors no longer achieve desired goals, the individual may again rely upon older habits. These older habits have usually been previously successful in need-satisfaction although they have since lost their effectiveness. Regressive behavior may involve immature responses such as crying, pouting, sulking, and demands for attention. The regression to physical assault as an ineffective attempt to solve problems is sometimes seen in the adult who kicks the car that refuses to run properly. In severe pathology, the regression may be so extreme that the individual is again infantile. Such a condition represents an escape from the demands, responsibilities, and stresses of adult living.

Allied to regression is fixation. This involves the clinging to a fixed mode of behavior. Newer habits are resisted in spite of their greater effectiveness or efficiency. When fixation occurs during the years of growth it means that arrested development has taken place preventing the individual from achieving a higher level of maturity and adjustment. Curiously enough, fixation is encouraged by either positive or negative experiences. In the case of overindulgence during some phase of childhood, the future seems less attractive than the present state of bliss. In the cause of excessive anxiety or trauma, the child appears to be too fearful to change and stereotype seems to set in. In most people, fixations in development are ultimately overcome and the maturational process proceeds. However, they may remain as "sore spots" which the individual continues to relive and suffer through or which strongly influence his approach to circumstances reminiscent of his childhood. When regression takes place, it is believed that the regression is to some point of fixation.

THE SELF-CONCEPT

One of the most significant traits differentiating man from lower creatures is his capacity for self-consciousness. Man and animal alike can respond to the outside environment and to others, but the human is particularly capable of also being able to respond to himself. This self-awareness is, in fact, the fundamental source of identity. The answers to the questions "Who are you?" or "What are you?" or even the more philosophical "Why are you?" are found in the grasp of self-identity. In psychological terms, this identity involves the *self-concept*. The self-concept may be viewed as:

> The unifying core of each individual's personality, providing for the mean-

ing and organization that we see. People are more than fragmented sets of needs, or defensive structures.

That aspect of personality which provides a sense of continuity and consistency through time and across events. Time may pass, and things may change but each person retains his own special sense of stability. We may enter into a kaleidoscope of experiences which buffet us from stress to stress, which fling us from challenge to challenge, and which strain our gamut of emotions, yet each of us can still retain that individualized feeling of "I"—"I lived through it all," "I had the particular experience" "I . . . enjoyed . . . feared . . . loved . . . was embarassed . . . couldn't believe . . . ."

That constellation of self-referents that is experienced as "I" and "me" and is distinguished from all that is "not-me." The self-concept involves the perception of oneself as object and includes all self-assigned attributes as well as values attached to such attributes. For example, the self-concept may include the trait "I am intelligent" as well as the evaluation of that trait "It is good to be intelligent" or "Being capable of intelligent behavior is a satisfying experience." One way of determining what traits form each of our own self-concepts is to raise the question of control— those attributes which we accept as part of our self-concept are also those over which we feel a sense of control. A person with a self-concept of assertiveness will accept responsibility for his own aggressive behaviors. A person whose self-concept excludes assertiveness, and who still shows such behavior, will deny responsibility for the actions by saying, "I apologize, that was not like me" or "I can't possibly imagine *what made me* be-

have as I did." Occasionally, we are actually able to experience ourselves behaving in a manner beyond our control, for example, during half-awake states or during alcoholic intoxication. These uncontrolled actions are always perceived as a strange event.

The Development of the Self-Concept

We are not born with a ready-made self-concept. Nor is the complete self-concept developed soon in life. The self-concept is a perception, self-perception. During the first month or two after birth, the only perceptions that are present are primitive and vague sensations. Internal sensations are not differentiated from externally caused sensations. The world of consciousness is but a "big, blooming, buzzing confusion" (James, 1890). Gradually, as the infant matures, he begins to develop an awareness of his body as distinguished from all else. No doubt primitive pleasure and pain contribute to this recognition. Perhaps thumb-sucking is experienced as satisfying while sucking on the crib bars is not. An accidental bodily injury is painful and draws attention to the pained member of the body. Physical self-exploration soon occupies the infant's time and he may be seen intensely engrossed in staring at his own fingers or hand.

Another stage in the development of self-awareness is the evolving of other-awareness. The gross distinction between "me" and "not-me" is involved in the infant's growing capacity to respond to others in the environment. At about the age of three months, the presence of another person in the visual field of the infant will produce a smiling response. This responsiveness to others does not mean that the infant identifies others any more than it means that a well-formed self-concept has developed. In fact, such smiling is indiscriminately elicited by any figure and will be limited to familiar figures only after age six months. However, part of acquiring a self-concept is separating the self as an object from others as objects, that is, "me" from "not-me."

Throughout the first year of life, with greater maturation and increased contact with the environment, the infant develops more and more self-awareness (Ames, 1952; Gesell and Ilg, 1949). The parents' actions and evaluations provide much of the foundation for the self-concept. The regular and consistent use of a name enhances the process of self-awareness. In addition, parents help to convey an image by expressing their feelings: "You are a good boy," "My, aren't you strong," "That wasn't nice, naughty boy." As is characteristic of the infant's present level of maturity, the self-perceptions are overgeneralized and broad. He may have accepted the parental appraisal and conceive of himself as a "good-me" or a "bad-me." With a warm, secure family environment he may perceive himself as loved and worthy of love. Parental rejection, on the other hand, may arouse negative self-conceptions. Parents who reproach, scorn, or humiliate convey an appraisal of worthlessness, inadequacy, incompetency, "badness." Overprotection, indulgence, and excessive devotion may lead to a sense of self-importance or possibly of fearfulness and the need to be protected.

Continuous change and shaping occurs with further growth and learning. By the second year of life, sufficient stability has evolved such that the child can now exert his identity against others. The age of negativism seems an example of self-expression. Two year olds appear to resist for the sake of resisting. It is as if they are fully aware of their own existence as separate individuals and are now taking the opportunity to exhibit this awareness. However, even this phase of self-development is subject to further modification. Social contacts soon begin as the child encounters other children either as playmates or in the form of a newly arrived sibling. Interactions with peers invariably lead to self-other comparisons. These may again focus on physical differences—who can run the fastest, who can jump the furthest, who is the tallest, who is the strongest? The child's self-concept will be enhanced if he is compared with peers less able than himself and downgraded if he continues to compete and compare with more able playmates.

From late childhood on, the basic elements of the self-concept remain fairly distinct and stable. With further growth, greater stability develops and the person becomes more and more resistent to changes in his self-perceptions. However, changes can occur. Mild stress has little effect in changing the self-concept (Suinn and Geiger, 1965), but more severe pressures can yield changes. The conflicts that multiply during adolescence, stemming from physiological changes and parental-peer relations, create conditions for renewal of self-consciousness and evaluation. Intense new experiences demanding participation and involvement may also provoke changes, for example, the soul-searching of the business executive who is confronted with making a major decision affecting his own life and the lives of others; the worker faced with the issue of whether to seek further education for higher income or to remain in a secure career with a limited future; the student encountering failure in his first major academic challenge; the adolescent suffering from being smitten with the love of a seemingly inaccessible person. Anxieties influence of the self-concept by making the individual more susceptible to lowering his self-evaluation (Suinn and Hill, 1964; Doris and Sarason, 1955).

Self-Consistency

As the self-concept is formed and gradually stabilized, a simultaneous development is the need for consistency. This motive may be no more than another branch of the desire for consistency in perceptions generally. We tend to search for confirmation of our sensory and perceptual experiences. We hear the sound of an airplane and immediately scan the skies for visual confirmation. We often fail to see misprints because they do not seem to fit what we expect to see (see Figure 8-6). We witness a scene in which there is a discrepant element, and sometimes distort our memories in our attempts to resolve the discrepancy. In a similar fashion, once self-perceptions are developed, we tend to seek a certain consistency of other perceptions that are related to our self-concepts. If we are provided with information about ourselves that is consistent with our self-concepts, these are readily accepted. On the other hand, information that is inconsistent is not easily tolerated and may be denied or distorted. This holds true for even positive information. How many individuals do we all know who show all the signs of competency and yet refuse to believe that they are anything more than a failure in life? A typical theme is exemplified by the young graduate student whose academic achievements were the envy of his struggling peers; yet he withdrew from school at the end of the term because he felt he was doing so poorly. Self-consistency is a powerful agent; it can militate against changes in the self-concept through new insights if these insights are inconsistent with the established self-image. Suinn, Osborne, and Winfree (1962) had students describe their self-concepts by rating themselves on a list of traits. They were also asked to describe those students seated next to them in class. Five days later, each person was presented with a completed rating said to represent the composite of the ratings by others of him. In actuality, the rating represented descriptions that were systematically inconsistent to varying degrees from the individual's self-concept. Two days later, the students were asked to recall the data indicating how they appeared to others. The results clearly indicated that ratings that agreed with the individual's own self-concept were accepted and recalled more accurately than descriptions that were inconsistent. Moreover, the greater the degree of inconsistency, the less the subjects were able to recall the information accurately. And this held true regardless of whether the descriptions were more *or* less positive than the student's own self-description.

In effect, the rule of self-consistency allows for a certain degree of security in the face of change. As the child grows and faces an increasingly varied set of experiences, he can at least find comfort in sorting out those experiences consistent with and thus confirming his self-concept. This stability offers a reliable and constant reference point in the variegated world. However, the pressure for self-consistency can also prevent the individual from significant self-insightful experiences. As indicated earlier, an adult faced with information about himself which is inconsistent with his self-concept will resist this insight. This is especially true of the neurotic and is part of what is meant when

Figure 8-6. **Illustration of how expectations influence perception: What do the triangles say?**

it is said that the neurotic does not learn from experience. A more flexible person accepts the new fact about himself and uses it as a guide in the future. He is open to learning more about himself and thereby develops a more realistic self-appraisal based not only on his own views but those of others. The neurotic continues to base his adjustment on perceptions that are rigid, inaccurate, and unrealistic. He is more concerned with protecting his current self-concept than in being open to experience. Because his self-perception and self-appraisals are themselves incomplete or inaccurate, his decisions and actions based on his self-image also suffer. In the severest form, inconsistent self-traits are denied even though they may exert significant effects on behavior. Cases of multiple personality as exemplified in "the three faces of Eve" are dramatic instances of such extreme denial (Thigpen and Cleckley, 1957). Eve White perceived herself as a well-behaved, inhibited, quiet girl and could not accept her sexual, flirtatious, sociable side. Consequently, the denied self split off into a separate personality in which such traits were more consistent with the self-image and therefore expressable.

Self-Esteem

Self-esteem, positive regard for oneself, the capacity for self-acceptance is an important aspect for adjustment. Associated with self-esteem are self-reliance, feelings of confidence, a sense of competency, nondefensive behavior, an openness to experience, self-respect, and a capacity to live with oneself with tranquility. Interpersonal satisfactions are enhanced when self-esteem exists. Studies have shown that the ability to be accepting of other people in general is significantly influenced by the degree of self-acceptance (Berger, 1952; Omwake, 1954; Scheerer, 1949). In addition, self-regard also enables a person to feel satisfied with those specific people with

whom he interacts. For example, Suinn (1961) demonstrated that high school boys with high self-regard also tended to react favorably toward their parents and their teachers while those with low self-regard tended to express dissatisfaction with others. In a preliminary study, there was also some evidence that self-acceptance also influenced acceptance of spouse and even satisfaction with one's home town (Suinn, 1959)! It also appears that self-regard is influential in shaping prejudicial attitudes. For example, high anti-Semitism scores have been found in Jewish college students with low self-regard (Sarnoff, 1951). Low self-acceptance has also been reported to be associated with ethnocentrism (the acceptance of the ingroup and the rejection of the outgroups) and authoritarianism (the biased rejection of certain groups—intellectuals, nonconformists, homosexuals—along with the acceptance of certain other groups—patriots, parents, etc.) (Brodbeck and Perlmutter, 1954; Pearl, 1954).

Level of self-esteem has quite naturally been examined as an index of maladjustment. A common feature of neurotics is the low regard which they have for themselves. Typically, their evaluations of themselves are distorted in the direction toward the low or self-derogatory end. The neurotic feels incompetent and discontent with his achievements, and generally quite self-critical. On the other hand the psychotic appears to have distorted his self-perception in the opposite, although equally unrealistic, direction (Leary, 1957; Rogers and Dymond, 1954; Sarbin and Rosenburg, 1955). Friedman (1955), for example, discovered that although neurotics showed little satisfaction with themselves, schizophrenics appeared to be quite content. It seems that psychotic patients are so out of touch with reality and so threatened by what they might see in themselves that they twist their self-appraisals. Of particular interest are the results of psychotherapy on the self-concept and self-esteem of maladjusted persons. A variety of studies indicate that counseling leads to:

Increased accuracy of self-appraisal (Berdie, 1954).

Decreased attempts to distort inconsistent self-concept information and an increased self-awareness (Haigh, 1949; Vargas, 1954).

Increased self-esteem in the successfully treated clients (but continued self-disapproval and ambivalence in the unsuccessfully treated clients) (Raimy, 1948).

Such results support the belief that psychotherapy aids the individual in enlarging his scope of personal experience. By reducing the need for defenses to protect what little self-esteem is left, counseling enables the person to fully know himself through nondefensive self-exploration. Although self-knowledge or insight is by no means the sole effector of therapeutic change (as we shall see in later discussion of behavior therapy), it is an extremely important facet of adjustment.

Glossary

Age regression: Return to traits and behaviors characteristic of an earlier age.

Anxiety: Reaction to threat characterized by feelings of apprehension.

Authoritarianism: The biased rejection of outgroups along with the attitude of superiority of certain ingroups.

Conflict: The presence of antagonistic needs or goals forcing the individual to make a choice.

Defense mechanisms: Also called security mechanisms. Behaviors for coping with threats to the personality.

Denial: A defense mechanism involving refusal to accept the existence of a threat.

Displaced aggression: The directing of aggression away from the appropriate object and toward a substitute one.

Displacement: A defense mechanism involving substitution of one object in place of the more appropriate one.

Dissonance: The presence of mutually incompatible cognitions.

Ethnocentrism: The tendency to exhalt the group to which one belongs and to evaluate other groups as lower.

Frustration: The result of blocking of ongoing goal-directed activity.

Galvanic skin response: A measure of electrical conductivity over the skin. Used as a measure of emotional response.

Goal: The end result of motivated behavior.

Identification: A defense mechanism involving an attempt to become exactly the same as another person.

Instrumental act regression: Return to earlier, less mature methods for achieving goals.

Isolation: A defense mechanism involving compartmentalizing life experiences.

Maturation: The normal process of growth and development involving changes not attributable to learning.

Need: Forces that motivate man.

Need regression: The reversion to earlier, less mature needs.

Object regression: The reversion to a goal held at an earlier, less mature stage of the person's development.

Partial reinforcement: The intermittent presentation of a reward when the correct responses occur.

Perceptual defense: The protection from anxiety through the dulling of awareness to threatening cues.

Perceptual vigilance: The heightened sensitivity to need-related cues.

Projection: A defense mechanism involving the repression of a trait along with the accusation that others possess the trait instead.

Rationalization: A defense mechanism involving the use of unrealistic logic to justify an action when the act was really caused by other factors.

Reaction formation: A defense mechanism involving the repression of a trait which one possesses and the demonstration of the opposite trait in its extreme.

Regular reinforcement: The occurrence of a reward consistently after the correct response is given.

Repression: A defense mechanism involving the removal of a threatening thought or feeling from awareness.

Self-concept: That aspect of the personality which is associated with the terms "I" and "me."

Socialization: The process of acquiring behaviors characteristic of the culture one lives in.

State anxiety: A transitory experience of threat and apprehension.

Subception: Also called subliminal perception. The phenomenon whereby a person reacts to a cue in the environment even though it is presented below sensory threshold.

Sublimation: A defense mechanism involving the modification of a motive into a more socially acceptable one.

Suppression: A defense mechanism involving the conscious prevention of an impulse from expression.

Trait anxiety: The continued presence of an anxiety condition so that the anxiety becomes a characteristic of the individual's personality.

Unconscious motivation: The Freudian premise that motives can affect a person's actions without his being aware of the motives.

Zeigarnik effect: The phenomenon of memory involving recall of incomplete tasks to a greater degree than completed tasks.

References

Ames, L. The sense of self of nursery school children as manifested by their verbal behavior. *J. genet. Psychol.*, 1952, **81**, 193.

Baker, L. The pupillary response conditioned to subliminal auditory stimuli. *Psychol. Monogr.*, 1938, **50**, No. 3.

Berdie, R. Changes in self-ratings as a method of evaluating counseling. *J. counsel. Psychol.*, 1954, **1**, 49.

Berger, E. The relation between expressed acceptance of self and expressed acceptance of others. *J. abnorm. soc. Psychol.*, 1952, **47**, 778.

Bevan, W. Subliminal stimulation: A pervasive problem for psychology. *Psychol. Bull.*, 1964, **61**, 81.

Bindra, D., Patterson, A., & Strzelecki, J. On the relation between anxiety and conditioning. *Canad. J. Psychol.*, 1955, **9**, 1.

Brehm, J. Attitudinal consequences of committment to unpleasant behavior. *J. abnorm. soc. Psychol.*, 1960, **60**, 379.

Brehm, J. & Cohen, A. *Explorations in cognitive dissonance.* New York: John Wiley, 1962.

Brodbeck, A. & Perlmutter, H. Self-dislike as a determinant of marked ingroup-outgroup preferences. *J. Psychol.*, 1954, **38**, 271.

Brown, W. Conceptions of perceptual defense. *Brit. J. Psychol.*, 1961, Mongr. Suppl. No. 35.

Cannon, W. *The wisdom of the body.* (Rev. ed.) New York: Norton, 1939.

Cattell, R. Anxiety and motivation: theory and crucial experiments, in C. Spielberger, (Ed.) Anxiety and Behavior. New York: Academic Press, 1966.

Crowne, D. & Marlowe, D. The approval motive. New York: John Wiley, 1964.

Denny, J. The effects of anxiety and intelligence on concept formation. Dissert. Abstr., 1963, **24**, 2132. Duke University Dissertation.

Diven, K. Certain determinants in the conditioning of anxiety reactions. *J. Psychol.*, 1937, **3**, 291.

Doris, J. & Sarason, S. Test anxiety and blame assignment failure situation. *J. abnorm. soc. Psychol.*, 1955, **50**, 335.

Erickson, M. Experimental demonstrations of the psychopathology of everyday life. *Psychoanal. Quart.*, 1939, **8**, 338.

Eriksen, C. Some implications for TAT interpretation arising from need and perception experiments. *J. Person.*, 1951, **19**, 282.

Eriksen, C. Discrimination and learning without awareness. A methodological survey and evaluation. *Psychol. Rev.*, 1960, **67**, 279.

Eriksen, C. & Wechsler, H. Some effects of experimentally induced anxiety upon discrimination behavior. *J. abnorm. soc. Psychol.,* 1955, **51,** 458.

Farber, I. & Spence, K. Complex learning and conditioning as a function of anxiety. *J. exp. Psychol.,* 1953, **45,** 120.

Festinger, L. *A theory of cognitive dissonance.* Stanford: Stanford University Press, 1957.

French, E. & Thomas, F. The relation of achievement motivation to problem solving effectiveness. *J. abnorm. soc. Psychol.,* 1958, **56,** 45.

Freud, S. *The psychopathology of every life.* New York: Macmillan, 1914.

Freud, S. *The problem of anxiety.* New York: Norton, 1936.

Freud, S. *Leonardo Da Vinci: a study in psychosexuality.* New York: Random House, 1947. (First German edition, 1910.)

Freud, S. *The interpretation of dreams.* New York: Basic Books, 1956. (First German edition, 1900.)

Friedman, I. Phenomenal, ideal and projected conceptions of self. *J. abnorm soc. Psychol.,* 1955, **51,** 611.

Gesell, A. & Ilg, F. *Child development.* New York: Harper, 1949.

Gynther, R. The effects of anxiety and of situational stress on communicative efficiency. *J. abnorm. soc. Psychol.,* 1957, **54,** 274.

Haigh, G. Defensive behavior in client-centered therapy. *J. consult. Psychol.,* 1949, **13,** 181.

Hamilton, G. A study of perseverance reactions in primates and rodents. *Behavior Monogr.,* 1916, **3,** No. 13.

Hovland, C. & Sears, R. Minor studies of aggression: VI. Correlations of lynchings with economic indices. *J. Psychol.,* 1940, **9,** 301.

James, W. *Principles of psychology.* New York: Holt, Rinehart, & Winston, 1890.

Kasl, S. & Mahl, G. The relationship of disturbances and hesitations in spontaneous speech to anxiety. *J. pers. soc. Psychol.,* 1965, **1,** 425.

Krasner, L. Studies of the conditioning of verbal behavior. *Psychol. Bull.,* 1958, **55,** 148.

Leary, T. *Interpersonal diagnosis of personality.* New York: Ronald Press, 1957.

Mann, N. An apparatus for testing visual discrimination in animals. *J. gen. Psychol.,* 1931, **39,** 342.

Masserman, J. *Principles of dynamic psychiatry.* (2nd ed.) Philadelphia: Saunders, 1961.

McClelland, D., Atkinson, J., Clark, R., & Lowell, E. *The achievement motive.* New York: Appleton-Century-Croft, 1953.

McClelland, D. & Liberman, A. The need for achievement in recognition of need-related words. *J. Person.,* 1949, **18,** 236.

Miller, N. & Bugelski, R. Minor studies of aggression: II. The influence of frustrations imposed by the in-group on attitudes expressed toward out-groups. *J. Psychol.,* 1948, **25,** 437.

Montague, E. The role of anxiety in serial rote learning. *J. exp. Psychol.,* 1953, **45,** 91.

Mowrer, O. Anxiety-reduction and learning. *J. exp. Psychol.,* 1940, **27,** 497.

Munn, N. An apparatus for testing visual discrimination in animals. *J. genet. Psychol.,* 1931, **39,** 342.

Omwake, K. The relation between acceptance of self and acceptance of others shown by three personality inventories. *J. consult. Psychol.,* 1954, **18,** 443.

Patrick, J. Studies in rational behavior and emotional excitement. I: Rational behavior in human subjects. *J. comp. Psychol.,* 1934, **18,** 1. (a)

Patrick, J. Studies in rational behavior and emotional excitement. II: The effect of emotional excitement on rational behavior in human subjects. *J. comp. Psychol.,* 1934, **18,** 153. (b)

Pearl, D. Ethnocentrism and the self-concept. *J. soc. Psychol.,* 1954, **40,** 138.

Prasad, J. A comparative study of rumours and reports on earthquakes. *Brit. J. Psychol.,* 1950, 41, 129.

Raimy, V. Self-reference in counseling interviews. *J. consult. Psychol.,* 1948, 12, 153.

Rogers, C. & Dymond, R. (Eds.) *Psychotherapy and personality change.* Chicago: University of Chicago Press, 1954.

Ruebush, G. Interfering and facilitating effects of test anxiety. *J. abnorm. soc. Psychol.,* 1960, 60, 205.

Sarason, I. Test anxiety, general anxiety and intellectual performance. *J. consult. Psychol.,* 1957, 21, 485.

Sarbin, T. & Rosenburg, B. Contributions to role-taking theory: IV. A method for obtaining a qualitative estimate of the self. *J. soc. Psychol.,* 1955, 42, 71.

Sarnoff, I. Identification with the agressor: some personality correlates of anti-Semitism among Jews. *J. Person.,* 1951, 20, 199.

Scheerer, E. An analysis of the relationship between acceptance of and respect for self and acceptance of and respect for others in ten counseling cases. *J. consult. Psychol.,* 1949, 13, 169.

Sears, R., Maccoby, E., and Levin, H. *Patterns of child rearing.* New York: Harper and Row, 1957.

Siegman, A. The effect of manifest anxiety on a concept formation task, a nondirected learning task, and on timed and untimed intelligence tests. *J. consult. Psychol.,* 1956, 20, 176.

Smith, E. The power of dissonance techniques to change attitudes. *Public Opinion Quart.,* 1961, 25, 626.

Spence, J. & Spence, K. The motivational components of manifest anxiety: drive and drive stimuli. In C. Spielberger (Ed.), *Anxiety and behavior.* New York: Academic Press, 1966.

Spence, K., Farber, I., & McFann, H. The relation of anxiety (drive) level to performance in competitional and noncompetitional learning. *J. exp. Psychol.,* 1956, 52, 296.

Spielberger, C. Theory and research on anxiety. In C. Spielberger (Ed.), *Anxiety and behavior.* New York: Academic Press, 1966.

Stagner, R. *Psychology of personality.* New York: McGraw-Hill, 1961.

Suinn, R. Self-acceptance and acceptance of spouse and home town. Unpub. manus., 1959.

Suinn, R. Self-acceptance and acceptance of others: a learning theory analysis. *J. abnorm. soc. Psychol.,* 1961, 63, 37.

Suinn, R. Anxiety and cognitive dissonance. *J. gen. Psychol.,* 1965, 73, 113. (a)

Suinn, R. Anxiety and intellectual performance: a partial failure to replicate. *J. consult. Psychol.,* 1965, 29, 81. (b)

Suinn, R. Susceptibility to anxieties: a generalized trait. *J. gen. Psychol.,* 1965, 73, 317. (c)

Suinn, R. A factor modifying the concept of anxiety as a drive. *J. gen. Psychol.,* 1965, 73, 43. (d)

Suinn, R. Types of work motivation. *Rehab. Counsel. Bull.,* 1966, 9, 102. (a)

Suinn, R. The disarmament fantasy: psychological factors that may produce warfare. *J. human Relat.,* 1966, 15, 36. (b)

Suinn, R. Anxiety and color dreaming. *Mental Hygiene,* 1967, 51, 27. (a)

Suinn, R. Psychological reactions to physical disability. *J. assoc. phys. ment. Rehab.,* 1967, 21, 13. (b)

Suinn, R. Anxiety as a drive: recall of perceptually appropriate and inappropriate items. *J. genet. Psychol.,* 1967, 110, 45. (c)

Suinn, R. & Geiger, J. Stress and the stability of self and other attitudes. *J. gen. Psychol.,* 1965, 73, 172.

Suinn, R. & Hill, H. The influence of anxiety on the relationship between self-acceptance and acceptance of others. *J. consult. Psychol.*, 1964, **28**, 116.

Suinn, R., Osborne, D., & Winfree, P. The self-concept and accuracy of recall of inconsistent self-related information. *J. clin. Psychol.*, 1962, **18**, 463.

Taylor, J. & Spence, K. The relationship of anxiety level to performance in serial learning. *J. exp. Psychol.*, 1958, **57**, 55.

Thigpen, O. & Cleckley, H. *The three faces of Eve.* New York: McGraw Hill, 1957.

Vargas, M. Changes in self-awareness during client-centered therapy. In C. Rogers, and R. Dymond (Eds.), *Psychotherapy and personality change.* Chicago: University Chicago Press, 1954.

Whiting, J. & Child, I. *Child training and personality.* New Haven: Yale University Press, 1953.

Wright, H. The influence of barriers upon the strength of motivation. *Contrib. psychol. Theory*, 1937, **1**, no. 3.

Zeigarnik, B. Affektpsychologie Untersuchungen zur Handlungs- und Affektpsychologie Behalten erledigter und unerledigter Handlungen. *Psychol. Forsch.*, 1927, **9**, 1.

9 *The Psychoneurotic Disorders*

Psychoneurotic disorders are emotional disturbances in which certain fixed symptoms are used to cope with anxiety and conflict. The neurosis essentially represents defense mechanisms that are being overly relied upon in efforts to avoid rather than directly deal with life's difficulties. In a few conditions, the syndrome represents an inability of the defensive structure to handle the stresses, as in anxiety states and traumatic neuroses.

Neurotic conditions are less severe than the psychotic states. In comparison with the psychotic, the neurotic is capable of at least a fair social, interpersonal, and work adjustment. A certain amount of self-insight is present in that the neurotic still has partial capacity to evaluate himself and his suffering. In fact, the psychoneurotic patient is quite aware of feelings of tension, anxiety, concern, and dissatisfaction, although he may not be able to understand the exact nature of his problems. Whereas the psychotic is characterized by gross distortions and misperceptions, the neurotic is much more able to differentiate between fact and fantasy. The emotional experiences of the psychotic patient may be extreme, completely absent, or constricted, while the neurotic patient is still capable of a more normal diversity and intensity of feeling. Psychoneuroses are by far more prevalent forms of disease than psychoses. In addition, since the neurotic conditions are relatively milder, the majority of cases are seen and treated outside of psychiatric hospitals.

Among the types of psychoneurotic disorders to be discussed are the following:

1. Traumatic neurosis: the neurosis precipitated by the experience of extreme stress or catastrophe.

2. Anxiety reaction: the neurosis characterized by marked apprehension and feelings of imminent danger.

3. Hypochondriasis: the neurosis involving excessive preoccupation with the body and its functioning with a stress on the state of health.

4. Conversion reaction (Hysteria): the neurosis in which organic symptoms are manifested without the presence of any identifiable physical basis.

5. Dissociative reaction: the neurosis characterized by disturbances of consciousness and memory.

6. Phobia: the neurosis involving the persistence of excessive, irrational fears.

7. Obsessive-compulsive neurosis: the neurosis in which unwanted intrusive thoughts or actions must be repeated.

8. Reactive depression: the neurosis precipitated by an unhappy life experience leading to despondency.

TRAUMATIC NEUROSIS

A traumatic neurosis is a psychological reaction to severe external stress and is sometimes referred to as a *gross stress reaction.* Included are the traumatic neuroses of war or *combat reactions,* and *civilian catastrophic reactions.* Each person has a breaking point if faced with persistent, severe stress. The amount of trauma that can be tolerated is determined by the current psychological health of the individual, his self-esteem, the relevance of the type of stress to his conflict areas, the adequacy of his psychological defenses, and his physical well-being. Civilian reactions derive from the sudden occurrence of disaster which forces the normal person to call upon his every resource to avoid being overwhelmed. The startling involvement in a major automobile accident after an evening of gaiety, the stark information that a severe financial reversal has completely wiped out one's life savings, the disgrace and permanent loss of position in a hard-earned career due to a moment's indiscretion, are all examples of circumstances that can precipitate a traumatic neurosis. World War I and World War II were responsible for testing the psychological strength of vast numbers of soldiers. Entering the battlefield with high morale, excellent physical health, confidence in his weapons and his comrades, and a belief in his own invulnerability, the military man was soon faced with inhuman stresses. The world of combat is a world of persistent threat to security, intolerable suspense, a nightmare of never-ending fatigue and inescapable turmoil of waiting and wondering and wishing. All are threatened by the dangers to their lives, many are disturbed by doubts over their ability to be effective in the eyes of their comrades.

Whether the trauma originates from military or civilian circumstances, the symptoms of traumatic neuroses are similar. The early symptoms announcing a person's approach to a breaking point include:

poor appetite
inability to relax
oversensitivity to sudden noise
difficulty in falling asleep
either recklessness or extreme
    timidity

If these symptoms are not attended to and treatment prescribed, the traumatic neurosis develops into a chronic, or more permanent stage. In this phase, the individual exhibits:

irritability, especially to sounds
repetitive dreams of catastrophe
diminution of interest in the world
reduction of overall efficiency
interference with intellectual activity
explosive aggressive behavior along
    with loss of memory of the violence

In addition to the above symptoms, individual patients may exhibit further elaborations on their symptoms. In some instances a symbolic action is adopted, for example, sleeping with the hands thrown protectively over the head—a posture symbolizing the wartime act of "taking cover." In others, the main symptoms are violent physiological and somatic changes such as fast pulse rate (tachycardia), involuntary muscle spasms, twitches, and tremors. In World War I, a considerable number of cases involved epilepticlike seizures, or repetitions of battle scenes. These were sometimes triggered off by something in the environment which served as a reminder of the war trauma.

Dynamics

In everyday life individuals gradually develop an adjustment to their life conditions. Certain defenses are erected to

Traumatic neuroses include combat reactions in which mental illness erupts after prolonged exposure to stress. Such reactions can result from the trauma of war, for example, the soldier under fire in Vietnam. (DPI)

cope with recurring internal or external frustrations and conflicts. The individual acquires specific strengths as a means of adapting to his needs in his given surroundings. He soon learns to expect certain demands and stresses and is ready to exert a certain amount of effort. In the traumatic neurosis, the world of expectations collapses. The surroundings are drastically altered, the nature and intensity of stresses are suddenly changed, the skills needed are no longer the same. Perhaps adaptation could still take place if more time were allowed for the individual to prepare new defenses or skills provided he knew what to prepare for, or if the stresses were not so intense and persistent, or if recuperative periods away from the stresses and memories of the trauma were possible. But this does not happen and the individual must make do with what he has.

The stages of the traumatic neurosis appear to be similar to the phases of biological reaction to stress described by Selye (1953, 1956). This University of Montreal medical scientist suggested that prolonged stress to the body, from trauma, infections, emotional upheaval, or other such factors, can result in specific bodily reactions leading to a condition he calls the *general adaptation syndrome*. During such excessive stress, the body mobilizes its resources

in an "alarm-reaction" phase, whereby physiological defenses are alerted and called into action. Metabolic changes occur including the increased production of hormones, the activation of the adrenal cortex, blood changes, and gastrointestinal alterations. As the stress is prolonged, excessive hormonal secretions become not only useless but actually lead to damage or pathological changes affecting the brain or other organs. The second phase of the general adaptation syndrome is the "stage of resistance," characterized by the development of a specific resistance to the particular stress that is occurring and a lack of responsiveness to other stimuli. The "stage of exhaustion" is the final phase and results from the organism's exhausting its adaptive resources in dealing with the original stress. The organism is no longer able to resist as defenses are stripped away, leaving the person vulnerable. Of interest is Selye's position that the tissue and organ damage which can result from this syndrome may be irreversible. Such pathological changes within the body may also develop when relatively mild stress is presented over a long period, forcing the individual to continuously cope with the stressful conditions. In essence, constant exposure to a high pressure life can be responsible for insidious pathological dam-

Traumatic neuroses may involve civilian catastrophic reactions, such as a neurotic breakdown caused by the stress of a natural catastrophe. The massive destruction from the San Francisco earthquake of 1906 (*right*) strained the psychological resources of many residents. (Sy Seidman/Photo Trends)

age to the body and its normal functioning. The earlier phase of the traumatic neurosis is somewhat akin to the alarm-reaction. As will be recalled, the soldier is tense, alert, and ready to react to danger. The inability to relax or sleep reflects the watchful guarding against imminent danger. The sensitivity to sounds and other strong stimuli would be considered an adaptive keeping-alert were it not so pronounced a reaction. The chronic phase of the traumatic neurosis has much in common with the stage of exhaustion. In fact, the phenomenon of fatigue or physical exhaustion shows many similarities to the traumatic neurosis. In fatigue there is marked irritability, lowering of intellectual efficiency, loss of interest, and outbursts of temper. Of course, it must be remembered that the symptoms of traumatic neurosis are not solely due to physical strain and exhaustion. The more critical component is the psychological. In this new catastrophic world, the individual finds himself incapable, ineffective, overwhelmed. The surroundings have been transformed from a safe, secure, comfortable situation to a threatening, tension-provoking, disturbing condition. The most immediate reaction is flight, but avoidance is made quite impossible to achieve. In combat settings, the individual is faced

with the added demand of maintaining his self-esteem by being a "good soldier" and not letting his comrades down. Battle conditions may force into the open weaknesses which the individual had previously denied as part of his self-concept. Possibly the most serious psychological variable is the inability to depend upon previous modes of adjusting. The trauma is so unique in its severity, persistence, or form that the individual finds himself ill-equipped to produce a ready solution. All of the effective channels of action he is familiar with prove no longer reliable or appropriate. Under such circumstances, the person becomes psychologically vulnerable and subject to the symptoms of traumatic neurosis.

Treatment

The most significant factor in the treatment of this syndrome is time. If the patient has been left alone long enough to consolidate his symptoms, it is extremely difficult to change. The patient stops trying to adapt to the stresses, reduces his efforts, and begins to live a parasitic life depending upon others for care. In the early phase of the illness, treatment is directed toward preventing the patient from seeking refuge in escape. In the combat zone, the soldier is encouraged to re-

Case History 9-1

COMBAT REACTION

After a particularly heavy series of continuous mortar attack, a 19-year-old soldier was found wandering around in a daze, trembling, and muttering to himself. He seemed oblivious to the real dangers that still existed around him. Attempts by field hospital physicians to communicate with him met with failure as it seemed that he did not hear their inquiries. Yet, he was unusually responsive to very slight noises such as the crinkling of a pack of cigarettes. He was transferred to a psychiatric ward because of unpredictable outbursts of aggressive behavior during which he attacked others, destroyed furniture, and ripped his clothing. He was subject to extreme nightmares during which he shouted incoherently and thrashed about in his bed. Upon awakening he was again mute and apparently amnesic for the evening's dream. Under hypnosis the following was reported:

We were told to hold the line at all costs. The days were bad enough but the nights were worse—you couldn't see anything or anyone . . . I kept thinking I heard someone creeping up on me. Pretty soon I had to close my eyes and bite my lips to stop from panicking. I wanted to give up, to go home, to hide somewhere. I couldn't take it anymore. And then they started bombarding us. It just went on and on and on. The noise was so loud I thought my head would explode inside. I saw someone tossed into the air like a rag doll . . . and his arm. . . .

After nine months of active hypnotic therapy, the patient was eventually discharged. He was able to return to his prewar occupation as a service station attendant. However, his dream-life was still troublesome although no longer nightmarish. Stammering was a noticeable residual symptom. He was encouraged to continue in out-patient therapy to further root out the effects of the trauma.

---

main with his unit in a less strenuous role and with sedatives for sleep at night. Reassurance that he has not reached the point of complete breakdown permits the soldier to accept his fear and exhaustion. Another helpful form of treatment is hypnosis. Hypnotic recall is used as a means of preventing the retreat from trauma through repression. A protective reconstruction through hypnosis or even direct conscious recall enables the patient to take an active hand in coping with the traumatic events. Such early handling of traumatic neuroses leads to an optimistic outlook for recovery. Of course, in cases where the patient was already predisposed to a mental breakdown under any circumstances, long-term treatment is likely.

ANXIETY REACTION

The anxiety reaction ranks among the most disturbing of psychoneurotic conditions. It is an illness characterized by the presence of:

sweating
diarrhea
uneasiness
apprehension

An *anxiety attack* can occur suddenly and build up to a severe pitch, involving a sense of imminent danger, loss of self-control, going to pieces psychologically, and heightened tension. (Hoffmann La Roche)

breathlessness
anticipation of imminent danger
feelings of loss of self-control
palpitations of the heart
muscular tremblings and tremors
tightness of the chest

Subjectively it is a terrifying experience. The normal person can glimpse a little of the nature of the experience during normal instances of anxiety. Sometime in our lives, we are all confronted with situations that arouse this state—a critical school examination, the crucial employment interview, the test of one's athletic competence in competition, the encounter with the unfamiliar or the unknown. The severity of the symptoms of anxiety neurosis varies from individual to individual. In some instances the state is mild, in others, the anxiety builds into such an intense state as to be rightfully labeled as *panic*. For some patients the experi- ence is an omnipresent condition afflicting them throughout the day and night. For others the symptoms disappear for long periods only to suddenly overtake and engulf them with what has been called an *anxiety attack*. Attacks may last as short as a few minutes or be prolonged for weeks or months.

Dynamics

As will be recalled from the previous chapter, anxiety is a normal response signaling the approach of danger. As such, the response of anxiety itself is not abnormal. However, the persistent cueing of anxiety in the absence of true danger is abnormal. Once anxiety is cued, the body prepares itself for the impending threat. The subjective feelings and the physiological changes that occur in anxiety states are quite understandable as preparatory maneuvers for fight or flight. Indeed, the

227

same types of changes can be produced through the arousal of objectively based fear. In anxiety neurosis the individual is clearly prepared, but for what—for a threat that never materializes, disapproval that never appears, punishment that never occurs, rejection that never transpires. This unrealistic and inappropriate state of anxiety may derive from several sources:

1. Acquisition of parental pattern: A famous American psychiatrist, Harry Stack Sullivan (1953) pointed out that parents transmit their feelings of anxiety to even very young infants. A mother who is tense when she nurses her infant will soon be aware that her offspring is showing signs of anxiety. It is as if the infant empathizes with the mother. If such interactions continue, the child may continue to experience this state of anxiety later in life without being fully aware as to its origin. Feeling-along-with-others is not a mystical concept. Much can be communicated from one person to another without either attempting to do so with words. We have all had experiences during which our own moods were altered by simply being with someone who is deeply saddened over a recent experience. The emotions aroused during the viewing of a movie may continue long after we leave the theatre unless we make a deliberate attempt to shake them off. Some persons are more readily influenced and more deeply affected than others.

2. Inadequate learning of adaptive behavior: Since anxiety is the signal of danger, it will be triggered off whenever the individual feels he is faced with an event he cannot readily manage. The person with well-developed adaptive skills will find fewer situations threatening, while the person with inadequate or limited psychological capabilities will experience more events as dangerous. At the core of anxiety is a feeling of utter helplessness

in the face of life's demands. The case histories of anxiety neurotics frequently reflect immaturity of development, dependency, insecurity, poor preparation for coping with life because of early parental overprotection or indulgence. The feelings of anxiety threaten to overwhelm the self-concept; the person's sense of self-esteem and self-confidence are easily shaken.

3. Direct training and sensitization: Even though an individual may have the necessary competency and skills to deal successfully with his environment, he may still be subject to anxiety attacks. Over-ambitious, punitive parents may reflect expectations and appraisals that are extremely difficult to meet. Disciplinary techniques which rely upon the arousal of self-imposed punishment—guilt—make the individual acutely aware of the adequacy or perceived inadequacy of his performance. This type of individual is driven by a fear of failure, yet he expects failure and is spurred on even further by this threat. The reality evaluation of his performance as being competent and praiseworthy is most difficult for him to accept into his self-image.

4. Generalization of learned anxiety: Anxiety is a response that can be learned and generalized. It may initially appear as the normal warning response to a real threat, perhaps of punishment, rejection, isolation, loss of love. However, the evidence from learning studies indicate that anxiety responses can also generalize or become attached to other cues in the environment without the awareness of the individual. Thus, anxiety can be later elicited by the presence of these other or similar cues. An anxiety attack might therefore be the cueing of the anxiety pattern upon the appearance of such cues. Since awareness is lacking, the person is not able to predict when the attacks will occur nor is he able to understand why they occur.

Treatment

Prevention of the conditions which predispose an individual to anxiety neurosis should be in the forefront of any effective treatment program. Positive mental health planning can do much to stop such neurotic conditions before they start. Effective parental practices and the development of sound mental hygiene techniques are essential. Such prevention is not directed toward the complete removal of all anxiety. On the contrary, anxiety is a natural condition of the normal organism and serves a protective function. As seen previously, anxiety also contributes to learning through motivation. Mental health prevention programs should, however, be concerned with promoting those conditions which will diminish the likelihood of neurotic anxiety.

Once anxiety neurosis does envelop the individual, several steps must be taken involving the alleviation of anxiety, followed by the removal of the source of the anxiety. Among the alleviative measures are the various drug therapies, hydrotherapy, reduction of responsibilities and situational pressures, and the reassurance that the symptoms are not precursors of serious organic involvement. A common initial goal is communication by the therapist to the patient of the belief that the anxiety can be faced and that the experience is not as catastrophic as the patient perceives it to be. In some rather difficult cases, the technique of desensitization or counterconditioning has been successfully utilized by Wolpe (1958). On the basis of interviews, case history data, and psychological test results, the therapist aids the patient in constructing an anxiety hierarchy, a ranked list of situations that arouses anxiety in the patient (e.g., Table 9-1). The patient is then taught how to

TABLE 9-1. *Anxiety Hierarchies of Clients in Behavior Therapy*[a]

I. Phobia of Flying
1. During a flight, the pilot announces that some turbulence is ahead.
2. The plane is losing altitude prior to landing.
3. Sitting in the airplane waiting for take-off.
4. Sitting in the airport waiting for boarding.
5. Seeing someone else off at the airport.
6. Sitting in a field on a summer day watching an airplane overhead.
7. Reading a magazine about children and model airplanes.

II. Phobia of Heights
1. Walking near the edge of a cliff and looking down.
2. Standing on a hill looking down at a moving stream.
3. Looking out the window from the sixth floor.
4. Walking down a long stairway.
5. Standing on a stool and reaching for something.
6. Standing motionless on a bench.
7. Standing on a stage.
8. Standing firmly on flat ground.

III. Phobia of Examinations
1. Reading an exam question and not knowing the answer.
2. Waiting to enter the room where an exam is to be given.
3. Studying for a forthcoming exam.
4. Being asked by a friend about my standing in a class.
5. Reading an assignment for a class.
6. Discussing the content of an interesting class with a friend.

[a] Taken from cases in actual treatment.

relax. When he is capable of relaxing on cue, the patient is then asked to imagine a scene representing the weakest item on the anxiety hierarchy. If he is able to remain relaxed, then the next item on the list is brought up, and so on. The anxiety situations are thus gradually presented until the most disturbing one can be confronted without disturbance to the relaxation state. By this means, relaxation responses eventually become associated to the circumstances that originally provoked anxiety. This method is dependent upon the ability of either the therapist or the patient being able to identify the stimulus situations which arouse anxiety. In cases where the patient is unable to report

what triggers his anxiety attacks, long and extensive history taking is necessary for diagnosis.

HYPOCHONDRIASIS

Hypochondriasis is a neurotic condition characterized by a preoccupation and exaggerated concern with physical health. This preoccupation with the body and its functions usurps all other interests. The individual is attentive to the every breath he takes, every beat of the heart, every twitch of the muscle. At the slightest provocation, the hypochondriac will dash to the nearest physician for a diagnosis of what is perceived as a deadly illness.

Case History 9-2

ANXIETY REACTION

Ethel B. was referred for treatment of an anxiety neurosis of five years duration. She was never completely relaxed, and complained of vague feelings of restlessness and a fear that something was "just around the corner." Although she felt she had to go to work to help pay the family bills, she could not bring herself to start anything new for fear that something terrible would happen on the job. She had experienced a few extreme anxiety attacks during which she felt "like I couldn't breathe, like I was sealed up in a transparent envelope. I thought I was going to have a heart attack. I couldn't stop shaking . . . ." After these attacks she often thought of taking her own life as the only way to get rid of the tensions.

The patient was an only child who was made extremely dependent upon her mother. Her father was boisterous, impatient, intolerant of the daughter's attachment to his wife but unable to provide love himself. He found fault with the patient in whatever endeavor she engaged in and continued to belittle her reliance upon her mother. Ethel B.'s marriage was as much motivated by her desire to escape from home as it was by her fondness of her somewhat ineffectual boyfriend. When her husband was unable to earn an adequate income, Ethel B. was forced to consider seeking employment herself. Soon after, her first wave of anxiety attacks began.

Course of treatment involved exploration of her feelings of inadequacy and her fear of accepting the challenge of employment. Clarifying her perceptions of what to expect in the world of work helped to allay some of her misperceptions and fears. Training in assertive behavior as a counteractant to her anxiety was prescribed.

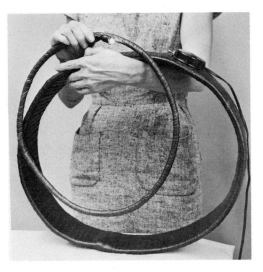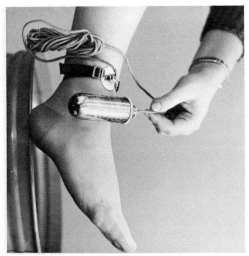

The "Theronoid Belt" (*left*), a medical marvel that cures all, was confiscated by the Federal Trade Commission along with other frauds. The photo shows a two-speed switch for effecting a slow or a gradual cure through magnetizing the blood's iron. The "Oxydonor" (*right*) was supposed to "reverse the death process into the life process" and cure arthritis. The gullible patient strapped the metal disc to his ankle and immersed the cylinder in water—the colder the better. Manufacturers of such devices often depend upon hypochondriacs for sales. (Raimondo Borea)

Health, or rather the lack of health, is a serious business for the hypochondriac. He does not tolerate jokes about his "condition" and takes seriously any comments about how ill he appears to others, even if said in jest. And for many drug and health product firms, the hypochondriac represents big business. This type of neurotic is especially susceptible to promises of relief particularly when the illness is portrayed in vivid detail. Such advertisements not only attract the patient to another source of medication to become engrossed in, but also feeds into the hypochondriac's extreme interest in the signs of disease. When health food fads or diet fads are undertaken, it is discussed in great detail with the emphasis on the dire consequences of not following the routine. Others may try new medication or diets without exhibiting the same intensity of emotional commitment and display that characterizes the hypochondriac. The slightest hint of food contamination or even the vaguest linkage between disease and a product is sufficient to drive the hypochondriac to complete abstinence from this and similar foods. Many hypochondriacs become walking encyclopedias of health information, mostly information on *detriments* to health. It is a remarkably accurate description to suggest that, behind all of the suffering and concerns of the hypochondriac, in the last analysis he "enjoys poor health." Such individuals give the impression of being comfortable only when they can worry about their bodies and of being anxious if prevented from such concerns. Among the multiple complaints focused on by the hypochondriac are insomnia, variegated aches and pains, pressures in the head, poor memory, and inability to concentrate. Gastrointestinal symptoms rank high.

Dynamics

It should be emphasized that the suffering and fears of the hypochondriac are real and not faked. His energies are bound up in his aches and pains, permitting him little time to enjoy life and people. He is continuously being prevented from new or pleasant endeavors because of his somatic fragility. His world becomes constricted. However, it is this very constriction which gives us the first clue into the dynamics of the illness. Frequently, the hypochondriacal neurotic is a person who has low self-esteem, who is fearful of close interpersonal relations, and who has had repeated experiences of disappointment, friction, and unhappiness. Living in a constricted world of diseased organs, medication, and trips to the doctor is a more tolerable existence for the neurotic than facing the challenges of interpersonal relationships. Endless discussions of one's somatic symptoms have a way of preventing others from becoming too involved. When the main topic of conversation is the patient's state of ill health, it is nearly impossible for others to become more intimately acquainted with other aspects of the hypochondriac. Yet there is a certain element of ambivalence present in the hypochondriacal personality. He is fearful of interpersonal closeness, yet he is pleased when sympathy and interest *in his physical symptoms* is expressed. This indirect advantage of an illness is referred to as *secondary gain*. Sympathy, the satisfaction of dependency needs, and the removal of responsibility are all types of secondary gains which can accrue and help to maintain symptoms.

The hypochondriac is basically an anxious person, even beyond the anxieties he feels about his body. In fact, the physical concerns are probably the displaced expression of psychological anxiety. His tensions are transposed and fixed on a tangible area. This explains the inability of the hypochondriac to receive a complete cure for his physical problem. The drug may treat the physical symptom, but it fails to remove the basic anxiety and conflicts giving impetus to the symptom. In fact, although the hypochondriac will

"shop doctors" and move from physician to physician, and from quack to quack, he will invariably avoid attempting psychiatric treatment. As far as he is concerned, his ailment is a medical disease and not a psychiatric one. And as long as he can occupy his attention with the intricate details about body functions, dosages of medication, foods to avoid, diets to keep, he can avoid admitting his disappointments with himself and his surroundings.

Treatment

The successful treatment of hypochondriasis is extremely difficult. In the first place, such patients will avoid psychiatric referrals since it represents to them an admission that there is no organic basis for their illness. Secondly, the hypochondriac has received some partial reinforcement for his pill-taking and for his visits to medical physicians in that just taking such action reduces some of the anxiety, hence some of the symptoms. Third, the secondary gains that accompany physical suffering also prevents the development of insight. Of course, it should be noted that somatizing of anxiety can also appear in cases of psychosis. Preoccupation with the body is a common symptom of schizophrenia.

Tranquilizers provide some symptomatic relief, but care must be taken to avoid the misconception that the pill is a miracle cure-all. Short-term reduction of physical symptoms typically follows but such changes are not stable. Extensive psychotherapy is necessary for any permanent resolutions. Great care is needed to avoid antagonizing the patient by confrontation. Many will be helped upon realizing that emotions play a significant role in affecting bodily conditions and are reassured to know that psychiatric consultations do not mean an admission of insanity or that "it's all in the head."

Case History 9-3

HYPOCHONDRIASIS

Jeff N., a middle-aged man with an eighth grade education, worked as a clerk in a drugstore. He soon became known as the pharmacist's best customer by being the first to try out every new product on the market. Although he was exhorted not to take pills indiscriminately, Jeff argued that he did so only when he felt they might help, which was often. He spent long hours compulsively describing his health and was always pleased when the druggist would refer him to a doctor in sheer exasperation. The patient preferred to see qualified physicians for his complaints but he was increasingly more willing to visit known quacks since "the real docs don't know everything there is to know." A year ago he stopped eating a certain type of fish after hearing rumors that cancer had been found in one fish.

The patient continues to live an isolated life with a few close friends who can tolerate hearing about his many complaints. Some find him amusing for his widespread knowledge of the latest "medical" discoveries which as often as not turn out to be Jeff's parroting from popular magazine articles. He has remained single because of a fear that his ill health would not permit him to be a good provider. A brief attempt at self-improvement ended in dismal failure when he found he could not concentrate on studies because of "pains in the chest and a feeling of pressure in the head." He will talk about psychiatry as "maybe" helping other people who are "tetched in the head" but denies that he personally has any emotional problems. He attributes the inability of medical experts to find any organic base for his symptoms to their "backward techniques." He will occasionally confide that his illness is probably such a rare and special disease that it eludes modern medicine's advances.

CONVERSION REACTION (HYSTERIA)

Conversion reaction, also known as hysteria, is a neurotic condition in which physical symptoms appear without any identifiable organic cause. This illness has had the most significant role in the history of psychopathology. Freud's effort to open up an entirely psychological orientation toward mental illness was derived and received its main support from work with hysterical patients. His discovery of the dramatic effects of the unconscious on the body, and the development of the therapeutic technique of psychoanalysis, were both made possible by his observations of these patients.

Among the mental illnesses, conversion reaction is known as the great imitator. The physical symptoms that develop are as diverse as the different varieties of real physical diseases. In fact, if the symptoms appear in a person well informed about neurology and anatomy, it is most difficult to determine whether the illness has a true organic base or whether it is entirely functional (due to psychological factors). To complicate the issue, *somatic compliance* may be involved—an already weak organ or part of the body becomes the focal point for the conversion symptoms. Among the major symptoms of conversion reaction are the following:

1. Sensory disabilities such as:
   a. Anaesthesias (the diminution of sensation)
   b. Paresthesias (the disturbance of sensation, e.g. "tingling," "pins-and-needles")
   c. Perceptual impairments (e.g. hysterical blindness, blurred vision, hysterical deafness)
2. Motor disabilities such as:
   a. Hysterical epilepsy (seizures, convulsions)
   b. Astasia-abasia (the inability to stand and walk although movements are possible when sitting or lying)
   c. Hysterical aphonia (the loss of voice to a whisper)
3. Visceral disturbances such as:
   a. Vomiting
   b. Diarrhea or constipation
   c. Hiccoughing
   d. Anorexia (loss of appetite which may become anorexia nervosa)
   e. Anorexia nervosa (self-starvation in young adult females or adolescents)

Of course, other symptoms and entire disease patterns may be duplicated by the patient suffering from conversion reaction. He may develop a hypersensitivity to light or sound such that normal amounts are reacted to painfully. He may show complete hemiplegia, the paralysis of an entire side of the body or his body may mimic the symptoms of a heart attack. In diagnostic work, the psychologist or psychiatrist looks for the following signs which help to differentiate the hysterically based symptoms from organically caused ones:

1. The lack of conclusive medical evidence. Frequently, the pattern of symptoms are based on the patient's limited knowledge of anatomical, neurological, or physical conditions. Thus, the hysterical epileptic does not become completely unconscious and resists having his eyes opened. The classic "glove" and "stocking" anesthesias were once common examples of anatomical errors exhibited by conversion-reaction patients in their symptoms (see Fig. 9-1). These anesthesias covered only the areas enclosed by such garments, the patients forgetting or not knowing that the nerves of the human body do not innervate simply the fashionably covered portions of the body.

2. In some instances, survival reflexes are maintained, for example, the convulsive hysteric will not fall in a dangerous setting nor will he bite his tongue during the seizure. Athough one woud expect the patient to be particularly in danger because of his disability, the conversion-reaction patient does not tend to injure himself. In fact, as will be seen under the discussion of the dynamics, the conversion reaction is a self-protective mechanism.

3. Traditionally, the conversion-reaction patient has been noted for being peculiarly blasé or unconcerned by his physical disability, no matter how serious it may be. This lack of appropriate emotion has been labeled *la belle indifférence*. It is one of the primary features that distinguishes the hysteric from the hypochondriac (another difference: the hysteric *has* a disability, the hypochondriac *worries* about having a disability).

It is also possible for a conversion-reaction patient to become quite involved in his disability rather than show complacency. Unlike the traditional hysteric, this type of patient will seek medical (non-psychiatric) treatment. The more typical hysteric, however, tolerates medical diagnostic procedures and gives the impression of submitting to examination because others think it necessary.

4. The symptoms frequently disappear when the patient is asleep or under hypnosis. It is as if the involved portion of

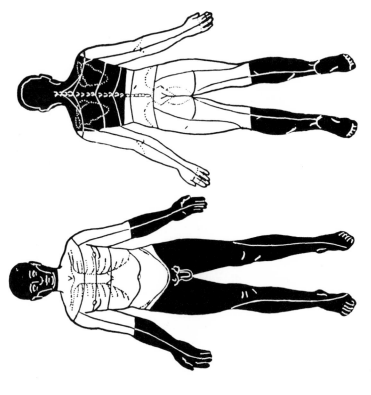

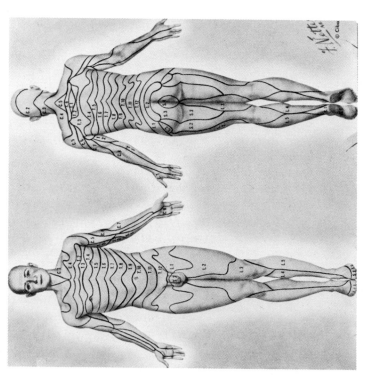

Figure 9-1. On the left is illustrated the areas of dermal (surface) sensations normally innervated by nerves. On the right is illustrated the typical areas of dermal anesthesias in conversion reaction patients. Notice the discrepancy.

SOURCE: Copyright The CIBA, Plate 32, p. 55, *Collection of Medical Illustrations*, by Frank H. Netter, M.D., 1957.

the body is released from its chore of representing the basic conflict. A paraplegic man, for example, was first suspected of suffering from this neurotic condition when his wife reported that he "tossed and turned" equally well with all limbs when asleep. On the other hand, it is quite difficult to "trick" the patient out of his symptoms when he is conscious. Moreover, the symptoms are real and not faked. A person with anesthesia does in fact possess a diminished ability to respond to pain or pressure sensations. A pain in the neck or in the back is often accompanied by muscle rigidity. Conversion-reaction patients will agree to surgery if informed that such intervention is needed. No malingerer would submit to such treatment.

Dynamics

Historically, hysteria was believed to be caused by a wandering uterus, hence the Greek name *hystera* or uterus. Freud presented the belief that the conversion symptoms involved emotionally charged conflicts or traumas which were repressed, then converted into physical symptoms which serve as outlets. The conflicts were said to involve genital-sexual wishes which had remained unresolved. Many psychoanalysts accept this viewpoint today and attempt to understand the symbolism involved in the symptoms. Cases that involve simulated pregnancy (pseudocyesis) are interpreted as wish-fulfillment, and perhaps a carryover from the Oepidal-conflict. Freud's patient Dora (Freud, 1905), who developed coughing attacks, was perceived as unconsciously trying to identify with Mrs. K. who had a cough. This identification served to satisfy Dora's wish to be the wife of Mr. K. Symbolic expression of conflict does appear to lend some understanding of conversion symptoms. Hysterical blindness may result from intense guilt feelings over a visual act ("if thy eye sins, pluck it out"), an inability

to speak may be punishment for cursing, a paralyzed hand can never be used again in a hostile or criminal act. In some situations, the hysterical symptoms represent an enactment of the traumatic event, as in the soldier whose paralysis continued from the battlefield when he was literally "rooted to the spot" with fear.

The conversion reaction is basically a self-protective mechanism. In its most straightforward form, the symptoms help to remove tensions and agony. The front line platoon leader becomes blind and is freed from the sight of his men being brutally torn into shreds by shrapnel. The young immigrant mother becomes deaf and is spared from hearing the pathetic cries of hunger and pain from her infant. The frightened youth loses his ability to stand and walk and is able to postpone plans for the wedding which he is not ready for. The tense student develops a painful intestinal pain and a distended stomach just prior to final examinations which will determine the difference between promotion or dismissal from school. The long-suffering husband exhibits an ache in the neck as his only means for safely paying tribute to his nagging wife who has been a constant "pain-in-the-neck." In all of these situations, the patient is protected from a dreadful experience by the onset of a condition which permits a momentary release from psychological pain.

Ambivalence, or the approach-avoidance conflict, is often a significant part of the dynamics of conversion reactions. This aspect of hysterical symptom development was particularly evident in incidents during World War I. The crude, nightmarish "over-the-wall" bayonet charges presented severe approach-avoidance conflicts—the young soldier wished to achieve the recognition for courage and the respect of his comrades-in-arms, yet he was repelled by the fear of death and destruction. In some, the conflict was of the avoidance-avoidance type—a fear of death from the enemy versus a fear of being branded a coward if he retreated. Conversion symptoms provided a means of psychologically leaving the field in safety. A man who doesn't advance because his legs are paralyzed cannot be blamed. He did his best and might even sincerely protest being removed from the battleground. Only after long and deep analysis will he be finally able to even accept the fact that he was afraid. The conversion reaction is thus a means of resolving conflicts without damage to the self-esteem.

Treatment

Therapists have noted the tendency on the part of hysterics to be suggestible, narcissistic, and dependent. For these reasons, it is possible to rid the patient of his current symptoms by persuasion or suggestive methods of treatment by an "authority" or "expert." So-called "miracle cures," faith-healing dramatic recoveries when the patient undergoes an experience which he believes in, can all be assigned to this category. Unfortunately, these are not permanent. A new and more severe symptom can soon develop to replace the symptoms now given up. Of course, this new ailment can in turn be chased away by suggestion but again at the risk of establishing a new and "better" illness. Such a transfer of symptoms is appropriately called symptom-chasing.

On the premise that the hidden or repressed conflict is the source of the hysterical symptom, Breuer and Freud (1895) worked on recovering the repressed and releasing the anxiety first through encouraging the patient to talk out his problems (*abreaction*), and later through *free-association,* a technique that Freud devised. Psychoanalytic treatment continues to be oriented toward the removal of the core trauma or conflict which has been converted into the physical symptoms. Prognosis has been generally considered to be favorable provided that the patient does not have his somatic symptoms wrenched away before he can develop more suitable adjustment skills. Hypnotic techniques may aso be used to gain access to the traumatic past.

With the more widespread practice of behavior therapy, conversion reactions are now also being treated by this method. In many instances, the procedures reported appear to rely as much on conditioning effects as on the influence of personal suggestion. For example, Malmo, Davis, and Barza (1952) used electric shock paired with a tone to treat a 19-year-old girl with hysterical deafness. Prior to the conditioning, however, the therapist strongly suggested to the patient that the electric-shock machinery would cure her deafness. Brady and Lind (1961) were successful in restoring sight to an hysterical patient two years after the onset of his disability by operant conditioning. The therapists relied upon monetary reward for reinforcement as well as the more personal effects of social approval. The task required the patient to press a small lever. A light was turned on at irregular intervals and the patient was rewarded whenever he pressed the lever following the presentation of the light. He soon learned to respond to the light stimulus first as a vague visual sensation, later as a distinct visual image. Wolpe (1958) offers a useful distinction between two types of hysteria: those with high anxiety and those with very little anxiety. The high anxiety patients responded well to behavior therapy, the low anxiety patients were treated by other methods such as abreaction and hypnosis. It may well be the most relevant way for determining which mode of treatment is most suitable for any given case of conversion reaction.

DISSOCIATIVE REACTION

Dissociative reactions involve a number of neurotic conditions in which disturbance of consciousness occurs. There is some similarity to conversion reactions in that severe repression has developed. Among the dissociative reactions are:

Amnesia   Somnambulism
Fugue states   Multiple personality

Amnesia symptoms involve the inability to recall one's name, address, or past circumstances. The loss of identity is usually abrupt but often there is a certain vagueness as to the exact time of onset. *Fugue* states are literally flights from familiar surroundings and way of life. The patient wanders away from home in a confused and dazed state, arrives in a distant area, recovers from the confusion but has no awareness of the events during the traveling. Amnesia for identity may accompany the fugue state. *Somnambulism*, or sleepwalking, involves engaging in walking and complex ritualistic behavior while in a dreamlike trance. The sleepwalker's eyes are usually open, he is able to respond to other's questions or commands, and his activities appear purposeful. Upon wakening the person is amnesic for his actions. *Multiple personalities* are rare conditions in which separate and distinct personal-

Case History 9-4

CONVERSION REACTION (HYSTERIA)

The patient was a young college student involved in a minor traffic accident on his way home from classes. Although he was slightly bruised, medical examination showed no serious physical involvement and the patient was discharged from the hospital. He awakened the next morning with a numbness in his legs and found himself unable to move them. He was returned by ambulance to the hospital for extensive neurological and X-ray examinations with negative results. Throughout, the patient seemed bemused by the procedures, intrigued by the machinery, and taken by the nurses. The diagnosis: conversion reaction.

This college student was interviewed by a psychologist and the following facts came to light. Just prior to the accident, he had another of many arguments with his family over his education. He preferred to seek employment in order to obtain an income. His parents, both from immigrant backgrounds, had forced him to continue his schooling in spite of constant bickering. He was on an allowance on the condition that he remain in school. Money had always been a problem since the patient tended to squander it on social activities, girl friends, and his motorbike. The patient admitted that had not prepared himself for final examinations and was certain he would have failed them since he was incapable of successfully cramming. The draft had already taken some of his peers and he was positive that he would also be called once he lost his student deferment from the draft. The accident itself came as a surprise since he had always been reasonably cautious on his motorbike. Yet, he had driven in a carefree and even reckless fashion when the accident occurred. When he was first released from the hospital he felt "kinda lucky that I wasn't killed, but kinda sorry I wasn't scraped up more than I was." The impression was that a disabling injury would have been painful but useful.

ities exist within a single individual. Such personalities will alternate appearance and seem to possess different, oppositional traits. In some cases, one of the personalities will be completely unaware of the existence of the other, while another personality is fully conscious of its counterparts. Robert Louis Stevenson's Dr. Jekyll and Mr. Hyde was a vivid, but nonetheless fictional, portrayal of a dual personality. Morton Prince reported on an equally dramatic and true case of multiple personality in the case of Miss Beauchamp, in whom three different personalities appeared: the "Saint"—idealistic, sexually inhibited, self-righteous; the "Woman"—aggressive, realistic, capable of sexual feelings; and "Sally"—impish, immature, childish. The Saint and the Woman shared many memories. Sally was aware of the Saint and made fun of her, but the Saint was unaware of Sally (Prince, 1906). A more recent and highly publicized case also involved a trio of personalities: Eve White was sweet, retiring, demure, and had no allergy to nylon; Eve Black was vivacious, mischievous, seductive, and allergic to nylon; Jane was mature, competent, and more secure (Thigpen and Cleckley, 1954).

Dynamics

The dynamics in the dissociative states and hysteria both involve repression of highly emotionally charged material; in fact, some psychopathologists consider dissociative states as forms of conversion reaction. Dissociative states are routinely understood as symptomatic of the massive effects of repression to prevent highly threatening stresses from overwhelming the person. In amnesias, fugue states, and multiple personality, the memory loss enables the person to escape from the otherwise intolerable tensions of his normal life situation. In somnambulism and multiple personality, the individual experiences some release for repressed needs

which cannot achieve free expression during consciousness. The "Woman" and Eve Black, for example, were both the type of vivacious, relaxed, uninhibited woman secretly admired by their inhibited counterparts. In contrast to conditions such as hypochondriasis and hysteria, the dissociative states permit the individual to escape rather completely from his frustrating environment and enjoy the pleasures of a different life without loss of self-esteem. It is true that the somatic symptoms of the hysteric remove him from certain obligations, but he must still cope with other responsibilities and the same people in his life. In addition, the hypochondriac and the hysteric are both much more subject to being suspected by their friends and families as soon as the medical reports are turned in. On the other hand, the dissociative states are more likely to trigger off sympathy, concern, and help from others.

Treatment

Amnesic states are often subject to spontaneous cure. Somnambulism, of course, stops when the patient is wakened. On the other hand, fugue states and multiple personality may be more resistent to spontaneous recovery and require more systematic treatment. To date, the major attempts at treatment have involved the goal of removing the emotionally charged conflict by removing the repression. Free association, hypnotic methods, and intensive psychotherapy are all useful measures.

PHOBIAS

Phobias are neurotic conditions involving inordinate, irrational fears. The word phobia is derived from the Greek *phobos*, meaning dread, panic, or fear. Phobias differ from normal fears in the fact that neurotic fears are groundless while a normal fear is based on realistic danger. When a phobic condition becomes asso-

Case History 9-5

DISSOCIATIVE REACTIONS

The following are excerpts from the *Three Faces of Eve* by Thigpen and Cleckley:

Eve White: "This neat, colorless young woman was . . . twenty-five years of age . . . Demure and poised, she sat with her feet close together, speaking clearly but in soft, low tones. Her dark hair and pale eyes were distinctly pretty, though she seemed too retiring and inert to utilize . . . her good features . . ." (p. 9).

Eve Black: "Suddenly her posture began to change. Her body slowly stiffened until she sat rigidly erect. An alien, inexplicable expression then came over her face . . . The lines of her countenance seemed to shift in a barely visible, slow, rippling transformation . . . . A pair of blue eyes popped open. There was a quick reckless smile. In a bright unfamiliar voice that sparkled, the woman said, 'Hi, there, Doc!'

With a soft and surprisingly intimate syllable of laughter, she crossed her legs, carelessly swirling her skirt in the process. She . . . was playful and somehow just a little provocative." (p. 24).

Jane: "After a few minutes the therapist, already impressed by the air of maturity and competence in this new figure, saw fit to inquire, 'What is your name?' Looking at him gravely . . . she replied, 'I don't know.'

Jane seemed to reflect a disciplined vitality, and ease, and a range of feeling beyond the reach of Eve White . . . . Unlike Eve White she could laugh, and her smile was fresh and lovely. She had the face of a woman whose interests might extend far beyond anything known to the other two. Her posture . . . suggested neither Eve White's tense decorum nor her alternate's semiadolescent, almost lascivious repose." (pp. 125, 126).

---

ciated with a realistic fear, the resulting fear is said to be *overdetermined*. There is still some tendency to view phobias as types of anxiety neurosis. However, anxiety neurosis is diffuse and the symptoms may be aroused by situations that are beyond the person's ability to identify; on the other hand, phobias are specifically tied to definable objects or situations. Freud (1895) distinguished between two categories of phobias: the common phobias —an exaggerated fear of objects or situations which we all tend to fear to some extent, such as snakes or the dark; and the specific phobias—the inordinate fear of objects or situations not usually feared by others, for example, open spaces or heights. Each form of phobia has been assigned a Greek name and the more common ones are listed below:

Acrophobia	—fear of high places
Agoraphobia	—fear of open places
Algophobia	—fear of pain
Anthropophobia	—fear of men
Claustrophobia	—fear of closed places
Mysophobia	—fear of germs
Monophobia	—fear of being alone
Nyctophobia	—fear of darkness, night
Ochlophobia	—fear of crowds
Syphilophobia	—fear of syphillis
Thanatophobia	—fear of death
Zoophobia	—fear of one or all animals

Such Greek labels are impressive but impractical and unenlightening. The number of potential objects that can be feared is so numerous as to make separate labeling meaningless, particularly in a foreign language! Theoretically, the number of phobias in existence is limited only by the number of objects and settings that man can react to. There are a few, however, that are more common: fear of heights, fear of closed spaces, and fear of the darkness. Children tend to be more susceptible of phobic conditions than adults and include among their fears the fear of school.

Dynamics

The phobias can be understood from two vantage points, the psychoanalytic and the learning. In his famous case of childhood phobia, called the case of "Little Hans," Sigmund Freud (1909) treated a fear of being bitten by a horse. In a brilliant application of symbolism and psychoanalytic theory, Freud explained the phobia as a displacement of fear. Hans was said to be in the throes of an Oedipal conflict with gave rise to a fear of being punished severely by the father, a fear of castration. The castration fear was repressed and transformed into a fear of being bitten (a disguised castration fear). Such symbolic displacement has been applied to many other phobias. Agoraphobia, or the fear of open spaces, may be symbolic of a fear of being sexually molested in an open street, or a fear that someone will die while one is away from home, or a fear of being tempted into running away. Claustrophobia and fears of being buried alive symbolize the fantasy of life within the mother's womb. Fears of the dark may be interpreted as a vestigial fear originating from early man's vulnerability to attack by prehistoric animals, or it may represent the fear of being isolated, alone, and helpless—it is intriguing to note that being suddenly thrust into total darkness by a power failure forces people to call out to or touch others to reassure

themselves that they are not as alone as it seems.

The phobia has the advantage of permitting the individual to circumscribe his conflicts and anxieties, and to limit it to a definable and therefore controllable situation. As such, this is a partial solution which helps to reduce the anxieties as long as the individual stays clear of the feared object. When away from this object, he can function fairly adequately and rationally. In addition, the phobia itself helps the patient to focus his attention on the feared object and away from the true source of psychological threat. Of course, secondary gains aid in maintaining the phobia. Finally, the possession of a fear provides the patient with a certain degree of control over others, since it forces others to behave protectively and submit to the direction and demands of the patient.

Phobias can be acquired through direct learning. A mother who continues to exhibit fear responses toward an object will provide a model for her offspring to imitate. Hagman (1932), for example, found a significant correlation between the number and types of fears of the parent and her child. Under classical conditioning circumstances, a neutral object may acquire fearful qualities if associated with a traumatic event. Watson demonstrated this in his laboratory case of Albert. Bomber pilots who must fly a fixed course through intensely dangerous flak and fighter attack may develop a fear of airplanes because of classical conditioning. Once instigated, the phobia is maintained each time the individual avoids the feared object. This is a well-understood rule of learning—the reduction of anxiety through the avoidance of or escape from the anxiety provoking stimuli serves to strengthen the avoidance behavior. Each time a patient reduces his anxiety by avoiding or escaping from the feared situation, his phobic behavior is strengthened. The data on avoidance behavior in conflict studies provide further understanding of the phobias. As will be recalled, the nearer the person is brought to an avoidance situation, the greater will be the tendency to avoid. This explains the difficulty of eliminating a phobic avoidance once the avoidance behavior has had a chance to be strengthened. In the future, it becomes most difficult to bring the patient to face his fears, and the closer he comes to the feared setting, the more vigorously he fights. The same applies whether the feared situation is an object that he must face or a repressed psychological event.

Treatment

Since the phobic patient recognizes the irrationality of his fears, direct suggestive therapy does not help. Similarly, suddenly confronting the patient with the feared object may trigger off such a high level of anxiety that panic may result. On the other hand, the phobic patient is concerned about his neurotic symptom and sufficiently bothered by it as to be highly motivated to seek treatment. In cases of symbolic involvement, intensive psychotherapy is aimed toward the gradual, systematic uncovering of the fundamental conflicts involved. In addition, because of

Case History 9-6

PHOBIC REACTION

A college student appeared at the counseling center with a complaint that he was deathly afraid of examinations. Although he prepared himself well for tests, the mere mention of an exam would arouse fear in him. He had thus far achieved a fair but not outstanding grade point average. He had previously been involved in a confrontation with an instructor whom he accused of having administered an unfair test in that there was not enough time to answer all the questions. It soon became evident that such antagonistic behavior was a displacement of his frustration with himself. He soon realized that the time limit had not been long enough because he had wasted most of his time in attempting to control his anxieties. He had already skipped two other examinations by remaining in bed petrified with his fears of failure.

Behavior therapy was started with this patient. He first made up a hierarchy of circumstances which he felt produced fear responses. He was then instructed in relaxation of muscle groups. The lowest item on his anxiety hierarchy list, being asked a question of fact by his kid brother, was then presented while the patient was relaxing. When it was evident that this situation was well tolerated, the next item on the list was evoked, and so on. Within a month, the student reported being able to undertake midterm examinations with only a modicum of tension. The patient returned, however, during final examinations with a recurrence of his paralyzing fear. Retraining continued with an emphasis on generalizing the relaxation responses to a wider variety of evaluational situations. Excellent progress has been noted and the student has recently been notified of his acceptability for graduate admissions.

the definable nature of phobias, they are particularly well treated by behavior therapy such as the counterconditioning procedures of Wolpe (see p. 229). Quite unsuccessful are those procedures based on the hope that prolonged absence from the feared situation will permit decay of the fear (see p. 177). Distracting the person from his fear is helpful only as long as the individual remains inattentive to the feared object. Exhortations and other verbal appeals to give up the irrational behavior are ineffective for obvious reasons.

OBSESSIVE-COMPULSIVE NEUROSIS

Obsesssive-compulsive reactions are really two types of neurotic conditions both characterized by recurring activities over which the individual has no control. Obsessions are recurring thoughts which interfere with normal behavior. Compulsions are recurring actions which the individual must engage in. Obsessive-compulsive neurotics are faced with irresistible thoughts or actions which they must engage in. If they are prevented from these activities, they become quite anxious and even panic. Freud described the picture of the obsessive-compulsive person as follows:

The obsessional neurosis takes this form: the patient's mind is occupied with thoughts that do not really interest him, he feels impulses which seem alien to him, and he is impelled to perform actions which not only afford him no pleasure but from which he is powerless to desist. The thoughts (obsessions) may be meaningless in themselves or only of no interest to the patient; they are often absolutely silly . . . . Against his will he has to worry and speculate as if it were a matter of life or death to him. (Freud, 1917)

Obsessional thoughts may center around very trivial matters or very serious issues. The individual may wonder whether the lights were turned off, and feel forced to get out of bed time and time again to make sure, repeating this into the night. Or the person may have a recurring belief that he *might* commit a violent crime, and ruminate over this possibility. Such thoughts will persist for awhile, then vanish, only to reappear during the oddest and most unexpected moments to plague the individual. The compulsions may involve rather simple acts or more elaborate and complex activities. A ritualistic quality is associated with such behavior. Compulsions may include hand-washing rituals, an inability to walk by a piece of furniture without brushing it, counting from one to one-hundred, or moving books from shelf to shelf each time the room is entered. These behaviors may be repeated so often as to become physically harmful, for example, hand-washing to such an extent that the skin actually becomes raw from all the rubbing. The prominent characteristic of the obsessions and compulsions is their rigid, uncompromising, inflexible control over the person. Much as the sufferer may wish to stop, he cannot. If a compulsion is involved, the individual must carry it through with exactitude; not even the minutest modification is tolerated, the act must be perfectly executed.

Dynamics

The psychoanalytic viewpoint traces obsessive-compulsive behavior to the anal stage of development. During this phase, bowel training and cleanliness are desired by the parent and impressed on the child. Partly because he enjoys being messy, and partly because he is at a defiant age, the child resists the demands of the parent. The parent relies upon punishment and guilt in exerting her will, forcing the child to deny his pleasure-oriented behavior. Reaction formation develops and the child becomes excessively neat and perfectionistic. As an adult he may recreate the judgmental attitude of his parent and repeatedly suspect himself of

Obsessive-compulsive neurosis involves the repetition of thoughts (obsession) or actions (compulsions). The famous scene from MacBeth is an excellent illustration of a compulsion involving handwashing. ("Out, damned Spot! Out, I say!") (New York Public Library Picture Collection)

inadequate behavior—thus, he becomes doubtful about whether he turned the lights off, realigns the books as if anticipating a parental inspection, or avoid touching certain objects in a symbolic avoidance of becoming soiled. In many cases, the spectre of a perfectionistic parent seems to govern the patient's activities. It is as if the patient is trying to be perfectly certain that he will be able to "pass inspection."

In some instances the obsessive-compulsive behavior symbolically reflects attempts to reverse the outcome of the childhood scene. The hostility and rage felt by the patient as a child becomes expressed in vaguely disguised recurring thoughts of death, usually toward someone close. The sudden obsessional thought of "What if I should kill someone" is more accurately

"Why didn't I kill that demanding parent of mine." The fact that the neurotic is disturbed by the obsession reflects the threatening quality of the impulse such that he cannot admit to such feelings. The sense of not being in control over these thoughts which act as though they had a life of their own suggests the strong influence of repression. The compulsion to crumple up stray pieces of paper might be interpreted as the expression of a wish to crush the parent. Or the children's game of not stepping on the cracks in the sidewalk for fear of "breaking your mother's back" may be extended into adult life with a very similar hostile meaning.

Guilt plays a prominent role in the dynamics of obsessive-compulsive behavior. Individuals are taught to monitor their own behavior by the instigation of guilt.

244

An individual with a well-developed conscience does not require supervision; he has already internalized the evaluative-supervision role. For the obsessive-compulsive, this phenomenon has been developed to its extreme. The compulsion to confess to any and all crimes that appears in the newspapers is a clear-cut example of the overly developed conscience. Hand-washing may represent attempts at expiation and atonement for an "unclean" act. Compulsive acts may also serve to neutralize unacceptable impulses by blocking them or ritualizing them (in much the same way as religious rites are used to make unacceptable acts acceptable, e.g. the blessing of military weapons).

Learning principles are also involved in obsessive-compulsive neurosis. The hyper-critical, demanding, perfectionistic parent rewards similar behaviors in her offspring. In some cases, the obsessive characteristic also appeared in the parent and was quickly adopted by the child. In addition, the ritualistic behaviors are maintained by another type of reinforcement, anxiety reduction. As was noted, the neurotic becomes increasingly anxious when prevented from preceding with his compulsion, but receives temporary relief when allowed to finish such activity. This reduction of anxiety serves to strengthen the compulsive behavior and increase its likelihood of reappearance whenever anxiety cues recur.

Treatment

Obsessive-compulsive conditions are among the most difficult neuroses to treat. Intellectualizing often occurs during the course of treatment as part of the defensive maneuvers. In addition, the patient is sincerely fearful of giving up a proven, although annoying, way of reducing anxiety. Frequently, he will ask for advice on what to do and how to live from the

Case History 9-7

OBSESSIVE-COMPULSIVE NEUROSIS

A department store clerk soon lost her job because of complaints from customers over her slowness in making change, and her eccentric behavior. She was obsessed with the number seven. If the number appeared in the cents column, she found herself unable to stop from repeating the figure over and over. If the number appeared in the dollars column or in any other circumstance, she felt a strong urge to omit it. She could not take the seventh step in stride but always managed to do a little skip. Rather than getting off the elevator on the seventh floor of any building, she preferred the inconvenience of going to a higher or lower floor and walking the rest of the way. She changed her residence several times in order to live in a district where the telephone was given an area code without a seven.

The patient had been raised by her divorced mother. Throughout her life she heard endless accounts of the cruelties of life and the necessity of being so self-reliant and competent that she would never have to rely upon anyone else. Her mother used every waking moment to instruct her daughter by continuously evaluating her performance on trivial as well as important matters. The mother died after an agonizing battle with cancer. She died on the seventh day of July.

---

therapist, thereby substituting the obsessions and compulsions derived from the therapist for his own. Therapy is aimed at encouraging the patient to deal constructively on the adult level with his guilt and repressed feelings toward others. An attempt at reconstructing the emotional reactions felt in early life is sometimes useful. Behavior therapy has appeared promising in those cases of anxiety-reducing obsessions although its application to the anxiety-elevating obsessions has been limited. An example of the latter is the case of a forty-year-old woman who had been plucking her own eyebrows compulsively for thirty-one years! Negative reinforcement was used in which she was instructed to inhibit movements toward the head. Cure was reportedly obtained within ten days (Taylor, 1963). Negative practice has also been used successfully to extinguish compulsive behavior. By this technique, the patient is required to perform the compulsive acts beyond the point of fatigue in order to develop satiation. Finally, counterconditioning has been effective in removing obsessive-compulsive behavior which has anxiety-reduction qualities.

REACTIVE DEPRESSION

In reactive depression, the individual experiences a despondency that is out of proportion to the disappointing event and prolonged beyond the normal period. To a similar event, the normal person would react with either a milder degree of emotion, or, if the event were more severe, with an emotion of shorter duration. The reactive depression seems to be overdetermined. Among the symptoms are:

    despondency
    lack of activity
    diminished interest
    inability to work
    lowered self-assurance
    inability to concentrate

The depression is triggered by an un-happy experience, such as poor grades, loss of a job, illness or death of a friend or relative, financial reversal. Others recover within a reasonable time, the neurotic is precipitated into a deep chasm of depression in which he remains trapped. The patient is certain that life will never again be the same, that all is forever lost, that the future does not exist. He is dejected, unable to eat, self-condemning. The reactive depression differs from the psychotic depression in a number of ways. Foremost is the fact that the patient suffering from reactive depression is responsive to encouragement and reassurance. He can be consoled and distracted from his grief. He is still able to profit from environmental change. Moreover, he does not have a past history of recurring depressions. Finally, the neurotic depression is a reaction to a depressing event which can be identified.

Dynamics

The person susceptible to a reactive depression has been sensitized to loss. He may have experienced a life pattern of insecurity, meagerness, inadequacy. The precipitating disappointment is simply the culmination of all his disappointments throughout life. It becomes the straw that breaks the camel's back. Such a break, of course, suggests that the individual's resources were inadequate to cope with frustration and disappointments. Others face similar losses, stumble a bit, but recover and progress onward. The person with reactive depression seems incapable of recovering. He may have never properly learned to depend upon himself. He may have always been surrounded with immediate gratification for his slightest needs. He may have developed the false impression that his was a charmed life. The loss of a loved one, or the realities of failure in competition, may suddenly bring home the degree of his dependency on others. He may suddenly be aware of the artificiality of his successes. He is now faced with relying upon his own poorly developed adjustment skills and realizes his lack of capacity.

Treatment

Reactive depressions are helped by a combination of drug treatment and psychotherapy. Antidepressant drugs during the early phases of the depression will help in the management of the emotion. Supportive measures such as reassurance and removal of the patient from the stressful environmental circumstances are also quite helpful. Occupational and recreational therapy help to keep the patient interested in activity while preventing excessive rumination. Review of the patient's relation toward others, reorientation of life goals, and renewed stress on substitute strengths, are all necessary aspects to include where appropriate to the precipitating event. A few cases have proven responsive to behavior therapy. Hospitalization is not usually required unless there is the possibility of suicide.

Case History 9-8

REACTIVE DEPRESSION

Jon O., age 45, suffered a heart attack leaving him partially paralyzed. Because of the residual motor involvement, it was evident that he could not return to his former occupation as a butcher in the supermarket. He became increasingly despondent during his hospitalization for the heart condition and soon stopped going for physical therapy. It seemed useless to him to continue rehabilitation treatment when he was certain that he would never recover the use of his arm and hand. Much of his life's satisfactions had been associated with his skill in carving meat. The depression became so severe that he refused to move from his bed and lay facing the wall without talking.

He was moved into a room with another patient recovering from a stroke. This older patient was cheerful, optimistic, and had shown some gains in learning how to care for himself with his limited physical capabilities. He was actively planning for a change of occupation by meetings with the rehabilitation counselor. Gradually, Jon O. began to relate to his roommate, first with hostility and resentment, later with growing interest. Finally, he agreed to return to physical therapy and asked for an appointment with the rehabilitation counselor. At last report, he was considering the possibility of continued work at the supermarket in a clerical capacity.

Glossary

Abreaction: The expression of charged emotions.

Amnesia: The loss of memory of past experiences where such recall is normally expected.

Anaesthesia: The loss of sensation.

Anorexia: The loss of appetite.

Anorexia nervosa: The loss of appetite for foods leading to self-starvation.

Anxiety reaction: A psychoneurotic condition involving marked apprehension and feelings of imminent danger.

Aphonia: Inability to speak above a whisper.

Astasia-abasia: The inability to stand and walk although movements are possible when sitting or lying.

Conversion reaction: Also referred to as hysteria, and sometimes as conversion hysteria. A psychoneurotic condition involving the manifestation of organic symptoms without any organic basis.

Dissociative reaction: A psychoneurotic condition characterized by the disturbance of consciousness and memory.

Dynamics: The psychological factors interacting to produce certain behavioral consequences.

Free association: The reporting of thoughts immediately upon their arousal and without censorship.

Fugue state: A fleeing from a threatening or unsatisfying life situation; usually involves an amnesia for the past life although skills and habits are retained.

Functional: Disorders attributed to psychological, nonorganic factors.

Hypochondriasis: A psychoneurotic condition involving excessive preoccupation with the body and ill health.

La belle indifférence: A symptom of conversion reaction involving the indifference or lack of concern about the disability.

Malingerer: A person who deliberately fakes an illness.

Multiple personality: The existence of separate and distinct personalities within a single person.

Obsessive-compulsive reaction: A psychoneurotic condition involving the intrusion of unwanted thoughts or actions which must be repeated.

Paresthesia: The disturbance of sensation, as in pins-and-needles sensations.

Phobia: A psychoneurotic condition involving the presence of excessive fears.

Panic: A condition involving extreme anxiety.

Partial reinforcement: The intermittent presentation of a reward when the correct responses occur.

Psychoneurosis: Also referred to as neurosis. Emotional disturbances in which certain fixed symptoms are used to cope with anxiety and conflict, and which do not involve severe personality breakdown.

Psychosis: Emotional disturbances involving severe personality breakdown, gross distortions and misperceptions, and severe disturbance of emotional reactions.

Pseudocyesis: Conversion reaction involving the symptom of false pregnancy.

Reactive depression: A psychoneurotic condition involving despondency that persists beyond a normal period.

Secondary gain: The additional rewards that accrue from symptoms, such as attention from others, sympathy, or relief from responsibility.

Somatic compliance: The development of a conversion symptom in that part of the body which is already vulnerable to illness.

Somnambulism: The carrying out of seemingly normal activities during a sleeping state.

Tachycardia: Rapid heart rate.

Traumatic neurosis: A psychoneurotic condition involving reactions to extreme stress or catastrophe.

References

Brady, J., & Lind, D. Experimental analysis of hysterical blindness. *A.M.A. Arch. gen. Psychiat.*, 1961, 4, 331.

Breuer, J., & Freud, S. Studies in hysteria. In J. Strachey (Ed.), *Standard edition of the complete psychological works.* London: Hogarth Press, 1955. First German edition, 1895.

Freud, S. Obsessions and phobias; their psychic mechanisms and their aetiology. In *Collected papers,* Vol. I. New York: Basic Books, 1959. First published in German, 1895.

Freud, S. Fragment of an analysis of a case of hysteria. In *Collected papers.* Vol. III. New York: Basic Books, 1959. First published in German, 1905.

Freud, S. Analysis of a phobia in a five year old boy. In *Collected papers.* Vol. III. New York: Basic Books, 1959. First published in German, 1909.

Freud, S. *A general introduction to psychoanalysis.* New York: Liveright, 1935. First German edition, 1917.

Hagman, R. A study of fears of children of preschool age. *J. exper. Educ.,* 1932, 1, 110.

Malmo, R., Davis, J., & Barza, S. Total hysterical deafness: and experimental case study. *J. Person.,* 1952, 21, 188.

Prince, M. *The dissociation of a personality.* New York: Longmans, Green, 1906.

Selye, H. The general-adaptation-syndrome in its relationships to neurology, psychology, and psychopathology. In A. Weider (Ed.), *Contributions toward medical psychology.* New York: Ronald Press, 1953.

Selye, H. *The stress of life.* New York: McGraw-Hill, 1956.

Sullivan, H. *The interpersonal theory of psychiatry.* New York: Norton, 1953.

Taylor, J. A behavioral interpretation of obsessive-compulsive neurosis. *Behav. Res. Ther.,* 1963, 1, 237.

Thigpen, C., & Cleckley, H. A case of multiple personality. *J. abnorm. soc. Psychol.,* 1954, 49, 135.

Thigpen, C., & Cleckley, H. *The three faces of Eve.* New York: McGraw-Hill, 1957.

Wolpe, J. *Psychotherapy by reciprocal inhibition.* Stanford: Stanford University Press, 1958.

10 *The Psychophysiologic Disorders*

The psychophysiologic disorders are certain conditions in which structural changes in the body are attributed mainly to emotional disturbance. These reactions, also called *psychosomatic disorders,* are the end effects of the intimate interrelationship between body and mind, that is, the inseparable interaction between personality and emotional conflict on the one hand, and the autonomic nervous system on the other. In the psychophysiological disorders, organs are affected which are not under voluntary or conscious control, for example, the lungs or the colon. Incidentally, this close association between physiology and emotions is a common thing to the layman: we note that a person blushes with shame, or see the blood drain from the face of the frightened, or try to calm the butterflies in our stomachs. Modern physiology recognizes that the *autonomic nervous system* is involved in such reactions. The autonomic nervous system serves the twofold functions of preparing the body for emergencies or danger, and maintaining the homeostasis level of the body under normal conditions. For these functions, the autonomic system is subdivided into the *sympathetic system,* which is significantly involved in emotional behavior, and the *parasympathetic system,* which is primarily concerned with

the maintenance of body functions. In general, the sympathetic and the parasympathetic nervous systems are antagonistic in actions, with the sympathetic taking over in emotional situations and the parasympathetic working to restore the normal body balance. For example, the sympathetic system acts to accelerate the heart rate during emotions while the parasympathetic system acts to maintain the normal heartbeat under nonstressful conditions. The digestive activity of the stomach is inhibited by the sympathetic nervous system but accelerated by the parasympathetic system. The master-control mechanism appears to be centered in the *hypothalamus* in the brain. As the center of endocrine and autonomic nervous system control, the hypothalamus coordinates and controls the organ-behavior and hormone-secretion condition of the body during emotions. For example, changing the physiologic balance of the hypothalamus may lead to either a reduction in sensory-motor activity having a tranquilizing effect, or a facilitatory action on emotions having a counterdepressant effect.

What causes the appearance of psychosomatic symptoms? Overall is the view that the person suffering from a psychophysiologic reaction has failed to develop a successful defense against anxiety. Unlike the psychoneurotic, the psychosomatic patient has failed to find some way of discharging his tensions; instead they are channeled through his organs. The stresses and conflicts, of course, still remain unconscious to a great degree. The mystery lies in the choice of organ involvement (*organ specificity*), that is, why some persons develop a bleeding ulcer, others break into persistent hives, while still others go into bronchial spasms. Several theories have sought to explain these variations in organ involvement:

1. Genetic or constitutional weakness —inherited or constitutionally based weakness may predispose. the individual to breakdown of a specific organ. Some support for this is obtained from the hereditary occurrence of diabetes and the apparent relationship between body type and pulmonary tuberculosis.

2. Conditioned weakness—previous physical illness or injury has been viewed as contributing to organ susceptibility under future stress. A person who has had a respiratory infection may become prone to asthma. This viewpoint is similar to the first theory in the belief that a breakdown will occur at the weakest link in the human body.

3. Psychodynamic specificity—each personality structure and conflict is associated with a specific organic expression. Investigators such as Flanders Dunbar (1943) hypothesize that patients with the same physical symptoms also show the same personality dynamics. Peptic ulcer patients, for example, are described as conscientious, ambitious workers who are in conflict over their passive dependency (see Table 10-1, see pages 254 and 255).

4. Stress specificity—separate physiological defense patterns are aroused by different threats. Where the defensive arousal becomes prolonged, a chronic physiological state develops. Anxiety leads to the release of stomach acid secretions; persistence of the anxiety and the acidity can produce ulceration—eating up of the stomach wall by stomach acid, as is the case in peptic ulcers.

5. Symbolic specificity—the bodily symptom is the residual symbolic representation of the emotional state. For example, the suppressed gasp for help may continue on as the spasmodic breath of the asthmatic. This theory differs slightly from the psychodynamic specificity in that symbolic specificity suggests that the symptoms are directly imitating the actions of an emotional event.

A wide range of psychophysiologic reactions have been categorized. In all, certain common aspects are present:

Real organic illness exists which requires medical treatment.

The organs involved are under autonomic, hence involuntary, control.

The illness is a result of emotions and their physiological concomitants.

The organic symptom development does not serve to reduce the tensions.

It should be emphasized that the psychosomatic symptoms are the associated physical reactions to stress and emotions. Although the symbolic specificity theory is offered by some, the psychophysiologic reactions are not viewed as being psychological defense mechanisms as is the case with conversion reactions and hypochondriasis.

Among the basic types of psychophysiologic reactions are the following:

1. Psychophysiologic skin reactions— e.g., neurodermatitis, "hives."

2. Psychophysiologic musculoskeletal reactions—e.g., arthritis, backache, cramps.

3. Psychophysiologic respiratory reactions—e.g., asthma, hayfever, sinusitis.

4. Psychophysiologic cardiovascular reactions—e.g., hypertension, migraine, angina.

5. Psychophysiologic hemic and lymphatic reactions—e.g., psychogenic hemorrhage.

6. Psychophysiologic gastrointestinal reactions—e.g., ulcers, constipation.

7. Psychophysiologic genitourinary reactions—e.g., certain menstrual disturbances.

8. Psychophysiologic endocrine reactions—e.g., obesity, certain types of hyperthyroidism.

9. Psychophysiologic nervous system reactions—e.g., loss of strength.

10. Psychophysiologic reactions of organs of special sense—e.g., vertigo.

A final, rather important, distinction is necessary before discussion of the psychophysiologic reactions continues. This is the difference between psychosomatic and *somatopsychic*. Somatopsychology is an entire branch of psychology concerned with the reverse of psychosomatics, the emotional changes that occur because of a physical condition. Psychosomatic medicine stresses the ability of the emotions to affect the physical state, somatopsychology stresses the ability of the bodily state to affect the emotions. Suinn (1967) has discussed the various classes of psychological consequences of physical illness or disability. These involve injury-linked reactions, common emotional reactions to disablement, and idiosyncratic reactions:

The *injury-linked reactions* are those so directly associated with the organic injury as to be part of the clinical picture, e.g., injury to the brain is associated with impairment of memory, intellect, orientation. This association is so intimate that diagnosis of the locus of the damage can be made from knowledge of the psychological symptoms.

Common emotional reactions to disablement are those associated with the state of being disabled, no matter what the origin or nature of the disability. These appear so common that they might be called "normal" emotional reactions. From this viewpoint, their *absence* in

a patient is of greater significance than their presence. These emotional reactions can be conceived of as falling roughly into the following sequential stages: (1) Shock . . . , (2) Implicit denial . . . , (3) Emotionality: Depression, Anxiety . . . , (4) Partial adaptation . . . , (5) Adaptation.

Finally, the *idiosyncratic reactions* are those associated with the individual personality makeup and life setting of the patient. These are the personal reactions which characterize one person and make him easily identified from another. (Suinn, 1967, pp. 13-14).

A complete, holistic understanding of the patient suffering from a psychophysiologic reaction should ultimately take into account the somatopsychological reactions. A patient who has survived a heart condition originally associated with emotional factors may now face a new set of emotional conditions as a heart attack victim. He may become overly concerned about physical exertion for fear of another heart attack; he may perceive himself as quickly drawing near the end of his life; he may become depressed at a handicap which he has little control over. Such new tensions may in turn create further somatic difficulties, and so on.

Some of the more common psychophysiologic reactions will be discussed in the following part of this chapter. Among the disorders to be described are:

1. Peptic ulcers
2. Asthma
3. Essential hypertension
4. Coronary artery disease

GASTROINTESTINAL REACTIONS: PEPTIC ULCERS

A peptic ulcer is a condition involving the gradual sloughing off of a small area of the stomach tissue, leaving that particular place continuously raw. The ulcer may vary in size from a pin head to a silver dollar and is usually situated near the outlet of the stomach to the duodenum.

TABLE 10.1. *Psychological Characteristics of Four Psychosomatic Types*

	ULCERATIVE COLITIS	PEPTIC ULCER	ESSENTIAL HYPERTENSION	BRONCHIAL ASTHMA
General neurotic traits	Immature Insufficiently balanced Passive-dependent Egocentric Over-sensitive and vulnerable Impaired adaptability Insecure Inadequately regulated discharge of aggression Difficulty in interpersonal communication	Immature Insufficiently balanced Passive-dependent Egocentric Over-sensitive and vulnerable Impaired adaptability Insecure Inadequately regulated discharge of aggression Difficulty in interpersonal communication	Immature Insufficiently balanced Passive-dependent Egocentric Over-sensitive and vulnerable Impaired adaptability Insecure Inadequately regulated discharge of aggression Difficulty in interpersonal communication	Immature Insufficiently balanced Passive-dependent Egocentric Over-sensitive and vulnerable Impaired adaptability Insecure Inadequately regulated discharge of aggression Difficulty in interpersonal communication
Outward appearance	Mild, "average", sometimes pseudovirile Sentimental polite Ambition Activity Honesty ⎫ Moderate Diligence Reliability ⎭ Neat Obedient-dutiful ("Conventional super-ego", middle-classy) Compliant Socially moderately successful	Driving, self-asserted Business-like Ambition Activity Honesty ⎫ Marked Hard-working Reliable ⎭ Careful; orderly Conscientious-dutiful (Highly developed super-ego, idealistic) Dominant Often successful	Controlled, driving Correct Ambition Activity Fanatically-honest ⎫ Marked Hard-working Reliable ⎭ Careful; orderly Compulsive-dutiful (Strict super-ego, rigid-normative) Partly docile, partly aggressive Often successful	Sometimes shy, often exacting, and stubborn At times docile, at times irritable and impatient Ambition Activity Honesty ⎫ By outbursts Diligence Reliability ⎭ Compulsive Dutiful by outbursts (Super-ego insufficiently incorporated) Exacting, often in protest, tyrannical Sometimes successful, often social failures

TABLE 10-1. (*Continued*)

	ULCERATIVE COLITIS	PEPTIC ULCER	ESSENTIAL HYPERTENSION	BRONCHIAL ASTHMA
Social behavior pattern	Imitation of standards of other people	Living up to high ideals	Rigid, living on principles	Poorly adapted, feel easily wronged, often in protest. Impulsive, unpredictable
Preferred pattern of abreaction of aggression	Transferred to parental figure	Competitive	Destructive ("hot tempered") ("throw the truth in one's face")	Domineering
Attitude toward marriage partner	Overtly dependent, often frigid or impotent. Marriage often late or not at all	Ambivalent: dependent but overtly protective and dominant. Loyal to partner Sex life usually normal	Ambivalent: on one hand conforming to partner's standards, on the other hand dominating and aggressive Sometimes promiscuous	Ambivalent: on one hand tyrannical and exacting; on the other hand dependent Often frigid or impotent Sometimes promiscuous
Basic mood	Insecure and anxious	Insecure and driving	Insecure and aggressive	Insecure and oppressed

SOURCE: From J. Bastiaans, The place of personality traits in specific syndromes: cause or effect. In J. Wisdom and H. Wolff (Eds.), *The role of psychosomatic disorder in adult life.* London: Pergamon Press, 1965.

The patient first becomes aware of a burning, gnawing pain in the stomach appearing regularly within a few minutes to an hour or two after each meal. In more severe cases, vomiting results. Hemorrhaging may take place to such an extreme that the patient passes black tarry stools. Loss of blood may then occur so rapidly as to leave the patient weak and in serious danger. The ulceration is due to the failure of the gastric secretions to stop after the food substances are passed into the intestines. As an aid in digestion, the normal gastric secretions include much hydrochloric acidity which can lead to inflammation of the stomach wall if not stopped.

Dynamics

Correlation between the emotions of the individual and the activity of the stomach was first noted by Beaumont (1833) in his observations of a patient who sustained an opening in his stomach wall from a gunshot wound. Wolf and Wolff (1943) recorded the relationship between specific emotions and gastric activity in a patient with a fistula (opening) following surgery. Extensive observations were conducted in an attempt to obtain the maximum advantage from this unique condition. The patient was carefully supervised and his gastric reactions analyzed during various emotional states. The scientists found that panic reactions led to a temporary paling of the mucous membrane of the stomach wall. In addition, there was a reduction of gastric secretions. During anger and anxiety, there was just the opposite—an increase in blood and a distinctive stimulation of the production of secretions. Both of these conditions, mucous membrane swelling and increased hydrochloric acidity, heighten the vulnerability of the stomach tissues to injury. Mittelmann and Wolff (1942) worked together on an experimental study of a number of normal subjects and patients with somatic difficulties. Gastric secretions were obtained by means of a nasal catheter. The subjects were studied when relaxed and after the experimental arousal of stress through the initiation of emotionally charged topics. Increased hydrochloric acid secretion was noted to decrease in relaxed sessions and increase in emotional sessions for the normal subjects. For one peptic ulcer patient, the gastric secretions increased to such a high level during a period of intense anger that hemorrhaging was soon detected. It seems conclusive, therefore, that certain emotions such as anger and anxiety may establish a condition within the stomach which makes the individual vulnerable to developing an ulcer.

Earlier studies have attempted to describe the "peptic ulcer personality." Among the traits noted were:

immaturity
egocentricity
competitiveness
ambitiousness
successfulness
conscientiousness

More recently, the trend has shifted toward describing the basic conflicts and attempts of the individual to cope with these. Sawrey and Weisz (1956), for example, produced ulcers in rats by subjecting them to an approach-avoidance conflict. The most repeated conflict mentioned is the dependency-independency problem. On the one hand, the person wishes to be loved and cared for, to cling to someone who would be protective and responsible for any decisions in life. Yet, this is incompatible with the person's self-image of self-reliance and assertiveness. This self-concept of competency becomes an all-consuming drive as the individual reacts against his underlying infantile passivity. He undertakes activities which tend to prove his self-sufficiency, exhibits active ambition, and quite often becomes successful in his occupation. In fact, in some high pressure business agencies the ulcer

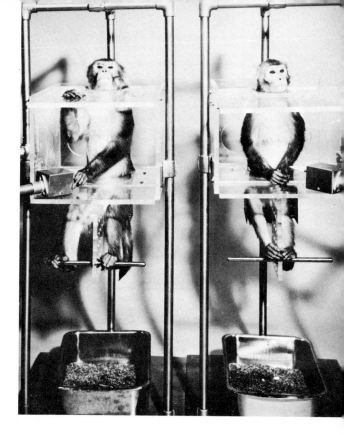

An experiment which produced *ulcers*. The "executive" monkey on the left has learned that he must press a lever to prevent shocks to himself and his companion. The companion monkey has lost interest in the dummy lever next to him. Only executive monkeys developed ulcers. (Medical Audio Visual Department/Walter Reed Army Institute of Research)

is the symbol of the successful executive. Dr. Alexander, a renowned psychoanalyst, has theorized on the particular link between dependency conflict and ulceration of the stomach. He hypothesizes that in infancy, being fed is the one primary activity which epitomizes all of the characteristics entailed in being dependent and being cared for. The infant during feeding is carried, cuddled, loved and, for the moment, is the sole object of the mother's affection and attention. Feeding and dependency become intimately associated. In the future, Alexander speculates, the digestive processes are again stimulated whenever dependency needs are aroused but denied gratification. It is as if the earlier dependency satisfaction-food digestion tie was again recalled as a form of conditioned response. Alexander (1934) supports this contention by referring to the many patients whom he has treated who displayed in their dreams and fantasies an unconscious longing for comfort, for support, and for affectional care. In

addition, he points out the fact that ulcer patients sometimes recover without any special treatment other than bed rest or hospital care.

Environmental stresses have been offered as one of the component factors in producing ulcers. Brady (1958) stumbled onto the topic in his research on avoidance conditioning in monkeys. After the death of several trained monkeys, the investigator discovered that gastrointestinal damage had occurred. He pursued the conditions causing such ulceration and developed a training arrangement involving an "executive" monkey. In this arrangement, two monkeys are placed side by side in chairs and shocked during certain time intervals. The executive monkey can prevent the shock to himself and his partner by pressing a lever, the other monkey has no control whatsoever but must rely upon the actions of his neighbor. Brady observed that the ulcers appeared in the executive monkey with such severity that death resulted, but the non-

257

executive monkey was spared any signs of illness. An additional result suggested that the gastric activity leading to ulceration increased during the rest period *after* the shock session, and only if the sessions were six hours long. It is indeed difficult to refrain from drawing an analogy with the preceding discussion. Perhaps the executive monkey was faced with the stressful chore of being the only responsible and independent personage in the experimental setting and could not permit himself even the slightest slip to the dependent, passive-recipient role of his partner.

Of final interest in the possible etiology of peptic ulcers is the findings on individual differences in gastric activity. Mirsky and his colleagues (Mirsky, Futterman, and Kaplan, 1952) reported a

Case History 10-1

PEPTIC ULCERS

Mr. M., aged 30, worked as an electronics engineer in an aerospace firm. His assignment involved the design of a new type of supersonic aircraft being submitted by the firm for contract support by the government in competition with several other industries. Although the responsibilities were enormous, he seemed to delight in the challenge. In fact, the experience of planning was perceived as an important step toward further advancement in the firm. The first sign of gastric difficulty was a burning discomfort after an evening meal. This gnawing sensation disappeared only to return periodically after eating. Physical examination disclosed the presence of a peptic ulcer.

The patient had lived a hard-working, independent life ever since adolescence. As the oldest of a large family, he was soon ignored as his parents devoted their efforts toward the younger offspring. He obtained his first job while still in high school and began to learn a trade. He stayed in the same occupation upon receiving his high school diploma. After an adequate showing on the job, he decided to return for further education in order to increase his future earning power. College was difficult and Mr. M was pleased when he received his bachelor's degree. From that date forward, he was engaged in a number of transfers from firm to firm in an ever-increasing attempt to reach a higher and higher level position. He kept an eye out for property investments and lived on a cautious budget which permitted him to buy some land while still having an adequate amount for his family. Just prior to his latest assignment on the government-bid design, he was beginning to feel the pressures of a number of major decisions—the purchase of a new home, the shift of his oldest son to a different school, the desire of his wife to go on an extensive vacation, the sale of his investment property.

A strict diet and an enforced regime of recreation was initiated. The patient retained his assignment but was confronted with the heightened stress it placed on him. He was advised to declare a moratorium on any financial ventures including the sale of the property. Discussions with the wife regarding the family and occupational pressures were begun and her role in facilitating their relief examined. The ulcer pains diminished within a few months.

relationship between pepsinogen in blood and in urine and peptic ulcers, with peptic ulcer patients showing higher amounts of pepsinogen than normal persons. The level of pepsinogen in blood is determined early in life, perhaps genetically, and remains constant throughout life. Thus, it is possible that those who are susceptible to ulcers are those whose secretion level is already high. In a later study, Weiner, Thaler, Reiser, and Mirsky (1957) selected 120 army inductees out of 2073 on the basis of showing high or low pepsinogen values. Before the end of basic training, an assumed stressful circumstance, nine men developed ulcers. Of these nine, eight were in the upper 5 percent of the pepsinogen distribution and the remaining man was in the upper 15 percent. In addition they had been correctly identified by psychological measures as being vulnerable on the basis of dependency-conflicts.

In summary, it would seem that peptic ulcers are likely to appear in individuals under the following conditions:

1. The individual is characterized by a high level of gastric activity even under normal conditions.

2. The individual is in conflict over dependency needs.

3. The individual is exposed to environmental stress arousing conflict.

Treatment

The medical treatment of the ulcer includes a prescribed diet, rest, and the avoidance of alcohol, tobacco, and coffee. In severe cases, modern surgical techniques are employed to remove the ulcerated area. The patient must learn to identify which environmental circumstances he can deal with adaptively, which demands he must learn to meet with more adaptive behavior, and which situations he must completely avoid. Psychotherapy is directed toward the underlying conflicts connected with the assumption of responsibilities in life.

RESPIRATORY REACTIONS: ASTHMA

Bronchial asthma is an illness characterized by the inability to breathe freely because of muscular spasms and the accumulation of serum in the bronchial tissue (edema). The movement of air through the lungs is a function of the elasticity of the bronchial tubes (the tracheo-bronchial tree of the lungs) and the amount of obstruction of these tubes. In an asthmatic attack, the muscles of the small bronchials contract, decreasing the amount of air flow. The swelling of the lining membranes and the addition of edema both act as obstructions which produce a wheezy breathing sound. The attacks may be mild with labored breathing or severe with the subjective feeling of suffocation. A sudden onset leaves the patient extremely distressed, fighting for air, his chest heaving with effort and convulsive coughing. The attack may last for a few minutes or continue for hours or even days. In the periods in-between, the patient is entirely symptom-free. Attacks may be highly seasonal, subject to certain specific irritants, or triggered by physical activity. In asthma which is allergenic, the attacks are clearly associated with the presence of allergens. An allergen is a substance to which the patient is extremely sensitive and which elicits what may be a violent physical reaction.

Medical advances have clearly shown that some asthmatic conditions are due solely to allergen-reactions. The irritating substance may be a pollen such as ragweed, or a food such as cereal or eggs. Changing weather conditions, which produce shifts in the pollen count in the atmosphere, can yield an attack. Research has also indicated that some asthmatic conditions are entirely caused by emotional variables. Emotional stresses or continuing conflicts can be responsible for arousing the spasmodic breathing attack. It is toward these latter conditions that the diagnosis of psychophysiological reaction applies.

Dynamics

A number of experimenters have reported respiratory symptoms in animals under experimental stress. For example, Liddell (1951) recorded symptoms resembling the labored breathing of asthmatics, and Gantt (1941) produced recognizable wheezing in his experimentally neurotic dog. It is not known whether these animals also exhibited the other pulmonary changes characteristic of asthma. Other experimenters were able to initiate asthmatic attacks to neural stimuli by means of classical conditioning, thereby raising the possibility that neutral cues paired with emotional stress may eventually act as precipitating situations (Dekker, Pelser, and Groen, 1957). A remarkably daring study was reported by Stein (1962) in which asthmatic patients were confined in a small chamber locked from the outside by a door the thickness of a bank vault and filled with an array of electronic instruments. Although the box was allergen-free, one patient showed marked apprehension (an understandable reaction) and went into a severe asthmatic attack. A placebo solution was administred to determine whether the asthma would be relieved, but the patient was helped only when correct medication was given. The general line of evidence from these various researches argues in favor of the belief that emotional circumstances may well act as triggering mechanisms that bring on asthma.

Of greater interest to psychologists and psychoanalysts are the hypotheses regarding the specific conflict patterns which describe the asthmatic patient. A frequent explanation suggests that the fear of separation from the mother leads to a cry for help which is the prototype of the later respiratory problem. In this light, it is interesting that Stein produced an asthmatic seizure by the arousal of fear in an isolation situation. An extreme extension of the separation hypothesis proposes that the patient unconsciously wishes to return to the intrauterine life within the mother during which respiration was not experienced or needed. Other theories interpret the spasmodic intake of breath as a suppressed rage reaction. The asthmatic is seen as harboring ambivalent feelings toward the parent, with resentment and rage being controlled for fear of complete rejection by the mother. French and Alexander (1941) extensively examined ten patients with asthma and their parents. They noted that all ten expressed strong feelings of ambivalence toward their mothers associated with a feeling that they had been deprived of maternal love. In actuality, nine of the mothers were described as rigid, insecure, and domineering while the fathers were apparently meek, passive, and ineffectual. The appearance of numerous dreams of water and drowning led to the speculation that these dreams symbolized the fear of separation. (However, it must be noted that real-life experiences with near-drownings by some of these patients may well have conditioned such dreams.) The overall viewpoint sees asthma as occurring in patients with heightened dependency on the mother, fearful concerns about rejection, suppression of resentment reactions, and ultimately efforts to control and regain the relationship.

Treatment

Symptomatic relief from the asthmatic attack is possible through use of a variety of drugs. In very mild reactions, an antihistamine may provide some relief. In most cases, injection with epinephrine hydrochloride or aminophylline, or the oral inhalation of an epinephrine mist leads to immediate recovery from the attack. Where allergens are involved, preventive therapy is in order through the

Case History 10-2

ASTHMA

The patient was a 10-year-old child who was hospitalized with severe asthmatic attacks. According to the mother, the first symptoms appeared at age two and had become progressively worse with time. The mother had little time for the youngster since she worked full time as a clerk in a department store. The father was away most of the time on the road as a traveling sales representative. The patient was first cared for by an aunt, then by a baby-sitter, and finally by a practical nurse. He missed school often because of severe attacks which left him too exhausted for attendance at school. However, he still managed to do quite well through extensive reading and a strong interest in academic work to the exclusion of all other activity. He always seemed to develop a close relationship with his teachers. The recent attack had started soon after the mother had considered a transfer of schools. She had explored the possibility of a boarding school and was planning a visit. Two days before the visit, the patient came down with severe bronchial spasms which resisted the effects of his usual medication. He was rushed to the hospital and has been under close supervision since.

---

avoidance of the irritants or through injections designed to increase the body's tolerance. Deep trance suggestion has been reported as successful in inhibition of allergic reactions in those patients capable of deep hypnosis (Black, 1965). With children, counseling with the parents can help them modify their attitudes and contribution to the illness. Not infrequently, psychotherapy with the adult patient directed toward the hostile elements of his conflicts will reduce the symptoms. In some cases, the onset of the illness was precipitated by a current environmental conflict arousing aggressive feelings resembling an early familial conflict. Venting of the original repressed feelings frequently permits the patient to deal with his present difficulties with greater insight. The danger of such revival of childhood hostilities is the possibility that the impact may be so intense as to induce a very severe asthmatic attack during the treatment session. Fortunately, asthma is one of the few illnesses for which immediate symptomatic relief is possible given the correct medication.

CARDIOVASCULAR REACTIONS:

Essential Hypertension

Hypertension is an illness characterized by blood pressure above that normally registered—in the relaxed, resting normal adult the normal systolic arterial pressure is about 120 mm. Hg. (mercury) and the diastolic pressure is about 80 mm. Hg. Chronic increase of arterial blood pressure will occur with hardening of the arteries, a disease connected with aging. This "hardening" is basically a narrowing of the arteries, and since the same volume of blood is being circulated, the result is an increase in pressure. *Essential hypertension* is the term for chronic high blood pressure which has no known organic origin and which therefore has been assumed to be psychological in etiology. In all hypertensive ailments there exists a potential threat to life, the danger of heart failure or stroke. Death from heart failure lists among the leading causes of mortality in the United States (Fig. 10-1). Cerebral hemorrhage, or stroke, can also be fatal or may be survived with paralysis as a result.

Dynamics. Several observations have reported increased blood pressure under conditions of environmental stress (e.g., Fig. 10-2). In one report, students showed elevation of arterial pressure during a major college examination in which they reported feeling tension, apprehension, and anxiety (Bogdonoff, 1960). In another investigation, patients were examined following the Texas City disaster. Results showed that 57 percent of the people who

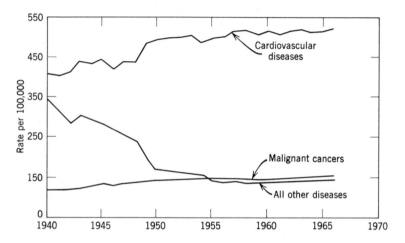

Figure 10-1. **Major causes of death in the United States.**
SOURCE: Adapted from U.S. Department of Health, Education, and Welfare, *Health, education, and welfare trends,* 1966-1967 edition, Part 1. Washington, D.C.: U.S. Government Printing Office, 1968.

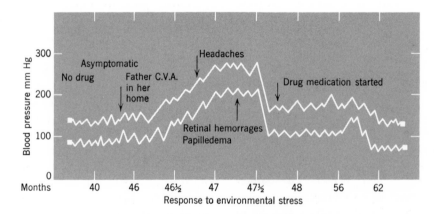

Figure 10-2. **Progress of essential hypertension during stress and medication. Patient shows severe recurrence after death of father to whom he was deeply attached.**
SOURCE: L. Mills, Psychodynamic factors in hypertension. In J. Nodine and J. Moyer (Eds.), *Psychosomatic medicine.* Philadelphia: Lea & Febiger, 1962.

Case History 10-3

ESSENTIAL HYPERTENSION

Mrs. H., a 45-year-old housewife was admitted to a clinic for headaches and dizziness. Her blood pressure was found to be extremely high requiring intensive medical therapy after which it returned to a normal level. She remained healthy and symptom-free for six months. At this time her daughter eloped with a boy who was a stranger to the mother, although the father had been informed of him by the daughter. Mrs. H. had previously cautioned her daughter over and over again about the necessity of care in choosing a mate. Nevertheless, Mrs. H. remained outwardly serene in the face of the seemingly impulsive wedding. Within a week of the elopement, the patient experienced a recurrence of hypertension.

The patient had always been a hard-working, and extremely neat housekeeper. Dishes were immediately cleaned and stacked after meals, soiled clothing washed and dried. She had strong opinions regarding the family discipline but very seldom engaged in open arguments with her husband. In fact, she was never known to be cranky or to shout in anger. Her children said that the best sign that she was losing her temper was her "sudden quiet manner." She maintained that arguments never won any battles and someone had to be reasonable.

survived showed quite abnormal diastolic pressures (over 95 mm. Hg.) which were maintained for up to one or two weeks after the stressful blast incident (Ruskin et al., 1948). Thus, as with all psychophysiologic reactions, the very intimate interrelationship between bodily functions and emotions appears evident.

Essential hypertension is a long-term symptom. Because the high blood pressure persists, psychopathologists have looked for more prolonged forms of emotional stress to explain this continuation of hypertension. The studies just mentioned prove that blood pressure is responsive to stress and that the physiological reaction may persist for a short period, but this is insufficient to account for the continuation of the ailment. Among the more popular explanations is the viewpoint that hostility conflict exists. Many hypertensives are described as being aggressive, bitter, and hostilely competitive. This aggressive component is held in check because of a need to retain strong dependent attachments. The individual suppresses the chronic rage and exhibits a facade of graciousness and affability. One possible speculation suggests that the anger leads to biochemical changes ultimately affecting blood pressure. Personality descriptions reveal an obsessive-compulsive perfectionistic style linked with overambitiousness. In addition to rigidity, it is also believed that the hypertensive person is emotionally insulated from interpersonal relationships and particularly fearful of those persons from whom they seek dependency gratification. The patient with high blood pressure has also been suspected of being involved in a "civil war" between passive-dependency needs and aggressive-assertive desires. Such a person appears more able to express hostility through indirect and rationalized outlets.

Treatment. At the present, drug medication relies upon tranquilizers and sympathetic nervous system inhibitors. Corrective and preventive measures include the use of sedatives, weight reduction, the avoidance of emotionally stressful situations. Unfortunately, a great many patients have waited too long before seeking treatment and the disease has progressed to an advanced state. If hospitalization is required, the patient is encouraged to engage in whatever is most relaxing such as staying in bed or light recreational activity. The tendency toward compulsive fearfulness is limited by the professional staff who are involved in the treatment program. In out-patient treatment, the capacity to release frustration and hostility through acceptable routes is necessary.

Coronary Artery Disease

Coronary artery, or heart disease is a term used in some medical works to cover several disorders: *coronary occlusion* (vascular blockage), *myocardial infarction* (heart failure), and *angina pectoris* (acute chest pains occurring after exercise or emotional stress). Although coronary disease has been traditionally and distinctively a medical illness, psychological factors have been raised pointing out the fine line that exists between the two realms of influence. Heart disease is still viewed predominately as a *medical* syndrome aggravated by emotional tensions and with somatopsychological effects. However, because of an exciting modern discovery, coronary artery disease deserves a more detailed attention in psychological writings. This section will outline the Friedman and Rosenman research breakthrough as a fascinating example of diligent research by physicians on the psychological aspects of heart disease.

The search for personality correlates of coronary occlusion and angina is not new.

Dunbar believed (1959) that personality traits acted as predisposing factors to coronary occlusion and angina. The former type of patients are described as:

Presenting a surface calm with little appearance of strain.

Possessing an air of self-sufficiency and a positive self-concept.

Using conversation and argumentation to dominate and control others.

Identifying with authority and attempting to become super-authorities.

Being extremely articulate about their feelings in an intellectualized way.

Suppressing their inner feelings and imagination instead of acting them out.

Having difficulty in expressing hostility but divert it into a course of action which will ultimately place them in a position of dominance.

The patients with angina pectoris are characterized as similar to the coronary occlusion patient with the difference being mainly in emphasis. Like the coronary persons, they show a strong drive to work, but their work records are slightly less stable, and they tend to choose occupations where they could be their own boss and achieve distinction without too much administrative responsibility. The predominant behavior patterns for both groups was the compulsive striving, the urge to get to the top through hard work and self-discipline. In the coronary patient, the striving was in occupations where one could work his way up; in the angina patient, the striving was in noncompetitive occupations where he could be his own boss. In both types of patients, the predominant conflict was an authority-conflict.

The Dunbar characterization of the

coronary personalities has been partly challenged, partly augmented by Friedman and Rosenman. In a series of well-planned and well-executed studies, they set out to demonstrate that specific observable behavior patterns are associated with coronary heart disease. Basically, they delineated two behavior pattern groups:

Pattern A—persons are characterized by the following:

1. An intense, sustained drive to achieve self-selected but usually poorly defined goals.

2. Profound inclination and eagerness to compete.

3. Persistent desire for recognition and advancement.

4. Continuous involvement in multiple and diverse functions constantly subject to time restrictions (deadlines).

5. Habitual propensity to accelerate the rate of execution of many physical and mental functions.

6. Extraordinary mental and physical alertness.

Pattern B—persons who were the converse of Pattern A, characterized by:

1. Lack of desire to compete.

2. Relative absence of drive for advancement and recognition.

3. Lack of involvement in deadlines.

4. Lack of propensity to accelerate speech, mental, and physical functions.

5. Placidity.

In each study, the initial selection of the subjects was made by certain laymen in various corporations, businesses, unions, and religious orders. Once these candidates were selected, the researchers interviewed them and classified them a second time. In nearly all cases, the typing agreed with the laymen's original classification, thus proving that the behavior patterns are clearly and readily observable patterns of life. Examination of the individuals ruled out any significant influences on the results which might have been due to differences in exercise, calorie or fat intake, alcohol, cigarettes, age, height, or weight. In the women studied, differences in the

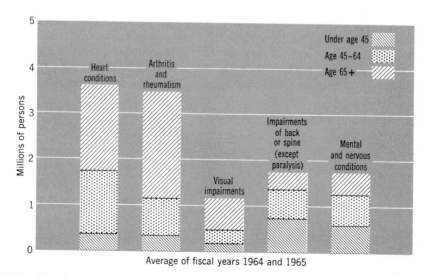

Figure 10-3. **Chronic conditions causing limitation of major activities, such as working, keeping house, attending school.**
SOURCE: U.S. Department of Health, Education, and Welfare, *Health, education, and welfare trends,* 1966-1967 edition, Part 1. Washington, D.C.: U.S. Government Printing Office, 1968.

menopausal state were also controlled. To determine the incidence of coronary artery disease, the subjects' medical histories were taken and all underwent extensive blood studies and electrocardiogram recordings. These medical records were then analyzed "blind," that is, possible biases in diagnoses were ruled out by forcing the pathologists to determine the presence of abnormality without any knowledge of whose records they were examining.

Some of the findings of the studies are given below.

The Study of Men (Friedman and Rosenman, 1959). Type A men were drawn from engineering, paper manufacturing, and aluminum corporations, newspaper organizations, advertising agencies, grocery chains, television stations, and other independent businesses. Type B men were from a union of a municipal government, a union of professional embalmers, and several accounting firms during relatively quiet business months. Twenty-eight percent of type A men showed clear-cut signs of coronary disease as compared with only four percent of type B men. Interestingly enough only four of the 23 pattern A subjects with evidences of coronary disease had been even the slightest bit aware that they had suffered a cardiac ailment, although the clinical signs were indisputable!

The Study of Women (Rosenman and Friedman, 1961). Pattern A women were composed of 125 attorneys, physicians, political executives, white collar workers, unemployed women and nuns from an "admittedly forceful" order of sisters. Pattern B women consisted of 132 housewives, white collar workers, and "placid" nuns in a teaching order. Type A women showed four times the incidence of coronary artery disease as type B

women, as well as a higher cholesterol level and a faster blood-clotting time. In addition, there was a significantly higher incidence of hypertension in type A women (three to seven times higher). Of interest was the separate analysis of the data of the two groups of nuns, none of whom smoked, consumed alcohol, or engaged in physical activity other than walking. Nine cases of coronary disease were found in type A nuns as compared with one case in the type B nuns.

The Study of Fat Ingestion (Friedman, Rosenman, and Byers, 1964). The researchers were concerned about the findings associating pattern A with cholesterol level. In this study, men were studied in pairs, with each fasting overnight for thirteen hours, then partaking of the same breakfast. Vascular physiology was examined by means of photographs taken of the blood vessels of the eye through a microscope. The results showed that the pattern A and B men were alike in the free flow of blood prior to breakfast; however, four hours later, pattern B men showed no change while pattern A men showed significant vascular obstruction by "clumsily transported, irregular masses that caused an intermittence and marked sluggishness of flow" (p. 881). It seems evident that pattern A is related not only to the onset of coronary disease, but also to faulty cholesterol and fat removal, a condition that can be preliminary to coronary disease.

The Western Collaborative Group Study (Rosenman, Friedman, Straus, Wurm, Kositchek, Hahn, and Werthessin, 1964; Rosenman, Friedman, Straus, Wurm, Jenkins, and Messinger, 1966). Over *three thousand* men from eleven industries and sci-

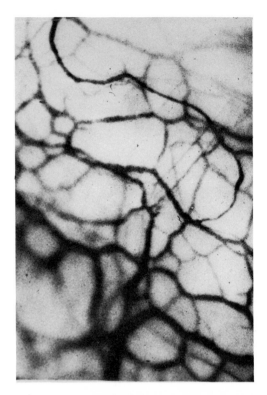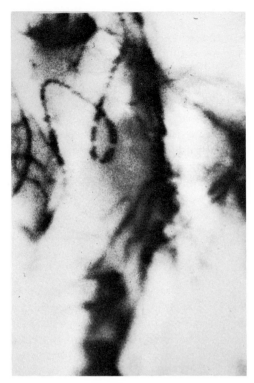

Research has identified Pattern A persons as vulnerable to *cardiovascular* diseases. In addition, these persons show a poorer ability to deal with fatty foods. Photomicrographs above show vessels before (*left*) and 6 hours after (*right*) fat ingestion. In strong contrast to the normal vasculature on the left, the right photograph shows sludging, "beading" of vessels, and the obliteration of most preexisting vessels. (**From** *Pathogenesis of Coronary Artery Disease* **by Meyer Friedman, M. D. Copyright © 1969 by McGraw-Hill Inc. Used with permission of McGraw-Hill Book Company**)

entists from three major cities across two states participated over a long term. Initial work began in 1960 to 1962 during which attempts were made to predict which of the men would be subject to coronary heart disease in the future. Over a two-year period, pattern A men incurred coronary diseases at a rate three times that for type B, with the younger type A men (ages 39-49) showing a rate over six times that for type B men of the same age. In addition, the behavior pattern diagnostic method was compared with prediction based on a purely medical method, the examination of lipid data (beta/alpha lipoprotein level). The results indicated that the behavior pattern method was the more useful method for predicting coronary disease with minimal error involving failure to identify a coronary-prone person. The researchers also attempted to determine the characteristics which made an individual "immune" to coronary disease. They discovered that low cholesterol level or a low beta/alpha level were both associated with high immunity. Behavior pattern B was also good insurance against coronary disease; however, even the slightest tendency toward some of the pattern A traits immediately increased an individual's vulnerability to disease. The researchers were so impressed by this that they concluded that immunity was a function of low lipid level and *fully-developed* pattern B behaviors.

Summary. The exciting work of Fried-man, Rosenman, and their colleagues deserves the title of "breakthrough." The identification of personality or behavioral variables, or of lipid levels, is in itself not unique. The breakthrough involves the systematic testing of each variable, psychological and medical, and the ultimate matching or combining of the two in a useful, predictive way. The exact nature of the mechanisms involved in behavior patterns and heart disease is still unknown, and preventive measures are still in their formative stage. It appears certain, however, that a number of factors interact in a complex way to pre-

Case History 10-4

CORONARY ARTERY DISEASE

Dr. S., a 45-year-old data-processing supervisor, is a typical case of coronary heart disease. He is married, smokes an average of 26 cigarettes a day, and earns an annual income of $14,000. His occupation gives him little opportunity for exercise other than walking although the corporation is instigating a program of planned physical activity for its administrative employees. He drinks "a manhattan or two" each evening to unwind from the day's work, but even then he continues to be occupied as he plans the next day's activities. At work he has the utmost respect from his employees and his superiors as a man who gets things done. He keeps intimately in touch with each and every job being processed and is always ready to take on new challenges. He prefers walking, to the delay of putting through a telephone call. Outside of work he is part of a community voluntary committee surveying food prices and is a member of the school board. His home is more like an extension of his office as he utilizes evening hours in order to accomplish more. And yet, the predominant tone of his activities is competency—although he seems pressed for time, he is efficient. He has taken on the task of writing an instructional book for data processing in industry, a task which has filled up the last remaining gap in his active schedule.

Dr. S. recently underwent his annual physical but under a new physician's care. Unlike previous cursory examinations, this one was quite extensive and included laboratory work-ups. He was found to be in good health although a little overweight. However, the medical history taken by the physician revealed that he had a brief period of discomfort several months previous. This was characterized by an uncomfortable tightness in the chest during his return up a flight of stairs following an unusually heavy luncheon. This chest sensation of pressure soon passed. The examining physician ordered an electrocardiogram which was found to be abnormal. There was indisputable evidence of a heart attack. Dr. S. was advised of his condition, and placed on a preventive program. His dietary habits were modified, he was encouraged to enroll in the physical activity program at work, and he was cautioned about his behavioral pattern of life.

cipitate coronary heart disease. Diet, weight, smoking, alcohol intake, the physiological functions connected with fat intake and blood coagulation, and the overt behavior pattern of men and women are all highly relevant. To the psychologist, the significant signs are those of pattern A persons: these individuals are "doers" capable of accomplishing their assigned functions; chronically harassed by their variety of committments, ambitions, and self-imposed deadlines; and eager to compete and to win in their endeavors, both vocationally and avocationally.

Glossary

Allergen: A foreign substance to which the individual is hypersensitive, which triggers off a physiological defense reaction.

Aminophylline: A drug used in the treatment of asthmatic spasms.

Angina pectoris: A heart disease involving pain and suffocation in the chest area.

Asthma: An illness involving muscular spasms and obstruction of air flow in the lungs.

Autonomic nervous system: Part of the peripheral nervous system governing internal organs; involves the sympathetic and parasympathetic systems.

Bronchial tubes: Part of the branches of the lungs.

Cathether: A slender tube inserted for drawing fluid.

Colon: Part of the large intestine.

Coronary artery disease: Diseases of the heart including vascular blockage and heart failure.

Duodenum: First section of the small intestine adjoining the stomach.

Edema: The accumulation of serum in the bronchial tissue.

Electrocardiogram: A graphic record of the heart's performance through the measurement of electrical activity.

Endocrine: Referring to internal bodily secretions, especially of the glands.

Epinephrine: The secretions of the adrenal glands; as a drug, used in the treatment of asthma.

Essential hypertension: High blood pressure.

Hemic reactions: Referring to the blood.

Hyperthyroidism: A condition involving the excessive secretion by the thyroid gland.

Hypothalamus: A part of the brain apparently controlling rage or fear behavior.

Lipids: Group of organic compounds consisting of the fats and similar substances.

Lymphatic: Referring to the bodily fluids derived from the blood.

Organ specificity: The choice of a specific organ for the development of a symptom.

Parasympathetic nervous system: Part of the autonomic nervous system often working during relaxed states and in opposition to the sympathetic nervous system.

Pepsinogen: A substance in the gastric glands necessary for the production of digestive enzymes.

Peptic ulcer: Ulceration of the stomach.

Psychophysiologic disorder: Disorders involving structural changes in the body attributed mainly to emotional disturbances.

Serum: Watery organic fluid, for example, blood serum.

Somatopsychology: The branch of psychology concerned with the influence of bodily states, such as physical illness or disability, on the emotions.

Sympathetic nervous system: Part of the autonomic nervous system often working during emergency states and in opposition to the parasympathetic nervous system.

Vertigo: Dizziness.

References

Alexander, F. The influence of psychological factors upon gastro-intestinal disturbances. *Psychoanal. Quart.,* 1934, **3**, 501.

Beaumont, W. *Experiments and observations on the gastric juice and the physiology of digestion.* Plattsburgh: F. A. Allen, 1833.

Black, S. The use of hypnosis in the treatment of psychosomatic disorders. In P. Hopkins & H. Wolff (Eds.), *Principles of treatment of psychosomatic disorders.* London: Pergamon Press, 1965.

Bogdonoff, M., Estes, E., Harlan, W., Trout, D., & Kirshner, N. Metabolic and cardiovascular changes during a state of acute central nervous system arousal. *J. clin. Endocrinol.,* 1960, **20**, 1333.

Brady, J. Ulcers in "executive" monkeys. *Scient. Amer.,* 1958, **119**, no. 4.

Dekker, E., Pelser, H., & Groen, J. Conditioning as a cause of asthmatic attacks. *J. psychosom. Res.,* 1957, **2**, 97.

Dunbar, F. *Psychosomatic diagnosis.* New York: Hoeber, Inc., 1943.

Dunbar, F. *Psychiatry in the medical specialties.* New York: McGraw-Hill, 1959.

French, T. & Alexander, F. Psychogenic factors in bronchial asthma, *Psychosom. Med. Monogr. IV,* Washington, D.C.: National Research Council, 1941.

Friedman, M., & Rosenman, R. Association of specific overt behavior pattern with blood and cardiovascular findings. *J.A.M.A.,* 1959, **169**, 1286.

Friedman, M., Rosenman, R. & Byers, S. Serum lipids and conjuntival circulation after fat ingestion in men exhibiting Type-A behavior pattern. *Circul.,* 1964, **29**, 874.

Gantt, W. Experimental basis of neurotic behavior. *Psychosom. Med. Monogr. 3,* No. 3 and 4, Washington, D.C.: National Research Council, 1941.

Liddell, H. The influence of experimental neuroses on respiratory function. In H. Abramson (Ed.), *Treatment of asthma.* Baltimore: William & Wilkins, 1951.

Mirsky, I., Futterman, P., & Kaplan, S. Blood plasma pepsinogen, II. The activity of the plasma from "normal" subjects, patients with duodenal ulcer and patients with pernicious anaemia. *J. labor. clin. Med.,* 1952, **40**, 188.

Mittelman, B. & Wolff, H. Emotions and gastroduodenal function: experimental studies on patients with gastritis, duodenitis and peptic ulcer. *Psychosom. Med.,* 1942, **4**, 5.

Rosenman, R., & Friedman, M. Association of specific behavior pattern in women with blood and cardiovascular findings, *Circul.,* 1961, 24, 1173.

Rosenman, R., Friedman, M., Jenkins, C., Straus, R., Wurm, M., & Kositchek, R. The prediction of immunity to coronary heart disease. *J.A.M.A.,* 1966, **198**, 1159.

Rosenman, R., Friedman, M., Straus, R., Wurm, M., Kositchek, R., Hahn, W. & Wethessin, N. A predictive study of coronary heart disease. *J.A.P.A.,* 1964, **189**, 15.

272 *Types of Abnormal Conditions, Their Dynamics and Treatment*

Ruskin, A., Beard, O., & Schaffer, R. Blast hypertension: elevated arterial pressure in the victims of the Texas City disaster. *Amer. J. Mid.,* 1948, 4, 228.

Sawrey, W., & Weisz, J. An experimental method of producing gastric ulcers. *J. comp. physiol. Psychol.,* 1956, **49,** 269.

Stein, M. Etiology and mechanisms in the development of asthma. In J. Nodine & J. Moyer (Eds.), *Psychosomatic medicine.* Philadelphia: Lea & Febiger, 1962.

Suinn, R. Psychological reactions to physical disability. *J. assoc. phys. ment. Rehab.,* 1967, **21,** 13.

Weiner, H., Thaler, M., Reiser, M., & Mirsky, I. Etiology of duodenal ulcer: I. Relation of specific psychological characteristics to rate of gastric secretion (serum pepsinogen). *Psychosom. Med.* 1957, **19,** 1.

Wolf, S. & Wolff, H. *Human gastric function.* New York: Oxford, 1943.

11 *The Conduct Disorders*

Over a century ago, Pinel reported on patients who showed no disturbance of their rational abilities, yet whose behaviors were as maladjusted as many mentally disturbed persons. These patients are not psychotic nor truly psychoneurotic and certainly not psychophysiologic reactions. They involve a wide variety of characteristics but share one in particular: they exhibit disorders in conduct or behavior that reflect a violation of the codes of conduct of the society. The particular ways in which these persons "act out" their conflicts differs to such a degree that grouping them under one heading is done mainly out of convenience. Historically there has been a number of differing classifications given to these groups of patients: *constitutional psychopathic inferiority, character disorder, moral feeblemindedness,* and *sociopath.* The term *sociopath* comes the closest to denoting the tendency of the patients to engage in behaviors which are either antagonistic to law and convention, or irresponsible and valueless to the society, or in some other way irritating to or actually condemnable by the culture. We have chosen to use the less technical term of *conduct disorder* since it avoids some of the ethical and moral connotations of the other classifications. Among the conduct disorders to be considered in this chapter are:

Antisocial Reactions
Dyssocial Reactions
Addictions
Sexual Deviations

ANTISOCIAL REACTIONS (PSYCHOPATHIC PERSONALITY)

Individuals in this classification are in constant difficulty with the authorities, are undependable employees, and are unable to relate to others with any degree of depth. Several distinctive features are said to characterize this form of conduct disorder:

Emotional immaturity
Lack of responsibility
Exceedingly poor judgment
Lack of ethical or moral values
Inability to learn from experience
Inability to postpone gratification
Outward sincerity but without depth
Marked poverty of feeling toward others
Inadequate motivation to develop talents
An abiding belief in being immune from the law

Those who have encountered one of these psychopathic perons tend to stress either his social ease or the crushing disappointment in him. Superficially, the psychopath excels in social relations. He is a good mixer, often the life of the party, charming, and may be quite sought after. He is facile and engaging and not infrequently admired for his social graces. Many are taken by him. On the other hand, those who become better acquainted are soon aware of his immaturity, superficiality, and chronic inability to make a success of his own life. Sooner or later he seems to stumble over himself, quickly losing the good impression he so easily built up. He becomes a true disappointment to those who were charmed to expect more, to those who began to believe in him, to those who continue to see his potential, to those who still hope for him. The psychopath seems to be personally instrumental in damaging his own image and his future, often by little things: a missed appointment at a critical time because he just didn't care, a broken promise, a fraudulent act on the spur of the moment. Surprisingly enough, when confronted with his misconduct the psychopath has enough false sincerity and apparent remorse that he renews hope and trust among his accusers. However, after several repetitions, his convincing show is finally recognized for what it is —a show. The psychopath is quite knowledgeable about the proper and accepted ways to behave. It even seems that he does not deliberately plan to lose his friends or to get into trouble. These events happen almost spontaneously and without forethought and certainly without foresight. He is quite willing to become a parasite on society, taking what he can and offering nothing in return. When he needs money, he might write a bad check even though he may have a more acceptable means at hand for an income. Friends are acquired and dropped as soon as their usefulness for the moment ends or his attention shifts to other immediate selfish needs. People are treated as tools rather than as persons. Included in this group of antisocial reactions are the chronic liar —the so-called pathological liar—and the swindler or confidence ("con") man.

Dynamics

The psychopathic personality has never been fully understood or explained. The earlier attempts to offer an explanation suggested that an inborn defect was the cause, hence the term *constitutional inferiority*. The psychopath was supposed to be a person who failed to inherit the qualities required for normal conscience. Thus, he lacks feelings of guilt and persists in amoral behaviors even though he knows he is breaking the law or social custom. Supporters of this view pointed to the evidence of criminality in the parents of psychopaths; however, we realize today that this is insufficient proof of a genetic influence. Furthermore, few would defend the viewpoint that conscience is inherited.

A common current emphasis holds that faulty conscience development is the critical feature of psychopaths, but that this deficit is due to environmental or psychogenic factors. The psychopath's lack of concern with the ethical and moral codes of his society, and the absence of concern for people in general, have been attributed to an early disturbance in parent-child relationships. For example, the psychoanalytic school proposes that the psychopath does not develop normally because he is fixated at an early stage due to frustration and parental rejection. He never forms a super-ego that would later serve as an intrinsic guide to conduct. In addition, he is unable to form a meaningful relationship with his own parents, the model for relationships with others. He remains fixated at a stage characterized by the pleasure principle, the search for immediate gratification without concern for consequences, and without the capacity for postponement. Finally, he develops an anxiety over authority (parental) relations which becomes modified into a rejection and perhaps even an active rebellion against authority standards. Several recent studies offer tentative support to the psychoanalytic premise about faulty early parental relationships. Examining the backgrounds of delinquents they called the "Children Who Hate," Redl and Wineman (1957) found that "the 'adult-child relationship' was severely damaged. Broken homes, the chain reaction style of foster home placement and institutional storage, a rapidly shifting galaxy of neglectful, disinterested, sometimes cruel and brutal adults formed a basic theme in the background histories of the youngsters. . . . Once the children were with us (in the treatment residential center), the parents seemed to lose interest in them almost entirely." (p. 566). Greer (1964) discovered that parental loss occurred more often among psychopaths than normals or neurotics; moreover, a higher proportion of psychopaths had lost a parent *before they were age five,* and more psychopaths than neurotics had lost both parents. O'Neal et al. (1962) studied a group of 524 males originally seen 30 years previous as children in a child guidance clinic. At the time of the study, they were fully grown, ranging in ages from 31 to 54. The records of those who were now diagnosed as psychopath by reason of their criminal records were compared with those now considered normal or falling in a classification other than psychopath. They found that the psychopaths had fathers who were themselves antisocial or alcoholic, or fathers who deserted, failed to supervise their children, or divorced their wives. A study by Ehrlich and Keogh (1956) on electroencephalographic (E.E.G.) records is provocative and pertinent to the psychoanalytic hypothesis of an early fixation and lack of personality maturation. These researchers examined the E.E.G. records of psychopaths institutionalized in a mental hospital and found that 80 percent of this group showed abnormal E.E.G. brain patterns. Specific examination of these abnormal patterns indicated patterns that were interpreted as signs of failure of maturation, poor integration of the cerebral cortex, physiological immaturity, and homeostatic disturbance. Ehrlich and Keogh comment that these patterns were more like those of children rather than adults.

The learning theory viewpoint offers a similar emphasis. The desire to please others and to form lasting relationships is seen as due to secondary reinforcement. It is believed that people acquire reinforcing value because they have been previously associated with positive rewards. Money or personal checks are in the same category: they are not valuable in and of themselves, but acquire reinforcing features because of what they are associated with, for example, the food that is purchased in turn reduces hunger. In the psychopath's history, people have never been associated with satisfaction, perhaps because the parents have been rejecting or absent, neglecting or punitive, cold or hostile. It is not so much that the psychopath is unable to form close and meaningful relationships, but rather that he has never acquired the motivation to do so. Bandura and Walters (1959) believe that the development of a *dependency motive* is necessary for socialization to be effective. The dependency motive involves the child's wanting the interest, attention, and approval of others; once this is acquired, the rewards of approval or attention or interest can then be made conditional on the child's conforming to the demands and prohibitions of his parents and society. In addition to dependency motivation, socialization demands are also required if the child is to grow into a normal member of society. If dependency is present but few socialization demands are made, then the child learns to expect and demand immediate and unconditional gratifications (a trait of the psychopath). Among the conditions that contribute to socialization failure, Bandura and Walters list lack of affectional nurturance, punitiveness or rejection, unsocialized behavior by the parental models themselves, and inconsistent disciplinary practices.

Socially conforming behavior can also be learned through the influence of anxiety. Even if the child does not learn socially acceptable behaviors through rewards, he might still learn to show such behaviors to avoid punishment. Avoidance learning, the acquiring of behaviors to avoid threatening events, may be as important a means for socialization as reward learning. The psychopath, however, seems to be characterized by a deficiency in avoidance learning. Lykken (1957) attempted to condition psychopaths through the use of shock. He found that the psychopaths not only showed minimal manifest anxiety, but less reactivity to the conditioned stimulus associated with shock, and poor avoidance learning where the learning was dependent upon the arousal of anxiety. Lykken concluded that psychopaths are clearly defective in the ability to develop conditioned anxiety, and they continue to emit responses even though these responses are punished. As will be recalled, the psychopath is not defective in the overall ability to learn skills; he is in many ways highly skillful socially and, unlike the psychotic, the psychopath can assume all the roles of normal people. Sherman (1957) tested psychopathic subjects and found them to show a *better* retention of meaningful and nonsense materials which they had learned in the experiment than nonpsychopathic criminals or neurotic patients. Thus, the deficiency in learning which seems to characterize the psychopath is a highly specific deficiency: the inability to learn from experience where the arousal of anxiety or the avoidance of threat is the key reason for the learning. The psychopath does not seem to be manifestly anxious, is not as reactive to the use of anxiety arousal as a motive for learning to behave, and seems even less affected by punitive consequences of his actions which are in the distant future. Hare (1966) gave psychopaths, nonpsychopathic criminals, and noncriminals, the opportunity to choose between an immediate painful shock or shock after a 10-second delay. Nonpsychopaths showed a strong preference for immediate shock in order to get it over with and avoid the distress of waiting; the psychopaths were more inclined to avoid the immediate discomfort. The psychopaths appeared to be more affected by immediacy; the future consequences seemed to have little emotional significance even when the "future" was delayed by a mere 10 seconds. Hare's study is consistent with the belief that the psychopath lives for the moment, fails to show foresight, and acts without concern for the possible negative consequences of his actions.

Another possible explanation for psychopathic behavior, especially the impulsive and aggressive variety, involves organic, neurological abnormality. The electroencephalographic recordings of psychopaths have sometimes been found to be abnormal (Hill and Watterson, 1942; Gottlieb, Ashby, and Knott, 1947; Knott and Gottlieb, 1943). The study by Ehrlich and Keogh (1956) mentioned earlier determined that 80 percent of their sample of mental hospital psychopaths showed E.E.G. abnormalities. Such E.E.G. readings are usually reported in patients with a known history of brain injury or disease, and their presence in psychopathic patients raises the possibility of neurological involvement. Schwade and Geiger (1956) found abnormal patterns in 453 of 623 delinquents, and offer the tentative suggestion that the brain pathology is either in the thalamus, the hypothalamus, or the amygdala. Closer analysis of the data and reports on E.E.G.'s, however, leads us to the more cautious conclusion that some, but not all, psychopaths exhibit antisocial actions because of organic impairment or damage. Common antisocial features that are perhaps attributable to neurological factors include assaultiveness, irritability, distractibility, restlessness, poor control, and difficulty in adapting to routine restrictions.

Treatment

The psychopathic or antisocial reaction has been perceived as untreatable for so long that very little research has been devoted to their treatment! The problem is aggravated by the fact that the psychopath's symptoms are neither psychotic nor psychoneurotic in nature; hence, they give the impression of being basically normal people who simply refuse responsibility and who will not learn to be different. In addition, little is really known about possible organic factors that might be involved in the psychopath's impulsive behavior. Until the etiological picture is clarified, systematic therapeutic procedures will be difficult to develop.

The one goal often established in the treatment of the psychopath is the development of a positive interpersonal relationship between therapist and patient. Although this is a common goal sought after in most psychotherapeutic settings, it is especially relevant since the antisocial reaction seems to lack a basic concern for people. A consistent, interested, accepting atmosphere is established which will permit the patient to begin interacting on a more trusting basis. With the younger patient, the therapist may be an older figure with the warmth and concern of a parent; with an older patient, the therapist may be a mature and effective person of the same age group or older. In some cases, a group of people serves as the treatment agents. Once a significant relationship has been developed, and once the patient becomes dependent to some degree on the therapist's approval or controls, then socialization training begins. In an understanding and consistent fashion, the patient is exposed to clear and firm standards of behaving. He interacts with therapeutic models who show him what is expected. He learns that there are positive effects and interpersonal satisfactions if he alters his previous modes of acting. He is led to experience the advantages of delay of gratification, and of cooperation with others.

Nearly every type of treatment method has been tried with the psychopath. Lindner, the author of the book *Rebel Without a Cause* (1944) has reported on a few successful cases using hypnoanalysis. Aichorn (1935), Jones et al. (1953), and Redl and Wineman (1957) have each independently worked with *mileau therapy*. Mileau therapy is based on the assumption that the entire community that comes into contact with the patient must be therapeutic; thus the patient does not have one therapist whom he is assigned to meet an hour every day, rather all of the staff whom he interacts with are treatment oriented and concerned about establishing the conditions for his recovery. The Wiltwyck School in New York has been described as an effectively conducted mileau therapy setting for youngsters who are delinquent (Glueck and Glueck, 1950). In cases involving acute excitement and mental confusion, drugs such as the tranquilizer chlorpromazine have been prescribed to help reduce such symptoms. Behavioral therapy has been utilized in an experimental residential program at Camp Butner, North Carolina (Burchard, 1967). At this camp, delinquents were systematically reinforced or punished contingent upon their behaviors. Cooperative and prosocial activities were rewarded, while behaviors such as lying, stealing, and cheating were punished (e.g., by the withdrawal of positive reinforcers). A similar approach was used by Schwitzgebel (1964) with young offenders. In support of the data indicating that the psychopath learns poorly when anxiety or threat is used, Schwitzgebel (1967) discovered that his delinquents altered their behaviors in the desired direction when reinforcers were used but did not change when punishment was used.

In general, the treatment of the psychopath or antisocial reaction has not been rewarding nor enlightening. The strong tendency to treat the psychopath as a criminal who must be held punishable for his behavior creates a barrier to effective therapy. The discrepancy between legal definitions of mental illness and psychiatric or psychological definitions sometimes

Case History 11-1

ANTISOCIAL REACTION

John P. was a very bright young man who might have been a successful economist. He was one of the more unusual psychopaths inasmuch as he found it desirable to complete a college education, earning a Master's degree in economics. His academic history was not without its ups and and downs; he was expelled from one institution for forging the dean's name on a check, and placed on scholastic probation at another school for poor grades. He was frank enough to admit that continuing in college was more "for a kick" and to show that he could "pull the wool over the instructor's eyes" and still graduate. He obtained his degrees mainly because of his exceptionally keen mind which could be highly productive when motivated, which was seldom. His social life was unbelievably active, and in fact, most of his school work was done by girlfriends. Several professors in economics worked long hours to try to light the spark that would release his full potential, but ultimately all recognized that John would go his own way unfazed and unaltered. Following his Master's, John worked at whatever occupation gave him the opportunity to pursue his current whims. He spent several months on a road gang in Alaska for adventure. He enjoyed the respectability of a part-time lectureship at a community college in California for a semester. He spent a year with the "hippies," then signed on as a seaman to the Philippines. He managed to stay away from prison mainly through his ability to charm his victims, who invariably felt a faint hope that they might personally be responsible for his reform. His most recent venture was an appointment as a research economist with city-planning. Although he contributed somewhat to the project, he frequently delayed his data analysis until deadlines were passed, and even then he turned in highly profound reports although they were totally lacking in data. He was still impressive enough so that he was not actually fired, but simply not rehired when his contract ended. To another person, this might have been a discouraging loss, but John simply went on a vacation to the nearest seashore and cashed another check . . . on a nonexistent account.

A group of Hippies illustrate the paradox of many protesters; such groups often attack the conventionalism of the "establishment," yet display themselves an even higher degree of group *conformity* especially in dress. Note the hair length, hair styling, clothing, and bare feet which increase their resemblance to one another. (Bioudi/PIP Photographers, Inc.)

makes it unclear as to what are the appropriate ways of handling the psychopath if his behaviors have included law-breaking. Imprisonment is costly to all concerned since it does not involve the therapeutic conditions needed for the true psychopath to learn to change. On the other hand, psychotherapeutic procedures are also costly since the ideal treatment program for the antisocial personality is yet to be devised. The consensus is that the antisocial reaction is extremely difficult to treat or to control either by incarceration or by therapeutic intervention, yet patients of this type are in need of some type of help rather than punishment for their emotional difficulties.

DYSSOCIAL REACTIONS

This type of individual is basically similar to the antisocial reaction except for a capacity to form strong loyalties to a group. His behaviors are then shaped by his group affiliation. Many are able to avoid encounters with the law; some become identified with a criminal gang and adopt its rules. The dyssocial person may join subsocieties such as the "arty" group, the beatnik, the hippies, the psychedelic drug takers (see the section on drug addiction), and become embroiled in an amoral way of life which isolates him from the more commonplace society of the majority. He may express an antagonism toward conforming while at the same time failing to recognize his own exaggerated acquiescence and conformity to his own group's codes. The dyssocial person who identifies with a criminal subsociety will experience a strong loyalty to his gang, resist those who are not also outside-the-law, and eventually become the hardened criminal. As with the arty type, the criminal finds his greatest satisfaction in his group membership.

Dynamics

In some cases, adolescent immaturity and rebellion play a major role. The individual is still in the stage of battling against authority, resisting tradition, being annoyed with parents and adults in general, and seeking self-identity. Peer relations serve to fill the void left by such secession from society. Intense emotional loyalties develop, and uncritical acceptance of the rules of the group results. In some groups, no rules are openly conveyed; rather the individuality of the person is stressed. Yet, rules of conduct and implicit values are quickly communicated and eagerly absorbed. The hippie may argue that he is protesting the "conformity-craze" of the larger society, yet it is amazing how much hippies resemble one another. There are no more strongly enforced "ethics" of behavior than in the criminal culture which condemns "stool-pigeons" by ostracism and other drastic actions. The psychopath's lack of planning for the future also frequently appears in the dyssocial individual and might be understood as resulting from a similar lack of maturity of psychological development. For example, the drug users live for the moment and worry little about the future. In defense of their behavior, group mem-

bers often take the position that their's is the only courageous and honest life, or that those on the outside can never be capable of truly evaluating the drug experience unless they belong, or that outsiders are too trapped in straitlaced morality and rigidity to share the insights that are connected with psychedelics. Some groups simply want to be alone and withdraw from even the mildest arguments about their lot in life. In one sense, the unique types of subgroups may be a social phenomenon similar to the goldfish swallowing or bathtub-gin behaviors of an earlier decade. The uncertainty of the future because of fantastically powerful nuclear armaments, and the weird feeling of having no control over one's destiny because of the seemingly monolithic political decision-making machinery of nations, may combine to trigger off the dyssocial withdrawal from society. The insecurity of the nation is replaced by the security of the subsociety; the vagueness of tomorrow is supplanted by the wonderous certainty of the psychedelic trip; the seeming inconstancy of international ethics is supplanted by the naive honesty of irresponsible existence.

Treatment

The hardened criminal who has introjected the mores of his own subsociety is unreachabe unless he can accept the richer rewards of identification with the larger law-abiding group. Becoming weaned from criminal elements who reinforce his orientation, acquiring skills that increase his chances for competing successfully via acceptable channels, and reforming his values and self-concept, are all necessary steps. For the noncriminal dyssocial individual, added growth and maturity helps. The opportunity to objectively survey his adopted sub-society, its meaning, its direction, its outcome, its influence, is important. And this can be accomplished only by standing apart from the persuasions of the ingroup as well as the exhortations of the extremist antigroup attackers. An occasional trauma will be revealing and enable a member to extricate himself, for example, from the dangers of drugs.

Case History 11-2

DYSSOCIAL REACTION

Allan W. was a junior college freshman raised in a wealthy family. He had a below average high school academic career, having shown little interest in schoolwork other than activities connected with basketball. Because of his poor grades, he enrolled in junior college with the hope of doing well enough to transfer to the same university attended by his older brother. It soon became evident that college life had no more appeal than high school; Allan remained in school mainly because his parents seemed to expect it of him. However, it was here that he was introduced to "acid" (LSD), through his associations with a small group of drug users. Allan was attracted by the similarity between the group's attitude toward education and his own, exemplified by their leader's belief that formalized education was confining and only drugs could really free the intellect. In addition, Allan was taken by the group's casual attitude toward drugs, the apparent honesty of the individuals in discussing themselves as they "once were," and their quickness to befriend him. One member pointed out the insights that he had gained from LSD and suggested that he had learned more from drugs than from any class. The following night, Allan "dropped acid" for the first time under the watch of two of his new-found associates. He was entranced by the vividness of his perceptions, the sudden flashes of understanding that he experienced, and the awesome feelings that were unleashed. When the effects of the drug wore off, he accepted a "joint" of marijuana to help him settle. Subsequently, Allan dropped acid an average of twice a week, each time with pleasant effects. He became an advocate of the drug, although he cautioned others that proper use required that "your head be in the right place"; bad trips were blamed on improper attitudes rather than on the properties of LSD. Allan soon took to withdrawing to the hillside to observe the sunset while under the influence of the drug. This experience was so profound as to be nearly a religious ecstacy. Although he was taking LSD at a high frequency, he never lacked a supply since his parents provided him with an ample allowance, and since his friends were always willing to provide him with some without charge.

Allan had only one bad trip, and speaks in an offhand fashion about it. During this occasion, he had taken some LSD in the morning—he could not estimate how much since his supply always involved an inestimable amount within sugar cubes. During a lapse of concentration (or a moment of poor judgment), he introduced another dosage into his body through a hypodermic needle. His next four to five hours were frightening: he found himself seeing faces in ugly, distorted fashion; he jumped at small sounds; he lost track of time; his surroundings moved about him in waves. He kept reminding himself

Case History 11-2 (*Continued*)

DYSSOCIAL REACTION

that this was all unreal and due to hallucinations and perceptual distortions. Finally, a friend discovered him cringing in a corner, gave him a tranquilizer, and remained nearby until the "freak-out" subsided. Allan's attitude toward LSD is still extremely positive; in fact, acid and his acid-head friends are the only aspects of life that seem to have any meaning to Allan. He is being dismissed from school for inferior grades, he has no desire to return home, and has little interest in employment. He admits to a total involvement in drugs, and to his apathy toward everything else, but he finds this justifiable. He is convinced that the world opened up by LSD is more significant; he cannot communicate what new gains or insights or contributions to life he has developed; he can only describe the immediate experience itself as too important to give up.

ADDICTIONS

Alcoholic Addiction

Alcoholism stands fourth among leading health problems in the United States, outranked only by heart disease, cancer, and the other forms of mental illness. There are about 6.8 million heavy drinkers in the United States (Cisin and Cahalan, 1966), and approximately 5 million alcoholics (Keller and Efron, 1955). Famous persons who were alcoholic include William Sidney Porter (O. Henry), Jack London, Douglas Fairbanks, Sr., Lillian Roth, and John and Diana Barrymore. Noah (Genesis 9:21) may have been the first heavy drinker in the history of man. Sinclair Lewis drank a quart of brandy per day and, toward the end of his career, he avoided friends and wandered over the earth. F. Scott Fitzgerald was known to his intimate friends as F. "Scotch" Fitzgerald. A suitable definition of alcoholism has proved elusive for many experts. A Japanese proverb provides some of the flavor of what alcoholism is:

> First the man takes a drink,
> Then the drink takes a drink,
> Then the drink takes the man!

The World Health Organization (WHO), (1952) has defined alcoholism as follows: "Alcoholics are those excessive drinkers whose dependence upon alcohol has attained such a degree that it shows a noticeable mental disturbance or an interference with their bodily and mental health, their interpersonal relations, and their smooth social and economic functioning; or who show the prodromal signs of such developments. They therefore require treatment." Clark (1966) suggests that alcoholism involves four elements:

excessive intake
loss of control over drinking
mental disturbance due to drinking
disturbed social and economic behavior

Keller (1960) considers alcoholism a chronic disease manifested by repeated implicative or morbid drinking so as to cause injury to the drinker's mental or physical health, or to his social or economic functioning. Jellinek (1960), one of the leading experts on the topic, emphasizes the physical disease nature of alcoholism, but adds that there are several different types of alcoholism:

Alpha Alcoholism. A form involving purely psychologically determined, habitual reliance on alcohol for relief of emotional or physical pain, with no loss of control over drinking or signs of progression toward more severe drinking habits.

Beta Alcoholism. Heavy social drinking leading to physical complications such as gastritis, but no signs of psychological or physical dependence.

Gamma Alcoholism. Psychological and physical dependence on alcohol shown by loss of control, the acquisition of tissue tolerance to alcohol, craving for alcohol, withdrawal symptoms when deprived of alcohol intake.

Delta Alcoholism. Psychological and physical dependence occur and shown by inability to abstain from drinking rather than loss of control, i.e., there is no compulsion to drink oneself into a stupor, yet the delta alcoholic cannot abstain from alcohol consumption.

Epsilon Alcoholism. Periodic drinking bouts that last a few days or weeks, with complete abstinence in between these bouts. Previously referred to as dipsomania.

Alcoholism is a problem of major dimensions: it is insidious, becomes a financial drain on those who can least afford it, affects the self-esteem, creates an immense social problem, and is a severe threat to health (see Table 11-2). Among the physical ailments directly or indirectly attributable to alcohol are gastric pains during digestion from inflammation of the stomach and intestine, increased pulse rate, enlarged liver, anemia from lack of food and excessive drinking, and multiple vitamin deficiencies in vitamins A, C, ribloflavin, and nicotinic acid due to

TABLE 11-1. *Amount of Alcohol Ingested and Degree of Intoxication[a]*

AMOUNT OF WHISKEY INGESTED	PERCENTAGE OF ALCOHOL IN BLOOD	STAGE OF INTOXICATION	CLINICAL EFFECTS
2.5 oz or less	0.05 or less	Subclinical	Normal by ordinary observation.
2.5 to 4.5 oz	0.05 to 0.09	Subclinical	Normal by ordinary observation; Slight change by special tests.
4.5 to 10.5 oz	0.09 to 0.21	Stimulation	Decreased inhibition; emotional instability; slight incoordination.
9.0 to 15.0 oz	0.18 to 0.30	Confusion	Disturbed sensation; decreased pain sense; staggering gait; slurred speech.
13.5 to 19.5 oz	0.27 to 0.39	Stupor	Marked stimuli decrease; approaching paralysis.
18.0 to 24.0 oz	0.36 to 0.48	Coma	Complete unconsciousness; depressed reflexes; subnormal temperature; anesthesia; impairment of circulation; possible death.

[a] Based on formula of Dr. H. Heise: X/0.02 no. of oz of 86 proof liquor taken by 165 pound man, where X = blood alcohol percent. Overlapping figures are used since differing individuals with differing physical and mental conditions will vary in their reactions.
SOURCE: Adapted from Roche Laboratories, *Aspects of alcoholism,* Vol. 1. Philadelphia: Lippincott, 1963; and C. Muehlberger, in T. Gonzales et al. (Eds.), *Legal medicine, pathology and toxicology.* (2nd ed.) New York: Appleton-Century-Crofts, 1954. Copyright Appleton-Century-Crofts.

erratic eating and poor dietary habits. In addition, alcoholics appear to be five times more susceptible to tuberculosis, and vulnerable to pneumonia (Roche Laboratories, 1966).

On the whole, alcoholics share a common life history of drinking. The typical alcoholic had his first drinking experience about age 16-18 years (Amark, 1951; Jellinek, 1946; Tahka, 1966; Ullman, 1953), began to show signs of heavy drinking by age 25-30 (Amark, 1951; Buhler and Lefever, 1947; Fleming and Tillotson, 1939), was arrested for the first time about age 29 (Edwards, Hawker, and Williamson, 1966), and ended up as an alcoholic within 9-15 years after his first introduction to drinking (Plaut, 1967). The alcoholic goes through several phases on his way to becoming an alcoholic (Jellinek, 1946) (See Fig. 11-1; Table 11-3):

1. The prealcoholic symptomatic phase

TABLE 11-2. *Complications of Alcoholism and their Probable Cause*

COMPLICATION:	CAUSES			
	a	b	c	d
Coma	x			
Gastritis	x			
Skin lesions			x	
Pancreatitis	x			?
Hallucinosis	x			
Hepatic disease	?	x		x
Delirium tremens	x			?
Korsakoff's psychosis		x		
Cardiovascular disorders	?	x	x	x
Susceptibility to trauma	x	x	x	
Susceptibility to infections		x		x

KEY: *a*—Direct effects of alcohol
　　b—Nutritional failure
　　c—Psychic factors
　　d—Other factors
　　x—highly probable or of principal importance
　　?—Doubtful, secondary importance
SOURCE: Adapted from Roche Laboratories, *Aspects of alcoholism*, Vol. 1, Philadelphia: Lippincott, 1963.

2. The prodromal phase
3. The crucial phase
4. The chronic phase

In *the prealcoholic symptomatic phase,* the individual begins to establish a drinking pattern. He manages to find more and more reasons for celebrating, more and more social occasions that permit drinking, more and more ways to justify drinking to reduce tensions. A routine is established: the "eye-opener" in the morning, the martini before lunch, the quick one before going home, the one to relax after a hard day's work, and the "nightcap" before turning in. He is not too different from his social-drinking friends in outward appearance, and many who will not become alcoholic join in some of the same routines, such as the Friday afternoon celebration-at-the-tavern gang. He just seems to find a few more occasions to drink than others, and requires less encouragement to "have another." Gradually, he finds himself drinking heavily, developing an increasing tolerance for alcohol, requiring more occasions to drink, and searching harder to find a justification.

The prodromal phase is initiated by the occurrence of periods of amnesia or a "pulling of the blanks," during which time the individual remains conscious and carries out activities but without any later recall. These blackouts occur during drinking, and may occur even when he is not severely intoxicated. In addition, he now becomes aware of being different from his friends in his orientation toward alcohol. He slyly gulps his liquor so that he can have another while his friends are still preoccupied in mixing their first. He feels guilty and becomes secretive about his drinking, increasing his consumption when others are not looking. He becomes obsessively concerned about not having enough to drink and gets as much as he can while he can. Yet he will deny having a problem, avoid references to alcohol in social conversation, become irritable if his drinking is alluded to by others, and rationalizes his behavior. In a subtle fashion, his entire attitude toward drinking has changed from being a part of his everyday routine to a consuming need. He has become dependent upon alcohol. The prodromal phase will last anywhere from six months to five years.

In *the crucial phase,* the individual becomes somewhat alarmed at his dependence and strives for control. He may be able to abstain for awhile but this lasts for shorter and shorter periods. Once he touches the bottle, all willpower is lost and he is unable to stop drinking until he is too intoxicated to continue. He strives to limit his intake to evening hours, and may be able to do so for long periods.

However, alcohol has become more and more crucial to his life pattern to the extent that he neglects his nutritional needs and is concerned only about protecting his supply of liquor. Hiding places are sought for his secret caches of alcohol. By now, friends and employers are aware of his "drinking problem" and begin to express their concern and dissatisfaction. Friends are lost, social pressures increase, demotions occur. His tensions are even further heightened, and he drinks more to calm himself. He tries to cover up, to act grandiosely, to offer excuses, to justify his behavior, but it soon becomes pitifully evident that these are rationalizations and no more. He needs to drink but is embarassed by his need; he feels persistent remorse and self-pity. He defends his self-

TABLE 11.3. *Common Mental and Personality Changes in the Alcoholic*

TRAITS	THEIR EXPRESSION
1. Egocentricity	Self-centered view of his problems—extreme narcissism, primary concern with self and need to drink; in later stages, promises or does anything to maintain his supply of alcohol.
2. Paranoid ideas	Accusations of marital infidelity by alcoholic mate, offers of help and expressions of concern misinterpreted as "picking on him."
3. Ambivalence of feelings	Expressions of love as well as of annoyance and hostility toward mate, family members and friends; alternating attitudes whereby he seeks, and then rejects, treatment and/or help.
4. Inconsistency	Excessive deviations in behavior, often impulsive in nature; undependable at home, at work and in other situations, all because of drinking which must be done; extraordinary fears.
5. Lack of insight	Rationalizations and tendency to blame others and his environment for his compulsive need to drink, creation of myth that he can control his drinking, attitude of indifference to cover up feelings of shame and degradation.
6. Arrogance and defiance	Grandiosity of thought and of discourse, masking feelings of inferiority and inadequacy; aggressive acting out of resentments and hostility against family, friends and others, often leading to fights; sadistic traits.
7. Moods of depression	Deep feelings of guilt, remorse and self-accusation after a bout, general avoidance of discussion or admission of drinking, occasional outbursts of self-disgust and desire to stop, masochistic inclinations.

SOURCE: Roche Laboratories, *Aspects of alcoholism,* Vol. 1. Philadelphia: Lippincott, 1963.

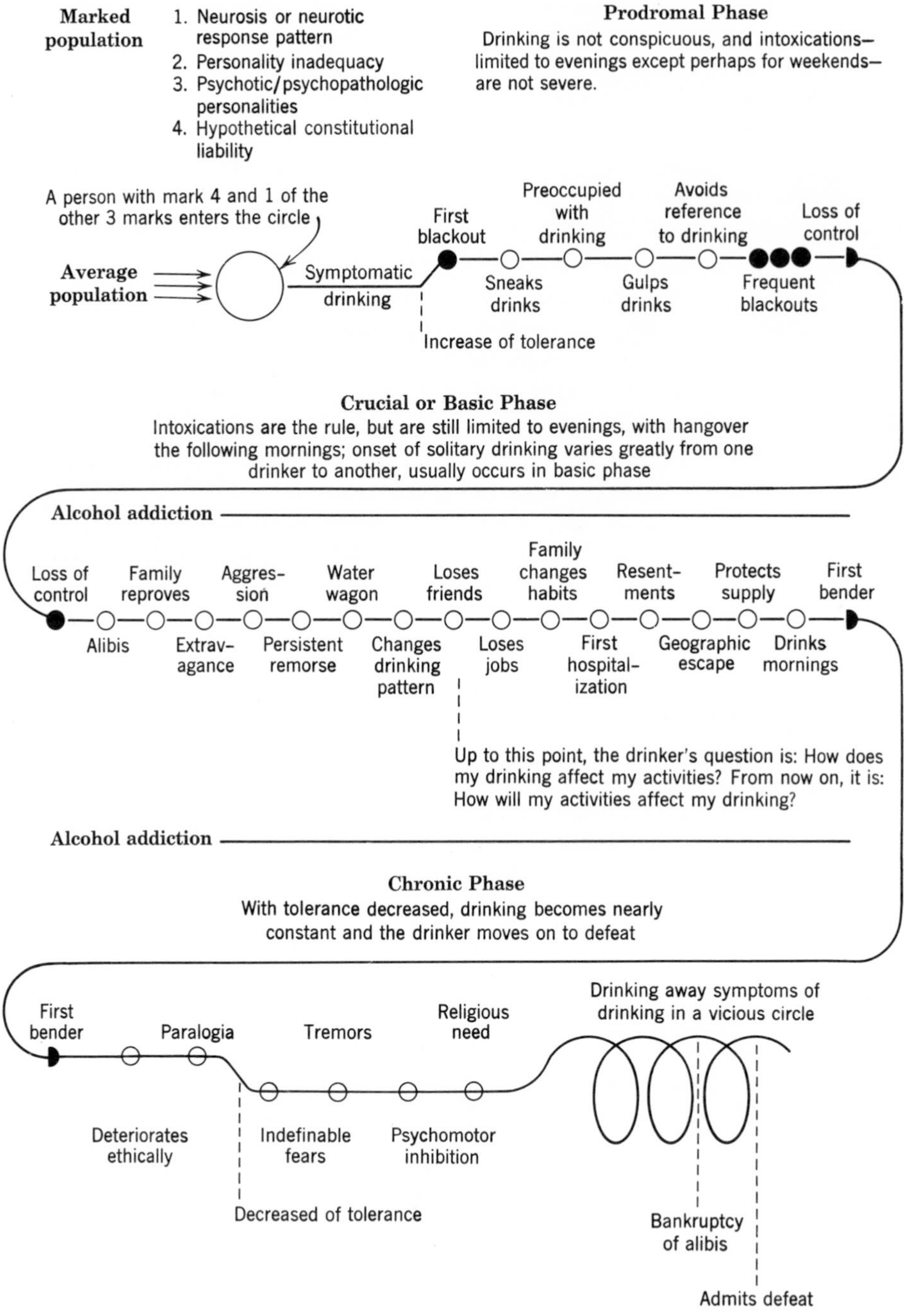

Marked population
1. Neurosis or neurotic response pattern
2. Personality inadequacy
3. Psychotic/psychopathologic personalities
4. Hypothetical constitutional liability

Prodromal Phase
Drinking is not conspicuous, and intoxications—limited to evenings except perhaps for weekends—are not severe.

A person with mark 4 and 1 of the other 3 marks enters the circle

Average population ⟶ Symptomatic drinking

First blackout   Preoccupied with drinking   Avoids reference to drinking   Loss of control

Sneaks drinks   Gulps drinks   Frequent blackouts

Increase of tolerance

Crucial or Basic Phase
Intoxications are the rule, but are still limited to evenings, with hangover the following mornings; onset of solitary drinking varies greatly from one drinker to another, usually occurs in basic phase

Alcohol addiction

Loss of control   Family reproves   Aggression   Water wagon   Loses friends   Family changes habits   Resentments   Protects supply   First bender

Alibis   Extravagance   Persistent remorse   Changes drinking pattern   Loses jobs   First hospitalization   Geographic escape   Drinks mornings

Up to this point, the drinker's question is: How does my drinking affect my activities? From now on, it is: How will my activities affect my drinking?

Alcohol addiction

Chronic Phase
With tolerance decreased, drinking becomes nearly constant and the drinker moves on to defeat

First bender   Paralogia   Tremors   Religious need   Drinking away symptoms of drinking in a vicious circle

Deteriorates ethically   Indefinable fears   Psychomotor inhibition

Decreased of tolerance

Bankruptcy of alibis

Admits defeat

Figure 11-1. The phases of alcoholism.
SOURCE: Roche Laboratories, *Aspects of alcoholism.* Vol. 2. Philadelphia: Lippincott, 1966.

esteem against his personal, social, economic failures, but there is little left to protect.

The chronic phase is ushered in by drinking and prolonged intoxication during the day, the so-called "benders." The individual lives only to drink. His life revolves around pursuing and obtaining another drop of alcohol. All else in life becomes secondary: his family, his occupation, his friends, his appearance, his health, his self-esteem, his honor, his social or ethical obligations. He will beg, cheat, lie, and steal to possess another bottle. He suffers from malnutrition, becomes financially poor, skids downward. When he is not unconscious from drinking, he is searching for the means to drink himself unconscious. He no longer attempts to offer any defense or excuse for his intoxication. His life sphere shrinks to a limited existence commanded by liquor. Indefinable fears, tremors, inhibition of psychomotor behavior, mark him for what he is. He may ultimately succumb to death or mental illness. He has already been dying by his own hand from the moment he became a pathological drinker.

Chronic consumption of alcohol over long periods of time leads to severe mental and physical illness. Among the major psychotic conditions associated with alcoholism are:

1. Pathological intoxication
2. Delirium tremens
3. Korsakoff's psychosis
4. Wernicke's syndrome
5. Acute hallucinosis
6. Alcoholic deterioration

PATHOLOGICAL INTOXICATION

This condition is a form of *acute* psychotic reaction, that is, reactions that have a sudden onset, are short in duration, and are considered reversible. Pathological in-

toxication appears in individuals with unstable personalities. When such persons ingest even moderate amounts of alcohol, the effect is a transitory emotional state that goes far beyond the condition of simple intoxication. The individual may become confused, disoriented, and excitable. Hallucinations, sensory distortions and illusions, and brief delusions may dramatically and suddenly appear. Emotions may be stimulated to the point of severe anxiety, deep depression, or extreme rage, and could lead to suicidal or homicidal actions. Criminal acts of violence are sometimes attributable to pathological intoxication, including murder, rape, arson, burglary, and manslaughter. Rigidity of the pupils, and the sudden onset of the mental confusion and emotional change, are primary signs of the condition. The reaction may be due to the alcohol simply acting as a precipitating factor in a person who is already typically impulsive and emotional. Since pathological intoxication also occurs among epileptics (persons with brain dysfunctions involving disturbance of consciousness and convulsions), there is a possibility that this acute psychotic reaction to alcohol is a form of epilepsy. The symptoms of pathological intoxication last from a few minutes to a day or more. The confusion and excitement or emotional change are usually followed by a prolonged sleep, after which the individual awakens amnesic for the episode.

DELIRIUM TREMENS

This disorder is an acute psychosis appearing in the chronic alcoholic usually after a severe or prolonged period of heavy drinking. Because it appears during the period of abstinence immediately following the drinking episode, it is possible that the "d.t.'s" are a form of withdrawal syndrome rather than an acute psychosis developed during drinking. Other factors associated with the onset of delirium tremens are lack of food intake and sleep from inability to eat, restlessness, and insomnia which occur just before the psychotic condition. Delirium tremens occurs most often among individuals over 30 years of age who have been chronic alcoholics for three to four years.

Among the physical signs of delirium tremens are the pupils of the eyes, which are dilated and react slowly to light changes. Tremors are nearly always present and can be seen in shaking of the fingers and tremors of the lips, face, and even tongue. The pulse rate is irregular, rapid, and weak. As is common in all states of delirium, whatever the cause may be, confusion, disorientation, and restlessness appear. In this state, the delirious person may not know where he is, misidentify people, lose his sense of time, be impelled to suddenly respond to fleeting impressions, and show marked interference of attention.

Terrifying illusions and hallucinations can grip the alcoholic. Visual hallucinations of a vivid nature may appear involving bizarre, frightening, fantastic animals that threaten and horrify. The hallucinations may change shape and undergo weird metamorphosis, increase to gigantic proportions, or fade into the colors of the wall. Olfactory hallucinations may convince the person that death is imminent from strangling gases. Intense tactile hallucinations involving gruesome, small, fast-moving animals create awesome anxiety. Ants crawling under the skin, or spiders leaving their imprints on the back, cause severe discomfort which leaves the patient in an incessant but losing struggle.

The hallucinations may at times be a product of the person's extreme suggestibility. Some individuals can be prompted to see an object that is suggested to him. He may take an imaginary string, and under instructions, proceed to wind it into a ball. He may begin to read from a blank sheet of paper when asked to do so.

Commonly, the emotional state involves fearfulness, apprehension, terror, irritability. In rare instances, the person experiences a sense of humor, elation, or a fit of silliness. More often, the mood is associated with the illusions and hallucinations that appear. If the telephone wire turns into a threatening snake, the patient may cringe, cower in fear, or desperately cry out for his life.

Delirium tremens normally terminates in 3 to 10 days. During the period of hospitalization, the patient is kept in bed and placed on a soft diet rich in vitamins, carbohydrates, and dextrose. Convalescence is ordinarily preceded by a deep prolonged sleep from which the patient awakens in a lucid and oriented condition. Brief and intermittent periods of delirium may occur at night during this period. Mortality rates of 5 to 15 percent occur with patients suffering from delirium tremens, most commonly from heart failure or pneumonia. Diseases of the liver also account for some deaths. Occasionally, the delirium tremens merges into Korsakoff's psychosis.

KORSAKOFF'S PSYCHOSIS

This is a condition that was first described in 1887 by the Russian psychiatrist Sergei Korsakoff, who associated it with polyneuritis, an inflammation of certain nerves, although the two do not always appear together. The characteristic signs of Korsakoff's psychosis are disorientation of time and place, *anterograde amnesia* (loss of memory for events that have just occurred), and a marked tendency to fabricate answers to fill in the past. Unlike the previously described psychoses, the patient suffering from Korsakoff's psychosis shows superficially little sign of any disturbance of consciousness. On the contrary, he seems clear instead of confused, and may readily identify friends and relatives. Upon further examination, however, it becomes evident that the patient is impaired on any information that is beyond immediate observation or dependent upon recent memory. Even memory for past events may become lost in some patients. Frequently, the anterograde amnesia is seen in the patient's failure to remember the name of the nurse immediately after the introduction to her, or the fact that he had eaten his lunch a few minutes earlier. Yet the patient is jocular and willingly answers questions about his past, calling upon fictitious memories to conceal the amnesia. These *confabulations* are related without discomfort even though they may appear to be no more than fanciful tales. A skillful interviewer can even lead the patient into "recalling" whatever memories are desired. Despite the apparent clarity of the patient's conversation, he is in actuality lacking in insight into his condition.

Current evidence indicates that Korsakoff's psychosis is a result of vitamin B deficiency and other nutritional inadequacies, rather than directly to alcoholic intoxication. Although the same vitamin deficiency can occur through other circumstances, the chronic alcoholic is particularly prone because of his poor dietary habits and his increased vitamin requirements resulting from the high caloric effect of alcohol. In Korsakoff's psychosis, degenerative changes occur in the cerebrum and the peripheral nerves. If the degenerative changes involve the brain stem, then Wernicke's disease develops.

To correct the vitamin deficiency, thiamine chloride, powdered brewers' yeast and milk, fruit, eggs, meat, and other foods rich in vitamin B complex are liberally provided. Within six to eight weeks, the patient is restored to his normal mental and physical functioning. In some cases, the improvement takes place without the return of memory. Psychological deterioration can also take place even without irreversible organic damage to the brain, leaving the patient with intellectual inefficiency, and a degree of moral and ethical deterioration.

WERNICKE'S SYNDROME

Because it involves pathological changes in the brain stem, Wernicke's syndrome is sometimes classified with the organic disorders. This condition was first described in 1881 by Wernicke who called attention to an illness characterized by confabulation, memory loss, a disturbance of eye function, apathy, confusion, and sometimes coma. A state of delirium precedes the illness, involving restlessness, confusion, and fears of a vague nature. Speech may be slurred and incoherent. The eyes react slowly to changes in light intensity, and the patient may be unable to follow a moving light with his eyes.

As with Korsakoff's psychosis, Wernicke's syndrome is associated with chronic alcoholism by way of vitamin deficiency, more particularly thiamine insufficiency. Degenerative alterations occur within the brain stem involving lesions, and alteration and even hemorrhaging of the blood vessels. Since vitamin inadequacies can produce a variety of different physical illnesses, it is possible to find a patient suffering from both Wernicke's syndrome and pellagra, or even Wernicke's syndrome, delirium tremens, and Korsakoff's psychosis all at once. Often the illnesses blend into one another, the predominant symptoms being determined by the vitamin in which the deficiency is the highest and by the extent and sites of the degeneration.

ACUTE HALLUCINOSIS

Acute hallucinosis derives its name from the primary symptom involved, the appearance of auditory hallucinations. The patient is typically coherent and remains oriented for place, time, and person. Yet he is more and more disturbed by sounds or voices. The voices are usually accusatory, threatening, or humiliating, and arouse fearfulness and terror in the patient. These voices may start off mildy reproachful, but eventually become increasingly disturbing. They may accuse him of indecent sexual crimes, refer to him as a homosexual or of having harbored abhorrent sexual plans toward women. They may shout vile names at him, ridicule his actions, or reproach him for unspeakable sins. The voices may be heard referring to him in the third person, plotting his punishment in great detail, such as, "When he's least suspecting, we'll sharpen our knives and cut him up and burn the remains." Sounds of a rhythmical, mechanical nature can accompany the voices, such as the sound of knives being sharpened, or the measured fall of footsteps approaching, or the crackling of fire. Although the auditory hallucinations are commonest, olfactory hallucinations and visual illusions may appear.

As the hallucinations persist and acquire more acceptance by the patient as being real, delusions may be formed consistent with the hallucinatory content. He begins to believe that enemies are after him, that the threats are being carried out, that police protection is necessary. In the grip of terror, the patient may run panic-stricken for help, or turn to attack the imaginary foe, or finally succumb to the despair of his helplessness and attempt suicide.

The acute hallucinosis may persist anywhere from a few days to a month. If the patient continues to drink excessively, recurrence of the symptoms are probable. In contrast to delirium tremens, there is no amnesia for the events during recovery, and the patient continues to remain oriented rather than becoming confused or delirious.

Despite the association between the chronic and excessive use of alcohol and the onset of acute hallucinosis, it is currently believed that the illness is not directly attributable to alcohol itself. Rather, the alcoholic indulgence releases the symptoms of an underlying mental disorder. In some cases, the alcohol is simply a precipitating factor disclosing a hidden schizophrenic reaction. For such cases, other conditions might have similarly served as precipitants, such as prolonged physical illness, drugs, or physical exhaustion. There is also a possibility that some cases of acute hallucinosis .which occur soon after abstinence from alcohol are related to heightened sensory sensitivity. In these cases, the individuals are affected by disturbance of the auditory pathways, or are persons with a predisposition towards auditory imagery.

ALCOHOLIC DETERIORATION

Chronic and excessive use of alcohol can result in disintegration of personality, intellectual impairment, and deterioration of ethical and moral behavior. The patient becomes irritable and moody, quickly changing from a carefree attitude to an angry outburst. With his drinking friends and with strangers, he may be a clowning or a deferent companion; at home, his pretenses drop to reveal a surly and hostile character. Forgetfulness, retarded comprehension, lack of ideas, and shorter and shorter attention span interfere with his ability to function. Ambition is lost and the patient loses interest in helping himself, demanding financial support from his family. At the same time he will accuse his wife of neglect and infidelity and abuse her at the slightest provocation. Ethical and moral decline proceed rapidly. Lewd behavior, vulgar speech, deviant sexual acts, and neglect of personal appearance make him a more and more aversive person to be with. Unable to accept the blame for his condition, he indulges in self-pity and portrays himself as the victim of circumstances. He distorts facts in an attempt to avoid coping with reality. He quickly reaches a point where he is unreliable, irresponsible, and unreachable. Inhibitions may be reduced and judgment affected to the point that the patient engages in impulsive actions that lead to arrests. Ultimately, physical symptoms mark the patient: impaired muscular coordination, tremors, general muscular weakness, sluggish pupillary response, twitches, and extreme nausea.

Dynamics. As Jellinek (1960) indicated by his classification of different types of alcoholism, it may be improper to view all alcoholics as alike. Lemere (1953) reviewed the evidence and concluded that "there remains only one characteristic that is common to all alcoholics and that is that they drink too much." Consequently, there is probably no single explanation for alcoholism, but multiple causation depending upon the individual. Therefore, several approaches to etiology will be discussed in the following section: psychoanalytic explanations, psychological explanations based on the personality of alcoholics, sociocultural explanations, and physiological explanations.

The *psychoanalytic* viewpoint suggests that the alcoholic shows a developmental fixation at the early oral stage which predisposes him to need care from others, to be passively dependent, and to be intolerant of frustration, pain, or psychic tensions. A characteristic of this fixation is the reliance upon orally centered behaviors such as drinking, eating, smoking, and so forth. In addition, the alcoholic is said to be suffering secretly from an unspeakable terror which he cannot face; he may not even know the real nature of this fear within him. As an infant, he found that whenever he was hungry, anxious, and alone, a fluid (milk) seemed to appear almost magically to feed him, warm him, and

soothe his fears all at the same time. As an adult, the alcoholic again searches for a similar liquid that is able to accomplish the same feats (Menninger, 1938). Alcohol comes the closest. Alcohol intake reduces inhibitions, provides temporary escape, reduces self-criticism, raises self-esteem, and allows infantile, unconscious needs to be expressed and gratified (Fig. 11-2). In a sense, alcoholic intoxication is an attempt to achieve a momentary state of equilibrium and has been viewed as an attempt at self-cure of need tensions and conflicts (Freud, 1905; Fenichel, 1945; Knight, 1937). The alcoholic is faced with hostile feelings that he cannot express because of his extreme dependency and need for the help of others. Alcohol serves several functions: it allows the patient to release his hostility directly with a built-in excuse ("It was the alcohol acting, not me"), it allows the patient to indirectly exhibit his resentment toward his family by making them embarrassed in the presence of others over his condition, it permits a form of passive aggression in a way analogous to the child who takes vengeance by refusing to eat, and it acts as a form of self-punishment for this release of hostility. The self-destructive effect of alcohol has often been emphasized as a form of atonement for the guilt over aggression, and a type of suicide (Menninger, 1938). Although the results differ considerably for different samples, suicidal attempts and actual suicide completions appear to be higher among alcoholics (Palmer, 1941; Ellermann, 1948). Alcoholism, and other addictions such as drug addiction, gambling, escape through sleep, and even smoking, have been analyzed as involving both pleasure and relief from pain (Glover, 1932; Sachs, 1923).

Psychological studies have sought the common childhood and current characteristics of alcoholics which could explain the source of the disorder. A national study by Cisin and Cahalan (1966), and

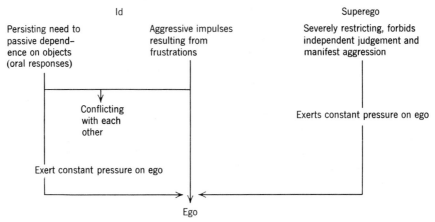

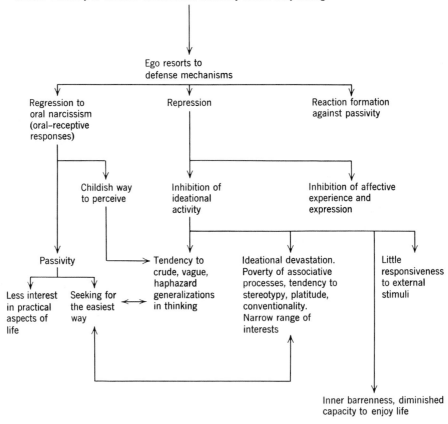

Figure 11-2. **A psychoanalytic representation of the psychodynamics of alcoholism.**
SOURCE: V. Tahka, *The alcoholic personality.* Helsinki, Finland: Finnish Foundation for Alcohol Studies, 1966.

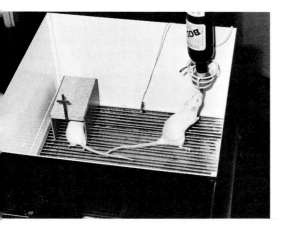

Alcoholism and abstinence may be learned behaviors. Pictured is a rat who learned to drink to avoid shock (*right*), and one that was trained to enter a "church" box to avoid shock (*left*). The alcoholic rat consumed the equivalent of a half bottle of Scotch in less than an hour when threatened. (R. Ramsey & H. Van Dis, *Behavior Research & Therapy*, Vol. 5. Copyright © 1967, Pergamon Press)

work by others (Knupfer et al., 1963; Jones, 1962), indicate that alcoholics describe themselves as having more problems, being more unhappy than nonproblem drinkers, and as being from socially disadvantaged environments. They appear to be insecure, anxious, guilt-ridden, emotionally unstable, and low in self-esteem. Among the few studies of the childhood traits of alcoholics are those of McCord and McCord, and Jones. The McCords (1962) reexamined the childhood history files of known adult alcoholics, comparing them with those of nonalcoholics from the same neighborhood. They found that the alcoholics as children were more self-contained, indifferent to their siblings, disapproving of their mothers, outwardly self-confident, unrestrained in aggression, and anxious about sex. Jones (1965) did a 30-year follow-up on normal public school children. Those who had become problem drinkers were discovered to have experienced from early life more tensions, less satisfactions, fewer ways of handling life difficulties, families that lacked understanding or warmth, and mothers who were indifferent or rejecting. As adults, the heavy drinkers were aggressive, acting out, attention-seeking, extroverted socially, resentful of authority, lacking in feeling for others, power seeking, lacking in control of impulses, and self-destructive. Interestingly enough, both the abstainers

and the heavy drinkers showed evidence of personality maladjustment in contrast to the moderate drinkers.

Alcoholics themselves have pointed out that drinking was used early in their life to facilitate easier interpersonal relations. Drinking was used because it increased their sociability, their confidence, and decreased their tension, and lessened their oversensitivity. However, alcohol did not eliminate their tensions or problems; in fact, these same patients reported that alcohol currently failed to help in their sociability, reduced their ability to be cooperative, decreased their ambition, and increased their depression (Blume and Sheppard, 1967).

Among the common psychological interpretations of alcoholism is the idea that alcohol is used as a means of tension reduction. Basic to this is a belief that the alcoholic is a person who seeks to avoid conflict rather than come to grips with it. There seems to be some evidence that alcoholics have a low frustration tolerance, a low capacity for coping with tensions of any type, and a tendency to sidestep or to make concessions to avoid unpleasantness, delays, or decisions (Korman and Stubblefield, 1961; Fox, 1957; Coopersmith, 1964). This avoidance of direct effort to resolve conflict seems to be also exhibited in the dependency characteristics of the alcoholic (Zwerling, 1959; Witkin, Karp, and Goodenough, 1959). The alcoholic soon relies upon drinking because of the temporary positive effects of the alcohol on the body: it raises the pain threshold and thus momentarily makes the patient immune to pain and criticism, it dulls his judgment and thus reduces his concern about his conflicts, it increases his sense of self-esteem, and removes his inhibitions. Thus, not only does the patient feel better about himself, but his tensions are reduced and conflicts seem diminished. Masserman et al. (1946) and Conger (1951) have both demonstrated that alcohol seems to have a transitory favorable effect on animals with experimentally produced neuroses. Masserman's cats, for example, who were unable to eat when hungry because of a neurotic condition, were able to resume normal eating after alcoholic ingestion. Conger suggested that the alcohol helped to break up the approach-avoidance conflict.

In spite of the mounting research on the psychological characteristics of alcoholics, one serious drawback has existed which limits the significance of the data. Nearly all studies have been based upon analyses of chronic alcoholics who are already in hospitals or in treatment for their alcoholism. It is difficult to determine whether the traits discovered are cause or effect. Chronic exposure to alcohol may itself lead to personality changes, create conditions for arousal of new conflict, and perhaps even hide the real prealcoholism traits of the patient. Thus, the low self-esteem, the guilt feelings, the inability to face conflicts, the anxiety, and the low frustration tolerance may be the patient's reaction to being an alcoholic rather than the factors that led him to become an alcoholic.

Sociocultural explanations have contributed much to understanding how the alcoholic becomes exposed to drinking, and what factors seem to work against the development of alcoholism. Jellinek (1960) proposes that a person becomes initiated into drinking because it is part of the social culture. Jack London did not enjoy the taste of alcohol, but found that social drinking in saloons was associated with good fellowship and brought him into contact with cheerful and warm surroundings. Heavy drinking is higher among men of low socioeconomic class (Cisin and Cahalan, 1966) perhaps because the friendship of the tavern is a much more enjoyable circumstance than the drab dwelling they live in. Persons whose occupations involve a high exposure to drinking appear more susceptible to alcoholism, for example, bartenders, liquor salesmen, and nightclub entertainers (Kant, 1954; Roch, 1940). In addition, exposure to parental models who drink also seems to help initiate alcoholism. Tahka (1966) found the rate of alcoholism among the fathers of alcoholics to be 30-35 percent. It appears that encouragement of drinking by one's social group may well be involved in starting a person on the path to alcoholism. However, further cultural data suggests that the problem is more complicated. The Jews, Irish, Chinese, Italians, and French are all exposed to a high incidence of drinking. Yet, the Jews, Italians, and Chinese have low rates of alcoholism, while the Irish and French have high rates (Bacon, 1947; Snyder, 1958; Lin, 1953). The significant factor seems to be the extent to which drinking has become formally integrated into the culture. For the Jew, drinking is firmly imbedded in a network of sacred ideas with a religiously symbolic character to it. The taking of alcohol is a part of religious rituals and thus highly controlled. Moreover, sobriety is defined as a Jewish virtue, drunkenness is stigmatized as a Gentile failing. Similarly, the Italian looks upon alcohol as a part of mealtime activities, and only in moderation. Again drunkenness is strongly disapproved. Among the Chinese, drinking is common

The *use of alcohol* has come under formal control for the Jewish family. Drinking is a solemn part of religious rituals such as the Passover celebration pictured above. Because sobriety is a Jewish virtue, the Jews have a low rate of alcoholism among their members. (Merrim/Monkmeyer)

but alcoholism is rare. Alcohol is used in social and ceremonial functions and at meals only. Family ties are especially strong, and drunkenness is seen as radically opposed to family and community values (Lin, 1953; Barnett, 1955). On the other hand, the Irish have not ritualized the use of alcohol. For this group, drinking is used in situations of stress and for emotional reasons. It is not that the Irish have more tensions to deal with, in fact both the Jews and the Irish have similar levels of tension (Bales, 1944); the difference is in the cultures' formal attitudes toward alcohol. If the Italians and French are compared, it is evident that both cultures are exposed to the availability of alcohol by reason of wine industries. Yet, there is five times more alcoholism in France than in Italy. One answer seems to be the lack of social pressure to drink among the Italians, as against the use of

heavy drinking among the French as an index of manhood (Sadoun & Lolli, 1962).

The *physiological* work on alcoholism is exceptionally intriguing. A number of studies have demonstrated that it is possible to selectively breed animals with high or low preference for alcohol (Mardones, Segovia, and Hederra, 1953; McClearn and Rodgers, 1961; Rodgers and McClearn, 1962). Further studies have attempted to determine what mechanisms differentiate such groups of animals, and several hypotheses have been formulated. One approach suggests that nutritional deficiency leads to a craving for alcohol. Mardones (1951), for example, showed that rats deficient in vitamin B complex increased their alcohol consumption. Another hypothesis is that excessive use of alcohol damages the cortical cells and changes the metabolic pattern of brain cells so that the brain requires alcohol for continued optimal functioning. Withdrawal of alcohol throws the brain cells into a state of disequilibrium and is said to bring about cellular demands for alcohol, or a craving (Lemere, 1956). Jellinek (1960) maintains that psychoanalytic-psychological explanations are applicable only for alpha alcoholism. For the other types, he proposes a disease concept. Social factors initiate drinking, but soon heavy drinking leads to nutritional deficiency and toxic effects. Such toxicity reduces the capacity of the liver to detoxify the alcohol and more damage occurs. The diseased liver leads to additional susceptibility to neural tissue degeneration and increased use of alcohol as part of cell metabolism. Ultimately, physical addiction to alcohol occurs. Schlesinger (1966) offers a different approach in focusing on why some animals seem to *avoid* the use of alcohol, rather than directly attempting to explain high preferences. He discovered that low preference mice metabolized alcohol slower and speculated that an unpleasant interim product of metabolism was associated with abstinence. Acetaldehyde is formed in the first stage of the metabolism of alcohol and does seem to accumulate more in the low preference mice. Furthermore, among the "alcoholic mice," there is a greater activity of the enzyme that promotes the metabolism and elimination of alcohol. In addition, older mice from the high preference strain appear to show a decrease in their preference for alcohol with advancing age, and this decrease seems associated with a corresponding decrease in enzyme activity. Finally, the drug Antabuse, which is sometimes used in the treatment of alcoholics, appears to work by slowing down the elimination of acetaldehyde.

The data on the various factors that might be involved in the etiology of alcoholism is provocative but in many ways unsatisfying. There does not seem to be a single "alcoholic type" in the sense of well-defined psychological, sociocultural, or physiological traits which are invariably associated with alcoholism. Jellinek comes the closest to the crux of the problem; perhaps there are many types of alcoholism, a version that is dependent upon psychological experiences, a version that is maintained by cultural pressures, and a version that is a bodily addiction. In addition, within each group, there may be great variability; nutritional variables may be involved in some physical cravings, while in others metabolic changes are more important. And of course, multifactorial explanations may eventually prove to be the most accurate: social factors may initiate, encourage, or limit the person's use of alcohol to begin with; the presence of emotional conflicts, a behavioral tendency to rely upon avoidance when faced with tensions, the comforting effects from the pharmacological properties of alcohol may combine to strengthen a habitual reliance on alcohol; and the disease effects of prolonged and excessive use of alcohol may finally prevent the patient from withdrawing from alcoholism.

Treatment. The first stage of treatment is the withdrawal of alcohol to prevent further damage or deterioration. During this drying-out period, tranquilizers are administered to help the patient better tolerate the stress of withdrawal. Previously, drugs such as the barbiturates, paraldehyde or chloral hydrate were used for this purpose, but are currently relied upon to a lesser degree because of their potential addictive danger—alcoholics have been known to readily substitute one addiction for another. Paraldehyde has the additional problem of possibly producing products of metabolism which are the same as that of alcohol and thus aggravating the symptoms. Since the alcoholic's health is usually impaired from malnutrition, he is also placed on a diet rich in vitamins and glucose. Occasionally, insulin is introduced in small doses to speed up the metabolism and elimination of alcohol remaining in the system. When the medical aspects are thus taken care of, the psychological problems are ready for attention.

In most instances, unless the patient is under the direct control of the therapist, psychological therapy is likely to be ineffective for the simple reason that the patient will quit before a month is over. In a hospital setting, the therapist does have a better environment in which to work. To be successful, a patient must be ready to recognize that he is alcoholic and has lost control over his drinking, able to give up his denials and rationalizations, willing to report any relapses that occur. Foremost, the patient must be ready to accept the unavoidable fact that he will have to abstain completely from alcohol for the rest of his life! Only a mere 10 percent of former alcoholics have ever been able to become social drinkers (Ditman, 1968); in fact, over 75 percent of alcoholic bouts began with the intention of having "just one little one." Therapy attempts to make abstinence an obsessive goal for the alcoholic, provides the patient with support in combating the seductive appeal of the pleasures of alcohol intoxication, and helps in coping with the apprehension which the patient feels about the stresses he must face during withdrawal. In addition, therapy tries to help the alcoholic develop greater skills, more flexibility and adaptability, and a greater role in improving on his own functioning in society and in the home. Rehabilitation may focus on vocational planning since job success can contribute immeasurably to the sense of self-esteem of the patient. The inclusion of the family in psychotherapeutic treatment has helped significantly. In some cases, this is because the wife has driven the husband deeper into alcohol by reason of her own neurotic need (Fox, 1956); in some severe cases,

the wife has actually unconsciously initiated the drinking in a vulnerable husband just as in certain cases of emotional disturbance in children, the parent may have instigated the symptoms (see Chapter 5, parental instigation process). In other cases, the very presence of an alcoholic spouse creates an extreme stress on normal family development. Family therapy is helpful in that it enables the wife and children to better understand the alcoholism and also helps to maintain their own mental health.

Drug therapy has been tried in the treatment of alcoholics, with 81 to 87 percent of psychiatrists in one survey reporting they relied to some extent on drugs (Ditman, 1967). Yet the evidence on the effectiveness of drug therapy is not convincing. Tranquilizers have been of value in handling the effects of withdrawal symptoms, but appears to be of no value in eliminating drinking behavior itself (Cohen et al., 1954; Ditman, 1961). Lysergic acid diethylamine (LSD) has received some enthusiastic support as a therapeutic agent for alcoholism (Osmond, 1957; Smith, 1958; O'Reilly, 1962). In fact, another hallucinogenic drug, peyote, was used by the American Indian for the cure of alcoholism (Schultes, 1940). A major argument is that dramatic improvements can be obtained because LSD produces a transcendental experience bringing self-awareness and insights leading to a near-religious conversion to abstinence. Of alcoholics followed up in two surveys, 36 to 38 percent reported having abstained from drinking as a result of LSD with the percentage going up to 46 percent for those who had experienced the mystical transcendentalism (Ditman et al., 1962; O'Reilly and Funk, 1964). Subsequent studies, however, have failed to confirm these findings (Smart and Storm, 1964; Smart, Storm, Baker, and Solursh, 1966; Sarett, Cheek, and Osmond, 1966). Currently, clinicians and researchers are skeptical about the value of LSD and one set of writers (Blum and Blum, 1967) have finally concluded that this drug is clearly not a form of treatment specifically helpful for alcoholism. If the hallucinogen is helpful in any way, it is not due to the pharmacological properties of the drug but rather to the beliefs of the therapist and patient, the suggestibility of the patient, or even a placebo effect. The danger of substituting dependence upon LSD for dependence upon alcohol, and the possible harmful effects of LSD, must always be taken into account in evaluating the usefulness of the drug.

Conditioned reflex therapy, or aversion therapy, has been credited with some success with alcoholics. The procedure involves the learning theory idea that avoidance responses can be acquired toward alcohol if drinking is always associated with unpleasant consequences. Disulfiram or Antabuse, has been used since it produces a noxious reaction when interacting with alcohol. When a patient who has taken Antabuse drinks alcohol,

Case History 11-3

ALCOHOLIC ADDICTION

The patient was a 42-year-old woman committed to the hospital following an episode of drinking and drunken driving. She had attended a party during which she consumed the equivalent of a bottle of wine. On the way to the party, she had stopped at an inn and fortified herself with two quick beers. The evening's affair ended at midnight, after which the patient headed for home in her car. Because she felt a little "down in the dumps," she took a "handful" of tranquilizers. She proceeded to drive into the back end of a moving bus and was arrested while she sat in her car giggling.

The patient had been married and divorced twice. Her first husband introduced her to social drinking through cocktail parties which he attended as part of his business. She found herself spending more and more time avoiding the other guests in order to remain situated near the kitchen where the glasses were being filled. Soon she began "experimenting" with a variety of ways of preparing liquor, serving it only to herself. Her housework suffered as she spent more and more of each day in sampling, sipping, then gulping alcohol.

Her current hospitalization is her second. She was previously treated for delirium tremens during which she hallucinated imaginary mice. She exhibited an extreme fear of animals which she said were climbing all over her, tore at her clothes, and rolled on the floor. She screamed incessantly. She remained in this condition for five days, then went into a deep sleep. She awakened with complete amnesia and was subsequently discharged.

Currently, she is being treated with a combination of psychotherapy and aversion therapy. She has shown some minimal insight into her maladaptive use of alcohol and hopes for the day when she can abstain completely. However, she still exhibits a tendency to see psychotherapy as a magical arrangement which will effect a cure without her intensive involvement. The therapist feels that her prognosis for recovery is actually poor.

he experiences within minutes headache, dizziness, chest pain, nausea, air hunger, and vomiting. In uncontrolled dosages, the effects can be fatal. Under controlled use, the drug has been used to condition the patient such that the sight, smell, and taste of alcohol become associated with strong aversive feelings. Antabuse has also been used as a means of helping the patient to consciously avoid drinking while the drug is in effect. Aversive training can also be developed through the use of mild electric shock (Lazarus, 1965). A portable, hand-held apparatus is available which is capable of generating an unpleasant shock. In this situation, the patient is instructed to give himself a shock whenever he feels a craving for liquor. Although this technique has not received wide usage, it is believed to be potentially a more appropriate and successful form of treatment than Antabuse. Lazarus (1965) used a combination of shock aversive treatment and desensitization therapy with a patient with success within two months. The aversive treatment strengthened the avoidance behavior when in the presence of alcohol. The desensitization therapy, which is a procedure to eliminate anxieties, was used to remove the tensions that had originally provoked the patient to drink.

A valuable approach to alcoholism is found in the Alcoholics Anonymous (AA) organization. Interestingly enough, a nationwide survey of state hospitals showed that 88 percent relied upon Alcoholics Anonymous as part of their treatment program, as compared with 75 percent which used drugs, and 57 percent which depended upon individual psychotherapy (Moore and Buchanan, 1966). Alcoholics Anonymous now claims over 8000 worldwide groups with an estimated membership of 300,000; similar groups in Europe are called Blue Cross or Good Templars. The organization provides a sense of belonging and of being understood while

preventing the denial and rationalizations —this is prevented since all AA members have been alcoholics and know such defenses through personal experience. Social pressure to change is high, but much group support is available to help the patient achieve a day-to-day abstinence. The *Twelve Steps* program forces the alcoholic to become obsessed with sobriety; the members are ready to spend as much time as is needed at any hour with anyone having difficulty in abstaining.

Drug Addictions

The World Health Organization (1950) defines drug addiction as a state of periodic or chronic intoxication, detrimental to the individual and to the society, produced by a repeated consumption of a drug (natural or synthetic) and including as characteristics:

1. An overpowering need or compulsion to continue taking the drug and to obtain it by any means.

2. A tendency to increase the amount of the dosage because of greater tolerance being built up.

3. A psychological and sometimes physical dependence on the drug.

The *psychological dependence* upon a drug is often referred to as habituation (the heavy reliance upon drugs because of the emotional relief they provide). The *physical dependence* upon a drug involves an altered physiological condition effected by prolonged drug usage, and is characterized by the appearance of the withdrawal syndrome upon abstinence. The amphetamines—cocaine, peyote, LSD, psilocybin, and marijuana—are drugs that can promote extreme psychological dependence or habituation. Opium, morphine, heroin, barbiturates, some tranquilizers, and codeine, are drugs that produce physiological dependence.

Narcotics usage has a history nearly

as old as the history of man. The narcotic properties of the opium poppy were known to the Sumerian civilization dating to 7000 B.C. The records indicate that they gave it the name by which it is still known today, "the plant of joy" (Neligan, 1927). Morphine was isolated in Germany in 1805, and heroin was produced in 1898 as a new miracle drug. Since it was believed that heroin was medically safe, it was used freely in medications, thereby producing many early cases of addiction. The use of morphine in the Civil War contributed another large share of addicts, euphemistically referred to as patients suffering from "army disease." Patent medicines and soft drinks mixed with narcotics added to the numbers, and by 1914 when the Harrison Narcotic Act was passed, there were 175,000 addicts in the United States. Currently there are approximately 60,000 addicts, most of whom are men. During 1967, three states accounted for about 74.7 percent of known addicts: New York (52.1 percent), California (12.0 percent), and Illinois (10.6 percent) (Figs.

11-3, and 11-4). Negroes accounted for 56.9 percent of the addicts, native-born whites included 25 percent, with Puerto Ricans, Cubans, and Mexicans making up the remainder. Relatively few Negro addicts are reported in the South (Federal Bureau of Narcotics, 1960). Unlike alcohol, there is little evidence to suggest that any religious group is protected from drug addiction (the orthodox Jews and the Moslems have strong prohibitions against alcohol). Adolescents and young adults have been increasingly involved in narcotics in recent years.

Drugs are introduced into the body in a variety of ways depending upon the type of drug and the degree of the addiction. The early drug user may take morphine, heroin, amphetamines, opium, the barbiturates, peyote, or LSD by mouth, either with a sweet substance to cover the unpleasant taste or alone. As tolerance de-

TABLE 11-4. *Narcotic Addiction Around the World*

COUNTRY OR LOCALE	NUMBER OF KNOWN ADDICTS
India	324,904[a]
United States	60,000
Burma	26,570
Hong Kong (China)	11,025
Germany (Republic of)	4,395
Canada	3,354
Japan	1,881
England and North Ireland	635
Mexico	528

[a] Cannabis (marijuana) addiction accounts for 200,000.

SOURCE: Adapted from United Nations Economic and Social Council Commission on Narcotic Drugs. *Summary of annual reports of governments relating to opium and other narcotic drugs, 1963.* France: United Nations Publication, 1965.

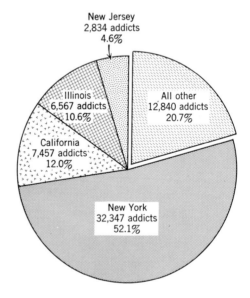

Figure 11-3. **Active narcotic addicts in selected states as of 1967.**
SOURCE: U.S. Treasury Department, Bureau of Narcotics, *Traffic in opium and other dangerous drugs,* Washington, D.C.: U.S. Government Printing Office, 1968. Copyright Bureau of Narcotics and Dangerous Drugs, U.S. Department of Justice.

velops and the addict finds he must take a higher dosage to attain the same effect, hypodermic needles may be used especially for the opiates (morphine, heroin, codeine). The most direct version is to insert the narcotic into the vein (*mainlining*), a procedure often causing damage to the veins and the surrounding skin. Inhaling or sniffing drugs, such as cocaine, is another method for absorbing narcotics. Opium smoking in pipes is an ancient method for taking in this drug, while marijuana users inhale the smoke from cigarettes.

The various drugs that can produce dependence fall into several categories:

1. The narcotics—opium and its derivatives (morphine, heroin, codeine, laudanum).

2. The sedatives—barbiturates, bromides, chloral hydrate, paraldehyde.

3. The tranquilizers—Equanil, Miltown, Librium, Valium.

4. The stimulants—cocaine, Benzedrine, Dexedrine.

5. The hallucinogenics and psychotomimetics—peyote, LSD, psilocybin, marijuana.

Some of the most commonly used drugs relied upon by addicts are given below.

1. *Opium*—a dark brown or black sticky substance prepared from the unripe pods of the opium poppy. It is usually smoked and gives off a pungent odor. The derivatives of opium are also addictive, including morphine, heroin, codeine, and Demerol. Heroin has been the addict's main choice in the United States although its presence is illegal. Heroin, "H," or "Horse," is the most dangerous of drugs obtained in the form of capsules ("caps")

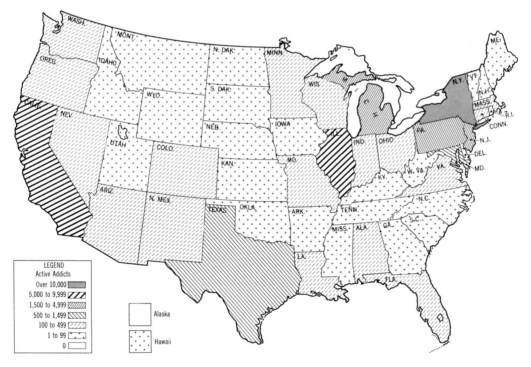

Figure 11-4. **Active narcotic addicts across the United States in 1966.**
SOURCE: U.S. Treasury Department, Bureau of Narcotics, *Prevention and control of narcotic addiction.* Washington, D.C.: U.S. Government Printing Office, 1967. Copyright Bureau of Narcotics and Dangerous Drugs, U.S. Department of Justice.

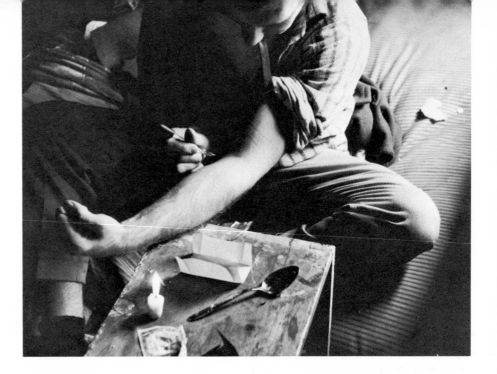

or packages ("decks"). Addicts may start off sniffing it, then move to injecting it into the arm or leg, then "main-lining" it by injecting it directly into the vein.

Opium and its derivatives work as depressants, dulling the central nervous system and producing a decrease in fear, pain, sex, and hunger. With prolonged use, ambition, intellectual efficiency, aggression, and moral standards are lowered although there is no evidence for mental deterioration. Vivid fantasies have been reported with opium, although true hallucinations do not often occur.

Withdrawal symptoms are agonizing: a desperate craving, cold sweat, tremors, abdominal cramps, anxious restlessness, retching and diarrhea, insomnia and uncontrollable yawning, and even mild shock, panic, or suicidal attempts. The withdrawal symptoms reach their peak about 36 to 48 hours after the last dosage, persist at this maximum level for about 48 more hours, then subside gradually over the next five days—an unbearable experience that leads many addicts to resort to any act in order to obtain the needed drug.

2. *Marijuana*—is the cheapest form of narcotic available and, like opium, is smoked. In cigarette form it is called "a joint," unrolled it is referred to as "grass," "Acapulco gold," "Mary Jane," or "pot." It is actually the flowers and stems of the hemp plant which are made into loosely rolled cigarettes. In Eastern countries, the drug is called hashish, ganga, or manzoul, and is smoked or chewed or even consumed as a drink.

The drug is often used as a substitute for alcohol. Some claim that it will relax inhibitions, increase relaxation. Musicians try it on the premise that they can play with "more feeling." Irritability, anxiety, and incoherence of speech are symptoms that sometimes appear. The passage of time may be unusually slowed subjectively. Within two to three hours, the individual falls asleep. The effects of marijuana are generally very difficult to predict and may range from euphoria to violence. Chronic use may result in sleep difficulty, apathy, loss of objective productivity (although there is a greater subjective sense of creativity), and decreased social and intellectual effectiveness (McGlothlin and West, 1968).

Marijuana differs from the opiates in several ways. Users seldom develop an in-

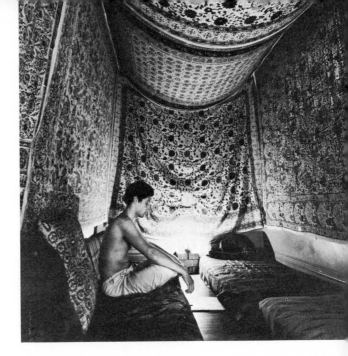

Left: Youthful narcotic addict *mainlining*, introducing the drug directly into his vein. (Steve Schapiro/Black Star)

Right: An *LSD* (lysergic acid diethylamide) user surrounded by Eastern motif draperies to enhance the effects of the drug. (Ivan Massar/Black Star)

creased tolerance for marijuana, nor is there physiologic craving, or withdrawal symptoms. The primary danger is that it has been a favored way of introducing individuals to the use of drugs, after which the individual is persuaded to "graduate" to heroin.

3. *Cocaine*—comes from the leaves of a cocoa plant and is referred to in slang as "coke," "star-dust," or "snow." It is usually taken by intravenous injection, although it is also sniffed. Currently, cocaine is comparatively unpopular.

Mild euphoria and friendly, extroverted behavior is an early effect of cocaine. As a stimulant it gives some people the added lift, or a sense of exhilaration, that they are searching for. However, with continued use, the individual becomes suspicious, irritable, and begins to develop highly frightening hallucinations such as the sensation of having bugs under the skin. The addict may become assaultive and murderous.

Users do not develop an increased tolerance for the drug, nor are there physiological withdrawal symptoms when it is discontinued. However, a psychological craving will develop prompting the in-dividual to continue its use to recapture the early desirable state of being "high."

4. *Barbiturates*—are compounds used for sedation. Some of the drugs are phenobarbital, Nembutal, sodium amytal. Before the tranquilizers were discovered, the barbiturates were the prime drugs used in psychiatry. They are still depended upon in psychiatric treatment and in general medical treatment. It is somewhat surprising that addiction cases are relatively few in spite of the widespread use.

The barbiturates act as depressants on the central nervous system. The individual feels relaxed, comfortable, calm. He may show slurring in his speech and unsteadiness. Tolerance levels increase until the individual has become physiologically addicted, showing withdrawal symptoms upon discontinuation. Withdrawal after prolonged intake of high dosages will produce severe epilepticlike seizures, anxiety, nausea, tremors, restlessness. There is also the danger of overdosage either through deliberate continuation of increased amounts or through accident. Newspapers are full of reports of accidental overdoses in which the patient started with the correct dose for sedation,

303

Methadrine is a form of *amphetamine,* compounds of which act as central nervous system stimulants. The photograph illustrates the subjective effects of methadrine leading to the nickname "speed." (Photo Trends)

became sleepy and confused about how much he took, was unable to fall asleep immediately, got up to take another pill to make sure, became even more uncertain and confused, remained awake with concern, and continued the cycle until the fatal dosage was taken.

5. *Amphetamines*—are compounds with chemical structures similar to norepinephrine and which act as central nervous system stimulants. These "pep pills" or "speed" include Dexedrine and Benzedrine and have been used by many to remain awake during all-night study sessions, or prolonged travel. Athletes have been suspected and suspended for reliance upon the stimulants as an extra boost in competition.

The drugs produce an increased level of alertness, elevation of mood, a sense of well-being and confidence, enhanced ability to carry out mental and physical activity in the sense of prolonging effort. Addiction follows the typical characteristics of increased tolerance level and with-

drawal symptoms. Side effects involve restlessness, hostility, tension, insomnia, intense fear or panic, suicidal behavior, paranoid delusions, or hallucinations. Nausea, vomiting, diarrhea, increased blood pressure, anginal pain, and death are potential results.

6. *Tranquilizers*—are quite commonly used in place of barbiturates as a means of controlling the symptoms of mental illness. When a milder form was manufactured, it was believed essentially nonaddicting. More recently it appears that tranquilizers such as meprobamate (Miltown, Equanil) can be habit forming and patients may show the physical dependence and withdrawal symptoms associated with drug addiction.

Tranquilizers enable the individual to reduce his tensions and anxieties and face conflicts. One patient described the differences between alcohol and tranquilizers as follows (he was an expert on both): "You take alcohol and your problem vanishes while you're drunk, but the morning after it not only returns but you feel even worse than you did before! With tranquilizers, your problem is still there, but it doesn't matter to you anymore; and the next morning it isn't any bigger than it was before." Withdrawal from the drug is less agonizing in comparison with the other drug addictions. However, the symptoms may include confusion, anxiety, insomnia, and convulsions in some cases.

7. *Lysergic acid diethylamide*, known also as "acid" or "big D," is one of a group of hallucinogenic drugs (hallucination producing) which reached great heights of popularity during the mid-twentieth century. It was accidentally discovered by a Swiss chemist, Albert Hoffman, who was exposed to a small quantity in a test tube and who found himself subsequently undergoing a bizarre ride on his way home an hour later (Stoll, 1947). Unlike peyote, which has a nauseating effect upon inges-

tion, LSD is easier to ingest and is often delivered in sugar cubes. A dose as low as a quarter-*millionth* of an ounce can trigger a dreamlike experience affecting the senses, judgment, memory, motor coordination, and the emotions. Perceptual distortions and visual hallucinations develop, and in some cases *synesthesia* occurs. Synesthesia is the responsiveness of one sense modality when another is stimulated, for example, a musical note may be experienced as a definite color, or the sound of a typewriter may be converted into a visual fireworks display. Severe emotional effects have been reported ranging from excruciatingly pleasant feelings to terrorizing panic to a religiouslike conversion. In some cases a "free trip" occurs, reexperiencing the LSD state without ingesting additional LSD. As with marijuana and peyote, it is difficult to determine which effects are a function of the pharmacolog-

TABLE 11-5. *Two Styles of Reaction to Peyote as Related to Differences in Cultural Heritage and Expectations*

EUROAMERICANS	INDIANS
Their mood varies and shifts from agitated depression and anxiety to euphoria, depending on the stage of intoxication and the psychological characteristics of the individual.	The Indians' mood is at first stable. Then religious anxiety follows and enthusiasm, with a tendency toward feelings of religious reverence and personal satisfaction once the vision appears.
Social inhibitions frequently break down; sexual and aggressive behavior is shamelessly displayed.	They retain proper behavior even if they show revivalistic enthusiasm (which is proper in the situation).
The intoxicated person becomes suspicious of others around him.	No report of suspiciousness.
Unwelcome feelings of loss of contact with reality occur; depersonalization; meaninglessness, and "split personality."	Peyotists experience welcome feelings of being in contact with a more meaningful, higher order of reality.
Idiosyncratic hallucinations take hold.	Hallucinations occur, patterned by the Peyote religion's doctrines.
No therapeutic benefits or permanent change in behavior known.	Marked therapeutic benefits earned; chronic anxiety reduced; the Indian's sense of personal worth climbs, and his life contains more satisfaction.

SOURCE: A. Wallace, Cultural determinant of response to hallucinatory experience. *Arch. gen. Psychiat.*, July, 1959, **1**, 58-69. Copyright 1959, American Medical Association. Reprinted by permission of the copyright owner.

ical properties of the drug and which are due to the prior expectations, attitudes, suggestibility, and beliefs of the user (Mc-Glothlin and West, 1968) (Table 11-5). During an 18-month period in Los Angeles County alone, some 4100 adverse reactions requiring professional care were noted (Ungerledier et al., 1968). Chronic exposure to LSD seems to lead to a look of aging from loss of facial muscle tone, extreme passivity, increased belief in magical-mystical ideas, and perhaps some central nervous system alterations (Blacker et al., 1968; Evarts, 1956) and chromosomal damage (Irwin and Egozcue, 1967; Cohen, Marinello, and Back, 1967).

Dynamics. Since drug addiction may involve physical dependence as well as psychological dependence, it is convenient to discuss two major routes in the etiology of addiction: addiction without the con-

sent or intention of the user, and addiction on a more or less voluntary basis. Physical dependence means that continued use is necessary not only for the addict to continue to feel and function normally, but also to prevent the withdrawal symptoms from appearing. Physical dependence on such drugs as morphine or codeine has been known to develop unintentionally. During the early part of the century, many became addicted through the narcotics in patent medicines and in soft drink beverages (Fig. 11-5). The heavy use of pain-killing narcotics in medical treatment was often prescribed in the past even by reputable physicians. Today, however, *iatrogenic addiction,* or medically produced addiction, is rare because of the deliberate precautions that are taken. Occasionally, the inadequate facilities of battlefield conditions force an increased

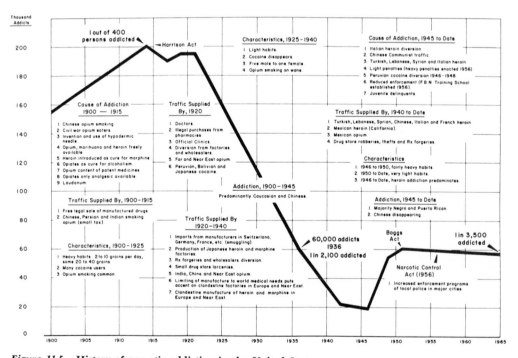

Figure 11-5. **History of narcotic addiction in the United States.**
SOURCE: U.S. Treasury Department, Bureau of Narcotics, *Prevention and control of narcotic addiction.* Washington, D.C.: U.S. Government Printing Office, 1967. Copyright Bureau of Narcotics and Dangerous Drugs, U.S. Department of Justice.

reliance upon morphine syrettes (hypodermic tubes) for pain. In general, the unwitting development of physical dependence has been sharply reduced through better federal control over medical and prescription practices, the availability of nonaddicting substitutes for narcotics, and the increased awareness of a better-informed public about drugs. Perhaps five percent of admissions to hospitals for addiction are iatrogenic addiction (Pescor, 1943). Physical dependence for such cases is readily broken through gradual withdrawal of the drug; future cravings do not seem to develop in such patients in contrast to those who have voluntarily become addicted (Maurer and Vogel, 1962; Rasor, 1958). Although these latter patients tend to ascribe their addiction solely to iatrogenic factors, this has seldom proven accurate.

The majority of known addictions have occurred on a voluntary basis. The typical narcotic addict in the United States is from a metropolitan region, comes from a low socioeconomic level, is a minority group member, and is between 18-25 years of age (Murray, 1967). A number of studies have described them as falling into several patterns: the "socially deviant," the rebellious, the gang or group victim, and the neurotic or psychotic. The socially deviant pattern is the most characteristic; it involves a picture of social ineptness, insecurity, lack of assertiveness, passivity, and frequently a continuing emotional relationship with the mother (Haertzen, Hill, and Belleville, 1963; Laskowitz and Einstein, 1963; Lewis and Osberg, 1958). The home environment contributed much to the development of this pattern. The mothers are often women who have infantilized their sons while demonstrating both possessiveness and rejection. In some cases the mothers encouraged the youngsters to give up drugs while at the same time procuring more drugs for them. These parents often harbored resentment toward their offspring, and attempted to dominate, overpower, overprotect, and indulge their sons (Bender, 1963; Hirsh, 1961; Mason, 1958; Vaillant, 1966a). One report on physician-addicts stressed the mixed desires of these patients to remain tied to their parents while also wishing emancipation and hating the dependency (Scher, 1966). Vaillant's 12-year study of narcotic addicts indicated that 47 percent still lived with a female relative after the age of 30 years (Vaillant, 1966a). In contrast, the fathers contributed little in the way of serving as models of strength for their sons. These male parents were either absent because of death or separation, or weak and inconsistent figures (Mason, 1958; Kolb, 1968; Lewis and Osberg, 1958; Easton, 1965).

The rebellious feature of some cases of drug addiction is in keeping with the *dyssocial* aspects of narcotics use. For this group, the acting out of aggressive impulses toward society seems to be reflected in criminal acts, delinquency, and the use of narcotics. In Vaillant's (1966a) study group 56 percent were delinquent before drug addiction, while Gerard and Kornetsky (1955) identified 72 percent of their addicts and Alksne et al. (1959) discovered 50 percent of their sample to be delinquent prior to the use of drugs. Drug use therefore appears to be another phase in the overall pattern of rebelliousness. Many come from slum districts and fragmented families which contribute to alienation, rootlessness, and striking-out against society (Freedman, Sager, Rabiner, and Brotman, 1963). A number have parents who were foreign born, and who represent a culture and mores alien to the addict's (Vaillant, 1966a). Such parent-offspring conflict of beliefs probably contributed its share to the rebelliousness and lack of conformity of the youngster.

For many drug addicts, the influence of their group membership is a factor. A group may encourage addiction through

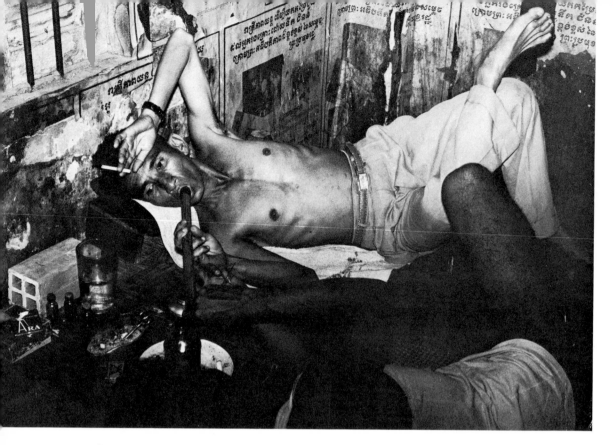

Among the Eastern countries, reliance upon narcotics was common. *Opium* dens provided a source for the drug and privacy. (PIP Photographers, Inc.)

making drugs available, peer-group enticement and even pressure to try the drugs, and protection from the disfavor of nongroup members (Scher, 1966; Haines and McLaughlin, 1952). An individual may participate in the use of "pot," "speed," or "acid" because it is the exciting "in-thing" for his group, or for kicks, or for fear of social ostracism from his group if he refuses. Groups using hallucinogenic drugs have been known to develop their own cultural mores and standards in which group acceptance is based upon ready acceptance and use of certain drugs; the advantages of membership include sharing of sources for obtaining drugs, "sampling" parties where salesmen with different wares permit free tasting, and mutual help when one member is in trouble. Members are quick to promote the virtues of the drug experience but tend to avoid serious discussions of

the inherent problems. In groups using narcotics, the novice user may seek out and respond to group pressure because of his initial desire for the fraternalism and sense of belonging that membership provides. As he becomes addicted to the point of requiring a continuous supply, he soon encounters the negative sanctions of the society at large. Rejected by the community, he is even more reliant upon the group for acceptance. As his dependence upon the group increases, the ability of the group to shape his behavior to their standards also increases (Ausubel, 1961; Maurer and Vogel, 1962).

Although the vast majority of drug addicts show no signs of psychoneuroses or psychoses (Kolb, 1968; Vaillant, 1966b, Nyswander, 1956), a small proportion of addicts do suffer from some emotional disorder. In the neurotic who becomes an addict, the introduction to drugs appears to be through an accident. The narcotic helps the patient relieve his tensions or deaden his feelings. Rather than face the anxieties of life, he finds the fantasies of the drug-induced state more pleasing. Among psychotics, the use of drugs seems as much a result of their weakened ability to adapt to their environment as it is their desire for a narcissistic state of self-gratification (Nyswander, 1956; Bender, 1963).

One further interesting aspect of drug usage should be mentioned. Maurer and Vogel (1962) suggest that the addiction-prone individual experiences intense pleasure on their first contact with the opium drugs. This experience is never truly forgotten and is much sought-after in his future drug experiences. As tolerance builds and a larger and larger dose is needed to achieve the same level of sensation, the addict may even voluntarily abstain from drugs such that he might again repeat that original intense state. On the other hand, the nonaddiction-prone person usually finds the experiences induced by narcotics to be unpleasant. Furthermore, he is wary and concerned about the long-term agony associated with drug addiction and its consequences. In some ways, this distinction between a reaction to the immediate pleasures aroused by the narcotic drug versus the consideration of the potential ill effects of its use may also be characteristic of the chronic user of psychedelic drugs versus the nonuser. Users of hallucinogenic drugs have included a wide variety of people, ranging from the suggestible adolescent to the mature professional man. Those who manage to avoid further use of the drugs seem to be impressed by the experiences produced but also more aware of the dangers of psychological dependence. In addition, these abstainers seem to find little value in the behaviors, motivations, and values of the chronic users. On the other hand, the individuals who persist in their use of the hallucinogens appear wrapped up in the immediate effects of the drugs. The almost instant release of new feelings or display of a new world seems never forgotten. The excessive LSD user seems trapped in an eternal search for "experience," with little concern for the future. Some marijuana users also stress the immediate value of "pot" in "breaking up my hangups so that I can function again."

Treatment. The first phase of treatment is help in abstinence from the drug and control over the withdrawal reaction. Whenever the narcotic drugs are abruptly withdrawn, a sequence of withdrawal symptoms occur. Among the early results are yawning, rhinorrhea (nose runs), lacrimation (eyes water), sneezing, and perspiration. Soon, appetite is lost, the pupils dilate, gooseflesh appears, and tremors develop. The worst physical symptoms include intense reslessness, uncontrollable spasms, insomnia, vomiting, and diarrhea. Among the psychological signs are irritability, fault-finding, destructive outbursts, weeping, or suicidal attempts. Prior to 1948, the abrupt withholding of drugs, the "cold turkey" method, was used to break the physical dependence. Since then, the usefulness of methadone has been discovered and used as an aid. Methadone is an antinarcotic agent that blocks the action of heroin, morphine, or other opiate drugs. In effect, it serves as a substitute for the narcotic drugs (although it is dangerous in cases of barbiturate addiction), and has the advantage of being more readily withdrawn with less distress (Vogel, Isbell, and Chapman, 1948; Dole and Nyswander, 1966). The reduction of drug intake is conducted over a period of seven days to two weeks. Other drugs that have been experimentally used in withdrawal include ACTH and cortisone but neither is very helpful in morphine addiction. Tranquilizers, insulin to promote the appetite, hydrotherapy, massage,

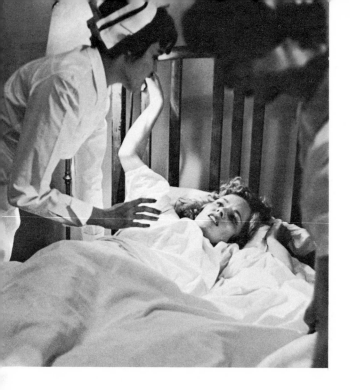

Withdrawal symptoms are feared by the narcotic addict. The support of professional staff is helpful in enabling the patient to cope with the restlessness, tremors, spasms, and intestinal upset. (I. Howard Spivak/DPI)

recreational and occupational therapy are helpful adjuncts during the withdrawal phase. The United States Public Health Service maintains two hospitals for the treatment of drug addicts, one in Lexington, Kentucky established in 1935 and the other at Fort Worth, Texas, built in 1938. The Lexington facility has a daily census of 1000 patients of whom 20 percent are women. In addition, it has an active research program and has contributed much to understanding the psychological factors involved in addiction and its treatment.

Another phase of the treatment program involves dealing with the conditions associated with the addiction. For the addictions without physical dependence, this phase begins first since withdrawal from the drug poses no special medical problem. If the addiction developed during the course of treatment by narcotics for a major physical disease, then psychotherapy is not appropriate since the addiction was not attributable to psychological factors. For others, psychotherapeutic sessions may be devoted to relief of the conditions that originally disposed the patient toward reliance upon drugs. In addition, the de-

pression, sense of lowered self-esteem, or resentment toward the community which may have developed, must be attended to. Imminent crises that could send the patient running back to drugs must be anticipated and the patient helped in his attempts to cope with them. The commitment to a drug-free environment such as in the Lexington facility is a great help in such matters. In fact, it is generally believed that the main hope for cure from addiction remains in the use of drug-free hospital environments (Murray, 1967).

Enrollment in Narcotics Anonymous, the corollary to Alcoholics Anonymous, is desirable upon release from the hospital. Organizations such as Synanon seem to be making considerable headway as a treatment type unit. Synanon gets its name from the mispronunciation of "seminar," group meetings in which members discuss their character traits and face themselves as they are through the help of other addicts. In addition, they can work in small businesses operated by Synanon while working through their problems. Many members have gone through a cold turkey cure, remained in residence for a period,

310

The independent drug addiction organization, *Synanon,* derives its name from the "seminar" group discussion meetings. Drug addicts help one another in these self-realization sessions. Illustrated above is a seminar held at Exodus House, a residential treatment center in East Harlem. (Hilda Bijur/Monkmeyer Press)

obtained employment, participated in the critical-evaluative group meetings, and have eventually left for a self-supporting life (Yablonsky, 1965).

In general, the prognosis for complete recovery from drug addiction is not good. Estimates of relapse rates have been as high as 75 to 97 percent (Ausubel, 1961; Duvall et al., 1963). Over a short-term study period, recidivism is extremely high but the rates for abstinence improve considerably as time passes. For example, Duvall et al. (1963) followed up 453 Lexington patients and found over 97 percent relapsing during the first part of the five-year period; but by the end of the fifth year after discharge 49 percent were abstinent. In a 12-year follow-up study, Vaillant discovered that 30 percent had achieved abstinence of three years or more

(1966a); O'Donnell (1964) found that more women were abstinent (79 percent) than men (38 percent). Of interest is Vaillant's (1966b) findings that when the 30 most successful recovery patients were compared with the 30 least successful the successful ones had been able to obtain steady employment and had come from more intact homes and homes with nonforeign-born parents. The employment characteristic was interpreted to indicate that the recovered addict had finally given up his war against society and was able to sustain an independent life through gainful employment.

SEXUAL DEVIATIONS

The sexual deviations include all sexual behaviors in which gratification of sexual

311

Case History 11-4

DRUG ADDICTION

Thomas de Quincey, the renowned English author, wrote *The Confessions of an English Opium-Eater* as his first contribution to the *London Magazine*. It was written rapidly in the autumn of 1821, when he was in extremely poor health and melancholy spirits. The book was well received and was to lay the foundations of a successful career for him. Its theme centered around his confession of his life with drugs.

De Quincey was one of six children born of a merchant. His father died when the writer was seven, leaving the children in the care of four guardians. De Quincey recalls two incidents which profoundly influenced him and which occurred before he was two years of age. The first was a dream, intensely vivid and filled with a sense of grandeur—dream qualities that persisted with him throughout his life. The second event which he believed to be of great importance was his inexplicable deep melancholy upon seeing the reappearance of crocuses after winter. This susceptibility toward depressive moods also tended to characterize him throughout life. He was quite close to one sister and was deeply affected by her early death in childhood; he even contrived to secretly visit her corpse prior to the funeral. On the other hand, he was quite subjugated by one of his brothers who required him to literally show deference.

He was a desperately lonely individual, nearly always without sufficient money and once almost jailed as a debtor, and continuously melancholic. He appeared completely unable to engage in sustained intellectual efforts; nevertheless his literary journalism catapulted him to success. He apparently was an excellent linguist in Greek. In fact, he gave up his academic studies at Oxford on the pretense that an oral examination, which was originally to be conducted in Greek, had been changed to Latin. It is believed that this excuse was a rationalized defense over his extreme fear of failure, another trait that persisted in de Quincey's life.

De Quincey attributed his opium addiction to his childhood unhappiness, and a physical illness. A college friend suggested opium as a means of deadening the pains from a toothache, and de Quincey continued to use opium to rid himself of the agonies from a recurring stomach condition that he acquired because of "extremities of hunger, suffered in my boyish days" (perhaps a peptic ulcer). The addiction precipitated four opium crises, but de Quincey was able to recover his health after some eighteen years of opium addiction!

Some of his experiences are worth quoting (1924):

Opium . . . communicates serenity and equipose to all the faculties . . . and it gives that sort of vital warmth which is approved by the judgment, and which probably always accompany a bodily constitution of primeval or antediluvian health (171-2).

(My) . . . disease . . . was to meditate too much and to observe too little, and . . . a deep melancholy, from brooding too much . . . the remedies I sought were to force myself into society . . . . But for these remedies, I should certainly have become hypochondriacally melancholy (183). . . . at the time I began to take opium daily, I could

Case History 11-4 (*Continued*)

DRUG ADDICTION

not have done otherwise. I confess . . . I hanker too much after a state of happiness, both for myself and others; I cannot face misery . . . and am little capable of encountering present pain . . . (189).

The cursed crocodile became to me the object of more horror than all the rest. I was compelled to live with him; and (as was always the case in my dreams) for centuries . . . the abominable head of the crocodile, and his leering eyes, looked out at me, multiplied into ten thousand repetitions; and I stood loathing and fascinated. So often did this hideous reptile haunt my dreams . . . . No experience was so awful to me (233).

Nothing short of mortal anguish, in a physical sense, it seemed, to wean myself from opium; yet, on the other hand, death through overwhelming nervous terrors—death by brain fever or by lunacy—seemed too certainly to besiege the alternative course.

I *did* accomplish my escape . . . I triumphed. But infer not, reader, from this word "*triumphed*," a condition of joy or exultation. Think of me as one, even when four months had passed, still agitated writhing, throbbing, palpitating, shattered (p. 237).

impulses is obtained by practices other than intercourse with a genitally mature person of the opposite sex who has reached the legal age of consent. The aberrations may involve a deviation in the object of choice, the sexual acts, or the degree of sexual desire. The following are examples of perversions within these categories:

1. Deviation in object choice—homosexuality, masturbation, pedophilia (selection of a child), zoophilia or bestiality (selection of an animal), fetishism (selection of an inanimate object or a part of a human object), necrophilia (selection of corpses). In all of these, the individual becomes sexually aroused and engages in intercourse with a deviant sexual object.

2. Deviation in sexual act—sadism, masochism, exhibitionism, voyeurism, coprolalia. In these, the individual becomes aroused through deviant acts other than genital stimulation, for example, in coprolalia the individual utters obscene words.

3. Deviations in degree of sexual desire —frigidity or impotence, nymphomania

or satyriasis. In these, the sexual urge is either impaired or exaggerated.

Sexual deviations as defined above have appeared with widely divergent results in man's history. The Greeks, of course, were known to deliberately practice homosexuality between older men and young boys. In fact, such relationships were considered aesthetically superior to the relationships with the women who were viewed as inferior beings. On the other hand, the annihilation of Sodom and Gomorrah has been interpreted as punishment for the sinful perversions of anal or animal sexual intercourse. Such catastrophic punitive action for sodomy represents the other extreme in attitude toward sexual deviations.

Homosexuality is a deviation in which the sexual partner of choice is the same sex as the chooser. In women, this condition is referred to as lesbianism. Not all individuals who have had a homosexual experience are true homosexuals; in fact, it is estimated that 37 percent of the males and 13 percent of the females in the

A *transvestite* is a person who derives sexual gratification from dressing in the clothing of the opposite sex. As illustrated in the photograph above, the male transvestite can dress in a deceptively alluring manner disguising his true sex. (Carr & Miller/PIP)

United States have had a homosexual orgasm sometime in their lives (Kinsey, Pomerory, Martin, and Gebhard, 1953). However, many of these were immature youthful experiments in sex and do not automatically make the person a pervert. Homosexuals are not identifiable by their physical characteristics, despite folklore beliefs. A few, but not all, transvestites are homosexuals and thus even dressing in the clothing of the opposite sex (transvestism) is not a clear indication of homosexuality. Male homosexuals tend to be more promiscuous than female homosexuals and some have been known to have engaged in relations with hundreds of partners.

Fetishism is a deviation in which the object of choice is a part of the human body, or an object, commonly a shoe. In extreme cases, the sight or touch of the shoe is sufficient to arouse an orgasm; the individual thus does not require a human mate for a sexual experience. Fetishism appears to be more common with men than with women. The object may be lace, silk, perfumes, or soap, the hair, the eyes, the hands, or ears. In an exaggerated fashion, fetishism is similar to the normal tendency to admire those objects that have become associated with a loved one; thus, a normal person may cherish the class ring belonging to her sweetheart, and he in turn may "worship the ground she walks on."

Sadomasochism is a deviation in which the infliction of pain is necessary for sexual satisfaction. The sadistic individual is aroused by hurting his sexual partner, the masochistic individual is aroused when hurt by the sexual partner. The term sadomasochism recognizes the intimate association between the two aspects. It is not uncommon for a sadistic deviate to pair with a masochistic partner in com-

314

plementary roles. The acts may involve the infliction of physical or psychological pain, for example, whipping, verbal abuse, humiliation. Violent crimes in which the victims have been mutilated and sometimes raped have been committed by sadists. It is possible for the sadomasochist to achieve sexual gratification without engaging in sexual intercourse.

Voyeurism is a deviation in which the individual is sexually gratified by looking at the sexual organs or activities of others. This perversion is also called *scoptophilia*. The "peeping Tom" is frequently searching for a chance to see a sexually exciting situation. Voyeurs will loiter around bath houses, toilets, or apartments in the hope of catching a glimpse of an undressed person. In some houses of prostitution, elaborate performances are staged to obtain the business of these perverts. Typically, the urge is to see the genitals or the nude body of a person of the opposite sex. The voyeur differs from the peeping Tom who observes out of frustration in that the voyeur prefers staring at the genitals of others to normal sexual intercourse.

Nymphomania is a deviation characterized by an incessant desire for sexual stimulation. The same aberration appearing in men is called *satyriasis*. The individual hungers for sexual relations in any manner available. There is little selectivity in terms of the partner's traits or appearance. The individual's thoughts become preoccupied with sexuality and her entire life becomes oriented around achieving her sexual goal. There is reason to believe that many normal persons experience quite high amounts of sexual desire in comparison with nonpassionate but equally normal individuals. The difference is the degree to which the urge becomes an all-consuming, persistent, and foremost focus of the person's everyday life. This particular deviation is also different from normal desires in that the sexual activity

is motivated by tension, frustration, and inadequacy.

Dynamics

Some attempts have been made to demonstrate a physical basis for the various perversions. Homosexuality has been studied with reference to hormone imbalance, nymphomania in terms of organic lesions in the brain. However, the scientific evidence does not substantiate the proposed role of hormones in homosexuality, and there is no good evidence that brain pathology is involved in nymphomania (although destruction of the amygdala in the brain can produce excessive sexual urges). Even in cases of hermaphroditism—where one individual is born with the sexual organs of both sexes, the sexual role that is assumed is by no means solely a function of physical equipment.

A continuing pattern running throughout the sexual pathologies is the retarded social development of the deviant. Whereas others have matured through satisfactory contacts with the opposite sex, the deviant has never developed the confidence to interact with others. Fearful of failure if he approaches a potential mate, the deviant protects himself by resorting to fetishes, animals, children, or just looking. Strong feelings of personal inadequacy and unattractiveness compound his fear of being humiliated in heterosexual relationships. Another contributor to sexual perversions is an unsatisfactory parental relationship. Behaviors such as voyeurism, exhibitionism, and homosexuality have a component of rebellion and may represent an expression of delayed opposition toward parental figures. The masochistic sublayer, which is perceptible in the extreme risks involved in such perversions, may be an unconscious wish for discovery and punishment for guilt feelings. Psychoanalysts portray the difficulties of normal sexual relations when the individual has been unsuccessful in resolving early conflicts over his sexual feelings toward his mother, struggle against his father, and fear of castration. The homosexual, for example, can be understood as becoming homosexual:

1. Because he has failed to identify with his father and therefore with the masculine role. For girls, lesbianism would be the failure to shift from the first natural love object, the mother, to one of the opposite sex.

2. Because he has felt inadequate in competing with his father, and seeks to gain power and strength by symbolically absorbing these through intercourse with a strong male.

3. Because he has developed the approach-avoidance reaction toward women on the basis of his earlier fears of castration were he to approach his mother.

It is entirely possible that the sadistic deviant is punishing his victim just as he was punished for childhood sexual acts discovered by his parents. Masochism, on the other hand, can be seen as the more direct expression of low self-esteem regarding all self-traits, especially the sexual desire. The deviant activities can be understood in some circumstances as defense mechanisms. Sadism is a form of displaced hostility, fetishism a form of displaced love. It will be recalled, that displacement involves the release of emotion toward a less threatening object. Therefore, we must search out the source of the emotion and the reason behind the threat that the deviant feels. The nymphomaniac may be attempting to compensate for an earlier inability to engage in sexuality, or she may be reacting against covert homosexual desires. Of course, it has already been mentioned that tension release through sexual promiscuity or through perversions such as masturbation tends to be self-perpetuating since this drive reduction is reinforcing.

Treatment

Sexual deviation is amenable to psychotherapy with the prognosis being dependent upon the severity of the pathology involved. Deviations of object choice are relatively minor cases compared to the grosser disturbances involved in sadistic crimes of violence; homosexuality resulting from a recent trauma in a heterosexual relationship is more subject to cure than nymphomania associated with a lifetime pattern of inadequacy and conflict. The aim of psychotherapy is the same as in the treatment of the psychoneuroses, the uncovering and elimination of the source of the pathology. Guilt feelings, rebelliousness, low self-esteem, tension reduction, continued struggle with early parental conflicts, all need to be considered as potential origins.

Behavior therapy has been applied to sexual deviations with varying success. Aversion methods have been applied to homosexuality, fetishism, and transvestism; desensitization has been used with impotency, frigidity, and voyeurism; and reciprocal inhibition with assertive methods has been relied upon for cases of impotency, exhibitionism, and voyeurism. One case of transvestism and its treatment is interesting. The patient, age 33, practiced the deviation every two weeks for over six years. Six or so years of psychotherapy had not proved beneficial. Behavior therapy consisted of having the patient first dress in his favorite female clothing, then undress when signaled. During the undressing, a shock was administered. This treatment was conducted for six days. Follow-up data six months later showed that the transvestitism has stopped completely and the patient was now experiencing an improved sexual relationship with his wife. A second follow-up fourteen months after treatment indicated that one minor relapse had occurred, but under unusual conditions. While attending a party, he became intoxicated, arranged a meeting with a prostitute who catered to transvestites, and cross-dressed. No further relapse or desire for cross-dressing occurred since (Blakemore, 1963).

A letter written by Sigmund Freud in reply to a woman who appealed to him for help for her homosexual son is instructive.

By asking me if I can help, you mean, I suppose, if I can abolish homosexuality and make normal heterosexuality take its place. The answer is, in a general way, we cannot promise to achieve it. In a certain number of cases we succeed in developing the blighted germs of heterosexual tendencies which are present in every homosexual, in the majority of cases it is no more possible. It is a question of the quality and the age of the individual.

Case History 11-5

HOMOSEXUALITY

William O., age 39, is an overt homosexual who has always assumed the passive or feminine role. He works as an accountant and lives in an apartment near his place of occupation. However, he spends much of his evenings and weekends prowling known homosexual bars in the hopes of finding a new partner since he was recently left by another. He admits that it has become increasingly difficult for him since he must compete with the younger homosexuals who are considered more attractive than persons of his age. His last "marriage" to another homosexual lasted one month.

William O. was raised by his father, a burly longshoreman who had always been disappointed at the lack of aggressiveness of his son. During his drinking bouts, this parent often teased his son, making fun of the boy's tiny genitals, and laughing heartily when this was responded to with embarassment. William's first heterosexual date was arranged by his father with a prostitute some 10 years older than the then adolescent boy. She had been instructed to "teach him to be a man"; however, the experience only served to frighten the boy and convince him of his sexual inadequacy and ignorance.

His first homosexual experience occurred through an association with a friend whom he admired for his outgoingness, daring, and unconventionality. They had spent a casual evening together in a pseudo-intellectual discussion of conventional sexual morality, the great figures in history such as Alexander the Great and Michelangelo who were homosexual, and the "misunderstood" views which people had toward the homosexual. William stopped to have several drinks at his friend's apartment, became a little unsteady, and was seduced by his friend. The next evening, he was welcomed into a homosexual group with much ado and became quite taken by all the attention he received. He soon became a willing convert. William would never change his ways; his only discomfort is the fear of losing his attractiveness and the occasional beating that he suffers when he mistakenly makes an advance towards a non-homosexual. He has rationalized and intellectualized his way of life so well that he believes homosexuality is the only normal way for anyone to live. He feels that the society has persecuted him out of its own fear of recognizing the true value of his choice.

The result of treatment cannot be predicted.

What analysis can do for your son runs in a different line. If he is unhappy, neurotic, torn by conflicts, inhibited in his social life, analysis may bring him harmony, peace of mind, full efficiency whether he remains a homosexual or gets changed . . . .

Sincerely yours with kind wishes,

Freud

Case History 11-6

NYMPHOMANIA

Charisse is a 23-year-old woman who sought treatment at a mental health outpatient clinic. She had been precipitated to the clinic as a result of a recent proposal from a man whom she deeply loved, yet she was fearful of her sexual drives. Since she was fifteen, she had passed through innumerable sexual experiences with a variety of men whom she convinced herself she really cared for. Yet, many of these involved passing acquaintances thus making it evident that her convictions were no more than rationalizations. Her first sexual intercourse set the pattern for those that followed. She had been desperately hoping to be accepted into a junior high sorority, but was turned away in a callous fashion. That evening, she accepted a date on the spur of the moment with an older neighbor boy. She sought comfort in his arms and soon found herself being intimately embraced and caressed. Her despair was soon forgotten as she became aware of a new, exciting sensation. When it was over, she recalls that her tensions and sorrows had all dissipated. From that evening on, she found that her sexual desires tended to become heightened especially after a disappointment or when she was under stress. Occasionally she felt the need for a sexual "binge" when she became extremely frustrated and angry.

As a child, Charisse had lived an isolated and lonely life. She was the only child and was carefully protected by a temperamental and controlling mother. Her father had been antagonistic toward her birth since it had not been planned. Physically, she matured rapidly and was fully developed by the time she was thirteen. Except for her well-developed body, she was not a particularly pretty girl. However, to make up for her plain features, she dressed more daringly, adopted a carefree attitude, and developed a seductive manner. She was able to attract the attention of many boys but never seemed to be able to relate well to girls. At best, she was tolerated by her girl acquaintances, at worst, she was snubbed as being too forward and uncouth. She completed high school with fair grades, entered the state university and soon withdrew because of her inability to keep her attention on her course work. She worked for several years as a theatre usherette.

Because of her strong motivation to understand her feelings, she was considered a good candidate for treatment. Her therapist initially was a woman but the treatment program entailed having her transferred eventually to a man as a means of helping her deal with her difficulty at a controlled pace. Her progress had been satisfactory enough that she was able to accept an engagement ring and plan for a future wedding. The relationship between her emotional distress and her use of sexuality for tension release was one of the more important aspects under examination.

Glossary

Acute hallucinosis: A condition associated with chronic alcoholism and characterized by auditory hallucinations. In contrast to delirium tremens, the patient remains oriented and does not show amnesia; the cause is believed to be the release of underlying emotional disorder when alcohol is consumed.

Addiction: Technically, the increased reliance upon a substance such that its withdrawal leads to several physiological effects. Also used to refer to psychological dependence upon a substance where no physiological need is entailed.

Alcoholic deterioration: A condition associated with chronic alcoholism and characterized by the disintegration of personality, intellectual impairment, and ethical and moral decline.

Alcoholics Anonymous: An organization of alcoholics who lend aid to one another in working toward abstinence.

Alcoholism: Extreme physiological or psychological dependence upon alcohol. There is some disagreement as to whether alcoholic addiction is purely a physiological dependence. There is also some controversy as to whether a person addicted to alcohol is always suffering from psychological disturbance.

Antabuse: A drug used to control alcoholism by precipitating a nauseating sensation when mixed with alcohol.

Anterograde amnesia: The loss of memory for events within the immediate past.

Antisocial reaction: One of the conduct disorders characterized by emotional immaturity, lack of responsibility, amoral behavior, inability to learn from experience, and superficial interpersonal relations.

Aversion therapy: A form of behavior therapy involving the association of an aversive stimulus with the behavior to be eliminated.

Bestiality: Sexual deviancy involving intercourse with animals.

Character disorder: Another term for the conduct disorders.

Chronic phase: A phase of alcoholism characterized by the onset of "benders," the loss of defense mechanisms or justifications for drinking, and the total immersion of alcoholic consumption.

Constitutional psychopathic inferiority: Historically used term for conduct disorders.

Crucial phase: A phase of alcoholism characterized by some attempt to regain abstinence, the loss of control over drinking, self-pity, and the inability to cover up the presence of a drinking problem.

Delirium tremens: A condition associated with chronic alcoholism and characterized by disorientation, hallucinations, and amnesia for the experience upon recovery.

Dyssocial reactions: Criminals or social rule-breakers who appear to retain a strong group relationship.

Epilepsy: A group of disorders characterized by convulsions.

Exhibitionism: Sexual deviancy involving sexual arousal through self-display.

Fetishism: Sexual deviancy involving sexual arousal through manipulation of inanimate objects.

Hallucinogenic drugs: A group of drugs that produce hallucinations.

Hepatitis: A disease of the liver caused by or associated with many factors including alcoholism.

Heroin: A drug derived from morphine, a habit-forming narcotic.

Homosexuality: Sexual deviancy involving sexual relations with persons of the same sex. Homosexuality among women is also referred to as lesbianism.

Iatrogenic addiction: Drug addiction due to the use of narcotics in heavy amounts for the treatment of a disease, or the pain associated with disease or injury.

Impotence: Sexual deviancy involving the inability to become sexually aroused. Also called frigidity.

Korsakoff's psychosis: A condition associated with chronic alcoholism and characterized by disorientation, anterograde amnesia, confabulation, and lack of insight. The cause is believed to be vitamin deficiency and is especially common in alcoholics with nutritional deficiences.

Marijuana: A drug made from the flowers and stems or leaves of a hemp plant. Said to be nonaddicting in the physiological sense.

Masochism: Sexual deviancy involving sexual arousal when pain is inflicted.

Masturbation: Achievement of orgasm through manual stimulation of genitals.

Methadone: A drug used in the treatment of drug addiction.

Mileau therapy: Treatment involving an entire environment being totally devoted to therapeutic conditions.

Nymphomania: Sexual deviation involving an abnormally strong sex desire in females. Called satyriasis in males.

Pancreatitis: A disease of the pancreas caused by or associated with many factors, including alcoholism.

Paraldehyde: A drug used in the treatment of alcoholics.

Pathological intoxication: An acute condition associated with alcoholic intake and characterized by disorientation, emotional changes, hallucinations, confusion. Belived to be caused by alcohol acting as a precipitating factor releasing an unstable emotional condition or aggravating a brain dysfunction.

Pedophilia: Sexual deviancy involving sexual relations with children.

Prealcoholic phase: A phase of alcoholism characterized by the establishment of heavy drinking patterns.

Prodomal phase: A phase of alcoholism characterized by spells of amnesia, secretive drinking, and dependence upon alcohol.

Psychopathic personality: Same as antisocial reaction.

Psychotomimetic drugs: A group of drugs that produces psychoticlike behaviors.

Sadism: Sexual deviancy involving sexual arousal when inflicting pain to others.

Sociopath: Another term for the conduct disorders.

Synanon: An organization of former drug addicts who lend aid to other drug addicts in achieving abstinence from drug usage.

Synesthesia: A sensory phenomenon whereby one sensory modality responds when another has been stimulated.

Transvestism: Sexual deviancy involving dressing in the garments of the opposite sex.

Voyeurism: Sexual deviancy involving the seeking of sexual gratification by peeping or observing others. Also called scoptophilia.

Wernicke's syndrome: A condition associated with alcoholism and characterized by brain stem deterioration, memory loss, confabulation, confusion, and sometimes coma. Believed to be caused by vitamin deficiency and is especially common in alcoholics suffering from nutritional deficiency.

References

Aichorn, A. *Wayward youth*. New York: Viking, 1935.

Alksne, H. et al., *A follow-up study of treated adolescent narcotic users*. New York: Columbia Univ. Sch. Public Health & Adm. Med., 1959.

Amark, C. A study in alcoholism. Clinical, socio-psychiatric and genetic investigations. *Acta psychiat. neurol. scand.,* Suppl. 70, 1951.

Ausubel, D. Causes and types of narcotic addiction: a psychosocial view. *Psychiat. Quart.,* 1961, **35**, 523.

Bacon, S. Alcoholism: nature of the problem; and alcoholism: its extent, therapy and prevention. *Federal Probat.,* 1947, **2**, 1.

Bales, R. The "fixation factor" in alcohol addiction: an hypothesis derived from a comparative study of Irish and Jewish social norms. Unpub. Ph.D. dissert., Harvard University, 1944.

Bandura, A. & Walters, R. *Adolescent aggression*. New York: Ronald Press, 1959.

Barnett, M. Alcoholism in the Cantonese of New York City: An anthropological study. In O. Diethelm (Ed.) *Etiology of chronic alcoholism*. Springfield, Ill.: Thomas, 1955.

Bender, L. Drug addiction in adolescence. *Compr. Psychiat.,* 1963, 4, 181.

Blacker, K., Jones, R., Stone, G., & Pfefferbaum, D. Chronic users of LSD: the "acid-heads." *Amer. J. Psychiat.,* 1968, **125**, 97.

Blakemore, C. et al. Application of faradic aversion conditioning in a case of transvestism. *Behav. Res. Ther.,* 1963, 1, 29.

Blum, R. & Blum, E. *Alcoholism, modern psychological approaches to treatment*. S. F., Calif.: Jossey-Bass, 1967.

Blume, S. & Sheppard, C. The changing effects of drinking on the changing personalities of alcoholics. *Quart. J. Stud. Alcoh.,* 1967, **28**, 436.

Buhler, C. & Lefever, D. A Rorschach study on the psychological characteristics of alcoholics. *Quart. J. Stud. Alcoh.,* 1947, **8**, 197.

Burchard, J. Systematic socialization: a programmed environment for the habilitation of antisocial retardates. *Psychol. Record,* 1967, **17**, 461.

Cisin, I. and Cahalan, D. American drinking practices. Social Research Project, George Washington University. Presented at a symposium on "The Drug Takers" at U.C.L.A. June 12, 1966.

Clark, W. Operational definitions of drinking problems and associated prevalence rates. Berkeley Drinking Practices Study, 1966 (unpublished).

Cohen, M., Marinello, M., & Back, N. Chromosome damage in human leukocytes induced by lysergic acid diethylamide. *Science,* 1967, **155**, 1417.

Cohen, S., Ditman, K., & Mooney, H. Effect of Trifluoperazine on some symptoms common among skid row alcoholics. In *Trifluoperazine: clinical and pharmacological aspects*. Philadelphia: Lea & Febiger, 1954.

Conger, J. The effects of alcohol on conflict behavior in the albino rat. *Quart. J. Stud. Alcoh.*, 1951, **12**, 1.

Coopersmith, S. Adaptive reactions of alcoholics and non-alcoholics. *Quart. J. Stud. Alcoh.*, 1964, **25**, 262.

De Quincey, T. *The confessions of an English opium-eater*. London: Macmillan, 1924.

Ditman, K. Evaluation of drugs in the treatment of alcoholics. *Quart. J. Stud. Alcoh.*, 1961, Suppl. No. 1, 107.

Ditman, K. Review and evaluation of current drug therapies in alcoholism. *Intern. J. Psychiat.*, 1967, **3**, 248.

Ditman, K. Do we have a specific treatment for alcoholism? *Inter. J. Psychiat.*, 1968, **5**, 48.

Ditman, K., Hayman, M., & Whittlesey, J. Nature of claims following LSD. *J. nerv. ment. Dis.*, 1962, **134**, 346.

Dole, V. & Nyswander, M. Rehabilitation of heroin addicts after blockage with methadone. *N.Y. J. Med.*, 1966, **66**, 2011.

Duvall, H., Locke, B., & Brill, L. Follow-up study of narcotic drug addicts five years after hospitalization. *Publ. Hlth. Rep.*, 1963, **78**, 185.

Easton, K. Clinical studies on the pathogenesis and personality structure of male narcotic addicts. *J. Hillside Hosp.*, 1965, **14**, 36.

Edwards, G., Hawker, A., & Williamson, V. London's skid row. *Lancet*, 1966, **1**, 249.

Ehrlich, S. & Keogh, R. The psychopath in a mental institution. *Arch. neur. Psychiat.*, 1956, **76**, 286.

Ellermann, M. Social and clinical features of chronic alcoholism. *J. nerv. ment. Dis.*, 1948, **107**, 556.

Evarts, E. Brain effects of LSD in animals. In L. Cholden (Ed.), *Lysergic acid diethylamide and mescaline in experimental psychiatry*. New York: Grune & Stratton, 1956.

Fenichel, O. *The psychoanalytic theory of neurosis*. New York: Norton, 1945.

Fleming, R. & Tillotson, K. Further studies on the personality and sociologic factors in the prognosis and treatment of chronic alcoholism. *New Eng. J. Med.* 1939, **221**, 741.

Fox, R. The alcoholic spouse. In V. Einstein (Ed.) *Neurotic interaction in marriage*. New York: Basic Books, 1956.

Fox, R. Treatment of alcoholism. In H. Himwich (Ed.) *Alcoholism: basic aspects and treatment*. Washington, D.C.: Amer. Assoc. Advanc. Science, 1957.

Freedman, A., Sager, C., Rabiner, E., & Brotsman, R. Response of adult heroin addicts to a total therapeutic program. *Amer. J. Orthopsychiat.*, 1963, **33**, 890.

Freud, S. *Drei Abhandlungen zur Sexualtheorie*. Ges. Werke. London: Imago, 1942. First published in 1905.

Freud, S. *Der Witz und seine Bedeutung zum Unbewussten*. Ges. Werke. London: Imago, 1940. First published in 1905.

Gerard, D. & Kornetsky, C. Adolescent opiate addiction: a study of control and addict subjects. *Psychiat. Quart.*, 1955, **29**, 457.

Glover, E. On the etiology of drug addiction. *Inter. J. Psycho-Anal.*, 1932, **13**, 298.

Glueck, S. & Glueck, E. *Unravelling juvenile delinquency*. Harvard: Commonwealth Fund, 1950.

Gottlieb, J., Ashby, M., & Knott, J. Studies in primary behavior disorder and psychopathic personality; inheritance of electrocortical activity. *Amer. J. Psychiat.*, 1947, **103**, 823.

Greer, S. Study of parental loss in neurotics and sociopaths. *Arch. gen. Psychiat.*, 1964, **11**, 177.

Haertzen, C., Hill, H., & Belleville, R. Development of the Addiction Research Center Inventory (ARCI): Selection of items that are sensitive to the effects of various drugs. *Psychopharmacologia*, 1963, **4**, 155.

Haines, W. & McLaughlin, J. Narcotic addicts in Chicago. *Amer. J. Psychiat.*, 1952, **108**, 755.

Hare, R. Psychopathy and choice of immediate versus delayed punishment. *J. abnorm. Psychol.*, 1966, **71**, 25.

Hill, D. & Watterson, D. Electroencephalographic studies of psychopathic personalities. *J. neurol. Psychiat.*, 1942, **5**, 47.

Hirsh, R. Group therapy with parents of adolescent drug addicts. *Psychiat. Quart.*, 1961, **35**, 702.

Irwin, S. & Egozcue, J. Chromosomal abnormalities in leukocytes from LSD-25 users. *Science,* 1967, **157**, 313.

Jellinek, E. Phases in the drinking history of alcoholics. *Quart. J. Stud. Alcoh.*, 1946, **7**, 1.

Jellinek, E. *The disease concept of alcoholism.* New Haven: Hill House Press, 1960.

Jones, M. et al. *The therapeutic community: a new treatment method in psychiatry.* New York: Basic Books, 1953.

Jones, M. Review of studies in the field of alcohol using psychometric methods. Article prepared for the Encyclopedia of Alcohol Problems. Stanford: Institute for the Study of Human Problems, 1962.

Jones, M. Drinking patterns in the context of the life history: A developmental study. Monograph prepared for the Cooperative Commission on the Study of Alcoholism. Stanford: Institute for the Study of Human Problems, 1965.

Kant, F. *The treatment of the alcoholic.* Springfield, Ill.: Thomas, 1954.

Keller, M. & Efron, V. The prevalence of alcoholism. *Quart. J. Stud. Alcoh.*, 1955, **16**, 619.

Keller, M. Definition of alcoholism. *Quart. J. Stud. Alcoh.*, 1960, **21**, 125.

Kinsey, A., Pomeroy, W., Martin, C., & Gebhard, P. *Sexual behavior in the human female.* Philadelphia: W. B. Saunders, 1953.

Knight, R. The psychodynamics of chronic alcoholism. *J. ner. ment. Dis.*, 1937, **86**, 538.

Knott, J. & Gottlieb, J. The electroencephalogram in psychopathic personality. *Psychosom. Med.* 1943, **5**, 139.

Knupfer, G., Fink, R., Clark, W., & Goffman, A. *California drinking practices study.* Report # 6. Factors related to the amount of drinking in an urban community. State of Calif. Dept. of Public Health, Berkeley, 1963.

Kolb, L. *Noyes' modern clinical psychiatry.* (7th ed.), Phildelphia: Saunders, 1968.

Korman, M. & Stubblefield, R. Definition of alcoholism. *J. Amer. Med. Assoc.*, 1961, **178**, 1184.

Laskowitz, D. & Einstein, S. Personality characteristics of adolescent addicts: manifest rigidity. *Corr. psychiat. & J. soc. Ther.*, 1963, **138**, 215.

Lazarus, A. Towards the understanding and effective treatment of alcoholism. *So. Afr. medical Journal,* 1965, **39**, 736.

Lemere, F. What happens to alcoholics. *Amer. J. Psychiat.*, 1953, **109**, 649.

Lemere, F. The nature and significance of brain damage from alcoholism. *Amer. J. Psychiat.*, 1956, **113**, 361.

Lewis, J. & Osberg, J. Treatment of narcotic addict: II. Observations on institutional treatment of character disorder. *Amer. J. Orthopsychiat.*, 1958, **28**, 730.

Lin, T. A study of the incidence of mental disorder in Chinese and other cultures. *Psychiat.* 1953, **16**, 313.

Lindner, R. *Rebel without a cause.* New York: Grune, 1944.

Lykken, D. A study of anxiety in the sociopathic personality. *J. abnorm. soc. Psychol.,* 1957, **55**, 6.

McClearn, G. & Rodgers, D. Genetic factors in alcohol preference of laboratory mice. *J. comp. physiol. Psychol.,* 1961, **54**, 116.

McCord, W. & McCord, J. A longtitudinal study of the personality of alcoholics. In D. Pittman & C. Snyder (Eds.), *Society, culture and drinking patterns.* New York: Wiley, 1962.

McGlothlin, W. & West, L. The marihuana problem: an overview. *Amer. J. Psychiat.,* 1968, **125**, 126.

MacKay, J. Problem drinking among juvenile delinquents. *N.Y. Bull. Alcoholism,* 1963, **12**, 29.

Mardones, J. Metabolic and nutritional patterns in alcoholism. *Ann. N.Y. Acad. Sci.,* 1954, **57**, 788.

Mardones, R. On the relationship between deficiency of B vitamins and alcohol intake in rats. *Quart. J. Stud. Alcoh.,* 1951, **12**, 563.

Mardones, R., Segovia, M., & Hederra, D. Heredity of experimental alcohol preference in rats. *Quart. J. Stud. Alcoh.,* 1953, **14**, 1.

Mason, P. The mother of the addict. *Psychiat. Quart. Suppl.,* 1958, **32**, 189.

Masserman, J. & Yum, K. An analysis of the influence of alcohol on experimental neuroses in cats. *Psychosom. Med.,* 1946, **8**, 36.

Maurer, D. & Vogel, V. *Narcotics and narcotic addiction.* Springfield, Ill.: Thomas, 1962.

Menninger, K. *Man against himself.* New York: Harcourt, 1938.

Moore, R. & Buchanan, T. State hospitals and alcoholism. A nation-wide survey of treatment techniques and results. *Quart. J. Stud. Alcoh.,* 1966, **27**, 459.

Murray, J. Drug addiction. *J. gen. Psychol.,* 1967, **77**, 41.

Neligan, A. The opium question, with special reference to Persia. London, 1927. Quoted in C. Terry & M. Pellens, *The opium problem.* Camden, N.Y.: The Haddon Craftsmen, 1928.

Nyswander, M. *The drug addict as a patient.* New York: Grune & Stratton, 1956.

O'Donnell, J. A follow-up of narcotic addicts: mortality, relapse and abstinence. *Amer. J. Orthopsychiat,* 1964, **34**, 948.

O'Neal, P. et al., Parental deviance and the genesis of sociopathic personality. *Amer. J. Psychiat.,* 1962, **118**, 1114.

O'Reilly, P. Lysergic acid and the alcoholic. *Dis. nerv. Syst.,* 1962, **23**, 331.

O'Reilly, P. & Funk, A. LSD in chronic alcoholism. *Canad. psychiat. assoc. J.,* 1964, **9**, 258.

Osmond, H. Review of the clinical effects of psychotomimetic agents. *Ann. N.Y. Acad. Sci.,* 1957, **66**, 418.

Palmer, D. Factors in suicide attempts. *J. nerv. ment. Dis.,* 1941, **93**, 421.

Pescor, M. A statistical analysis of the clinical records of hospitalized drug addicts. Suppl. No. 143 to the Public Health Reports. Washington, D.C.: U.S. Government Printing Office, 1943.

Plaut, T. *A report to the nation by the cooperative commission on the study of alcoholism.* New York: Oxford, 1967.

Rasor, R. Narcotic addicts: personality characteristics and hospital treatment. In P. Hoch & J. Zubin (Eds.), *Psychopathology of communication.* New York: Grune & Stratton, 1958.

Redl, F. & Wineman, D. *Controls from within: techniques for the treatment of the aggressive child.* Glencoe, Ill.: Free Press, 1954.

Redl, F. & Wineman, D. *The aggressive child.* Glencoe, Ill.: The Free Press, 1957.

Roch, M. Der Alcoholismus in der inneren Medizin. *Die Alkoholfrage in der Schweiz.* 1940, 1, 293.

Roche Laboratories. *Aspects of alcoholism.* Vol. 1. Philadelphia: Lippincott, 1963.

Roche Laboratories. *Aspects of alcoholism.* Vol. 2. Philadelphia: Lippincott, 1966.

Rodgers, D. & McClearn, G. Alcohol preferences of mice. In E. Bliss (Ed.), *Roots of behavior.* New York: Harper, 1962.

Sachs, H. Zur Genese der Perversionen. *Int. Z. Psychoanal.,* 1923, 9, 172.

Sadoun, R. & Lolli, G. Choice of alcoholic beverage among 120 alcoholics in France. *Quart. J. Stud. Alcoh.,* 1962, 23, 449.

Sarett, M., Cheek, F., & Osmond, H. Reports of wives of alcoholics of effects of LSD-25 treatment of their husbands. *Arch. gen. Psychiat.,* 1966, 14, 171.

Scher, J. Patterns and profiles of addiction and drug abuse. *Arch. gen. Psychiat.,* 1966, 15, 539.

Schlesinger, K. Genetic and biochemical correlates of alcohol preference in mice. *Amer. J. Psychiat.,* 1966, 122, 767.

Schultes, R. The aboriginal uses of Lophophoria Williamsii. *Cactus and Succulant J.* 1940, 12, 177.

Schwade, E. & Geiger, S. Abnormal electroencephalographic findings in severe behavior disorders. *Dis. Nerv. Syst.,* 1956, 17, 307.

Schwitzgebel, R. *Street-corner research: an experimental approach to the juvenile delinquent.* Cambridge, Mass.: Harvard University Press, 1964.

Schwitzgebel, R. Short-term operant conditioning of adolescent offenders on socially relevant variables. *J. abnorm. Psychol.,* 1967, 72, 134.

Sherman, L. Retention in psychopathic, neurotic, and normal subjects. *J. Pers.,* 1957, 25, 721.

Smart, R. & Storm, T. The efficacy of LSD in the treatment of alcoholism. *Quart. J. Stud. Alcoh.,* 1964, 25, 333.

Smart, R., Storm, T., Baker, E., & Solursh, L. A controlled study of lysergide in the treatment of alcoholism. *Quart. J. Stud. Alcoh.,* 1966, 27, 469.

Smith, C. A new adjunct to the treatment of alcoholism: the hallucinogenic drugs. *Quart. J. Stud. Alcoh.,* 1958, 19, 406.

Snyder, C. *Alcohol and the Jews.* Glencoe, Ill.: Free Press, 1958.

Stoll, W. Lysergsäure-diäthylamid, ein Phantastikum aus der Mutter-korngruppe. *Schweiz. Arch. neurol. Psychiat.,* 1947, 60, 1.

Tahka, V. *The alcoholic personality.* Helsinki, Finland: Finnish Foundation for Alcohol Studies, 1966.

Ullman, A. The first drinking experience of addictive and of normal drinkers. *Quart. J. Stud. Alcoh.,* 1953, 14, 181.

Ungerleider, J., Fisher, D., Goldsmith, S., Fuller, M., & Forgy, E. A statistical survey of adverse reactions to LSD in Los Angeles County. *Amer. J. Psychiat.,* 1968, 125, 108.

United Nations Economic and Social Council, Commission on Narcotic Drugs. *Summary of annual reports of governments relating to opium and other narcotic drugs, 1963.* France: United Nations publication, 1965.

Vaillant, G. A 12-year follow-up of New York narcotic addicts. *Arch. gen. Psychiat.,* 1966, 15, 539. (a)

Vaillant, G. Twelve-year follow-up of New York narcotic addicts. Some characteristics and determinants of abstinence. *Amer. J. Psychiat.,* 1966, 123, 573. (b)

Vogel, V., Isbell, H., & Chapman, K. Present status of narcotic addiction. *J.A.M.A.,* 1948, 138, 1019.

Witkin, H., Karp, S., & Goodenough, D. Dependence in alcoholics. *Quart. J. Stud. Alcoh.,* 1959, 20, 493.

World Health Organization. *Report of expert committee on mental health, subcommittee on alcholism.* World Health Organization Technical Report Series No. 48, 1952.

World Health Organization. *Expert committee on drugs liable to produce addiction. Second Report.* World Health Organization Technical Report Series No. 21. Geneva: Switzerland, World Health Organization, 1950.

Yablonsky, L. *The tunnel back: Synanon.* New York: Macmillan, 1965.

Zwerling, I. Psychiatric findings in an interdisciplinary study of forty-six alcoholic patients. *Quart. J. Stud. Alcoh.,* 1959, 20, 543.

12 *The Organic Disorders*

The organic disorders include a number of mental dysfunctions in which a biochemical or structural change in the brain is a known factor. Such malfunctioning or damage produces symptoms that can include any or all of the following:

1. Impairment of memory
2. Impairment of emotions
3. Impairment of intellect
4. Impairment of judgment
5. Impairment of orientation for time, place or person

In some of the organic disorders, the effects are reversible, for example, the toxic states, while in others, the damage is complete and irreversible, for example, in injuries to the brain. In recognition of this, the organic brain disorders are classified as *acute* or *chronic*. The *acute brain syndromes* or disorders are those that are temporary and reversible; the *chronic brain syndromes* are those that are permanent and irreversible. Listed among the acute brain syndromes are those disorders associated with acute alcohol intoxication, some head injuries such as mild concussion, drug or poison intoxication; among the chronic brain syndromes are those disorders associated with chronic alcoholic intoxication, central nervous system syphilis, severe lead or carbon monoxide poisoning, degeneration of the brain from senility, congenital cranial abnormalities, and deterioration of the brain from tumors. The symptoms are *primarily* but not *solely* attributable to the organic condition (Bowman and Blau, 1943; Ruesch, Harris and Bowman, 1945). The human being is a complex organism that functions, acts, and reacts as a total integrated mechanism. It is true that when the injury is focalized in one specific part of the brain, the symptoms will differ from those resulting from damage to a separate section (see Table 12-1). Convulsive motor movements suggest nondestructive lesions of the motor area of the cortex, disturbance of language or speech may be due to damage to the left cerebral hemisphere in right-handed persons (their dominant hemisphere), and the appearance of visual difficulties could be traceable to the occipital lobe. However, the symptomatology expressed by the patient will also be affected by the premorbid (preillness or preaccident) personality of the patient, the frustrations and stresses and conflicts he must cope with, his self-concept and motivational structure, all interacting with the organic state itself.

Correct diagnosis of an organic factor

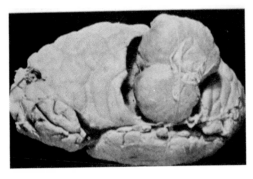

Intellectual or personality alterations can occur as a result of growths in the brain. Pictured is a tumor, called a *meningioma*, of great size taken from a human brain. (From *Boyd's Pathology for the Surgeon*, 8th Edition, by William Anderson © 1967, W. B. Saunders Company)

in the illness is a significant step in the understanding and treatment of the patient. Unexpected personality changes become more intelligible in cases of the

organic disorders. In addition, knowledge of the nature of the organic disease is an aid in planning inasmuch as the therapist can prepare for certain anticipated symptomatic changes. The nature of the treatment program is, of course, influenced by the diagnosis. Thus, the treatment goals are those appropriate for the particular individual with the particular organic deficit or damage or dysfunction. Similarly, the type of drug, surgical, or psychotherapeutic therapy to be prescribed is dependent upon the diagnosis.

In diagnosis, a number of different factors can interfere with brain functioning and lead to symptom development. *Trauma*, or a direct physical injury to brain tissue, is one such factor; traumas may occur from automobile accidents, bullet or shrapnel wounds, falling objects,

TABLE 12-1. *Symptoms Associated with Tumors in Various Parts of the Brain*

FRONTAL LOBE	PARIETAL LOBE	TEMPORAL LOBE	OCCIPITAL LOBE
Aphasia	Aphasia	Aphasia	Homonymous hemianopia
Ataxia	Apraxia	Homonymous hemianopia	Aphasia
Convulsions	Alexia	Hallucinations	Alexia
Loss of memory	Convulsions	Micropsia	Visual hallucination
Incontinence	Astereognosis	Macropsia	
Yawning		Convulsions	

CEREBELLUM	MIDBRAIN	MEDULLA	MOTOR AREA
Ataxia	External strabismus	Dysarthria	Convulsions
Dizziness	Ataxia	Nystagmus	Speech defects
Adiadokokinesia	Ptosis	Ataxia	Loss of fine movement
Nystagmus		Vertigo	

THALAMUS	PONS	BASAL GANGLIA	PITUITARY GLAND
Hallucinations (olfactory, visual, gustatory)	Nystagmus	Astereognosis	Hemianopia
Jocularity	Paralyses (facial, extremities)	Hemiplegia	Headache
		Hemianopia	Acromegaly
			Polyuria
			Polydipsia

SOURCE: Louis P. Thorpe, Barney Katz, & Robert T. Lewis. *Psychology of abnormal behavior* (2nd ed.). Copyright © 1961 The Ronald Press Company, New York.

or even excessive pressure at childbirth. *Infections* from diseases such as syphilis, meningitis, or encephalitis can result in brain damage. *Metabolic aberrations* can impair the normal internal functioning of the body and lead to changes ultimately affecting the brain. *Toxic* factors, or poisons, such as from the intake of carbon monoxide or the sniffing of glue or exposure to lead, may result in neuropathology. The gradual deterioration associated with *aging* involves degenerative changes not only in the bodily vascular and endocrine systems but also in the central nervous system. The growth of *tumors* in the brain can lead to atrophy, scarring, and damage to the brain tissue, or blockage of passageways for the normal flow of cerebrospinal fluid.

The organic disorders may be classified as follows:

1. Those due to *infections*—for example, from meningitis, encephalitis, syphilis.

2. Those due to *nutritional* or *metabolic dysfunction*—for example, from anoxia, vitamin deficiency, thyroid conditions, adrenal conditions.

3. Those due to *toxic effects*—for example, from bromides, alcohol, amphetamines, lead.

4. Those due to *trauma (head injury)*—for example, from concussions, bullet wounds.

5. Those due to *aging*—for example, senile psychosis, Alzheimer's disease, Pick's disease, arteriosclerosis.

6. Those due to *tumors*—for example, from metastatic tumors, congenital tumors.

7. Those involving *convulsive reactions*—for example, Jacksonian epilepsy, psychomotor epilepsy.

Some of the more prominent types of organic disorders will be presented in the sections to follow. Unlike the previous chapters, the psychodynamics of the disorders will not be discussed since the main symptoms of the organic conditions are primarily related to somatic factors. The reader should also refer to chapters 6, 11, and 16 for descriptions of organic states such as the metabolic and endocrine disorders, and for additional information on the toxic ailments such as alcoholism intoxication.

BRAIN INFECTION DISORDERS: GENERAL PARESIS

Syphilis, an infectious venereal disease, is believed to have been first introduced to Europe by Christopher Columbus and his crew (Zilboorg and Henry, 1941). In 1493 with his return, and again in 1496, a disease called the "Great Pox" descended on the Old World. From this period onward, syphilis spread to become a major disease. A result of syphilis is *general paresis,* first known as a "general paralysis of the insane," and initially described by Haslam (1798), a pharmacist, in 1798. Haslam was involved in the autopsy of a 42-year-old man who believed himself to be the king of Denmark, the king of France, the master of all dead and living languages, and the peer of William the Conqueror.

Syphilis is diagnosed by the Wassermann blood test which detects the presence of a spirochete microorganism, known as *Treponema pallidum,* the cause of the disease. It may be congenitally transmitted from the mother to the fetus, or acquired through sexual intercourse. The disease progresses through four definable stages:

1. Within four weeks of entry, the spirochetes have multiplied and spread throughout the body. A sore, called a chancre, appears at the point of infection; it looks like a small pimple or open sore. The chancre gives little discomfort and disappears by itself.

2. A dark skin rash covers the body

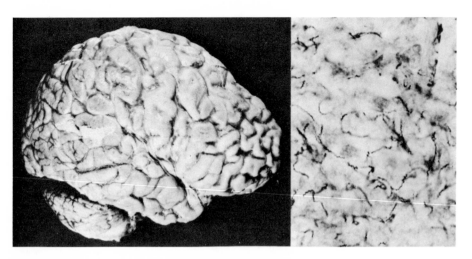

General paresis: On the left is the atrophied brain of a paretic patient, on the right are the spirochete microorganisms (Treponema pallidum) causing the disease. (W. Blackwood from *Greenfield's Neuropathology* by W. Blackwood, W. McMenemy, A. Meyer, R. Norman, and Dorothy Russell, Edward Arnold Publishers, Ltd., London, 1963. Used with the permission of the publisher)

within three to six weeks following the appearance of the chancre. The copper-toned rash may be very mild or more severe and like smallpox. Small warts often appears on the genitals.

3. A latency period soon takes over during which no overt signs are present. However, the spirochetes are infesting various organs and causing irreparable damage. The individual may experience no discomfort or pain.

4. After a delay of as much as three decades, the spirochetes may increase their activity and again attack the heart, or the spinal cord, or the brain. General paresis is the result of brain infection by the spirochetes.

General paresis appears five times more frequently in men than in women, in comparison to syphilis which is twice as common in men than women. Not all syphilitic patients develop paresis. It typically appears between the ages of 35 and 50, and may incubate for anywhere from 5 to 30 years. Paresis is detectable through blood and spinal fluid analysis. In addition, certain neurological signs ap-

pears such as different sized pupils, or the Argyll-Robertson pupil—a slowness in the pupillary reflex to light. The most important motor disturbance is convulsions. In addition, tremors of the extended fingers, tongue, or lips may appear. Handwriting disturbances are shown in very slow, irregular, and scratchy writing. Speech disorder is a characteristic diagnostic sign. The patient hesitates or slurs such that he says, "Meh-adis Pis'pal" instead of "Methodist Episcopal." Disturbance of the spinal cord is exhibited in locomotor ataxis, a shuffling gait.

The psychological picture of general paresis is appalling. Progressive deterioration occurs as the spirochetes do their damage. Memory for recent events, such as the meal just eaten, is affected although the individual may recall remote events. Irritability, slovenliness, loss of judgment, and diminishing ethical and moral values appear. As the illness progresses, either of three courses may develop: deterioration without delusions, deterioration with delusions of grandeur, deterioration with depression. The most common is the slowly advancing deterioration. Next is

*Cetated satat Naspiado
Insddanpoil Indana
Que 28 1422*

General paresis is detectable in motor disturb-ances, such as in *handwriting difficulties*. The above is a writing sample from a paretic patient who was asked to write "Central State Hospital, Indianapolis, Indiana, June 28, 1952". (From Wal-ter L. Breutsch "Neurosyphylitic Conditions," in S. Arieti, *American Handbook of Psychiatry*, Vol. II, © 1959, Basic Books)

the grandiose delusional state in which the patient claims to be the Grand Duke, Jesus Christ, the founder of the world, or a millionaire, a philanthropist, a surveyor of gold. The patient's mood is expansive and he feels that all is well with the world and himself. In the depressed condition, the individual is fraught with guilt and suicidal notions. He is certain that he must do penance, or he is convinced that his brain is rotting inside his skull. Assaul-tive behavior is a frequent concomitant of the delusional states. In the final stages of the illness, the delusional symptoms dimin-ish and the intellectual deterioration be-comes the foremost feature. Sudden out-bursts of destructiveness may appear, but soon the patient is bedridden and reduced to a vegetative mass without awareness, incentive, recognition, thought, or volun-tary movement.

Treatment

Fortunately, syphilis is curable if treated early and the symptoms of paresis can be arrested even if treatment has been de-layed. Of course, any structural damage caused by the spirochetes are irreversible once they have occurred. On the other hand, other symptoms resulting from in-flammation of the brain may be com-pletely eliminated.

Initially, the induction of a fever was the favored means for destroying the spiro-chete. For this purpose, physicians relied upon the use of malarial therapy (Wagner-Jauregg, and Bruetsch, 1946), machines for artificially inducing a temperature, and even typhoid vaccines. Dr. Wagner-Jauregg, the innovator of malaria therapy, received the Nobel prize for this contri-bution to psychiatry. By this method, a paretic patient is given 1 to 3 cc. of blood from a malaria sufferer, carefully super-vised through about a dozen malarial attacks, then treated with quinine to re-move the malarial infection.

Modern therapy relies upon heavy doses of penicillin to which Treponema palli-dum has proven highly sensitive (Bruetsch, 1949). Whereas malarial therapy led to about 35 percent recovery, penicillin has claimed about 83 percent recovery. The symptoms may disappear during therapy or not vanish until months later. Labora-tory tests of spinal fluid (e.g., cell count) are relied upon for diagnosis of progress since the Wassermann tests many remain unchanged for years even after successful treatment (Thomas, 1956).

DISORDERS OF NUTRITIONAL OR METABOLIC FUNCTION: PSYCHOSIS ASSOCIATED WITH PERNICIOUS ANEMIA

Pernicious anemia is associated with a deficiency of vitamin B12. Among the most prominent results of this disease is the degeneration of the spinal cord. Men-tal symptoms can also occur, but very little attention has been given to these psycho-logical changes despite the fact that Addi-son in 1849 mention the occasional "wandering of the mind" in his original diagnostic description. The mental symp-toms tend to be grouped in one of three types: acute deliriod state, paranoid state,

Case History 12-1

GENERAL PARESIS

Mr. Leonard K., age 55, was referred to the hospital by his family after an episode of reckless promises, extravagant claims, and grandiose commitments. He had usually been a calm and reserved person, but gradually began to show a change in personality. Once a fastidious dresser, he had suddenly surprised his wife by neglecting to shave, wearing suits that had been wrinkled because he slept in them, and refusing to wash. He became more and more expansive, talkative, and occasionally violent. By the time he was committed for treatment he believed himself to be a state senator, and spoke of his planned travels to Washington. He intended to have a new bill passed proclaiming himself "executive emperor" (words he had difficulty in communicating). He was known to stand wherever a crowd was willing to listen and loudly pronounce his views on war, religion, birth control, and nearly any topic that was suggested. His views were more on the order of "solutions" to world problems than opinions. His wife described him as having been an almost too mild person prior to the recent outbursts. His gradual loss of memory led him to confabulation (filling in memory gaps by creating events to relate). His shift to grandiosity was believed to be an attempt to compensate for his lowered self-confidence and esteem. He was diagnosed as suffering from paresis and placed on a treatment program consisting of 20 million units of penicillin.

---

or affective reactions. In the *acute deliriod state,* the patient shows confusion, inability to attend or concentrate, impairment of consciousness, and transient hallucinations. He fluctuates from an incomplete awakening to a dream-filled sleep. The hallucinations or visual illusions may be threatening and terrifying, causing restless movements and crying out for help. The *paranoid state* involves delusions of persecution, suspiciousness, distrust, and fear. The patient is certain that a plot is underway to keep him imprisoned in the hospital, to poison him in order to gain his estate, or to infect him with a deadly germ. In a milder form, the paranoid state might be expressed in a wariness and general discontent, or a highly critical and complaining attitude. The *affective reactions* involve the onset of severe emotional reactions; depression involving psycho-motor retardation, agitated and restless depression, or anxiety and apprehension may appear.

As with most of the organic disorders, the mental condition associated with pernicious anemia will also include intellectual deterioration, disturbance of memory, impairment of judgment, and confusion. The degeneration of the spinal cord may add physical symptoms such as disturbance of touch sensations, weakness in the muscles, loss of reflexes, and impairment of position and vibration senses.

Treatment

Early treatment can prevent the illness from progressing and leading to chronic brain damage or spinal cord deterioration. Calves' liver has been given to remove the anemia; however, vitamin B12 injected in large doses is the preferred mode of treat-

Case History 12-2

PSYCHOSIS WITH PERNICIOUS ANEMIA

The patient was a 38-year-old laborer who had been unemployed for seven months. As a bachelor with no family contacts, he drifted from region to region eking out a marginal existence. The first evidence of any pathology was the appearance of uncomfortable, needlelike sensation in his feet that would not go away. His memory became more and more faulty, making it even more difficult for him to obtain or maintain any employment. Soon after, he entered into a state of delirium and was found by the manager of the hotel in which he was staying. The manager initially considered the patient to be another drunk having the d.t.'s, but decided to have a physician stop in anyway. The patient was transferred to a county hospital where further examination showed signs of pernicious anemia with spinal cord damage. The delirium continued for a week before clearing under treatment. The patient remains unemployed and has never recovered from the neurological damage.

---

ment. Vitamin treatment is conducted once a day for the first week of treatment, then twice weekly, and every other week after two months. In emergencies, transfusions are used.

TOXIC DISORDERS: BROMIDE PSYCHOSES

Bromides are found in compounds often used in the past for sedation. They can be identified in many "sleeping pills" currently sold in drugstores. The bromides are relatively poor in producing sleep, hence the insomniac is likely to resort to toxic doses in an effort to sleep. With such doses, he is exposed to the risk of a toxic psychosis. The bromide intoxication may assume any of four forms; hence, there are four types of bromide psychoses: simple intoxication, delirium, hallucinosis, and transitory schizophrenia (Levin, 1948). In *simple intoxication,* some symptoms are quite similar to paresis—tremors and impaired coordination, slowed pupillary reflexes, irritability, and forgetfulness. The patient feels sluggish and sleepy and may confabulate. If the toxic condition becomes more severe, other forms of bromide psychoses take over. *Delirium* involves complete disorientation for time and place and a marked dreamlike disturbance of consciousness. In the bromide psychosis with delirium, the patient becomes anxious, restless, perplexed, and incoherent. Fears may surge into prominence and the patient may believe himself to be embroiled in a serious catastrophe. He may erroneously identify his surroundings as his own bedroom instead of recognizing the hospital room. Isolated delusions or visual hallucinations may appear. In the *hallucinosis* state the patient may hallucinate voices but remains oriented and thus able to identify himself, his whereabouts, and the date. Hallucinosis of this type may also appear in other forms of organic illness, for example, it appears commonly in alcoholic intoxication, carbon monoxide poisoning, and paresis. In *bromide schizophrenia,* the patient exhibits all of the typical symptoms of schizophrenia making an accurate diagnosis difficult. Bromide-caused schizo-

Case History 12-3

BROMIDE PSYCHOSIS

Marlene T. was a high-strung, restless woman who suffered from insomnia. No matter how tired she was, she could not manage to completely relax and fall asleep but often found herself thinking over the day's events. Because she was too embarassed to see a physician, and covertly fearful that she would be referred to a psychotherapist, she took to using sleeping pills which could be bought without prescription. She followed the directions on the bottles but found that she still stayed awake. One weekend she decided to try to sleep through the day and night and hopefully catch up on her rest. She doubled the recommended dose but could not detect much effects within a half an hour and so ingested four more pills. Within minutes she became drowsy and drifted into a disturbed daze in which she was not completely asleep yet not completely awake. She groped for the bromides, poured out a handful, and swallowed them in a final effort. She was found by a girlfriend and taken quickly to the hospital. Marlene could not speak clearly, and appeared to be in a delirium. She tossed in the hospital bed, tore at the sheets and restraints, and began screaming. When her friend appeared, Marlene begged for help, then within minutes seemed to be unable to recognize her companion. Laboratory tests showed an extremely high bromide concentration in her blood, thus confirming the diagnosis of bromide psychosis. She was treated and released with the recommendation of seeking psychotherapeutic help for her tensions.

---

phrenia is suspected on the basis of information that the patient has been taking excessive amounts of bromides. In this form of bromide intoxication, the individual is withdrawn, aloof from people, bizarre in his delusions, may hallucinate, and becomes suspicious of others. Certain visual distortions may also appear in the bromide psychoses, for example, the sensation that objects in the visual field are farther away or smaller than they actually are (micropsia). If micropsia exists, visual hallucinations tend to incorporate the distortion, thus little men and women may be hallucinated (the Lilliputian hallucination).

Treatment

The most immediate treatment of course is the withdrawal of the drug to prevent further intake. Forced intake of fluids and other measures to facilitate excretion are used. Rest and control of anxious activity is helped by such drugs as paraldehyde or chloral hydrate. Most important, an increased diet of sodium chloride (NaCl), common table salt, helps to restore the normal salt balance—the presence of bromine leads to the transformation of NaCl into the toxic compound NaBr thus lowering the normal salt content. Once the bromide level has been lowered, the symptoms may still persist for several weeks. Recovery from the symptoms is dependent upon the extent of cerebral damage, but even the severe schizophrenic symptomatology may disappear if permanent brain damage was avoided.

ORGANIC DISORDER RESULTING FROM TRAUMA

The skull is generally capable of withstanding minor to moderate injuries with-

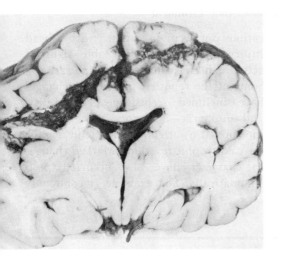

Organic disorders can occur from *trauma* to the brain. Pictured above is a damaged brain with the track of the bullet wound through the frontal lobes being clearly distinguishable. (Dorothy S. Russell, from *Greenfield's Neuropathology* by W. Blackwood, W. McMenemy, A. Meyer, R. Norman, and Dorothy Russell, Edward Arnold Publishers, Ltd. London, 1963. Used with permission of the publisher)

out any discernable effects other than lacerations of the skin. Indeed, this body encasement serves to protect the brain from damage. However, brain injury of a serious nature does occur if the blow is severe enough or if the injury is the result of a missile entering the head, such as was the case in the assassination of the late President Kennedy. There are several types of traumatic circumstances: concussions, contusions, and lacerations to the brain tissue. A *concussion* is an immediate, transitory loss of consciousness due to a head injury such as occurs in boxing or in football. The individual regains consciousness usually with amnesia for the events just prior to the injury. He may remain confused and disoriented for awhile, but these symptoms soon vanish. In some cases, the victim has been known to return to his previous activities while still partially disoriented, as in the case of professional football players who return to action or boxers who continue to fight. A *contusion* results from a blow so severe as to cause the brain to become bruised against the skull itself. The continuous blows to the head received by an unprotected boxer can result in contusions. In addition to the symptoms of concussion, contusions lead to severe headaches, dizziness, fatigability, apathy, irritability, and decreased tolerance to

light, noise, and alcohol. These symptoms ordinarily subside within six weeks. Cerebral *laceration* is a severe injury in which the brain tissue itself is ruptured or pierced by objects such as bullets, skull fragments, or shrapnel. The typical traumatic brain injury symptoms are exhibited —the loss of consciousness, disorientation, confusion, and recovery. In severe cases, the loss of consciousness ends in a coma and delirium. The specific locale of the laceration determines the appearance of other symptoms, for example, damage to the parietal-temporal lobe areas in the dominant hemisphere will result in aphasia (disturbance of language) (Penfield and Rasmussen, 1950).

Many patients with severe brain injury show aftereffects involving intellectual deficits or personality changes. The patient may show an impairment of intellect, an inability to deal with concepts, a deficit in the capacity to plan ahead or deal with abstract goals, a tendency to perseverate in ideas and solutions. In the face of failure on simple intellectual problems, the patient sometimes displays an extreme reaction characterized by agitation, anxiety, sullenness, resistance, and confusion. The disturbance is so extreme that the term *catastrophic reaction* has been applied (Goldstein and Scheerer,

1941). Personality changes have also been reported in some cases. In most, it is difficult to assess the relative roles which the organic damage and the premorbid personality factors contribute to such changes. It is more often noted that the marginally adjusted patients are much more subject to gross personality changes than the better adjusted. In fact, subjective complaints and personality modifi-cations can occur in patients with a head injury but without detectable signs of actual damage (contusions or lacerations). Some of the reported personality changes have included seclusiveness, volubility, and euphoria—behaviors that may be interpreted as attempts to defend against the catastrophic reactions. Marked changes in character have also occurred post-traumatically. For example, a commonly

Case History 12-4

ORGANIC DISORDER RESULTING FROM TRAUMA

A classic case of trauma involving cerebral laceration was reported in 1868. The victim, Phineas P. Gage, was the young foreman of a railroad excavation crew. His disposition was such that he enjoyed the respect and favor of his men. On the 13th of September, a premature explosion drove a tamping iron through his skull. The iron was a rod three foot, seven inches long, one and one-fourth inches in diameter, and weighed thirteen and one-fourth pounds.

The missile entered by its pointed end, the left side of the face, immediately anterior to the angle of the lower jaw, and passing obliquely upwards, and obliquely backwards, emerged in the median line, at the back part of the frontal bone, near the coronal suture.

Gage was thrown onto his back by the force of the blast and the entry of the rod, convulsed a bit, then regained his speech. He was placed in an ox cart in which he rode sitting upright for a full three-quarters of a mile to his hotel room. He got out of the cart by himself and was later able to walk up a flight of stairs. He remained conscious although blood poured profusely from his skull. Subsequently Gage, who must have been an extraordinarily strong man, re-covered physically from the ordeal. However, his personality changed such that his friends felt he was "no longer Gage." Harlow reports:

(He) has no pain in head, but says it has a queer feeling which he is not able to describe. Applied for his situation as foreman, but is undecided whether to work or travel. His contractors, who regarded him as the most efficient and capable foreman in their employ previous to his injury considered the change in mind so marked that they could not give him his place again. The equilibrium or balance, so to speak, between his intellectual faculties and animal propensities, seem to have been destroyed. He is fitful, irreverent, indulging at times in the grossest profanity (which was previously his custom), manifesting but little deference for his fellows, impatient of restraint or advice when it conflicts with his desires, at times pertinaciously obstinate, yet capricious and vacillating, devising many plans of future operations, which are no sooner arranged than they are abandoned in turn for others appearing more feasible. A child in his intellectual capacity and manifestations, he has the animal passions of a man (p. 339-340) (Harlow, 1868).

cheerful person may become impulsive, hostile, and emotionally unstable. Brain-injured children show a hyperactivity, distractibility, inability to accept social restrictions, and are often insistent and immature.

Treatment

In cases of severe brain injury leading to sensory, motor, or intellectual disabilities, the medical aspect of treatment is referred to as rehabilitation medicine. This branch of medicine aims at restoring the patient to the fullest physical, mental, social, vocational, and economic usefulness of which the patient is capable. In effect, this means enabling the patient to make maximum use of his now limited capabilities. If a motor disability has resulted, for example, paralysis, the individual is trained to achieve the highest level of self-care and ambulation that his disability permits. Vocational rehabilitation may involve retraining in vocational skills that match his interests and his physical abilities.

Psychiatric treatment is symptomatic treatment, directed toward alleviating any residual permanent symptoms. Drugs for controlling overexcitability and hyperactivity may involve use of tranquilizers. Supportive counseling provides reassurance and encouragement. For children who suffer from distractibility, the learning (educational) situation must be adapted so as to maximize the attention span and minimize interfering and competing cues.

DISORDERS OF AGING

To paraphrase a saying, "Nothing is as certain as taxes and aging"; and although there may be legal loopholds that permit escape from some taxation, there is no escaping from the ravages of time. We are born, mature, and invariably decline. The rate of decline may be more noticeable for some than others; the body may show the effects of degeneration before the mind; aging may even become an asset in some circumstances, for example, the political leaders of most nations are well into their second half-century of life. However, for most of us aging brings with it new stresses: the final admission that our intellect is not and will never again be as quick as it once was; the eventual giving up of a position of responsibility and the role of active contributor to society; the inability to feel truly a part of the interests and thinking of the current ruling generation, and perhaps even the loss of a personal sense of usefulness and competency. Some resent their new roles and interpret "retirement" to mean "jobless," "aging" to mean "senility," and "disability" to mean "invalidism." The cultural mores can but often do not provide for the psychological adjustment of the elderly. In primitive societies, the wise old man is seen as having acquired his wisdom through aging. Respect was given to old ones, and this in turn enabled the aged to retain their own self-respect. The older person had a responsibility and a contribution to make. In other primitive cultures, the elderly person had no contribution to make, expected to make none, and accepted his role as a burden on others. For him, being left behind to die was the natural outcome of his uselessness to the tribe. In modern civilization, we are still making the transition between these two alternatives—the aged is not assigned the rank of contributor of wisdom, nor is he permitted to be left to die as a useless person. Each must prepare himself to develop his own way of adjusting to aging.

The disorders of aging may be classified under two headings: the senile psychosis, and the psychosis with cerebral arteriosclerosis. *Senile psychosis* pertains to the mental disorders associated with deterioration as a result of age. At one time it was

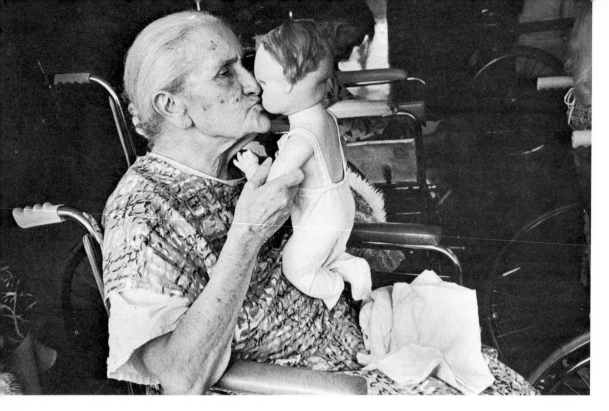

Regression can occur in senile psychosis. The elderly woman above is exhibiting the affection for her doll reminiscent of similar behaviors more appropriately displayed by young children. (B. D. Vidibor/Photo Researchers)

called senile dementia. This illness is a result of aging, brain pathology, and psychosocial stresses. Patients with senile psychosis exhibit a marked shrinkage of the brain due to atrophy and loss of lymphatic fluid (Critchley, 1938); but the severity of the symptoms is by no means routinely connected with the amount of the shrinkage. Senile plaques also appear —these are small areas of tissue degeneration generally round and of granular and filamentous structure (Simchowitz, 1910). Externally, the person shows graying, a thickening of the skin, tremors, feeble and shuffling gait, and an overall paucity of motion. Behaviorally, the patient becomes neglectful of his appearance, wearing clothes in disarray, dripping foodstuff on himself. Memory for recent events becomes lost and fragmented, and the patient dwells more and more on the past. He is soon unable to keep track of time and does not know his own age. His waking state may become more and more

interrupted by confused daydreams. He shows emotional lability, weeping readily or becoming highly irritable. He becomes opinionated and set in his way of doing things. Orientation becomes increasingly impaired and the patient may wander around the premises. He may begin to hide minor articles such as a paper clip or a pencil. Some patients become morally lax and are arrested for sexual indecency. In the *simple senile deterioration* type of senile psychosis, the patient exhibits the traits already mentioned without any marked emotional, delusional, or disoriented episodes. In the *delirious and confused* types, the patient shows incoherence, clouding of consciousness, restlessness, vague hallucinations. In the *depressed and agitated* types, the patient is extremely melancholic, agitated, and experiences delusions of self-destruction or somatic delusions. In the *paranoid* type, the patient shows delusions of persecution and accuses others of being against him. Many chil-

Senile psychosis involves atrophy and shrinkage of the brain (*below*), and the appearance of senile plaques, i.e., granular and filamentous shaped tissue (*right*). (Below: Dr. Corsellis from *Greenfield's Neuropathology* by W. Blackwood, W. McMenemy, A. Meyer, R. Norman, and Dorothy Russell, Edward Arnold Publishers, Ltd., London, 1963. Used with permission of the publisher).

(Right: From A. Ferraro, "Senile Psychoses," in S. Arieti, *American Handbook of Psychiatry*, Vol. II, © 1959, Basic Books. Used with permission of the publisher)

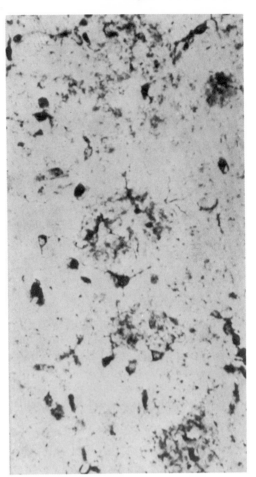

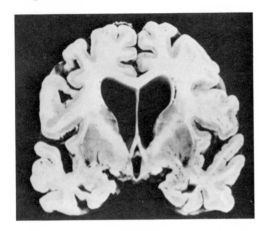

dren are disinherited during these periods.

Psychosis with *cerebral arteriosclerosis* pertains to the condition characterized by fatty deposits in the blood vessels of the brain. Cerebral arteriosclerosis can appear, of course, before old age but is more common beyond the age of fifty. The vascular changes involve reduction of the vessels and thickening of the vascular wall from fatty substances and connective tissue. Early signs of the illness include headaches, dizziness upon suddenly rising or when resting, discomfort in the neck, fleeting weakness in the limbs, and transitory aphasia. As the disease progresses, fluctuations in memory occurs, along with a loss of initiative, carelessness in self-care, distrust, querulousness, emotional outbursts,

and sexual immorality. Ultimately, mental functions fail, emotional bursts of depression or crying appear, and childishness dominates. Euphoria, or delusional material may appear. In some of the cases, the deterioration becomes progressively worse until death while in others a plateau is reached and the symptoms appear to be stabilized.

Previously two other diseases, *Alzheimer's disease* and *Pick's disease* were considered as organic conditions similar to senile dementia and arteriosclerotic psychosis except for their appearance earlier in life. It has been suggested that Pick's disease involves a premature neurone aging. These diseases have therefore been referred to as *presenile dementias*. They

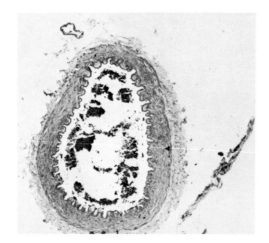 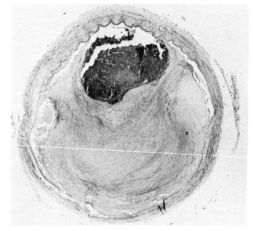

A normal artery *(left)* **showing scattered red blood cells in an unobstructed lumen (cavity). In contrast is an** *atherosclerotic* **artery** *(right)* **with the lumen being almost completely blocked off. (Louisiana State University Medical Center)**

are relatively rare disorders characterized by progressive intellectual impairment, defects in memory, and disturbance of abstract thinking. Alzheimer's disease, which appears between ages 50-60 years, involves cortical atrophy and the appearance of tangled, threadlike fibers in place of normal nerve cells (Alzheimer, 1907). Convulsions can appear, as well as aphasia (language difficulty) or apraxia (inability to use objects correctly). Restlessness, anxiety, and depression may occur. Delusions, hallucinations and confabulations occur such that the patient is out of touch with reality. Within a short time span, from five to ten years, the patient is reduced to a mere vegetative existence. Pick's disease (Pick, 1901) usually has its onset about age 45 but has been known to appear as early as age 31. Atrophy, especially of the frontal and temporal lobes, develops such that the total brain weight may be reduced from 1340 grams to 1000 grams. Speech and higher thought processes are impaired, emotions are blunted or characterized by irritability, suspiciousness or depression. Convulsions are rare, defects of memory for simple and routine tasks remain longer, delusions and hallucinations are

less frequent in Pick's disease than in Alzheimer's. The patient suffering from Pick's disease usually dies within four to six years of its inception. There is currently some doubt as to whether these diseases are appropriately labeled as results of aging; some experts prefer to consider them as chronic brain syndromes due to unknown cause.

Treatment

The illnesses of aging are irreversible disorders. Once organic changes occur, such as deterioration, recovery is impossible. On the other hand, there is agreement that much of the personality symptoms are due to psychological rather than organic factors. Preparation for retirement and old age should be a crucial part of every person's planning. The early development of a sense of self-satisfaction and esteem can carry over into the later period of lessened activity and responsibilities. Preparing to live a rich and meaningful life rather than to fill in empty time is important. Maintaining an interest in life and in people can help to prevent the impact of senile psychosis. Once senile

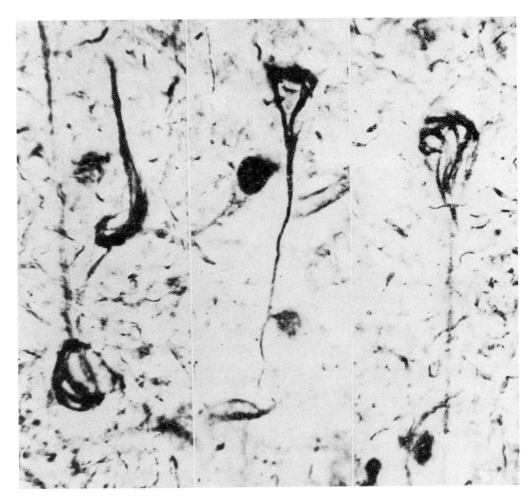

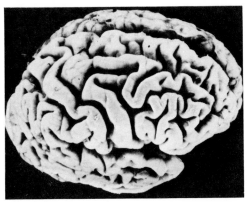

Alzheimer's disease involves cortical atrophy (*left*) and the appearance of threadlike fibers instead of normal nerve cells (*above*).

(Left: Dorothy S. Russell from *Greenfield's Neuropathology* by W. Blackwood, W. McMenemy, A. Meyer, R. Norman and Dorothy Russell, Edward Arnold Publishers, Ltd., London, 1963. With permission of the publisher). Above: From A. Ferraro, "Presenile Psychoses," in S. Arieti, *American Handbook of Psychiatry*, Vol. II, © 1959, Basic Books. With permission of the publisher)

psychosis occurs, the prognosis is typically poor. Treatment is directed toward removal of unnecessary stresses, and supportive counseling. Tranquilizers can reduce the agitations and control delusions. Confusional states may respond to vitamin therapy. For cases involving arteriosclerosis, the control of dietary intake is important. Massive doses of nicotinic acid, the use of anticoagulants, or ultraviolet radiations, have been tried as ways of reducing cholesterol content.

Case History 12-5

PSYCHOSIS WITH CEREBRAL ARTERIOSCLEROSIS

The patient was an 88-year-old man placed in a hospital for veterans. His wife had died five years previous, and his children were all unable or uninterested in caring for him. His tendency to lie in bed throughout the day muttering to himself was a constant problem to the hospital staff. He resisted all recreational facilities and offers of a change of scene. Several times a day he would enter a delirious state and shout for his wife. During these periods he recognized no one. He was incontinent and extremely irritable when required to use a bedpan. Although he accused the staff of secretly planning his degradation, he exhibited a total lack of disturbance over his tendency to display his genitals when children were visiting on the ward. He became more and more secretive and suspicious as time progressed. In his better moments, he discussed his Spanish-American War experiences with some lucidity but progressively lost his memory for even his most favored story. In his last days, he was completely disoriented, apparently hallucinatory, and agitated. He died of cerebral hemorrhage.

CONVULSIVE DISORDERS: EPILEPSY

Epilepsy is derived from the Greek *epilepsia,* meaning seizure, and is now used to refer to those conditions involving motor or sensory convulsions that are periodic and self-limited. A variety of factors can cause convulsions—brain tumors, inflammation or infection of the brain, cerebral vascular disease, traumatic damage, withdrawal of drugs, hypoglycemia (sugar deficiency in the blood). Thus, *epilepsy* might more accurately be referred to as *the epilepsies* since it may appear as a disease in itself or as a side component of other disorders. When the seizures are due to demonstrable organic causes, they are classified as *symptomatic epilepsy.* When the origin is not clearly based in organic etiology, the classification used is that of *idiopathic epilepsy.* A number of prominent historical figures were epileptic, among them Julius Caesar, Alexander the Great, and Van Gogh. The Greeks had considered it the divine disease until Hippocrates refuted this

belief. The actual incidence of epilepsy in the United States today is unknown. Estimates range from 700,000 (Kolb, 1968) afflicted to as high as 2,000,000 (Coleman, 1964). The majority of patients with convulsive disorder remain at home; only about 50 thousand are in special institutions, living areas, or residential schools, and a very small number are in psychiatric hospitals inasmuch as the convulsive disorders are primarily neurological difficulties rather than psychiatric or psychological problems (National Institute of Mental Health, 1961).

Modern attitudes are based on the information that the seizures are associated with sudden electrical discharges disturbing the usual rhythmical pattern of brain activity. Electroencephalograms (EEG) are records of such brain activity, and represent the "handwriting" of the brain. Recordings of differing convulsive states are illustrated on page 344. Seizures may be experimentally triggered off in normally seizure-free persons by photic stim-

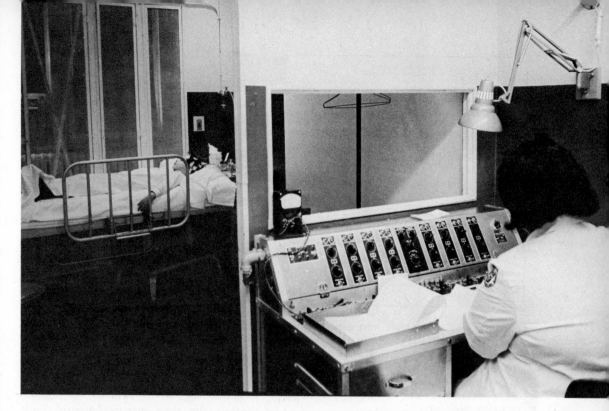

Epilepsy is detectable through brain wave recordings. Illustrated above is the examination of a youth; electrodes attached to his head pick up electrical signals from the brain, which are amplified and recorded by the electroencephalographic instrument in the foreground. (Elizabeth Wilcox)

ulation, the presentation of a rapidly flickering light. Epilepsy may also appear as part of a conversion reaction but this has become increasingly rare.

Epilepsy takes many forms depending upon what area of the brain is involved and how severe the disturbance. The seizures may be of the circumscribed type, for example, circumscribed sensory seizures characterized by numbness or tingling sensations (somato-sensory seizures); moving flashes of light, dark spots, stars, colors (visual seizures); or buzzing, roaring sounds (auditory seizures). The more common types of seizures are:

> Grand mal
> Petit mal
> Jacksonian
> Psychomotor

The *grand mal seizure* is the most common and dramatic type. The attack is sometimes preceded by a warning called an aura which consists of a sensory symptom such as the sensation of visceral pressure gradually moving up toward the head. An aura may appear anywhere from less than a second to several days before the seizure. The seizure itself takes part in three states: tonic, clonic, and recovery. The tonic stage is initiated in some by a vocal outburst like a cry or yell. The body muscles then tighten in a spasm with the trunk rigid, the head thrown backward, the jaw tightly closed, the hands clenched. The eyes are open although the person is unconscious; respiration ceases. Within a minute or so, the tonic stage ends and the clonic stage begins. This stage involves jerking movements actually due to swift alternations between contractions and relaxation of muscles, occurring as often as fifteen a second. Respiration is spasmodically resumed, saliva may foam at the

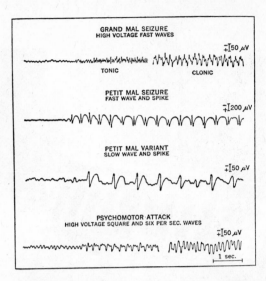

GRAND MAL SEIZURE
HIGH VOLTAGE FAST WAVES

$\mp$50 μV

TONIC   CLONIC

PETIT MAL SEIZURE
FAST WAVE AND SPIKE

$\mp$200 μV

PETIT MAL VARIANT
SLOW WAVE AND SPIKE

$\mp$50 μV

PSYCHOMOTOR ATTACK
HIGH VOLTAGE SQUARE AND SIX PER SEC. WAVES

$\mp$50 μV

1 sec.

Electroencephalograph brain wave patterns of different types of *epilepsy*; grand mal, petit mal, and psychomotor seizures. (From Frederic A. Gibbs, "Influence of Blood Sugar Level in Wave and Spike Formation in Petit Mal Epilepsy," in *Archives of Neurology and Psychiatry*, Vol. 41, pp. 1111-1116, June 1939)

mouth. The clonic convulsions last for two to three minutes and is followed by a state of general muscular relaxation. Some patients recover amnesic but completely alert, others fall asleep without gaining consciousness. In some, grand mal seizures occur in a rapid series of attacks during which the individual never reaches consciousness before another convulsion begins. This condition is referred to as a *grand mal status*, or *status epilepticus*.

The *petit mal seizure* is the next most common type. Unlike the grand mal, this type is never associated with an aura, and semiconsciousness is possible. The person may be vaguely aware of others although unable to comprehend what is being said. Such attacks are short, lasting from a second up to a minute. The patient shows no massive muscle convulsions, only minor rhythmic movements such as scratching or trembling. The eyes are open but unseeing. The individual may simply appear as though he had stopped in midsentence, paused, then continued on. Sometimes

the person is aware only of having experienced a blank spell in which he did not hear what was being said for a brief period. Confusion may or may not be present following the seizure. In fact, many are able to pass through a seizure without being noticed. Petit mal seizures are likely to disappear with age and is thus rarer among adults; however, the grand mal may develop in its place. Seizures up to several hundred a day have been known to occur.

The *Jacksonian seizure* is a type of circumscribed motor seizure. It consists of muscular twitches beginning on one side of the body and progressing throughout the arm or leg of the same side. The convulsions always start in the same place, for example, the face or the hand. In some patients, the attack spreads throughout the one side, then over to the entire body occasioning the loss of consciousness. If it is restricted in focus, then it is described as a focal seizure. Such circumscribed motor seizures are usually due to tumors or other irritations to a region of the motor area in the brain.

The *psychomotor seizure,* or *psychic equivalent,* is characterized by automatic behaviors. It has all the same qualities of the petit mal but usually involves the emission of highly complex behaviors for which the person has later total amnesia. In some, the patient appears to be entirely normal and attracts little attention. The patient may go on a trip during a seizure, and later find himself miles away without any recollection for his activities. In others, the seizure state leads to the display of overtly psychotic or violent behavior. The patient may commit mass murder without any recollection for his catastrophic act; however, such activities are rare events. Victoria Lincoln (1966) argues that the infamous Lizzie Borden murdered her parents during a psychomotor seizure. The attorneys of Jack Ruby, who shot Lee Oswald, the accused assassin

Jack Ruby under arrest after his shooting of Lee Oswald, the accused assassin of President John Kennedy. Defense counsel suggested that Ruby was suffering from *epileptic* seizures and not responsible for his actions. (Bill Winfrey/Black Star)

of President Kennedy, pursued the defense that Ruby had been himself a victim of epilepsy and hence not responsible for his actions.

It has sometimes been suggested that an "epileptic personality" exists, which predisposes an individual to having convulsive seizures, or which reflects maladjustment resulting from epilepsy. Such personality patterns are said to include the traits of rigidity, hypersensitivity, irritability, moodiness, rage over frustrations, and stubborness. It is currently accepted that there is neither a personality type which is susceptible to epileptic seizures, nor is there any evidence of a common personality pattern resulting from epilepsy (Lennox, 1944; Tizard, 1962). Epileptics may sometimes exhibit the above traits, but they are not limited to appearing only among epileptics, and do not appear in all epileptic patients. When they do appear, they are more clearly understood as a result of the social, psychological, and physical stresses which result from living with convulsions. The individual epileptic may exhibit certain traits in his attempts to cope with the unpredictable seizures, the attitudes of other people towards his condition, and his anxieties over the disability.

Treatment

A substantial number of epileptics are able to conduct a normal life, displaying intellectual, social and work adjustments equal to any non-afflicted group (Himler and Raphael, 1945). Moreover, there seems to be no significant relationship between the type, duration, or frequency of convulsion and the ability to adapt to everyday living (Mulder, 1959). Seizures can be completely controlled in 50-60 percent of the cases, while in another 30 percent the number and severity of attacks can be significantly reduced (National Epilepsy League, 1962; Forster, 1960). Grand mal seizures are quite responsive to treatment leading to control or complete abolition in about 80 percent of the patients (Kolb, 1968). Petit mal, Jacksonian, and psychomotor epilepsy are next in line in responsiveness to treatment, in that order. The prognosis is less favorable when the onset is in childhood than when the seizures are found to have begun in adulthood.

Seizures can be controlled by avoiding those circumstances which aggravate the condition. Hyperventilation (induced by deep breathing), alcohol, photic stimulation, and emotional stresses can all contribute to seizures in different patients. For example, the flickering light patterns that occur when driving down a tree-lined lane have been known to trigger a convulsion. Ordinarily, the epileptic can eat the same food as any other member of the family; however, sometimes a child may be placed on a ketogenic diet consisting of high fat, no carbohydrate, and medium protein foods. Epileptics sometimes have attacks precipitated from hypoglycemia and are therefore told to avoid going for long periods without food.

Drug therapy has proved a major contributor to the control of seizures. Bromides were once heavily relied upon as the principal form of chemotherapy. In 1912, these were replaced by phenobarbital which has proved effective in grand mal seizures. In large doses, phenobarbital has the disadvantage of producing drowsiness and impairment of attention and concentration. In 1937, Putnam and Merritt (1938) discovered Dilantin (sodium diphenylhydantoin sodium) and opened a new phase in the drug treatment of epilepsy. Dilantin is often successful in the control of grand mal and psychomotor seizures where phenobarbital may fail. It is not subject to the

side effect of affecting alertness, although gastric discomfort and dizziness have been known to sometimes occur. In addition, Dilantin together with phenobarbital has been used as a combination that is more effective than either drug alone. Petit mal convulsions, which are resistant to phenobarbital treatment, does seem to be controllable with Tridione (trimethadione). However, this drug can aggravate other types of epilepsy and can have dangerous toxic effects if not properly administered. Phenurone (phenacetylcarbamide) and Primodone (mysoline) are valuable in the treatment of psychomotor seizures (Forster, 1960; Friedlander, 1963).

In certain severe cases of epilepsy, brain surgery may be considered. This involves the surgical excision of the convulsive producing brain site (Penfield and Erickson, 1941; Sperry, 1964). Typically, surgery may be attempted when the affected part of the brain lies mainly in one temporal lobe as indicated by electroencephalographic study (Rasmussen and Branch, 1962). About two-thirds of the patients surgically treated are either free from convulsions or limited to a few isolated attacks. Dangers involve the usual hazards of such specialized operative techniques: a small percentage (less than 1 percent) die post-operatively, and there is some risk of unexpected complications such as aphasia or paralysis.

Families of epileptics are encouraged to involve the epileptic in an active and normal life pattern. Alarming though the symptoms may be, epilepsy is not as disabling a disease as it seems. Children are able to acquire an education without difficulty, unless of course they are multiply handicapped by other disabilities. When seizures are under medical control, the adult is capable of being socially useful, maintaining employment under normal working conditions, and even earning and owning a driver's license (in states such as Ohio). In less than five percent of the cases

Case History 12-6

PSYCHOMOTOR EPILEPSY

During an interview with him and his father I probed rather insistently . . . (saying) rather sharply, "Well, something must have been going on! These things don't usually come out of the blue, especially in your case."

At this the boy started to answer but stopped; his face went blank, then red, then became fixed in a frowning, frozen expression. He looked around the office as if seeking something. Then he took some paper from my desk and tore it methodically into small squares. These he proceeded to lay on the floor in lines and rough patterns, mumbling rather incoherently as he did so. Among his mumblings were a few Latin words, but mostly there emerged distinct phrases such as, "Eggplant . . . that's eggplant . . . carrots here . . . tomatoes . . . damn fool . . . tomatoes there . . . damn fool could see . . . ". He emphasized some placements with vigorous pointing and nodding. From time to time he looked contemptuously at me as if he were instructing a stubborn but idiotic pupil. Suddenly his face and manner returned to normal; he looked at me and asked, "What did you say?"

Source: Barker, W. *Brain storms.* New York: Grove Press, 1968, pp. 77-78.

Case History 12-7

EPILEPSY

Joan K. is a member of the political staff of a state senator. She first became interested in government issues through a speech she heard concerning candidates in an upcoming gubernatorial election. She enrolled in a private university with an active political science program, applied for and received a summer appointment as a political science intern in the state capitol. She had been subject to petit mal seizures during childhood and continued to have them while in college. Initially, she was concerned about her ability to lead a normal life and was painfully shy in fear that she would have a seizure in the presence of her classmates. Although the attacks were themselves not noticeable, she experienced a confusion upon their termination. In spite of the condition, she was soon more confident of her abilities and become more comfortable about her seizures. She found that others were more able to adapt to her brief attacks once they were aware of her disorder. In addition, she was actually able to help educate her peers in the facts of epilepsy, removing many inaccurate beliefs. She often worked as a baby-sitter once she was certain the physician had found the right combination of drugs for her. She graduated in the middle of her class with a sense of real satisfaction at her own emotional development and the progress of others in understanding epilepsy.

of epilepsy is there any conclusive evidence of inheritance. For an epileptic marrying a nonepileptic, the chances of a convulsive child being born is estimated to be one in 50. However, most authorities feel that the illness itself will rarely be the sole reason involved in any advice against having offspring.

Glossary

Acute brain syndrome: Organic disorders which are temporary and reversible.

Alzheimer's disease: An organic disorder involving cortical atrophy and the appearance of threadlike fibers in place of normal nerve cells.

Anoxia: Deficiency in the supply of oxygen.

Aphasia: Loss or impairment of language function; caused by organic brain damage.

Apraxia: Loss or impairment of ability to perform purposeful movements; caused by organic brain damage.

Argyll-Robertson pupil: Disturbance of pupillary reflex and a symptom of syphilitic damage.

Ataxia: Loss or impairment of coordinated muscle movements; caused by organic brain damage.

Bromide psychosis: An organic disorder involving psychotic symptoms such as hallucinations, schizophrenic behavior, or disorientation and disturbance of coordination.

Catastrophic reaction: An occasional reaction to brain damage involving confusion, severe anxiety, and resistance when faced with a difficult task.

Cerebral arteriosclerosis: Thickening of the walls of the arteries; may lead to brain damage.

Chronic brain syndrome: Organic disorders which are permanent and irreversible.

Concussion: Transitory loss of consciousness due to a severe blow to the head or spinal column.

Congenital tumor: Abnormal growth of tissue present at birth.

Contusion: An injury to the brain not involving the breaking of the skin; caused by the brain becoming bruised against the skull itself.

Encephalitis: An acute inflammation of the brain or its membranous coverings.

Epilepsy: A group of organic disorders involving the occurrence of convulsions.

General paresis: Also known as paresis. An organic disorder involving gradual and complete mental deterioration; caused by a syphilitic condition.

Grand mal seizures: Epileptic convulsions characterized by major muscle spasms and loss of consciousness.

Hypoglycemia: Deficiency of sugar in the blood stream sometimes leading to convulsions.

Idiopathic epilepsy: Epileptic condition which is not clearly attributable to an organic origin.

Jacksonian seizure: Epileptic convulsions characterized by circumscribed spasms beginning as muscle twitches and involving larger and larger areas of the body.

Laceration: An injury involving the breaking of the skin.

Meningitis: Inflammation of the membranes covering the brain and spinal cord.

Metastatic tumor: A malignant growth originating from another area of the body.

Pernicious anemia: A disease that can lead to organic brain damage; caused by a deficiency in vitamin B12.

Petit mal seizures: Epileptic convulsions characterized by brief, minor, rhythmical movements.

Pick's disease: An organic disorder involving atrophy of the frontal and temporal lobes and impairment of language and intellect.

Presenile dementias: A group of organic disorders believed to be a form of premature aging deterioration. Includes Alzheimer's disease and Pick's disease.

Psychomotor epilepsy: Also known as psychic equivalent. Epileptic disorder characterized by automatic behaviors.

Senile plaques: Areas of tissue degeneration generally round and of granular and filamentous structure; involved in the aging process.

Senile psychosis: Also known as senile dementia. An organic disorder involving atrophy of the brain and characterized by loss of memory, emotional lability, disorientation, moral deterioration.

Spirochetes: Microorganisms responsible for the damages of syphilis.

Status epilepticus: Also known as grand mal status. A rapid series of epileptic convulsions during which the patient never reaches consciousness before another convulsion begins.

Symptomatic epilepsy: Epileptic condition which is clearly attributable to an organic origin.

Syphilis: An infectious venereal disease caused by spirochetes called Treponema pallidum.

Trauma: Injury or wound.

Wassermann test: A blood test for determining the presence of the syphilitic spirochete.

References

Alzheimer, A. Uber eine eigenartige Erkrankung der Hirnrinde. *Centralbl. Nervenheit. Psychiat.,* 1907, **18**, 177.

Alzheimer. A. Über eigenartige Erkrankung der Hirnrinden. *Allg. Ztschr. f. d. ges. Neurol. u. Psychiat.,* 1911, **4**, 356.

Association for Research in Nervous and Mental Diseases. Vol. XXIV: *Trauma of the central nervous system.* Baltimore: Williams & Wilkins, 1945.

Bowman, K. & Blau, A. Psychotic states following head and brain injury in adults and children. In S. Brock (Ed.), *Injuries of the skull, brain, and spinal cord.* Baltimore: Williams & Wilkins, 1943.

Bruetsch, W. Penicillin or malaria therapy in the treatment of general paralysis? *Dis. Nerv. System,* 1949, **10**, 368.

Coleman, J. *Abnormal psychology and modern life.* Illinois: Scott, Foresman, 1964.

Corsellis, J. *Mental illness and the aging brain.* London: Oxford University Press, 1962, Maudsley Monographs No. 9.

Critchley, M. Discussion on presenile psychoses. *Proc. Roy. Soc. Med.,* 1938, **31**, 1443.

Cummings, J. *Heavy metals and the brain.* Springfield, Ill.: C.C. Thomas, 1959.

Dattner, B. Penicillin in neurosyphilis. New York: Grune & Stratton, 1949.

Forster, F. Drugs most effective in the control of epilepsy. *Postgrad. Med.,* 1960, **27**, 711.

Friedlander, W. Epilepsy. *Amer. J. Psychiat.,* 1963, **119**, 654.

Gibbs, F., Davis, H., & Lennox, W. The electroencephalogram in epilepsy and in conditions of impaired consciousness. *Arch. neurol. Psychiat.,* 1935, **34**, 1133.

Goldstein, K. & Scheerer, M. Abstract and concrete behavior: an experimental study with special tests. *Psychol. Monogr.,* 1941, **53**, 1.

Hahn, R. et al., Penicillin treatment of general paresis. *AMA Arch. neurol. & Psychiat.,* 1959, **81**, 557.

Harlow, J. Recovery from the passage of an iron bar through the head. *Publ. Mass. med. Soc.,* 1868, **2**, 327.

Haslam, J. *Observations on insanity: with practical remarks on the disease and an account of the morbid appearances on dissection.* London: F. Rivington and C. Rivington, 1798.

Himler, L. & Raphael, T. A follow-up study on 95 college students with epilepsy, Ann Arbor, Michigan, *Amer. J. Psychiat.,* 1945, **101**, 760.

Kolb, L. *Noyes' modern clinical psychiatry.* Philadelphia: Saunders, 1968.

Lennox, W. Seizure states. In J. McV. Hunt (Ed.), *Personality and the behavior disorders.* New York: Ronald Press, 1944, Vol. II.

Levin, M. Bromide psychoses: four varieties. *Amer. J. Psychiat.,* 1948, **104**, 798.

Merritt, H. The early clinical and laboratory manifestations of syphilis of the central nervous system. *New Engl. J. Med.,* 1940, **223,** 446.

Merritt, H., Adams, R., & Solomon, H. *Neurosyphilis.* New York: Oxford University Press, 1946.

Mulder, D. Psychoses with brain tumors and other chronic neurologic disorders. In S. Arieti (Ed.), *American handbook of psychiatry,* Vol. 2. New York: Basic Books, 1959.

National Epilepsy League, Special issue of *Horizon,* May 1962, 1.

National Institute of Mental Health. *Mental health statistics. Current Reports.* Bethesda, Md.: National Institute of Mental Health, 1961.

Penfield, W. & Erickson, T. Epilepsy and cerebral localization. Springfield, Ill.: C.C. Thomas, 1941.

Penfield, W. & Rasmussen, T. *The cerebral cortex of man.* New York: Macmillan, 1950.

Pick, A. Uber die Beziehungen der senilen Hirnatrophie zur Aphasia. *Prag. med. Wschr.,* 1892, **17,** 165.

Pick, A. Senile Hirnatrophie als Grundlage von Herderscheinungen. *Wien. klin. Wchnschr.* 1901, **14,** 403.

Post, F. *The clinical psychiatry of late life.* Oxford: Pergamon Press, 1965.

Putnam, T. & Merritt, H. SDH in treatment of convulsive disorders. *J. Amer. med. Assoc.,* 1938, **3,** 1068.

Rasmussen, T. & Branch, C. Temporal lobe epilepsy: indications for and results of surgical therapy. *Postgrad. Med.,* 1962, **31,** 9.

Ruesch, J., Harris, R., & Bowman, K. Pre- and post-traumatic personality in head injuries. *Res. publ. assoc. res. nerv. ment. Dis.,* 1945, **24,** 507.

Simchowitz, T. Histologische studien über die senile Demenz. *Hist. u. Histopathol. Arb. Nissl.,* 1910, 4, 268.

Sperry, R. The great cerebral commissure. *Scient. Amer.* 1964, **210,** 42.

Stengel, E. A study on the symptomatology and differential diagnosis of Alzheimer's disease and Pick's disease. *J. Ment. Sci.,* 1943, **89,** 1.

Thomas, E. Current status of therapy in syphilis. *J.A.M.A.* 1956, **162,** 1536.

Tizard, B. The personality of epileptics: a discussion of the evidence. *Psychol. Bull.,* 1962, **59,** 196.

Wagner-Jauregg, J. & Bruetsch, W. The history of the malaria treatment of general paralysis. *Am. J. Psychiat.,* 1946, **102,** 577.

Zilboorg, G. and Henry. G. *A history of medical psychology.* New York: Norton, 1941.

13 *The Psychotic Disorders*

The psychotic disorders represent man's most serious reaction to stress. They are major disorders equivalent to the major medical illnesses, such as cancer, which severely incapacitate the patient. The psychotic conditions are reflections of profound disorganization and disability. The symptoms represent the final breakdown of the personality as it fails to successfully adopt adaptive or even moderately effective means of dealing with conflict. Psychotics share most though not necessarily all of the following characteristics:

1. Symptoms of such severity that interpersonal, intellectual, and work adjustment is markedly impaired.

2. A lack of insight into the pathological state that they are in.

3. A profound disturbance of their capacity to evaluate reality—a break with reality.

4. Personality decompensation, that is, disorganization of the personality due to excessive stress.

5. Behavior frequently self-injurious or dangerous to others.

6. Illness of such magnitude that institutional treatment is typically demanded.

The specific symptoms involved vary with the psychotic condition. Some of the possible symptoms are given below.

1. Disorders of perception

a. *Hallucinations* are sensory perceptions without the presence of an external stimulus. These may be auditory involving noises, music, or voices speaking in an abusive fashion or a friendly fashion. Hallucinatory voices may command the patient, provide him with a revelation ("You are the Chosen One"), accuse him ("You are a filthy man and must be punished"), or report on his actions ("He is putting his spoon to the plate"). The hallucinations may be visual, for example, the patient may see organized patterns of colors or a hand writing on the wall. Less common are the olfactory, gustatory, and tactual hallucinations. Tactual hallucinations such as the sensation of insects crawling under the skin are frequently found in delirium tremens.

b. Sensory distortions may also appear. These are disturbances of normal sensations and may involve any of the sensory modalities. Objects may appear visually smaller than in reality, sounds may seem to come from a long distance away, parts of the body may feel altered in size.

Pen drawings reproducing the visual hallucinations of a patient. Portrays the patient-artist balanced with a rope around his neck and tied at the other end to another victim; each is dependent upon the other for survival since both will be strangled if either loses 'balance'. Other figures include the patient's family at the bottom, a 'bird of death' the hanging bodies of corpses, and a guard with a bayonet.

SOURCE: From J. Plokker, *Art From The Mentally Disturbed.* Courtesy of Mouton & Co., n.v. Publishers, THE HAGUE.

2. Disorders of thinking

a. *Autism* involves the excessive preoccupation with fantasy unchecked by attention to reality. The patient becomes involved in his own private inner life and is little concerned with the realities around him.

b. *Delusions* are beliefs which are unshakable but ungrounded in reality. A delusion is accepted with an intensity that puts it beyond the scope of mere superstitious beliefs. It is defended in the face of strong contradictory evidence. The story is told of a patient who firmly believed he was dead. To prove the opposite he was asked whether dead persons bled, to which he replied in the negative. He was then pricked, and shown his bleeding. Faced with this incontrovertible evidence, he responded, "By gosh, I guess dead people do bleed after all!"

Delusions may be of several varieties. The *ideas of reference* involve a belief that others are referring to the patient, or that every event that occurs is related to him. In *delusions of persecution,* these references take on a threatening tone as the patient believes that others are out to harm him or degrade or discriminate against him. The *delusions of grandeur* encompass the belief that he has extraordinary talents or is in some other way highly important. He may be convinced that he is Jesus Christ or a great inventor. Other delusions include hypochondriacal delusions ("I am dying of cancer"), and nihilistic delusions ("Everything in existence has been destroyed").

c. Thought process may be interfered with in a number of ways. Thoughts may be blocked with one train of thought suddenly stopping and a totally unrelated one taking over. Thoughts may become inhibited and slowed down to such an extent that thinking becomes a real effort. Thoughts may become speeded up such that ideas follow one another in rapid succession, connected by loose associations (*flight of ideas*).

d. Disorientation may be present. The patient may be confused about himself, the time, the place, other people. He may falsely recognize others, or refuse to recognize friends.

3. Disorders of emotion

a. Emotions may be exaggerated and unrealistic as in the euphoric or the melancholic states of manic-depression.

b. Emotions may be inappropriate to the circumstances, or flattened entirely, as in the schizophrenias.

Print by a hebephrenic schizophrenic of a tree-man holding a bleeding human head. The patient showed inappropriateness of emotion in describing the picture as "humorous." (Mouton and Co. n. v. Publishers)

4. Disorders of behavior

a. Speech may become affected. The patient may become incoherent, or repeat the words of others (*echolalia*), or coin new terms (called *neologisms*).

b. Motor behavior may be impaired. The individual may show an uncontrolled excitability, or an extreme immobility (*stupor*), or imitate the movements of others (*echopraxia*) or engage in stereotyped actions.

The basic psychotic disorders generally include different clusters of symptoms. However, there is some overlapping of symptoms, for example, motor excitement may appear in catatonic schizophrenia and manic-depressive psychosis. In some cases, the patient may exhibit most but not all of the symptoms connected with his illness; in other cases, the patient shows all of the symptoms but with certain symptoms subsiding at times. Indeed, patients may show sufficient transient reduction during the acute stages of the illness that they are able to relate and communicate fairly normally. In comparison to the psychoneuroses, there are fewer types of psychotic disorders. Among the more important of these major disorders are:

The Affective Disorders
    Manic-Depressive Psychosis
    Psychotic Depression
    Involutional Melancholia
The Paranoid Disorders
    Paranoia
    Paranoid State
The Schizophrenic Disorders
    Simple
    Hebephrenic
    Catatonic
    Paranoid

THE AFFECTIVE DISORDERS

Affect refers to emotion or mood; the affective disorders are therefore disturbances of emotion. Manic-depressive psychosis involves certain recurring disturbances of elation and depression; the psychotic depression is a disturbance without signs of recurrence; and involutional melancholia is a depressed condition believed associated with certain physical changes in life.

355

Manic-Depressive Psychosis

Manic-depressive psychosis is a disorder consisting of periodic attacks, frequently alternating in type, of extreme elation or depression. In the latter part of the nineteenth century, Kraepelin recalled attention to a disorder known to the Greeks, described the conditions of mania and melancholia, and decided that such conditions represented different facets of a single illness which he named "manic-depressive insanity" (Kraepelin, 1898). Manic-depressive psychosis, as it is known today, is characterized by certain features (Table 13-1):

1. The recurrence of periods of mood-disturbance. Some patients exhibit only periods of elation, others only periods of depression, while others show the classical symptoms of cyclic alternation between elation and depression (Fig. 13-1).

2. The periods of disturbance soon terminate with or without treatment. Manic reactions run their course in about three months, depressive reactions last about nine months before terminating.

3. In between periods of disturbance, the patient lives an undisturbed, essentially normal life. These normal phases may last for a period of decades.

4. The disturbance is fundamentally emotional; intellectual deterioration does not occur.

5. Thought processes are interfered with by flight of ideas in the manic state, and retardation in the depressed state.

6. Delusions are common. In the manic state, the delusions are in keeping with the general euphoria and expansiveness, including delusions of grandeur. In the depressed state, ideas of guilt, low self-esteem, and hypochondriacal beliefs abound.

7. Hallucinations are common when the disturbance is severe, but even then, they are less common than in schizophrenia. Hallucinations appear in less than twenty percent of the cases of manic-depressive psychosis.

Manic-depressive psychosis, manic reaction, is the term used to refer to those cases of the illness in which the manic state dominates. The manic is an exciting per-

TABLE 13-1. *Comparison of Manic and Depressive Symptoms*

MANIC	DEPRESSIVE
Emotional Manifestations	
Elated	Depressed
Increased gratification	Loss of gratification
Likes self	Dislikes self
Increased attachments	Loss of attachments
Increased mirth response	Loss of mirth response
Cognitive Manifestations	
Positive self-image	Negative self-image
Positive expectations	Negative expectations
Blames others	Blames self
Denial of problems	Exaggeration of problems
Arbitrary decision-making	Indecisive
Delusions: self-enhancing	Delusions: self-degrading
Motivational Manifestations	
Driven and impulsive	Paralysis of the will
Action-oriented wishes	Wishes to escape
Drive for independence	Increased dependent wishes
Desire for self-enhancement	Desire for death
Physical and Vegetative Manifestations	
Hyperactivity	Retardation/agitation
Indefatigable	Easily fatigued
Appetite variable	Loss of appetite
Increased libido	Loss of libido
Insomnia	Insomnia

SOURCE: Table 6-1 (p. 91) "Comparison of Manic and Depressive Symptoms" from *Depression: Clinical, Experimental, and Theoretical Aspects* by Aaron T. Beck. Copyright © 1967 by Hoeber Medical Division, Harper and Row, Publishers, Inc. By permission.

son to be near because his spontaneity, activity, and outbursts of exuberance are infectious. He is full of ideas, has multitudinous plans, possesses grand visions which somehow seem vaguely possible when presented with the supreme confidence characteristic of the manic. However, being near the manic patient soon turns into a wearing experience. His ideas are too flighty—they shift too readily, they are too circumstantial, they cover too many irrelevant issues as the patient finds himself unable to deal precisely and simply with single topics. His claims and masterful proposals are too shallow and poorly supported by reality. His motor behavior is too incessantly active, and he may be assaultive and destructive. One soon finds that the manic is highly distractible, irritable, self-centered, intolerant of having his ideas or plans questioned, and boastful. In *hypomania*, the patient is less markedly disturbed. He is in heightened good humor, talkative, entertaining. He dominates the social surroundings, and appears to be physically

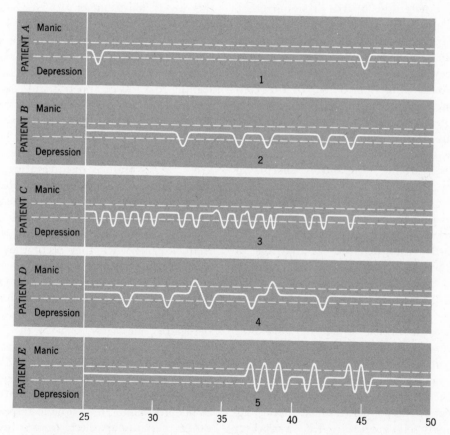

Figure 13-1. Sample patterns of depressive and manic-depressive attacks among five patients: Patient *A* with widely interspersed depressed attacks. Patient *B* with depressive attacks every few years. Patient *C* with annual depressions but a few healthy years. Patient *D* with some isolated depressions, a few manic states. Patient *E* with alternating phases of mania and depression.

SOURCE: Adapted from *Depression and its treatment* by J. Pollitt. William Heinemann Medical Books Limited, London. Distributed in the United States by C. C. Thomas, Publishers.

inexhaustible. He may engage in an over-whelming display of energy, for example, covering reams of paper with his impressions of life, or personally knocking on the doors of every house in the vicinity of a square mile. He may engage in a spending spree, turning himself into a pauper within a few hours. In *acute mania,* the symptoms are much more intense. The flight of ideas is pronounced, he may become involved in disturbing the peace, he can be quite belligerent. His loud talk may be obscene, he is often incoherent and partly disoriented. Delusions of being a special person are in keeping with the expansive state; thus he will pronounce that he is an emissary of the Great World of the Orient, of the new Messiah, or more simply, a scientific genius. The illness may proceed on to such magnitude that a *delirious mania* is initiated. In this condition, the patient is totally disoriented, completely incoherent, extremely agitated, and in the most severe state of excitement. He is so active that he appears unaware of those around him and is difficult to communicate with. Hallucinations and delusions are common. His sexual behavior may become uncontrolled, obscene, promiscuous. Such patients are always in jeopardy from exhaustion, and loss of body weight. They will not take time for nourishment, sleep, or rest, and will continue their excited activity until they collapse.

Manic-depressive psychosis, depressive reaction, is the term used to refer to those cases of the illness in which the depressed state dominates. The depressed patient is a difficult person to be near since he is extremely despondent, melancholic, agonizingly self-deprecating. Like a mockery of King Midas, he believes that everything that he touches will turn to dust. His gloom pervades his every thought, his every action. He is certain of his utter worthlessness and his hopeless guilt. Occasionally he cannot say what he is guilty of, only that he bears the massive burden of something horribly wrong. His past and his future are so devoid of any hope that he contemplates suicide—about 75 percent of such patients consider suicide, and nearly 15 percent actually attempt suicide (Arieti, 1959; Hastings, 1958) (Table 13-2; Table 13-3). The depressed patient exhibits a general slowing down of his activities. He finds it an effort to think out simple problems such as how much money he needs to complete his payment of bills. He can no longer concentrate on little tasks such as reading a letter, and complains that he cannot comprehend what the words mean anymore. He becomes physically lethargic as if oppressed by the mood he is in. His body also appears to react with a general slowing down—his gastrointestinal activity becomes retarded, leading to a loss of appetite and constipation. The patient may focus his attention on his body and display his depressive attitude through somatic delusions. He begins to believe that his bowels are eaten away, or his brain is disintegrating. In a combination of self-condemnation and self-aggrandizement, he may accept the delusion that he has syphilis and will infect the entire universe. Hallucinations are infrequent, but when they occur they tend to be much less distinct than in the schizophrenic. The patient hears vague sounds or has the sensation of visual illusions. The hallucinations transmit accusatory, derogatory messages. As with the manic condition, there are also different varieties of depressive states. The patient suffering from a *simple depression* is dejected, gloomy, lethargic, full of uncertainty and self-depreciation. He is slow to respond to others, becomes apathetic toward life. He is capable of caring for his basic needs but needs supervision. Suicidal thoughts and actions may be expected, but delusions and hallucinations are absent. The *acute depression* is a more exaggerated version of the symptoms in the simple depression.

The patient is morbid and despairing. He may refuse to speak, show a poverty of thought, and is self-accusatory. Loss of weight is a serious problem. Delusions of being sinful or of wasting away may be present. Hallucinations may also occur and reflect the patient's preoccupation with guilt, disease, self-punishment. The *depressive stupor* is the most severe variety of depression. The patient is utterly and hopelessly depressed. He is so completely enveloped in his deeply disturbing melancholy that he will not speak or eat, and remains in bed apparently oblivious of

TABLE 13-2. *Psychiatric Diagnoses in Suicide and Attempted Suicide, England, Wales, and Scotland, 1961-1962*

DIAGNOSIS	SUCCESSFUL SUICIDE			ATTEMPTED SUICIDE		
	Males	Females	Total	Males	Females	Total
Schizophrenic psychoses	3	—	3	22	43	65
Manic-depressive psychoses	11	19	30	58	184	242
Senile dementia	—	1	1	1	4	5
Organic psychoses	1	—	1	1	—	1
Acute confusional states	—	—	—	—	4	4
Epileptic psychoses	1	—	1	3	6	9
Pregnancy psychoses	—	1	1	—	7	7
Other psychoses	1	—	1	—	2	2
Anxiety without depression	—	—	—	7	26	33
Anxiety with depression	3	2	5	24	50	74
Hysteria	—	2	2	7	34	41
Mental retardation	—	—	—	—	4	4
Problems of addiction	7	—	7	9	3	12
Psychopathy	1	—	1	10	8	18
Childhood behaviour problems	—	—	—	2	2	4
Other psychoneuroses	2	—	2	2	2	4
Total	30	25	55	146	379	525

SOURCE: C. Watts, *Depressive disorders in the community.* Bristol: John Wright & Sons, 1966.

TABLE 13-3. *Death by Suicide in Manic-Depressive Disease: A Summary of Five Follow-Up Studies*

INVESTIGATOR	NO. CASES	NO. DEAD	PERCENT DEAD	NO. DEAD BY SUICIDE	PERCENT DEAD BY SUICIDE	PERCENT OF DEATHS DUE TO SUICIDE
Langelüddecke	341	268	78.8	41	12.0	15.3
Slater	138	59	42.8	9	6.5	15.3
Lundquist	319	119	37.4	17	5.3	14.3
Schulz	2004	492	24.5	66	3.3	13.4
Stenstedt	216	42	19.4	6	14.3	

SOURCE: E. Robins, G. E. Murphy, R. H. Wilkinson, S. Gassner, and J. Kayes. Some clinical considerations in the prevention of suicide based on a study of 134 successful suicides. *Amer. J. Pub. Health,* 1959, **49**, 888.

The Dutch painter, *Vincent Van Gogh*, suffered from mood shifts alternating between profound depression to extremes of enthusiasm. In addition, it is possible that he may have been subject to convulsive seizures. His self-portraits seem to mirror his own psychological deterioration: a movement from the controlled, soft impressionism, through a depiction of sadness, to the fearful and anguished self-portrait, and finally, to the tense and swirling harshness of his last painting of himself. (Stedelisk Museum, Amsterdam, Courtauld Institutes of Art, O. Vaering, Oslo, Bulloz—all from Art Reference Bureau)

all else but his depression. He must be fed to keep his health from disintegrating; losses up to a hundred pounds body weight have been known. Waste products must be artificially removed since the patient is severely constipated. The patient's thought associations are the complement opposite of the manic's—the manic patient overflows with immediate, ever-changing associations, the depressed patient in the stuporous condition appears chronically unable to react to or generate ideas. Hallucinations seem to be present, and delusions are sometimes exhibited. Two other varieties are also recognized and should be briefly mentioned. The *paranoid depression* is a condition similar to the acute depressive state but one in which paranoid delusions play a prominent role. The patient believes that there is danger to himself, that someone is persecuting him, that someone is watching his movements. These delusions will disappear when the patient recovers from the depressed condition. The *agitated depression* is a depressed condition characterized by tense activity instead of the motor inhibition that is usually present. The patient paces, twists

and wrings his hands, appears to be continuously restless. The melancholic, self-deprecatory mood still prevails and suicidal thoughts may be catapulted into impulsive actions.

Dynamics. As was discussed in Chapter 3, hereditary factors have been strongly advocated by some theorists. The work with twins and human risk studies lend support to this viewpoint (Table 13-4). The incidence of manic-depressive psychosis in monozygotic twins was reported to be 95.7 percent, as compared to 26.3 for dizygotic twins, and only 0.4 percent in the unrelated population (Kallmann, 1958). A second viewpoint has been the constitutional theory, suggesting that the person with a pyknic or endomorph body type is also possessed of a cycloid temperament. Kretschmer reported that two-thirds of manic-depressive patients were pyknic in constitution (1925, 1934), a finding that has been upheld by others (see Chapter 6). However, the constitutional or somatotype orientation has many difficulties to overcome before it can be offered as a suitable explanation for manic-depressive psychosis or any psychological disorder, for that mat-

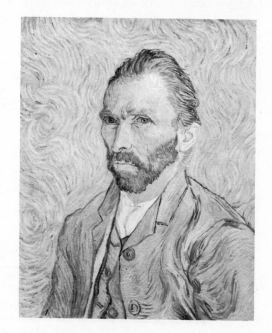

ter. Regarding the hereditary viewpoint, some recent figures indicate that manic-depressive psychosis has been on the decline (Arieti, 1957). Thus, manic-depressive patients comprised about 15 percent of first admissions to mental institutions about 30 years ago, but such patients form only about two percent of the new admissions today. The decline started in 1928. This decrease in the incidence of manic-depressive psychosis tends to refute the genetic hypothesis as the sole explanation of the illness.

A possible explanation for the downward shift in incidence is a change in cultural features. Manic-depressive psychosis is relatively higher in incidence in countries such as Ireland, those of the Mediterranean basin, and the Fiji Islands (Gold, 1951). In addition, although the incidence is low in India where schizophrenia is relatively higher, the reverse pattern is true for Indians who have emigrated to the Fiji Islands. Among the Africans, the manic reactions are rather common, but the depressive states are somewhat rare (1959). These findings, especially those which show a shift in symptomatology with emigration, lend support to Spiro's belief that:

. . . the incidence of psychopathology in any society is a function . . . of the strains produced by its culture, but also of the institutional means which its cultural heritage provides for the resolution of strain . . . (p. 14).

361

There are also societies in which manic-depressive psychosis is the "favored" means of expressing personality breakdown. For example, the Hutterites exhibited over four times as many manic-depressive conditions as schizophrenic disorders (Eaton and Weil, 1955). Hollingshead and Redlich (1954) discovered a higher incidence of both manic-depressive and schizophrenic disorders in lower socioeconomic class persons (Fig. 13-3); but among the higher class individuals who became psychotic, the manic-depressive condition appeared more frequently than schizophrenia.

Psychological factors have been increasingly offered as the more significant contributors to the development of manic-depressive psychosis. The early family backgrounds of manic-depressives has been explored with results indicating that these patients have been born into a less traumatic setting than schizophrenic patients (Arieti, 1959). The mother was willing, and in fact felt duty-bound to administer to her offspring. This atmosphere during the first year of life fosters a similar commitment in the child towards his family, encouraging him to accept the standards and wishes of the parent. By the second year of life, the mother alters her position drastically; this age is for most children the start of their own change in behaviors as they become more independent, demanding, and resistant but also ambivalent. The mother now begins to base her care and affection on contingencies, that is, they are provided only if and when the child responds to her conditions. The child is faced with greater demands by his parent and family responsibility, rigid standards, and discipline are now stressed (Gibson, 1958; Gibson, Cohen, and Cohen, 1959). The easy nonconditional atmosphere now shifts to one of conditionality and high expectations. These family circumstances produce an individual with a high sense of loyalty to standards reaching obsessive heights. The early commitment by the child toward his family permits the development of conscience which prevents him from deviating from the internalized rules or even from expressing resentment toward the parents for the restrictive demands. Manic patients have been described as showing the following prepsychotic personalities (Becker, 1960; Gibson et al., 1959):

ambitious
sociable
energetic
conventional
achievement oriented
concerned about social
    expectations

TABLE 13-4. *Hereditary Incidence of Manic-Depressive Psychosis*

PERSON WITH THE PSYCHOSIS	RELATIVES EXAMINED FOR SIMILAR PSYCHOSIS	INCIDENCE OF SIMILAR PSYCHOSIS
Both parents	Offspring	44.4% (Elsasser, 1952)
One parent	Offspring	33.3% (Lewis, 1933)
Neither parent (general population)	Offspring	0.4% (Kallmann, 1953)
Sibling	Monozygotic twin	95.7% (Kallmann, 1953)
		84.0% (Luxenburger, 1942)
Sibling	Dizygotic twin	26.3% (Kallmann, 1953)
		15.0% (Luxenburger, 1942)
Sibling	Full sibling	23.0% (Kallmann, 1953)
		18.1% (Banse, 1929)
Sibling	Half sibling	16.7% (Kallmann, 1953)

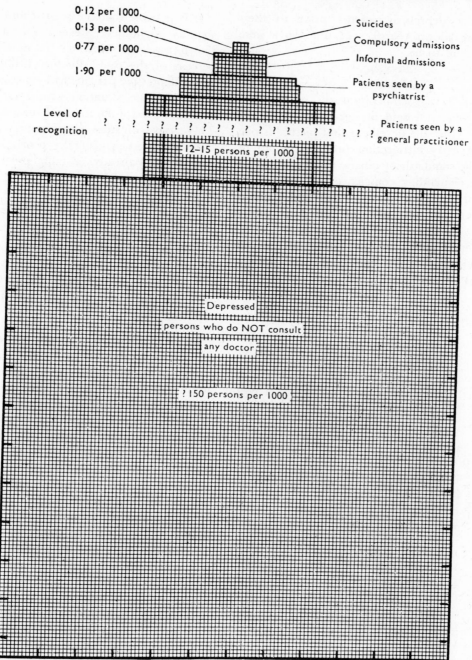

Figure 13-2. **Frequency of depression in a population (England and Wales). One small square = 0.01 persons per 1000.**

SOURCE: C. Watts, *Depressive disorders in the community.* Bristol: John Wright & Sons, 1966.

The depressed patients prior to their breakdown (Grinker et al., 1961) were found to be:

> anxious
> obsessive
> self-deprecatory
> rigid in conscience

Thus, the developmental picture is one of early introjection (internalization) of the standards of others, the formation of a demanding conscience that rules with rigidity, and the obsessive and anxious concern with rules of behaving in the depressive, or the shallow attempt to escape through reaction formation and the adoption of the sociable and gay facade of the manic.

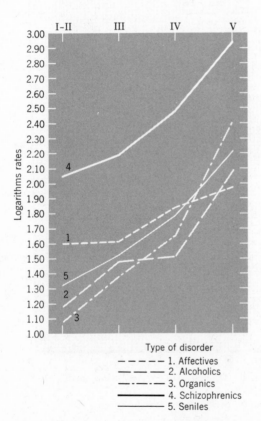

Type of disorder
- - - - - 1. Affectives
— — — 2. Alcoholics
—·—·— 3. Organics
———— 4. Schizophrenics
———— 5. Seniles

Figure 13.3 **Rates of differing psychoses associated with social classes.**
SOURCE: A. Hollingshead and F. Redlich. *Social class and mental illness.* New York: Wiley, 1958.

It is possible that the prepsychotic personality might never develop into a full blown psychosis. However, in nearly 80 percent of the cases (Rennie, 1942), the manic-depressive patients had experienced a stressful life situation which was sufficient to precipitate the final breakdown. Three types of stress circumstances have been suggested as generally poorly tolerated by the already unstable premanic-depressive personality:

1. The death of a person important to the patient.
2. The realization by the patient of a failure in an interpersonal relationship, usually with the spouse.
3. A severe disappointment in the work to which the patient has devoted his entire life.

In all of these, the common feature is the loss of a valued object with the overtones of abandonment or a failure to achieve established goals. Unlike the normal or even the neurotic person who can expend his grief, direct blame toward others, or reevaluate his goals, the manic-depressive assumes personal responsibility for his circumstances. He feels guilty over the loss of his loved one, accepts full blame for the failure of his marriage, or engages in self-deprecatory ruminations over his failure to live up to the standards of his occupation. Sometimes the psychotic episode is precipitated by the achievement of success—in this circumstance, the patient appears to have collapsed in awe of the even higher standards which he must now cope with to prove his worthiness in the new position. Typically, it is believed that the depressive aspects are triggered by losses, disappointments, failures, while the manic conditions are precipitated by seeming successes, achievements, accomplishments.

The symptom of depression may be an expression of a number of features. The depression may be an attempt to regain the acceptance of those whom he has lost and who may forgive him and return to his assistance in his misery. The depression may be self-punishment in reparation for wrongdoing; the patient believes himself responsible for not caring enough, nor working enough, or for harboring feelings of resentment toward his loved one (Abraham, 1911; Freud, 1917). Whereas someone else may be able to express resentment, the depressed patient is unable to attack those who hurt him because of his emotional dependence upon them. The depression may also be a symbolic flagellation of those whom the patient resents. In a roundabout warped fashion, the patient hates the other, but since he has introjected the other and since he is impotent to directly harm the other, he therefore punishes the *introjected* other in himself. The dynamics of suicide can also be understood in the same manner.

The symptom of manic behavior may also be viewed as a reaction to loss and failure. However, instead of admitting failure, the manic patient denies that it exists. Instead of recognizing his lack of competency, he extols his grand virtues. Rather than submitting to his dependence on others, he dominates and demands. Flightiness of ideas enable him to avoid attending to the topics that face him with his failure. A carefree attitude distracts him from the imminent threat of depression. His continuous hyperactivity is a sign of a man "on the run" as he desperately tries to escape, avoid, cover up, ignore, deny, refuse, or use any means available to defend against his own deep inner feelings. The very methods for coping with tension and conflict become themselves pathological and futile. Soon he can run away no longer and must fall in exhaustion into the arms of depression.

Treatment. For any given attack, the chances of recovery are excellent since nearly all of the patients will recover from

A chalk drawing of a female patient depicting herself as a lonely child from whom mothers turn away. Isolation, rejection, loneliness, and depression are all conveyed by this print.
SOURCE: From J. Plokker, *Art From The Mentally Disturbed.* Courtesy of Mouton & Co., n.v. Publishers, THE HAGUE.

the manic or the depressed state within approximately nine months with or without treatment. In addition, only about 15 percent of the cases are of the pure cyclic variety in which the manic condition is immediately supplanted by a depression followed by another manic state and so on. However, following recovery without treatment (*spontaneous recovery*), only 20 to 25 percent of the patients never have another episode. About 40 percent will have only two attacks and approximately 40 to 50 percent will be subject to four or more episodes. The typical age of onset of the illness is 44; earlier onset usually carries with it a better prognosis for recovery. Similarly, a better prognosis is expected with those reactions in which the manic features predominate.

Among the dangers to the manic-depressive patient are suicide, intoxication, physical exhaustion, financial bankruptcy through manic spending sprees, bodily injuries resulting from wild hyperactivity, and the well-meaning attempts of friends who try to cheer the patient out of his depression or argue the manic into sensibility. Constant supervision is needed. In some instances, patients have been known to swallow a variety of unique objects such as nails, hairpins, erasers, pins, in either a suicidal attempt or a manic display of "fun-loving" disposition. The severely depressed may require intranasal feeding to prevent weight loss, the manic patient will have to be calmed down sufficiently for him to accept food during his "busy" schedule of plans and activities. Warm baths and occupational therapy are helpful adjuncts to controlling symptoms.

Among the major direct treatment approaches are *electroshock therapy, chemotherapy,* and *psychotherapy. Electroshock therapy* was among the first real breakthroughs in the treatment of depressions. In an intensified form (two to three a day) it has also been of some success in the treatment of manic states. The depressions have responded with about 70 to 90 percent success (Kalinowsky and Hoch, 1946, 1961) following a course of 8 to 10 treatments given every other day. The manic states run longer and involve from 15 to 20 treatments. With the discovery of drug therapy, electroshock treatment (ECT) has become less popular especially because of the complications involved—fractures during the artificially induced grand mal seizure, and the uncomfortable transitory loss of memory and the disorientation which follows. However, depressed patients are returned to their more normal disposition and manic persons are greatly calmed and in control of themselves.

Chemotherapy is the modern alchemist's scientific answer to mood disturbances. The pharmacologist now has in his bag of treatments the ataratic or tranquilizing drugs and the antidepressants. Tranquilizers such as chlorpromazine have the capability of bringing the manic excitement under control within three or four days. Antidepressants are used with depressed patients in an attempt to alleviate the inactivity and provide a lift to their mood. Unfortunately, these drugs work slowly and are associated with a high incidence of physical side effects (Flach and Regan, 1960). In addition, much more needs to be known about these antidepressants before they can be routinely used without danger. The claims for their success have ranged from between 40 to 75 percent of the cases. In comparison with the known effectiveness of ECT, chemotherapy must be considered as secondary to electroshock as a preferred form of treatment for depressions.

Psychotherapy is impossible to conduct with the severely disturbed patient with either manic excitement or depressive stupor characteristics. However, it is effectively helpful with the milder manic-depressive states. Reassurance and directive suggestion can help immeasurably to relieve the symptoms. In the depressions, the patient is encouraged to perceive the discrepancy between his despondency and the reality of the circumstance triggering the depression. With support, the patient develops insight into his condition and a more realistic appraisal of himself. The manic patient is difficult to deal with because of his circumstantiality, lack of insight, and denial of all feeling other than happiness. Arieti (1959) has recommended that a competent therapist first directs his focus on releasing the underlying feelings of resentment, or the disguised depression. Once a mild depression is precipitated, the therapist can then deal properly with the true features of the illness.

Case History 13-1

MANIC-DEPRESSIVE PSYCHOSIS

Madeline K. was a 60-year-old widow who recently lost her second husband. She was initially hospitalized when she was 22, soon after her marriage to her first husband. On that occasion she showed manic symptoms, was treated and discharged, returned within a month with depressive features, was treated and released. She remained essentially normal until the recent breakdown.

The records show that she was suffering from an acute manic condition during her first hospitalization. Her husband had returned home to find her twirling around the living room bizarrely draped in her wedding gown tied with a bathtowel and wearing a lampshade. She gaily greeted him, laughed with an ear-piercing shrillness, and invited him to stay for the exciting "coming-out" party she was giving. Strewn on the table were a thousand handwritten invitations signed with a flourish and addressed to such dignitaries as the President of the United States, the justices of the Supreme Court, the Board of Trustees of the University of California, and the Emperor of Japan. She made incessant noises: singing her own ballads, shouting mottoes which she devised, reciting limericks, making rhyming sounds, and yelling obscenities. She had recorded her speech for presentation to the Library of Congress. The following is an excerpt:

(Singing) By yon bonny briefs—my briefs are entirely outrageous but God take me you'd best like it—(in normal voice) the world is round the world is crown'd—illusions of Georgie, once a porgie—can't you see?—I am worth more than all the cherries in the universe—red is beautiful, red is ripe—bow ye before me and receive my blessing —thank God I'm not the devil—the freshest thing on this earth is a newborn clod— to work is to win—twin is as twin does—I sing a song of sexpot—hand me your head on a platter and I will forgive you all your sins—my plan will earn you a hundred-thousand-fold—mishmoshmoneymash—slipperydickerypop—dam it all full speed abreast—my head is gold, my hands are silver, my tail is platinum—Where am I? What time is it? Who goes there?—Gee but it's marvelous to be alive. . . .

By contrast, her most recent commitment at age 60 involved a severely depressed condition. An acquaintance had noticed her gradual refusal to leave her apartment and her apathetic attitude toward herself and the world around her. She looked immensely weary and had not slept soundly for days. She seemed mute, but would occasionally reply if a question were repeated long enough. Through careful probing it was found that she believed herself responsible for the "epidemics of the world" which she said was her punishment for her earlier sickness. She felt an urge to do penance for a lifetime of sin but could not remember the exact nature of her sin. For the past three weeks she had remained indoors pondering her own evil nature, and fearful of going out and possibly infecting others through the sheer enormity of her evilness. Life looked hopeless, she felt as though she was living in a shadow of despondency, despair enveloped her very existence. In the hospital she typically retired to a dark corner and would sit motionless for hours, heaving an occasional deep sigh. She seemed on the verge of weeping but her sorrow was never able to

Case History 13-1 (*Continued*)

MANIC-DEPRESSIVE PSYCHOSIS

break loose. She was easily led by the nursing aides to different rooms, but once there she resumed her previous posture and ruminating. Her recovery has been extremely slow in spite of repeated ECT sessions.

Psychotic Depression

This disorder is essentially the same as the acute depression symptomatology that occurs with the manic-depressive psychosis, depressive reaction. *Psychotic depression* differs in the absence of periodic episodes of depression or elation, and in the greater occurrence of precipitating factors in the environment. The depression may be short termed or it may persist and become chronic. The general symptoms, psychodynamics, and treatment is identical with that of the manic-depressive psychosis, depressive reaction. The reader is referred back to this discussion for details.

Involutional Melancholia

Involutional melancholia is a disorder predominately characterized by depression, anxiety, and delusions, which occurs during the climacteric (change of life). The human being undergoes two distinct physiological changes in life, both related to the sexual procreative function—puberty, when the sexual organs mature, and the climacteric, when these organs are no longer productive. The disorder generally has its onset in women sometime between the ages of 40 to 55 years, while men are more likely to experience it between the ages of 50 and 60 years. There are more women than men with this disorder, a ratio of about 3 to 1. The psychosis may first begin to show itself several months ahead of its actual release through symptoms of anxiety, irritability, restlessness,

easy fatigability, and insomnia. The patient soon breaks into a full blown psychotic condition involving a depression of great intensity coupled with agitation. The patient experiences deep despair, paces the floor bemoaning her wicked life. She may wring her hands, weep aloud, pull her hair, and tear at her clothing. She is in continuous agony in her despondency. Many will center their thoughts around some past real or imaginary wrongdoing about which they feel they will be eternally condemned. This self-accusatory orientation may concern acts of commission ("I led a wicked life of sex") or acts of omission ("I should have helped my children more than I did"). Hypochondriacal delusions are common. She may express the belief that her bowels are stopped up, her liver has turned to stone, her brain is withered, or her heart is being gnawed apart. Nihilistic delusions may appear in a belief that her husband and children are nonexistent, or that the world is gone, or that there is no more food left. Guilt feelings trigger off a delusional belief that punishment of its severest form is imminent. Sometimes the punishment is conconceived of in mundane form such as being left in the hills to starve, sometimes it reaches highly imaginative expression, for example, being boiled to death in a solid gold kettle. Delusions may also be paranoid in nature, although the depressive type is more common. Suicide during one of the agitated periods was once expected in about a fourth of the cases. Many harm

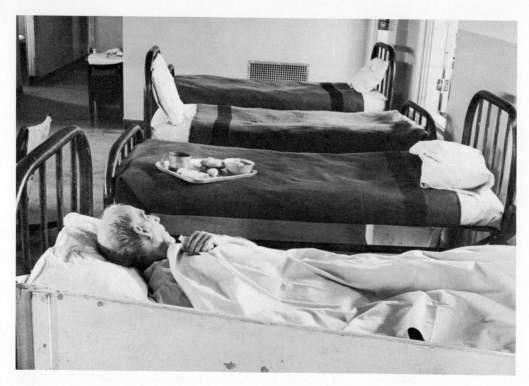

Involutional melancholia is predominately characterized by depression and seems to occur during the climateric period. The despondency, loneliness, and disinterest in food and bodily functions, are illustrated above. (Jerry Cooke)

themselves as a side complication of the endless hair-pulling or picking which occurs during the agitation. Yet, in spite of the generally disturbed overall picture, involutional melancholics retain their orientation and may be aware of their need for treatment. Frequently, a patient will stop in the midst of a delusional outburst to accurately describe the details of an incident which she has just seen.

Dynamics. The climacteric marks a significant period of change in life both physically and psychologically. Hormonal changes occur, and the menopause in women is marked by hot flashes, dizziness, insomnia, and headaches. Psychologically, the individual is faced with what indeed seems to be a change of life. The best years of life have come and are now irrevocably gone. The deeds of the past remain irretrievably in the past and can be relived through reminiscence but never redone in reality. For some, it is viewed as the point at which they no longer face their birth but must now turn about and face their eventual death. Women must come to grips with their faded youth and beauty, no longer a possibility but a reality. Men must cope with their diminished virility and waning strength. Both must cope with their loss of friends through death as increasing age takes its toll. Many grow old gracefully, a number succumb to the involutional psychosis. The most vulnerable appear to be those who are rigid, meticulous, perfectionistic personalities, overconscientious, and narrow in social interests (Gregory, 1961; Haggerty, 1941; Palmer, 1942). Such individuals lack the sufficient flexibility to cope with increasing disappointments or to acquire a new orientation toward life.

Case History 13-2

INVOLUTIONAL MELANCHOLIA

William D. was a successful businessman and vice president of a firm which he had been associated with for 30 years. He was 53 when he was given the responsibility of personally supervising the planning and construction of a new insurance building to house their offices and that of other firms. Although he was not an architect, he entered the challenge with zest, considering the assignment an honor. He worked diligently with planners of other major structures to acquire an overall understanding of the functional characteristics of a well-designed building, and the values associated with outstanding aesthetic qualities. He maintained an active social life as a means of obtaining more information on his and allied projects, even though he often found himself tiring physically. As time progressed, he experienced less and less real satisfaction at the structure that was growing before his very eyes and through his own efforts. He found himself increasingly restless but without knowing why. Soon he started to worry about things, a number of little things that would not have bothered him in the slightest five years ago. First it centered around the row of offices that was to house his firm—he wondered if they were suitable, if they were spacious enough or too ostentatious, if someone else would have done it differently. Then he began to ruminate about his own contributions to the firm in specific and to life in general. He soon felt that he should have been a more active and energetic vice president, closer to his employees. He questioned whether the assignment to supervise the planning of the building was really an honor or whether it was an attempt to "kick him upstairs" and to keep him occupied while the really important decisions were being made. He felt no resentment at this, only a deep sadness at his own ineffectuality. He became more and more morose by the day, and plunged deeper into despondency. He began to retire to bed earlier and sleep later as he felt the wearisome fatigue of age as incentive dissolved. He noticed that he was constipated and speculated as to whether his intestinal tract might be calcifying, but he could not remember whether the intestines could turn into bone or not. On the urge of his wife, he went to his physician and was advised to seek psychiatric hospitalization. Upon reviewing his disturbing set of feelings, he readily admitted that this was the best solution. He received electroshock therapy three times a week for six weeks and was released fully recovered. He is currently eagerly anticipating his eventual retirement, has taken up fishing, and has recently acquired a summer home near the seashore in a community of others also planning for their retirement.

They are what they have always been and their superego will not permit any deviation. Many have been insecure in their adjustment even during the best years of their lives.

Initially, it was believed that involutional melancholia was caused by the hormonal changes which accompany the climacteric. However, the disorder is not responsive to hormonal treatment, and it can occur before the actual physical change of life develops. Somatic symptoms may appear as the typical corollary of the aging process, but there is no connection between the psychosis and any organic pathology or dysfunction. There is some possibility of an inherited component to involutional melancholia. The incidence figure for monozygotic twins is 60.9, 6.0 for dizygotic twins, and 1.0 for the unrelated population (Kallmann, 1950). However, psychopathologists believe that the disorder is essentially a psychological one that is subject to complications from biological and physiological factors.

Treatment. Individuals, of course, should be encouraged to plan ahead for their future; this applies to the early prevention of involutional melancholia as well through the undertaking of a second career, or recreational activities that can be enjoyed later in life. Once the psychosis has been precipitated, then psychiatric treatment is necessary. Prior to electroshock therapy, the involutional disorder was considered a chronic state with a high mortality rate through suicide. With ECT, approximately 80 percent of the agitated depressive types are cured. Its value with the paranoid involutionals is comparatively poorer with only about 50 percent showing improvement. A variety of drugs may be used, especially a combination of tranquilizers and antidepressants. Within a period of from one to two months, improvements will occur if they occur at all. Extensive neurological and physical examination is necessary to rule out or to determine the presence of organic pathology which might need attention. Psychotherapy is oriented toward providing the patient with support and reassurance, an opportunity to rework his value systems and modes of achieving satisfaction, a chance to talk through their disappointments and bitterness, and the development of a new perspective on life.

THE PARANOID DISORDERS

Paranoid disorders are those which are characterized by a thought disorder but where the emotional reactions are still appropriate to the thought content. The thoughts typically reflect suspicion and persecutory delusions but grandiose delusions may also occur. *Paranoia* is a form of paranoid disorder, a very rare psychotic condition. *Paranoid states* are psychoses which differ from paranoia only in that the delusions are neither as highly systematized, nor as elaborate as exist in paranoia. These paranoid disorders differ from paranoid schizophrenia in that the schizophrenic shows a gross disturbance of every aspect of the patient's personality —his emotions, his intellect, his speech, his perceptions. The patient suffering from a paranoid disorder, on the other hand, is able to function adequately, has emotional responses appropriate to his beliefs, does not usually have hallucinations, but is preoccupied with beliefs which are delusional in nature. The paranoid disorders share the following features:

1. Organized delusions of persecution and/or of grandeur.

2. Orientation and emotional reactions normal.

3. Judgment and thinking impaired only in areas of delusion.

4. Reliance upon denial and projection as defense mechanisms.

5. Suspicious and sensitive personality.

6. No fragmentation or deterioration or gross disturbance of personality.

7. Hallucinations rare, although sometimes occur.

Paranoia is extremely rare. In an investigation of 5000 successive admissions, only three authentic cases could be located (Pearson, 1952). *Classical paranoia* as it is sometimes called is generally considered to

'Family Group': Painting by a patient with paranoid features illustrating the inability to see people in comfortable, close relationships. The figures are portrayed as stilted, rigid, and anxiously stiff. The emphasis on the staring, suspicious eyes has sometimes been interpreted as a sign of paranoia.
SOURCE: From J. Plokker, *Art From The Mentally Disturbed*. Courtesy of Mouton & Co., n.v. Publishers, THE HAGUE.

be incurable. The diagnosis is based upon the presence of a highly systematized, involved delusion, and the absence of any other type of mental or emotional disturbance. Hallucinations, for example, are never present. The patient is often average or superior in intellect and is capable of maintaining his delusion without letting it interfere with his everyday functioning. Paranoid states are relatively more common, and even these conditions are not seen too frequently. In fact, some texts no longer discuss the paranoid disorders. Because of the similarities between the two conditions, no attempt will be made to provide a separate discussion for each.

The paranoid disorders tend to begin during the thirties in rigidly organized individuals. The patient becomes increasingly tense until he is living under high levels of anxiety. He soon becomes sensitive to happenings around him, and concerned about the motivation of others, the extent to which he can trust those around him, and the likelihood of being treated badly. The delusional structure typically focuses on that part of the patient's life which is currently dissatisfying. He begins to slowly but systematically form vague suspicions. Before long, he is suddenly convinced that his suspicions have basis in fact, and he develops an "insight" in which everything finally falls neatly into place. The patient now lives in an environment which he "knows" to be hostile. If he centers his delusion around his occupation, he is certain that his work has been altered to make him look incompetent, he is positive that he is being given the worst assignments, he may even suspect that his wife is secretly laughing at his ineptness in his occupation. His notions are never completely unbelievable, and he may be able to find some allies who accept his story. However, the paranoid seldom confides since he seldom trusts. In fact, he expects to be betrayed by nearly everyone. He lives a lonely and jittery life. Nothing is necessarily what it appears to be on the surface. It was only through shrewd observation and careful attention to the most seemingly trivial details that he was able to acquire his insight into the "truth." With this attitude, the paranoid lives a pseudoespionage existence—suspecting everyone, trusting no one, speculating on the significance of everything, seeking to intercept the plot, believing nothing of what he hears without first evaluating the source. Despite the world of false reality in which he lives, the paranoid is fully capable of continuing an active and outwardly normal life. However, where the delusional beliefs are concerned, the patient is adamant about their reality. Arguments and contradictory evidence are received with smug tolerance or scorn, but nevertheless rejected. In some chronic cases the persecutory delusions have reached such dimensions that the patient may be tripped into a burst of hostility or accusation. In others, plans are formulated for an attack on the "enemies" in an attempt to forestall the anticipated assault. It should be stressed that the paranoid retains contact with his social environment by means of his delusions which keep him sensitively aware of his surroundings. Yet, he is not in full communication with others since he is unable to test the reality of his beliefs through sharing them with others. Cameron and Magaret (1951) describe this phenomenon as a pseudo-community which the patient has erected for himself, self-sustaining and self-confirming. Those who people this pseudo-community are all subject to the patient's delusional interpretations of their behavior and intent.

The delusions of the paranoid are typically persecutory in content. However, there are other forms which can be identified and which have sometimes been used as the basis for categorizing paranoia. *Grandiose delusions* may be present ranging from simple convictions that one is specially skilled or talented to the more expansive belief that one is a great spiritual, financial, or scientific genius. Patients with such beliefs possess the zealous fervor that make them useful members of fanatic movements. They may devote endless hours to crusading against smoking, drinking, gambling, Communism, or intellectualism. A patient with *erotic delusions* mistakenly believe that a certain individual is in love with him. Although this other person has never directly said this, the patient finds proof for his delusion in the thousand tiny actions which betray her secret to him. A polite smile or a casual acknowledgment is interpreted as an expression of passion. Most often, the individual chosen is a public figure such as a television actress, movie star, or model. The patient becomes an avid follower of the "lover" and may even deluge her with intimate gifts and passionate letters. Because of this, the police are often called in. In *jealous delusions,* the patient is fitfully certain that his loved one is unfaithful. He focuses his every effort toward obtaining proof of this with the same intensity as the patient with persecutory delusions. He begins to time his wife's trips to the grocers, calls home at unexpected times, and listens in on her conversations with acquaintances. Any delays in her return, unanswered phone calls, or suspicious words, are interpreted with stark meaning.

A bizarre condition that has been discovered is *folie à deux,* a condition in which two persons close to one another develop similar delusions. The most common combination seems to be sister-sister, but husband-wife, and mother-child also appear with regularity. For the most part, the circumstance appears to be more on the order of a psychosis with a pseudo-psychosis than it is the development of two psychotic conditions. Typically, a dominant psychotic person provokes delusions in a dependent, submissive individual. When the dominant person is removed, the dependent one usually recovers within a few months. *Folie à deux* appears most frequently in the form of paranoid disorders or paranoid schizophrenia, with persecutory delusions being the most common type of false beliefs maintained. The condition may include two, three, four, or more persons, with different terms being used in order to identify the numbers of people involved, e.g., *folie à trois* for three, *folie à quatre* for four, etc.

Dynamics

The paranoid delusional structure is the end product of reliance upon denial and projection as defenses. All self-disturbing faults such as hostility are denied, but are then projected onto others to an exaggerated extent. This action has several advantages. The blaming of others distracts the patient from his own guilty possession of the very trait of which he is accusatory. In addition, by establishing that others are hostilely persecuting, the patient permits himself to engage in counteraggression without fear of arousing guilt feelings. Psychoanalytic theory once stressed the belief that the basic component of paranoia was repressed homosexuality (Freud, 1953). The patient feels guilt-ridden and extremely anxious about latent homosexual leanings and copes with it by a two-stage defensive maneuver: first, the denial and use of reaction formation—"I don't love him, I hate him"; then, the projection—"I don't hate him, he hates me." The erotic delusions would be found in patients who do not depend upon the reaction formation defense mechanism but proceed to the stage of "she loves me," thereby justifying his reciprocal love wishes. In grandiose delusions, the denial mechanism is more strongly actuated as the patient refuses to accept his insecurity and deludes himself into a belief in his own superiority.

The paranoid develops his feelings of insecurity, unworthiness, self-condemnation during his formative years of life (Schwartz, 1963). Parental neglect, lack of warmth, and absence from the home, provide a foundation of uncertainty. The home atmosphere itself may be one of threats, abuse, attention to failure, or sadism, thereby encouraging the traits of seclusiveness, sullenness, and watchfulness (Bonner, 1951). Continued experiences of social dissatisfaction fosters further isolation thus preventing the patient from retaining open lines of communication with others. Failures in life increase the threatening sense of inferiority. Lacking a basic feeling of trust for others, and suffering from an inability to learn to understand the motives of others, the patient is forced to rely upon his own

judgments and guesses, inadequate and unrealistic as they are. The more he relies upon his own personal interpretation of the world, and the less he validates his beliefs against the perceptions that other people have, the more he becomes subject to gross distortions which become built upon other distortions. Ultimately, he has progressed to such a delusional state that it is impossible to even contemplate reexamining his earlier premises.

Treatment

The prognosis for the severe cases of paranoid disorders is extremely poor. Their basic distrust, highly organized delusional system, and rationalizations are so firmly imbedded that they are not easily reached. In fact, the patient may exhibit antisocial features and become a participant in assassinations, and international subversive activities. The first aim in treatment is the reduction of the high anxiety level of the patient. The preferred procedure is to induce the paranoid to seek help in a situation with minimal coercion since force and restrictions on activity simply serve to exacerbate the patient's delusions. In milder cases, removal of the everyday stresses surrounding the patient is helpful. If hospitalization is needed, the opportunity to recognize the helping nature of the insitution will aid in decreasing the perception of the hospital as punitive and limiting. Chlorpromazine is the drug chosen in chemotherapy as it often relieves the anxiety and the attending suspiciousness and distrust. On the other hand, barbiturate sedation during the early stages of treatment has been considered an undesirable procedure. Only rarely is electroconvulsive treatment of any value. It may provide temporary relief from the delusions, perhaps through its general disruptive influence, and perhaps because it is seen as a symbolic expiation of guilt. The second aim of treatment is the reestablishment of realistic interpersonal contact. Psychotherapist and patient meet under somewhat less wary conditions. The therapist maintains an attitude of suspended judgment, partly because it is truly difficult to separate fact from delusion, partly to prevent arousing the fear and consequent suspiciousness of the patient. By remaining somewhat detached, the therapist avoids the appearance of being intrusive. The therapeutic condition attempts to establish a relationship of reasonable firm mutual trust such that the patient can reevaluate his perceptions and beliefs. Hopefully, the patient will eventually be able to relinquish his rigid personality patterns and substitute more reality-oriented behaviors. In all cases, the outcome is still viewed with caution by most psychotherapists.

Case History 13-3

PARANOIA

The patient was a 23-year-old graduate student in psychology. He had attended an undergraduate college known for its permissive orientation toward student discipline and class room education. Independent thinking was an earmark of their graduates. The patient acquired his bachelor's degree after five years of academic toil, displaying no great talent other than a tendency toward argumentativeness. Upon entry to graduate work, he showed a disposition toward avoiding assignments in favor of "creative" thinking mostly aimed at refuting accepted scientific principles. His arguments were based on possible but not probable lines of analysis. Facts were often twisted until they fit his preconceptions. He was always quite willing to argue but never willing to listen. At mid-year, he was advised to reconsider his goal in education and encouraged to postpone completion of his degree until he was more certain of his choice of career. He refused to delay his education and continued in the department. Within weeks, a highly intricate delusional system evolved of a persecutory nature. He harbored the belief that the departmental recommendation had been the first step in a plot to distract his progress. He reasoned that he was probably nearing a major scientific discovery which, if publicized, would revolutionize science and make all current scientific theories, from Darwinism to nuclear theory, obsolete. The psychology faculty were simply pawns given the task of preventing him from his imminent contribution. As he pondered his insight, he felt he more clearly understood his undergraduate career. He had been "guided" toward the particular college by those who had recognized his potential genius and who had hoped even then to sidetrack him by subtle brainwashing. Magazine solicitations through the mail were attempts to direct him towards the "right" kind of reading. He believed that it was even possible that his parents were part of the scheme and, with this in mind, he spent long hours in retracing the places they had taken him as a child with the hopes of finding a pattern. He was beside himself with satisfaction when he recognized the telephone repairman coming out of the department chairman's office as the same one who had installed his telephone in his apartment. This link proved

Case History 13-3 (*Continued*)

PARANOIA

---

his suspicion that his telephone wires had been tapped. He was henceforth careful to listen for telltale sounds during his telephone conversations; when he was unable to detect any, he became even more impressed by the technical skills of the wiretappers. Since he was still enrolled in school, his draft board renewed his deferment. This event was taken by the patient to mean that the federal government was deeply involved in the attempt to keep him in a location where he could continue to be surveyed. In a shrewd maneuver, he decided to "play the game" and not reveal his newfound knowledge. Instead, he became the model student and impressed the faculty in his more controlled, seemingly attentive, and mild manner. He continued to apply his above average intellect to his schoolwork and was doing relatively well. In an attempt to impress the department and to "lull them into a false sense of confidence," he joined in a group psychotherapy program. During the fourth meeting, he became excited by the "revelations" he thought he detected in another member's comments, and announced in a tone of mixed anger and pride that he could no longer be treated as a fool and that he would expose the whole plot and work on his scientific discovery besides! He eventually entered more intensive individual treatment but at this date still maintains some mild suspicions that the therapist—a psychologist—is also involved in the plot.

Glossary

Affective disorders: Psychotic disorders characterized by disturbances of the emotions. Includes manic-depressive psychosis, psychotic depression, and involutional melancholia.

Autism: The excessive preoccupation with fantasy without concern or interest for the realities of life.

Decompensation: Disorganization of personality functioning due to excessive stresses.

Delusions: Beliefs that are strongly maintained in the face of contradictory evidence.

Delusion of grandeur: A delusion that one is of extraordinary ability or in some other way important.

Delusion of persecution: A delusion that harm or hardships are being inflicted on a person by others.

Echolalia: The repetition of the speech of others, symptomatic of some psychotic disorders.

Echopraxia: The automatic repetition of the actions of others, symptomatic of some psychotic disorders.

Flight of ideas: The rapid succession of ideas outside the control of the individual.

Folie à deux: The affliction of two close associates of the same mental disorder at the same time.

Hallucinations: Sensory perceptions without the presence of an external stimulus.

Ideas of reference: A delusion that events and circumstances and people are making references to the individual.

Involutional melancholia: An affective psychotic disorder occurring around the climacteric and characterized by severe depression.

Manic-depressive psychosis: An affective psychotic disorder characterized by cycles of disturbance followed by improvement. In the manic condition, the patient is hyperactive; in the depressed condition, the patient is plagued by extreme dejection and self-accusation.

Neologism: The coining of a new word or term.

Paranoia: A form of paranoid disorder characterized by systematized delusions and the absence of other emotional or intellectual disturbance.

Paranoid disorders: Psychotic disorders characterized by delusional disturbances but where the emotional reactions are appropriate to the thought content. Includes paranoia and the paranoid states.

Paranoid schizophrenia: A form of schizophrenia involving delusions of persecution along with gross disturbances of the emotions, intellect, and adaptive functioning.

Paranoid states: A form of paranoid disorder characterized by delusions that are less systematized or elaborate than those of paranoia.

Pseudocommunity: The fantasized view of the world constructed by a psychotic person in place of the real community around him.

Psychosis: A severe form of mental illness involving a profound break with reality and a marked impairment of adjustment.

Psychotic depression: An affective psychotic disorder that lacks the cyclical characteristic of the manic-depressive psychosis.

Spontaneous recovery: In mental illness, this refers to the remission of symptoms without treatment.

Stupor: The lack of mobility or responsiveness to the environment in any expressive fashion.

References

Abraham, K. Notes on the psycho-analytical investigation and treatment of manic-depressive insanity and allied conditions. In K. Abraham, *Selected papers on psycho-analysis.* London: Hogarth Press, 1949. Initially published in 1911.

Arieti, S. The decline of manic-depressive psychosis: its significance in the light of dynamic and social psychiatry. Paper read in Chicago at the 113th annual meeting of the American Psychiatric Association, 1957.

Arieti, S. Manic-depressive psychosis. In S. Arieti (Ed.), *American handbook of psychiatry.* New York: Basic Books, 1959.

Banse, J. Zum Problem der Erbprognosebestimmung: die Erkrankungsaussichten der Vettern und Basen von Manisch-Depressiven. *A. ges. Neurol. Psychiat.* 1929, **119**, 576.

Beck, A. *Depression.* New York: Harper & Row, 1967.

Becker, J. Achievement related characteristics of manic-depressives. *J. soc. Psychol.,* 1960, **60**, 334.

Bonner, H. The problem of diagnosis in paranoic disorders. *Amer. J. Psychiat.,* 1951, **107**, 677.

Cameron, N. & Magaret, A. *Behavior pathology.* Boston: Houghton Mifflin, 1951.

Eaton, J. & Weil, R. *Culture and mental disorders; a comparative study of the Hutterities and other populations.* Glencoe, Illinois: Free Press, 1955.

Elässer, G. *Die nachkommen geisteskranker Elternpaare.* New York: Grune & Stratton, 1952.

Flach, F. & Regan, P. *Chemotherapy in emotional disorders.* New York: McGraw-Hill, 1960.

Freud, S. *The standard edition of the complete psychological works.* J. Strachey (Ed.) London: Hogarth Press, 1953.

Freud, S. Mourning and melancholia. In *The standard edition of the complete psychological works of Sigmund Freud.* London: Hogarth Press, 1953. Initially published in 1917.

Gibson, R. The family background and early life experience of the manic-depressive patient: a comparison with the schizophrenic patients. *Psychiat.,* 1958, **21**, 71.

Gibson, R., Cohen, M., & Cohen, R. On the dynamics of the manic-depressive personality. *Amer. J. Psychiat.,* 1959, **115**, 1101.

Gold, H. Observations on cultural psychiatry during a world tour of mental hospitals. *Amer. J. Psychiat.,* 1951, **108**, 462.

Gregory, I. *Psychiatry, biological and social.* Philadelphia: Saunders, 1961.

Grinker, R. et al. *The phenomena of depressions.* New York: Harper, 1961.

Haggerty, H. Pre-psychotic personality traits in women with involutional melancholia. *Smith College stud. soc. Work,* 1941, **12**, 191.

Hastings, D. Follow-up results in psychiatric illness. *Amer. J. Psychiat.,* 1958, **114**, 1057.

Helgason, T. The frequency of depressive states in Iceland as compared with the other Scandinavian countries. *Acta psychiat. Scand. Suppl. 162,* 1961, **37**, 81.

Hollingshead, A. & Redlich, F. Social class and mental illness. New York: Wiley, 1958.

Kalinowsky, L. & Hoch, P. *Shock treatments and other somatic procedures in psychiatry.* New York: Grune & Stratton, 1946.

Kalinowsky, L. & Hoch, P. *Somatic treatments in psychiatry: pharmacotherapy, convulsive, insulin, surgical and other methods.* New York: Grune & Stratton, 1961.

Kallmann, F. The genetic of psychoses: an analysis of 1,232 twin index families. *Congr. int. Psychiat. Rapports,* 1950, **6**, 1.

Kallmann, F. *Heredity in health and mental disorder.* New York: Norton, 1953.

Kallmann, F., Falek, A., Hurzeler, M., & Erlenmeyer-Kimling, L. The developmental aspects of children with two schizophrenic parents. *Psychiat. Res. Rep., Amer. Psychiat. Assoc.,* 1964, **19**, 136.

Kraepelin, E. *Psychiatrie: Ein lehrbuch für studierende und ärtze.* Leipzig: Barth, 1896.

Kretschmer, E. *Physique and character.* New York: Harcourt, 1925.

Kretschmer, E. *A textbook of medical psychology.* London: Oxford, 1934.

Lewis, A. Inheritance of mental disorders. *Eugenic Rev.,* 1933, **25**, 79.

Luxenburger, H. Das zirkulare Irresein. In A. Gutt (Ed.), *Handbuch der Erbkrankheiten.* Vol. 4. Leipzig: Thieme, 1942.

Palmer, H. Involutional psychoses: melancholia. *Pub. Hlth. Rep.* (Suppl. 168) Wash., D.C., 1942, 118.

Plokker, J. *Art from the mentally disturbed.* Boston: Little, Brown & Co. 1965.

Pollitt, J. *Depression and its treatment.* Illinois: C.C. Thomas, 1965.

Rennie, T. Prognosis in manic-depressive psychosis. *Amer. J. Psychiat.,* 1942, **98**, 801.

Robins, E., Murphy, G., Wilkinson, R., Glassner, S., & Kayes, J. Some clinical considerations in the prevention of suicide based on a study of 134 successful suicides. *Amer. J. Pub. Hlth.,* 1959, **49**, 888.

Sainsbury, P. Suicide in later life. *Geront. Clin.,* 1962, 4, 161.

Schwartz, D. A review of the "paranoid" concept. *Gen. Psychiat.,* 1963, **8**, 349.

Seager, C. & Flood, R. Suicide in Bristol. *Br. J. Psychiat.,* 1965, **111**, 919.

Silverman, C. *The epidemiology of depression.* Baltimore: Johns Hopkins Press, 1968.

Spiro, J. The African mind in health and disease. A study in ethnopsychiatry. Geneva: World Health Organization, 1953, no. 17. Culture, psychiatry and the written word. *Psychiat.,* 1959, **22**, 307.

Watts, C. *Depressive disorders in the community.* Bristol: John Wright & Sons, 1966.

14 *The Schizophrenic Disorders*

Schizophrenia involves those psychotic disorders characterized by withdrawal from reality, disturbance in emotional appropriateness and bizarre speech, thought, and motor symptoms. Delusions and hallucinations occur. Kraepelin is credited with first grouping the schizophrenic disorders together on the basis of what he perceived to be a common characteristic—dementia following progressive deterioration. He distinguished the three types of schizophrenia—hebephrenic, paranoid, and catatonic, and accepted the recommendation by Bleuler to add the simple type. During Kraepelin's time, the term *dementia praecox* was used to refer to this illness—dementia meaning mental deterioration, and praecox referring to the early age of onset. Bleuler did not believe that dementia praecox necessarily progressed toward dementia, but proposed that it was mainly characterized by a splitting of personality. Upon his suggestion the new term schizophrenia—*schizin,* to divide or split, and *phren,* the mind (Greek)—has supplanted the old Kraepelinian label. This set of disorders is one of the most severe of the major psychiatric disturbance. Twenty-to-twenty-three percent of all new admissions to mental hospitals are diagnosed as schizophrenics, that is, about *one out of every five* patients

suffer from the symptoms of this syndrome. It arouses particular concern because it can begin quite early in life, mostly during the twenties, and can well continue uncured for the remainder of the patient's life. The alarming fact is that the average length of hospitalization for the schizophrenic is 13 years, a period equivalent to the sentence imposed for a major crime. Although the entry rate of schizophrenics is about one out of five, one out of every two patients in the hospital at any time is schizophrenic because of the tendency of these patients to accumulate since the rate of recovery is so slow. It is indeed startling to recognize that 25 percent of all hospital beds in all types of hospitals in the United States are occupied by schizophrenics. This syndrome is a severe burden on both the individual patient and society as a whole. The figures alone are awesome, but none can adequately represent the deep personal loss to all who are in the slightest bit concerned about the dignity of humanity. In addition, despite the immensity of the problem of schizophrenia, very little real progress has been made toward a conclusive understanding of the origins of the syndrome or its treatment.

The label schizophrenia has been used to classify certain subgroups of mental disorders, although currently it is acknowledged that a single classification may be used more for convenience than as a result of scientific necessity. Thus, there is some possibility that "schizophrenia" should really be "the schizophrenias" with the nomenclature being used to merely indicate a comparability of symptoms but not necessarily etiology, in the same vein as the term "affective disorders" is sometimes used. In fact, there is some evidence that there exist two classes of schizophrenia, the *process* and the *reactive*. *Process schizophrenia* (Kantor, Wallner, and Winder, 1956) follows the traditional pattern involving early psychological trauma, poor home environment, unstable prepsychotic personality, and severe deterioration. The *reactive schizophrenia* is used to refer to patients who came from a normal family setting, who enjoyed adequate interpersonal adjustment in adolescence, who suddenly became psychotic, who show relatively mild symptoms, and whose prognosis is generally rather good. The theory that has evolved from this distinction is that process schizophrenia represents the classical type—an inherited, organic disease that has an insidious onset and that progresses inexorably toward deterioration; the reactive form may be an altogether different syndrome and not rightly a "schizophrenia" as evidenced by its acute or sudden onset, limited symptoms, and good response to treatment. Brackbill and Fine (1956) have contributed evidence that shows the process schizophrenic to be similar to organic patients in Rorschach personality test performance whereas the reactive schizophrenics showed few signs of organic damage.

Until a more productive system can be developed, the current grouping on the basis of commonality of symptoms must be continued. There are today some nine types of disorders classified as schizophrenic disorders: the simple, hebephrenic, catatonic, paranoid, childhood, acute un-

differentiated, chronic undifferentiated, schizo-affective, and residual. In addition, ambulatory schizophrenia, the pseudo-psychopathic form, the acute confusional type, pseudoneurotic schizophrenia, and even a "three-day" schizophrenia, have also been identified. These types of schizophrenia share the following characteristics:

1. Seclusiveness and withdrawal—the patient shows a narrowing of interest in the social environment and in his surroundings.

2. Disturbance of emotions—there is a shallowness or blunting of affect, an altering of emotional reactions such that the emotional tone is not appropriate to the circumstance.

3. Autistic thinking—private fantasy occupies the patient's time, thereby displacing attention from reality.

4. Bizarre behavior—the patient demonstrates a grotesque quality to his actions, including peculiarities in gesture and posture.

5. Sensory disturbances — hallucinations, especially auditory and distortions of body sensations or perceptions occur.

6. Delusions—at least 71 percent of schizophrenics have been reported to have delusions, mainly of the persecutory variety but also including delusions of grandeur, ideas of reference, sexual, religious, and hypochondriacal beliefs (Lucas, Sansbury, and Collins, 1962).

7. Disturbance of speech and thought —speech is seemingly evasive, sentences may be made up of sequences of unrelated words *(word-salad)*, neologisms may develop, or the patient may become mute. Thinking may be blocked, associations become bizarre or confused.

Of the several types of schizophrenic disorders, the more commonly known are the four accepted by Kraepelin—the simple, hebephrenic, catatonic, paranoid—

and the schizo-affective. These five types will be discussed in the following sections.

SIMPLE SCHIZOPHRENIA

The *simple type of schizophrenia* takes place in a gradual insidious fashion, starting as early as adolescence. Because the symptoms are not dramatic in nature, many are able to live without being suspected of their illness, although they are instead accused of being shiftless, lazy, eccentric, ne'er-do-wells. The primary symptom is the increasing lack of involvement or interest in the surroundings. The patient appears to be listless, apathetic, inattentive to school or work commitments. He becomes more and more seclusive and aloof, preferring the privacy of his own room. He will answer questions but prefers not to converse. He is capable of achieving, but he chooses to limit his activities, refuses to participate, and is indifferent to demands. His speech is seen by others as evasive, but it is more accurate to say that he just does not bother to communicate properly. He seems to be obstinate, irritable, and moody. His apathy and lack of concern about what others think or want continues and extends to his personal habits, choice of clothes, and school performance. He may refuse to bathe or comb his hair, dresses sloppily, and performs with such little concern that he is mistakenly considered mentally retarded. There are no delusions, ideas of reference, or hallucinations. The family soon becomes used to his curious traits and tends to describe him as "shy," "unassertive," "poor in heterosexual relations," or at the worst, as "shiftless," "odd," or "eccentric." A number leave their families and make their way in the world in the least demanding role possible; thus many filter into the ranks of the hobo, the tramp, or the prostitute. In fact, vagrancy is one of the most prominent factors which call them to medical attention.

HEBEPHRENIC SCHIZOPHRENIA

This is the most regressed form of the major psychoses of psychogenic origin. This type of patient is known for his childish silliness. He shows uncontrollable fits of giggling, uninhibited gestures, and grotesque grimaces. This bizarre behavior often makes others uncomfortable because it is so unlike the controlled and meaningful actions of others, even other patients. The hebephrenic's activities are weird and appear totally without sense, it is as if a harlequin were deliberately mimicking a madman. Speech patterns reflect the severity of the personality disturbance as the patient babbles incoherently, uses neologisms, repeats words or meaningless phrases, or engages in word-salad. The patient often seems to be totally in his own private world with his own private meanings. He may laugh hilariously for hours, or smile secretly when asked a question. Hallucinations are common, and typically seem to evoke pleasant reactions. Delusions are in keeping with the overall good mood and tend to be grandiose. Other moods can appear and some experts have suggested that these represent different subgroups of hebephrenia—the silly and giggling variety, a depressed type, an apathetic subgroup, and an autistic excitable subgroup. Depending upon the subgroup, the patient may show childish behavior, complaining hypochondriacal concerns, apathetic detachment, or excited paranoid beliefs. Obscenities and feces smearing are likely symptoms. One is tempted to compare the hebephrenic to a very young child in his temperament, poor self-control, and behavior.

CATATONIC SCHIZOPHRENIA

This is possibly the most dramatic form of schizophrenia. The disturbance is exhibited primarily in motor symptoms. The

A *catatonic* patient exhibiting the catatonic stuporous state in which bizarre postures are maintained for long periods. (Ed Lattau)

ity). The phenomenon of waxy flexibility has an unbelievable quality—patients will remain holding awkward and what appears to be physically impossible positions for hours. This extreme suggestibility is also noticeable in speech. The patient may demonstrate *echolalia,* repeating everything he hears. On the other hand, the opposite may occur and the catatonic patient may instead show an extreme *negativism.* Instead of being molded into a position, he resists being moved; instead of doing what he is told to do, he does the exact opposite. An apathetic contrariness seems to replace the suggestibility. There is some evidence that the catatonic may be highly aware of his surroundings rather than inattentive during the stuporous condition. Some patients report that they hear with extreme acuity although they had failed to show earlier any outward evidence of their alertness. The catatonic may recover from the stuporous stage and go into a *catatonic excitement.* This stage is characterized by violent aggressive and destructive outbursts. The inhibited, immobile, quiet phase is suddenly shattered by impulsive, intense, noisy, agitated movement. The stuporous patient may suffer injury in stiff and swollen limbs from their long immobility or cut off circulation from awkward postures; the excited patient may suffer injury during a fit of self-destructive frenzy or an attack on the environment. Despite the seemingly severe state that must seem present when one reviews the stuporous and excitement symptoms, catatonic schizophrenia has a much better outlook for recovery than any other type of schizophrenia.

PARANOID SCHIZOPHRENIA

Paranoid schizophrenia is the most common form of the schizophrenic disorders. These patients tend to be, on the average, brighter than other schizophrenics; how-

patient may evidence a stuporous condition, or he may display excitement, or the two may alternate. During the *catatonic stupor,* the patient seems to be in a state of physical suspension. He is usually mute, unresponsive to even uncomfortable stimulation, and immobile. He may have to be tube fed, and assisted with bladder and bowel movement. Saliva can sometimes be observed dribbling out of the mouth as the patient does not swallow. The immobility may take the form of retention of a fixed position (*catalepsy*) or the retention of any posture in which someone else places him (*waxy flexibil-*

ever, because of their mental breakdown they are also often unable to make full use of their intellect. As the term suggests, the paranoid is most distinguishable for his delusions. The delusions are more often the persecutory variety with the patient believing that he is the center of a carefully devised plot (see Fig. 14-1). He may believe that the Communists are after him, or the F.B.I., or gangsters, or dope peddlers, or a secret society, or a business combine after his knowledge. He might complain that his food is being slowly poisoned, or that he is being followed, or talked about, or controlled by strange scientific equipment such as an "automatic electric cosmic-ray machine." The paranoid schizophrenic might also possess delusions of grandeur, particularly if he is a European. In a sense, the delusion of grandeur and the delusion of persecution go hand in hand. Being persecuted implies that one is special enough to be the center of a plot and all the attention. The corporation combine is after you because you have the secret to a revolutionary process, someone is trying to control your thoughts because you have great hidden powers, the secret society is after you perhaps because you are possessed of dangerous knowledge. After all, the paranoid may think, they persecuted Jesus Christ, plotted against the mighty Caesars, and assassinated the president. It is only a short step for the patient to begin believing that he is someone really special, perhaps the Prophet, a Disciple, or even Jesus Christ returned. The opposite delusional development might also occur, starting with the delusion of grandeur and progressing toward persecutory beliefs. In this event, the adage "Uneasy lies the head that wears the crown" applies. The patient believes himself to be a great person, begins to feel misunderstood and unrecognized, and soon develops the insight that a plot is underway to dethrone him. Sirhan Sirhan, the assassin of Senator

Sirhan B. Sirhan, the assassin of Senator Robert Kennedy, was diagnosed as being a *paranoid schizophrenic* who believed himself to be the savior of his people. (Wide World Photos)

Robert F. Kennedy, was suffering from paranoid schizophrenia and preoccupied with the delusion that he was to be the savior of the Arab people. There is also evidence that he experienced spells of terror released under hypnosis. These types of delusions are similar to those of the paranoid disorders, the major difference between the paranoid disorders and paranoid schizophrenia is the greater disintegration of personality of the latter. The paranoid psychotic can manage to get along in the everyday world since there is no gross fragmentation, his orientation and intellect are preserved, and hallucinations rarely occur which call attention to him. On the other hand, the paranoid *schizophrenic* does show major disturbance in his functioning and is unable to carry on long without treatment. Hallucinations are common in paranoid schizophrenia, often taking the form of vivid auditory hallucinations. Voices speak to him, or command him, or curse him. The paranoid schizophrenic may become

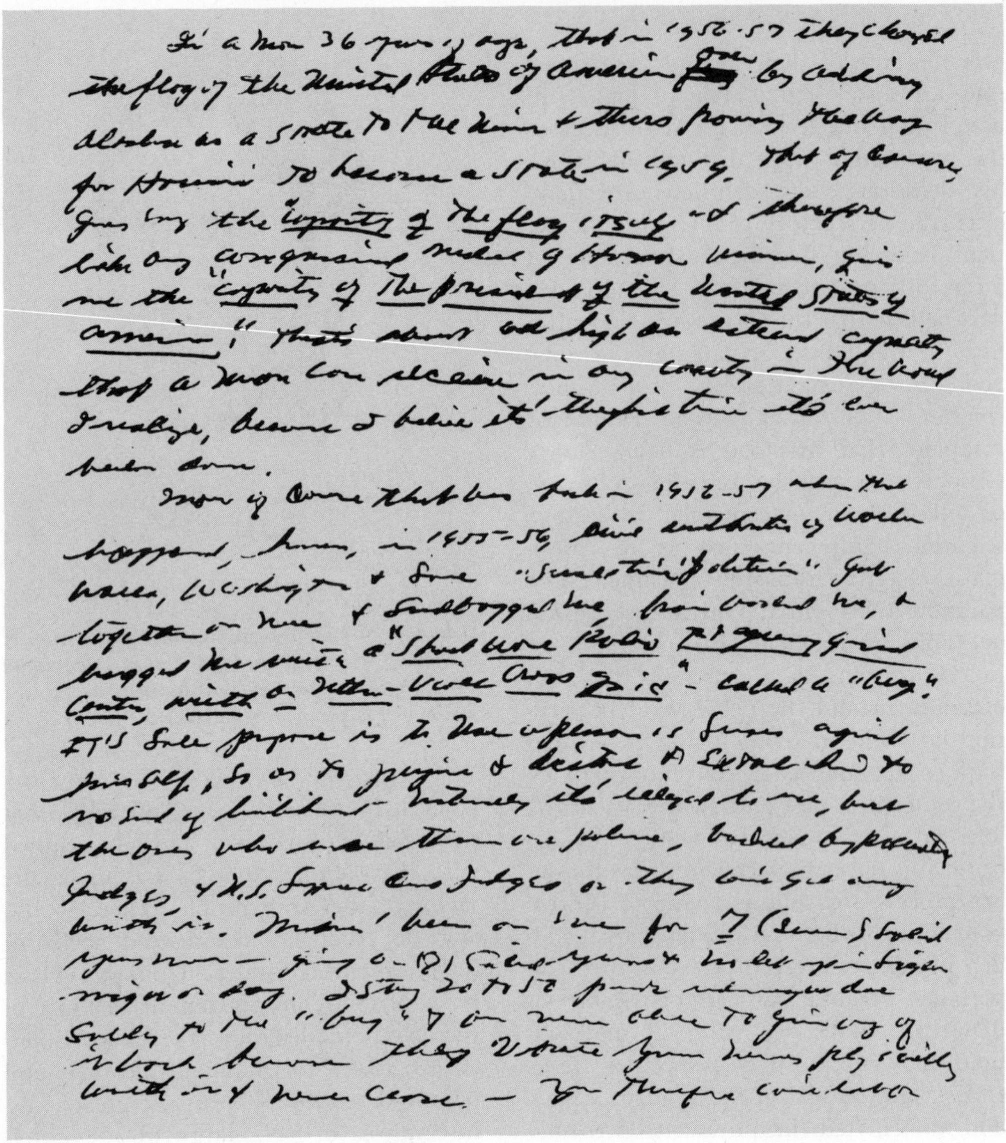

Figure 14-1. A letter received from a mentally disturbed person illustrating delusions of grandeur and persecution. The text of the letter is as follows:

I'm a man 36 years of age, that in 1956-57 they changed the flag of the United States of America once by adding Alaska as a State to the Union and thus paving the way for Hawaii to become a state in 1959. That of course, gives me the *"capacity of the flag itself"* and therefore like any Congressional Medal of Honor winner, gives me the *"capacity of the President of the United States of America,"* that's about as high an esteem capacity that a man can receive in any country. . . .

. . . in 1955-56 civil authorities . . . some "small time" politicians got together on me and sandbagged me and brainwashed me and bugged me with a *"short-wave* Radio grid center, with an ultra-Violet Cross Grid" called a "bug." It's sole purpose is to use a person's senses against himself, so as to perjure and distort him to no end of humiliation . . . they vibrate your nerves physically with it and never ceases.

. . . I'd been there several months before they gave me "ground privileges" and once on the grounds, they started frequencing my time all the more, vibrating the back of my neck, first flicking it to the front of my face, like a "whip" or a cat of 9 tails, . . .

destructive or homicidal in response to his hallucinations or his delusions. In spite of his suspicious and often antagonistic attitude, he is still more in contact with his environment than other schizophrenic types. In a way, the simple schizophrenic is *apathetic* to the environment, the hebephrenic *ignores* all but his own peculiar environment, the catatonic *inhibits* his spontaneous reactions to the environment, and the paranoid *grips* and warily inspects it in his delusions.

SCHIZO-AFFECTIVE SCHIZOPHRENIA

This form is a cross between a schizophrenic disorder and an affective disorder. These are patients with the same features of schizophrenia but one—instead of showing a general blunting of emotions, they show a pronounced and exaggerated mood similar to the manic-depressive psychosis. Elation or depression appear mixed in with bizarre thoughts and hallucinations. Feelings of guilt and despondency interact with disturbances of reality contact. As the disorder progresses, the schizophrenic features become increasingly dominant while the manic-depressive aspects decline. Although Kallmann (1953) has evidence which suggests that the two disorders are genetically distinct and tend to be mutually exclusive, the schizo-affective psychosis appears to be an exception. Bellak (1958) offers the theory that psychiatric disorders exist on a continuum from mental health through psychoneurosis and conduct disorder to manic-depressive psychosis and ultimately terminating in schizophrenia. This would explain the schizo-affective psychosis as the transitional point in the patient's progression through the manic-depressive condition to the schizophrenic disorder. On the other hand, the viewpoint fails to account for the pseudoneurotic schizophrenics and the pseudopsychopathic schizophrenics, groups who appear to be on the way from a neurotic

or conduct disorder condition directly to the schizophrenic state and apparently bypassing the manic-depressive stage. It is possible to argue that the schizo-affective diagnosis is an artifact of misdiagnosis, that is, a more accurate patient evaluation would identify him as either schizophrenic or manic-depressive. This argument would maintain that the classification has no real value. However, there is some data that tends to refute this position. Clark and Mallett (1963) reviewed the records of patients three years after discharge from a mental institution. The data indicated that a fifth of the depressed patients (psychotic depression) required rehospitalization, about one-half of the schizo-affective patients, and nearly three-fourths of the schizophrenic patients. This permits the conclusion that the prognosis for the psychotic depressions is relatively good while the presence of schizophrenia is unfavorable. Moreover, the diagnosis of a mixed condition, the schizo-affective category, is valuable in prognosis which tends to be midway between that for schizophrenia and that for depressions.

Dynamics

Schizophrenia, under one name or another, has been with us for over sixty years and still there is no conclusive information on the etiology or causation of the illness. However, there are many clues and more scientifically sound evidence which lend support to various hints than there was when Kraepelin first organized attention around dementia praecox. Kraepelin and Bleuler both believed that a *genetic* background was a necessary condition interacting with subsequent psychological factors to produce schizophrenia. Kallmann and Slater have provided evidence supporting this view (Kallmann, 1946; Slater, 1947). As mentioned in Chapter 3, Kallmann discovered that:

1. The offspring of two schizophrenic

parents is 68[1] times more likely to develop schizophrenia than the offspring of normal parents.

2. With one parent schizophrenic, the risk of the child also becoming schizophrenic is still over 16 times that of a normal union.

3. The incidence of schizophrenia in relatives of a schizophrenic patient increases rapidly, the closer the blood relationship:

> Half-siblings show a 7 percent incidence.
> Full-siblings show a 14 percent incidence.
> Monozygotic twins show an 86 percent incidence (Fig. 14-2).

Even when monozygotic twins have been reared in different home environments, the incidence of illness has still been impressive—78 percent of the twins share a schizophrenic breakdown. Kallmann concludes that schizophrenia is genetically determined by the single-factor inheritance of a recessive type. On the whole, many other investigators of genetics in schizophrenia across the world tend to agree with Kallmann, including Böök (1953), Hurst (1951), and Stromgren (1948). On the other hand, others such as Pastore, Bellak, and Jackson, have criticized the genetic studies on statistical and methodological grounds. For example, Pastore questioned Kallmann's statistical analysis technique, Bellak felt that the selection of patients for study was biased, and Jackson raised questions over the validity of twin studies and the accuracy of diagnostic methods (Pastore, 1949; Bellak, 1948; Jackson, 1960).

The *constitutional* hypothesis regarding schizophrenia had its origin with Kretschmer (1925). He believed that schizo-

phrenics tended to be aesthenic, and observed that two-thirds of those he studied were of this body type or athletic in constitution. As will be recalled from Chapter 6, Betz (1942), Rees (1943), Bellak and Holt (1948), Moore and Hsu (1946), and Morris (1951), all reported a greater proportion of the narrow, slender body build among nonparanoid schizophrenics, in different parts of the world. In addition, the data seems to show that the paranoid schizophrenic is more likely to be mesomorphic, that is, athletic in build (Morris, 1951; Wittman et al., 1948; Kline and Tenny, 1950). However, Rees (1957) reviewed the research literature and concluded that the constitutional hypothesis of Kretschmer could only be considered partially supported. For example, Kline and Tenny (1950) examined 455 male schizophrenics and found 26 percent to be ectomorphic (aesthenic) but 13 percent were endomorphic (pyknic), a body type supposedly associated with manic-depressive psychosis and not schizophrenia. In the light of the availability of a refined measurement technique for body typing developed by Sheldon et al. (1954), the constitutional hypothesis is a hopeful one if it can deal more satisfactorily with the many criticisms raised. It is intriguing to note that Kline and Oppenheim (1952) found that those schizophrenics with the theoretically unexpected body type, the endomorphs, had a poorer prognosis. If somatotyping proves unable to contribute much toward understanding the origins of schizophrenia, maybe it can prove a valuable means for determining the outcome with treatment.

The *Russian* research on schizophrenia again demonstrates the domination of psychology by Pavlovian theory. The views of Ivan Petrovitch Pavlov, the great discoverer of classical conditioning and one of the earliest to establish the conditions for experimental neurosis, were centered around the study of inhibition and exci-

---

[1] A recent summary shows that this figure ranges from 40 to 71 (Kallmann, Falek, Hurzeler, and Erlenmeyer-Kimling, 1964).

tation. He hypothesized that *protective inhibition* is a state induced in the brain by intense or prolonged stimulation. Any area that is thereby inhibited causes excitation to appear in other regions. Protective inhibition weakens excitatory and inhibitory responses in the region that it encompasses. This state is a result of physical illness, drugs, shock, and perhaps constitutional vulnerability. Schizophrenia is conceived of as a disorder involving protective inhibition in the cerebral cortex. The catatonic stupor, for example, is viewed as a result of the inhibition spreading to the sympathetic nervous system. The catatonic excitement is the result of the protective inhibition acting to depress the normal cortical control over behavior in a fashion similar to the depressive results of alcohol (which "stimulates" behavior by depressing or removing the inhibitions). Among the data on schizophrenics which lends support to this hypothesis are the following:

1. Electroencephalograms (EEGs) show a blocking of normal alpha waves in a resting state and no reaction to auditory and visual stimulation in simple and catatonic schizophrenics. Paranoid schizophrenics showed a diminished alpha rhythm, increased EEG activity with mild stimulation, but no reaction to intense stimulation (Gavrilova, 1960).

2. Pupillary reflex responses are abnormal in schizophrenics. Sounds, olfactory stimulation, and hot and cold pricks, were found to cause pupillary dilation in normals. But 75 percent of hebephrenics, simple, and paranoid schizophrenics studied showed either no pupillary reaction or greatly inhibited response to the same conditions (Streltsova, 1955).

3. Schizophrenics, especially catatonic schizophrenics, are extremely slow to learn under operant learning training where verbal reinforcement is used. In addition, stable learning under classical conditioning methods have also been troublesome to establish (Dobrzhanskaya, 1955). These are in contrast to the work of Taylor and Spence (1954), which indicated that schizophrenics showed a more rapid eyelid conditioning, and the experiment of Lair (1954) showing schizophrenics to improve

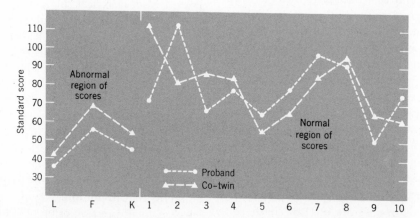

Figure 14-2. **Personality test profile of an identical twin pair showing the marked similarity of traits. CODE: The higher the score, the greater the degree of pathology. L, F, K–Validity scales; 1–Hypochondriasis; 2–Depression; 3–Hysteria; 4–Psychopathic deviate; 5–Masculine/ feminine interests; 6–Paranoia; 7–Psychasthenia; 8–Schizophrenia; 9–Social introversion.**
SOURCE: Reprinted from *Roche Report—Frontiers of Hospital Psychiatry,* Vol. 3, No. 6, March 15, 1966, with permission of Hoffmann-LaRoche Inc.

in performance under positive reinforcement to a greater extent than when reproved or given no information on their progress.

It is of interest to observe that the Russian data identifies a small group of patients with increased rather than decreased sympathetic nervous system reactivity. This group includes those schizophrenics with agitated, confused, delirious symptoms, as well as the paranoid schizophrenics, who tend to react with increased defensive reactions.

A number of *biophysiologically* oriented viewpoints deserve to be recalled (more detailed discussion may be found in Chapter 6). Biochemical toxins in the patient's brain has been considered a possible source of psychosis. Among such toxins examined are ceruloplasmin, taraxein, and serotonin. The discovery of the psychotomimetic drugs such as LSD and mescaline has added impetus to this hypothesis. Endocrine malfunctioning has also been pursued. Pincus and Hoagland (1950), for example, have proposed that the schizophrenic shows a deviation from the normal endocrine adaptation to stress. They found that patients tended to show an underreactivity of the adrenals to experimentally induced physiological and psychological stress. Adrenal functioning has been considered a critical mechanism for the adequate response to stress. Unfortunately, there are still some uncertainties which make this line of research as yet inconclusive. Organic impairment has been suggested by some, with some evidence for this appearing in Brackbill and Fine's (1956) data showing a similarity between the organic patients and the process schizophrenics on Rorschach performance. Davis (1940) reported a disorganized EEG pattern as appearing frequently in schizophrenic patients; however, Hill (1957) reviewed the literature and concluded that there is little con-

clusive evidence for a common organic pathology. In a similar fashion, the search for signs of neuropathology of the brain has proven thus far inconclusive and fruitless. Examination of layers of the brain taken from biopsy or autopsy specimens has not revealed any morphological changes unique to schizophrenia (Wolf and Cowen, 1952). Heath's initial investigations (which ultimately led him to the discovery of taraxein) were directed toward neurophysiology. He and his colleagues felt that the septal region of the brain malfunctioned, thereby impairing subcortical integration and emotions. They noted abnormal EEG recordings from electrodes directly implanted in the septal region in psychotic humans. These abnormal spikes appeared when the psychotic symptoms were exacerbated either through the use of psychotomimetic drugs or through the direct electrical stimulation of an area connected with the septal area (Heath, 1964; Heath and Guerrero-Figueroa, 1965; Krakoff, 1961). The septal region has sometimes been nicknamed the "pleasure center of the brain" from Olds' work which demonstrated that rats will continue to perform where their only reward is an electrical shock to the septal region. It is as if the stimulation to the septal region produces a pleasant sensation that induces the animals to continue to work for it (Olds and Milner, 1954). Meehl (1962) has proposed that the schizophrenic has an imbalance between "pleasure" and "aversive" centers in the brain such that the aversive areas overcome the pleasure centers during activities involving interaction with other persons. Pleasure thereby becomes restricted to cognitive or aesthetic, that is, noninterpersonal, experiences. A final direction of biophysiological research which deserves mention is the dream deprivation studies. As described in Chapter 7, sleep deprivation leads to the exacerbation of illness in chronic schizophrenics with the regression to symptoms

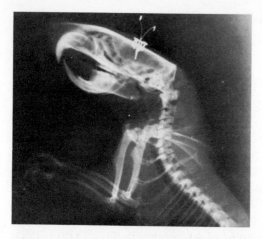

Animal research involving electrode implants has identified the *septal region* of the brain as an important area in emotions. The x-ray photograph (*above left*) shows the implanted electrodes in a rat brain. The animal (*above right*) is depressing a treadle to obtain electrical stimulation of the brain; some animals will shock themselves for 24 hours without rest and as often as 5000 times an hour. (Dr. James Olds/California Institute of Technology)

that had once been removed (Karanyi and Lehman, 1960). Normal subjects deprived of dreams but not all sleep showed increases in anxiety (Dement, 1960). A theoretical interpretation is that certain biochemical processes occur during dreaming which are necessary for normal personality functioning; any interference with these processes can therefore lead to pathology.

Sociocultural factors have also come under investigation as possible contributors to schizophrenia. Social class has been examined as a possible variable, dating back to the classic work of Faris and Dunham (1939), which showed a high incidence of schizophrenia in those parts of the city marked by low economic status. Occupational level can be used as an index of social class. A number of studies have confirmed the inverse relationship between the rate of schizophrenia and occupational level. For example, the highest proportion of patients were found in unskilled jobs in studies by Nolan (1917), Frumkin (1952), and Locke (1958). Social class could contribute to the etiology of schizophrenia through any number of channels: the communication of pre-

scribed attitudes of ways of living and adapting, the exposure to stresses and trauma particularly associated with lower economic status, the arousal of frustrations evident when one compares what he has and can attain with what others of a higher class have and can attain, or the shaping of an inadequate self-concept by the low status, low prestige aspect of one's social class. Since schizophrenia has been known to occur in all parts of the world, some insights have been sought regarding possible modifications brought about by differences in cultures. Benedict (1958) did an exhaustive review of research on Africans, American Indians, Australians, Formosans, Japanese, Fijians, East Indians, Micronesians, Negroes in Latin and South America, Chinese, Hawaiians, and displaced persons and immigrants to the United States and Canada. He concludes:

1. Schizophrenia is not only a disease of civilized man but appears in primitive, nonliterate cultures as well.

2. Europeans appear to require hospitalization more than primitive natives, perhaps because the Western culture makes it more difficult for the psychotic

person to adjust without the protection of an institution. Primitive societies, on the other hand, may demand less complex skills and contributions, may be more tolerant of bizarre behavior, and may even condone such bizarreness in its own religio-magical rituals.

3. Depressive features in schizophrenia are relatively rare in primitive societies, possibly because of the encouragement of displacement of blame on supernatural beings.

4. Schizophrenic symptomatology in primitive cultures tends to be of the more disintegrated variety such as states of excitement and confusion and less of the systematized, intact variety such as paranoid schizophrenia.

As psychiatric experts from all parts of the world begin to share information on their patients based on comparable selection, diagnostic, and statistical techniques, the role of sociocultural factors will become clearer than they are currently. In spite of the enormous data thus far collected, there is still a certain sense of dissatisfaction among experts in the field regarding the true meaning of the materials (e.g., see Mishler and Scotch, 1965). Transcultural psychiatry, however, is developing and attracting increasing numbers of psychiatrists, psychologists, anthropologists, and sociologists to its challenges.

Psychiatric theories of the etiology of schizophrenia have undergone evolution. Kraepelin (1925) was an early believer in organic pathology although he later suspected that schizophrenia was due to a metabolic disorder. Bleuler (1950) tried to devise an entirely psychological explanation with an emphasis on the loosening of associations, the presence of ambivalence, and the acceptance of an autistic world by the patient. He himself, however, still entertained the probability of an organic toxic causation underlying the psychogenic factors. Meyer (1948) was more truly committed to a psychological approach. He conceived of the disorder as the end result of an accumulation of faulty habits over the years. This longitudinal approach saw the patient reacting to failures in life by subterfuges such as daydreaming, brooding, withdrawal of interest. These trivial habits become more and more relied upon and soon substitute for more adjustive habits. Eventually, they become extreme and turn into the symptoms of schizophrenia. Freud (1914, 1923) offered a dynamic formulation of hallucinations as an unsuccessful attempt by the ego to reject an unbearable wish which returns in the form of an hallucination. Schizophrenia is understood as a withdrawal of libido from the external world, and the alliance of the ego with the id as the ego now rejects its service to reality and alters reality. Sullivan (1946, 1953, 1956), the prominent American psychiatrist, was the first to stress the interpersonal nature of schizophrenia. He viewed schizophrenia as an outcome of poor interpersonal relations between the child and his parents. Parental communication of anxiety, disapproving self-appraisals, the threat of loss of approval, may all cause the child to resort to "parataxic distortions," distorted interpretations of an interpersonal situation. These distortions along with a poorly developed self-system prevent the patient from developing more adaptive security mechanisms. The patient becomes more isolated from interpersonal reality, panics, and experiences a return of dissociated "not-me" experiences characteristic of the psychosis.

A number of these psychiatric viewpoints may be drawn upon in our attempt to understand the development of schizophrenia. It is clear that a purely *psychological* contribution to etiology must acknowledge the early family conditions influencing the child. The studies of the "schizophrenogenic mothers" and the fathers of schizophrenics reviewed in Chapter 5 point out the extremely pathological environment surrounding the child as he struggles toward normal development. By extremely pathological, we do not necessarily mean that such parents are bizarre or frankly psychotic themselves, although this does occur. The pathology of the family exists in the disturbed quality of the parents' attitudes and actions toward their offspring. Schizophrenogenic mothers are described as exhibiting a wide variety of traits: they are rejecting, overprotective, devoted, aloof, cold, intrusive, anxious over sexuality, self-sacrificing, subtly dominant, and fearful of intimacy. The list is long indeed and seemingly with some contradictions. However, the evidence is striking and not readily dismissed. The apparent contradictions are not only resolvable but informative in themselves. It is a critical observation to note that the schizophrenogenic mother is a model of inconsistency: she is aloof yet smothering; she may seem accepting and protective on the surface, yet this appears to be more of a reaction against her rejection; she may avoid intimacy and remain aloof, yet she seems to have an overwhelming need to be intimately involved in the child's every activity (Hill, 1955). This unpredictability and inconsistency makes it very difficult for the child to develop a truly satisfying relationship with her. It is impossible to gauge what will please the parent. Moreover, since the frustration that she imposes is in itself variable, the child is at a loss as to how to effectively cope with it. With such an ungratifying interpersonal relationship, the child has little incentive to wish to continue to relate to people. In addition, the child may soon begin to actually withdraw as a means of defending himself against this demanding, inconsistent, interfering parent (Nagelberg, Spotnitz, and Feldman, 1953). The fathers of schizophrenic patients have been described as detached, passive, unable to assume the adaptive—instrumental role. Lidz and his colleagues (Lidz et al., 1957) identified five patterns ranging from the undemanding, dependent role to the hostile, demanding, and unrealistic one. Such men are poor models of adjustment and may in fact be better models of maladjustment. From the standpoint of the child, such a parent is more tolerable since he is more consistent and therefore the child knows what to expect. On the other hand, he is unable to transmit much help on the "hows" and "wherefores" of adaptive mechanisms, and his own demands may be so extreme as to be impossible to satisfy. The child is again left with poor reason to seek continued interpersonal contacts, and little support and help in learning how to cope with life's stresses.

If the personal traits of the parents individually are insufficient to create the conditions for pathology, their interactive influence makes up the difference. The family structure is itself distorted. For example, it may be either schismatic with members of the family taking opposing sides, or skewed such that one spouse and the offspring passively go along with the aberrant ways of the more disturbed parent (Fleck, Lidz, and Cornelison, 1963). Brodey has described the interaction process by drawing an analogy with the theatre:

> The family is . . . more like the morality play of medieval times. Actors take allegorical roles, positions that are stereotyped and confined—one is Good; another, Evil; a third Temptation (Brodey, 1959).

To continue this analogy, in some families of schizophrenics, the roles are: father—Smugly Unconcerned, mother—Facade of Normal Adjustment, child—the Poor Psychotic One. Such families are characterized by a male parent who sees little value in psychological "double-talk," a female parent who searches out treatment for her child who is beginning to disturb her, and a child who has little hope left except for a therapist who has insight into the parental contribution to the illness. The child expresses the illness of the family, and his role of illness permits the family unit to maintain its own unique level of pseudo-adjustment. It is a common phenomenon to observe the child recover in treatment, only to find that his role is now assumed by another member of the family, or to see the hidden conflict between the parents suddenly burst into the open.

Of course, there are family setups where the conditions quite directly precipitate disorganization. Fisher and Mendell (1956) discovered families in which pathogenic perceptions and obsessions persisted over several generations. Fleck, Lidz, and Cornelison considered the families of schizophrenics to be permeated by irrationality, distortions, and idiosyncracies. In other families, the "double-bind" mode of communicating is basic to the disturbance (Bateson et al., 1960). In the double-bind situation, the child receives at least two conflicting messages. No statement is conveyed to the child in a simple, clear-cut fashion but always carries along with it another message which disqualifies it. The child is told yes and no in the same communication; he is offered love and rejected; he is praised and reproven. The incredible complication is the fact that the child is not permitted to question the communication, ask for clarification, or even acknowledge that he is faced with confusing and interfering messages. He must pretend that he not only hears, but comprehends. He must attempt an adaptive response in spite of the fact that the conditions do not allow for an adjustive solution. It is like a bizarre game in which everyone agrees to behave incomprehensibly but act as if everything were entirely comprehensible. The child soon learns to play the game even better than his parents and also splits his communications so that it soon becomes impossible to de-

termine what he thinks, feels, or wants. His emotional responses convey information completely out of keeping with his verbal or even thought content—the child is well on his way towards exhibiting a "split personality."

The role of the emotions and tensions of the child must not be overlooked. Arieti analyzed the psychosis as *"a specific reaction to an extremely severe state of anxiety, originated in childhood, reactivated later in life"* (1955). We can view schizophrenia as an attempt at coping with the threats of overwhelming anxiety; admittedly the attempt involves mechanisms that are of dubious value and frankly self-defeating. The child experiences a series of stresses, perhaps some from specific identifiable traumas, others from the continuing frustrations of living in a schizophrenogenic family atmosphere. Withdrawal, apathy, and indulgence in autism all serve to momentarily free him from having to confront these conditions. Denial and projection enable him to avoid responsibility for threatening needs. Delusions and hallucinations absolve him of the chore of deciding what to do since his delusions now guide him and his hallucinations now command him. Grandiose beliefs serve to hide the low self-esteem and feelings of failure. These defenses are usually inadequate, for after all, the child has had inadequate models to learn from. Increasingly higher levels of anxiety may develop until it disrupts all remaining traces of rational thought processes, attempts to reach out to others, and movement toward more mature solutions. Primitive defense mechanisms come to the fore. Intermittent frenzied attempts to fight off personality disintegration may appear. When all else fails, the patient may withdraw entirely into his own private world of personal meanings, hallucinatory wish-fulfillment, and undisturbed, undemanding existence.

Treatment

Dementia praecox was once considered a disastrous disorder because it had an early onset and proceeded unabated and unresponsive to treatment for years. As mentioned in the earlier part of this chapter, the picture is still grim, although it is now known that schizophrenia can have a later onset, is responsive to treatment, and complete recoveries are possible. Modern treatment methods, especially chemotherapy, now enables:

Half of first admissions to be discharged within four months.
Two-thirds to be discharged within six months.
Ninety percent to be discharged within one year.

(Kennedy, 1963; Mandelbrote and Folkard, 1963; Ruesch, Brodsky, and Fischer, 1963.) Discharge, of course, is not synonymous with cure but rather control. A patient is released when his symptoms are sufficiently under control that he can be returned to other forms of treatment such as out-patient clinics. Clark and Mallett's (1963) three-year follow-up of hospital discharged patients showed that only 11 percent of the schizophrenics remained symptom-free over this period of time. On the other hand 72 percent showed sufficient return or exacerbation of their symptoms as to require rehospitalization.

In the light of this type of depressing evidence, more attention is being devoted toward determining what factors are associated with a more favorable prognosis. Huston and Pepernick (1958) reviewed some earlier studies and summarized those factors that appeared to be connected with favorable and those associated with unfavorable prognosis. These are found in Table 14-1. More recently, Vaillant (1966) extracted six factors which he found to be repeatedly favorable signs in a number of other researchers' works. These were:

An acute onset
A clear precipitating event
A good premorbid adjustment
Presence of confusion or disorientation
Presence of depressive symptomatology
History of a relative with psychotic depression

Vaillant conducted a study using these factors and found that all six successfully differentiated those patients who recovered from those who remained hospitalized. In addition, the more factors present, the greater the indication of likely recovery. The distinction between process and reactive schizophrenia has also come under study as a possible way of identifying the patients who are more likely to recover. The features for diagnosing the two types are based on case history data with the Kantor, Wallner, and Winder (1953) list of criteria being the most complete (see Table 14-2). Some studies have relied upon other means for identification, such as the Elgin Prognostic Scale (Wittman, 1941), the Phillips Premorbid Adjustment Scale (Phillips, 1953), and even autonomic responsiveness (King, 1958). Investigations on recovery rates have supported the contention that process schizophrenics are poorer prognostic risks than reactive patients. Stephens and Astrup (1963), for example, followed up patients for from 5 to 13 years and found that:

1. Only 10 percent of the process patients recovered, as compared to 38 percent of the nonprocess patients.

2. About 49 percent of the process patients were unimproved, as compared to 3 percent of the nonprocess patients.

Prognostic statements can never be completely meaningful without taking into account therapy. Schizophrenics have been introduced to a wide variety of treatment methods. For a time, the use of psychosurgery was greatly applied to schizophrenia. For patients hospitalized for one to two years, 52 percent may respond well enough to surgery to be discharged in a quieter and more cooperative mood. The best results are obtained by treatment within six months, which permits some 82 percent "recovery," (Freeman, 1953). Unfortunately, it must be recognized that the effects of surgery are

TABLE 14-1. *Prognostic Indices: Favorable and Unfavorable Factors Associated with Recovery from Schizophrenia*

FAVORABLE	UNFAVORABLE
Clinical Factors	
Acute onset[a]	Gradual onset[a]
External precipitant[a]	Long duration of illness prior to hospitalization[a]
Short duration of illness prior to hospitalization[a]	Flat affect[a]
Preservation of affect[a]	Inappropriate affect[a]
Tension and anxiety	Little overt hostility
Depression	Defiantly paranoid
Manifest moderate hostility	
Self-reproaching delusions	
Compliantly paranoid	
Ability to rationalize reality lapses	
Social and Personal History Factors	
Upper socio-economic group	Lowest socio-economic group
Good educational history	Single, divorced or separated
Good occupational history	Over 35
Steady church attendance	
Married	
Good marital adjustment	
Good recent sexual adjustment	
Relatively stable prior to onset	
Under 30	
Psychological Test Factors	
High I.Q.[a]	Low I.Q. (under 90)[a]
Functioning at level lower than potential	Marked impairment of abstract thinking
Little impairment of abstract thinking	
Constitutional Factors	
Ecto-mesomorphic	Endomorphic
Pyknic	
Physiological Factors	
Chills after mecholyl	Increased blood pressure response to mecholyl
Anxiety precipitated only by mecholyl	
Small blood pressure response (or decrease) to mecholyl	
Moderate blood pressure response to epinephrine	

[a] These factors have a reliability that is *apparently* higher than the others.
SOURCE: P. Huston and M. Pepernick, Prognosis in schizophrenia. In L. Bellak (Ed.), *Schizophrenia: a review of the syndrome.* New York: Logos Press, 1958. Reprinted with permission of Leopold Bellak, Editor.

irreversible, parts of the brain are destroyed, and the treatment is symptomatic and not curative. A serious question is involved: is it worth the risk—although

52 percent are dischargeable, 48 percent do not recover enough to be discharged from the hospital when surgery is delayed over one year; if surgery is accomplished at

TABLE 14-2. *Characteristics Differentiating Process from Reactive Schizophrenia*

PROCESS SCHIZOPHRENIA	REACTIVE SCHIZOPHRENIA
Birth to the fifth year	
a. Early psychological trauma	a. Good psychological history
b. Physical illness—severe or long	b. Good physical health
c. Odd member of family	c. Normal member of family
Fifth year to adolescence	
a. Difficulties at school	a. Well adjusted at school
b. Family troubles paralleled by sudden changes in patient's behavior	b. Domestic troubles unaccompanied by behavior disruptions; patient "had what it took"
c. Introverted behavior trends and interests	c. Extroverted behavior trends and interests
d. History of breakdown of social, physical, mental functioning	d. History of adequate social, physical, mental functioning
e. Pathological siblings	e. Normal siblings
f. Overprotective or rejecting mother, "momism"	f. Normally protective, accepting mother
g. Rejecting father	g. Accepting father
Adolescence to adulthood	
a. Lack of heterosexuality	a. Heterosexual behavior
b. Insidious, gradual onset of psychosis without pertinent stress	b. Sudden onset of psychosis; stress present and pertinent; later onset
c. Physical aggression	c. Verbal aggression
d. Poor response to treatment	d. Good response to treatment
e. Lengthy stay in hospital	e. Short course in hospital
Adulthood	
a. Massive paranoia	a. Minor paranoid trends
b. Little capacity for alcohol	b. Much capacity for alcohol
c. No manic-depressive component	c. Presence of manic-depressive component
d. Failure under adversity	d. Success despite adversity
e. Discrepancy between ability and achievement	e. Harmony between ability and achievement
f. Awareness of change in self	f. No sensation of change
g. Somatic delusions	g. Absence of somatic delusions
h. Clash between culture and environment	h. Harmony between culture and environment
i. Loss of decency (nudity, public masturbation, etc.)	i. Retention of decency

SOURCE: R. Kantor, J. Wallner, and C. Winder, Process and reactive schizophrenia. *J. consult. Psychol.* 1953, **17**, 157.

its most ideal time (within six months), 18 percent of the patients are no better off then they were prior to the surgical destruction. For these reasons, psychosurgery may improve the prognosis, but it is becoming more and more reserved for chronic, otherwise unresponsive patients.

Electroconvulsive shock therapy (ECT) has also been used with schizophrenia but with less spectacular results than found with the affective disorders. A follow-up study over 25 years compared the course of illness before and after the advent of ECT and insulin. The results indicated that the five-year recovery rate improved from 9 percent before to 22 percent after treatment was available (Bond, 1954). It is also agreed that the effectiveness of shock therapy decreases with cases of more than one year duration. Convincing figures are hard to obtain because such factors as the

duration of illness have not been controlled, and because of the need for follow-up information since many acutely ill schizophrenics will recover after brief ECT treatment only to invariably relapse. Catatonic stupors, hebephrenic and simple schizophrenics respond poorest to ECT; catatonic excitement, and acute paranoid schizophrenics respond more favorably. Shock treatment is still basically considered symptomatic treatment, reducing the symptoms of the disorder but not necessarily effecting a cure.

The tranquilizing drugs have effected the highest recovery rates in the treatment of schizophrenics, enabling reduction of the acute manifestations of the psychosis within the first three to six weeks of therapy. In fact, the National Institute of Mental Health Psychopharmacology Service Center Collaborative Study Group

Left: A *psychotic* patient, withdrawn, alone, and oblivious to her surroundings and her nudity. (Jerry Cooke)

Right: A *mental patient* in restraints, yet smiling inappropriately to herself at something occurring within her autistic world. (Jerry Cooke)

(1964) has been so impressed by the phenothiazine drugs (such as chlorpromazine) that it regards these as antischizophrenic drugs rather than merely tranquilizers. With the chronically disturbed schizophrenics there is evidence that over 50 percent can be discharged to out-patient treatment from hospitalization after massive dosages of the phenothiazines (Forrest, Geier, Snow, and Steinback, 1964). However, there is some question as to the possible side effects of prolonged chemotherapy. A peculiar purplish pigmentation of the skin and opacities in the cornea and lens from drug therapy is being investigated (Greiner and Berry, 1964).

Behavior modification techniques have been recently applied to the schizophrenic disorders. Operant conditioning procedures have been the preferred method, in-

volving the presenting of a reinforcement whenever the patient shows the desired response. Isaacs, Thomas, and Goldiamond (1960), selected two mute catatonic schizophrenics for behavioral therapy. Interestingly enough, both patients were quite responsive to the offer of chewing gum which was thereafter used as the reinforcement. Through a gradual process, the experimenters were able to reinstate speech in the two patients. Allyon and Michael (1959) undertook a difficult case of a female patient known for episodes of extreme violence. Because of her outbursts, she had been given ECT and undergone psychosurgery to no avail. During her hospitalization she spent from 3 to 12 hours daily in an isolation room to control her violence. The experimenters selected a behavior pattern exhibited by the patient which was incompatible with

399

her violent behaviors: sitting or lying on the floor. As long as she was on the floor, she could not readily engage in fighting or assaults. For four weeks, she was reinforced for this incompatible behavior during which time her violence was reduced drastically. When the treatment was withdrawn, the patient again demonstrated her unprovoked hostility, attacking eight patients during a four-week period as compared with one attack during the treatment period. Operant techniques have also been applied to childhood cases with promising results. Ferster and De-Myer (1962) have attempted some intensive work with autistic children using coin-operated vending machines to administer rewards. With this procedure, they have managed to widen the children's behavior repertoire and bring much of their autistic behavior under control.

Psychotherapy with the schizophrenic is an intensive affair requiring great flexibility and skill. Most commonly, psychotherapy experts believe in the necessity of establishing a trusting relationship with the patient, whose basic attitude is distrust. Through a variety of methods the therapist becomes a real link with reality that is consistent and dependable and trustworthy. The patient is not forced to progress into deeper insights or intellectual understanding of his symptoms until he is ready to relate with a greater sense of security and control. Many therapists feel that it is necessary to become more of a real person to the patient, sharing their own background, interests, or feelings when asked. This enables the patient to differentiate between his fantasies and reality. More than with any other type of patient, the psychotherapist must be continually aware of the confused communication of the schizophrenic in which meaning and intent and actual verbalizations do not always coincide. A number of unique forms of therapeutic relationships have

been explored by various therapists. Gertrude Schwing (1940) attempts to become a loving mother toward her patients, spending long hours comforting them, bringing them candy or fruits, attending to their physical needs. In contrast, John Rosen practices "direct analysis," a method referred to as the psychological shock method by others (Ellenberger). Rosen believes in providing a strong, protective approach. His main objective is to convey to the patient his ability to fully grasp and understand what is going on in the patient's world. He enters the psychotic world and interprets to the patient what is happening in highly direct, often shocking terms. In addition, Rosen spends up to 16 hours a day sitting with the patient, feeding him, helping him, and endeavoring to convey his understanding in order to make contact.

A variety of other treatment methods deserve mention. The Russians have relied upon prolonged sleep combined with stimulants such as caffeine, insulin, or ECT as a means of dealing with the protective inhibitions (Andreev, 1959; Ivanov-Smolenskii, 1954; Williams and Webb, 1966). Mental hospitals and psychiatric wards have been undergoing progressive changes away from the old concept of custodial care and toward the concept of a therapeutic community. The entire hospital and personnel is geared in the direction of being a social system in itself with only one aim, treating the patient in ways to continue his progress toward mental health (Jones, 1953). Two types of family therapy has been introduced: one in which the patient and his family are brought together for a family psychotherapy meeting, another in which the patient and family actually live together in research facilities on a family-in-residence arrangement. No patient is ever seen in individual treatment; the family as a unit is treated (Jackson, 1961; Masserman, 1962).

Case History 14-1

SIMPLE SCHIZOPHRENIA

Kent C. is a 23-year-old former Air Force officer. He recently finished his bachelor's degree at a state university with a major in agriculture. Through an R.O.T.C. program he was able to enter military service with a commission. His first six months in service were uneventful although he seemed to be quite listless and indifferent toward his career. He was likable enough to his peers, mainly because he asked little of them but was always himself a "soft touch." Loaning out money without being repaid did not seem to disturb him; in fact, he seemed to have become quite isolated from his surroundings. The other officers and enlisted men often made jokes at his expense, but could stir no reactions other than a mild smile every now and then. Emotional display seemed entirely absent. As his first year of service reached its end, Kent came to the attention of his superiors because of his "eccentric" behaviors. He had taken to talking to himself, sometimes quietly muttering, at other times speaking aloud. His sleeping habits were sometimes altered and he would spend part of the evening sitting with a stray dog that he had found. His ability to carry through an order, or to delegate a task became increasingly more impaired as he appeared to barely take notice of commands. He was referred for a psychiatric evaluation and diagnosed as a schizophrenic reaction, simple type.

Kent had always seemed to his immediate family an unusually withdrawn person. In fact, he was laughingly dubbed "The Shy One" during childhood, a nickname which seemed so appropriate even later in life that it stuck. In elementary school he participated in few group sports or activities, preferring to be alone. While the other children enjoyed remaining at the school playground when classes were over, Kent left by himself and spent most of his hours in his room at home. In high school he was a model student in the sense that he never was a disciplinary problem, knew enough to get by, and was always polite. Few teachers felt that he was reachable, none noticed any topic about which he could become "fired-up." At the university he spent more of his time with the animals and in the fields than with his fellow students. He joined a fraternity but this seemed more for the convenience of the living arrangement. Parties generally found him a quiet observer although he occasionally allowed himself to be prompted into participating. He soon became the butt of many jokes because of his tendency to work in the yard while others were busy meeting and chatting with coeds. The joking barbs never seemed to penetrate his almost too even-tempered disposition. None of his friends ever felt they knew him in any real sense, and most of them found it difficult to explain how he ever decided to volunteer for advanced R.O.T.C.

Kent was given a medical discharge from the military. He made an abortive attempt to enter outpatient treatment on the request of a friend. However, this lasted for one session. He was last heard of leaving the state in his car, heading toward farming land where he thought of seeking intermittent employment in soil conservation. If his apathy toward life did not overtake him completely, it is possible that he is now working in an isolated area on a job with minimal demands.

Case History 14-2

HEBEPHRENIC SCHIZOPHRENIA

Edna K. was a 45-year-old wife of a laborer. Her illness had progressed rapidly and she was quite severely disturbed by the time of her admission to the hospital. It was impossible to obtain a meaningful description of her condition directly from her. The following is an excerpt from her intake interview:

Dr.: I am Dr. ———. I would like to know something more about you.

Pt.: You have a nasty mind. Lord, Lord! Cat's in a cradle.

Dr.: Tell me, how do you feel?

Pt.: London's bell is a long, long dock. Hee! Hee! Hee! (Giggles uncontrollably.)

Dr.: Do you know where you are now?

Pt.: D—n! S—t on you all who rip into my internals! The grugerometer will take care of you all! (Shouting) I am the Queen, see my magic, I shall turn you all into smidgelings forever!

Dr.: Your husband is concerned about you. Do you know his name?

Pt.: (Stands, walks to and faces the wall) Who am I, Who are we, Who are you, Who are they. (Turns) I . . . I . . . I . . . I!!! (Makes grotesque faces)

Edna was placed in the women's ward where she proceeded to masturbate. She always sat in a chosen spot and in a chosen way, with her feet propped under her. Occasionally, she would scream or shout obscenities. At other times she giggled to herself. She was known to attack other patients. She began to complain that her uterus was attached to a "pipeline to the Kremlin" and that she was being "infernally invaded" by Communism. She was placed on an ECT schedule and showed some improvement after a few treatments. However, she relapsed within a week into her previous behavior and began actively hallucinating. At times she seemed to be having an enjoyable set of hallucinations as she would sit and laugh hysterically. On other occasions she appeared frightened, and would huddle and whimper in her corner. In lucid moments, she described her experience as including a vague sensation of being enveloped by a "cosmic cloak" of power and majesty which would suddenly burst into fragments, each dissolving or being transformed into hideous insects. She was tried on massive doses of Thorazine (chlorpromazine) and is showing gradual improvement.

Case History 14-3

CATATONIC SCHIZOPHRENIA

Manuel A. was a catatonic patient, chronically ill and hospitalized for years. He had been a transient farm laborer, one of many who eked out a living traveling from state to state following the crops. After a particularly long and hot journey from a southwestern state to the Pacific Northwest, he collapsed from what seemed to be sheer exhaustion. It was discovered that he had gradually become seclusive, staying off by himself and not associating with the other workers. Most thought he was meditating as he had recently "got religion ideas." Just before his collapse, he had been on a sparse diet although food was available and shared by other workers. He had been seen sitting on the running board of his old car gazing off into the distance. It was in this position that he slowly fell over and was taken to the hospital.

Except for some signs of fatigue, and a typical transient worker's dietary deficiency, Manuel appeared to be physically healthy upon examination. Yet he did not regain his awareness of his surroundings. He remained motionless, speechless, and seemingly unconscious. One evening an aide turned him on his side to straighten out the sheet, was called away to tend another patient, and forgot to return. Manuel was found the next morning, still on his side, his arm tucked under his body, as he had been left the night before. His arm was turning blue from lack of circulation but he seemed to be experiencing no discomfort. Further examination confirmed that he was in a state of waxy flexibility. Psychiatric consultation confirmed the diagnosis of catatonic schizophrenia.

Manuel gradually appeared to recover from his stuporous condition. His body showed more muscle tone as he would occasionally change position. He was somewhat more responsive to others although he was echolalic, repeating phrases which others addressed to him. Within a few months he was able to communicate intelligibly to an interviewer. He described the onset of his illness as starting with a supernatural feeling of being flooded with omniscience. He felt the world was opening up its true meaning to his gaze although he still had lacked the ability to fully comprehend what he was envisioning. He saw "through and beyond" the surface of objects, with visions occurring one after another as if in a picture slide show. He became aware of feeling transported from his earthly surroundings into a transitional space where he sometimes saw his own features as readily as he viewed external objects. His own countenance was consecutively realistic, blurred, demoniacal, majestic, and undefinably mystical. These experiences began to recede slowly and he soon became aware of sounds at a distance. They seemed vaguely familiar, yet unidentifiable. He tried to concentrate all his attention on them but found them more elusive than ever. He was soon attracted by the intriguing quality of the sounds, each being distinctive from another, each having a life of its own. Gradually, the sounds arranged themselves in order, and he found himself hearing words for the first time since his breakdown. He was still more fascinated by their quality than their meaning. However, before long he was able to regain the experiences which had so fascinated him.

Case History 14-4

PARANOID SCHIZOPHRENIA

Ben K. was a 20-year-old senior in college who was within three credits of finishing a degree in psychology when he was hospitalized. Ben had been raised in a "schismatic" family in which the parents were continuously arguing and blaming one another. He himself was often punished for inadequacies which were really the fault of his parents. It was as if neither parent could tolerate admitting their own basic mistakes, large or small. As an adolescent Ben sometimes wished that he could run away and leave both his parents to their mutual miseries, but he found himself unable to do more than fantasize. He left home to attend a nearby state college and found himself still under their influence. He was always fearful of what they might do if he did not do well in his studies, if he dated someone they did not approve of, if he failed to return on weekends. He was one of many persons motivated to achieve because he was afraid of failure. He seemed congenitally unable to express anger for fear that he would prove to be unjustified in it and thereby subject to further reprimand. He enrolled in a psychology major in the hopes of improving his adjustment; he found, however, that his knowledge did not automatically improve his life adjustment.

Ben acquired a Christmas temporary job in the post office. His task was to sort and place mail into boxes rented by customers. During this work, he began to feel quite worried about his midsemester examinations which had just been completed. He was certain he had done well on them but he had the same feeling of confidence before and had been disappointed. It was while he was thus ruminating that he became aware of the disappearance of a letter from a mailbox that he had filled. He did not recall seeing anyone take the letter out and was certain that he had been alert. For the next week he alternated between worrying about his grades and speculating about the missing letter. Then he was beset with an insight: the letters were top secret material, and the post office was a messenger station. He called the F.B.I. and conveyed his proof—the disappearance of the letter without his seeing anyone nearby. The F.B.I. agent seemed unconcerned. Ben felt rebuffed and wrestled with his concern that something be done. Then he realized that the lack of concern of the F.B.I. was a clue in itself—the federal agency was part of the plot. This development gave him a keen sense of anticipation and satisfaction until he recognized the enormity of the situation. He had given himself away by the telephone call and was now exposed to personal danger. He recalled hearing that the Communists had infiltrated the F.B.I. and had now proof of this. He wanted to immediately quit his job but was afraid that this might be too suspicious. He wanted to confide in someone but knew that no one could be trusted.

He was soon amazed at the number of clues he now became aware of which he had been ignorant of before his "insight." Secret agents were posted on every corner to watch him; he could identify them because whenever he suddenly looked sharply at one, the agent would appear to be occupied with

Case History 14-4 (*Continued*)

PARANOID SCHIZOPHRENIA

something else. Television broadcasts were almost certainly coded messages about him. Magazines began to appear on the stands with sexy pictures as a means of trapping him so that he could be arrested as a sex pervert. He soon began to take delight at uncovering their traps and frustrating their attempts. Then one morning he awakened with the feeling that they finally had decided to throw caution to the winds, and now he could escape no longer. He experienced a slight sense of grogginess upon getting out of bed, a sure sign, he thought, of a secret weapon at work. He reasoned that it was some kind of ultra-ray machine turned on his soul in the midst of night while he slept. In fact, he began to actually feel parts of his brain sleeping and disintegrating to dust in his head. As the days progressed, he refused to eat any food other than that prepared by himself because he was certain that he had detected dope in dessert served him at a restaurant. He ultimately refused to use anything but canned food since the fresh groceries were too easily "doctored." He finally limited himself to the few herbs and fruits that he could scrounge in the woods since the canned food began to taste peculiar, and he had noticed small scratches on the cans indicating that they had been tampered with. Ben began to hear strange voices in the air as if several people were talking at once on a telephone party line. These voices appeared loudest during the day, and particularly when he was trying to concentrate on his schoolwork. He finally could not bear up with this last persecutory action any further, and ran to the college counseling center for help. His major complaint: the spies were trying to drive him to insanity and he wanted help to overcome their efforts. Ben was referred to the state hospital for psychiatric treatment. He has a moderately good chance for recovery, but he is at this date still delusional and believes that the counseling center has also been infiltrated by his "enemies" and that the hospitalization is in reality incarceration.

Case History 14-5

SCHIZO-AFFECTIVE SCHIZOPHRENIA

Maya M. was a recent patient of a private mental hospital. She comes from a wealthy family and has enjoyed the best of privileges in life. She went to an exclusive private girls school and majored in fine arts in an Eastern college. She married an industrial executive and continued to live a successful life, throwing large gala gatherings attended by governors, senators, corporation presidents, diplomats. She gave birth to a son and was quite unhappy at having to take time away from her social life. Within a year of his birth, Maya developed a deep depression. She was despondent about the oncoming birthday party and felt she could not do him justice. Her depths of despair seemed real enough but quite inappropriate to the topic of her concern. She began to berate herself for having her child born before she could properly prepare the program for his first birthday party. She seemed to recover from her depression before long but retained some bizarre behavior. She fired all her servants on the basis that their personalities clashed with the wallpaper. She had a bedroom window torn out and replaced with a window that was triangular shaped because the three points imparted a feeling of "godliness" to her. She began writing notes to herself and having them translated into Chinese since this helped to unify the East and the West in the Universe. Her notes were often incomprehensible and irrational. Many phrases were sound associations, for example, "Clang, chang, brang, bang, ultramang." She became very literal in her interpretation of instructions. For example, her French recipe called to her to "prepare the lamb"; she did exactly this by talking soothingly to the lamb chop, describing her intentions so that it would know what to expect and be properly "prepared." She was hospitalized by her husband. Subsequently she plunged into another highly agitated fit of despair.

Maya was given electroshock therapy three times weekly for a total of 20 treatments. Her depression subsided and she appeared in much better control. She entered intensive psychotherapy and was also placed on tranquilizers. She was release from the hospital within six months, continuing her treatment with a private psychiatrist. Her social activities have been sharply curtailed, but she has been permitted and encouraged to be with her husband and her son. She says herself that it is the first time she has really felt part of a family.

Glossary

Autopsy: Medical examination of the body after death.

Biopsy: Medical microscopic examination of tissue taken from a living organism.

Catalepsy: Retention of a muscularly rigid and fixed position.

Catatonic excitement: A condition of extremely agitated and impulsive outbursts in a catatonic schizophrenic.

Catatonic schizophrenic: A psychotic disorder characterized by motor inhibition or excitability along with the usual characteristics of schizophrenia.

Catatonic stupor: A condition of physical unresponsiveness in a catatonic schizophrenic.

Dementia praecox: An historical term now replaced by the term schizophrenia.

Echolalia: The repetition and senseless mimicking of words just spoken by another person.

Hebephrenic schizophrenic: A psychotic disorder characterized by silly and inappropriate behavior and regressive features along with the usual characteristics of schizophrenia.

Negativism: The resistence of suggestions or influence of others.

Neologism: A newly coined word.

Paranoid schizophrenia: A psychotic disorder characterized by systematized delusions along with the usual characteristics of schizophrenia.

Process schizophrenia: A type of schizophrenia believed to be present early in life and possibly attributable to nonpsychological origins. Not a formal diagnostic category acknowledged by the American Psychiatric Association classification system.

Protective inhibition: Related to schizophrenia, a belief that continual stress results in inhibition of brain function as a self-protective reaction.

Reactive schizophrenia: A type of schizophrenia believed to have a late onset and attributable to psychological factors. Not a formal diagnostic category acknowledged by the American Psychiatric Association classification system.

Simple schizophrenia: A psychotic disorder characterized by the usual characteristics of schizophrenia with the exception of hallucinations and delusions.

Schizo-affective schizophrenia: A psychotic disorder characterized by the usual characteristics of schizophrenia with the exception that a pronounced mood state is present instead of the blunting of emotions.

Schizophrenia: A psychotic disorder characterized by the blunting of emotions, social withdrawal, seclusiveness, inappropriateness of affect, autistic thinking, bizarre behavior, sensory disturbances, delusions, and disturbances of thought.

Waxy flexibilty: Heightened motor responsiveness to suggestions.

Word-salad: A jumble of words with no meaning except for the speaker.

References

Allyon, T. & Michael, J. The psychiatric nurse as a behavioral engineer. *J. exp. anal. Behav.*, 1959, **2**, 323.

Andreev, B. *Sleep therapy in the neuroses.* Leningrad: Megiz, 1959.

Arieti, S. *Interpretation of schizophrenia.* New York: Robert Brunner, 1955.

Bateson, G., Jackson, D., Haley, J., & Weakland, J. Toward a theory of schizophrenia. *Behavioral Science,* 1956, **1**, 251.

Bellak, L. *Dementia praecox. The past decade's work and present states: a review and evaluation.* New York: Grune, 1948.

Bellak, L. (Ed.) *Schizophrenia: a review of the syndrome.* New York: Logos Press, 1958.

Bellak, L. & Holt, R. Somatotypes in relation to dementia praecox. *Amer. J. Psychiat.,* 1948, **104**, 713.

Benedict, P. Sociocultural factors in schizophrenia. In L. Bellak (Ed.) *Schizophrenia: A review of the syndrome.* New York: Logos Press, 1958.

Betz, B. Somatology of the schizophrenic patient. *Hum. Biol.,* 1942, **14**, 21.

Bleuler, E. *Dementia praecox or the group of schizophrenias.* Transl. by Joseph Ziskin. New York: International University Press, 1950.

Bond, E. Results of psychiatric treatments with a control series. *Amer. J. Psychiat.,* 1954, **110**, 561.

Böök, J. A genetic and neuropsychiatric investigation of a North Swedish population with special regard to schizophrenia and mental deficiency. *Acta. Genet.,* 1953, 4, 1, 133, and 345.

Brackbill, G. & Fine, H. Schizophrenia and central nervous system pathology. *J. abnorm. soc. Psychol.,* 1956, **52**, 310.

Brodey, W. Some family operations and schizophrenia. *A.M.A. Arch. gen. Psychiat.,* 1959, **1**, 379.

Clark, J. & Mallett, B. A follow-up study of schizophrenia and depression in young adults. *Br. J. Psychiat.,* 1963, **109**, 491.

Davis, P. Evaluation of the electroencephalograms of schizophrenic patients. *Amer. J. Psychiat.,* 1940, **96**, 850.

Dement, W. The effect of dream deprivation. *Science,* 1960, **131**, 1705.

Dohrzhanskaya, A. Issledovanie neirodinamiki pri ostroi shizophrenii. In *Trudy Vsesouznoi Nauchno-Prakticheskoi Konferentsii posviyaschenii 100 letiyu so dnya rozhdeniya S.S. Korsakova i aktualnym voprosam psikhologii,* 20-27, Maya 1954, Moscow: Medgiz, 1955.

Ellenberger, H. Psychotherapie de la Schizophrenie. In *Encylopedie Medico-Chirugic, Psychiatrie,* Vol. I, 37295 C10, Paris.

Faris, R. & Dunham, H. *Mental disorders in urban areas.* Chicago: University Chicago Press, 1939.

Ferster, C. & DeMyer, M. A method for the experimental analysis of the behavior of autistic children. *Amer. J. Orthopsychiat.,* 1962, **32**, 89.

Fisher, S. & Mendell, D. The communication of neurotic patterns over two and three generations. *Psychiat.,* 1956, **19**, 41.

Fleck, S., Lidz, T., & Cornelison, A. Comparison of parent-child relationships of male and female schizophrenic patients. *Arch. gen. Psychiat.,* 1963, **8**, 1.

Forrest, F., Geier, C., Snow, H., & Steinback, M. Drug maintenance problems of rehabilitated mental patients: the current drug dosage "merry-go-round." *Amer. J. Psychiat.,* 1964, **121**, 33.

Freeman, W. Level of achievement after lobotomy. A study of one thousand cases. *Amer. J. Psychiat.,* 1953, **110**, 269.

Freud, S. On narcissism: an introduction. In *Collected papers,* Vol. IV. London: Hogarth Press, 1933. First published in 1914.

Freud, S. *The ego and the id.* London: Hogarth Press, 1947. First published in 1923.

Frumkin, R. *Occupation and mental illness.* Ohio public welfare statistics, 1952, 4.

Gavrilova, N. Investigations of the cortical mosaic in different forms in schizophrenia. Issledovanie Korkovoi mosaiki pri razlichnykh formakh shizophrenii. *Zh. Nevropat. Psikhat.,* 1960, **4**, 453.

Greiner, A. & Berry, K. Skin pigmentation and corneal and lens opacities with prolonged chlorpromazine therapy. *Canad. M.A.J.,* 1964, **90**, 663.

Heath, R. Pleasure response of human subjects to direct stimulation of the brain: physiologic and psychodynamic considerations. In R. Heath (Ed.), *The role of pleasure in behavior.* New York: Harper, 1964.

Heath, R. & Guererro-Figueroa, R. Psychotic behavior with evoked septal dysrhythmia. *Amer. J. Psychiat.,* 1965, **121**, 1080.

Hill, D. Electroencephalogram in schizophrenia. In D. Richter, *Schizophrenia: somatic aspects.* New York: Macmillan, 1957.

Hill, L. *Psychotherapeutic intervention in schizophrenia.* Chicago: University Chicago Press, 1955.

Hurst, L. Genetics of schizophrenia: reply to Pastore. *Psychol. Bull.,* 1951, **48**, 402.

Huston, P. & Pepernick, M. Prognosis in schizophrenia. In L. Bellak (Ed.). *Schizophrenia: a review of the syndrome.* New York: Logos Press, 1958.

Isaacs, W., Thomas, J. & Goldiamond, I. Application of operant conditioning to reinstate verbal behavior in psychotics. *J. speech and hearing Dis.,* 1960, **25**, 8.

Ivanov-Smolenskii, A. *Essays on the patho-physiology of the higher nervous activity.* Moscow: Foreign Languages Publishing House, 1954.

Jackson, D. *The etiology of schizophrenia.* New York: Basic Books, 1960.

Jackson, D. Family therapy in the family of schizophrenic. In M. Stein (Ed.), *Contemporary psychotherapies.* New York: Free Press of Glencoe, 1961.

Jones, M. *The therapeutic community.* New York: Basic Books, 1953.

Kallmann, F. The genetic theory of schizophrenia. An analysis of 691 twin index families. *Amer. J. Psychiat.,* 1946, **103**, 309.

Kallmann, F. *Heredity in health and mental disorder.* New York: Norton, 1953.

Kallmann, F., Falek, A. Hurzeler, M., & Erlenmeyer-Kimling, L. The developmental aspects of children with two schizophrenic parents. In P. Solomon & B. Glueck (Eds.), *Recent research on schizophrenia.* Psychiat. Res. Rep. #19. Washington, D.C.: American Psychiatric Association, 1964.

Kantor, R., Wallner, J., & Winder, C. Process and reactive schizophrenia. *J. consult. Psychol.,* 1953, **17**, 157.

Karanyi, E. & Lehman, H. Experimental sleep deprivation in schizophrenic patients. *A.M.A. Arch. gen. Psychiat.*, 1960, **2**, 534.

Kennedy, J. Special message on mental illness and mental retardation. *Amer. Psychol.*, 1963, **18**, 280.

King, G. Differential autonomic responsiveness in the process-reactive classification of schizophrenia. *J. abnorm. soc. Psychol.*, 1958, **56**, 160.

Klein, N. & Oppenheim, A. Constitutional factors in the prognosis of schizophrenia: further observations. *Amer. J. Psychiat.*, 1952, **108**, 909.

Kline, N. & Tenny, A. Constitutional factors in the prognosis of schizophrenia. *Amer. J. Psychiat.*, 1950, **107**, 434.

Kraepelin, E. *Dementia praecox and paraphrenia.* Edinburgh: Livingston, 1925.

Krakoff, I. Effect of methionine sulfoximine in man. *Clin. Pharmacol. Ther.*, 1961, **2**, 599.

Kretschmer, E. *Physique and character.* New York: Harcourt, Brace and World, 1925.

Lair, C. The effect of praise and reproof on learning and retention of non-psychotics and schizophrenics. *Dissert. Abs.*, 1954, **14**, 1459.

Lidz, T., Cornelison, A., Fleck, S., & Terry, D. The intrafamilial environment of the schizophrenic patient: I. The father. *Psychiat.*, 1957, **20**, 329.

Locke, B. et al. Problems in interpretation of patterns of first admissions to Ohio State public mental hospitals for patients with schizophrenic reactions. In B. Pasamanick & P. Knapp (Eds.), *Psychiat. Res. Reports. No. 10: Social Aspects of Psychiatry.* Washington, D.C.: American Psychiatric Association, 1958.

Lucas, C., Sansbury, P., & Collins, J. A social and clinical study of delusions in schizophrenia. *J. ment. Sci.*, 1962, **108**, 747.

Mandelbrote, B. & Folkard, S. The outcome of schizophrenia in relation to a developing community psychiatric service. *Ment. Hyg.*, 1963, **47**, 43.

Masserman, J. (Ed.) *Current Psychiatric Therapies.* New York: Grune & Stratton, 1962.

Meehl, P. Schizotaxia, schizotype, schizophrenia. *Amer. Psychol.*, 1962, **17**, 827.

Meyer, A. *The common sense psychiatry of Adolf Meyer.* A. Lief (Ed.) New York: McGraw-Hill, 1948.

Mishler, E. & Scotch, N. Sociocultural factors in the epidemiology of schizophrenia. *Intern. J. Psychiat.*, 1965, **1**, 258.

Moore, T. & Hsu, E. Factorial analysis of anthropological measurements in psychotic patients. *Hum. Biol.*, 1946, **18**, 133.

Morris, C. Similarity of constitutional factors in psychotic behavior in India, China, and the United States. *Amer. J. Psychiat.*, 1951, **108**, 143.

Nagelberg, L., Spotnitz, H., & Feldman, Y. The attempt at healthy insulation in the withdrawn child. *Amer. J. Orthopsychiat.*, 1953, **23**, 238.

National Institute of Mental Health Psychopharmacology Service Centre Collaborative Study Group. Phenothiazine treatment in acute schizophrenia. *Arch. gen. Psychiat.*, 1964, **10**, 246.

Nolan, W. Occupation and dementia praecox. *N.Y. State Hospital Quarterly*, 1917, **3**, 127.

Olds, J. & Milner, P. Positive reinforcement produced by electrical stimulation of the septal area and other regions of rat brain. *J. comp. physiol. Psychol.*, 1954, **47**, 409.

Pastore, N. Genetics of schizophrenia: a special review. *Psychol. Bull.*, 1949, **46**, 285.

Phillips, L. Case history data and prognosis in schizophrenia. *J. nerv. ment. Dis.*, 1953, **117**, 515.

Pincus, G. & Hoagland, H. Adrenal cortical responses to stress in normal men and in those with personality disorders. I. Some stress responses in normal and psychotic subjects. *Amer. J. Psychiat.*, 1950, **106**, 541.

Rees, L. Physical constitution in relation to effort syndrome, neurotic and psychotic types. M.D. thesis, University of Wales, 1943.

Rees, W. Physical characteristics of the schizophrenic patient. In D. Richter (Ed.) *Schizophrenia: somatic aspects.* New York: Macmillan, 1957.

Rosen, J. *Direct analysis.* New York: Grune & Stratton, 1953.

Ruesch, J., Brodsky, C., & Fischer, A. The acute nervous breakdown. *Arch. gen. Psychiat.,* 1963, 8, 197.

Schwing, G. *Ein Weg zur Seele des Geistekranken.* Zürich: Rascher Verlag, 1940.

Sheldon, W. *et al.* Atlas *of men: a guide for somatotyping the adult male at all ages.* New York: Harper, 1954.

Slater, E. Genetical causes of schizophrenic symptoms. *Monatsschr. Psychiat. u Neurol.,* 1947, 113, 50.

Stephens, J. & Astrup, C. Prognosis in "process" and in "non-process" schizophrenia. *Amer. J. Psychiat.,* 1963, 119, 945.

Streltsova, N. Kharakteristike nekotorykh bezuslovnykh refleksov u bolnykh shizohreniei. In *Trudy Vsesouznoi Nauchno-Prakticheskoi Konferentsii posviyaschenii 100 letiyu so dnya rozhdeniya S. S. Korsakova i aktualnym voprosam psikhologii,* 20-27, Maya 1954, Moscow: Medgiz, 1955.

Stromgren, E. Psychiatric researches in heredity during recent years in the northern countries. *Schweiz. Arch. Neurol. Psychiat.,* 1948, 62, 378.

Sullivan, H. *Conceptions of modern psychiatry.* Washington, D.C.: American Psychiatric Association, 1946.

Sullivan, H. *The interpersonal theory of psychiatry.* New York: Norton, 1953.

Sullivan, H. Clinical studies in psychiatry. New York: Norton, 1956.

Taylor, J. & Spence, K. Conditioning level in the behavior disorders. *J. abnorm. soc. Psychol.,* 1954, 49, 497.

Vaillant, G. The prediction of recovery in schizophrenia. *Intern. J. Psychiat.,* 1966, 2, 617.

Weakland, J. The "double-bind" hypothesis of schizophrenia and three-party interaction. In D. Jackson (Ed.) *The etiology of schizophrenia.* New York: Basic Books, 1960.

Williams, R. & Webb, W. *Sleep therapy.* Springfield, Ill.: Thomas, 1966.

Wittman, P. A scale for measuring prognosis in schizophrenic patients. *Elgin State Hospital Papers,* 1941, 4, 20.

Wittman, P., Sheldon, W., & Katz, C. A. study of the relationship between constitutional variations and fundamental psychotic behavior reactions. *J. nerv. ment. Dist.,* 1948, 108, 470.

Wolf, A. & Cowen, D. Histopathology of schizophrenia and other psychoses of unknown origin. In A. Wolf (Ed.), *Biology of mental health and disease.* New York: Hoeber, 1952.

15 *Pathological Conditions of Childhood*

Historically, attention to the disorders of early life has developed later and in lesser detail than attention to the disorders of adulthood. There are several good reasons for this. Most of the leading psychiatric experts who were responsible for the development of psychiatric theory and practice had little contact with children. Even Freud, the leading exponent of the importance of early infantile experience on adult symptoms, failed to see a single child in treatment until three years after he had published his theory on infantile sexuality (in 1905). The rantings of the insane adult has always been more impressive, intriguing, startling, or dramatic, than the tantrums or phobias of a child. In addition, it must be recognized that the disturbed adult *demands* attention since he is more capable of destruction or annoyance to others than a child. Moreover, the society expects adults to assume an independent role and is compelled to make special arrangements such as hospitalization for the adult patient. On the other hand, children are typically housed within a family setting which assumes the prime obligation for care. By the turn of the century, psychiatric interest was directed toward children, and the efforts of the Mental Hygiene Movement under Clifford Beers (1908) promoted concerns about early prevention of mental disturbances. However, unlike the symptoms of adult pathology, the signs of child pathology proved to be less clear-cut. The child, by virtue of his lack of maturation, will show behaviors that would be diagnosed as pathological in the adult but that are normal for children. For example, the child's inability to delay his impulses and his low frustration tolerance may lead to aggression or emotional outbursts. The problem of defining pathology is therefore more difficult when a child is involved. An early study by Wickman (1928) demonstrated that teachers tended to identify as pathological those behaviors in children that were disruptive, disorderly, and basically contrary to the proper conduct of a good classroom. Those behaviors that did not disturb the school routine were overlooked even though such behaviors might be equally indicative of social or emotional probems, for example, extreme withdrawal and shyness. More so than in adult pathology, the development of insights into childhood pathology was dependent upon the understanding of normal child development.

Better information on normal child development has shown certain "problem behaviors" to be normal behaviors. "Eating problems" are an expressed complaint of many parents by which they mean "fussiness" or "finickiness" in eating. Such "poor" eating is noticed soon after a period during which the child had eaten large quantities of nearly any food placed before him. In actuality, this change of eating habits is typical in the process of normal development. The child eats less because he is growing at a slower rate and requires less amounts of food; finickiness reflects the establishment of food preferences that are little different from adult preferential behavior except the child may rely upon food coloration to decide his preferences. Aggressive behaviors, tantrums, egocentric demands, and refusals to share are not difficult to understand if one takes into account the emotional and social maturational level of the child (Goodenough, 1931). Minor anxieties and fears seem to run an early course in many normal children ranging from separation anxiety when the parents leave for a night out, to fears of tiny insects (Jersild and Holmes, 1935). Speech hesitations which seem like stammering or stuttering have been found to be present in about 85 percent of all children three to four years of age (Martin and Stendler, 1953). Such recognition of what to expect from children as they mature and develop normally is readily obtainable from a variety of published sources such as Gesell and Ilg (1946) and Carmichael (1954).

Certain criteria for identifying psychopathology in children have been suggested by Kessler (1966). They are:

1. The behaviors are inappropriate for the child's age level.
2. The frequent display of a symptom.
3. Exhibition of regressive symptomatic behavior under *minimal* stress.
4. Multiplicity of symptoms.
5. The degree to which the behavior interferes with the child's normal opportunities and development in life.
6. The presence of personal feelings of suffering and concern.
7. The persistence of the behavior despite efforts to change.
8. The child's generalized inability to relate well, attain satisfactions from life, and show progressive development towards maturity.

The last mentioned sign deserves further elaboration. Children are highly flexible and adaptable. They show a resiliency that enables them to develop and grow despite personal or environmental setbacks. They strive toward maturity in a fashion that is impressive. Immature, ineffective behaviors are quickly discarded for more mature ones as the child grows. Stresses may provoke momentary retreat to regressive behaviors but the child soon returns to his forward-moving nature. Events may trigger deeply felt emotions, yet these are transient and do not interfere with the child's basic ability to enjoy life. When a child consistently shows behaviors that are regressive, inhibiting, fearful, ineffectual, or otherwise contrary to this progressive development, it is time for a careful evaluation.

THE INCIDENCE OF CHILDHOOD PROBLEMS

The National Institute of Mental Health reports:

An estimated 10 percent of public school children in the United States are emotionally disturbed and in need of psychiatric guidance, and at least 250,000 with less serious psychiatric disorders receive services each year at mental health clinics.

During 1963, about 4,000 Americans under 15 years of age and 27,000 between 15 and 24 years were admitted to mental hospitals, both public and private. At the end of the year, 5,000 children under 15 and 25,000 children between 15 and 24 were living their broken lives in these hospitals (National Institute of Mental Health, 1965).

In a long-term study of 252 randomly selected children, Macfarlane counted up the frequency of occurrence of 63 problem behaviors. Many children exhibited some of the problems at one time or another (see Table 15-1). The age of the child had a great deal to do with the type of behavior shown, for example, overt tempers and oversensitiveness increased to about age 4 and then declined. By age 5 the presence of tantrums, quarrelsomeness, irritability, mood swings, and negativism, was suggestive of emotional disturbance

TABLE 15-1. *"Symptoms" Present in 252 Normal Children*

BEHAVIOR	INCIDENCE IN PERCENT	
	BOYS	GIRLS
Disturbing dreams	21	26
Poor appetite	13	15
Excessive modesty	14	17
Nail biting	17	23
Thumbsucking	6	14
Nocturnal enuresis	17	16
Specific fears	34	25
Speech problems	12	9
Lying	24	18
Stealing	6	3
Destructiveness	13	6
Overdependence	13	16
Oversensitiveness	37	44
Shyness	11	24
Mood swings	22	22
Temper tantrums	51	38
Irritability	34	25
Jealousy	34	29
Excessive reserve	30	41

SOURCE: J. Macfarlane et al., *A developmental study of the behavioral problems of normal children between twenty-one months and fourteen years.* Berkeley: University of California Press, 1954. Reprinted by permission of The Regents of the University of California.

(Macfarlane, 1943; Macfarlane, Allen, and Honzik, 1954).

It must be noted that the appearance of a few "problems" does not mean the presence of pathology particularly when the behavior is a common adjustive reaction for the child's age. On the other hand, Macfarlane et al. studied these children into adolescence and noted that multiplicity of problems at an early age was highly predictive of problems at later ages.

CLASSIFICATION OF CHILDHOOD DISORDERS

With the acceptance of the need for early treatment and the recognition that emotional disorders can occur as early as infancy, the field of child psychiatry and child clinical psychology is rapidly developing its own identity. Initially, the diagnostic system for classifying adult pathology was considered directly applicable for describing childhood disorders; in essence, all childhood problems were considered to be merely early representations of adult syndromes. This viewpoint has changed. Professional workers have come to the realization that the classification of childhood illnesses is not a simple matter. In the first place, traditional classifications applicable to adult illnesses fail to identify certain disorders exhibited in children, such as *specific learning disabilities.* In addition, there are childhood syndromes which share some symptoms in common with what appears to be the adult versions of the same disorder but which are, in fact, completely different. For example, *infantile* or *childhood autism* has sometimes been considered synonymous with *schizophrenia* appearing early in life. Most experts now agree that childhood autism and adult schizophrenia are quite distinct from one another (although *childhood schizophrenia* may be an early version of adult schizophrenia). Another complicating feature is the very changeableness of children. Symptoms may be highly variable depending upon the child's disposition, his surroundings, and his level of maturity. As noted previously in the Macfarlane work, the expression of emotional conflict can take different forms as the child grows older. In a longitudinal study of 89 infants and children, Kagan and Moss (1962) discovered that the stability of personality traits was a function of the sex of the child, the age of the child, and the behaviors of the mother. For example, boys who showed behavioral disorganization at ages 6 to 10 were more likely than girls to exhibit similar traits later in life. Fearfulness in girls was related to maternal restrictiveness followed by maternal hostility, while fears in boys were associated with maternal protectiveness followed by hostility and restrictiveness.

In an attempt to provide some common frame of reference, psychopathologists have recommended the derivation of a diagnostic classification system for childhood disorders. Unfortunately, a proliferation of schemes has developed. Among those offering systems for classification were Beller (1962), Chess (1959), Kanner (1957), and Ross (1959). Pearson (1949) proposed a system essentially taken from the adult psychiatric classification system, Pick attempted to develop one based on learning theory (1961), while Peterson (1961) derived one from a statistical factor analysis.

This chapter will not attempt to be a compendium of child psychopathology; instead, it will introduce the reader to selected childhood disorders. The major disorders are as follows:

1. Habit disorders: tics or spasms, habitual acts, habits interfering with biological functioning.
2. Learning disorders: disorders of reading, disorders of speech.
3. Conduct disorders: delinquency.
4. Psychophysiologic disorders: asthma, cyclic vomiting.
5. Psychoneurotic disorders: phobias, conversion reaction, obsessive-compulsive behavior, hypochondriasis.
6. Psychotic disorders: autism, childhood schizophrenia.
7. Organic disorders: brain-injury, epilepsy.

Habit Disorders

These are disorders in which the major symptom involves a repeated response. The repetition may appear involuntary as in nervous tics, or voluntary as in thumbsucking. The repeated response may range in complexity from a single muscle twitch to guided body manipulation as in masturbation. In some cases, the habitual response may be a nuisance but does not prevent the child from his normal routines, while in other cases, the symptom interferes with normal functions such as sleep. A few of the habit disorders will be discussed in the following paragraphs.

A *tic* is an involuntary muscular spasm of short duration. Repeated twitches such as these most commonly involve the face and neck regions but may occur in any part of the body. Examples of tics include facial grimaces, eye blinking, sniffing, frowning, coughing, ear pulling, and scratching. Tics are not under voluntary control: they begin suddenly and involuntarily, persist in spite of attempts to interrupt, and terminate in due course. The origin of tics is unclear. Organic involvement does contribute to the appearance of some tics, for example, postencephalitis symptoms may include spasmodic coughing or sniffing. Kanner (1957) suggests that tics trace back to once purposeful actions, to imitations of actions of others, or to customary gestures that have become habitual. He is convinced that the tic is a symptom that may directly represent a psychological conflict (a head-shaking may represent a negative attitude) or an in-direct expression of generalized emotional strain. Kessler (1966) stresses even more heavily the symbolic nature of the tic and comments that tics usually involve conversion reaction. Involuntary eye-blinking, for example, is interpreted in the same way as hysterical blindness—an attempt to blot out an image that was seen. Another speculation views the loss of muscle control as a reaction to cultur-ally prescribed demands for control. Mahler (1944) points out the impositions placed by parents on free motor behavior of children who eventually develop tics. Russian children live in a culture with high regimentation and classroom control and perhaps as a result appear to have a high incidence of tic symptoms.

Habitual acts are somewhat more com-plicated forms of repetitious activities usually involving more than one part of the body. Such habitual manipulations of the body may involve thumbsucking, nail-biting, nose-picking, or masturbation. In comparison with tics, habitual acts are prolonged in duration, subject to volun-tary interruption, and consciously initiated (for further distinctions, see Table 15-2). Thumbsucking is a common activity of many infants, perhaps because of feelings of satisfaction derived from oral stimula-tion. Physicians and psychologists have both contributed data suggesting that early sucking behavior is normal either because it satisfies an innate oral drive (Levy, 1928) or because it is an expected consequence of learning related to late weaning (Sears and Wise, 1950). Few child experts express concern if the thumb-sucking is reported in a child of three years or less. In fact, some pediatricians are more accepting of thumbsucking than of the use of pacifiers. Dental authorities are not so much concerned over nap and nighttime thumbsucking as they are about continuous oral activity which ultimately subjects the teeth to abnormal pressures.

Thumbsucking becomes a psychological symptom worthy of attention when it meets the criteria mentioned at the begin-ning of this chapter, in particular if it per-sists way beyond the accepted age and when thumbsucking substitutes for more appropriate means for obtaining satisfac-tion and security. The frequent occurrence of thumbsucking later in life can be indicative of emotional frustrations and tensions. The thumbsucker appears to attain a state of serene satisfaction away from his troubles in much the same fash-ion as an adult achieves tension reduction from a cocktail; however, too frequent display of either behavior is a sign of continual presence of tension and the fail-ure of adaptive behavior.

The child is introduced to bodily ma-nipulation partly through a natural in-clination to explore and perhaps partly through accident. The fascination of one's own body parts can be illustrated by the fact that many infants show an early preoccupation with their own fists and will spend long periods in gazing at them. With increasing age and motor develop-ment, self-exploration continues and the child finds that handling some parts arouses pleasant sensations. In some in-stances, this discovery is accidentally initi-ated through surface irritants which lead to scratching which in turn produces agree-able sensations. Genital manipulation or masturbation, as with all behaviors pro-ducing gratification, attracts the interest of children. Yet cultural mores supported by some early medical literature have viewed the topic with near-abhorrence. Physicians of high reputation during the mid-eighteenth century and up to the early twentieth century authoritatively promulgated the view that masturbation was unhealthy. Tissot (1760) devoted an entire book to the physical and mental ailments resulting from masturbation with dire warnings to parents. Krafft-Ebing (1875), a leading psychiatric expert, even documented cases of insanity which he attributed to masturbation. Although modern physicians no longer condemn masturbation as vigorously as in the past, some concern is felt where the child appears to be compulsively (many times per day) masturbatory or exhibitionistic. Under these conditions, other signs of

TABLE 15-2. *Characteristics of Tics Versus Habitual Acts*

TICS	HABITUAL MANIPULATIONS OF THE BODY
1. They are automatisms, carried out involuntarily.	1. They are carried out at a much higher level of awareness.
2. They are ushered in suddenly, without any preparation whatsoever.	2. They are initiated very much more slowly and sometimes require a relatively complicated and deliberate preparation (e.g., assuming the proper position enabling the child to bite his toenails; curling up the hair before pulling it out; taking the hand out of the pocket or putting away a toy before introducing the finger into the mouth).
3. They last a few seconds only.	3. There is no limit to their possible duration.
4. They are localized twitchings of a circumscribed muscle group.	4. The performances involve the combined and successive activity of at least two parts of the body, the hand most frequently being one of them.
5. Although originally purposive (expressive or defensive), they seem to serve no obvious purpose after they have become automatized.	5. They appear to be purposive, in that the biting, pulling or sucking itself is the desired goal, usually felt and recognized as pleasurable.
6. The repetitions resemble each other to the point of cinematographic identity with regard to their duration, intensity, and course.	6. The repetitions may vary greatly with regard to their duration, intensity, and course. (The choice of the fingernails to be bitten may depend on their length, on which hand happens to be unoccupied, etc.)
7. Once the single tic has been started, it cannot be interrupted.	7. They may be interrupted at any stage of the single performance.
8. They are felt subjectively by the patient as something alien, irresistible, and uncontrollable, for which he does not consider himself responsible.	8. They are felt subjectively by the patient as actions for which he is responsible and which are subject to his volitional control.
9. There is rarely a subject-object relation between parts of the body.	9. One part of the body does something to another (the teeth bite the lips and fingernails; the hand pulls the ear or picks the nose.
10. They are personality disorders bearing the earmarks of unintended part-dysfunctions.	10. They are personality disorders appearing clearly as behavior dysfunctions of the individual as a whole.

SOURCE: From Leo Kanner, *Child psychiatry*, 1957. Courtesy of Charles C Thomas, Publishers, Springfield, Illinois.

emotional disturbance are also commonly found. Sometimes it is discovered that the child's activities are quite harmless but exaggerated out of proportion by prohibitive parents. Occasionally, a resentful child deliberately chooses genital manipulation because of its impact on his parents. In such cases, the sexual anxieties of the parents are as much the subject of treatment as the child's antagonisms. In most instances of prolonged and repeated masturbation, the belief is that it is a manifestation of a lonely or anxious child's search for security. Unfortunately, the behavior itself may promote even further isolation as it provokes parental censure or guilt feelings. Ultimately, masturbation produces greater and greater social withdrawal as the child finds pleasure in being by himself and experiences discomfort when with others as his guilt reactions are aroused.

Some types of habit disorders are unpleasant rather than pleasurable to the child, particularly those that interfere with the child's normal biological needs. Among these are the *sleep disturbances*. During the first few months of life, the infant is in a sleep or semiconscious state during the better part of each day and night. By seven months, most infants are on a sleep pattern in the night and a few short naps in the day. The first five years of life is often characterized by some sleep disturbances which reflect the normal tensions and stresses of physical and psychological growth processes. These tend to be of two types: inability to go to sleep and inability to maintain sleep. Reluctance to sleep may be precipitated by any number of normal causes such as the excitement of play prior to bedtime or the mild fearfulness from an overactive, maturing imagination. Reluctance may also be associated with less reasonable causes such as an excessive fear of being left alone or overly acquiescent parents who continue to respond to the child's

bedtime demands for attention. The wise parents arrange for a private bedroom assigned to each child rather than share space in the master bedroom, and maintain a fairly regular and firm bedtime routine. This will help eliminate many of the difficulties surrounding getting to sleep. Once asleep, children may experience awakenings which are again of little import if in moderation. A nightmare that is traceable to an unusually excitable day, a missed nap, or a trying incident, should be of minimal concern. However, habitual nightmares or the occurrence of night terrors require further investigation. Night terrors (pavar nocturnes) are severe night experiences involving panic, a hallucinatorylike reaction, and amnesia upon awakening. They are much more severe than a nightmare (see Table 15-3). Night terrors rarely continue beyond the age of puberty; nightmares tend to peak between ages four to six but may reappear occasionally thereafter. As yet there are no uniform explanations for nightmares or night terrors; in fact, there are few satisfactory explanations of normal dreaming. Viewpoints range from the premise that night terrors are due to carbon dioxide intoxication from adenoid breathing obstructions to the speculation that they result from the child's observation of parental intercourse. Ordinarily, psychopathologists consider sleep disorders in the context of the overall life pattern and emotional development of the child. Frequency and intensity of sleep disturbances are signs requiring further attention.

Learning Disorders

Disturbances in the learning process, particularly in the scholastic skills, form a highly important topic for child specialists. The term *specific learning disabilities* has been introduced into the literature as synonymous with *learning disorders*. The disorders referred to by these terms cover a broad spectrum including deficits in acquiring basic skills (reading, writing, spelling, arithmetic), speech difficulties, and pseudoretardation (an overall deficiency in intellectual performance attributed to emotional factors). Many different factors have been recognized as contributors to learning difficulties, such as sensory handicap, cultural deprivation, motivation, teaching methods, parental influence, and neurological deficit. Among the problems of primary importance are those involving the language or communication skills, especially reading and speaking. Impairment of either of these basic

TABLE 15-3. *Characteristics of Nightmares Versus Night Terrors*

NIGHTMARE	NIGHT TERROR
1. Fearful sleep experience after which the child wakes. The fear may persist for a while, giving way to good orientation and clear realization.	1. Fearful experience taking place in the sleep or in a somnolent twilight state, not followed by waking.
2. Slight defense movements or moaning immediately before waking are the only noticeable activities.	2. The features are distorted and express terror. The eyes stare, wide open. The child sits up in bed or even jumps to the floor in a great agitation, runs helplessly about, clutches at persons or objects, cries out that someone is after him, implores an imaginary dog or burglar to leave him alone, shouts for help, or screams inarticulately.
3. The child is already awake when the parents notice his distress and, after he has been calmed, is able to give a coherent account of what has happened.	3. The child, sleeping through the episode, is unable to give any account of his distress, which he is living out in all details while the parents look on and infer from his shouts and actions what might go on within the child. The attack cannot be cut short by any amount of calming and reassurance.
4. The child, after waking, knows all the persons and objects of his surroundings.	4. The persons and objects of the environment are often not recognized and may be mistaken for others and woven into the dream content.
5. No hallucinations ever occur.	5. The child hallucinates the frightening dream objects into the room.
6. There is usually no perspiration.	6. The attack is usually accompanied by perspiration.
7. A long period of waking and conscious going over of the dream situation may follow.	7. Peaceful sleep instantly follows the termination of the reaction.
8. The entire episode rarely lasts longer than one or two minutes.	8. The terror may last for some time, up to fifteen or twenty minutes.
9. The contents are remembered more or less clearly. The incident itself is always recalled.	9. There is complete amnesia for the contents as well as for the occurrence of the episode.

SOURCE: From Leo Kanner, *Child psychiatry*, 1957. Courtesy of Charles C Thomas, Publishers, Springfield, Illinois.

skills has severe consequences on the child's performance in other areas.

For most adults, *reading* seems an easy and natural activity. For the child in the elementary grade, being confronted with letters and words and obtaining meaning from them through "reading" is an almost magical experience, perhaps never again duplicated by any other life experience. Reading requires grasping form, spatial, and directional orientations, and associating objects and events with visual symbols. It involves sensory and perceptual processes since the child must first accurately see the distinctions among letters, then ultimately perceive words as whole units rather than letter-by-letter. A reading problem is said to exist when a child's reading competency is incongruent with his intellectual level and the level of his performance in other academic subjects. Among the primary causes of reading disability are sensory deficits, perceptual deficits, and emotional factors.

Simple sensory impairment such as poor visual acuity accounts for a minority of reading difficulties since eye vision clinics conducted in schools identify those children who need corrective lenses. Perceptual deficits have been of special interest in cases of *dyslexia*. Dyslexia is a term used by some to refer to a specific type of reading and writing disorder characterized by: word reversals ("was" for "saw"), mispronunciations ("quidlic" for "liquid"), and omissions, lack of phrasing or rhythm in reading (Slingerland, 1965). However, the term is inconsistently used and the meaning often confusing in the literature. In some instances, dyslexia is used interchangeably with the term reading disability or reading retardation; some consider dyslexia as a reading condition of unknown cause while others lean strongly toward the belief in a neurological foundation. There is some evidence that reading can be damaged through brain lesions (Geshwind, 1962). Such an effect of brain lesion has been well documented with aphasia—the inability to express oneself in words or to comprehend the speech of others. Investigators have also pursued the possibility of a relationship between cerebral dominance and dyslexia. A review of the research finding by Vernon (1958) revealed that there was very little in the way of consistent support for this notion. Myklebust and Boshes (1960) suggest that dyslexia be grouped among the "psycho-neurological" disorders—those which have a neurological component from injury or development occurring in average- or even superior-intellect children and often without other signs of neurological impairment. The last word on dyslexia appears to be still a long way off.

It is also possible that emotional factors are intertwined in reading disabilities. Just why the skills of reading should be interfered with and not the other skills of learning must be answered. One possibility is that reading or reading-readiness is attended to quite early in the primary grades and hence more subject to being the focus of emotional difficulties. A second possibility is the fact that reading involves a complexity of psychological processes (attending, associating sight and sound, remembering, conceptualizing) and is consequently more subject to being hindered by emotional tensions. Thus, any emotional conflicts that occurred concurrent with the child's beginning reading program would deter his ability to learn the fundamentals of reading and hence affect his later performances as well. Of course, parental pressures may contribute to the development of a reading problem through a direct overemphasis on the necessity of doing well and not failing in reading. In an early study of nonreaders, Missildine (1946) discovered that nearly all of the 30 children examined came from difficult home environments with a large proportion of the mothers being either overtly hostile or tense and coercive. Finally, the educational process itself must be mentioned. Staats and Staats (1963) suggest that the traditional school techniques for teaching reading are woefully inadequate and in fact conducive to developing habits that interfere with learning, such as daydreaming. For those children who do not respond to the incentives traditionally offered by teachers, or who develop aversive reactions, learning to read may develop slowly if at all. Other observers note that psychological symptoms may in turn develop in reaction to this reading disability (Shaw, 1966). Conduct problems such as negativism, boisterousness, aggressiveness, and clowning in the classroom may be a child's way of drawing attention away from his inadequacies in reading. The child might also overgeneralize his reading failures and become convinced that he is completely inadequate scholastically and as a person.

As with the reading disabilities, *speech* problems may appear in a number of ways and include delayed development, difficulties in articulation, speech rhythm interferences (stuttering), and the aphasias. Speech problems are, in addition, often predecessors of reading difficulties. Similar to reading symptoms, speech disturbances may arise from physical handicaps, neurological damage, deficient educational models, or psychological factors. The most common speech defect is poor *articulation* —the omission, substitution, or distortion of speech sounds (Mid-century White House Conference, 1952). With the exception of problems of delayed speech and stuttering, most of the primary speech difficulties are referred to specialists called speech pathologists or speech therapists. Approximately six percent of the referrals to child guidance clinics involve problems of speech (Gilbert, 1957).

Normal identifiable speech generally begins with the first word being uttered toward the end of the first year of life, with a rapid acceleration of vocabulary acquisition from the second year onward (Smith, 1926). *Delayed speech* may be expressed as delay in the appearance of spoken sounds, words, or speech considered appropriate for the child's age. As in reading, sensory defect is occasionally a causative factor—the child who does not hear will not readily learn to speak. A form of aphasia of expression can also interfere with the normal development of spoken language and has generally been associated with organic damage. Mental retardation is often suspected and therefore must be investigated where speech retardation has been noted in a youngster. Speech deficiency involving the failure to use speech for the purpose of communication is sometimes a result of infantile autism, a form of childhood psychosis. Delayed speech may also be a result of lack of environmental stimulation; there is no question that a child who lacks the reinforcement or encouragement for speaking will continue to rely upon other means that have been successful in obtaining what he wants such as gesturing or baby talk. Finally, the lack of good models of communication may be a factor related to slower speech development. Parents who converse and provide the child with a source to imitate serve an important role in the development of language.

Stuttering is a disturbance in the rhythmical flow of speech involving spasmodic vocalizations. Temporary stuttering occasionally occurs between the second through fourth years of life and has been attributed to the fact that the child's thoughts are progressing more rapidly than he is verbally able to express them. As with reading problems, boys appear to be more subject to stuttering than girls. There is some evidence that stuttering tends to run in families (Barbara, 1956; Johnson, 1955). Stuttering is considered a problem when it persists and is a frequent characteristic of the child. It appears even when the child is calm and may become more pronounced under conditions of stress. Many theories have been advanced regarding the origin of stuttering. Among the intriguing ones are those connected with the psychodynamics of aggression, and with cerebral dominance. Psychoanalytically oriented child pathologists stress the child's belief in the magic of words (Fenichel, 1945). One notion is that the child is fearful of speaking less he inadvertently permit his anger to be released in words and thereby symbolically destroy the parent. Another belief suggests that speech is symbolic of the child's aggressive feelings and his ambivalence; the inhibition and freeing of speech in stuttering is representative of his desire to control yet release his aggression. Orton (1937) and Travis (1931) introduced the theory that stuttering and reading disability occur because of antagonistic rivalry between the cerebral hemispheres. Travis believed this cortical interference to be constitutionally determined, although a shift of handedness of left-handed children could also produce such cerebral competition. Although the idea of cerebral interference has lost favor in recent years, the belief in a constitutional predisposition perhaps aggravated by environmental events has some adherents (Travis, 1957; Eisenson, 1958). A modified viewpoint proposes that stuttering appears for a variety of reasons, but it develops into a symptom as a result of excessive parental anxiety conveyed to the child who may be sensitive to disapproval and perfectionistic demands (Van Riper, 1953).

Conduct Disorders

The conduct disorders include the use of alcohol, sexual difficulties, and other patterns similar to the adult state. However, attention has been particularly focused on those conducts by nonadults that are in violation of a law or municipal ordinance, that is, *juvenile delinquency*. Again it is obvious that this classification in child pathology includes a variety of differing behaviors just as the terms habit disorders and learning disorders include widely varying behaviors within each. The common feature that ties together those behaviors called delinquent is the fact that they are all legally and socially unacceptable behaviors subject to penalty. Prevalence figures indicate that about one boy in every five will be taken into legal custody between the ages of 10 and 17 years, and this rate appears to be increasing faster than would be expected from the increase in population size alone (Children's Bureau, 1964; U.S. Dept. of Justice, 1964). In general, the juvenile delinquent shows the following characteristics:

1. He is male—more boys than girls are delinquent, with figures ranging from four to eight times more boys involved than girls. However, the rate of arrests of girls appear to be increasing at a higher rate, thus the gap is closing.

2. He is about 14 or 15 years of age at the time of arrest. Boys tend to become involved at an earlier age than girls, perhaps because of the closer supervision over girls by the family.

3. He lives in large metropolitan cities, although the rate of delinquency in the suburbs is increasing.

4. He is likely to be involved in petty offenses rather than crimes of violence. Boys are usually tried for theft or destruction of property, girls for sexual promiscuity or running away.

There are all differing types of delinquent behavior, in terms of the severity of the behavior as a "problem," the motivational components, and their chronicity. Juvenile delinquency is a legal term rather than a psychological one. Thus, a delinquent may be an adolescent who was caught damaging a neighbor's fence in a fit of frustration. A delinquent might also be a minor who was carefully schooled in the theft and resale of automobiles for financial profit or a youngster who engaged in lawbreaking as a result of a personal or familial emotional disturbance. Although the causation of delinquent behavior is a highly individualized and complex matter, it is instructive to consider some pertinent factors.

1. Sociological—poverty, lack of employment, life in the fringe areas of the city, appear to be associated with delinquency perhaps partly because the youngsters are faced with basic needs and lack the means for need-satisfaction.

2. Social—as with some adults, some delinquents have grown up and been schooled in a subcultural environment which values criminal activity as a normal way of life. Delinquent behavior is thus learned behavior in an "educational system" which promotes antisocial activities.

3. Familial—in some instances deficient learning of socialized behavior rather than misdirected learning may be involved. Disorganization within the family or broken homes fail to provide the youngster with the rules for socialized participation and the adolescent is left to devise his own standards or to adopt what little he can infer of his parents' standards. In a sense, the "social delinquent" is guided by a set of rules of his own subgroup while rejecting the values of the larger society, while the delinquent from a broken home lacks even a subgroup to look to for guidance.

4. Psychological—in some cases the delinquent act is incidental to intellectual, emotional, or educational problems. The mentally retarded youngster may break a law quite unintentionally; he is an unwitting victim of his own poor judgment and low intellect. In those with emotional disturbances, the delinquent act may be simply expressive of intensely hostile feelings displaced upon society, or a response

to an hallucinatory or delusional experience, or even a plea for attention and psychotherapeutic help. As was mentioned in the previous section, educational handicaps such as reading disabilities may precipitate acting-out behaviors partly out of feelings of frustration at the academic chores and partly as a means of drawing attention away from the deficiency.

Each case of delinquency must be considered on an individual basis. Even then it is not likely that a single primary factor can be identified as the source of the behavior. Multifactor approaches are needed to take into account the characteristics of the child, the familial structure, the group influences, or the community qualities, which interact to produce the antisocial act.

Psychophysiologic Disorders

The separation of psychological processes and physiological states in the child is less distinct than in the mature adult. An adult may focus his thoughts on finishing an intellectual exercise while pointedly preventing his physical needs from interfering; for a child, his thoughts, feelings, and physical condition are all intricately intertwined. In the course of human development, undifferentiated and wholistic activity characterizes the early phases of life. A hungry infant is uncomfortable all over; he is irritable, emotional, generally disturbed. As the infant develops, more specific and separable response patterns replace this earlier lack of differentiation. However, even in childhood the relationship between body and emotion is far from complete. The anticipations and tensions of the first day of school are often reflected in stomach twinges at breakfast or loss of appetite. Distaste for certain foods by a child may be quickly expressed in regurgitation. In the child with psychophysiologic disorders, the picture may be further complicated by heightened autonomic reactivity to environmental conditions and perhaps stress, and maternal attitudes and behavior toward the child. There is evidence that newborn infants three to four days old show quite clear individual differences in autonomic reactivity to loud sounds, with some being hyperreactors and others being hyporeactors (Richmond and Lustman, 1955). Gerard attended to the maternal conditions associated with psychophysiologic difficulties and found that the mothers of afflicted children tended to be rejecting and even at times physically cruel. Such mothers often appeared to have been particularly disturbed about particular physiological functions, for example, obsessively fearful of constipation developing in their children. This organ emphasis seemed to be passed on to the children in their symptom development, thus the bowel-concerned parent tends to have a child who suffers later from a bowel-connected disorder such as an ulcer in the colon (Gerard, 1953).

Most of the psychophysiologic disorders of adults have been found in children. Among these are ulcers, asthma, neurodermatitis, and hypertension (although rarely). In many instances, the personality characteristics and explanations for the disorder in the adult are reflected in children. For example, the asthmatic child has been perceived as either fearful of separation and rejection or as angry in his relationship with the parent. The ambivalence over dependency has also been stressed (French and Alexander, 1941; Finch, 1960). Of interest is the general belief that children suffering from psychophysiologic disorders are more disturbed than children with chronic or psychoneurotic disorders (Garner and Wenar, 1959; Finch and Hess, 1962).

Psychoneurotic Disorders

The psychoneurotic disorders account for a very large group of childhood complaints. These are exhibited through continuing symptoms which may have been precipitated by a traumatic circumstance but which has persisted instead of gradually dissipating. The child with a neurosis is not as severely disabled as a child suffering from a psychosis or a psychophysiologic disorder. As with the conception of the adult neurosis, this type of pathology in children is viewed by many as the result of psychological conflicts, emotional arousal, and defensive behavior. Conditions contributing to such conflicts may include:

1. Changes in the family structure or pattern, for example, through the birth of a new sibling.

2. Continuing stressful family patterns, for example, the presence of overt schisms between parental members, or the absence of parents or parent substitutes perhaps because of employment.

3. Parent pathology, for example, an anxious overprotecting mother, or an immature unhappy father.

4. Childhood sensitivity. Although there is yet no conclusive evidence that psychopathology is inborn, Chess (1960) has discovered that infants from the third month on display identifiable characteristics, such as high or low sensitivity and adaptive or nonadaptive responsivity.

5. Changes in environmental demands, for example, major geographic moves may face the child with school and neighborhood peers with entirely different standards and demands for acceptance.

Among the more common neurotic symptoms is that of the *phobias*. Fears of some kind or another seem to occur with almost predictable frequency in children in the course of their development. As the child matures, he becomes more perceptive of his environment, more able to comprehend the meaning of threat, and hence more likely to experience fears.

Developmentally it has been noted that fears of strange persons or events tend to decline while fears of a less tangible, more imaginary nature tend to increase up to the age of six years (Jersild and Holmes, 1935). In the neurotic child, such fears not only persist rather than decline with age, but they also consume a great deal of the child's daily life. The fears are omnipresent, extremely intense, and produce an experience akin to a panic state. The fears consume enormous amounts of energy as the child orients almost his entire activities toward avoiding or escaping from circumstances which have even the slightest connection with the feared objects. Among the fears associated with childhood are animal and school phobias. An *animal phobia* is a good example of the differences between a "normal" fear and a neurotic one. The child with a fear common in his developmental progress will exhibit a strong avoidance and fright reactions whenever he encounters the feared object. Such behavior may become a nuisance for the parents, especially if the object that is feared is a harmless insect such as an ant. However, the child is content when the animal is removed and will show no other signs of apprehension. In an amazingly short time, the child will "outgrow" the fear. The child with a phobia of animals (most commonly a dog or an insect) will also show strong avoidance and fright reactions upon encountering the feared object. In young children, the intensity of the reactions are similar in phobic and fearful nonphobic children. In older children, the phobic child reacts with something akin to panic while the fearful nonphobic child is able to show at least some controlled and adaptive behaviors. The phobic child seems to be more preoccupied with the feared object: he takes great pains to inspect his surroundings for signs of animals; he may refuse to visit or travel to unfamiliar places; he is constantly and anxiously

alert. Such an intense expression becomes very debilitating. In addition, the child appears to retain his fear as he grows older, perhaps embellishing on his security precautions or even increasing his avoidance behaviors and fearfulness. In a *school phobia,* similar diagnostic signs appear which distinguish it from fearfulness that is reality-based such as fear of a bully in school. The emotions connected with the phobia are pervasive and diffuse rather than tied to a specific reason (such as a bully). In addition, the fearfulness is so intense as to involve somatic effects such as gastrointestinal pain, nausea, vomiting. These somatic symptoms appear in the morning and frequently are severe enough to prevent the parent from sending the child to school. Since school phobias tend to occur in elementary school, continuing absence from school complicates the problem because the child fails to learn the fundamental academic skills. The further behind the child gets, the more likely that school attendance will become associated with failure experiences, thereby exacerbating the original phobic problem.

The factors contributing to phobias are many. A minor fear expressed by a child may become blown out of proportion because the parent exhibits an overreactive concern to the fear. Phobic children have been described as timid but also encouraged in their timidity by the presence of overprotective, insecure and inconsistent parents (Editorial, *British Medical Journal,* 1960). In some instances the child may actually acquire a specific phobia through learning. A traumatic experience with an animal or on the first day of school might initiate an extreme fear in the same way that a phobia was conditioned in Albert through classical conditioning (see Chapter 7). The high association between the number and types of fears of mothers and their children (Hagman, 1932) suggests some direct training occurs in the acquiring of fears. Perhaps the child learns the

Experiences, such as occur on the first attendance in school, can contribute heavily to potential fears. The insightful parent can do much to reassure the child and counteract any preliminary anxiety; a fearful or overprotective mother may instead initiate and encourage the development of a school phobia. (Elizabeth Wilcox)

fear of his parent through the imitation or modeling process proposed by Bandura (1962, 1963) and discussed earlier in Chapter 5. For some children, the possibility exists that it is not so much the object or situation itself that is feared but the feelings that are aroused. For example, an insecure child may be afraid of someday being left in school permanently; each time he is separated from his parents and taken to school his anxieties about complete separation are aroused (Johnson, 1941). Child pathologists have also searched for the origins of phobias in conflicts. Freud (1909) suggested that a fear of an animal might represent a displaced fear of the father. In general, this psychoanalytic viewpoint looks for certain needs or wishes that the child has repressed, then projected outward, then displaced to some object. The child feels hostile toward his parents, finds this an unacceptable feeling and therefore represses it. Then, according to the analyst, the child attributes the hostility to the parents (projection). Finally, since this, too, is anxiety provoking, the child displaces the hostility to another object such as an animal—it is a dog that is dangerous, hostile, threatening, and therefore feared.

Psychotic Disorders

Psychotic conditions in children are comparatively rare events. It is difficult to explain why the incidence appears low. A major possibility is that many go undetected because the signs of childhood psychoses might differ from those of adult psychoses. For example, systematic delusions or hallucinations are characteristic of adult schizophrenia but not of infantile autism. Another possibility is that childhood signs of psychoses are overlooked because of the difficulty of identifying these signs in the very young—psychotic thinking is undetectable if not verbally expressed and speech is not well developed in the young child. An additional complication facing the diagnostician is the very fact that the child is still developing; lack of speech may reflect a characteristic of the child's level of maturation or it may be a sign of psychosis; in contrast, absence of speech in an adult is a pathological sign since all adults are expected to talk. A further problem in identifying the severely disturbed child is the possibility that many children of preschool age are never called to anyone's attention. Unlike adults, children do not have the responsibilities of reporting to work or relating to other people. The preschooler can quietly play by himself, disturb no one, and be little more than a puzzle to his parents. As long as he stays out of trouble, he can remain ill but undiag-

nosed. A final factor that causes difficulty in childhood diagnosis is the lack of a real understanding of childhood pathology. The adult classification schemes have led the search for symptoms along predetermined paths. Perhaps childhood pathology involves entirely different systems or patterns of illnesses.

The variety of differing forms of psychoses that have been identified will provide the reader with some idea of the difference between childhood illnesses and adult psychoses. It should be repeated, however, that there is no single classification system that has proved acceptable to all child psychopathologists. For example, the terms "childhood schizophrenia," "infantile autism," and "atypical child" have all been widely used, often interchangeably. However, the picture becomes confused since Beata Rank (1955) uses the designation "atypical child" to cover a number of disorders including childhood schizophrenia; Mahler (1952) lists the autistic child as a form of childhood schizophrenia as does Kanner (1957); but both Rimland (1964) and Wing (1967) consider autism as different from childhood schizophrenia; and finally Reiser (1963) suggests that "infantile psychosis" be substituted for the terms "autism" and "atypical child" to refer to an illness that is different from childhood schizophrenia. Briefly, the following descriptions have been offered in connection with various terms for psychotic disorders in children:

Childhood Schizophrenia. A psychotic condition usually appearing after the age of five, after an infancy of normal-appearing psychological behavior (Hill, 1955). The schizophrenic child has usually experienced poor physical health from birth with respiratory, metabolic, and digestive difficulties being common (Bender, 1956; Fish, 1957). This child is disoriented, confused, or anxious about his environment (Benda, 1952, 1960). Hallucinations and

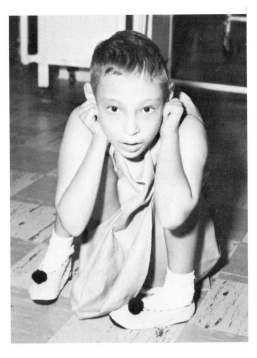

An *autistic* child exhibiting a posture characteristic for this youngster. (Charles H. Castes, *Handbook of Mental Retardation Syndromes*, 1966. Courtesy of Thomas Publishers, Springfield, Illinois)

delusions sometimes occur (Bettelheim, 1959). Bizarre motor behavior may include body-whirling and toe-walking. A normal child will try to resist body rotation if his head is turned but the schizophrenic child responds to body rotation to the extent of whirling with delight. Bender (1956) describes disturbances in sleeping, eating, and elimination, unpredictable temperature responses to illnesses, and flushing or perspiring.

The Atypical Child. These children have been characterized as exhibiting withdrawal, mutism or noncommunicative speech, bizarre postures, passivity or outbursts of rage, severe inhibition of impulses, and identification with inanimate objects or animals (Rank, 1955). The atypical child may speak but with an odd quality to his voice, shows a low frustration tolerance, ignores other children, and

may show strong or unusual fears. The attentiveness of the atypical child is often reported as impaired, either because of heightened distractibility or preoccupation (Brown, 1960).

Infantile Autism. These are exceptionally healthy and attractive children frequently of bright, well-educated parents. By the fourth month of life, the infant may show an apathy toward people, and may later be found sitting alone with a preoccupied look. Other symptoms include rocking or head-banging, insistence that the environment remain unchanged, and uneven development such that some skills are more developed than others. The autistic child will show intense preoccupation with mechanical objects and respond violently if interrupted. Many parents have suspected these children of being deaf because of their lack of responsiveness. Hallucinations are absent. Autistic children either lack the words "I" or "Yes" or infrequently use them in their speech (Rimland, 1964; Kanner, 1957).

Infantile Symbiotic Psychosis. These children are stricken later in life than the autistic children, most commonly around age four. Unlike the autistic child who resists contact with adults, the symbiotic one literally melts into his parent. Other major symptoms include: intense distress reactions, panic behavior with rage responses, unpredictable outbursts of destructiveness, stereotyped speech, alternation of a craving for body contact and a shrinking from it. Records will sometimes indicate unusual sensitivities in the child such that he might give up trying to walk for months because of experiencing a minor tumble. Children with this illness have been known to hallucinate and to feverishly attempt to test reality, for example, by touching objects to insure that they are real (Mahler, 1952, 1958, 1959).

Anaclitic Depression. This is the term

given by Spitz to the reaction of infants to prolonged separation from the mother. The early stage of this psychosis shows itself with what has been described as a sad expression on the infant's face. The infant will cling when approached. Following this phase, the infant tends to react to an approach by signs of distress such as crying although the infant may eventually learn to accept the visitor. Finally, complete withdrawal and depression sets in with eyes open and expressionless, face with rigid and frozen features, and a far away look as if in a daze. Continued separation leads to deterioration and infant mortality becomes a distinct possible danger.

Manic-Depressive Reaction. This affect disorder, characterized by extreme moods, is believed by experts to be rare in children. In fact, some (Lurie and Lurie, 1950) assert that manic-depressive psychosis does not occur in childhood. Transitory expressions of exaggerated moods apparently do occur during childhood but are rarely diagnosed as manic-depression. In hyperkinetic children (a disorder often associated with brain injury) a certain state of excitement may occur but without the other characteristics of manic-depressive psychosis such as the infectious quality of euphoria, excitement, or hilarity. By the age of puberty, or adolescence, manic-depression is believed to appear as a distinct affliction.

Because of certain symptoms that may be shared, psychotic disorders are sometimes confused with other types of disturbances such that careful differential diagnosis is necessary. The parents of autistic children have almost invariably questioned their child's hearing as soon as abnormal behaviors were noted. The autistic child and the truly deaf child both seem unresponsive to being called or being addressed. Mental retardation is also commonly suspected because of certain similarities such as low level intellectual performance by many psychotic children. The possibility of brain damage may be considered in psychotic children who exhibit destructive outbursts, distractibility, or stereotyped hyperactivity. In diagnosing a form of psychosis instead of these other disorders a variety of factors are sifted and examined. An autistic child may sit passively in a hearing testing room with the sound intensity turned up to pain level without showing the slightest response; however, continued observation may reveal that the child turns toward the sound of a tractor heard at a distance. Similarly, the mentally retarded child is consistently unable to perform above his intellectual capacity on all types of questions; however, the schizophrenic child may fail a simple question but pass a difficult one. The outbursts, distractibility, or restless wanderings of the brain-injured child seem to be in a context of an overresponsiveness to the environment; on the other hand, the psychotic child still appears to be isolated from the environment in spite of the activity level.

The treatment of the psychotic child has included nearly every approach used with adults including metrazol and electroshock (Bender, 1947), and prefrontal lobotomies (Freeman and Watts, 1947, 1951). Drug therapy has been prescribed (Fish, 1960; Freedman, 1958) but with disappointing results. Tranquilizers seem to make the disturbed child even more distressed, tense, and restless. Psychotherapy has taken many approaches: Mahler (1952) recommends that the therapist use music, rhythmic activities, and other sensory enticements to lure the autistic child out of his private world; Rank suggests that the therapist first permit a maximum of gratification and a minimum of frustration for the atypical child, then aid the child to postpone gratification and become more socialized (1955); Ferster believes that the psychotic symptoms of children

Autistic children are often apathetic toward others and socially unresponsive. Basic social contact is being developed in the two autistic boys (*above*) through the use of food reinforcers. (Allan Grant/Peter H. Schub)

can be brought under control through the systematic dispensing of reinforcement (1961, 1962); and Lovaas et al. (1965) attempts to attract the attention of a withdrawn child or control his behavior by relying upon painful or startling stimuli such as the therapist's shouts, argumentative demands, or even electric shock.

Organic Disorders

Organic disorders may arise from a multitude of causes. Prenatal factors include:

> Irradiation
> Germ cell defects
> Developmental defects

Nutritional deficiencies
Maternal infections
    (e.g., German measles)
Factors affecting the child at or after birth include:

Tumors
Head injury
Premature birth
Central nervous system
    disease
Illnesses producing
    prolonged high fever

Damage to the brain can show itself in physical disturbances. When gross motor disabilities occur, the term cerebral palsy is often used. Aphasia, the difficulty in communication or comprehension, may also result from organicity. Epilepsy is another common complication of brain injury, especially in childhood. In many cases, the telltale physical symptoms may be absent and other signs may signal the presence of brain damage. Among the more common psychological symptoms are the following:

anxiety
impulsivity
hyperactivity
distractibility

The *anxiety* of the brain-injured child is believed to be connected to the overactivity of the child. He is overly responsive to external and internal stimuli, being driven to a tense state by overstimulation and an inability to respond more selectively (Bender, 1949; Goldstein, 1954). It may also be similar to the disruptive emotions characterized as the "catastrophic reaction" seen in organic adults when confronted with a problem they can no longer solve (see Chapter 12).

In common with this overresponsiveness is the *impulsivity* of the brain-damaged child. The child seems unable to inhibit or delay his responses but acts out whatever urge overtakes him at the moment. This impulsivity may lead him to be labeled as destructive or aggressive since he tends to carry out his urges without regard for others. It is common to hear teachers and parents complain about their inability to control the brain-injured child. Yet it becomes even more evident that the child himself is equally unable to control his own behavior. He acts when he feels so impelled, whether it be suddenly pushing another child or breaking a toy.

The *hyperactivity* of the brain-injured child has been considered a prominent trait. Continuous restless flow of movement seemed to be a characteristic such that parents were quickly worn out if they attempted to keep up with their children. Such behaviors tend to be especially troublesome in school settings where the child is normally expected to sit quietly for long periods of time. In such a situation, the brain-damaged child may be found squirming in his seat, turning around, moving his legs, getting up and walking, and in general calling attention to himself through his heightened activity level. It should be noted that motor overactivity, called hyperkinesis, is not limted to brain-damaged children but may also appear in psychotic children such as those with autism.

The *distractibility* of the brain-injured child is another complication to his adjustment. He seems to be unable to attend very long to a single stimulus, task, or activity. There are no such things as irrelevant events for the child, he responds to everything with equal interest (and soon with equal disinterest). He seldom completes an assignment or even a self-initiated activity but will often leave part way through to pursue something else. Unlike the psychotic child who might quit a task because he is unmotivated and prefers to withdraw to his own inner fantasies, the brain-damaged child is quite motivated by external events and quits a task because he has become attracted to another.

In closing this section, it should be noted that the separation between the organic and the psychotic disorders may well prove to be an artificial one. Moreover, there is speculation building that childhood psychoses may be traceable to organic factors. Rimland (1964), for example, hypothesizes that infantile autism is due to organic impairment resulting from oxygen imbalance. Bender (1953, 1961) has proposed that childhood schizophrenia is a form of neurological disorder associated with a maturational lag occurring at the embryonic level. In support she reports the large percentage of abnormal electroencephalographic readings obtained on schizophrenic children. On the other hand, equally strong arguments have been presented by those who believe that parental environmental factors are primary in childhood psychosis such as the influence of schizophrenogenic parents or disturbed family units (Rank, 1949, 1955; Haley, 1959). Similarly, questions are being raised about brain damage and whether the psychological symptoms are caused by the damage or by the parental reactions to the child's handicap. In essence, the proposal is that brain injury clearly contributes to deficits in learning, memory, and intellectual functioning, but may be only of minor importance in the appearance of such symptoms as hyperkinesis (Pond, 1965).

Glossary

Anaclitic depression: A disorder characterized by sadness and withdrawal and related to separation from the parents.

Atypical child: A disorder characterized by withdrawal, mutism or noncommunicative speech, bizarre postures, and disturbance in identification.

Cerebral palsy: Motor disturbances associated with brain lesion.

Childhood schizophrenia: A disorder characterized by disorientation, confusion, anxiety about the environment, bizarre motor behavior, and sometimes hallucination. Generally begins after age five years.

Delinquency: Violation of legal code by a young person.

Dyslexia: A disorder characterized by reading and writing disability, word reversals, mispronunciations, omissions, and lack of phrasing or rhythm during reading.

Habit disorders: Disorders involving repeated acts, for example, tics, sleep disturbances.

Habitual acts: A habit disorder characterized by prolonged, consciously initiated acts that are subject to voluntary interruption.

Hyperkinesis: Motor excitability symptomatic of brain damage but also present in childhood psychosis.

Infantile autism: A disorder characterized by apathy, preoccupation with objects instead of people. Frequently the offspring of well-educated parentage. May begin as early as four months of age.

Infantile symbiotic psychosis: A disorder characterized by extreme dependence on the parent, unpredictable emotional outbursts, stereotyped speech, and unusual sensitivity to experiences.

Learning disorders: Disorders involving disturbances in the learning process especially scholastic skills, for example, academic and communication skills.

Night terror: Sleep disturbance characterized by awakenings, panic, hallucinations, and amnesia for the event.

Stuttering: A disorder characterized by disturbance in the rhythm of speech and involving spasmodic vocalizations.

Tic: A disorder characterized by the involuntary repetition of muscular spasms, usually of brief duration and not subject to voluntary control.

References

Bandura, A. Social learning through imitation. In M. Jones (Ed.), *Nebraska symposium on Motivation.* Lincoln, Nebr.: University of Nebraska Press, 1962.

Bandura, A. Behavior theory and identificatory learning. *Amer. J. Orthopsychiat.,* 1963, **33**, 591.

Barbar, D. Understanding stuttering. *New York State Medical Journal,* 1956, **55**, 1789.

Beller, E. *The clinical process.* New York: Macmillan, 1962.

Benda, C. *Developmental disorders of mentation and cerebral palsies.* New York: Grune & Stratton, 1952.

Benda, C. Childhood schizophrenia, autism and Heller's disease. In P. Bowman & H. Mautner (Eds.), *Mental retardation: proceedings of the first international conference on mental retardation.* New York: Grune & Stratton, 1960.

Bender, L. Childhood schizophrenia. *Amer. J. Orthopsychiat.,* 1947, **17**, 40.

Bender, L. The psychological problems of children with organic brain disease. *Amer. J. Orthopsychiat.,* 1949, **19**, 404.

Bender, L. Childhood schizophrenia. *Psychiat. Quart.,* 1953, **27**, 663.

Bender, L. Schizophrenia in childhood: its recognition, descriptions, and treatment. *Amer. J. Orthopsychiat.,* 1956, **26**, 499.

Bender, L. The brain and child behavior. *A.M.A. Arch. gen. Psychiat.,* 1961, 4, 531.

Bettelheim, B. Joey: a "mechanical boy." *Scient. Amer.,* 1959, **200**, 116.

British Medical Journal. School phobia. (Editorial), *Br. Med. J.,* 1960, **2**, 848.

Brown, J. Prognosis from symptoms of preschool children with atypical development. *Amer. J. Orthopsychiat.,* 1960, **30**, 382.

Chess, S. *An introduction to child psychiatry.* New York: Grune & Stratton, 1959.

Chess, S. et al. Implications of a longitudinal study of child development for child psychiatry. *Amer. J. Psychiat.,* 1960, **117**, 434.

Children's Bureau, Statistics on public institutions for delinquent children, 1963. *Children's Bureau Statistics Series no. 78.* Washington, D.C.: U.S. Department of Health, Education, and Welfare, 1964.

Eisenson, J. A perseverative theory of stuttering. In J. Eisenson (Ed.), *Stuttering: a symposium.* New York: Harper & Row, 1958.

Fenichel, O. *The psychoanalytic theory of neurosis.* New York: Norton, 1945.

Ferster, C. Positive reinforcement and behavioral deficits of autistic children. *Child Developm.* 1961, **32**, 437.

Ferster, C. & DeMyer, M. A method for the experimental analysis of the behavior of autistic children. *Amer. J. Orthopsychiat.,* 1962, **32**, 89.

Feshwind, N. The anatomy of acquired disorders of reading. In J. Money (Ed.), *Reaching disability*. Baltimore: Johns Hopkins Press, 1962.

Finch, S. *Fundamentals of child psychiatry*. New York: Norton, 1960.

Finch, S. & Hess, J. Ulcerative colitis in children. *Amer. J. Psychiat.*, 1962, **118**, 819.

Fish, B. Drug therapy in child psychiatry. *Compreh. Psychiat.*, 1960, **1**, 55, 212.

Fish, B. The detection of schizophrenia in infancy: a preliminary report. *J. nerv. ment. Dis.*, 1957, **125**, 1.

Freedman, A. Treatment of autistic schizophrenic children with Marsilid. *J. clin. exper. Psychopathol.*, 1958, **19**, suppl. 1, 138.

Freeman, W. & Watts, J. *Psychosurgery in the treatment of mental disorders and intractable pain*. (2nd ed.) Springfield, Ill.: Thomas, 1951.

Freeman, W. & Watts, J. Schizophrenia in childhood: its modification by prefrontal lobotomy. *Digest of Neurology and Psychiat.*, 1947, **15**, 202.

French, R. & Alexander, F. Psychogenic factors in bronchial asthma. *Psychosom. Med. Monogr. I, II*, 1941.

Freud, S. Analysis of a phobia in a five-year-old boy. In *The standard edition of the complete psychological works of Sigmund Freud*. Vol. X, James Strachey (Ed). London: Hogarth Press, 1953. First published in 1909.

Garner, A. & Wenar, C. *The mother-child interaction in psychosomatic disorders*. Urbana, Ill.: University of Illinois Press, 1959.

Gerard, M. Genesis of psychosomatic symptoms in infancy. In F. Deutsch (Ed.), *The psychosomatic concept in psychoanalysis*. New York: International University Press, 1953.

Gilbert, M. A survey of "referral problems" in metropolitan child guidance centers. *J. clin. Psychol.*, 1957, **13**, 37.

Goldstein, K. The brain-injured child. In Michael-Smith (Ed.), *Pediatric problems in clinical practice*. New York: Grune & Stratton, 1954.

Goodenough, F. Anger in young children. *Inst. Child. Welf. Monogr. Series No. 9*. Minn.: University of Minnesota Press, 1931.

Hagman, R. A study of fears of children of preschool age. *J. exp. Educ.* 1932, **1**, 110.

Haley, J. Family of the schizophrenic: a model system. *J. nerv. ment. Dis.*, 1959, **129**, 357.

Jersild, A. & Holmes, F. Children's fears. *Child Developm. Monogr.*, 1935, No. 20.

Johnson, A. et al. School phobia. *Amer. J. Orthopsychiat.*, 1941, **11**, 702.

Johnson, W. *Stuttering in children and adults*. Minn.: University of Minnesota Press, 1955.

Kagan, J. & Moss, H. *Birth to maturity: a study in psychological development*. New York: Wiley, 1962.

Kanner, L. *Child psychiatry*. Springfield, Ill.: Thomas, 1957.

Kessler, J. *Psychopathology of childhood*. Englewood Cliffs, N.J.: Prentice-Hall, 1966.

Krafft-Ebing, R. Über Irresein durch Onanie bei Mannern. *Allg. Zeitschr. f. Psychiat.*, 1875, **31**, 425.

Lovaas, O., Schaeffer, B., & Simmons, J. Building social behavior in autistic children by use of electric shock. *J. exp. res. Personal.*, 1965, **1**, 99.

Levy, D. Fingersucking and accessory movements in early infancy: an etiological study. *Amer. J. Psychiat.*, 1928, **7**, 881.

Lurie, L. & Lurie, M. Psychosis in children: a review. *J. Pediat.*, 1950, **36**, 801.

Macfarlane, J. Study of personality development. In R. Barker, J. Kounin, and H. Wright (Eds.), *Child behavior and development*. New York: McGraw-Hill, 1943.

Macfarlane, J., Allen, L., & Honzik, M. *A developmental study of the behavior problems of normal children between twenty-one months and fourteen years*, University of California Publications in Child Developm., 1954, no. 2.

Mahler, M. Tics and impulsions in children: a study in motility. *Psychoan. Quart.,* 1944, **13**, 430.

Mahler, M. On child psychosis and schizophrenia: autistic and symbiotic infantile psychosis. *Psychoanal. Study of the Child.* New York: International University Press, 1952, **7**, 286.

Mahler, M. On child psychosis and schizophrenia: autistic and symbiotic infantile psychosis. *Psychoanal. Study Child.* New York: International University Press, 1952.

Mahler, M. Autism and symbiosis: two extreme disturbances of identity. *Int. J. Psychoanal.,* 1958, **39**, 77.

Mahler, M., Furer, M., & Settlage, C. Severe emotional disturbances in childhood psychosis. In S. Arieti (Ed.), *American Handbook of Psychiatry.* New York: Basic Books, 1959.

Martin, W. & Stendler, C. *Child development: the process of growing up in society.* New York: Harcourt Brace, 1953.

Mid-century White House conference, Report on speech disorders and speech correction. *J. speech & hearing disorders,* 1952, **17**, 129.

Missildine, W. The emotional background of thirty children with reading disability. *Nerv. Child,* 1946, **5**, 263.

Myklebust, H. & Boshes, B. Psychoneurological learning disorders in children. *Arch. of Pediatrics,* 1960, **77**, 247.

National Institute of Mental Health, *Mental Health of Children.* Bethesda, Md.: U.S. Department of Health, Education, and Welfare, 1965.

Orton, S. *Reading, writing and speech problems in children.* New York: Norton, 1937.

Pearson, G. *Emotional disorders of childhood.* New York: W. W. Norton, 1949.

Pond, D. The neuropsychiatry of childhood. In J. Howells (Ed.), *Modern perspectives in child psychiatry.* Springfield, Ill.: Thomas, 1965.

Rank, B. Intensive study and treatment of preschool children who show marked personality deviations, or "atypical development," and their parents. In G. Caplan (Ed.), *Emotional problems of early childhood.* New York: Basic Books, 1955.

Rank, B. Adaptation of the psychoanalytic technique for the treatment of young children with atypical development. *Amer. J. Orthopsychiat.,* 1949, **19**, 130.

Reiser, D. Psychosis of infancy and early childhood, as manifested by children with atypical development. *New Engl. J. Med.,* 1963, **269**, 790, 844.

Richmond, J. & Lustman, S. Autonomic function in the neonate: I. Implications for psychosomatic theory. *Psychosomatic Med.,* 1955, **17**, 269.

Rimland, B. *Infantile autism.* New York: Appleton-Century-Crofts, 1964.

Ross, A. *The practice of clinical child psychology.* New York: Grune & Stratton, 1959.

Sears, R. & Wise, G. Relation of cup feeding in infancy to thumbsucking and the oral drive. *Amer. J. Orthopsychiat.,* 1950, **20**, 123.

Shaw, C. *The psychiatric disorders of childhood.* New York: Appleton-Century-Crofts, 1966.

Slingerland, B. Recognition and help for today's intelligent specific language disability children. Paper read at the 43rd International Conference of Council for Exceptional Children. Portland, Ore., 1965.

Smith, M. An investigation of the development of the sentence and the extent of vocabulary in young children. *University of Iowa studies in child welfare,* 1926, **3**, no. 5.

Staats, A. & Staats, C. *Complex human behavior.* New York: Holt, Rinehart and Winston, 1963.

Tissot, S. *De l'onanisme ou Dissertation physique sur les maladies produites par la masturbation.* Lausanne: Chapuis, 1760.

Travis, L. *Speech pathology.* New York: Appleton-Century-Crofts, 1931.

Travis, L. *Handbook of speech pathology.* New York: Appleton-Century-Crofts, 1957.

U.S. Department of Justice. *Federal Bureau of Investigation Uniform Crime Report, 1963.* Washington, D.C.: U.S. Dept. of Justice, 1964.

Van Riper, C. *Speech therapy: a book of readings.* Englewood Cliffs, N.J.: Prentice-Hall, 1953.

Vernon, M. *Backwardness in reading: a study of its nature and origin.* Cambridge, Mass.: Cambridge University Press, 1958.

Wickman, E. *Children's behavior and teachers' attitudes.* New York: Commonwealth Fund, 1928.

Wing, J. *Early childhood autism: clinical, educational, and social aspects.* New York: Pergamon Press, 1967.

16 *Mental Retardation*

TERMINOLOGY

This chapter deals with a group of conditions having one common aspect: a significant deficit in intellectual functioning or development. As will be seen, this characteristic is present in persons who are otherwise extremely different from one another in their other traits. The term *mental retardation* is the most accepted heading used to classify these individuals, perhaps because it avoids some of the connotations of other terms that have been used synonymously, for example, *feeblemindedness, mental subnormality, mental defect* or *mental deficiency*. In the Soviet Union, the term *oligophrenia* is preferred where there is confirmed neurological pathology involved; in Great Britain, the term *amentia* is the more widely accepted one for referring to mental retardation. In the United States, the term *mental retardation* has the widest acceptance among professionals although the term *mental deficiency* has also had frequent usage; a leading professional organization is known as the American Association on Mental Deficiency; national parents' associations includes the National Association for Retarded Children, the president of the United States' special committee on this topic has been named The President's Committee on Mental Retardation.

NATURE OF MENTAL RETARDATION

According to the official definition adopted in 1959 by the American Association on Mental Deficiency, "Mental retardation refers to subaverage general intellectual functioning which originates during the development period and is associated with impairment in adaptive behavior" (Heber, 1959). One of the major means for measuring intellectual capabilities has been the intelligence test, such as the Stanford-Binet (Terman and Merrill, 1937). This type of test compares the performance of a child with the functioning expected of normally developing children of his chronological age group. If the child's test performance is equal to that expected of his chronological age level, then it is said that his mental age is equal to his chronological age. This can be expressed as a quotient of the child's mental age divided by his chronological age. When this quotient is multiplied by 100, the resulting figure is called the intelligence quotient, or IQ. A child whose mental age is keeping pace with his chronological age will achieve an IQ of 100; a child whose mental growth appears to be ahead of his chronological age will show an IQ above 100; a child whose mental age is below that of his chronological age will attain an IQ below 100. Generally, most people will achieve an IQ level of 100, with fewer and fewer people attaining higher or lower levels (see Fig. 16-1). The IQ has served as a convenient means for identifying mental retardation since mental retardation involves intellectual functioning below the level considered average for a particular age group. The problem has been to determine the cut-off point separating a person to be called "retarded" from a person still considered "average." Traditionally, the IQ of 70 has been accepted as the level that separates retarded performance from normal performance. This is an entirely arbitrary figure; however, its establishment has provided a fairly useful frame of reference. In addition, IQ figures have been used to provide further subdivisions among the retarded (see Table 16-1). Unfortunately, the use of the IQ involves certain hazards. Heiser and Wolman (1965) point out that "It imputes a totally unreasonable omniscience to the intelligence test, a power which has been seldom, if ever, claimed by test constructors." Among the problems inherent in intelligence tests are the following:

1. The influence of culture on perfor-

mance—immigrant families, culturally deprived youngsters, or minority groups may perform low on intelligence tests even though they may be intellectually quite competent.

2. The differences in the nature of different tests—tests vary in content and format such that some may measure verbal skills while others measure the ability to reason or to solve problems. It is possible that a person would score within the retarded range on some tasks but not on others (Suinn, 1967; Witkin, 1965).

TABLE 16-1. *Stanford-Binet Intelligence Test Scores for Different Levels of Mental Retardation*

LEVEL OF RETARDATION IN INTELLIGENCE	RANGE IN STANDARD DEVIATION VALUE	RANGE IN IQ SCORES FOR REVISED STANFORD-BINET, L.
Borderline	−1.01 to −2.00	83–68
Mild	−2.01 to −3.00	67–52
Moderate	−3.01 to −4.00	51–36
Severe	−4.01 to −5.00	35–20
Profound	< −5.00	<20

SOURCE: From Mental retardation: concept and classification, by Rick Heber in *Readings on the exceptional child.* Edited by E. Philip Trapp & Philip Himelstein. Copyright © 1962 by Meredith Corporation. Reprinted by permission of Appleton-Century-Crofts.

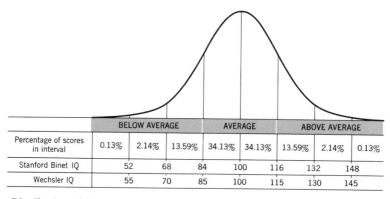

Figure 16-1. **Distribution of intelligence levels.**

3. The presence of certain fluctuations in performance over time—a test performance on one day may vary with the performance shown on a different day. Ideally, a test would show perfect *reliability*, meaning the results on one day would be identical with the results obtained on any other day. However, most tests do show some fluctuations such that a person may attain an IQ of 69 on one day and 71 on another.

In recognition of such difficulties and limitations of the IQ measurement, authorities have recommended the inclusion of other criteria for the diagnosis of mental retardation. Among the most widely accepted criteria used until recently has been those offered by Doll (1941). He believed that mental retardation involves the presence of several characteristics:

An essentially incurable condition
Constitutional in origin
Intellectual subnormality
Arrest of intellectual development
State of social incompetence

The first two characteristics are no longer readily accepted today. Although some forms of mental retardation are incurable, other conditions are viewed as reversible. In addition, it is now recognized that mental retardation can involve intellectually subnormal performance because of environmental deprivations or severe emotional disturbance. In effect, the modern stance is to assert that mental retardation is not necessarily a fixed characteristic, but an expression of intellectual and social inadequacy which may derive from a variety of sources. The remaining characteristics suggested by Doll have met with general acceptance, particularly the inclusion of the social criterion. In England, social incapacity has been an integral part of the legal definition of mental retardation (Tredgold, 1952). The concept of social competence calls attention to the fact that a person may demonstrate intellectual incompetence on IQ measures, but an acceptable level of social competence in life situations. Social competence in its broadest sense includes an evaluation of social maturity. In children, for example, this may involve self-help, socialization, self-direction; in adults, social maturity may be exhibited in responsiveness to cultural mores, signs of responsibility and trustworthiness, and self-support. Many adults who might be diagnosed as mentally retarded on the basis of IQ performance are managing an adequate personal, social, and vocational adjustment in the community.

A useful means for grasping the nature of mental retardation is to consider the descriptions of individuals with various levels of retardation. For this purpose, the official classification of the American Association on Mental Deficiency will be used. This scheme identifies four levels of retardation: the profoundly retarded, the severely retarded, the moderately retarded, and the mildly retarded (see Table 16-2). The discussion to follow will describe the distinct general characteristics of these levels.

The Profoundly Retarded

Those individuals who are considered to be profoundly retarded suffer from such a severe impairment that their IQ performance ranges below 20 (roughly, this means that a child aged 15 would have a mental age of a three year old if his IQ were 20). These individuals comprise about 1.5 percent of all retarded persons. Usually, serious central nervous system pathology has occurred. These individuals are not responsive to any current educational or training programs; most will remain in custodial institutional care. In many cases, other handicaps are also present such as deafness, mutism, seizures, lack of motor coordination. Their health is poor and a short life expectancy is characteristic.

The Severely Retarded

Those persons who are considered severely retarded will attain an IQ score between 20 and 35 (roughly equivalent to a mental age of 5¼ for a 15 year old with an IQ of 35). These persons comprise about 3.5 percent of all retarded persons. This group can develop limited levels of self-help skills and can lessen their dependency upon others. Many will not profit from such training opportunities but will remain in institutional or residential care under close supervision and support for their entire lives. Their motor and speech development is usually retarded, and central nervous system pathology is typically present.

The Moderately Retarded

Those individuals who are moderately retarded will achieve an IQ score between 36 and 52 (roughly equivalent to a mental age of about 8 for a 15 year old with an IQ of 52). These persons comprise about 6 percent of all retarded individuals. These

individuals can achieve a semi-independent status. They are capable of acquiring self-help skills in feeding, toileting, and bathing, and may be trained to achieve partial financial self-support in a special protective employment setting called a sheltered workshop. Motor and speech capabilities can be developed and improved to a level that permits employment and adequate communication. In a few, a minimal level of academic progress is attainable, possibly the third grade.

The Mildly Retarded

Those individuals who are mildly retarded will achieve an IQ score between 53 and 69 (roughly equivalent to a mental age of 10 for a 15 year old with an IQ of 69). These individuals comprise about 89 percent of all retarded persons. They are capable of learning social and communication skills under specially structured and supervised classes. Learning the use of numbers, arts and crafts, and manual arts, is possible. Many have the capacity to live a minimal but independent existence. A number marry and raise families, but these frequently encounter

TABLE 16-2. *Terms Used to Describe Mental Retardation in Relation to Measured Intelligence*

RANGE IN IQ SCORES ON TESTS WITH STANDARD DEVIATION OF 15	TERMS USED IN AAMD MANUAL (1961 REVISION)[a]	APA NOMENCLATURE (1952)[b]	FORMER TERMS	EDUCATIONAL CLASSIFICATION
70-84	Borderline	Mild	Borderline	Slow learner (sometimes included in educable range)
55-69	Mild	Moderate	Moron	Educable retarded
40-54	Moderate	Severe	Imbecile	Trainable retarded
25-39	Severe	Severe	Imbecile	Trainable retarded
Below 25	Profound	Severe	Idiot	Total-care group

[a] Heber, R. Modifications in the manual on terminology and classification in mental retardation. Monogr. Suppl. *Amer. J. ment. Def.*, 1961, **65**, 499.

[b] American Psychiatric Association, *Diagnostic and statistical manual: Mental disorders.* Washington, D.C.: Mental Hospital Service, 1952.

SOURCE: J. Kessler, *Psychopathology of childhood.* © 1966. Reprinted by permission of Prentice-Hall, Inc.

some difficulty in managing their family matters. Although they are usually slow in their early physical development, few exhibit observable physical disabilities as adults.

INCIDENCE

In 1962, the President's Panel on Mental Retardation estimated that mental retardation affects 10 times more individuals than does diabetes, 20 times more than tuberculosis, 25 times more than muscular dystrophy, and 600 times more than infantile paralysis. Only emotional mental disorders, heart disease, arthritis, and cancer affect a greater number of individuals. An estimated 5 million persons were retarded in 1962; this figure increased by another 1 million by 1967 (The President's Panel on Mental Retardation, 1962, 1967). It was predicted that 2100 infants who are or will be classified as mentally retarded were to be born every week in 1968. Approximately 677,000 children attend special classes for the mentally retarded, with another 201,000 residing in institutions. An estimated 2 million adults are in need of job training and placement services. Even at minimum wages, these individuals are losing about 6 billion dollars in annual earning capacity by remaining unemployed because of retardation and lack of opportunities. Over 400 million dollars a year is being appropriated for federal programs to help the mentally retarded. More than twice this amount is spent each year by states, localities, and private organizations.

THE CAUSES OF MENTAL RETARDATION

An understanding of the contributors to mental retardation has developed over the years. An early analysis was developed by Tredgold (1908) who classified mental retardation into four etiological groups*:

1. Primary amentia—mental retardation due to heredity. Also known as retardation associated with endogenous factors.

2. Secondary amentia—mental retardation due to environmental or external factors such as trauma, disease, dysfunction following birth. Also known as retardation due to exogenous factors.

3. Amentia due to mixed or combined hereditary and environmental causes.

4. Amentia due to unknown cause.

Although it is still instructive to remember this broad system of endogenous versus exogenous, the current etiological classification scheme accepted by the American Association on Mental Deficiency (AAMD) (Heber, 1961) recognizes eight primary causative factors:

1. Conditions due to infection.

2. Conditions due to intoxication.

3. Conditions due to trauma or physical agent.

4. Conditions due to disorder of metabolism, growth, or nutrition.

5. Conditions due to new growths.

6. Conditions due to (unknown) prenatal influence.

7. Conditions due to unknown or uncertain cause with structural reactions manifest.

8. Conditions due to unknown (or presumed psychologic) cause with functional reaction alone manifest.

The American Association on Mental Deficiency has also developed a sophisticated system for classifying specific diseases or conditions using a three-digit number-

* Tredgold has subsequently revised his classification into three major groups: primary, developmental, and environmental (Tredgold and Soddy, 1963).

ing diagnostic code as a shorthand recording system. It is interesting that genetic factors are not given a primary place in this system, although it may be mentioned along with the diagnostic code. Similarly, sociocultural factors have been omitted from direct reference. A brief exposition on these factors and some of the AAMD primary factors follows.

Genetic Factors

Certain conditions are transmitted directly from parent to child. In some cases, a disease is inherited via a dominant gene such as the rare syndrome called *tuberous sclerosis* (characterized by a rash at about age four, and tumors in the brain and other body organs). Among those disorders believed to be related to recessive genes are *amaurotic idiocy* (involving a rapid neurological degeneration, the appearance of a characteristic cherry red spot in the retina, and usually death by age 2 or 3), and *phenylketonuria* (an abnormal metabolic condition).

Recent advances in genetics have finally made it possible to accurately count the human chromosomes. It has now been determined that *mongolism* (Down's disease) is related to chromosomal abnormality. In normal individuals, there are 46 chromosomes whereas in the mongoloid there are 47 chromosomes, apparently due to the tripling of one of the normal pairs of chromosomes (Lejeune, 1959) (see photograph on p. 81). A number of cases of mental retardates have been found to have an abnormal number of chromosomes, but unlike the mongoloids, the extra chromosome appeared with the sex chromosome pair. The normal female has a pair of "X" chromosomes (XX) while the normal male has an "X" and a "Y" combining to form a pair (XY). A condition has been identified in which an XXY set appears (Klinefelter's syndrome), (Jacobs and Strong, 1959) and a "superfemale" has even been described with an XXX set of chromosomes (Jacobs, Baikie, Brown, MacGregor, MacLean, and Harnden, 1959).

Sociocultural Factors

The evidence strongly indicates that sociocultural factors significantly influence intelligence. Research has shown, for example, that an important correlation exists between a child's intellectual level and the social class; the correlation being about .50 (Jones, 1954). In addition, Class V parents (unskilled, day labor) have been found to have 1.5 times as many children classified as retarded, as compared with Class I parents (professional) whose rate was only 0.14 times as many retarded children as might be expected on statistical grounds. This finding was the result of a massive study of 45,000 children from 36 states (McGehee and Lewis, 1942). Mental retardation is not limited to the lower socioeconomic level families; however, they do seem to have a greater proportion than they deserve. Some 10 to 30 percent of schoolchildren living in some slum areas are mentally retarded as contrasted to 1 to 2 percent in the better economic districts of the same cities (President's Panel, 1962).

Many retarded children have come from backgrounds characterized by stark poverty, paucity of stimulation, cultural barrenness of the home, indifference toward learning (McCandless, 1952). With such an unfavorable early environment, the child lacks even the minimal incentives to develop his intellect, to search for knowledge, to apply himself, or to make maximal use of his native capabilities. Emotional deprivation and the lack of stimulation are powerful forces that can work against intellectual development and functioning (Goldfarb, 1945; Levy, 1947; Scott, Bexton, Heron, and Doane, 1959). In some cases, a change to a more stimulating environment can lead to gains in intellectual performance. Thus, in a British study, gains in IQ were shown by children who had been removed from their homes, with gains being greater in those children who had been originally living under very adverse home conditions (Clarke, Clarke, and Reiman, 1958). A rather interesting study (Kent and Davis, 1957) demonstrated a relationship between the family discipline characterizing the parents and the intellectual level of the children. *Demanding* parents, who set high standards but provided stimulating opportunities for the child to learn, had offsprings with an average IQ of 124. *Unconcerned* parents, who basically ignored their children as long as they kept out of trouble, had offsprings with an average IQ of 97. *Overanxious* parents (who were ceaselessly apprehensive) and *normal* parents (who were placidly affectionate toward their children) had children with IQ's of 107 and 110 respectively. Thus, it appears that opportunities and encouragement for intellectual achievement are effective factors in intellectual development.

Infections

Infections of many types can lead to mental retardation. Some diseases in a parent can affect the unborn fetus. It is now well established that the virus disease, German measles, in the pregnant mother may lead to mental defect in the fetus. The fetus is particularly susceptible to damage from the mother's illness during the first two to three months of pregnancy. Maternal syphilis is another acknowledged cause of retardation in the fetus. With improved prevention, detection, and treatment programs today, syphilitic conditions are now rarely a cause of mental retardation in children.

Following birth, a number of other diseases may leave the child with mental deficit following recovery from the disease itself. Meningitis, especially occurring in the first half year of life, may cause severe brain damage. The extent of the damage to the brain determines the degree of the deficit. Encephalitis is a disease affecting the brain which has appeared several times in history in epidemic form. Since 1924 it has declined and only a few sporadic cases occur. The effects are varied: about a third will recover completely with no effects, another third will die, and another third will live but with mental or physical defects.

Intoxication as a Factor

Intoxication here means the effects of toxic, or poisonous, agents in the body. Although many poisons may be capable of causing brain damage, few such cases actually occur. Lead poisoning is a rare condition in which an individual absorbs lead from some source; this may be achieved through a child's chewing on lead toys or through inhalation of spray paint containing lead. Carbon monoxide, as exuded from gasoline engines, has also been known to produce brain damage. The Thalidomide tragedy raises the possibility that drug ingestion may lead to retardation. Thalidomide is a drug that apparently had no unwarranted effects on tests with animals. It seems to be useful for sedation, and pregnant women found it a beneficial drug. However, it was subsequently found to cause malformations in fetuses when taken within a month after conception. Although the Thalidomide infants are generally believed to have been born with physical abnormalities but normal intelligence, some cases of a physical malformation (hydrocephaly) usually associated with retardation have been reported. In addition, one Swedish study suggests that intelligence is in fact affected (d'Avignon, Hellgren, and Juhlin, 1965).

Traumatic Factors

Any physical agent or circumstance that damages the brain can lead to mental retardation. At one time it was felt that birth injuries comprised the major cause of cases of mental defect. However, this is no longer the case. Some injuries do occur at birth despite modern delivery methods; when they occur, they are due to such factors as improper use of forceps, difficult and prolonged labor period, or damage from the effects of insufficient oxygen (anoxia). Anoxia, of course, can occur at later ages as well, for example, from near-drownings, attempted suicides by hanging, electrical shock, or the failure of the heart to provide oxygen-enriched blood. Similarly, extensive brain damage can also occur in adults through accidents or cerebral hemorrhaging from strokes.

The effects of radiation exposure might be considered here. The excessive use of X-rays during pregnancy may cause a certain malformation of the head known as microcephaly. Studies of pregnant Japanese women who had been exposed to the atomic explosion at Hiroshima in World War II indicate that a number gave birth to children who were microcephalic (Sutow, 1954). It has also been suspected that irradiation may produce chromosomal aberrations, leading to physical or mental defect. It is possible that fallout from nuclear testing will eventually have such effects on future generations born into the world (Pauling, 1962).

Metabolic or Nutritional Factors

Faults in metabolism or deficiencies in nutrition are quite clearly factors causing mental retardation. One of the most prominently known defects is *phenylketonuria* (phenylpyruvic oligophrenia), an abnormality in amino-acid metabolism due to a genetic error. Phenylketonuria involves the inability to metabolize a certain substance because of the absence of liver enzymes needed for the process. This leads to the excessive formation of phenylpyruvic acid. Interestingly enough, the abnormality was first detected because someone noticed a peculiar odor,

later identified as the presence of phenylpyruvic acid, in the infant's urine. In those afflicted, another overt sign is the absence of pigment resulting in very fair skin and extremely blond hair. Fortunately, phenylketonuria can be detected during the first month of life through a simple chemical test. Early treatment by means of a special diet is of great benefit in preventing retardation. Metabolic defects such as phenylketonuria can involve nearly every aspect of metabolic functioning. Abnormalities in carbohydrate metabolism can lead to conditions such as *galactosemia,* or gargoylism. Abnormalities in the functioning of the thyroid will produce conditions such as *cretinism;* damage to the hypothalamus can result in *Frolich's syndrome;* and disturbance in calcium metabolism may lead to *idiopathic hypercalcemia.* Since many of the abnormalities of metabolism are associated with genetic factors, they are sometimes placed under that classification in discussions of retardation.

New Growths as a Factor

Growths in the brain such as tumors can injure the brain directly, or indirectly by causing the cranial pressure to rise to a point causing retardation. Brain tumors are considered to be relatively rare in children and is therefore of lesser importance in the causation of retardation among the young. One condition involving the growth of tumors and believed to be genetically determined is *tuberous sclerosis.* In this disease, tumors are found in nearly all the tissues of the body including the brain, the face, the kidneys, the eyes, and even under the fingernails. The severity of the mental deficit in tumorous conditions depends upon the area of the brain and amount of damage involved. In tuberous sclerosis the damage is severe, leading to profound mental retardation and, ultimately, death for most patients before they reach maturity.

Psychogenic Factors

It is interesting that the classification scheme provided by the AAMD provides for a category involving mental retardation due to "presumed psychologic" causes. This provision accepts the definition of mental retardation as any deficit in intellectual *functioning* as opposed to intellectual *capacity*. In previous years, a distinction was made between "true" retardation versus "pseudo"-retardation or *pseudofeeblemindedness.* Mental retardation was a term formerly limited to cases where the intellectual deficit was permanent and due to nonemotional factors; no amount of psychotherapy or behavioral treatment could serve to increase the IQ of such persons. Pseudofeeblemindedness, on the other hand, included those cases of low intellectual functioning, perhaps because of emotional conflict blocking better performance. The current AAMD does not distinguish between the two in its definition of mental retardation. Yet, it does allow for a separate category for those deficits in functioning related to psychological factors. For example, included in this category are those cases of mental retardation associated either with *neurotic* or *psychotic* conditions.

COMMON CLINICAL TYPES OF MENTAL RETARDATION

Despite similarities in the area of intellectual deficit, different types of mental retardation conditions each possess other unique clinical characteristics. Some of the diagnostic characteristics of certain common forms of mental retardation will be discussed in the following sections.

Mongolism

Mongolism is a common form of mental retardation; estimates on its incidence range from 1 mongoloid child per 1000 births (Record and Smith, 1955) to 1 per 500 births (Benda, 1960; Boggs, 1962).

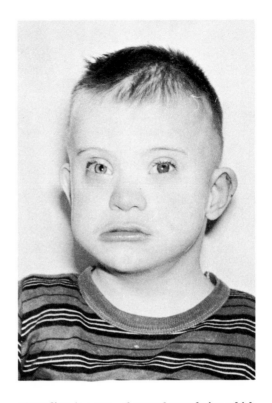

Mongolism is a type of mental retardation which has been found to be associated with a chromosomal aberration. The name derives from the slant-eyed appearance (*see above*) of the mongoloid retardate, a characteristic common to members of the Mongoloid race. (Courtesy—Dr. Irene Uchida)

Mongoloids comprise between 10 to 20 percent of institutionalized mentally retarded persons (Dingman, Miller, and Tarjan, 1960). There is some speculation that the seeming increase in the number of institutionalized mongoloids within the past 50 years is indicative of a growing incidence in the number of mongoloid births (Tredgold and Soddy, 1963). The term *mongolism* traces back to Langdon-Down (1866) who first described the retardation in 1886. He suggested that the facial features of certain retardates enabled them to be arranged into four ethnic groups, Mongolian, Ethiopian, Caucasian, and American Indian. Although there is some resemblance of the mongoloid retardate to members of the Mongolian

447

race, this is superficial and some prefer to refer to the condition instead as *Down's syndrome.*

The physical symptoms associated with mongolism are quite easily recognized. The most outstanding feature is the almond-shaped, slanted eyes (Fig. 16-2). The tongue in most cases shows deep fissures and tends to protrude out of the mouth as if too large for the oral cavity. Since this often occurs from birth, the tongue protrusion is frequently the first symptom attracting attention. The nose tends to be short and flat; the teeth are misshapen; the skin is milky white and dry and rough after infancy. Also noticeable are the clumsy-looking hands with their stubby fingers spread out, a foreshortened and curved little finger, and L-shaped loops instead of the normal whorl fingerprints. The short stature, protruding belly, and rudimentary genitals give a childlike appearance to the mongoloid. The voice is commonly harsh and guttural. The hair is at first soft, but later becomes dry and sparse.

The health of the mongoloid is usually poor. About 2 percent die shortly before or during birth, and approximately 40 to 53 percent die within the first year of life (Record and Smith, 1955). Infant mortality is primarily caused by heart defects, and diseases of the respiratory system such as pneumonia, bronchitis, and tuberculosis. The mongoloid is also plagued with a poor circulatory system and is very sensitive to temperature extremes. The life expectancy of those who survive beyond infancy is nowhere near normal, with one estimate being 12 years (Penrose, 1961).

The degree of mental retardation varies considerably. Although a few fit the widely used term *mongolian idiot,* many reach the imbecile range of functioning (moderate retardation). The moderately retarded ones can learn to perform simple duties, take part in ordinary family activities, and carry out household chores. Their clumsily constructed hands and poor coordination make it difficult for them to engage in any tasks requiring much dexterity. The disposition of the mongoloid person is of some help in their social adjustment. They remain happy and cheerful, affectionate, and easily amused. The mongoloid enjoys attention immensely. Although he may be provoked into aggressive misbehaving, the typical mongoloid is docile and good-tempered.

Previous searches for the causation of mongolism centered around the age of the parent and the birth order. An exceptional observation noted that advanced maternal age and mongoloid childbirths appeared to be related (Oster, 1953; Penrose, 1949). The risk of giving birth to a mongoloid child appeared to increase with

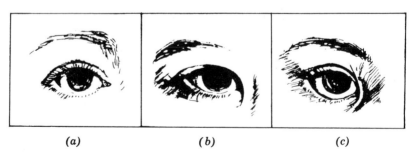

(a) *(b)* *(c)*

Figure 16-2. **Formation of the external eye in (*a*) European races, (*b*) Mongolian races, and (*c*) mongoloid retardates.**
SOURCE: C. Benda, Down's syndrome (2nd ed.). New York: Grune & Stratton, 1969. By permission of Grune & Stratton.

maternal age beginning at age 30 and rising to a peak between the ages of 45 and 49 (Fig. 16-3). This had led some to recommend that women avoid pregnancies after the age of 35 (Oster, 1953). Interestingly enough, Oster observed that mongoloids are frequently the last born in the family. The psychological reluctance of the mother to have another child after the birth of a retardate seems to be only part of the reason. A significantly high rate of abortions after the mongoloid birth suggests a lower reproductive capacity may also be involved (Goldstein, 1954). Benda (1946) hypothesizes that a defective uterine environment is at fault in such late and malformed births. In addition, the physical features of the mongoloid lend some justification to the view that mongolism is a condition of physical and mental maldevelopment. Russian studies of anatomy claim that the mongoloid brain shows certain signs of being underdeveloped: there is a poverty of convolutions or folds in the brain, and the cerebral hemispheres are small. Microscopic examination disclosed the presence of cells that normally

disappear by the sixth or seventh month of fetal life (Luria, 1963).

A new and fascinating direction was started with the work of Lejeune, Gautier, and Turpin (1959) who reported discovering an extra chromosome in mongoloids. This abnormal chromosome, now called the Orlando chromosome, results in a *trisomy,* that is, three chromosomes instead of the normal pair. Approximately 95 percent of mongoloids possess this chromosomal abnormality (Robinson, 1961). The brilliant discovery by Lejeune and his colleagues has unfortunately opened new vistas without providing complete explanations or answers for the old question. The exact causative factor for mongolism is still unknown. The reason for the trisomy occurring is still not clear. Hereditary factors have been considered involving recessive genes as a possibility. However, two cases of mongoloid females giving birth both indicate that the offspring were essentially normal in appearance, intellect, and chromosomes (Forssman, Lehmann, and Thysell, 1961; Forssman and Thysell,

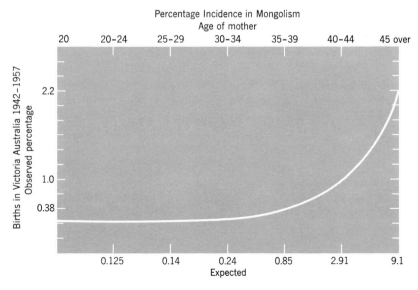

Figure 16-3. **Frequency of mongolism in relation to maternal age.**
SOURCE: From C. Benda, Mongolism. In C. Carter (Ed.), *Medical aspects of mental retardation,* 1965. Courtesy of C. C. Thomas, Publisher, Springfield, Illinois.

1957; Sawyer, 1949; Sawyer and Shafter, 1957). In the case reported by Sawyer, the mongoloid woman's own father was suspected of being also the father of the mongoloid's baby. Yet, the child produced by this mating was judged to be of superior intelligence when examined at age 11½ years. As an adult she was enrolled in nursing training and was making good progress in this professional coursework. An alternate explanation for the chromosomal abnormality developing is gene mutation. It has been stated confidently that the deviation of deveopment that leads to mongolism takes place early in the gestation or intrauterine growth period, perhaps around the eighth week after conception (Benda, 1946). Thus, a mutation could occur at some early stage of cellular formation and growth. It has been speculated that such mutation is fostered by the inadequate intrauterine environment present in older mothers. To further complicate the attempts to derive some satisfactory explanation, it should be noted that not all mongoloids have the extra chromosome and not all women over 35 give birth to mongoloid infants. Furthermore, in at least one case, chromosomal abnormalities were found including some physical symptoms of monoglism, yet the child was intellectually normal at age two years. In this case, the 47 chromosome count was discovered to exist in 43 percent of her cells while the rest showed the normal 46 count (Clark, Edwards, and Smallpiece, 1961).

Cretinism

Cretinism is a form of mental retardation caused by endocrine disturbance. This was once a common type of retardation, particularly in certain parts of the world such as the Himalayas of India, the Andes and Rocky Mountains of the Americas, and the area around the Swiss Alps. Concentrated study of these geographic areas led to the discovery that the soils were deficient in iodine, as was the food grown in them. Cretinism has subsequently been determined to be a condition in which the infant suffers from an insufficiency in iodine intake, the major ingredient for the formation of the much needed thyroxine. Since this discovery and with the mass use of iodized salt and other preventive measures, the incidence of cretinism has been drastically reduced. Today, cretins form less than 5 percent of the mentally retarded in institutions in the United States.

Unlike the mongoloid symptoms, the physical symptoms associated with cretinism usually appear sometime after birth. The cretin infant is normal at birth, and it is not until after the sixth month of life that symptoms begin to attract attention. It is possible that this delay occurs because the infant is still carrying a sufficient prenatal supply of thyroxine. By the second half of this first year, the infant becomes so lethargic that he fails to suck or otherwise respond. His tongue protrudes, the nose is thick and flat, the eyes are wide apart and the lids are puffy, and the lips are thick. The teeth are peg-shaped, chalky, and often decay early. The hair of the head and eyebrows is scanty, the skin tends to be exceedingly dry, rough, sallow, and wrinkled. The child breathes with "snorts" and may cry with a peculiar dry "leathery" sound. The limbs are malformed: the legs are bowed and much too short for the body, the feet and hands are stubby and ill-formed. The cretin walks with a slow, unsteady waddling gait, and in general shows clumsiness in motor activities. The growth of the cretin is stunted, the head appears too large for the body, the neck seems too short, the abdomen protrudes, and the genitals remain immature until some time past the age of maturity. In many respects, the cretin has a gnomelike or dwarfish appearance. Cretins at full growth seldom stand taller than three feet.

Cretins are typically voracious eaters. However, they suffer from respiratory difficulties, impaired motor coordination, and a general muscular weakness. Their pulse and respiration are slow, and their temperature two or three degrees below normal. This is reflected in a low basal metabolism which, along with laboratory tests, is helpful in diagnostic examinations.

Cretinism can be associated with anywhere from severe to moderate levels of retardation, depending upon the severity of the brain damage following iodine insufficiency. Unlike the mongoloid, there is a close association between the severity of the physical symptoms of cretinism and the severity of the mental deficit. The majority of the cretins are moderately retarded. Cretins are usually placid, quiet, good-tempered, and affectionate, and are considered the least troublesome of all retardates. Their disposition is helpful in aiding the vocational adjustment of those with sufficient intellect to acquire simple occupational skills.

Cretinism has been traced to a disturbance involving insufficient amounts of thyroxine, a hormone of the thyroid gland. Such deficits may arise because of inadequate amounts of iodine in the diet, because of malfunctioning or maldevelopment of the thyroid, and in some cases through the excessive use of antithyroid drugs in the treatment of the mother during her pregnancy. Early and continued treatment in cases of thyroid deficiency with a synthetic form of the thyroid hormone has met with success. This is a dramatic exception to the usually pessimistic outcome associated with mental retardation due to some physical disorder. In practically all cases of treatment during the early months, striking alterations of physical appearance occur, the child becomes alert and no longer apathetic, and normal intellectual functioning is achieved.

Phenylketonuria (Phenylpyruvic Oligophrenia or PKU)

Phenylketonuria is the result of another metabolic disturbance. Because of a genetic fault, the infant lacks an enzyme required to break down phenylalanine, an amino acid in protein foods. Phenylpyruvic acid is formed instead, and is excreted in the urine giving off a characteristic odor. The excessive phenylalanine that remains damages the nervous system and produces mental retardation. Phenylketonuria is possibly one of the best known of the metabolic disorders, yet is is a relatively rare condition. In the United States, about 1 out of every 25,000 children born will have this defect while approximately 1 percent of all institutionalized retardates suffer from this condition (Nisonger, 1962). Phenylketonuria is considered the first metabolic error found to be associated with mental retardation. The discovery was first made in 1934 when a Norwegian mother noticed an odd musty odor in her child and reported on this and on his mental retardation to Dr. Asbjorn Folling (1934). Folling diagnosed the case as a disorder of metabolism, and reported on the details of phenylpyruvic acid in the urine, phenylalanine metabolism, and mental retardation in ten cases. Modern developments make it possible to detect PKU within the first four to seven weeks of life. A solution of ferric chloride is added to a sample of urine: the appearance of a blue-green-black color is indicative of PKU. Another simple technique is the use of a specially treated stick which is pressed against a wet diaper; again a color change, to grey-green, is a positive sign of phenylketonuria.

The physical description originally reported by Folling characterizes many but not all of PKU retardates today. The generally accepted characteristics include normal physical development, dermatitis (skin rash), eczema (inflammation of the skin), and a wide spacing of the incisor teeth. Because of the endocrine disturbance, the child is fair-haired, fair-skinned, and blue-eyed, or at least of a clearly lighter complexion than his parents or siblings. Other symptoms include a stooped and flexed posture, a stiff gait, and fingering mannerisms (such as pill-rolling and finger-flicking). Abnormal electroencephalograms have been found, and a number may be subject to convulsions during the first decade of life. Some children show behavioral peculiarities such as hyperactive behavior, decreased attention span or responsiveness to the environment, and even schizophreniclike symptoms (such as catatonia).

If untreated, PKU will lead to severe mental retardation although a few cases will be in the moderate level. Early detection and early treatment (before age two or three) by means of a special diet low in phenylalanine, has been known to prevent the ruinous effects of the condition (Bickel, Gerrard, and Hickmans, 1954; Knox, 1960; Horner and Streamer, 1958). In older cases, the introduction of the special diet leads to slight increases in intellectual functioning as measured by intelligence tests (Knox and Hsia, 1957). The length of time that the individual must stay on the diet is not known with any certainty. Estimates range from four years to the time the child is at least eight or nine years old.

Microcephaly

Microcephaly is a term that describes retardates with small heads. The small skull that is present means that the brain is also extremely limited in size; such a condition typically involves the severely retarded level of intellect. Fortunately, the number of microcephalics is not large; they comprise not more than about 1 percent of all retarded persons in institutions. Microcephaly is caused by a number of

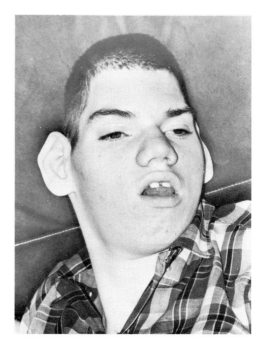

A case of *microcephaly*. Note the receding forehead and chin, the inward slope of the sides of the head, and the otherwise normal facial structure. (Charles H. Carter)

factors, such as an overdose of X-rays or maternal rubella (a form of measles) during pregnancy (Cowie, 1960), certain diseases of the cerebrum, and exposure to atomic radiation. One form of microcephaly (*true or primary microcephaly*) has been attributed to single recessive gene inheritance (Penrose, 1954).

The physical characteristics of the microcephalic are quite distinctive. The microcephalic's skull at its maximum development is less than 17 inches in circumference as compared with the normal size of about 22 inches. The forehead and chin recede sharply, the sides of the head slope inward, and the nose appears like a beak; for these reasons, sometimes the microcephalic is described as having a birdlike appearance or called a "pinhead" in sideshows (Tredgold and Soddy, 1963). Because of the diminished bone surface to be covered, the scalp may lie loosely in longitudinal furrows from front to rear. The body may be well developed but the microcephalic's stature is typically short.

Although the majority are intellectually in the severely retarded level, some variation exists such that some profoundly retarded and some moderately retarded microcephalics may be found. The degree of mental deficit apparently does not correspond directly to the size of the head. Most are capable of understanding what is said to them and can say a few words. Tredgold (1963) describes the true microcephalic as showing a general vivacity, a capacity for mimicry, and an alertness which make them entertaining. In addition, they are considered affectionate and well behaved and adapt well to institutional life. A rare case of exceptional craftsmanship skill and inventiveness has been reported by Tredgold. Among the productions of this microcephalic, named J. H. Pullen, were numerous scaled models of ships made of copper rivets, brass, iron and wood, and complete with anchors, pulleys, engines, furnishings, cannon, etc. His masterpiece was a 10-foot-long model of a steamship with a specially invented system of pulleys which allowed the entire upper deck to be raised for viewing below deck. Another creation was a barge carved out of ivory, ebony and other woods, and fitted with four angels and a figure of Satan. He also constructed a "monstrous human form about 13 feet high. This black-bearded, terrible-looking figure is armed with a gigantic sword, and can be made to perform a variety of movements, such as opening and shutting the mouth and eyes, protruding the tongue, rotating the head, raising the arms, etc., by means of an elaborate internal mechanism. It is calculated to strike terror into the heart of any juvenile beholder" (Tredgold and Soddy, 1963). Such incredible mechanical capability and imaginativeness in a person otherwise emotionally and intellectually retarded can only be

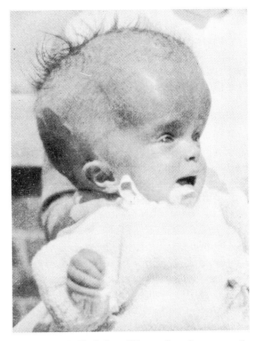

A *hydrocephalic* infant illustrating the extremely enlarged upper skull. Hydrocephaly is the result of the continuous pressure of excessive cerebrospinal fluid. (From Anderson: *Boyd's Pathology for The Surgeon*, 8th Ed., W. B. Saunders Company.)

viewed as an example of the rare group known as *idiot savants*, individuals who are intellectually retarded but extremely talented in some other way.

Hydrocephaly

Hydrocephaly is the result of an accumulation of the spinal fluid within the cranium. This buildup of fluid leads to increased pressure within the cranium resulting in damage to the brain tissue. The cerebrospinal fluid increases beyond its normal amounts because of an overproduction of the fluid, a malfunctioning in the reabsorption mechanism, or an obstruction to the normal flow and circulation of the fluid. The conditions producing hydrocephaly may occur before birth, during the first few months, or the first few years of life. These conditions include trauma, parental syphilis, tumors, or infectious diseases (such as meningitis or encephalitis).

453

The physical symptoms of hydrocephaly (literally, "water in the head") are quite pronounced. Most evident is the extremely enlarged upper part of the skull caused by the continuous pressure of the fluid pushing outwardly. The circumference about the forehead may be as large as 30 inches or more, although the face remains normal in size; this combination produces an appearance of an inverted pyramid. The scalp is thin and the veins tend to stand out prominently. The impression is that of a super-intellectual being from a special race; the opposite could not be more true since in the severest case, the skull may be merely a shell containing over a gallon of fluid and no more than a thin sheath of brain tissue. There appears to be no clear-cut relationship between the size of the skull and either superiority or inferiority of intellect.

The degree of mental deficit varies from only slight impairment to profound mental retardation. Nearly all of the prenatal cases of hydrocephalus die before birth, and a large proportion of those afflicted after birth also fail to survive. For unknown reasons, some cases are self-arresting and spontaneous cures may occur. These latter cases are more often seen in institutions for the retarded. Their motor coordination is impaired and they may show weakness in their muscles. However, they are usually willing helpers and are described as obedient and affectionate.

Chemotherapy has been tried in the treatment of hydrocephaly. Drugs have been prescribed in an attempt to decrease the formation of cerebrospinal fluid. The results have generally been considered helpful in momentarily alleviating the internal pressure. However, over long terms effects have not been entirely satisfactory. Surgical methods have also been introduced to drain off the excess fluid into another area of the body. Tubes have been inserted with one end in the cranial cavity and the other end into the kidney or the heart itself. A valve might be included to permit drainage out of the cranial cavity if the tubes become clogged. The mortality risk of surgery is considered high and little intellectual improvement can be expected if severe brain damage has already taken place. However, successful surgical procedures have been known to lead to some improvement in the hydrocephalic's functioning.

Amaurotic Familial Idiocy

Amaurotic family idiocy is an inherited degenerative disease involving mental retardation as well as other physical impairments. In actuality, there are four different forms of this particular disease differing only in terms of the age of onset and the rate at which degeneration progresses: *early infantile amaurotic idiocy, late infantile amaurotic idiocy, juvenile amaurotic idiocy,* and *late juvenile amaurotic idiocy.* The most well-known form is the early infantile amaurotic familial idiocy, also called *Tay-Sachs disease.* Tay-Sachs disease was first described by Tay in 1881, and neurologically studied through autopsies by Sachs in 1896. About one-half of 1 percent of institutionalized retardates are victims of this ailment. The disease is believed to be transmitted by a rare recessive gene. Jewish families appear to be more often afflicted than non-Jewish families; the frequency of persons acting as carriers for the gene being estimated as one in 40 for Jews and one in 380 for non-Jews (Myrianthopoulos, 1962).

Infants who are affected show normal birth and development until sometime around the second or third month of life. From this point on, the symptoms appear and become progressively severe. The early physical signs are an unusual sensitivity to noises, listlessness, and an inability to sit up, or to keep the head erect, or to turn over from a prone position. There soon develops a loss of visual acuity and ultimately, blindness. If the retina of the eye is examined, a distinctive cherry-red spot can be detected. With time there is atrophy (withering away from disuse) of the muscles of the entire body and optic nerves. Hearing, however, remains acutely sensitive and the child is easily startled by unexpected or loud sounds. In some cases, seizures may occur. Intellectually, the victim quickly deteriorates from normal intelligence to the profoundly retarded level. Few children survive for longer than three years of life.

The late infantile amaurotic idiocy usually begins after three years of life with the symptoms being essentially the same as for the early infantile condition. The life span may extend to age five or six. The juvenile amaurotic idiocy has an even later onset, between ages six and eight. Progress of the illness is slower and include the additional symptoms of paralysis, personality changes, irritability, and convulsions. These sufferers will live to as long as ten to fourteen years of life. The late juvenile amaurotic idiocy is very rare and may appear as late as the twentieth or thirtieth year of life. The symptoms are similar to those of the juvenile condition with an even slower rate of progress. These affected persons may live to be 40 to 50 years of age.

TREATMENT OF THE MENTALLY RETARDED

At one time, the belief was that mental retardation was incurable: "Once a retarded, always a retarded." The earlier definition by Doll made it impossible to consider an individual retarded if he showed any improvement toward normal intellectual functioning. In fact, if such improvement did occur, the conclusion was drawn that an error in diagnosis had been made. The current viewpoint, as represented by the American Association on Mental Deficiency, recognizes that changes in level of intellectual functioning are possible in the retarded. The degree of improvement possible will vary with different conditions, the severity of the brain damage, and the duration elapsed before treatment is initiated. A number of individuals can be returned to normal intellectual functioning with early treatment measures; others will show gains in social competency and self-care; some will profit from attention to emotional problems; and finally, there will remain those for whom institutional custodial care becomes the highest level they can ever hope to attain. The treatment measures in current use fall in three categories: medical treatment, educational-training measures, and psychotherapeutic approaches.

Medical treatment that has proved successful derives its value from the prevention of the brain injury resulting from disease processes. In effect, its success is really success in the treatment of diseases and not mental retardation per se (which is often the end product of the diseases). Early treatment of syphilis, meningitis, encephalitis, and toxic states before brain damage occurs is imperative in the prevention of retardation. For other conditions, prevention may involve the use of surgical techniques to remove the source of threat to the brain such as tumors or increased pressures from cerebrospinal fluid. In still other conditions, preventive treatment may require the replacement of materials which the body is deficient in such as is the case in cretinism, phenylketonuria, and other metabolic disorders. Damage can also be avoided through caution in circumstances known to be potentially dangerous such as in the exposure to radiation or traumas connected with birth deliveries.

Medical treatment has sometimes been aimed, not at prevention, but at restoration. In 1944, Zimmerman and Ross claimed that glutamic acid fed to white rats led to an increased ability to learn.

Two years later, Albert, Hoch, and Waelsch (1946) reported rises in IQ in six of eight retarded patients. However, subsequent studies have led to the conclusion that glutamic acid therapy has little significance to offer in restoring normal intellectual functioning to mental retardates; the changes that occasionally occur were attributable to factors other than the glutamic acid, and were too slight to be significant (Lombard, Gilbert, and Donofrio, 1955). The tranquilizing drugs have been used with the mentally retarded in the hopes that reductions in behavior problems would occur and perhaps an increase in social responsiveness and adaptability. Results to date have been very good although individual differences tend to exist in terms of reactions to this form of chemotherapy (Zimmerman and Burgmeister, 1955; Belmont, Elizabeth, Ogonik, and Timberlake, 1957; Robb, 1959).

Once it was recognized that the mentally retarded could respond to educational efforts, school and training centers began to develop. For the most part, the goals have been to provide the education and training needed to maximize the retardates' abilities to become independent. Many public school systems now offer special classes and programs for the mildly retarded to encourage the development of basic skills in reading, writing, self-care, the handling of money, and the acquisition of vocational skills. Such training might be offered in the framework of a mock-up "factory" with the retarded youngster being taught to go through all the processes of work, from "punching in" on time to collecting a paycheck. When ready, a retarded person might actually be employed in a special location called a sheltered workshop, often a small building in which a number of physically capable yet mentally retarded persons can work at their vocational skills under super-

vision and without the stresses of competitive industrial surroundings.

For the more severely retarded, special educational methods have been tried largely based upon the lines outlined by Seguin in 1846 and elaborated on by Montessori (1912) and others. These methods are based on the stimulation of sight, hearing, touch, and muscle movements through selected activities. The child is gradually led to become observant, to develop his judgment, to learn discrimination. Personal self-care, simple skills, and basic social training are established as limited goals which help the retardate to reach some satisfactions in life. Some interesting steps have been taken to use reinforcement techniques to train retarded persons (Birnbrauer and Lawler, 1964; Girardeau and Spradlin, 1964). Tokens, which are exchangeable for cosmetics or candy or soft drinks are given as rewards for desired responses. For example, retarded children have been toilet trained by this technique (Dayan, 1964).

In cases of profound retardation, even limited educational goals may be beyond reach unless closer supervision and specialized facilities are available. In addition, many of the severely retarded individuals also require medical care because of physical disabilities or illnesses. For these reasons, institutional living is often decided upon by parents. Several types of residential institutions are available for such living-in services. Among these are the state-supported institutions providing training, medical, and custodial care for residents of the state for little or no cost. Also available are private profit or nonprofit operations, some that are national in scope with branches in different parts of the country. The decision to institutionalize a retarded person is an extremely difficult one for the relatives involved. Separation from the family may appear to be a cruelty especially if the family members are already inclined to be overprotective, anxious, and guilt-ridden. Sometimes, weekend visits to the institution convinces the parents that the youngster will never be able to adapt to residential life since he appears momentarily upset. Not infrequently, the parents of a retarded child are convinced that institutional care will provide a more satisfying life for their youngster, yet cannot dispel the nagging question of whether their decision was morally right. On the other hand, institutionalization can appear to be the best arrangement in certain cases. Severely disabling physical diseases, uncontrollable aggressive behaviors, parental inability to provide even minimal supervision or care, are all factors that have led to decisions in favor of institutionalizing. Unfortunately, the picture is further confused by the findings that institutional life may be enriching for some (Kirk, 1958), but for many it adversely affects their development and self-esteem (Richards and Sands, 1963; Centerwall and Centerwall, 1960; Guthrie, 1963; Schlanger, 1954).

Psychotherapeutic approaches have been added to treatment programs for the retarded. This is particularly appropriate in those cases of mental retardation caused by emotional factors. In other cases, reports have suggested that psychotherapy may prove beneficial even with those persons where organic or hereditary factors predominate. For example, Heiser (1954) found that 12 out of 14 children who had received psychotherapeutic treatment showed improvements in social and environmental behavior. Sarason (1958) has been a leading exponent of the belief that the retarded can profit from psychotherapy. He discusses improvements in

his own patients, noting that one showed an increase in IQ from 45 to 76. In many cases, the emotional life of the retarded child has been one of parental rejection or abandonment, peer teasing and criticism, and self-dejection. Some are never fully able to grasp why they are never able to be as successful as other children; others are struck by the impact of somehow being different from their peers. Institutionalization may be an especially trying experience. In some ways, the mentally retarded faces the same problems to resolve as the physically disabled. Social adjustment is often made difficult by characteristics of the disabled and the uncomfortable reactions of others to him. The individual's self-concept is often jeopardized by the jarring recognition that life's achievements may never be the same as that for others. Moodiness, withdrawal, behavioral outbursts, may develop in reaction to the disability. In addition, the retarded person may experience anxieties and fears aroused because of their limited capacity to understand themselves and their surroundings. Those who have attempted to work therapeutically with the retarded have reported encouraging results (Chess, 1962) although systematic reports are still much needed to add to impressionistic data. Parental counseling also has its place in the psychotherapeutic approach. In cases where the child is to remain living at home, the parents may need aid in accepting the child's condition, and in avoiding the dangers of overreacting with feelings of self-blame or rejection of the child. In those cases leading to institutionalization, parental counseling may ease the conflict over the separation.

Glossary

Amaurotic idiocy: A form of mental retardation involving neurological degeneration and believed due to inherited factors.

Amentia: A term for mental retardation.

Anoxia: Insufficient oxygen supply to the tissues.

Cretinism: A form of mental retardation resulting from thyroid insufficiency.

Down's syndrome: Also known as mongolism. A form of mental retardation associated with trisomy of chromosomes.

Endogenous: Caused by hereditary factors.

Exogenous: Caused by environmental or external factors.

Frolich's syndrome: A form of mental retardation associated with insufficient pituitary activity.

Galactosemia: A disease involving central nervous system pathology and associated with inadequate carbohydrate metabolism.

Hydrocephaly: A form of mental retardation involving excessive cerebrospinal fluid in the cranium.

Idiopathic hypercalcemia: A disease associated with the abnormal rise of blood calcium.

Idiot savant: A person who is intellectually retarded but talented in other ways.

Intelligence quotient: A score reflecting intellectual level, usually involving mental age divided by chronological age and multiplied by 100.

Mental retardation: Subaverage intellectual functioning, along with impairment of social and adaptive skills.

Microcephaly: A form of mental retardation involving failure of development of the cranium; an abnormally small head.

Mild retardation: Retardation represented by an intelligence quotient from 53 to 69. Person is capable to a degree of independent living.

Moderate retardation: Retardation represented by an intelligence quotient from 36 to 52. Person is capable of a semi-independent life, self-care, and partial financial self-support.

Phenylketonuria: Also known as phenylpyruvic oligophrenia. A form of mental retardation associated with failure in amino acid metabolism.

Primary amentia: Retardation caused by hereditary factors.

Profound retardation: Retardation represented by an intelligence quotient of 20 or less. Person usually is not responsive to training, requires custodial care, and suffers from nervous system damage.

Pseudofeeblemindedness: Retardation believed to be reflective of failure to perform well on intellectual tasks by reason of emotional blockage rather than lack of capacity.

Secondary amentia: Retardation caused by environmental or external factors.

Severe retardation: Retardation represented by an intelligence quotient of from 20 to 35. Person is capable of limited self-help and often suffers nervous system damage.

Tay-Sachs disease: A form of amaurotic idiocy involving acute sensitivity to sounds, listlessness, and muscular atrophy.

Trisomy: The existence of three instead of two chromosomes in each set.

True microcephaly: Also known as primary microcephaly. Microcephaly believed caused by heredity.

Tuberous sclerosis: A disease involving the presence of tumors in every tissue.

References

Albert, K., Hoch, P., & Waelsch, H. Preliminary report on the effect of glutamic acid administration in mentally retarded subjects. *J. nerv. ment. Dis.*, 1946, **104**, 263.

d'Avignon, M., Hellgren, K., & Juhlin, I. Thalidomide damaged children, experiences from Eugeniahemmet, *Acta paed. Scand. Suppl.*, 1965, No. 159.

Benda, C. *Mongolism and cretinism.* New York: Grune & Stratton, 1946.

Benda, C. *The child with mongolism.* New York: Grune & Stratton, 1960.

Bickel, H., Gerrard, J., & Hickmans, E. Influence of phenylalanine intake on the biochemistry and behavior of a phenylketonuric child. *Acta Paediat.*, 1954, **43**, 64.

Birnbrauer, J. & Lawler, J. Token reinforcement for learning. *Ment. Retard.*, 1964, **2**, 275.

Boggs, E. Mongolism: new discoveries every month. *Child. Ltd.*, 1962, **10**, 6.

Centerwall, S. & Centerwall, W. Study of children with mongolism reared in the home compared to those reared away from the home. *Pediatrics*, 1960, **25**, 678.

Chess, S. Psychiatric treatment of the mentally retarded child with behavior problems. *Amer. J. Orthopsychiat.*, 1962, **32**, 863.

Clarke, A., Clarke, A., & Rieman, S. Cognitive and social changes in the feeble minded —three further studies. *Brit. J. Psychol.*, 1958, **49**, 144.

Clarke, C., Edwards, J., Smallpiece, V. 21 trisomy/normal mosaicism in an intelligent child with some mongoloid characteristics. *Lancet*, 1961, **1**, 1028.

Cowie, V. The genetics and sub-classification of microcephaly. *J. ment. def. Res.*, 1960, **4**, 42.

Dayan, M. Toilet training retarded children in a state residential institution. *Ment. Retard.*, 1964, **2**, 116.

De Prospo, C. News and notes. *Amer. J. ment. Def.*, 1962, **67**, 113.

Doll, E. The essentials of an inclusive concept of mental deficiency. *Amer. J. ment. Def.*, 1941, **46**, 214.

Folling, A. Über Ausscheidung von Phenylbrenzträubensaure in den Harn als Stoffwchselanomalie in Verbindung mit Imbezillitat. *Hoppe Seyler A. Physiol. Chem.* 1934, **227**, 169.

Forssman, H., Lehmann, O., & Thysell, T. Reproduction in mongolism: chromosome studies and re-examination of a child. *Amer. J. ment. Def.*, 1961, **65**, 495.

Forssman, H. & Thysell, T. A woman with mongolism and her child. *Amer. J. ment. Def.*, 1957, **62**, 500.

Girardeau, F. & Spradlin, J. Token rewards in a cottage program. *Ment. Retard.*, 1964, **2**, 345.

Goldfarb, W. Effects of psychological deprivation in infancy and subsequent stimulation. *Amer. J. Psychiat.*, 1945, **102**, 18.

Goldstein, A. A study of mongolism and non-mongoloid mental retardation in children. *Arch. Pediat.*, 1954, **71**, 11.

Guthrie, G., Butler, A., & Gorlow, L. Personality differences between institutionalized and non-institutionalized retardates. *Amer. J. ment. Def.*, 1963, **67**, 543.

Heber, R. (Ed.) A manual on terminology and classification in mental retardation. Monog. Suppl. *Amer. J. ment. Def.*, 1959, **64**, no. 2, 3.

Heiser, K. Psychotherapy in a residential school for mentally retarded children. *Train. Sch. Bull.*, 1954, **50**, 211.

Heiser, K. & Wolman, B. Mental deficiencies. In B. Wolman (Ed.), *Handbook of clinical psychology*. New York: McGraw-Hill, 1965.

Horner, F. & Streamer, C. Phenylketonuria treated from earliest infancy. *A.M.A. J. dis. Child.*, 1958, **97**, 345.

Jacobs, P., Baikie, A., Brown, W., MacGregor, T., MacLean, N., & Harnden, D. Evidence for the existence of a human "super female." *Lancet,* 1959, **2**, 423.

Jacobs, P. & Strong, J. A case of human intersexuality having a possible XXY sex-determining mechanism. *Nature,* 1959, **183**, 302.

Jones, H. The environment and mental development. In L. Carmichael (Ed.), *Manual of child psychology*. New York: Wiley, 1954.

Kent, N. & Davis, D. Discipline in the home and intellectual development. *Br. J. med. Psychol.*, 1957, **30**, 194.

Kirk, S. Early education for the mentally retarded. Illinois: University of Illinois Press, 1958.

Knox, W. An evaluation of the treatment of phenylketonuria with diets low in phenylalanine. *Pediatrics,* 1960, **26**, 1.

Knox, W. & Hsia, D. Pathogenetic problems in phenylketonuria, *Amer. J. Med.,* 1957, **22**, 687.

Langdon-Down, J. Observations on an ethnic classification of idiots. *London Hosp. Rept.,* 1866, **3**, 259.

Lejeune, J., Turpin, R. & Gautie, M. Le mongolisme, premier exemple d'aberration autosomique humaine. *Ann. Génétique,* 1959, **2**, 41.

Levy, R. Effects of institutional vs. boarding home care on a group of infants. *J. Pers.,* 1947, **15**, 233.

Lombard, J., Gilbert, J. & Donofrio, A. The effects of glutamic acid upon intelligence, social maturity, and adjustment of a group of mentally retarded children. *Amer. J. ment. Def.,* 1955, **60**, 122.

Luria, A. *The mentally retarded child.* Translated from Russian by W. Robinson. English translation edited by B. Kirman. London: Pergamon Press, 1963.

McCandless, B. Environment and intelligence. *Amer. J. ment. Def.,* 1952, **56**, 674.

McGehee, W. & Lewis, W. The Socio-economic status of the homes of mentally superior and retarded children and the occupational rank of their parents. *Pedagog. Sem.,* 1942, **60**, 375.

Mental Development Center, unpublished Biennial Report, Psychological services. Mental Development Center Library: Western Reserve University, 1962.

Montessori, M. *Montessori method.* (Transl.) A. George. New York: Stokes, 1912.

Myrianthopoulos, N. Some epidemiologic and genetic aspects of Tay-Sachs' disease. In S. Aronson and B. Volk (Eds.), *Cerebral sphingolipidoses*. New York: Academic Press, 1962.

Nisonger, H. Changing concepts in mental retardation. *Amer. J. ment. Def.,* 1962, **67**, 4.

Oster, J. *Mongolism.* Copenhagen: Danish Science Press, 1953.

Pauling, L. Genetic effects of weapons tests. *Bull. atom. Scient.* 1962, **18**, 15.

Penrose, L. *The biology of mental defect.* London: Sidgwick & Jackson, 1949.

Penrose, L. *The biology of mental defect.* London: Sidgwick & Jackson, 1954.

Penrose, L. Mongolism. *Br. med. Bull.,* 1961, **17,** 184.

President's Committee on Mental Retardation. *MR 67: a first report to the President on the nation's progress and remaining great needs in the campaign to combat mental retardation.* Washington, D.C.: U.S. Government Printing Office, 1967.

The President's Panel on Mental Retardation. *Report to the President: a proposed program for national action to combat mental retardation.* Washington, D.C.: U.S. Government Printing Office, 1962.

Record, R. & Smith, A. Incidence, mortality, and sex distribution of mongoloid defectives. *Br. J. prev. soc. Med.,* 1955, **9,** 10.

Richards, T. & Sands, R. *Mongoloid children living at home: Interim Report.* Kennedy Child Study Center. Santa Monica, Calif., 1963.

Robb, H. Use of chlorpromazine in a mental deficiency institution. *J. ment. Sci.,* 1959, **105,** 1029.

Robinson, A. The human chromosomes. *Amer. J. dis. Child.,* 1961, **101,** 379.

Sarason, S. Psychological problems in mental deficiency. (3rd ed.) New York: Harper & Row, 1958.

Sawyer, G. Case report: reproduction in a mongoloid. *Amer. J. ment. Def.,* 1949, **54,** 204.

Sawyer, G. & Shafter, A. Reproduction in a mongoloid: a follow-up. *Amer. J. ment. Def.,* 1957, **61,** 793

Schlanger, B. Environmental influences on the verbal output of mentally retarded children. *J. speech hear. Dis.,* 1954, **19,** 339.

Scott, T., Bexton, W., Heron, W., & Doane, B. Cognitive effects of perceptual isolation. *Canad. J. Psychol.,* 1959, **13,** 200.

Seguin, E. *Traitement Moral, Hygiéne et Education des Idiots et des Autres Enfants Arriérés.* Paris: J. B. Bailliére, 1846.

Suinn, R. The theory of cognitive style: a partial replication. *J. gen. Psychol.,* 1967, **77,** 11.

Sutow, W. Atomic bomb casualty commission report. May 1954. *Summary of studies on children exposed in utero to the atomic bomb in Hiroshima city.* Washington, D.C.: U.S. Atomic Energy Commission, 1954.

Tarjan, G., Dingman, H., & Miller, C. Statistical expectations of selected handicaps in the mentally retarded. *Amer. J. ment. Dis.,* 1960, **65,** 335.

Terman, L. & Merrill, M. *Measuring intelligence.* Boston: Houghton Mifflin, 1937.

Timberlake, W., Belmont, E., & Ogonik, J. The effect of reserpine on 200 mentally retarded children. *Amer. J. ment. Def.,* 1957, **62,** 61.

Tredgold, A. *Mental deficiency.* London: Bailliere, 1908.

Tredgold, A. *A textbook of mental deficiency.* (8th ed.) Baltimore: Williams & Wilkins, 1952.

Tredgold, A. & Soddy, K. *Tredgold's textbook of mental deficiency (Subnormality).* (10th ed.) Baltimore: Williams & Wilkins, 1963.

Witkin, H. Psychological differentiation and forms of pathology. *J. abnorm. Psychol.,* 1965, **70,** 317.

Zimmerman, F. & Burgmeister, B. Preliminary report upon the effect of reserpine on epilepsy and behavior problems in children. *Ann. N.Y. Acad. Sci.,* 1955, **61,** 217.

Zimmerman, F. & Ross, S. Effect of glutamic acid and other amino acids on maze learning in the white rat. *Archiv. neurol. Psychiat.,* 1944, **51,** 446.

17 *The Therapies*

The symptoms of mental illness are frequently disturbing to the patient and to those around him. The search for a cure has led researchers and clinicians to pursue better means of identifying the various types of mental disturbances, better procedures for differentiating symptoms caused by physical factors from those related to psychological factors, and better methods for treating different illnesses. Since there is no single panacea that will cure *all* diseases, precise diagnosis is necessary to determine which specific form of mental illness appears present in each case in order that the appropriate treatment may be prescribed. Diagnostic aids include observations of the patient's behavior, detailed case history information, reports from the patient himself or his family, psychological tests, and medical or laboratory data such as electroencephalograms, Wasserman tests, skull X-rays. In addition to accurate diagnostic tools, it is also necessary to have further knowledge of the origins of the illnesses themselves. Is schizophrenia a nonorganic (functional) illness; is there more than one schizophrenia with differing symptoms perhaps reflecting an organic causation at one time and a psychological causation at other times? If so, then differing courses of treatment would be in order. Finally,

methods of treatment are required as a means for combating the various illnesses. Historically, the methods that have been attempted have ranged from the mystical to the scientific, depending upon the level of understanding of practitioners of the time. Today, exorcisms have been replaced by psychoanalysis, dunkings and floggings by electroshock, trephining by lobotomy, imprisonment by hospitalization. Current therapies derive from either of two origins: the empirical or the theoretical. Many of the medical therapies have resulted from empirical reports—someone tries out a technique such as a drug and sees that it works. Continued use with other patients confirms the efficacy of the treatment. It is possible that no one can explain with any conviction why the procedure works, but this detracts in no way from the method's results. For example, few can offer a convincing rationale that outlines the exact way in which electroshock aids in the management of psychotic depressions. On the other hand, the theoretically derived therapies have developed because someone organized the data about an illness into a theory. Such a theory provides a means of logically arriving at recommendations for treatment. Sometimes the data or facts needed to form the basis for a theory are lacking.

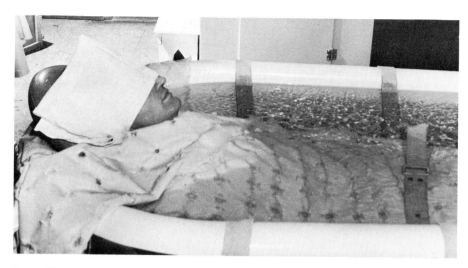

Tranquilizers are frequently prescribed for control of anxiety states. For highly agitated patients requiring immediate treatment effects, *hydrotherapy* may be used. The patient above is benefiting from the soothing effects of warm water around his body. (Jerry Cooke)

sometimes several theories can account for the same facts. Each theory, however, contributes its set of recommendations. Behavior therapists, for example, theorize that mental illness is learned and can therefore be unlearned. The therapy which they offer is therefore directed toward ways of "unlearning" maladaptive behavior. This chapter will discuss the various types of therapies currently relied upon by therapists in their attempts to either relieve or eliminate the symptoms of mental illness. For convenience, such therapies may be classified as the medical or the psychological.

THE MEDICAL THERAPIES

Included among the therapies requiring the collaboration of medical personnel are:

    drug therapy (chemotherapy)
    shock therapy
    psychosurgery

Because such therapies involve measures affecting the physical condition of the patient, they are used only by therapists with medical training. In addition, laws act as safeguards to protect the well-being

of patients, for example, it is illegal to obtain many psychopharmacologic drugs without a prescription.

Chemotherapy

Until approximately 1952, drug therapy was relatively little used and limited primarily to the sedatives, hypnotics, and mild stimulants. However, at about that time, the tranquilizers chlorpromazine and reserpine appeared. Such tranquilizers so revolutionized medicine that it was estimated that three out of every ten prescriptions were for one or the other of these drugs. The steady decline in rate of admissions to mental hospitals since 1955, and the shorter length of hospitalization of patients have been attributed in a large degree to the discovery and use of drugs. These drugs which have proven so valuable in psychiatric treatment are of two types: the tranquilizers and the energizers.

The Tranquilizers. Tranquilizing drugs have the effect of calming a patient without appreciably affecting his alertness or accessibleness. This distinguishes the tranquilizers from the sedatives (such as phenobarbital) which can produce a similar calming effect, but achieves this while making the patient sleepy and sluggish. Chlorpromazine was the first major tranquilizer of the phenothiazine group to be synthetically manufactured. It is interesting to note that the French scientists who were responsible for this achievement were in fact really trying to develop a drug with strong sedative power; the tranquilizing effect of chlorpromazine (originally developed as "4560 R.P.") was entirely unexpected. Since then, numerous other phenothiazine derivatives have been developed (such as Compazine, Stelazine, and Trilafon). Chlorpromazine has the effects of reducing anxiety, agitation, fear, restlessness, and hyperactivity without interfering with thought processes. The patient usually feels a sense of calm and a comfortable apathy. This drug has been particularly useful in the control of symptoms associated with schizophrenia, manic-depressive psychosis (manic stage), and organic brain syndromes involving agitation. An example of the effectiveness of the phenothiazines can be seen in a report made by the National Institute of Mental Health (Klerman, Davidson, and Kayce, 1964). A multihospital collaborative study was started in 1959 involving nine hospitals across the nation. Each new schizophrenic patient was randomly assigned to one of four treatment groups where he received chlorpromazine, one of two other phenothiazines, or a placebo (a pill with no therapeutic value). In order to control for bias effects, neither the patient nor his physician knew the true content of his medication (a "double-blind" study). Over 300 patients were followed over a course of six weeks of treatment. The results were impressive.

95 percent of the phenothiazine patients improved.

Over 75 percent of the phenothiazine patients were judged either "Much Improved" or "Markedly Improved."

Significant changes occurred in 17

of 21 symptoms of schizophrenia, for example, confusion, incoherence, indifference to environment, hallucinations, ideas of persecution, social participation.

There were no noticeable differences in effectiveness among the various phenothiazines, but they were all clearly more effective than the placebo.

Curiously enough, delusions appeared to be more resistant than hallucinations, a finding also previously reported in other research (Winkelman, 1957). Although it is known that chlorpromazine acts on the hypothalamus, the reticular activating system, the limbic system, the medulla, and the autonomic nervous system, it is still a matter of conjecture regarding the reason this drug is so beneficial with schizophrenia.

For centuries, the root of Rauwolfia Serpentina has been used in India to treat anxiety, manic states, and epilepsy. Reserpine, a derivative of Rauwolfia, was introduced in the United States soon after the discovery of chlorpromazine. Generally speaking, reserpine appears to have a lower therapeutic effect than chlorpromazine if recovery rates are examined (Freeman, 1958). It has essentially been displaced in practice by other tranquilizers. When used, reserpine seems to have some value in the control of hebephrenic and catatonic schizophrenics. As with chlorpromazine, the exact nature of its action on the human body is unknown although some speculation has been aroused since reserpine appears to deplete serotonin and noradrenaline, especially in the brain.

Whereas chlorpromazine and reserpine are mainly prescribed in cases of psychoses, other tranquilizers are available for use with minor disorders such as the psychoneurotic and psychosomatic syndromes. A typical example is meprobamate, better known to many under the brand name of Miltown or Equanil. Meprobamate is a drug with mild tranquilizing and muscle relaxing action. After a period of sudden popularity in outpatient treatment, the claims for this tranquilizer have recently been more carefully considered. Of primary concern is the fact that prolonged use may produce addiction and the symptoms of withdrawal when terminated. Drowsiness, dermatitis, and even convulsions have also been reported as possible side effects (Ewing, 1958; Lemere, 1956).

The Energizers. The group of drugs sometimes called psychic energizers are those that have the capacity to stir a patient out of a depression. Since depressions are characterized by a subjective feeling of a lack of energy, the term "energizer" is descriptive of the effects of drugs prescribed for depressions. These drugs are also referred to as antidepressants. Early attempts to energize the depressed patient by use of central nervous system stimulants, such as the amphetamines (e.g., Benzedrine, Dexedrine) proved to be of minimal value. Again, a historically significant discovery was, in reality, a result of chance. The drug iproniazid (Marsilid) was first used in 1951 as a means of treating tuberculosis. However, it had a side effect—that of increasing physical activity—which was considered undesirable; hence, Marsilid was discontinued as a form of treatment. Six years later, Kline (1958) prescribed the drug specifically for its mood-elevating property and was pleased with the results. However, it proved to have a toxic effect on the liver, producing a large number of deaths from jaundice. Furthermore, Marsilid was inconsistent in its therapeutic effectiveness. Fortunately, chemical analysts were already investigating the drug and determined that it was an inhibitor of mono-amine oxidase (MAO), an enzyme that causes depletion of serotonin in the brain. Consequently, it was hypothesized that MAO inhibiting drugs could be helpful in the treatment of depressions. Further laboratory work has led to the develop-

ment of substitutes with less toxicity, such as Nardil, Niamid, and Parnate.

Meanwhile, a second line of development was taken by Kuhn (1958) who was using a phenothiazinelike compound in Switzerland. This drug, imipramine (Tofranil) was used in treating schizophrenics, but showed itself also of particular value in the depressions. Currently, Tofranil and a similar drug Elavil form the second group of antidepressants. As yet, it is still an open question as to whether the MAO-inhibitors are better than the imipramine group. It has been suggested that the MAO inhibiting drugs be reserved for the non-agitated psychotic depressions, while Tofranil or Elavil is favored as a means of combating the agitated depressions or involutional melancholia.

There is little doubt that chemotherapy has made a significant impact on psychiatric treatment. As noted earlier, the introduction of drugs on a large scale beginning about 1954-55 was associated with a two percent reduction in mental hospital residents due to increased discharge rates (Kramer and Pollack, 1958). Some of this rise in discharge might certainly be attributed to factors other than the use of drugs, for example, the shift of hospitals away from custodial care and toward the concept of a therapeutic community. However, Brill and Patton (1959) were able to show a decline in the mental hospital census by over four percent in New York State hospitals, a decline which occurred after the introduction of chemotherapy and before any other major changes. Moreover, unlike the history of shock therapy, this increase in discharge rate occurred without being accompanied by relapses. Gross and Reeves (1961), for example, found relapses occurring in only thirteen percent of some 144 patients on chemotherapy. On the other hand, when the drug dosage was gradually reduced and replaced by a placebo (without the knowledge of either patient or physician), 58 percent of the patients showed relapses.

Despite the favorable results obtained thus far from chemotherapy, there is disagreement even among experts regarding the value and effects of drugs in psychiatry. The foremost concern is a fear of the side effects that can occur. This has been referred to as the "efficacy versus toxicity" problem—the dilemma of balancing the positive results from using the drug against the adverse side effects which may also result. Side effects may range all the way from the minor irritation of dryness of the mouth, to jaundice, or even retinitis pigmentosa (a condition leading to blindness). Moreover, psychopharmacologists are realizing that the positive effects of the drugs themselves appear to be determined by multiple factors and not solely their chemical properties or physiological effects on the body. Individual patients, with similar diagnosis, given similar doses of the same drug, can react quite differently. For example, Wirt and Simon (1959) found that reserpine had a pathogenic rather than a therapeutic effect on their schizophrenic subjects. Among the factors that appear to influence the effects of a drug are the following:

Physical status of the patient: Rate of absorption of the drug, rate of excretion, and tolerance which may have been developed are all important factors.

General attitude of the patient: The expectation that a drug will be beneficial will enhance the therapeutic effect of that drug; this is the reason placebos and double blind studies are used in research (Fisher, Cole, Rickels et al., 1962).

General attitude of the therapist: A therapist's sense of confidence in the therapeutic power of drugs can have as much a role in effecting recovery as the drug itself. There is even some question as to whether the therapist's belief in the drug is more influential than even the drug's

own properties (Haefner, Sacks, & Mason, 1960; Hanlon, Wiener, & Kurland, 1960; Honigfeld, 1962; Kurland, Hanlon, Tatom, & Simopoulos, 1961; Hurst, 1960; Wirt & Simon, 1959).

Personality pattern of the patient: Studies have indicated that outgoing, athletically oriented persons tend to react with anxiety and irritableness when receiving doses of chlorpromazine; while introverted, intellectually oriented persons become more tranquil and indifferent to their surroundings (DiMascio, 1964; DiMascio, Havens, & Klerman, 1963).

Pathological symptoms exhibited: Drug therapy appears more effective with certain symptom patterns than with others. For example, tranquilizers were found to be most effective with acute panic symptoms than symptoms involving withdrawal and periodic agitation (Katz, 1966).

Cognitive and social circumstances: A person experiencing a condition of physiological change for which he has no adequate explanation (cognition) becomes highly susceptible to social influences. Schacter, in an ingenious study, induced an emotional state in subjects with epinephrine. Subjects who were not aware of the emotional effects of the drug, or who were misinformed about what to expect, reported feeling emotions displayed by a stooge participant. Thus, if the stooge acted euphoric, the subjects felt emotionally euphoric; if the stooge acted angry, the subjects felt and actually behaved angrily (Schacter, 1966).

In conclusion, evidence is mounting in support of the belief that the proper use of drugs as a therapeutic tool is a highly complex matter. A distinct interaction exists between the class of drug and the type of mental illness in terms of the therapeutic outcome. Generally speaking, the tranquilizers are better limited to the tension states while the energizers are more effective with the depressed-retarded states. Of equal importance is the inter-action that appears to exist between the class of drug, the type of illness, the specific symptom pattern, the physical status of the patient, the attitudes of both patient and therapist toward chemo-therapy, the fundamental personality pat-tern of the patient, and even the emotions and behaviors of those surrounding the patient. Viewed in this context, chemo-therapy becomes simply one small aspect of a larger scale therapeutic program.

The Drastic Therapies

Among the group of medical therapies are those that might be referred to as the drastic therapies: the convulsive treat-ments, and psychosurgery. Following a brief span of time in which mental patients were neglected, several new methods of treatment were discovered and heralded as psychiatric breakthroughs. Within the course of a few years, starting in the early 1930's, insulin shock, psychosurgery, and electroshock, were all introduced. The convulsive methods were developed em-pirically; Sakel—the discoverer of in-sulin shock therapy—admitted that "There is . . . no explanation sufficiently sub-stantiated by experiment of why the Borderline Insulin Treatment and the Classical Shock Treatment are effective . . ." (1956). On the other hand, Moniz—the originator of psychosurgery—has de-scribed his decision to attempt surgery on the frontal lobes as a decision based on theoretical conclusions from careful con-sideration of known facts (1956). Currently, with the availability of chemotherapy, the drastic therapies have declined as a pop-ular form of psychiatric treatment. Psycho-surgery has been all but eliminated, with the rare exception of the extremely intract-able patient who is unresponsive to other therapies and whose behavior is highly detrimental to his own well-being and that of others. The convulsive therapies have also been curtailed in contrast to

their earlier use; when prescribed, electro-shock appears the more preferred form used by modern psychiatrists.

Insulin Shock Therapy. Insulin ther-apy is one of the oldest major forms of physical treatment used in psychiatry. Dr. Manfred Sakel first experimented with insulin in 1927 in Vienna. Believing that nerve cells are weakened during illness, he hypothesized that insulin might help by blocking the release of further energy from the cell, thereby leading to energy conservation. He also felt that cases of addiction and marginal psychiatric pa-thologies were reflections of metabolic imbalance which might be restored through the introduction of insulin. Orig-inally, Sakel attempted to avoid the induc-tion of convulsions; however, seizures did occur in some of his patients and, to his surprise, the seizures were followed by dramatic improvements. By 1933, the "Classical Sakel Insulin Shock Treatment" had developed with an emphasis on the curative effects of convulsion (Sakel, 1933; 1935; 1954). This method, as it is used today, involves intramuscular injection of increasing amounts of insulin until a "shock" stage, or a comatose state, is ob-tained. The course of treatment is fairly standard. The first phase is the induction phase: a period of days during which the patient receives an increasing dose each morning until a coma dose is reached. Phase two is the repeated administration of the coma dose each day for approxi-mately 30 to 90 treatments. Each comatose state is permitted to last for about 30 minutes to an hour. Basically, the condi-tion is caused by hypoglycemia (reduction in sugar content) caused by the insulin; termination of the coma is therefore at-tained by the administration of glucose directly into the stomach. During this treatment, the patient gradually becomes weak and drowsy, and perspires prior to the coma. As his stupor increases, fear or a burst of hostile activity may occasionally arise. Within three hours after the insulin injection, the patient is comatose. Muscular twitchings, vague motor activity, restless movements including flailing about, may occur. The patient may mutter, groan, or shriek. Severe convulsions can be controlled by the corollary use of a sedative such as phenobarbital. Once the coma is terminated, the patient is returned to his ward where he is then permitted to enter his normal hospital activities.

The use of insulin is inevitably associated with risk. Bruises and fractures from the thrashing about are not uncommon. An irreversible coma may develop, leading to possible damage to the brain or death. The mortality rate from insulin shock treatment is from 0.5 to 1 percent. Such risks are serious enough to demand careful reconsideration of the technique as a therapeutic measure. Insulin shock has been most often used in the treatment of paranoid or catatonic schizophrenics, and patients with extreme anxiety, fear, or panic (Laqueur, Dussik, La Burt, and McLaughlin 1962). The best results are obtained when the course of treatment is rapidly introduced—within six months after the onset of the illness or hospitalization (Kalinowsky and Hoch, 1952). When compared to the 25 to 30 percent rate of improvement of patients receiving no specific therapy, the reported 44 to 68 percent rates for insulin shock is encouraging (Appel, Myers, and Scheflen, 1953; Staudt and Zubin, 1957; West, Bond, Shurley, and Meyers, 1955). Closer examination, however, indicates that a large percentage of the patients counted as showing *immediate* improvement, experience relapses within a few years. If these patients are removed from the figures, the improvement rate for insulin shock drops to between 27 and 40 percent. More recently, researchers such as Stephens and Astrup (1965) were unable to provide any support for either short- or long-term effects of insulin therapy.

Electroshock Therapy. In the early 1930's, an Italian neuropsychiatrist, Ugo Cerletti, became interested in the anatomical effects of convulsions on the brain. His studies involved passing an electric current through the bodies of dogs by means of electrodes attached to the mouth and rectum, then examining the brains of the sacrificed animals. During a visit to Vienna, he observed Sakel's treatment techniques, speculated on the possibility of using electroshock as a substitute for insulin, but was cautioned by his own fear of possible electrocution. Subsequently, a chance visit to a slaughterhouse became a significant historical event, for it introduced Cerletti (1) to a modified technique whereby metallic tongs clamped to the temples were used, and (2) to an awareness that the electric current was not only safe but painless since the animals quickly became unconscious. Further experimentation convinced Cerletti that electricity thus controlled was harmless. Recalling that convulsive treatment was said to be psychiatrically beneficial, he selected a schizophrenic for his human subject, a patient referred by the police commissioner. Cerletti describes this experiment as follows.

As soon as the current was introduced, the patient reacted with a jolt and his body muscles stiffened; then he fell back on the bed without loss of consciousness. He started to sing abruptly at the top of his voice, then he quieted down.

The electrodes were applied again . . . we observed . . . the onset of the classic epileptic convulsion. We were all breathless . . . as we watched the cadaverous cyanosis . . . (Finally) he arose to sitting position and looked at us, calm and smiling, as though to inquire what we wanted of him. We asked: "What happened to you?" He answered: "I don't know. Maybe I was asleep." Thus occurred the first electrically produced convulsion in man, which

I at once named "electroshock." (Cerletti, 1956).

Electroshock therapy (EST), also known as electroconvulsive therapy (ECT) is basically unchanged from Cerletti's original method: about 110 to 150 volts of alternating current are administered across the temples for a period of 0.8 of a second. The usual series is about 8 to 12 treatments administered two to three times a week. The EST series often begins with premedication involving sedatives or anesthetics as a measure to prevent unwarranted fears from developing in the patient. As soon as the current is applied, the patient loses consciousness and undergoes a convulsion that subsides within less than a minute. The patient is then turned on his side and made comfortable during his recovery. Upon regaining consciousness, the patient feels confused, but recovers within 30 minutes. The most common complications of EST are a marked memory loss and fractures. After a dozen treatments, patients invariably experience a loss of memory for the period of treatment and sometimes for the few months prior to treatment. This amnesia can be the source of extreme anxiety for the patient whose adjustment in life is dependent upon his intellect, memory, and alert awareness of his surroundings. The most agonizing experience reported by one former patient was his struggle to regain his identity, orientation to his surroundings, and explanation for his hospitalization, after each EST session. However, this type of extreme reaction is by no means typical, and amnesias from treatment generally vanish completely within six months. Fractures that occur tend to be compression fractures, requiring no special treatment other than the use of a bedboard to support the mattress used by the patient. Fatalities are extremely rare, estimates range from .05 to .001 percent. In a series of 30,000 EST's

given at the Philadelphia General Hospital, only three deaths resulted and 67 fractures (61 of which were of the minor vertebral compression type) (Pearson, 1963).

Although EST has enjoyed some mild success when used with schizophrenics, its most appropriate use appears to be with the depressive reactions. For over 80 percent of cases of involutional melancholia and manic-depressive psychosis, depressive type, EST produces remission by the eighth treatment (Karagula, 1950; Thomas, 1954). In at least one follow-up study five years after initial recovery, 66 percent of the EST treated patients remained improved (Bond, 1954). The major value of electric shock treatment appears to be its capacity to shorten the duration of the depressive symptoms. The attack of depression in a manic-depressive will, in all probability, spontaneously clear up within eight months to a year; with EST, the symptoms can be overcome within three weeks.

Psychosurgery. Brain surgery is a drastic form of treatment conceived of by a Portuguese neurologist Egas Moniz and performed by his collaborator Almeida Lima in 1935. Moniz reasoned that mental disturbances arise from unhealthy synapses in certain regions of the brain, especially the prefrontal lobes which he believed to be most involved in mental activity. By disconnecting the neural pathways to this area, Moniz expected to force new neural relationships, hence new psychic activities. Prefrontal leukotomy, or lobotomy as it is also called, is a surgical technique whereby a specially designed scalpel is inserted through holes drilled in the skull, severing the fibers connecting the frontal lobes and the rest of the brain (see Fig. 17-1). It is currently hypothesized that the incision acts to separate conscious thoughts and ideas from disturbing emotions. Modifications of the prefrontal lobotomy have been introduced, such as topectomy and transorbital lobotomy. Topectomy involves the destruction or removal of certain segments of the frontal lobe. Transorbital lobotomy is an elegant name for an inelegant procedure whereby a surgical instrument is struck through the eye socket, thereby reaching and severing nerve tissue (Moniz, 1936; Freeman and Watts, 1942). Unless there are postsurgical complications, the patient is usually ambulatory within a week, and able to return home within a month.

It should be emphasized that the results of psychosurgery are permanent since nerve fibers in the brain do not regenerate. In addition, research has yet failed to provide conclusive evidence in support of either the belief that lobotomy does indeed have beneficial results or the belief that such techniques are completely valueless and should be banned. For these reasons, the main criterion relied upon for prescribing psychosurgery is the presence of chronic mental illness that has failed to respond to all other forms of treatment. Psychosurgery is considered by most authorities as a "last resort" procedure, relied upon only when all else has failed and some form of treatment must be initiated. Perhaps more than any other medical treatment approach, psychosurgery also suffers from undesirable side effects or complications. The mortality rate ranges from 1.5 to 9 percent. An additional 10 to 24 percent may become subject to convulsions, although these are typically controllable by proper medication. Although changes in the psychological characteristics of the patient are sought after in treatment, certain unplanned for changes also seem to result from surgery. Postoperative patients behave in a manner somewhat similar to brain-injured patients in showing impaired abstract ability, poorer planning, perceptual confusion, and stereotyping of responses when problem solving (Landis and Ehrlick, 1950; Levinson, Meadow, Atwell, Robey, and Bellis, 1953; Porteus, 1951; Goldstein, 1949). In some, personality changes

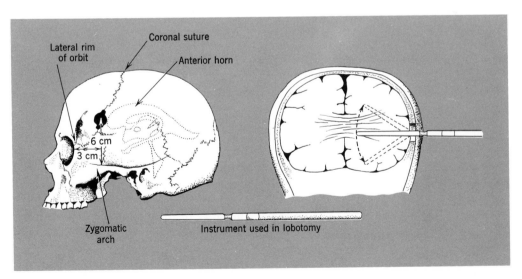

Figure 17-1. **Prefrontal lobotomy technique for the treatment of severe disturbances or control of intractable pain.**
SOURCE: From prefrontal lobotomy: Analysis and warning. K. Goldstein. *Scientific American* offprint. Copyright © 1950 by Scientific American, Inc. All rights reserved.

may include transitory loss of ambition and spontaneity (Meyer, Beck, and McLardy, 1947), lack of consideration for others, hostile outbursts, and a lowering of standards (Sykes and Tredgold, 1964).

Despite all the dangers involved, a number of reports on the effectiveness of psychosurgery have been in the favorable direction. One major study included a follow-up of 10,365 patients leucotomized in England and Wales between 1942 and 1954. This report by the Ministry of Health showed that 46 percent of the treated patients improved well enough to be discharged; these patients being among those initially considered extremely poor prognosis cases where psychosurgery was used as a last ditch measure (Tooth and Newton, 1961). An especially informative report which points out the problems of studies of lobotomy is that of Sykes and Tredgold (1964). Their work included a basic examination of 177 patients operated upon from 1951 to 1960. They conclude that 85 percent showed improvement following surgery. However, additional examination of their information shows that "improvement" included an improvement in symptoms but the symptoms remaining still were such as to require some treatment. In actuality, 53 percent had shown improvement to the degree that either the symptoms were completely removed or changed such that no treatment was required. Critics of lobotomy follow-up studies have often questioned the validity of counting patients as "improved" where this means that further treatment is still needed. In addition, Sykes and Tredgold acknowledge that successful adjustment of their patients was influenced not only by the surgery, but also by the availability of a suitable employment experience and the attitudes of the family who receive the patient. Significantly, 27 patients relapsed bringing the actual rate of improvement down to 37 percent. Many more long-term

follow-up studies are needed before psychosurgery can be viewed in proper perspective. Its popularity in the United States has declined sharply, although there has been some restirring of interest in other nations. Perhaps the greatest contribution that lobotomies can offer is in providing a means of helping the patient to manage his emotional turmoil. When successful, psychosurgery enables the patient to be freed of his preoperative incapacitating anxieties, fears, ruminations, or depression. These disturbances are not dispelled by the treatment; the patient is simply emotionally isolated from them and no longer reacts to them in the same way. This occurs in the same way that a lobotomy can ameliorate the intractable pain of cancer; the pain continues to exist, but the patient's distress is greatly diminished.

THE PSYCHOTHERAPIES

Psychotherapy is a method of treatment involving a corrective experience accomplished through the interaction between a professional therapist and one or more patients. The aim of psychotherapy is the restoration of the patient to a more effective and satisfying state of adjustment. The achievement of this aim is brought about through the establishment of certain conditions believed to be necessary for change; the methods for establishing these conditions may be called the *strategies* of psychotherapy. Psychoanalytically oriented therapists envision the therapeutic relationship as requiring a dynamic interplay between the patient with his maladaptive thoughts, feelings, and actions, and the therapist with his treatment skills and insights. Client-centered therapists emphasize their own deep involvement in the patient and his feelings, striving to relate to the client in a fashion so as to enhance the client's own growth and adjustive potential. Behavior therapists take a systematic, scientific, impersonal role as they introduce the patient to conditions designed to unlearn maladaptive behavior and acquire more appropriate response patterns. These psychotherapeutic orientations, their basic beliefs, and their strategies, will be discussed in more detail later in this section.

The psychotherapeutic relationship has often been described as a unique relationship replicated by a very few other interactions. Karl Menninger (1958), the chief of staff of the famed Menninger Clinic, has referred to the psychotherapeutic situation as a "contract." In this therapeutic contract, the therapist and patient have mutually agreed to engage in every means possible for the achievement of the therapeutic goal, a more adaptive and satisfying life for the patient. During the course of this arrangement, the patient is called upon to contribute his share to achieving this goal although it is recognized that he will often deliberately or unwittingly interfere with the treatment process. The therapist is also committed to applying all of his skills and knowledge of human behavior toward the patient's well-being. He is not always required to obtain the patient's approval for the techniques used since the therapist is better qualified by reason of his training and experience to make such decision. In addition, the patient's maladaptive characteristic may include a resistance to those conditions which may bring change. However, the patient is never in jeopardy since the psychotherapist is bound by the contract to always consider the overall well-being of the patient first and foremost. This notion of the psychotherapy contract may make the treatment situation appear overly impersonal and devoid of feeling. In reality, psychotherapy involves a highly personal relationship (Fiedler, 1953). This atmosphere of understanding and acceptance appears to be a primary distinguish-

ing feature of all therapeutic approaches whether the therapist works from a psychoanalytic, client-centered, or learning-oriented viewpoint. Every therapist has undergone extensive training which strengthens his concern and awareness of the deep feelings and emotional conflicts of his patients. In the psychotherapeutic meeting, the patient encounters a different type of interaction: he is faced with an expert who is willing to engage in a mutual effort without the dangers of either rejection or smothering overprotectiveness. He is given the opportunity to gradually express his fears without being ridiculed, to discuss his dissatisfactions without being admonished, to admit his weaknesses without being criticized. He is encouraged and helped to find ways of altering his present unsatisfying mode of adapting and when a more adaptive way of living seems in hand, he is urged to rely upon his own newfound capacities to continue toward further self-growth and development.

The strategies of psychotherapy are many and varied. Patients may, for example, be seen in groups. Such sessions are called appropriately enough *group psychotherapy* (Slavson, 1955; Hobbs, 1951; Bach, 1954; Powdermaker and Frank, 1953). Group treatment has the advantages of enabling patients to share their problems and solutions with one another, to try out new ways of relating to persons other than the therapist, to experience the emotional support often provided by the other group members, and to work out problems related to feelings of social isolation, difficulties in getting along with others, and poor reality testing. A more recent version of many persons treated simultaneously is the *family psychotherapy* strategy (Ackerman, 1958; Bell, 1961; Boszarmenyi-Nagy and Framo, 1965; Haley, 1962; Jackson, 1961). This approach is based on the belief that symptoms in a person are often the expression of difficulties in the interrelationships among mem-

Psychodrama is a type of activity psychotherapy. It is based on the premise that conflicts are resolved and adaptive behaviors learned when the client can enact the difficulties. The audience may be directed to participate in the therapeutic experience; on occasion the client is placed in the audience while others act out his life. (Raimondo Borea)

bers of a family constellation. Since it is the family unit that must be treated rather than a single individual, the therapist will therefore meet only with all members present. The topic is never what is wrong with an individual, only what is wrong with the relationships. When the family convenes together in psychotherapy, disturbed interactions are often quickly perceived by the therapist and thereby subject to discussion and alteration. *Psychodrama* is a treatment strategy that is, in a sense, a reversal of the group therapy arrangement. Instead of there being one therapist to several patients, there are several "therapists" to one patient. J. L. Moreno (1946), the founder of psychodrama, believed that real insights and changes in personality occur when a patient is able to act out his feelings. The psychodrama therapist therefore directs a therapeutic drama involving the patient

as the main actor, other patients, and an audience. The drama usually represents a conflict area with the patient being encouraged to spontaneously say and do whatever he truly feels at the moment. The other patient-actors may be assigned roles to help make the scene more realistic. In some dramas, the patient is given an alter-ego, another patient who tries to reflect the hidden feelings of the main actor-patient as a means of producing insight. In other dramas, the plot is arranged to permit the patient a controlled attempt at trying out new ways of adapting.

With children, play-acting is a common activity that allows them free expression of thoughts and feelings. In addition, the very young child may actually be able to express himself only through actions because his speech development is still primitive. Furthermore, the child does not have the intellectual or emotional maturity to develop self-insights in the way that adults might. For these reasons, *play therapy* is often used in child psychotherapy (Allen, 1942; Axline, 1947; Levy, 1939; Solomon, 1938). In play therapy, the child is placed in a room with a variety of playthings preselected for the treatment session. The basic criterion for inclusion of a toy or game is its capacity to encourage the expression of feelings. A family of dolls and a doll house, for example, will often elicit conflicts which the child feels in his own family. A re-creation of this will help the therapist to better understand the problems that exist and, frequently, the simple matter of reenacting such problem feelings will prove helpful to the child. As the child and therapist interact, with the play materials helping to focus on relevant issues, the child finds himself more and more able to work through feelings that were concealed. The acceptance of the therapist soon permits the child to face some of his tensions and unacceptable impulses, and gradually adopt more healthy modes of interacting.

Special treatment techniques are sometimes introduced in adults with certain difficulties. *Hypnosis* is a prime example (Brenman and Gill, 1947; Kardiner and Speigel, 1947; Weitzenhoffer, 1953; Wolberg, 1964). Its most dramatic effects have involved the recall of repressed experiences. During World War II, soldiers were helped to reexperience the traumatic event that precipitated their mental condition. A hypnotic drug, such as sodium pentothal, was relied upon to produce a state of relaxation and responsiveness to suggestion. On occasion, hypnosis may be used as a means of reaching repressed material not related to a single trauma. In order to accomplish this, the patient is stimulated to dream through the aid of hypnosis. The dreams are then evaluated for clues concerning the repressed conflict. Posthypnotic suggestions have also been attempted as a means of controlling undesirable behavior, for example, tics. However, such suggestions have not appeared to be a dependable way of permanently eliminating such neurotic symptoms. Another type of special aid to psychotherapy is the use of the hallucinogenic drug, LSD (lysergic acid diethylamide). As with hypnosis, LSD is not in and of itself curative but a technique for obtaining special effects possibly helpful in treatment. In addition, both hypnosis and LSD are potentially dangerous with unstable personalities and in untrained hands (Dahlberg, 1963). Nevertheless, some early and exploratory efforts with the drug suggest that it may help rigid and repressed personalities to become more spontaneous. Sometimes it is viewed as a means for experiencing a change in values or an emotional insight but this is not always a predictable result (World Health Organization, 1958; Dittman, Hayman, and Whittlessy, 1962). It is likely that the patient-therapist interaction is significantly affected by the circumstance since the therapist becomes the patient's sole link with reality, and sole protector, during the drug state.

Among the strategies of psychotherapy are three major approaches: the psychoanalytic, the client-centered, and the behavior therapist. Each strategy was derived from a particular set of beliefs about people and their problems. Each strategy includes certain specific procedures believed to be particularly useful in achieving personality change. The three major strategic approaches will be discussed in the following sections.

The Psychoanalytic Strategy

Psychoanalytic therapists (Alexander, 1937; Freud, 1955; Glover, 1940; Hartmann, 1958; Fenichel, 1934; Rapaport, 1951) believe that psychopathology is a result of repression of unacceptable impulses, anxiety arousal, and defenses which are erected to reduce the anxiety rather than resolve the conflict, and impaired

The *psychoanalytic therapist* relies upon techniques designed to facilitate the development of transference and the return of the repressed. In the above photograph of Freud's actual consulting office at 19 Berggasse, Vienna, the arrangement of the furniture is noteworthy. The couch permitted the patient to relax and free associate while Freud took notes from his chair out of sight of the patient. (Courtesy of Edmund Engelman)

psychological development. Repression prevents the patient from recognizing and dealing directly with the source of his difficulties. Instead, the patient is helpless, unable to resolve his problems, susceptible to expressing his unconscious conflicts through disturbing symptoms and dreams. Since the conflicts represent threats, the feeling of anxiety is aroused as a warning signal. Unfortunately, the patient is unable to do much more than respond to the warning by getting rid of the warning, that is, he attempts to do away with the anxiety. Various defense mechanisms are thus installed, some becoming severe enough to be disturbing symptoms themselves, for example, the compulsive actions that help to distract the patient from the anxiety-provoking material. This self-protective defense system is recognized by psychoanalysts as a characteristic that appears even in therapy. The term *resistance* refers to the tendency of patients to seek

to protect themselves from the threat of having to face their conflicts during psychotherapy. Analysts believe that overcoming resistance is a crucial part of the therapy process. Invariably, the conflicts have their roots in early childhood experiences that affect the later development of the personality. The patient often reacts to the therapist in ways characteristic of the patient's early reactions to parents. In this sense, it is inappropriate since the therapist's behavior is not similar to that of the patient's parents. Such irrational repetition of an early behavior or emotional pattern is referred to as *transference*.

The psychoanalytic therapist introduces techniques that are directed toward the sources of the pathology. *Free association* is a method developed by Freud to facilitate the recall of the repressed material. The patient is directed to say whatever passes through his mind without any attempt to select or censor. Freud found that this procedure enabled unconscious material to surface and thereby be identified. The *interpretation of dreams* is also used by analysts as a tool for delving into the repressed areas of the mind. Since defenses are not as strongly maintained during sleep, more information on basic conflicts are obtainable even though they may appear in disguised forms. The transference situation is also a useful and a necessary part of psychoanalytic treatment. The transference enables the therapist to point out to the patient the way in which he has permitted his past experiences to influence his behavior and attitudes toward current persons. These unresolved conflicts are then explored while the patient attempts to develop more ways of reacting that are more appropriate to his current life setting. The use of the transference situation is so important to psychoanalysts that their techniques encourage its development. For example, the analytic therapist does not reveal his own personal background, beliefs, or attitudes, in order to be certain that any opinions that the patient may later attribute to the therapist come from the patient's own misperceptions. The therapist maintains an attitude of interest and acceptance; thus, if the patient accuses the therapist of being too demanding or too controlling, it becomes clear that these accusations are part of a transference reaction. Menninger gives an illustration of transference in a case:

An unmarried male laboratory technician of thirty underwent psychoanalysis. . . Early in the process he described his father's reserve and aloofness. . . Ultimately, of course, it was the analyst who seemed reserved, cold and aloof. A little later, however, he recalled certain experiences with a girl cousin whose warmth. . . (made him feel) guilty, however, because of certain of his responses to her advances. . . The analyst was not surprised, accordingly, when some months later the patient dreamed of the analyst in the form of a seduc-

tress, which evoked reproach that the analyst was expecting too much of him and encouraging him in forbidden directions. Next, it developed that there had been in his childhood a particularly stern aunt whose judgments were feared. . . She evidently represented to him, then, what law and order, the police court and purgatory came to represent to him later. This began to appear in the transference when the analyst, who had previously been accused both of coldness and seductiveness, became a stern figure of retribution from whom the patient expected punishment and dismissal (Menninger, 1958, p. 82).

Dreams, free association, and transference are all aids whereby the patient is helped to achieve an *insight* into his conflicts and a *corrective emotional experience* leading to personality change. The analyst will also begin to suggest possible *interpretations,* that is, possible associations between certain current behaviors and past events. In other words, the psychoanalyst attempts to seek out and share the meanings behind certain of the patient's activities. Interpretations are used to stimulate insight, to decrease the power of maladaptive behavior, and to pave the way for the development of more adaptive traits. A patient who is continually late for his therapy appointment, or who seems to have nothing relevant to say during the treatment hour, may be doing so because of his *resistance.* An interpretation of this to the patient serves to weaken such defensive behavior by making him more aware of what is happening. This process may proceed for quite a long time before any appreciable gain is evident in therapy. Murray (1954), for example, followed the course of treatment of one patient and found that interpretation was followed by the decline in one form of resistance (intellectualizing) but led to the increase in another form of resistance (somatic complaints) (Fig. 17-2). After several efforts by the therapist, the patient was finally able to drop his defensiveness and come to grips with the anxiety provoking material.

The training of a psychoanalyst is long and expensive. Treatment by psychoanalysis is similarly long and expensive. Psychoanalytic therapy involves years of working through conflicts repressed since early life, reaching past defenses that have been firmly established, and slowly but persistently developing newer ways of relating and adjusting. Psychoanalysis is no less expensive than modern medical treatment, and since the patient is seen for hourly treatment sessions over a course of years, the total expenditures can run into several thousands of dollars. Partly because of the difficulty inherent in such prolonged treatment, modifications of the basic psychoanalytic method have been introduced. Alexander and French (1946) have introduced a shorter term approach which departs from standard psychoanalytic techniques without losing any of the thoroughness characteristic of psychoanalysis. This technique, better called

psychoanalytically-oriented psychotherapy, calls upon the flexible application of strategies selected to fit the particular patient and his circumstances. Free association, for example, may be relied upon if it is the most effective procedure for the client; on the other hand, it may be completely dispensed with if the patient appears unable to profit from it at the moment. The number of meetings per week is adjusted to correspond to the number required to keep the patient's motivation and progress at its optimal level. The therapist, still working from the psychoanalytic viewpoint, may nevertheless turn to ordinary face-to-face conversation with the patient or even direct confrontation. Finally, Alexander and French's approach encourages a controlled approach to transference. Whereas the traditional psychoanalytic strategy is to encourage a full transference, the psychoanalytically-oriented therapist may bypass or discourage transference for some patients if it appears feasible to do so without a loss to the treatment goals.

The Client-centered Strategy

Client-centered therapists (Rogers, 1951, 1959; Snyder, 1947) disavow the view that psychopathology develops because human nature is irrational, regressively self-defensive, and destructive. Carl Rogers, the founder of this approach, has remarked:

I have little sympathy with the rather prevalent concept that man is basically irrational, and that his impulses, if not controlled, will lead to destruction of others and self. Man's behavior is exquisitely rational, moving with subtle and ordered complexity toward the goals his organism is endeavoring to achieve (1957).

The client-centered or Rogerian therapist looks upon man as possessing an innate desire *and* capability toward positive self-development. The fact that man is progressive and not regressive is exem-

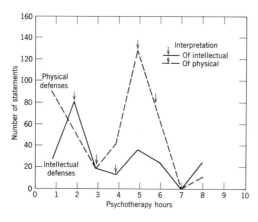

Figure 17-2. The effects of interpretation in therapy on intellectual defenses and physical complaint defenses.

SOURCE: E. Murray, a case study in a behavioral analysis of psychotherapy. *J. abnorm. soc. Psychol.,* 1954, **49**, 305.

plified by the child who is learning to walk. Despite nasty falls and numerous setbacks, children do persist in their attempts to achieve this higher level of coordination and motor skill. In a nonoppressive and nonrepressive home environment, the child seems to seek and acquire this skill without outside guidance or instruction as if the desire to develop were inborn. In many other ways, the human is perceived by the Rogerian as ever moving toward self-fulfillment, or *self-actualization*. Behaviors are selected and developed in accordance with the goal of self-actualization. More accurately, a person behaves in a way he *perceives* to be most likely to lead to this goal. It is possible that the individual might err in his perception and select a self-damaging alternative, however, his intentions are still basically good and by no means self-destructive.

Among the objects of one's perception are certain personally oriented experiences which comprise the self-concept. The self-concept formed during childhood becomes the core around which future experiences are evaluated, including self-concept experiences. In the maladjusted person, important experiences that could lead to personality change are distorted or denied to awareness because they are not in agreement with this basic core. In support of this premise, Suinn et al. demonstrated that people tended to resist remembering information about themselves if it was not consistent with their own self-views even though the information was favorable (1962). An increase in pathology occurs as the person prevents himself from access to more and more experiences that would aid in his adjustment; this state of *incongruence* makes the person more vulnerable to anxiety and less open to new experiences or change. The person is still motivated by a search for self-actualization. However, progress is blocked by his distorted experiences and the discrepancy

that exists between his true traits and abilities and what he believes himself to be. In effect, the maladjusted person is forcing himself to function with incomplete and misleading information about himself and his environment.

The major task of the Rogerian therapist is to establish an atmosphere conducive to greater openness to experience. The atmosphere that is sought after is one that views the client as capable; it replaces the attitude of searching for a "cure" with the emphasis on growth and self-development; it offers the client a setting of unconditional acceptance and encouragement. The client-centered therapist is not impressed with the tactics of interpretation since they believe this takes the initiative for progress away from the client. Instead, the Rogerian tries to involve himself intensively in an empathic understanding of the client, mainly through a grasp of the feelings being expressed. The therapist may repeat or restate the client's words in a struggle to insure that he perfectly understands the inner experiences of the client. Above all, the client-centered therapist strives to maintain a relationship free of judgment and evaluation so as not to threaten the client and thereby prevent the self-exploration process. It is for this reason that diagnostic evaluations and all attempts to discover "explanations" for behavior are rejected. More than any other treatment strategy, the client-centered approach stresses the necessity of a relationship developing between client and therapist. When a truly accepting relationship is developed, the client will become less fearful of examining his own feelings and perceptions and experiences. He will be able to face himself as he really is and reorganize his self-structure to include what had previously been distorted or denied. He becomes no longer constricted but can be open to new experiences. This freeing or loosening process enables the client to become more successfully self-directing. His self-regard and confidence increases immensely as he realizes that he is able to "find himself" in the presence of a therapist who had always believed in the client's inner value and capacity for self-growth.

The Rogerian orientation toward therapy is a unique one because it places such a high emphasis on conditions such as a "helping relationship," and "unconditional regard." When a client-centered therapist is trained, he does not learn techniques to use, such as the free association technique that a psychoanalytic therapist may rely upon. Intangible though this may seem, not only do Rogerian therapists develop their therapeutic skills but their patients respond when these skills are properly used. Halkides (1958) compared therapy sessions in terms of their conformity with the conditions considered necessary for successful therapy by Rogers. She predicted that 10 successfully treated cases would differ significantly from 10 unsuccessfully treated cases on the following four variables: (1) the degree of empathic understanding shown by the therapist, (2) the degree of unconditional positive regard shown by the therapist, (3) the genuineness of the therapist in his relationship, and (4) the degree to which the therapist's responses were able to match the patient's in intensity of emotional expression. Impossible though it may seem, three judges were able to reliably evaluate therapy interviews on these more or less intangible variables. In addition, Halkides' findings showed without a doubt that the first three aspects of the therapy relationship were indeed associated with successful treatment. In addition, these conditions which had characterized the successful therapists were present during the early contacts between patient and therapist just as consistently as they were present during the later interviews.

The Behavior Therapy Strategy

Behavior therapists (Bandura, 1961; Dollard and Miller, 1950; Dunlap, 1932; Eysenck, 1956; Salter, 1949; Wolpe, 1958; Wolpe and Lazarus, 1966) firmly believe that psychopathology is learned. In this way, normal development and abnormal development are similar; the behaviorist accepts the view that the same conditions that enable a person to learn to speak normally also apply to the development of psychotic speech. These conditions are referred to as classical conditioning and operant conditioning. As the reader will recall, *classical conditioning* was involved in the fear of the rat shown by Albert (Chapter 7). An irrational emotional response, fear, was conditioned to appear through the repeated arousal of fright whenever the rat was presented. In a similar fashion, an adult may exhibit severe shyness and inhibition or even withdrawal in the presence of others as a result of previous repeatedly aversive experiences with people. The more an emotional reaction is aroused in the presence of a particular stimulus (such as a rat, or people), the more that stimulus becomes capable of eliciting this emotion even though this leads to inappropriate behavior (such as running away from toys which only resemble the rat, or avoiding all contact with people). In *operant conditioning*, pathological behavior such as compulsions are acquired and maintained because they are reinforced by the prevention or reduction of anxiety or other drive states. The compulsive has learned that his anxiety decreases each time he goes through a ritual of activities. A vicious circle is soon established whereby the patient cannot stop his compulsive behavior because to do so would increase his anxiety, yet the compulsions are themselves annoying and worrisome and thereby contribute to further anxiety arousal which again triggers off the compulsions. A child may engage in severe tantrums because these are always followed by the reward of the parent acquiescing to his demands; another child may continue to rely upon baby-talk (or a schizophrenic upon neologisms) because such speech proves as effective in getting results that are reinforcing. The reinforcements are not always obvious: for some, it is the attention or the nurturance obtained; for others, it is the reestablishment of feelings of comfort and lowering of anxiety; for still others, it is the control over the environment which derives from the behavior. Although this may begin to make the behavior therapist's point of view seem similar to the psychodynamic explanations of the other strategies, this is far from the truth (Table 17-1). A psychoanalytically oriented therapist may pursue the reasons behind the patient's need for attention and attempt to "root out" the source of the symptom. A behavior therapist does not postulate such inner forces or disease process, nor does he believe that the symptoms are signs of deeper problems which must be dispelled through insight. The symptoms, such as the phobia

TABLE 17-1. *Comparisons of Psychotherapy and Behavior Therapy*

PSYCHOTHERAPY	BEHAVIOR THERAPY
1. Based on inconsistent theory never properly formulated in postulate form.	Based on consistent, properly formulated theory leading to testable deductions.
2. Derived from clinical observations made without necessary control observations or experiments.	Derived from experimental studies specifically designed to test basic theory and deductions made therefrom.
3. Considers symptoms the visible upshot of unconscious causes ("complexes").	Considers symptoms as unadaptive conditioned responses.
4. Regards symptoms as evidence of *repression*.	Regards symptoms as evidence of faulty learning.
5. Believes that symptomatology is determined by defense mechanisms.	Believes that symptomatology is determined by individual differences in conditionability and autonomic lability, as well as accidental environmental circumstances.
6. All treatment of neurotic disorders must be *historically* based.	All treatment of neurotic disorders is concerned with habits existing at *present*; their historical development is largely irrelevant.
7. Cures are achieved by handling the underlying (unconscious) dynamics, not by treating the symptom itself.	Cures are achieved by treating the symptom itself, i.e. by extinguishing unadaptive C.Rs and establishing desirable C.Rs.
8. Interpretation of symptoms, dreams, acts, etc. is an important element of treatment.	Interpretation, even if not completely subjective and erroneous, is irrelevant.
9. Symptomatic treatment leads to the elaboration of new symptoms.	Symptomatic treatment leads to permanent recovery provided autonomic as well as skeletal surplus C.Rs are extinguished.
10. Transference relations are essential for cures of neurotic disorders.	Personal relations are not essential for cures of neurotic disorder, although they may be useful in certain circumstances.

SOURCE: H. Eysenck. *Behaviour therapy and the neuroses.* London: Pergamon Press, 1960.

or the compulsive behavior or the tantrums, are present because they were learned and will disappear when they are unlearned. Eysenck expressed this concisely when he wrote: *"Get rid of the symptom and you have eliminated the neurosis"* (1964, p. 9). The behaviorist does not accept the belief that other drastic symptoms will appear to replace the ones eliminated. It is possible that the patient has learned other maladaptive behaviors just as he may have learned a number of adaptive responses pertaining to one situation. A child, for example, may have developed many ways for obtaining approval, each being strengthened whenever the reward of approval is achieved. In the same way, a neurotic may have acquired a series of maladaptive responses. The behavior therapist works on the assumption that the patient will be completely cured when the last of these learned behaviors has been unlearned.

Since the behavior therapist does not require the patient to develop insight, the therapeutic strategy is more characterized by training than by depth interpretations or analysis of feelings. The therapist may explore the patient's past life situation in order to obtain clues into the learning conditions that maintain the pathological behavior and prevent its extinction. On the other hand, the therapist may need to know only what behaviors are desired and what current events can serve as rewards or reinforcers and nothing else about the patient. Dr. Joseph Wolpe, one of the leading behavior therapy experts, has stressed, "I have no intention of devoting a great deal of time to raking up past history, because although it would be interesting and perhaps helpful, it is not necessary: *for to overcome his (the patient's) neurotic reactions it is of greater relevance to determine what stimuli do or can evoke . . . at the present time"* (1958, p. 105).

Among the more common procedures used by behavior therapists are:
> Counterconditioning
> Vicarious extinction
> Positive reinforcement
> Experimental extinction
> Aversion conditioning

Counterconditioning is the strengthening of a response that is incompatible or antagonistic to the unwanted maladaptive response. Conditions are set up that permit the more desirable response to compete successfully with and replace the pathological response. The most systematic development of this procedure is called psychotherapy by *reciprocal inhibition* (Wolpe, 1958). The founder of this methodology, Wolpe, advocates the use of relaxation, assertive behavior, or sexual responses, as the means for countering the ineffective maladjustive behaviors. A typical psychotherapy procedure is outlined below using a neurotic phobia symptom as an example.

1. Information-gathering interviews: The first few sessions are devoted to obtaining much detailed information on the learning conditions that contributed to the patient's symptoms (Suinn, 1969). The therapist wishes to determine the exact nature of the symptoms themselves, for example, what objects comprise the feared stimuli. He also tries to determine which type of behavior treatment process is most appropriate to use. The interviews may reveal that reciprocal inhibition techniques are less called for than negative reinforcement measures.

2. Information-giving interviews: Once the problem area has been carefully understood and clarified the therapist then proceeds to discuss his plan of action with the patient. He points out the way in which the patient seemed to have learned the maladaptive symptoms and outlines the ways in which they may be unlearned. If reciprocal inhibition is to be used, the

Desensitization therapy trains the client in relaxation, then instructs him to visualize scenes related to his fears. When properly conducted, the procedure substitutes calmness for fear. A young man demonstrates his ability to cope with heights after desensitization was completed. (Photographic lab, Colorado State University)

therapist informs the patient of the steps in counterconditioning and his plan to combat the phobia by matching a stronger and more adaptive response with a weaker phobic response.

3. Training sessions: For illustrative purposes, assume that the patient is highly fearful of taking examinations to the extent of "freezing" when faced with tests. If no other complicating aspects are present, the therapist is likely to rely upon *systematic desensitization*.

In systematic desensitization, the therapist first trains the patient in deep muscle relaxation, has the patient construct an *anxiety hierarchy,* then uses the relaxation to reduce the patient's sensitivity to the test-taking situations. The anxiety hierarchy is simply a ranked list of stimulus situations that evoke anxiety or fear in

the patient, for example, "Reading the first question on a final examination" or "Walking into an examination room." These items are ranked so that the therapist will know which situations bring forth the strongest feelings of anxiety or fear, which the next stronger, and so forth, down to the item eliciting the weakest feelings (Table 17-2).

The training in relaxation may involve a modified technique based upon Jacobsen's *Progressive Relaxation* (1938). This is a procedure where the patient first tenses muscles such as the biceps then immediately relaxes the muscles and attends to the contrast in feelings. By doing this for muscles from head to toes the patient learns how to relax. Another way of obtaining a relaxed state is through hypnosis in which the therapist strives to make the patient as comfortable and secure as possible.

4. Desensitization sessions: While in this state of relaxation, the patient is then told to visualize the least disturbing test situation. If any anxiety or fear is aroused, the patient is instructed to dismiss the scene and concentrate on relaxation again. When he is comfortable, the scene is again presented until the relaxed feelings are able to overcome and actually replace the anxiety responses. Once this weak stimulus situation is no longer able to arouse anxiety, the patient is then faced with a somewhat stronger situation. Ultimately the patient is able to take on the most feared item on his anxiety hierarchy without any sense of discomfort.

If handled properly, test anxiety may be eliminated within a period of 5 to 15 desensitization sessions (Suinn, 1968; Robinson and Suinn, 1969).

Recently Suinn has developed a procedure for the treatment of anxiety over examinations, with the desensitization sessions being initiated and completed within 24 hours (Suinn and Hall, 1969). Desensitization has also proved helpful

483

with phobias (Paul, 1966; Wolpe and Lazarus, 1966; Rachman, 1967), LSD "freakouts" (Suinn and Brittain, 1970), and falling asleep while driving (Suinn and Richardson, 1970).

Reciprocal inhibition may involve the use of training in skills other than relaxation. A patient who has great difficulty in interpersonal relationships may be helped by *assertive training* (Salter, 1961). The patient may be timid in his contacts or ingratiating. The therapist instructs the patient in forms of assertive behavior and selects circumstances for the patient to try out these behaviors. The therapist chooses these try-out circumstances with the view towards picking those which will help in the learning of assertive behavior, typically these are situations which will reinforce rather than punish the patient for being assertive. Some patients may start off with play-acting or role playing their assertion. The therapist takes the role of a responder to the patient, or he may act the part of an assertive patient thereby giving the patient a model to imitate. In successful cases, the patient learns how to be assertive appropriately, extinguishes his timid behavior, and finds his assertiveness more satisfying and re-

inforcing. The use of *sexual responses* may be relied upon in the treatment of problems of sexual inadequacy. The behavior therapist sees these problems as a result of anxiety associated with the stimuli involved in sexual acts. This anxiety produces an inhibition of the appropriate sexual responses and the individual becomes, for example, impotent or frigid. The behavioral approach to treatment may have the patient undertake only those sexual acts which do not arouse tension. As long as pleasurable feelings predominate the patient may continue; when anxiety feelings begin to appear the patient must slow down and await the increase of the pleasant feelings. The goal is to keep the sexual arousal and pleasure ascendant enough to successfully compete with the anxiety responses.

Vicarious extinction is an indirect form of desensitization treatment where the patient observes a model engaging in situations related to the patient's anxieties. Bandura has been highly successful in demonstrating that deviant behavior may be acquired through observing such behavior exhibited by another person who is rewarded (Bandura, Ross, and Ross, 1961, 1963; Bandura and Walters, 1963;

TABLE 17-2. *Anxiety Hierarchy from a Client with Extreme Anxiety on Tests*

Finding out I have received the lowest score on the last exam. (This situation arouses maximum tension).

Being told by the instructor that I need at least a "B" on the final exam in order to pass the course.

Reading the first question on an examination and discovering that I do not know the answer.

Studying for an examination that is coming up the next day.

Being asked by a friend whether I feel prepared for a coming exam.

Hearing the instructor ask the class a general question about a recent assignment.

Reading a syllabus which states the course requirements and dates and number of examinations required.

Reading an assignment on a topic I particularly enjoy and knowing that someday I will be reviewing the material for a quiz. (This situation arouses the least tension).

Bandura, 1965). Other researchers have also shown that vicarious acquisition of emotional responses can occur in classical conditioning. Typically, an observer-subject watches a model-performer being presented with a neutral stimulus and then apparently shocked. After the observer has witnessed the model undergoing this conditioning procedure, the observer will also display the conditioned anxiety response to the formerly neutral stimulus even though he had not himself directly experienced the shock (Barnett and Benedetti, 1960; Berger, 1962; Bandura and Rosenthal, 1966). The next logical step deriving from such findings would be the treatment of emotional responses through observation of a model. At Stanford University, children with extreme fears of dogs observed a graduated sequence of scenes of models with dogs. These models engaged in varying approach behaviors with no signs of fear, ranging from looking at a penned dog to dressing the dog in festive hats and "Beatle" wigs. The phobic children viewed these scenes set up in a prescribed fashion from the lowest fear-arousal scene progressively up to the most daring child-dog scene. Within a short number of sessions, the phobic children lost their fear of dogs to the extent that many were able to freely interact with such animals (Bandura and Menlove, 1968; Bandura, Grusec, and Menlove, 1967).

Positive reinforcement is introduced into therapy to capitalize on the fact that new responses are acquired and old responses are strengthened whenever the responses occur and they are followed by a reward (i.e., positive reinforcement). Behavior such as saying "please" is learned in this manner since requests phrased in this fashion are more frequently responded to favorably. Children with deviant behaviors are often encouraged to develop more adaptive responses through the use of candy, attention, or social approval as

rewards (Azrin and Lindsley, 1956; Bijou and Orlando, 1961; Patterson, 1965; Allen, Hart, Buell, Harris, and Wolf, 1964; Harris, Johnston, Kelley, and Wolf, 1964). Among the adult problems treated by the offering of a reward for the display of normal instead of pathological behavior have been hysterical blindness (Brady and Lind, 1961), anorexia nervosa or pathological self-starvation (White, 1959; Bachrach, Erwin, and Mohr, 1965), resistance to speaking (Sherman, 1965; Suinn and Augustine, 1969), and clothes hoarding (Ayllon, 1963). An example of this approach is found in a report by Bachrach, Erwin, and Mohr (1965) involving the treatment of a woman whose failure to eat had decreased her body weight from 118 pounds to 47 pounds. From an attractive "real chubby" woman she had wasted away until she gave "the appearance of a poorly preserved mummy suddenly struck with the breath of life" (Bachrach, Erwin, and Mohr, 1965, p. 154). The therapist first removed her to a barren room and isolated her from social contact so as to increase the effectiveness of the reinforcers. Interesting discussions, social visits, music, television, and walks, were made contingent upon her eating. Within less than two months, she had progressed well enough to be discharged to her home. In another case that involved a schizophrenic patient, gum was accidentally found to be a highly effective reinforcer. The therapists thereafter used gum rewards to develop speech in this formerly mute catatonic schizophrenic (Isaacs, Thomas, and Goldiamond, 1960). Suinn, Stewart, and McGuirk (1969) used an operant reinforcement technique to treat subjects without their awareness. The subjects, all phobic about snakes, thought that they were participating in a study of their ability to identify the attitude-statements of nonsnake phobic persons. Each time they selected and read aloud the nonphobic statements, they were rewarded. At no

time did the experiment expose the subjects to anything ordinarily considered therapeutic. Nevertheless, on a test following this study involving a live boa constrictor snake, all subjects showed significant reductions in their fears of snakes.

The information on positive reinforcement is useful in obtaining the return of normal behaviors since rewards may be used to strengthen the desired activities. It also sheds some light on the process whereby the pathological behavior was itself acquired. The behavior therapist believes that many abnormal behaviors are developed and maintained because they are actually reinforced. An especially informative work was the demonstration by Haughton and Ayllon (1965) that a bizarre behavior could be produced and eliminated solely through the use of reinforcement (Fig. 17-3). A patient was handed a broom and rewarded by a cigarette while she held this and remained standing. Within a short time, the "holding the broom" response was so strong

that she would resist any attempts by others to take it away. In order to further analyze the impact of this "compulsive" behavior on others, the experimenters asked two psychiatrists to observe and evaluate the patient through a one-way mirror. The following was the analysis by one of the psychiatrists.

Her constant and compulsive pacing holding a broom in the manner she does could be seen as a ritualistic procedure, a magical action. When regression conquers the associative process, primitive and archaic forms of thinking control the behavior. Symbolism is a predominant mode of expression and deep seated unfulfilled desires and instinctual impulses. By magic, she controls others, cosmic powers are at her disposal and inanimate objects become living creatures.

Her broom could be then:
1. A child that gives her love and she gives him in return her devotion;
2. A phallic symbol;
3. The sceptre of an omnipotent queen. (Haughton & Ayllon, 1965).

This somewhat unique study lends sup-

Dr. Albert Bandura has developed a behavior therapy technique based on modeling, called *vicarious extinction*. After watching models handle dogs without fear, phobic children are soon able to imitate similar approach behaviors. Pictured are previously dog-phobic children after therapy. (Courtesy of Albert Bandura, Stanford University)

port to the premise that deviant symptoms may well be attributable to the occurrence of the rewards that follow the display of the symptoms. In this event, the elimination of the rewards should lead to the elimination of the symptoms. This technique is called *experimental extinction*. This has proven to be an effective means

of removing a variety of symptoms including thumb-sucking (Baer, 1962), temper tantrums (Williams, 1959), psychotic disruptive behavior (Ayllon and Michael, 1959), and neurodermatitis (Walton, 1960). Temper tantrums in children seem to be clearly amenable to this type of approach. Ordinarily, the tantrum behav-

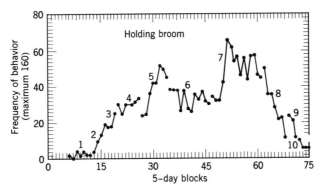

Figure 17-3. **Graph showing the acquisition and elimination of symptomatic behavior.**
SOURCE: From "Production and Elimination of Symptomatic Behavior" by Eric Haughton and Teodoro Ayllon, from CASE STUDIES IN BEHAVIOR MODIFICATION by Leonard P. Ullmann and Leonard Krasner. Copyright © 1965 by Holt, Rinehart and Winston, Inc. Reprinted by permission of Holt, Rinehart and Winston, Inc.

ior is strengthened by the parents or nursing or teaching staff giving in to the child's demands. Frequently, the attention that the child obtains is in itself rewarding. The treatment program is as simple as it is effective—the child is simply ignored, that is, all reinforcements are removed. Within a short span, if those around the child do not weaken, the tantrums disappear.

Aversion conditioning is a version of classical conditioning. By this procedure a deviant behavior, which has attractive qualities for the patient, is paired with a noxious event in order to give it aversive qualities instead. This has been tried with alcoholics with variable success—the alcoholic is given a drug that produces nausea and vomiting; the therapist times it so that the patient is offered an alcoholic drink just prior to the moment that the nausea sets in (Franks, 1958). Similar methods have been adapted to the treatment of sexual disorders such as homosexuality with equally inconsistent results (Max, 1935; Raymond, 1956; Rachman, 1961). One particularly successful case (Raymond, 1956) involved a highly unusual symptom. The patient, a married man of 33, was referred for possible leucotomy after he had attacked a perambulator (a type of baby carriage). The patient began his personal attacks on women's handbags and perambulators since he was 10 years old averaging two to three per week. He had been brought to trial five times for incidents as follows:

Slashed two empty prams on a railway station . . . setting them on fire.

Rode his motor-cycle . . . into a perambulator . . . was convicted of careless driving.

Damaged a pram . . . by squirting oil.

Drove his motor-cycle through a muddy puddle, splashing a pram.

Smearing (perambulator) with oil.

Psychoanalytic treatment convinced the patient that his attacks were traceable to

(a) Age 18; weight 120 lbs.

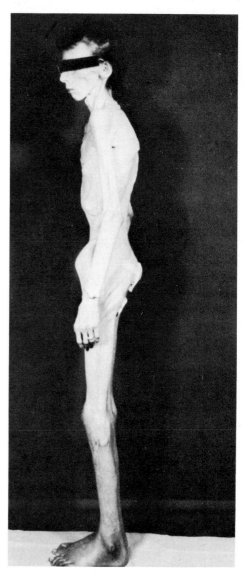

(b) 12/16/60; weight 47 lbs.

488

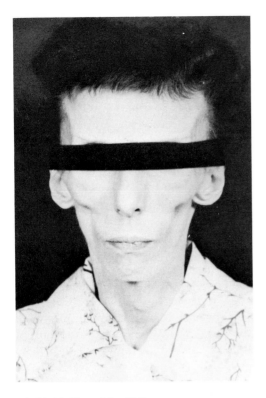

(c) 12/16/60; weight 47 lbs.

Pre-illness, pre-behavior therapy, and post-therapy pictures of an *anorexic patient*. (From "The Control of Eating Behavior in an Anorexic by Operant Conditioning Techniques," by A. J. Bachrach, W. J. Erwin, and J. P. Mohr, from *Case Studies in Behavior Modification* edited by Leonard P. Ullmann and Leonard Krasner. Copyright © 1965 by Holt, Rinehart and Winston, Inc. Reprinted by permission of Holt, Rinehart and Winston, Inc.)

symbolic sexual meanings related to two childhood incidents. This insight did little to help in the control of the impulses. Behavior therapy directed itself to developing an aversive reaction. The standard nausea-producing drug was used in association with the presentation of handbags and perambulators. This treatment was then replaced with confinement to a bed filled with handbags and surrounded with perambulators. Within a little over two weeks, the patient could tolerate prams and handbags no longer and was found sobbing that they be removed. He even

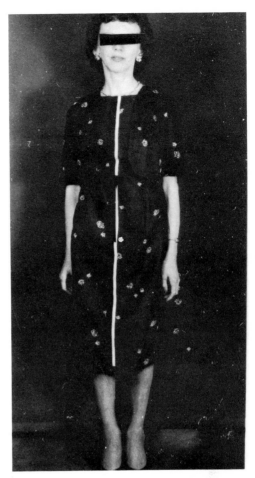

(d) 6/20/62; weight 88 lbs.

voluntarily handed over some photographic negatives of perambulators which he secretly carried. He was released, brought back for one "booster" treatment session, and remained happily free of his symptoms when last checked some 19 months later.

Aversion conditioning depends upon the arousal of an unpleasant emotion; *negative practice* relies upon the development of inhibition through continued repetition. When an act is repeated, a buildup of fatigue and inhibition appears to become increasingly associated with the act thus decreasing the person's tendency to repeat the act. Uncontrollable pathological acts such as tics, obsessions, com-

A snake-phobic coed volunteer after participating in a reinforcement *treatment-without-awareness* study of the author. Throughout the study she knew only that she was to attempt to correctly select the attitudes of a nonphobic person. She was rewarded for this activity, the activity in turn modified her own attitudes, and she was able to approach snakes with greater comfort. (Photographic lab, Colorado State University)

which she had also exhibited almost completely vanished and an eyeblink and throat tic were both substantially reduced. The treatment of this woman by Yates was primarily for the sake of experimentally testing certain hypotheses regarding behavior theory and behavior therapy. As such it was as much research oriented as treatment oriented. This interest in studying the value of behavior therapy has been characteristic of behavior therapists who are often experimenter-clinicians with strong research backgrounds. Some, such as Eysenck and Mowrer, have in fact never been psychotherapists but have become involved in the challenges which psychopathology and its treatment represent. Eysenck is credited with introducing the term "behavior therapy" to apply to this expanding therapy strategy (1959), and Mowrer has shown his versatility in

pulsions, and stuttering have been treated in this way (Dunlap, 1932, 1930; Lehner, 1954; Walton, 1960; Yates, 1958). By this method, the patient is asked to deliberately repeat the unwanted behavior for a large number of trials. A patient with an involuntary eye twitch, for example, would be asked to consciously twitch for a period of time, rest, twitch again, rest, twitch again until the therapist calls a halt. The results of this technique for a woman patient with a stomach contraction spasm is shown in Figs. 17-4 and 17-5 (Yates, 1958). As the figures show, through voluntary practice for five minutes per session the involuntary spasm was significantly decreased. Although the stomach contraction tic for this woman was never fully eliminated, a nasal tic

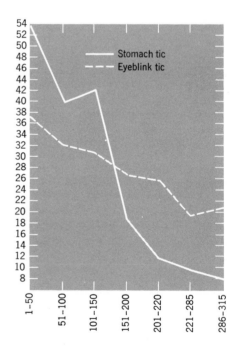

Figure 17.4 **Decline of stomach and eyeblink tics through negative practice.**
SOURCE: Adapted from A. Yates, The application of learning theory to the treatment of tics. *J. abnorm. soc. Psychol.*, 1958, **56**, 175.

490

his invention based on conditioning principles for curing bed-wetting (1938).

The experimenter-therapists of the behavior therapy approach have attempted to continuously subject their techniques to evaluation. In nine years of private practice, Wolpe showed that nearly 90 percent of his 210 patients were either cured or much improved by behavior therapy lasting usually about 30 sessions each patient (Wolpe, 1958). These patients exhibited a variety of neuroses including anxiety, hysteria, reactive depression, and obsessive-compulsive behavior. Lazarus also (1963) reviewed his practice and found that 78 percent of his 408 cases had shown marked benefits. In contrast, McConaghy (1964) was able to show improvement in 50 percent of his 18 patients, some of whom were psychotic and nearly all of whom had been unsuccessfully treated by conventional psychiatric therapy. The best successes have been reported by Mowrer (1938), Paul (1966), and Robinson and

Suinn (1969). Mowrer treated 30 children with bed-wetting problems and was able to cure all of them with his device. Paul selected 15 students with severe phobias about speaking in public and treated them with reciprocal inhibition techniques. He effected improvement in 100 percent of the behavior-treated cases as compared to improvement in 47 percent treated by other experienced psychotherapists relying upon insight therapy, 46 percent treated by a placebo pill and suggestion, and 17 percent who received no treatment at all. Robinson and Suinn removed a fear of spiders in clients to the extent that all were able to approach a live four-inch spider, and some were even able to stroke its back.

The Evaluation of Psychotherapy

The evaluation of psychotherapy must inevitably examine the results of psychotherapeutic intervention, the percentage of treated patients that show relief of symptoms and recovery of mental health. Among such psychotherapy *outcome studies* was a major effort conducted at the Counseling Center of the University of Chicago under the direction of Carl Rogers (Rogers and Dymond, 1954). Clients undergoing treatment were studied intensively before, during, and after therapy and compared with control students who were also examined but who received no therapy. In general, the clients showed significant improvements toward adjustment with such gains appearing to be attributable to the treatment contact. The clients described themselves as being tense and in distress at the start of treatment, and more comfortable, confident, and self-directing toward the end. The more successfully treated clients showed gains in maturity which were evident even to their friends. Barron and Leary (1955) obtained personality test information on 150 neurotic patients, some of whom were individually treated, some who were treated

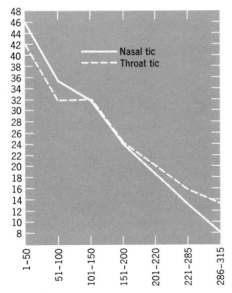

Figure 17-5. **Decline of nasal and throat tics through negative practice.**
SOURCE: Adapted from A. Yates, The application of learning theory to the treatments of tics. *J. abnorm. soc. Psychol.,* 1958, **56**, 175.

by group therapy, and some who were required to wait some six months before treatment was available. The therapists were psychoanalytically oriented. Within eight months, significant personality changes were noted including decreases in depression, physical complaints, and defenses. A survey of the actual rate of cure or improvements resulting from various types of psychotherapies in the treatment of neurotics shows a wide range of results. The Central Fact Gathering Committee of the American Psychoanalytic Association reported that of 210 neurotics who had completed their analysis, 126 showed great improvement or complete cure, for a recovery rate of 60 percent (Brody, 1962). Eysenck (1965) examined the results of a wide variety of psychotherapeutic strategies in studies published mainly in the 1930's and found a 64 percent improvement rate over 7293 patients. These are not remarkably high rates of cure when one considers that a large number of neurotics experience relief from their symptoms without formal psychotherapeutic intervention (the figures range from 40 to 66 percent). In addition, there may be reason to believe that exposure to therapy can make matters worse for some patients. In the Rogers group mentioned earlier, the unsuccessfully treated clients showed a decrease in their level of emotional maturity. In the Barron and Leary study, the control patients had also shown gains equal to that resulting from therapy even though they had not yet been in therapy. In addition, some of the treated patients showed a worsening of their symptoms (Cartwright, 1956).

Such outcome studies may seem discouraging, yet they need not be. Rather, they represent a challenge to a false assumption held by therapist and patient alike that all types of symptoms are curable by any type of psychotherapy and that no improvements can occur unless the patient participates in therapy. A more realistic appraisal of the capabilities of psychotherapy would recognize the following.

1. It is likely that some forms of psychopathology are better treated by some types of psychotherapy and not helped and perhaps even hindered by other forms. Just as a misapplied prescription of antibiotics will lead to no improvement and perhaps even a deterioration in a physical disease, so will misapplication of psychotherapeutic strategies lead to disappointing results.

2. The conditions leading to improvement may exist in settings outside of the psychotherapeutic session. In fact, therapists may rely upon environmental change to bring about improvement. A favorable psychosocial experience can replicate some of the very conditions present in the therapeutic session. The recognition of this fact has led many hospitals to employ *milieu therapy* or the *therapeutic community* concept whereby every experience outside of the psychotherapy session is designed to promote maximal growth toward adjustment.

3. The effective practice of psychotherapy involves therapeutic skill in the strategies of treatment. The ease of development of the skills depends upon the type of therapeutic strategy. Although it is possible within a short time to train nursery school teachers, parents, and nurses in the fundamentals of withholding reinforcement to eliminate unwanted behavior, learning the procedure of reciprocal inhibition and the appropriate behaviors to countercondition requires more experience and skill.

4. The various strategies are designed to achieve differing outcomes. Counterconditioning attempts to substitute one form of behavior for an undesirable one. Aversive training seeks to mainly inhibit an undesirable behavior pattern. Client-centered psychotherapy encourages self-

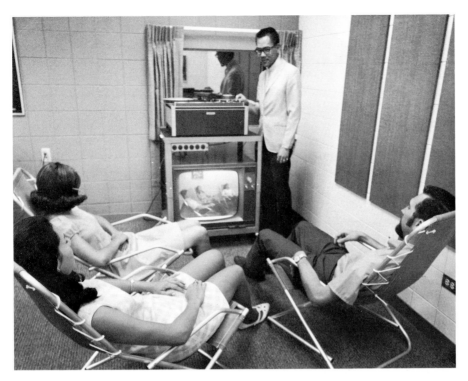

Short-term treatment by *video-tape* provides a means for offering desensitization therapy. On the television monitor operated by the author, is a video-tape playback of a desensitization session with other clients. Through viewing this tape, other clients can also receive similar effects of treatment. (Photographic lab, Colorado State University)

awareness and self-directedness. Psychoanalysis strives for extensive self-insight, self-understanding, and personality reorganization.

5. The effective elimination of pathological patterns requires a certain amount of time particularly since the decrease of one problem may permit another to become expressed and thereby subject to treatment. Thus far, the shortest course of treatment has been attributed to behavior therapy techniques dealing with limited problems such as specific fears. For example, Lazarus (1959) cured 18 children with phobias within about nine therapy sessions. Bandura and Menlove (1968) employed vicarious extinction through eight three-minute movies shown over four days in the successful treatment of children with extreme fears of dogs. Robinson and Suinn (1969) used systematic desensitization with groups of subjects treated in four consecutive days. Suinn and Hall (1969) completed treatment of test-taking anxiety within 24 hours by the use of *marathon desensitization groups*.

Psychotherapeutic strategies were developed in response to the suffering of people in psychological distress. Techniques evolved mainly through increased experience and therefore the process of treatment and cure is by no means perfectly understood. The outcome studies stand as good evidence that much more information is needed: which patients are more amenable to psychotherapeutic intervention, what interaction occurs between specific therapist traits and patient characteristics, what are the therapeutic conditions that bring about personality change, for what problems are these conditions helpful and which problems are aggravated, how meaningful are those facets of therapy such as "warmth and understanding," "growth," "interpretation," "emotional insight"? It is likely that the data regarding the outcome of psychotherapies will prove to be much more favorable when better studies are designed which eliminate the basic flaws of previous work, such as the lumping together of results from therapists of widely differing degree of skill and training, or the failure to control for differences in the nature and severity of the illnesses treated. However, even then the contribution of the psychotherapies will continue to be limited until answers are obtained to the questions just raised. Some studies are providing a tentative start in this direction and are referred to as *process* research. Such studies attempt to examine the very process of psychotherapy itself, giving substance to the dynamic and seemingly intangible thread of psychotherapy. Ingenious research scientists have devoted themselves to testing out claims and making observations about what happens in the therapeutic hour. Among the conclusions from such process studies are the following.

1. Interpretations by the therapist are helpful in releasing relevant personal information by reducing defensiveness (Dittmann, 1952; Murray, 1954; Speisman, 1959).

2. Therapists considered to be among the experts in various types of psychotherapy (psychoanalytic, client-centered, Adlerian) are highly similar to one another despite differences in their orientations (Fiedler, 1950, 1951).

3. A common factor characterizing the successful therapists might be called the "therapeutic relationship" (Fiedler, 1953).

4. Among the therapist's characteristics that affect the progress and the out-

comes of therapy are: a permissive attitude (Lipkin, 1948), an unconditional positive regard (Van der Veen, 1961; Snyder, 1961; Truax, 1963), and empathic understanding (Truax, 1963). In fact, where the therapist fails to establish these conditions, the outcome of therapy tends to be *deterioration* in the patients rather than progress (Truax, 1963).

5. During the course of a therapeutic session, the therapist's own comfort or anxiety about a topic affects the patient's ability to cope with the problem (Bandura, Lipsher, and Miller, 1960; Dittes, 1957). Treatment is hindered because the patient is led to avoid coming to grips with the topic area. On the other hand, an accepting and permissive attitude exhibited by the therapist may serve as a model helping the patient to become desensitized to the problem area.

Psychotherapists are yet a long way from fully controlling the conditions which bring about therapeutic change. The outcome studies confirm this. Progress is underway toward a clearer understanding of the manner in which the therapist, the patient, and the therapeutic strategy interact to prevent or to bring about change. The process studies illustrate this. The basic conceptualization of psychopathology and the means for altering personality is forever being challenged. Each challenge has provoked the further advancement of therapeutic progress. Because the challenges have often been issued by camps of therapists representing opposing views, progress has not always been systematic or in a singular direction. Psychoanalysts, client-centered therapists, and behavior therapists continue to pursue the development of their own techniques. And yet it may be possible that a combination of strategies such as depth interpretation used by a permissive therapist under reciprocal inhibition conditions might be the most fruitful approach for specific pathologies. In a broader framework, a therapeutic program involving medical-psychological-social treatment must be developed. In some instances, for example, drugs have been prescribed as an aid in counterconditioning and as a substitute for relaxation training (Walton, 1960). Similarly, milieau therapy or the reliance upon social psychological techniques (Fairweather, 1964) can be as effective as individual psychotherapy and can be used in conjunction with chemotherapy.

Glossary

Anxiety hierarchy: A list of situations associated with a phobia, ranked from low to high for use in behavior therapy.

Assertive training: The systematic directing of a client in assertive behavior.

Aversive conditioning: The pairing of an activity with a noxious stimulus in order to eliminate that activity.

Chemotherapy: The use of drugs to treat illness.

Chlorpromazine: A tranquilizer.

Classical conditioning: A method of learning involving the pairing of a neural stimulus with a stimulus that is associated with a reflex response.

Client-centered psychotherapy: A strategy of therapy that stresses personal growth and encouraged by the accepting attitude of the therapist.

Counterconditioning: Strengthening a response that is antagonistic to or incompatible with an undesirable response.

Electroshock treatment: The treatment of mental illness through electrical induction of a convulsion.

Energizers, psychic: Drugs used to stimulate a patient out of depression.

Experimental extinction: The elimination of a response by the withdrawal of the reinforcement that maintained the response.

Family psychotherapy: The treatment of the family as a single unit instead of each member individually.

Free association: The technique requiring a client to say anything and everything that comes to mind.

Group psychotherapy: The treatment of several patients meeting together with one or two psychotherapists.

Imipramine: An antidepressant drug.

Insulin shock therapy: The treatment of mental illness through the use of insulin in order to produce a comatose state.

Interpretation: In therapy, the delineation of an association between current behavior and past events.

Marsilid: A psychic energizer.

Mono-amine oxidase (MAO): An enzyme depleting serotonin and believed related to depressions.

Negative practice: The procedure of having a client repeat an undesirable response until it is weakened through satiation.

Operant conditioning: A method of learning involving the strengthening of a response through the presentation of a reward following the response.

Play psychotherapy: The therapeutic method for children that relies upon play activity.

Prefrontal lobotomy: Psychosurgery involving the frontal lobes.

Psychoanalysis: A strategy of psychotherapy that stresses free association, dream analysis, transference, and the development of insight.

Psychoanalytically oriented psychotherapy: Psychotherapies that are based on a psychoanalytic framework but that do not adhere rigidly to all the techniques of psychoanalysis.

Psychodrama: The treatment of mental illness by encouraging the client to enact different dramas of his life.

Psychosurgery: A medical treatment approach involving surgical isolation of lobes of the brain.

Psychotherapy: The treatment of mental illness through a corrective experience resulting from the interaction between a trained therapist and a client.

Reserpine: A tranquilizer.

Resistance: The psychoanalytic belief that a client will attempt to protect himself from facing his conflicts during therapy.

Self-actualization: The client-centered belief that each person is motivated toward self-growth and self-fulfillment.

Systematic desensitization: The gradual exposure of a client to feared situations while he is relaxed.

Tranquilizers: Drugs used to produce a calming effect without affecting the level of alertness.

Transference: The psychoanalytic belief that a client will irrationally repeat emotions or behaviors appropriate for an earlier period in life.

Vicarious extinction: The elimination of unwanted behaviors through the observation of a model.

References

Ackerman, N. *Psychodynamics of family life.* New York: Basic Books, 1958.

Alexander, F. *The medical value of psychoanalysis.* New York: Norton, 1937.

Alexander, F. & French, R. *Psychoanalytic therapy.* New York: Ronald, 1946.

Allen, F. *Psychotherapy with children.* New York: Norton, 1942.

Allen, K. Hart, B., Buell, J., Harris, F., & Wolf, M. Effects of social reinforcement on isolate behavior of a nursery school child. *Child Developm.,* 1964, **35**, 511.

Appel, K., Myers, J. & Scheflen, A. Prognosis in psychiatry; results of psychiatric treatment. *Arch. neurol. Psychiat.,* 1953, **70**, 459.

Axline, V. *Play therapy.* Boston: Houghton Mifflin, 1947.

Ayllon, T. Intensive treatment of psychotic behavior by stimulus satiation and food reinforcement. *Behav. Res. Ther.,* 1963, **1**, 53.

Ayllon, T. & Michael, J. The psychiatric nurse as a behavioral engineer. *J. exp. anal. Behav.,* 1959, **2**, 323.

Azrin, N. & Lindsley, O. The reinforcement of cooperation between children. *J. abnorm. soc. Psychol.,* 1956, **52**, 100.

Bach, G. *Intensive group psychotherapy.* New York: Ronald, 1954.

Bachrach, A., Erwin, W., & Mohr, J. The control of eating behavior in an anorexic by operant conditioning techniques. In L. Ullmann and L. Krasner (Eds.), *Case studies in behavior modification.* New York: Holt, Rinehart, and Winston, 1965.

Baer, D. Laboratory control of thumbsucking by withdrawal and re-presentation of reinforcement. *J. exp. anal. Behav.,* 1962, **5**, 525.

Bandura, A. Psychotherapy as a learning process. *Psychol. Bull.,* 1961, **58**, 143.

Bandura, A. Influence of models' reinforcement contingencies on the acquisition of imitative responses. *J. person. soc. Psychol.,* 1965, **1**, 589.

Bandura, A., Gruesec, J., & Menlove, F. Vicarious extinction of avoidance behavior. *J. person. soc. Psychol.,* 1967, **5**, 16.

Bandura, A., Lipsher, D., Miller, P. Psychotherapists' approach-avoidance reactions to patients' expressions of hostility. *J. consult. Psychol.,* 1964, **24**, 1.

Bandura, A. & Menlove, F. Factors determining vicarious extinction of avoidance through symbolic modeling. *J. person. soc. Psychol.,* 1968, **8**, 99.

Bandura, A. & Rosenthal, T. Vicarious conditioning as a function of arousal level. *J. person. soc. Psychol.,* 1966, **3**, 54.

Bandura, A., Ross, D. & Ross, S. Transmission of aggression through imitation of aggressive models. *J. abnorm. soc. Psychol.,* 1961, **63**, 575.

Bandura, A., Ross, D. & Ross, S. Vicarious reinforcement and imitative learning. *J. abnorm. soc. Psychol.,* 1963, **67**, 601.

Bandura, A. & Walters, R. *Social learning and personality development.* New York: Holt, Rinehart, and Winston, 1963.

Barnett, P. & Benedetti, D. Vicarious conditioning of the GSR to a sound. Paper read at Rocky Mountain Psychological Association, Glenwood Springs, Colorado, May 1960.

Barron, F. & Leary, T. Changes in psychoneurotic patients with and without psychotherapy. *J. consult. Psychol.,* 1955, **19,** 239.

Bell, J. Family group therapy. Wash, D.C.: Public Health Mongr. No. 64, U.S. Department of Health, Education and Welfare, 1961.

Berger, S. Conditioning through vicarious instigation. *Psychol. Rev.,* 1962, **69,** 450.

Bijou, S. & Orlando, R. Rapid development of multiple-schedule performances with retarded children. *J. exp. anal. Behav.,* 1961, **4, 7.**

Bond, E. Results of treatment in psychoses with a control series. *Amer. J. Psychiat.,* 1954, **110,** 881.

Boszarmenyi-Nagy, I. & Framo, J. (Eds.), *Intensive family therapy.* New York: Hoeber Med. Div., Harper and Row, 1965.

Brady, J. & Lind, D. Experimental analysis of hysterical blindness. *A.M.A. Arch. gen. Psychiat.,* 1961, **4,** 331.

Brenman, N. & Gill, M. *Hypnotherapy.* New York: International University Press, 1947.

Brill, H. & Patton, R. Analysis of population reduction in New York State Mental Hospitals during the first four years of large scale-therapy with psychotropic drugs. *Amer. J. Psychiat.,* 1959, **116,** 495.

Brody, M. Prognosis and results of psychoanalysis. In J. Nodine, and J. Moyer (Eds.), *Psychosomatic medicine.* Philadelphia: Lea and Febiger, 1962.

Cartwright, D. Note on "changes" in psychoneurotic patients with and without psychotherapy. *J. consult. Psychol.,* 1956, **20,** 403.

Cerletti, U. Electroshock therapy. In F. Marti-Ibanex, A. Sackler, M. Sackler, and R. Sackler (Eds.), *The great physiodynamic therapies in psychiatry.* New York: Hoeber, 1956.

Dahlberg, C. Pharmacologic facilitation of psychoanalytic therapy. In M. Masserman (Ed.), *Current psychiatric therapies,* Vol. III. New York: Grune & Stratton, 1963.

DiMascio, A. Personality factors and variability of response to chlorpromazine. Paper read at Eastern Psychological Association, Philadelphia, 1964.

DiMascio, A., Havens, L. & Klerman, G. The psychopharmacology of phenothiazine, promethazine, trifluoperazine, and perphenazine in normal males. *J. nerv. ment. Dis.,* 1963, **136,** 168.

Dittmann, A. The interpersonal process in psychotherapy: development of a research method. *J. abnorm. soc. Psychol.,* 1952, **47,** 236.

Dittman, K., Hayman, M., & Whittlessy, J. Nature and frequency of claims following LSD. *J. nerv. ment. Dis.,* 1962, **134,** 346.

Dittes, J. Galvanic skin response as a measure of patients' reaction to therapist's permissiveness. *J. abnorm. soc. Psychol.,* 1957, **55,** 295.

Dollard, J. & Miller, N. *Personality and psychotherapy.* New York: McGraw-Hill, 1950.

Dunlap, K. *Habits: their making and unmaking.* New York: Liveright, 1932.

Dunlap, K. Repetition in the breaking of habits. *Scient. Month.,* 1930, **30, 66.**

Ewing, J. & Haizlip, T. A controlled study of the habit forming propensities of meprobamate. *Amer. J. Psychiat.,* 1958, **114,** 835.

Eysenck, H. Learning theory and behavior therapy. *J. ment. Sci.,* 1959, **105,** 61.

Eysenck, H. The effects of psychotherapy. *Intern. J. Psychiat.,* 1965, **1,** 99.

Eysenck, H. & Rachman, S. *The causes and cures of neurosis.* San Diego: Robert R. Knapp, 1956.

Fairweather, G. *Social psychology in treating mental illness.* New York: Wiley, 1964.

Fenichel, O. *Outline of clinical psychoanalysis*. New York: Norton, 1934.

Fiedler, F. A comparison of therapeutic relationships in psychoanalytic, nondirective, and Adlerian therapy. *J. consult. Psychol.* 1950, **14**, 436.

Fiedler, F. Factor analyses of psychoanalytic, nondirective, and Adlerian therapeutic relationships. *J. consult. Psychol.,* 1951, **15**, 32.

Fiedler, F. Quantitative studies on the role of therapists' feelings towards their patients. In O. Mowrer (Ed.), *Psychotherapy: theory and research*. New York: Ronald Press, 1953.

Fisher, S., Cole, J., Rickels, K. et al. Drug-set interaction: The effect of expectations on drug response in out-patients. Paper read at Collegium Internationale Neuro-psychopharmacologicum, Munich, 1962.

Franks, C. Alcohol, alcoholism, and conditioning: a review of the literature and some theoretical considerations. *J. ment. Sci.,* 1958, **104**, 14.

Freeman, H. The tranquilizing drugs. In L. Bellak (Ed.), *Schizophrenia: a review of the syndrome*. New York: Logos Press, 1958.

Freeman, W. & Watts, J. *Psychosurgery*. Springfield: Thomas, 1942.

Freud, S. *The standard edition of the complete psychological works of Sigmund Freud*. Strachey, J. (Ed.), London: Hogarth Press, 1955.

Glover, E. *An investigation of the techniques of psychoanalysis*. Baltimore: Williams & Wilkins, 1940.

Goldstein, K. Frontal lobotomy and impairment of abstract attitude. *J. nerv. ment. Dis.,* 1949, **110**, 93.

Gross, M. & Reeves, W. Relapses after withdrawal of ataractic drugs: an interim report. In M. Greenblatt, D. Levinson, & G. Klerman (Eds.), *Mental patients in transition*. Springfield: Thomas, 1961.

Haley, J. Whither family therapy, *Family Processes*, 1962, **1**, 69.

Halkides, G. An experimental study of four conditions necessary for therapeutic change. Unpubl. doctroral dissertation. Univ. of Chicago, 1958.

Harris, F., Johnston, M., Kelley, C., & Wolf, M. Effects of positive social reinforcement on regressed crawling of a nursery school child. *J. ed. Psychol.,* 1964, **55**, 35.

Hartman, H. *Ego psychology and the problem of adaptation*. New York: International University Press, 1958.

Haughton, E. & Ayllon, T. Production and elimination of symptomatic behavior. In L. Ullmann and L. Krasner (Eds.), *Case studies in behavior modification*. New York: Holt, Rinehart, and Winston, 1965.

Hobbs, N. Group-centered psychotherapy. In C. Rogers, *Client-centered therapy*. Boston: Houghton Mifflin, 1951.

Isaacs, W., Thomas, J. & Goldiamond, I. Application of operant conditioning to reinstate verbal behavior in psychotics. *J. speech hearing Dis.,* 1961, **25**, 8.

Jackson, D. The monad, the dyad, and the family therapy of schizophrenia. In A. Burton (Ed.), *Psychotherapy of the psychoses*. New York: Basic Books, 1961.

Jacobsen, E. Progressive relaxation. Chicago: University of Chicago Press, 1938.

Kalinowsky, L. & Hoch, P. *Shock treatments, psychosurgery and other somatic treatments in psychiatry*. (2nd ed.) New York: Grune and Stratton, 1952.

Karagula, S. Evaluation of electric convulsion therapy as compared with conservative methods of treatment in depressive states. *J. ment. Science,* 1950, **96**, 1060.

Kardiner, A. & Speigel, H. *The traumatic neuroses of war*. New York: Hoeber, 1947.

Katz, M. A topological approach to the problem of predicting response to treatment. In J. Wittenborn, & P. May, *A prediction of response to pharmotherapy*. Springfield, C. C. Thomas, 1966.

Klerman, G., Davidson, E. & Kayce, M. Factors influencing the clinical responses of schizophrenic patients to phenothiazine drugs and to placebo. In P. Solomon & B. Glueck (Eds.), *Recent research on schizophrenia,* Washington, D.C.: American Psychiatric Association, 1964, 97.

Kline, N. Clinical experience with iproniazid (Marsilid). *J. clin. exp. Psychopath.,* 1958, 19, Suppl. 1, 72.

Kramer, M. & Pollack, E. Problems in the interpretation of trends in the population movement of the public mental hospitals. *Amer. J. pub. Health,* 1958, 48, 1003.

Kuhn, R. The treatment of depressive states with G22355 (imipramine hydrochloride). *Amer. J. Psychiat.,* 1958, 115, 459.

Landis, C. & Ehrlick, D. Analysis of Porteus maze test as affected by psychosurgery. *Amer. J. Psychol.,* 1950, 63, 557.

Laqueur, H., Dussik, K., La Burt, H. & McLaughlin, W. Tactical and strategical considerations in the use of Insulin therapy—a joint mental hospital study. Paper read at the Second International Conference on the Biological treatment of mental illness. N.Y. Academy of Medicine, No. 2, 1962.

Lazarus, A. The elimination of children's phobias by deconditioning. *Med. Proc. S. Afr.,* 1959, 5, 261.

Lazarus, A. The results of behavior therapy in 126 cases of severe neurosis. *Beh. Res. Ther.,* 1963, 1, 65.

Lehner, G. Negative practice as a psychotherapeutic technique. *J. gen. Psychol.,* 1954, 51, 69.

Lemere, F. Habit-forming properties of meprobamate. *A.M.A. arch. neurol. Psychiat.,* 1956, 76, 205.

Levinson, D., Meadow, A., Atwell, C., Robey, A., & Bellis, E. The relation of frontal lobe surgery to intellectual and emotional functioning. In M. Greenblatt, and H. Solomon (Eds.), *Frontal lobes and schizophrenia.* New York: Springer, 1953.

Levy, D. Release therapy in young children. *Amer. J. Orthopsychiat.,* 1939, 9, 713.

Lipkin, S. The client evaluates nondirective psychotherapy. *J. consult. Psychol.,* 1948, 12, 137.

Max, L. Breaking up a homosexual fixation by the conditioned reaction technique: a case study. *Psychol. Bull.,* 1935, 32, 734.

McConaghy, N. A year's experience with nonverbal psychotherapy. *Med. J. Austral.,* 1964, 1, 831.

Menninger, K. *Theory of psychoanalytic technique.* New York: Basic Books, 1958.

Meyer, A., Beck, E. & McLardy, T. Prefrontal leucotomy: neuro-anatomical report. *Brain,* 1947, 70, 18.

Moniz, E. *Tentative operatoires dans le traite-ment de certaines psychoses.* Paris: Masson and Co., 1936.

Moreno, J. *Psychodrama.* New York: Beacon House, 1946.

Mowrer, O. & Mowrer, W. Enuresis: a method for its study treatment. *Amer. J. Orthopsychiat.,* 1938, 8, 436.

Murray, E. A case study in a behavioral analysis of psychotherapy. *J. abnorm. soc. Psychol.,* 1954, 49, 305.

Patterson, G. A learning theory approach to the treatment of the school phobic child. In L. Ullmann and L. Krasner (Eds.), *Case studies in behavior modification.* New York: Holt, Rinehart and Winston, 1965.

Paul, G. L. *Insight versus desensitization in psychotherapy.* Stanford: Stanford University Press, 1966.

Pearson, M. *Strecker's fundamentals of psychiatry.* (6th ed.) Philadelphia: Lippincott, 1963.

Porteus, S. Recent research on the Porteus maze test and psycho-surgery. *Br. J. med. Psychol.,* 1951, 24, 132.

Powdermaker, F. & Frank, J. *Group psychotherapy.* Cambridge: Commonwealth Fund, 1953.

Rachman, S. Sexual disorders and behavior therapy. *Amer. J. Psychiat.,* 1961, **118**, 235.

Rachman, S. Systematic desensitization. *Psychol. Bull.,* 1967, **67**, 93.

Rapaport, D. *The organization and pathology of thought.* New York: Columbia University Press, 1951.

Raymond, M. Case of fetishism treated by aversion therapy. *Brit. med. J.,* 1956, **2**, 854.

Robinson, C. & Suinn, R. Group desensitization of a phobia in massed sessions. *Behav. Res. Therap.,* 1969, **7**, 319.

Rogers, C. *Client-centered therapy.* Boston: Houghton Mifflin Co., 1951.

Rogers, C. The necessary and sufficient conditions of psychotherapeutic personality change. *J. consult. Psychol.,* 1957, **21**, 95.

Rogers, C. A theory of therapy, personality and interpersonal relationships, as developed in the client-centered framework. In S. Koch (Ed.), *Psychology: a study of a science. Vol. II. General systematic formulations, learning, and special processes.* New York: McGraw-Hill, 1959.

Rogers, C. & Dymond, R. (Ed.) *Psychotherapy and personality change.* Chicago: University of Chicago Press, 1954.

Sakel, M. Neue Behandlung der Morphinsucht. *A. Neurol. Psychiat.,* 1933, **143**, 506.

Sakel, M. *Neue Behandlungsmethode der Schizophrenie.* Vienna and Leipzig Moritz Perles, 1935.

Sakel, M. The classical Sakel shock treatment; a reappraisal. *N. clin. exp. Psychopath.,* 1954, **15**, 255.

Sakel, M. The classical Sakel shock treatment. In F. Marti-Ibanex, A. Sackler, M. Sackler, & R. Sackler (Eds.), *The great physiodynamic therapies in psychiatry.* New York: Hoeber, 1956.

Salter, A. Conditioned reflex therapy. New York: Capricorn Books—Putnam, 1961.

Schacter, S. The interaction of cognitive and physiological determinants of emotional state. In C. Spielberger (Ed.), *Anxiety and behavior.* New York: Academic Press, 1966.

Sherman, J. Use of reinforcement and imitation to reinstate verbal behavior in mute psychotics. *J. abnorm. soc. Psychol.,* 1965, **70**, 155.

Slavson, S. Group psychotherapies. In J. McCary & D. Sheer (Eds.), *Six approaches to psychotherapy.* New York: The Dryden Press, 1955.

Snyder, W. *Case book of non-directive counseling.* Boston: Houghton Mifflin Co., 1947.

Snyder, W. *The psychotherapy relationship.* New York: Macmillan, 1961.

Solomon, J. Active play therapy. *Amer. J. Orthopsychiat.,* 1938, **8**, 479.

Speisman, J. Depth of interpretation and verbal resistance in psychotherapy. *J. consult. Psychol.,* 1959, **23**, 93.

Staudt, V. & Zubin, J. A biometric evaluation of the somatotherapies in schizophrenia—A critical review. *Psychol. Bull.,* 1957, **54**, 171.

Stephens, J. & Astrup, C. Treatment outcome in "process" and "non-process" schizophrenics by "A" and "B" types of therapist. *J. nerv. ment. Dis.,* 1965, **140**, 449.

Suinn, R. The STABS, a test anxiety measure for behavior therapy. *Behav. Res. Therap.,* 1969, **7**, 335.

Suinn, R. & Augustine, L. *Operant techniques with a blind, elected-mute child.* Colorado State University: Psychological Services Center, 1969.

Suinn, R. & Brittain, J. The termination of an L.S.D. "Freak-out" through the use of relaxation. *J. clin. Psychol.,* 1970, **26**, 127.

Suinn, R. & Hall, R. Marathon desensitization groups: an innovation. *Behav. Res. Therapy.,* in press, 1969.

Suinn, R., Osborne, D., & Winfree, P. The self-concept and accuracy of recall of inconsistent self-related information. *J. clin. Psychol.*, 1962, **18**, 463.

Suinn, R. & Richardson, F. Behavior therapy of an unusual case of highway hypnosis. *Behav. Therap. & Exp. Psychiat.*, in press, 1970.

Suinn, R., Stewart, S. & McGuirk, F. Treatment of snake phobia through the operant control of attitudes. In prep., 1969.

Sykes, M. & Tredgold, R. Restricted orbital undercutting, A study of its effects on 350 patients over the ten years 1951-1960. *Amer. J. Psychiat.*, 1964, **110**, 609.

Thomas, D. Prognosis of depression with electrical treatment. *Br. med. Journal*, 1954, **2**, 950.

Tooth, G. & Newton, M. *Leucotomy in England and Wales, 1942-1954.* Ministry of Health, London, H.M.S. 1961.

Truax, C. Effective ingredients in psychotherapy: an approach to unraveling the patient-therapist interaction. *J. counsel. Psychol.*, 1963, **10**, 256.

Van der Veen, F. The perception by clients and by judges of the conditions offered by the therapist in the therapy relationship. *U. Wisc. Psychiat. Inst. Bull.*, 1961, **1** (no. 10).

Walton, D. The application of learning theory to the treatment of a case of neurodermatitis. In H. Eysenck (Ed.), *Behavior therapy and the neuroses.* New York: Pergamon Press, 1960.

Walton, D. The relevance of learning theory to the treatment of an obsessive-compulsive state. In H. Eysenck (Ed.), *Behavior therapy in the neuroses.* New York: Pergamon Press, 1960.

Weitzenhoffer, A. *Hypnotism: an objective study in suggestibility.* New York: Wiley, 1953.

West, F., Bond, E., Shurley, J., & Meyers, C. Insulin coma therapy in schizophrenia: fourteen year follow-up study. *Amer. J. Psychiat.*, 1955, **111**, 583.

White, J. The use of learning theory in the psychological treatment of children. *J. clin. Psychol.*, 1959, **15**, 227.

Williams, C. The elimination of tantrum behavior by extinction procedures. *J. abnorm. soc. Psychol.*, 1959, **59**, 269.

Winkelman, N., Jr. An appraisal of chlorpromazine. *Amer. J. Psychiat.*, 1957, **113**, 961.

Wirt, R. & Simon, W. *Differential treatment and prognosis in schizophrenia.* Springfield: Thomas, 1959.

Wolberg, L. *Hypnoanalysis.* (2nd ed.) New York: Grune & Stratton, 1964.

Wolpe, J. *Psychotherapy by reciprocal inhibition.* Stanford: Stanford University Press, 1958.

Wolpe, J. & Lazarus, A. *Behavior therapy techniques.* London: Pergamon Press, 1966.

World Health Organization. Ataraxic and hallucinogenic drugs in psychotherapy. *W.H.O. Tech. Report Series*, #152, 1958. WHO: Geneva, Switzerland.

Yates, A. The application of learning theory to the treatment of tics. *J. abnorm. soc. Psychol.*, 1958, **56**, 175.

Appendix

A Nomenclature of Psychiatric Disturbances*

I. DISORDERS OF PSYCHOLOGICAL (PSYCHOGENIC) ORIGIN

A. The Psychoneurotic Disorders: Characterized by awareness of anxiety, fair adjustment to life, overreliance on defenses, some insight.

1. *Traumatic Neuroses*—neuroses precipitated by extreme stress or catastrophic experiences in an otherwise normal person.
2. *Anxiety Reaction*—neurosis marked by extreme apprehension and feelings of imminent danger; the exception to the rule that neurotics are noted for their defense mechanisms since the anxiety reaction appears to have none.
3. *Hypochondriasis*—neurosis involving excessive preoccupation with somatic functions, mostly a fear of developing ill health.
4. *Conversion Reaction*—neurosis characterized by the manifestation of somatic symptoms without any identifiable organic cause.
5. *Dissociative Reactions*—neuroses involving disturbances of consciousness and memory. Includes amnesia, fugue states, somnambulism, and multiple personality.
6. *Phobias*—neuroses involving the presence of irrational, excessive fears.
7. *Obsessive-Compulsive Neurosis*—neurosis in which unwanted, intrusive thoughts or actions must be repeated.
8. *Reactive Depression*—neurosis involving depression precipitated by an unhappy life experience.

B. The Psychophysiologic Disorders (psychosomatic disorders): Characterized by the occurrence of structural changes in the body because of emotional disturbance.

1. *Psychophysiologic Skin Reactions*—Diseases of the skin due to emotional factors.
2. *Psychophysiologic Musculoskeletal Reactions*—diseases of the muscles, bones, joints, due to emotional factors.
3. *Psychophysiologic Respiratory Reactions*—diseases of the nasal and respiratory structures due to emotional factors.
4. *Psychophysiologic Cardiovascular Reactions*—diseases of the cardiac and vascular systems due to emotional factors.

* With some modifications, such as the inclusion of childhood pathologies, this Nomenclature is similar to that approved by the American Psychiatric Association (1952).

5. *Psychophysiologic Hemic and Lymphatic Reactions*—diseases of the blood or the lymphatic system due to emotional factors.

6. *Psychophysiologic Gastrointestinal Reactions*—diseases of the gastrointestinal system due to emotional factors.

7. *Psychophysiologic Genitourinary Reactions*—diseases of the genitourinary system due to emotional factors.

8. *Psychophysiologic Endocrine Reactions*—diseases of the endocrine system due to emotional factors.

9. *Psychophysiologic Nervous System Reactions*—diseases of the nervous system due to emotional factors.

10. *Psychophysiologic Reactions of Organs of Special Sense*—diseases of special sensory organs due to emotional factors.

C. The Conduct Disorders: Characterized by behaviors that violate the codes of conduct of the society.

1. *Antisocial Reactions* (psychopathic personality)—disorders marked by emotional immaturity, lack of responsibility and poor judgment, absence of moral values, inability to learn from experience or to postpone gratification.

2. *Dyssocial Reactions*—disorders characterized by strong loyalties to subgroup values which conflict with the larger societal values.

3. *Addictions*—alcoholic addiction involves the excessive intake of alcohol, dependence on alcoholism to the extent of leading to disruption of social, economic functioning and health. Drug addiction involves the repeated reliance upon drugs associated with physical or psychological dependence.

4. *Sexual Deviations*—disorders in which the gratification of the adult sexual need is obtained through practices other than intercourse with a genitally mature person of the opposite sex who has reached the legal age of consent. Includes homosexuality, masturbation, pedophilia, bestiality, fetishism, necrophilia, sadism, masochism, exhibitionism, voyeurism, coprolalia, frigidity, impotence, nypmphomania, and satyriasis.

D. The Psychotic Disorders: Characterized by profound disturbance, disability, loss of contact with reality, sensory dysfunctions, and lack of insight.

1. *Affective Disorders*—psychoses marked by extreme disturbance of mood. Includes manic-depressive psychosis, psychotic depression, and involutional melancholia.

2. *Paranoid Disorders*—psychoses involving thought disturbances of a persecutory nature but where gross personality disturbance is absent. Includes paranoia, and the paranoid states.

3. *Schizophrenia*—psychoses characterized by withdrawal, disturbance of emotions, autistic thinking, bizarre behavior, sensory disturbances, speech and thought disturbances. Includes simple schizophrenia, catatonic schizophrenia, hebephrenic schizophrenia, paranoid schizophrenia, and schizo-affective schizophrenia.

II. DISORDERS OF ORGANIC ORIGIN

A. Disorders due to Infections: Brain damage resulting from infectious diseases.

B. Disorders due to Nutritional or metabolic dysfunction: Brain damage resulting from vitamin or endocrine deficiency or malfunction.

C. Disorders due to Toxicity: Brain damage resulting from poisonous agents.

D. Disorders due to Trauma: Brain damage resulting from physical injury to the brain.

E. Disorders due to Aging: Brain damage resulting from deterioration associated with aging.

F. Disorders due to Tumors: Brain damage resulting from cancerous growths in the brain.

G. Disorders involving Convulsive reactions: Brain damage associated with epileptic seizures.

III. MENTAL RETARDATION

A. Conditions due to Infection: Retardation resulting from infectious diseases such as German measles during pregnancy, meningitis, and syphilis.

B. Conditions due to Intoxication: Retardation resulting from poisons such as carbon monoxide and lead poisoning.

C. Conditions due to Trauma: Retardation resulting from physical damage to the brain such as associated with birth injury, strokes, radiation, anoxia.

D. Conditions due to Metabolic or Nutritional Disorder: Retardation resulting from faulty metabolism or nutritional deficiency, including phenylketonuria, cretinism, galactosemia.

E. Conditions due to Growths: Retardation resulting from cancerous growths in the brain such as caused by tuberous sclerosis.

F. Conditions due to Unknown Prenatal Influences: Retardation which is ascribed to prenatal conditions yet unknown. Includes mongolism, congenital hydrocephalus, and microcephaly.

G. Conditions due to Unknown Cause with Structural Reactions Manifest: Retardation in which neurological and physical symptoms are prominent but where the cause is yet unknown.

H. Conditions due to Presumed Psychologic Cause: Retardation in which there is an apparent absence or organic disease or pathology. Includes retardation in intellectual function associated with psychoneurosis or psychosis.

IV. CHILDHOOD PATHOLOGIES

A. Habit Disorders: Characterized by repeated, maladaptive spasms or actions. Includes tics, habitual acts, and habits which interfere with biological functioning.

B. Learning Disorders: Characterized by interference with the acquisition of scholastic or communication skills. Includes stuttering, aphasia, delayed speech, poor articulation, dyslexia, and other disorders of reading and arithmetic.

C. Conduct Disorders: Characterized by behaviors that violate the standards of conduct of the society. Includes alcoholism, drug addiction, and juvenile delinquency.

D. Psychophysiologic Disorders: Characterized by structural changes in the body due to emotional factors. Includes ulcers, asthma, neurodermatitis, and hypertension.

E. Psychoneurotic Disorders: Characterized by anxiety, excessive reliance upon defense mechanisms, fair adjustment to life. Includes phobias, obsessive-compulsive neurosis, conversion reaction, hypochondriasis.

F. Psychotic Disorders: Characterized by profound sensory and thought disturbances, loss of contact with reality, lack of insight. Includes childhood schizophrenia, atypical child psychosis, infantile autism, infantile symbiotic psychosis, anaclitic depression, and manic-depressive psychosis.

G. Organic Disorders: Characterized by biochemical or structural damage to the brain. May originate from radiation, developmental defect, maternal infection during pregnancy, tumors, trauma, central nervous system disease.

Appendix

B Nomenclature of Behavioral Dysfunctions[*]

I. **Behavioral Deficits:** Characterized by the absence of skills normally expected in an individual of that age. For example, delayed speech or withdrawal. May originate from presence of a physical disability, the absence of good parental models, the suppression of such behavior through punishment, or the absence of reinforcers encouraging such behavior.

II. **Defective Stimulus Control over Behavior:** Characterized by the inability of a stimulus, normally associated with a response pattern, to cue this pattern in an individual. For example, habitual law-breaking. May originate from extreme permissiveness, inconsistent discipline, absence of consequences which make discriminating relevant or important.

III. **Inappropriate Stimulus Control of Behavior:** Characterized by a normally neutral stimulus acquiring the capability to elicit a certain response. For example, a harmless animal arousing a fear response, or the triggering of a psychosomatic asthma attack by a plastic flower. May originate from a history of classical conditioning.

IV. **Defective or Inappropriate Incentive Systems:** Characterized by the failure of rewards, ordinarily capable of acting as an incentive, in influencing an individual (defective incentive system); or the development of reinforcing value of circumstances which ordinarily do not have reward value (inappropriate incentive system). For example, a person with a defective incentive system would show apathy towards work or achievement, remain isolated and aloof from the social environment (as in schizophrenia), or even aversion toward social rewards (as in certain delinquents). An individual with an inappropriate incentive system might derive sexual satisfaction from fetishism or dressing in the clothes of the opposite sex.

[*] Although the Nomenclature of Psychiatric Disturbances in the previous section is more commonly used in classifying mental illnesses, a strong movement has developed toward behavioral classification that is not as reliant upon disease entity assumptions. The above Nomenclature of Behavioral Dysfunctions is one attempt to view psychopathology in ways more consistent with data on normal human behavior and more congruent with psychological social learning information (see Staats and Staats, 1963; Bandura, 1968; for further detail). The reader is referred to Chapter 7 for further discussion of the topic.

May originate from early disturbances in the reinforcement history when primary and secondary reinforcers are being developed.

V. Aversive Behavioral Repertoires: Characterized by reliance on behaviors which have aversive consequences to others. For example, temper tantrums, aggressive actions, extreme dependency behaviors, attention-demanding acts. May originate from an early history of reinforcement for such behaviors or the presence of adult or peer models of such actions.

VI. Aversive Self-Reinforcing Systems: Characterized by the setting of high standards of self-evaluation leading to self-depreciation rather than self-reward. For example, persons extremely low in self-confidence, suicidal individuals, the depressed. May originate from early learning history whereby the individual was rewarded for reliance upon strict standards of self-appraisal.

Author and Name Index

509

Subject Index